Underst

Parricide

MW01088119

UNDERSTANDING PARRICIDE

WHEN SONS AND DAUGHTERS KILL PARENTS

Kathleen M. Heide, Ph.D.

Baker College of Clinton Twp Library

OXFORD
UNIVERSITY PRESS

Oxford University Press is a department of the University of Oxford. It furthers the University's objective of excellence in research, scholarship, and education by publishing worldwide.

Oxford   New York
Auckland   Cape Town   Dar es Salaam   Hong Kong   Karachi
Kuala Lumpur   Madrid   Melbourne   Mexico City   Nairobi
New Delhi   Shanghai   Taipei   Toronto

With offices in
Argentina   Austria   Brazil   Chile   Czech Republic   France   Greece
Guatemala   Hungary   Italy   Japan   Poland   Portugal   Singapore
South Korea   Switzerland   Thailand   Turkey   Ukraine   Vietnam

Oxford is a registered trade mark of Oxford University Press in the UK and certain other countries.

Published in the United States of America by
Oxford University Press
198 Madison Avenue, New York, NY 10016

© Kathleen Margaret Heide 2013

All rights reserved. No part of this publication may be reproduced, stored in a retrieval system, or transmitted, in any form or by any means, without the prior permission in writing of Oxford University Press, or as expressly permitted by law, by license, or under terms agreed with the appropriate reproduction rights organization. Inquiries concerning reproduction outside the scope of the above should be sent to the Rights Department, Oxford University Press, at the address above.

You must not circulate this work in any other form
and you must impose this same condition on any acquirer.

Library of Congress Cataloging-in-Publication Data
   Heide, Kathleen M.
   Understanding parricide: When sons and daughters kill parents / Kathleen M. Heide, Ph.D.
   p. cm.
   Includes bibliographical references and index.
   ISBN 978–0–19–517666–7 (pbk)
   1. Parricide.   2. Family violence.   3. Abused children.   4. Mentally ill children – Treatment.
   5. Juvenile homicide.   6. Parricide. – Case studies.   7. Family violence – Case studies.
   8. Abused children – Case studies.   9. Mentally ill children – Treatment – Case studies.
   10. Juvenile homicide – Case studies.   I.   Title.
   HV6542.H449 2013
   364.152'3 – dc23 2012014179

9 8 7 6 5 4 3 2 1
Printed in the United States of America on acid-free paper

To Eldra P. Solomon
and Fran Knowles
with deep appreciation
for your friendship,
support, and encouragement
over the decades.

Contents

Foreword

Socio-cultural taboos have had the function of keeping human aggressive and destructive drives in check since the beginning of civilization. Nevertheless, history is replete with acts of violence, including that which is the topic of this book, parricide. At present, such intra-familial violence, frequently fueled by terror or desperation in adolescent parricide offenders and often by feelings of humiliation and frustration in adult parricide offenders, might erupt in families that have become destabilized in a climate of progressive social change. In *Understanding Parricide: When Sons and Daughters Kill Parents*, Professor Kathleen Heide, in her usual objective and methodical way, describes the consequences of this climate within the family as she sheds light on the incomprehensible killing of parents by their children, the tragic shattering of a multi-millenial taboo and Biblical commandments. Even though she addresses both juvenile and adult parricide, her emphasis is on juvenile offenders, as their destructive behavior is more amenable to prevention and treatment.

Throughout the 16 chapters of this highly comprehensive book, Dr. Heide examines in a progressive way the problematic entity of parricide. The first chapter is fundamental to the understanding of parricidal offenders. Maltreatment and abuse, from emotional neglect to rape, are dealt with in Chapter 2. Their psychobiological consequences on the child/adolescent are pointed out in a concise and thorough way.

In the next several chapters, Professor Heide introduces psychological, biological, social, and legal views, especially when discussing the dangerously antisocial parricide offender and his or her characterological tendency toward violent behavior. She masterfully discusses the motivational dynamics, the legal issues, and the relevant defense strategies in various case studies. Her typology of adolescent and adult parricidal offenders, proposed in her first book, *Why Kids Kill Parents*, and validated throughout 20 years of professional and forensic experience, is highlighted in the extensive case studies presented in Chapters 8 through 13. The illustrative cases show the importance of a thorough assessment of the offender's personality and its development over years of maltreatment and abuse.

The various steps in the diagnostic process and the diagnostic criteria employed by Dr. Heide when examining these young offenders are of particular interest. They not only will captivate the interest of the studious reader, but also will enhance the diagnostic and treatment choices of many mental health and legal professionals. In addition, her clear and enlightening description of the various legal defense strategies based upon the mental state of the offender and recent national court dispositions in cases of parricide will be helpful to those attorneys who are called upon to defend these offenders.

One of the purposes of Professor Heide's book is to unravel the motivational dynamics behind parricide. Why and how did the killing take place, what were the feelings that preceded it, and what are the feelings now? These are among the questions she asks the offenders, many of whom she followed up on years after first evaluating them in connection with the homicides. The answers to her questions, especially those of young adult offenders, are reported verbatim, and with them she provides the reader with a better understanding of the types of parricide offenders and the abuse, neglect, and maltreatment that frequently contributed to chronic post-traumatic stress disorder.

The information given throughout the book, including the statistics concerning the offenders and the victims and the various case circumstances, is factual, comprehensive, and concisely presented. Dr. Heide's sources are multiple: the offender, the surviving family members, school records, socio-medical inputs, and law enforcement documents. In her assessments, she corroborates facts in order to establish the credibility of the offenders. Her diagnostic criminological acumen has a solid experiential basis: look for patterns, test hypotheses, verify previous findings, and review the reports of other scholars. Her clinical evaluations are invaluable to jurors and judges tasked with determining the culpability of the young perpetrators.

Her survey of the national and international literature on parricide points out that most research on parricide, although retrospective and descriptive, has contributed to the understanding of such crimes and the motivations behind them. It testifies to the ubiquity of parricide. It also puts into evidence the presence of mental illness in some of the perpetrators, who might suffer from schizophrenia, psychotic depression, or severe personality disorder, often associated with alcohol and drug abuse.

The importance of Professor Heide's book is that it is based on her hands-on professional experience as well as her extensive knowledge of the literature. It will significantly contribute to a better understanding of the problem of parricide, and it will be an invaluable asset to mental health professionals, lawyers, judges, and scholars working in this area. Her discussion of mitigating factors, as well as that of treatment considerations and risk assessment issues in the last three chapters, will be very helpful to prosecutors and defense attorneys in plea negotiations and to judges in handing down sentencing decisions. As a professional who frequently testifies in a court of law, she also presents to the reader the moral dilemma that the various court players face when debating the culpability and the legal disposition of these young offenders.

Understanding Parricide: When Sons and Daughters Kill Parents reads in a clear and easy manner, and with an intense humanness that Dr. Heide is able to transfer into her narrative. Her book is basically a criminological treatise. It is a thoughtful, lucid, and comprehensive presentation of parricide. Her argument that maltreatment of children must be stopped in order to prevent future parricides and ensure the development of physically and mentally healthy children has a strong scientific basis. In addition, the attentive reader will derive a more basic message from her book: the formative cell of society—the family—is fractured and needs prompt attention in order to return to its basic functions. Professor Heide rightly says that parricide represents the tip of an ugly iceberg, and, in my opinion, that iceberg can be melted only by a loving family.

George B. Palermo, M.D., M.Sc.Crim., Ph.D.
Clinical Professor of Psychiatry
University of Nevada School of Medicine
and
Medical College of Wisconsin
Editor-in-Chief
International Journal of Offender Therapy and Comparative Criminology

Dr. Palermo is the author of *The Faces of Violence* and *Severe Personality Disordered Defendants and the Insanity Plea in the United States*

Preface

It has been 20 years since my first book on parricide, *Why Kids Kill Parents*, was published by Ohio State University Press. Parricide offenders, particularly when they are young, continue to make front-page news. As I was writing this preface, one of the leading new stories involved a 10-year-old boy in Ohio who reportedly had killed his mother.[1] When the story broke, I received a call from a correspondent from *USA Today*. Her questions were ones I have been asked hundreds of times by reporters since the mid-1980s, when I started to study this phenomenon: How often do kids kill parents each year? Are boys and girls equally involved? What weapons do they commonly use? Are killings of parents by kids increasing? Always the caller on the other end wants to know, why? What would cause a young person to kill his or her own mom or dad?

I have written *Understanding Parricide: When Sons and Daughters Kill Parents* with these questions in mind. My goals are to put parricide in perspective in terms of its occurrence, to provide portraits of offenders and victims, and to elucidate the pathways that lead to murder. In this book, I discuss both juveniles and adults who kill parents. The focus of this book, however, is slanted more toward adolescent parricide offenders, because these cases of parricide, as we shall see, are the most preventable. I rely heavily on clinical accounts from the literature and my own cases in order to humanize and help readers understand individuals whom most people find incomprehensible. I provide detailed accounts of parents and their killers because, in the end, few crimes are as shocking or as intensely personal as the killing of one's parents.

Understanding Parricide: When Sons and Daughters Kill Parents is a more expansive work than my earlier book. I have included some material from *Why Kids Kill Parents*, but this book provides more in-depth coverage of parricide and synthesizes what I have learned over the years from my own research and the good work completed by other professionals. When the topic turns to children killing parents, I have found that almost all people—mental health professionals, lawyers, judges, journalists, parents, and the public at large—want some basic grasp of the numbers involved. I have taken care in this book to present factual information based on my analyses of thousands of sons and daughters who were arrested for killing their parents in the United States. I have done my best to present data clearly and concisely in the text. I have included more technical information in the Notes section for researchers or students who want to know more.

Given the interest in juveniles, and especially girls, who kill parents, I have presented statistical analyses of female and youth involvement in parricide. When appropriate, I have discussed findings in terms of parents and stepparents killed and of particular victim types (fathers, mothers, stepfathers, stepmothers). I have reported on killings involving multiple victims and multiple offenders, as well as those involving one parent killed by a son or daughter acting alone.

Understanding Parricide: When Sons and Daughters Kill Parents, similar to my earlier book, differs from many books and articles that have appeared in the popular press on adolescent parricide offenders (APOs). My work, unlike others, does not start with the premise that adolescents who have killed parents killed because they were severely abused, often were terrified, and saw no other way out of an intolerable situation. Although these dynamics seem to be the most commonly encountered among APOs, this determination is a scientific one. It can be made only after careful examination by a mental health professional who has extensive experience and expertise in evaluating child abuse, family violence, homicide, and adolescent homicide.

As a clinician frequently retained by defense counsel, and on occasion by the prosecution, my interest in parricide cases, as in other types of murder cases, has been to unravel the motivational dynamics that propel defendants to kill others. At this level of analysis, the individual is my primary focus of inquiry. The corroboration of facts is critical in determining the credibility of the defendant's statements. These youths, some as young as age 8, often face severe consequences in the United States. Under these circumstances, some defendants might be motivated to lie. If tried in adult court and convicted of first-degree murder, children under age 18 can be sentenced to long prison sentences and even life without parole (LWOP) under today's laws. In June 2012, the United States Supreme Court struck down *mandatory* life sentences for defendants convicted of murders they committed as juveniles; the Court did not hold in *Miller v. Alabama* that juvenile homicide offenders could not be sentenced to LWOP under any circumstances. Accordingly, in addition to clinical interviews with youths, I routinely interview family members and other pertinent parties (e.g., teachers, neighbors, friends) and study relevant materials, including school, medical, social services, and psychological records. I also examine law enforcement reports, autopsy findings, and depositions of key witnesses.

My task as a clinician is to understand the defendant and his or her role in the killing. When subpoenaed to testify at trial, my responsibility becomes one of helping judges and juries comprehend how the defendant makes sense of the world and identify what events led this individual to kill. At the sentencing hearing, I am typically asked questions regarding the defendant's risk to the community, what treatment would benefit the defendant, and what the prognosis is (that is, the likelihood that this individual could, at some point in time, be returned to the community).

My role as a scientist who has conducted assessments of well over 100 adolescent homicide offenders is broader than my role as a psychotherapist. As a university professor who has studied adolescent homicide and family violence for nearly three decades, I have examined these cases closely in order to look for patterns, test hypotheses, and verify previous findings. Every adolescent parricide case has allowed me, in varying degrees, depending upon the nature of my involvement, to assess to what extent the findings presented and conclusions drawn appear valid.

The 12 characteristics I identified in *Why Kids Kill Parents* as commonly found in cases of severely abused parricide offenders have since been reported in the works of others. The five factors I suggested as putting youths at higher risk of killing an abusive parent have also been identified in subsequent cases. In addition, the devastating effects of being a victim or a witness to violence have been demonstrated in many research studies, as well as in clinical evaluations conducted by myself and others.

In Part One (Chapters 1–7) of *Understanding Parricide*, I provide the foundation for understanding killings of parents. In Chapter 1, I discuss the phenomenon of parricide. Critical legal and developmental issues are reviewed, as parricide offenders include young children, adolescents, and adults. I then present the typology of parricide offenders that I proposed in 1992. Case examples are used to facilitate understanding of three types of parricide offenders: the severely abused, the dangerously antisocial, and the severely mentally ill. These three types have stood the test of time, as referenced in the publications of other researchers and clinicians. The chapter concludes by exploring evolving changes in society's response to APOs since the 1980s.

Chapter 2 provides an in-depth discussion of various types of abuse and neglect, given the pivotal role that child maltreatment plays in many cases of youths who kill parents. Examples from parricide cases are utilized to aid understanding. The psychological and biological effects of early and extreme childhood maltreatment are explained, given their significance in human development. Research showing that severe abuse and neglect compromise individuals' abilities to think logically, to calm themselves, and to respond adaptively, particularly in high-stress situations, might be very relevant in understanding and in defending APOs in the legal system.

I synthesize the literature on parricide in three chapters in order to make it more accessible to readers. Chapters 3, 4, and 5 present basic facts and discuss the literature targeted to key victim groups. Attorneys, judges, media representatives, mental health professionals, researchers, students, and surviving family members will find the organization of these three chapters helpful. Chapter 3 examines killings of parents (mothers and fathers combined) and stepparents (stepmothers and stepfathers combined). Special attention is focused on parricides and stepparricides involving youths under 18, females, multiple offenders, and multiple victims. This chapter also includes a discussion of research involving double parricides (the killing of both parents) and familicides (the killing of parents and other family members, such as siblings). Chapter 4 presents statistical analyses and reviews the literature on mothers and stepmothers. Chapter 5 does the same for fathers and stepfathers.

My review of the professional literature on parricide is comprehensive and documents the universal occurrence of parricide. I identify studies and clinical reports of mothers and fathers killed in Africa, North America, South America, Asia, Australia/Oceania, and Europe. The only continent without reported studies of parricide is Antarctica which reportedly has no permanent residents. Synthesis of dozens of scholarly accounts reveals commonalities of parricide victims, offenders, and incidents across cultures.

Legal issues are covered in Chapters 6 and 7. I discuss issues related to charging and prosecuting parricide offenders in Chapter 6; that chapter includes a discussion on juvenile parricide offenders who were sentenced to death when that was legally permissible in the United States. Portraits of these cases differ dramatically from the prototypical severely abused youth and provide clear examples of APOs who appeared dangerously antisocial. Life without parole is also addressed, and an example of an abused child sentenced to a mandatory LWOP sentence prior to the Supreme Court's decision in *Miller v. Alabama* is presented.

Issues pertinent to defending parricide offenders are covered in Chapter 7. The legal and psychological underpinnings of the battered child syndrome are discussed, given its relevance to children and adolescents who have killed abusive parents. Attention is focused on mental status defenses and on the doctrine of self-defense.

The next section of the book (Chapters 8–13) focuses on clinical assessment and case studies of parricide offenders. Chapter 8 discusses the need for a thorough assessment of parricide offenders by a mental health professional with expertise in domestic violence and homicide. The importance of personality development in understanding the involvement of offspring in the killings of parents is stressed. The discussion also includes ways of identifying parricide offenders whose destructive and violent behavior appears characterologically based, as these individuals represent a continuing threat to society. Chapter 8 serves as an introduction to the five chapters that follow it, which provide an in-depth look at APOs whom I evaluated.

The offenders in the cases presented fit the profile of severely abused, severely mentally ill, and dangerously antisocial parricide offenders. I also include a case in which drugs and anger proved to be a deadly combination. Long-standing anger, often the result of abuse and/or neglect, appears to depict the underlying dynamics of a possible fourth type of parricide offender; further research is needed in order to confirm this hypothesis. These case studies look at parricide offenders at several points in time, including before the killings, after their arrest for murder, and several years after the disposition of their case (through acquittal by insanity, conviction at trial, or a negotiated plea).

In the final section, society's response to parricide offenders is examined. In Chapter 14, I, joined by clinical psychologist Eldra P. Solomon, discuss treatment issues relevant to the three groups of parricide offenders. In Chapter 15, I provide long-term follow-up on 11 parricide offenders I evaluated years after they killed one or more parents. In Chapter 16, the final chapter of the book, I address risk assessment with respect to the three parricide offender types. The book concludes with a discussion of recommendations designed to prevent parricides. These efforts are targeted at reducing child maltreatment and at providing mental health services to individuals and families in need.

Parricide appears to be the tip of a very ugly iceberg. Over the years, I have been surprised by the number of therapy clients of mine, university students, and others familiar with my work in parricide who have told me that as adolescents they had seriously considered killing their abusive parents. In a study of women who had been severely abused, Dr. Eldra Solomon and I found that 50% reported that prior to age 18 they had seriously considered killing their abusive parents.[2] In addition to asking why some adolescents kill their parents, we need to be asking why more youths do not and what we can do as a nation to ensure that children today grow up in homes where they are loved and protected by their parents.

Kathleen M. Heide, Ph.D.
Professor of Criminology
University of South Florida

Acknowledgments

There are so many people who helped make this book possible. I want to thank the adolescent and adult parricide offenders who shared the most personal aspects of their lives with me when I evaluated them. I express my appreciation in particular to those who have kept in touch with me over the years and have given me permission to tell their stories using pseudonyms in the hope that sharing their experiences will help others. I also am indebted to the defendants' surviving family members and their friends, teachers, and employers who related their knowledge of the defendants and their life experiences even when it was so painful to do so.

I am grateful to the attorneys who have consulted with me on parricide offenders over the past three decades. I have been fortunate to have worked with many defense attorneys and prosecutors and to have testified before judges who believed in the fundamental principles of justice, had compassion for both offenders and victims, and were motivated to do the right thing. I learned a great deal from many of them.

Writing a book that is research based involves a great deal of work. I want to thank the many graduate and undergraduate students at the University of South Florida (USF) who assisted me over the years in searching the professional literature for studies on parricide, indexing articles, transcribing interviews, checking newspaper data bases, and developing a data base of the thousands of parricide offenders arrested in the United States. These students included Dr. Denise Paquette Boots, Brett Mervis, Rebecca Dimond, Sarah Sands, Carol Sedor Trent, Raleigh Blasdell, Mike Kinney, Jaclyn Cole, and Dr. Oliver Chan. I wish to acknowledge with gratitude several students who worked with me on parricide publications discussed in this book. These include Dr. Denise Paquette Boots, now a professor at University of Texas at Dallas; Jessica McCurdy, a graduate of Georgetown Law School and now working as a lawyer; and Autumn Frie, a doctoral student at USF. I want to express my appreciation to Andrew J. Atchison, a graduate of Florida State University Law School and now an attorney, who assisted me in updating the legal analysis of the battered child defense.

Special thanks to my colleagues in the Department of Criminology at USF for creating an environment where faculty and students are encouraged to pursue research. I appreciate the support of those who served as Chairperson of our department while I was writing this book: Dr. Tom Mieczkowski and Dr. Mike Leiber. I am grateful to the USF administration for their continued interest in my research, particularly Dean Catherine Batsch, College of Behavioral and Community Sciences, and Lara Wade, Media/Public Affairs Manager. I appreciate the assistance given by Claudia Dodd, USF research librarian, in doing a final check of the literature to make sure it was as up to date and accurate as possible. I acknowledge with gratitude my friend and former administrative assistant Mary Sweely, who for years did whatever was needed to help me as I was balancing my role as an active researcher with my responsibilities as a college administrator. I also thank Dr. Sandy Schneider, Professor of Psychology, for her friendship, support, and advice in research matters over the years.

I am indebted to Eldra P. Solomon, Ph.D., an internationally renowned psychologist and biologist, for her assistance in co-authoring the treatment chapter (Chapter 14), in reviewing the biological discussions in this book, and in reacting to the content of the entire book. Her insights and suggestions were invaluable. I am also very grateful to my dear friend Frances "Fran" Knowles for eagerly reading every chapter of the book; her excellent editorial suggestions and encouragement helped to keep me on track. I also want to acknowledge Brian Godcharles, a USF undergraduate Honors College student who read every chapter and critiqued it from the standpoint of an advanced college student. I also appreciate the meticulous reading of the page proofs by USF students Stephanie Bramm and Michelle Ingraham.

I am very grateful to the editors at Oxford University Press for their assistance and patience over the years while I was traveling to do follow-up interviews with parricide offenders and writing this book. I appreciate Maura Roessner for believing in this project and Nicholas Liu, Dana Bliss, Karen Kwak, and Vasuki Ravichandran for seeing the book through its production stages. I express my deep appreciation to several academic and professional reviewers; these include Sara G. West, MD, Case Western Reserve University School of Medicine; Craig Alldredge, criminal defense attorney and veteran public defender, Clearwater, Florida; and a third reviewer who wished to remain anonymous. This book is a stronger one because of the care with which they read the manuscript and the astute comments they made.

Last but not least, I remain indebted to my family for their love and presence in my life. In particular, I recognize with deep appreciation my mother, Eleanor Heide Halligan, who was a loving and devoted mother, and a powerful role model for all of us. The older I get, the more I realize how fortunate I was to have been raised in a home and to be part of a family in which children are loved, valued, and protected.

PART ONE
CLINICAL AND LEGAL ISSUES

1 The Phenomenon of Parricide

- St. Johns, Arizona—An 8-year-old boy fired multiple shots, killing his father and a boarder who lived with them in their home. The boy used a single action .22 caliber rifle that required reloading after each shot. His father had given him the rifle as a gift and taught him how to use it.[1]
- Conyers, Georgia—Twin 16-year-old sisters were charged with stabbing their mother to death. According to a neighbor, the girls' mother was afraid of the girls and feared something like this might happen.[2]
- Albuquerque, New Mexico—A 14-year-old boy admitted that he had shot his father and stepmother in the head after enduring years of physical and emotional abuse. He killed his 13-year-old stepsister so she would not tell on him. He buried all three bodies in a pile of manure on the ranch where he and his family lived.[3]
- Myakka City, Florida—A 20-year-old man bludgeoned to death his father, mother, 11-year-old brother, and grandmother on Thanksgiving night. He wrote a note saying he killed them not out of hatred, but rather from selfishness. He intended to take his own life and did not want to die alone.[4]
- Caratunk, Maine—A 24-year-old schizophrenic man bludgeoned his mother to death with a hatchet. He had been released two months earlier from a psychiatric hospital against the advice of his doctors. He reportedly killed his mother because the pope told him that she was involved with Saddam Hussein and Al Qaeda.[5]

These five cases, all shocking and tragic, are examples of *parricide*. The term "parricide" technically refers to the killing of a close relative, but it has increasingly become identified in the public mind with the murder of an individual's father (*patricide*) or mother (*matricide*). Media coverage of several cases in the United States in the 1980s in which adolescent sons and daughters acted alone or with others to kill parents who allegedly abused them generated widespread interest in this phenomenon. One of these cases—the Jahnke case—captured the interest and compassion of the nation.[6] In November 1982, a 16-year-old boy, Richie Jahnke, and his 17-year-old sister, Deborah, retrieved several guns from their father's arsenal of weapons. After methodically placing these weapons throughout their home, the two teenagers lay in wait for their father, Richard Jahnke, a 38-year-old IRS investigator, to return home with his wife from a dinner celebrating their 20th anniversary. As Mr. Jahnke walked toward the garage, Richie discharged a shotgun cartridge into his father's body, ending years of the father's verbal abuse against the whole family, physical abuse of his wife and son, and sexual abuse of his daughter.[7]

Interest in parricide cases extends beyond the United States.[8] An analysis of on-line media sources revealed that cases of children killing their parents become headline news across the globe. The media disproportionately cover the most disturbing cases of parricide—those perpetrated by children and adolescents, committed by females, and involving multiple victims.[9]

Homicides involving three or more victims are referred to as *multicides*; when those killed are family members, the mass murders are referred to as *familicides*.[10] News coverage was extensive, for example, in the case of 22-year-old Jeremy Bamber of Essex, England, who was charged and subsequently convicted of the 1985 killings of his adoptive father and mother, his stepsister, and her two six-year-old twin sons. Bamber reportedly shot them 25 times, mostly at close range, with a semi-automatic rifle. This case has continued to generate significant media attention over the past 25 years due to Bamber's appeals and the discovery of new evidence.

The public's fascination with parricide dates back thousands of years. The killing of fathers and mothers has been a recurrent theme in mythology and literature, as is evident in the stories of Orestes, Oedipus, Alcmaeon, King Arthur, and Hamlet.[11] Analyses of on-line archival data bases of the *New York Times* and the *Chicago Tribune* leave no doubt that the killings of parents were newsworthy events in the second half of the 19th century.[12] For several months in 1873, New Yorkers, "fed by front-page and multicolumned stories in the metropolitan press," for example, wondered whether the killing of a wealthy man who had repeatedly abused and threatened to kill his wife and children by his 19-year-old epileptic son was "a crime, the act of a madman, or a noble expression of filial duty?"[13] The case of Lizzie Borden, the 32-year-old daughter charged with killing her parents in 1892 remains notorious more than 100 years after the double parricide occurred.[14] The rhyme "Lizzie Borden took an axe and gave her mother forty whacks, and when she saw what she had done, she gave her father forty-one" has immortalized her for generations.[15]

The 1960 film *Psycho* is widely remembered more than 50 years after its release for its depiction of a mentally ill man who killed his mother, preserved her body, and adopted her persona to kill young women.[16] *Natural Born Killers,* a box office hit in 1994 and still a popular film today, chronicles multiple killings committed by two madly in-love adolescents. The killing spree begins with the boy killing the girl's sexually abusive father and neglectful mother, and it continues as the couple crosses the country.[17] Ronald DeFeo's slaughter of his entire family—mother, father, two sisters, and two brothers—in Amityville, New York, in 1974 led to the making of multiple films, including *The Amityville Horror* in 1979 and another with the same name more than 25 years later.[18] Songs extolling parricide have also appeared in recent years.[19] Numerous books in the true-crime genre have been written in the past four decades about adolescent sons and daughters killing their parents.[20]

Parricide and parricidal thoughts were major themes in the writings of Sigmund Freud, the founder of psychoanalysis.[21] His insights continue to be instrumental in the analyses of patricidal and matricidal acts and fantasies many decades later.[22] Why do parricidal acts both attract and repel at the same time? The killing of parents is considered taboo in all cultures.[23] It is in drastic contradiction to two biblical commandments: "Honor thy father and mother" and "thou shall not kill." Perhaps a major reason for people's interest in parricide since time immemorial is that all members of society are children (either minor or adult children) and many, if not most, are parents of (minor or adult) children. It is understandable that one might wonder whether "everyday people" are at risk of killing their parents or of being killed by their offspring.

PARRICIDE IN PERSPECTIVE

Despite the attention these cases garner, parricides are rare events in the United States and in other countries where this phenomenon has been studied.[24] In the United States, homicides reported to the Federal Bureau of Investigation by law enforcement agencies across the nation indicate that, on the average, between 200 and 300 parents are killed by their juvenile or adult offspring every year.[25] Mothers and fathers constitute about 2% of all murder victims in the United States,[26] Japan,[27] and Australia[28]; less than 4% of those in Canada[29] and Serbia[30]; between 2% and 3% of murder victims in France[31]; and between 1% and 5% of all homicides in Tunisia.[32] Although most parents killed are the biological parents of the murderers, parricide victims also include stepparents and adoptive parents. Arrest data indicate that over the 32-year period of 1976–2007, on the average, approximately 132 biological fathers, 115 biological mothers, 47 stepfathers, and 7 stepmothers were killed each year in the United States.[33] National data are not available on the number of adoptive parents killed.

Most parents and stepparents are killed in single-victim, single-offender incidents. Over the 32-year period of 1976–2007, 84% of offenders arrested in the United States for parricide killed a single parent or stepparent by themselves.[34] Nine percent used an accomplice to help them complete the murder. Only 7% of offenders arrested for parricide killed two or more victims by themselves (6.3%) or with the help of others (0.8%).

Many of the "children" who kill their parents in single-victim, single-offender situations are over the age of 18 and are technically adults from a legal perspective.[35] However, as shown in Table 1-1, more than one in five of those who take the lives of their parents or stepparents are minors in the eyes of the law (under age 18), and more than 30% are under 20 years old.[36] Close inspection of Table 1-1 reveals that of those arrested for parricides, there are higher percentages of adolescents up to age 20 involved in the killings of stepmothers (45%) and stepfathers (44%) than of biological fathers (33%) and mothers (20%).

If the age range for offenders is extended to include those through age 24, the percentage increases to nearly half of all parricide offenders arrested. More than half of individuals arrested for killing fathers and more than one-third arrested for killing mothers are under age 25. The percentages of those under age 25 who are arrested for killing stepparents are higher than percentages of those arrested for killing biological parents. Extending the offender age range to age 24 when discussing parricide offenders makes sense in two contexts. Many individuals live with their parents until their early 20s before they make their transition to independent living. In addition, scientific findings suggest that the brain is not fully mature until about age 25.[37]

TABLE 1-1 Offender age by parent type: single-victim, single-offender incidents, United States (1976–2007)

Offender Age (Years)	Father	Mother	Stepfather	Stepmother	Total
Under 18	798	392	411	52	1653
	(21.8%)	(13.3%)	(30.4%)	(33.8%)	(20.4%)
18–19	396	202	180	17	795
	(10.8%)	(6.9%)	(13.3%)	(11.0%)	(9.8%)
20–24	777	443	317	30	1567
	(21.2%)	(15.1%)	(23.4%)	(19.5%)	(19.3%)
25–29	561	451	171	15	1198
	(15.3%)	(15.3%)	(12.6%)	(9.7%)	(14.8%)
30–39	699	652	186	19	1556
	(19.1%)	(22.2%)	(13.7%)	(12.3%)	(19.2%)
40–49	334	459	65	9	867
	(9.1%)	(15.6%)	(4.8%)	(5.8%)	(10.7%)
50–59	79	259	24	7	369
	(2.2%)	(8.8%)	(1.8%)	(4.5%)	(4.5%)
Over 60	22	85	0	5	112
	(0.6%)	(2.9%)	—	(3.2%)	(1.4%)
Total	3666	2943	1354	154	8117
	(45.2%)	(36.3%)	(16.7%)	(1.9%)	(100.0%)

• Supplementary Homicide Report offender data, national estimates.

$\chi^2(21) = 690.307$; Cramer's V = .168; p < .001.

AGE: CRITICAL LEGAL AND DEVELOPMENTAL ISSUES

Age is an essential factor in evaluating offspring who kill their parents. Parricide offenders can be young children, adolescents, or adults. Cases exist of very young children killing parents, such as the 8-year-old boy mentioned earlier. Not surprisingly, cases of young children killing parents are very rare. During the 32-year period of 1976–2007, for example, 33 children under age 12 were arrested for killing parents in the United States.[38] These children killed 17 fathers, nine mothers, and seven stepfathers. With the exception of two matricide cases, the children involved acted alone. One perpetrator was 7 years old, two were age 8, three were age 9, 10 were age 10, and 17 were age 11.

Young children, particularly those 12 and under, are sometimes referred to in the professional literature as children, pre-adolescents, or preteens in order to distinguish them from adolescents or teenagers.[39] Precise definitions are rarely given because most of these terms have no specific ages attached to them. In this book, children under age 13 are referred to as young children so as to avoid confusion.

Two terms often used interchangeably in the literature are conceptually distinct: "juvenile" and "adolescent." *Juvenile status*, unlike "adolescence," is a legal term that clearly distinguishes childhood from adult status. In the United States, individuals are recognized as adults at age 18. By law, individuals aged 17 and under are considered children or juveniles unless a court rules otherwise. However, despite the fact that the age of majority is 18 according to federal law, the maximum age of juvenile court jurisdiction is not uniform across the 50 states. Thirty-seven states set it at age 17, 10 at age

16, and three at age 15. All 50 states and the District of Columbia have mechanisms for transferring juveniles to adult court.[40]

Adolescence is now typically defined as beginning at the time of puberty, the period of sexual development. This period is marked by significant physical, physiological, cognitive, and psychological development and is a turbulent time. The age at which children enter puberty varies by individual but now typically is about 10 to 12 years. By the time youths have reached age 13, almost all will be in their adolescent development period. In girls, puberty is completed by about age 14 to 16. For boys, puberty typically is completed by age 16 to 18.[41] From a biological perspective, in contrast to the legal definition of "juvenile," adolescence continues until the individual becomes a young adult, at about age 20 to 24.

More than 70 years ago, two psychiatrists recognized the importance of distinguishing between younger children and adolescents in understanding the motivational dynamics behind youths' involvement in murder.[42] Younger children typically do not fully appreciate the concept of death and have difficulty accepting that their actions led to an irreversible result. Clinicians have long observed that younger children frequently act impulsively without clear goals in mind.[43] They can be unduly influenced to engage in lethal action by mentally ill, unstable, or unscrupulous parents.[44] In addition, younger children who kill are much more likely to be severely disturbed than adolescents.[45] Adolescents, in contrast, are more likely to kill because of the lifestyle that they have adopted or in response to situational demands or environmental constraints that they believe parents or others have placed upon them.[46]

Older juveniles, unlike their younger counterparts, are typically charged when they kill parents. Under existing transfer policies, adolescent parricide offenders are likely to be prosecuted in adult court due to the seriousness of their crime. Adolescent parricide offenders (APOs) under 18 might shoot the same gun or wield the same knife as their adult counterparts, but equivalent weapon usage does not make the slayers equivalent players. Holding juvenile offenders as fully accountable as their adult counterparts has been successfully challenged in recent court cases involving juveniles sentenced to death for murder,[47] juveniles sentenced to life for nonlethal felonies,[48] and juveniles sentenced to mandatory life sentences for murder.[49]

APOs differ from adult offspring who murder their parents in several important ways. Adolescents, unlike adults, are at a higher risk of becoming parricide offenders when conditions in the home are unfavorable because of their limited options and alternatives. Unlike adults, adolescents cannot simply leave and set up residence elsewhere. Although running away is technically considered a status offense applying only to children, rather than a crime, it still subjects the youth to juvenile court intervention. Individuals who shelter a runaway without the parent's permission are guilty of a crime in some states.[50]

Typically, juveniles who commit parricide have considered running away. Unfortunately, many did not know of any place where they could seek refuge. Those who did run away usually either were picked up and returned home or went back voluntarily. Surviving on their own is hardly a realistic alternative for youths with meager financial resources, limited job skills, and incomplete education. State regulations invariably mandate their attendance at school, generally until age 16,[51] and federal law imposes strict limitations on when and how much juveniles, particularly those under 16, can work.[52]

Adolescents, as a group, also have far less experience than adults and cannot be expected to cope as well with deplorable environmental conditions. Adolescents are not as likely to see alternative courses of action and weigh different strategies; their cognitive development, judgment, and character are not equivalent to that of adults.[53] Research has established that the higher cortical areas (prefrontal cortex) of the brain associated with thinking and judgment are not fully developed until individuals are in their mid-20s.[54]

Because adults have more options and resources and are developmentally more mature than juveniles, an adult killing a parent would be expected to be an unusual occurrence. Logically, an emotionally and mentally healthy adult who found contact with his or her parents intolerable would simply leave the familial situation. One would expect to find more psychopathology, or severe mental illness, among adult offenders who kill their parents than among adolescents who commit the same act. Empirical studies and clinical case reports, discussed in later chapters, have confirmed this hypothesis.[55]

FOCUS OF THIS BOOK

Given these differences, discussing all parricide offenders as though they are the same is ill-advised. This book primarily focuses on juvenile and adolescent parricide offenders. As noted above, these terms are often used interchangeably in the professional literature. In general, children and adolescents who kill parents are more receptive to effective intervention and prevention strategies than their adult counterparts. Even after killing a parent, some young people might eventually become contributing members of society.

Although the spotlight is on young parricide offenders, information pertinent to adult offenders is presented throughout the book. Material on adult parricide offenders is included in order to enable readers to understand the differences between juvenile/adolescent and adult parricide offenders with respect to motivational dynamics, mental health histories and diagnoses, legal issues and defense strategies, treatment, and risk assessment. My synthesis of the existing literature on APOs and adult parricide offenders is intended to assist lawyers and mental health professionals who are tasked with representing and evaluating individuals who kill parents. It likely will be helpful also to judges involved in sentencing parricide offenders, legislators drafting legislation with respect to battered children, and social services providers developing policies regarding abused and neglected children. The discussion might prove useful to school guidance counselors and clinicians considering intervention strategies for individuals involved in extreme family conflict.

A TYPOLOGY OF PARRICIDE OFFENDERS

More than 20 years ago, I proposed a typology of parricide offenders based on my review of the professional literature and my own clinical evaluations. This typology was originally published in my 1992 book entitled *Why Kids Kill Parents: Child Abuse and Adolescent Homicide*.[56] I identified three types of parricide offenders: the *severely abused child* who kills to end the abuse, the *severely mentally ill child*, and the *dangerously antisocial child*. These three types have stood the test of time, as judged by cases referred to me for consultation or evaluation and the use of this typology by other clinicians and researchers.[57] Children and adolescents who kill parents tend to fall mainly into one of two categories: severely abused or dangerously antisocial (their adult counterparts usually are classified as severely mentally ill or dangerously antisocial). Not all cases fit neatly into these types; these cases are discussed briefly following the presentation of the three types. In this book, I refer to each type as a parricide offender rather than a child (e.g., severely abused *parricide offender* rather than severely abused *child*) in order to avoid confusion. Most offspring who kill parents, as noted above, are adults.

The Severely Abused Parricide Offender

This type is the most common one found among APOs. In these cases, an extensive and long-standing history of abuse is often easily corroborated through interviews with relatives, neighbors, and friends, and sometimes is documented by social service agencies. These youths increasingly come to perceive that their physical well-being or the lives of others are threatened, or that their psychological survival is at stake. They kill in response to terror or in desperation. They typically have sought help from others to no avail. They have often attempted to run away and sometimes have considered, or even attempted, suicide. From their perspective, there is no way out other than murder.[58]

In-depth portraits of youths who have slain parents have frequently suggested that these youths killed their parents because they could no longer tolerate conditions in the home environment.[59] These children, typically adolescents, were psychologically abused by one or both parents and often witnessed and/or suffered physical, sexual, and verbal abuse. They did not usually have histories of severe mental illness or of serious and extensive delinquent behavior. Close reading of these reports suggests that these youths often suffered from long-standing depression and *post-traumatic stress disorder (PTSD)*, although these disorders were not formally diagnosed in all cases. PTSD is an anxiety disorder that develops in some individuals when they are exposed to a traumatic, often life-threatening, event. Individuals with PTSD re-experience the traumatic event over and over through intrusive thoughts, images, flashbacks, or nightmares. They try to avoid people or events associated with the traumatic event and numb their feelings. In addition, they tend to be in a state of hyperarousal, easily startled, and on red alert for changes that might signal danger.[60]

Terry Adams (pseudonym), one of my earliest parricide cases, clearly fit this profile. Terry and his two older sisters had long been physically and emotionally abused by their parents, both alcoholics. When Terry's sisters reached the age of 18, they left the family home. Once they were gone, Terry became the sole target of the abuse. At the age of 16, Terry was caught in what he perceived as an endless cycle of torment inflicted by his parents. He decided there was no alternative other than to leave home and make it on his own.

At the time when Terry was making plans to run away, his parents' home was being renovated. Because of the construction, Terry had to go through his parents' bedroom to get out of the house. While he was attempting to escape through his parents' bedroom during the early morning hours, Mr. Adams woke up and confronted his son. Terry told his dad that he was tired of the way he was living, that he was old enough to make it on his own, and that he knew what he was doing. Terry maintained that he could quit school legally. Maybe he could not leave home legally, Terry told his dad, but he did not care; he was leaving anyway. Mr. Adams slugged his son, and the boy fell. When the youth got back up, his father pushed him hard, and he fell into a closet where several guns were kept, including a .22 caliber rifle. Terry grabbed the rifle and fired at his father. He remembered his father screaming, "Oh, my God!"

Terry recalled that his mother, who was in the bed when her husband was shot, woke up when the gun went off. Terry could not remember actually shooting his parents, particularly his mother. All he could remember was her face "when she sat up in bed…the agony within the terror …. The rest of it is more or less, sort of hazed out for me. I remember waking up completely. Standing there looking at two dead bodies. Two people. What have I done now, you know. Like it was a dream."

Court records revealed that four petitions alleging neglect, abuse, and physical abuse in the Adams home had been filed and investigated by the state social services agency. Three of these petitions targeted Terry as the victim; they had been filed in the two years preceding the homicides. The most recent referral was made when Terry was 15, when the state agency received a report that both parents were physically and emotionally abusing Terry. This investigation followed Terry's admission to a hospital for stomach problems. The hospital authorities could find no physical cause for the problems and decided that his ailments were caused by emotional problems related to the home situation. Terry was placed first in a foster care home, and then with his oldest sister and her husband, with whom he remained for three months. Thereafter the boy was returned to his parents under protective services supervision, which officially lasted nine months. Ten months after the state agency terminated supervision, Mr. and Mrs. Adams were dead, and Terry Adams was charged with two counts of first-degree murder.

Both killings were the reaction of a terrified youth who was trying desperately to get away from an abusive home environment. Terry's account suggested that he might have been so overwhelmed by the stress that in the moments when he fired the shots that killed his parents, he might have been unaware of what he was doing and, thus, not culpable. Despite Terry's documented history of abuse and the circumstances surrounding the killings, the youth was advised by his public defender to plead guilty to two counts of second-degree murder and was sentenced to life imprisonment. The judge who sentenced Terry to life was the same judge who had presided over the dependency proceedings alleging abuse. Upon being sentenced, Terry wrote the following "Request for Freedom":

I cry out at night, "I'm so sorry! I just couldn't take the fear and pain anymore, I won't hurt anyone again!" It doesn't matter what the degree of pain and fear was on me, all that matters is what I've done. I try to tell them I [am] so very young and have a lot to do with my life, but it doesn't matter. The public just says, "You shouldn't of done it, you shouldn't of done it!" I hear them lock the bars around me and I say to myself, "I can't stay in prison all my life, I've lived in a world of bounage [bondage] before and now once again." The world has no pity for me. They just don't understand. I couldn't take it anymore, I [am] human and make mistakes, I just made a big mistake and now I'm paying for it by doing life.

The Severely Mentally Ill Parricide Offender

Adult parricide offenders are often diagnosed as severely mentally ill. On occasion, adolescents who kill parents are also recognized as gravely mentally disturbed.[61]

These individuals typically suffer from a long history of serious mental illness that has been diagnosed and known to family members. Many of these individuals are diagnosed with psychotic conditions on the schizophrenia spectrum, particularly schizophrenia or schizoaffective disorder.[62] On occasion, they are viewed as having severe depression with psychotic features or bipolar disorder with psychotic features at the time of the killing.

The killing of the parent, for this type of parricide offender, is directly related to the mental illness. For example, the offender might have *delusions* (false beliefs that have no basis in reality) that Satan or God is commanding him or her to kill the parents. Offenders might have *hallucinations* (false sensory perceptions, such as seeing or hearing things that are not occurring), for example, that God is whispering to them and that choirs of angels are chanting, "You need to kill your father. Now is the time, time, time." Severely mentally ill parricide offenders frequently have been prescribed psychotropic medication to control their symptoms and might have spent time in a psychiatric facility. These killings often occur when psychotic individuals stop taking their medication.

In some parricide cases, severe mental illness is not mentioned, but close reading of the offender's behavior and the crime details suggests that the offender was severely disturbed at the time of the murder. The likelihood of severe pathology is particularly high when multiple family members are killed, extreme violence is used (e.g., decapitation of victims, dismembering of corpses), or unusual weapons are selected (e.g., swords or machetes). On occasion, the mental illness is so severe that prosecution is halted until the defendant is treated and restored to competency. *Competency* refers to an individual's ability to comprehend the nature of the criminal charges and to assist in one's own defense. In some cases, prosecution is not pursued because the judge determines, after reviewing the evaluations of mental health professionals, that the offender is unlikely to become legally competent. In these situations, individuals are civilly committed to mental hospitals where they will stay until they are no longer perceived as mentally ill and a danger to themselves or others.

The son of President Reagan's personal attorney, Michael Miller, made national news when, at age 20, he was charged with first-degree murder and rape after confessing to killing and sexually assaulting his mother. Mrs. Miller's nude and battered body was found sprawled in the master bedroom of her opulent home in March 1983. Available reports suggested that the Millers were a close-knit, religious family. However, evidence indicated that both of the Miller sons had suffered from mental illness. The older son, Jeff, had suffered a "nervous breakdown" while a student at Dartmouth College. Jeff committed suicide in 1981 while in a clinic that specialized in the treatment of schizophrenia. Michael was very upset by his brother's suicide, moved back to his parents' home, and sought psychiatric treatment.[63]

Court documents revealed that the psychiatrist who had been treating Michael for eight months prior to the matricide was "of the opinion that Miller has been and is presently suffering from severe mental disorders evidenced by manifestation of acute psychotic behavior and suicidal tendencies…and is in need of immediate and intensive psychiatric treatment and observation."[64] After hearing testimony from four mental health experts, the presiding judge found Michael incompetent to stand trial and committed him to a state mental health facility, suspending all criminal proceedings against him, until he was restored to competency.[65] Later, Michael was tried by a jury which acquitted him of the rape but found him guilty of first-degree murder. The judge subsequently set aside the jury verdict on the murder charge, found the defendant not guilty by reason of insanity, and sent him to a mental hospital.[66]

In other cases, mental illness presents no bar to prosecution, as was evident to me when I was consulted in the case of 19-year-old Jonathan Cantero, a psychotic matricide offender convicted of murder in the first degree. According to media accounts, the adolescent, pursuant to a detailed plan that he had drafted, stabbed his mother 40 times in the chest, stomach, and back, and slit her throat.[67] He told police that he tried to cut off his mother's left hand to demonstrate his allegiance to Satan but was too scared to collect his mother's blood in a vial as he had planned. After the killing, Jonathan had etched a pentagram (a five-pointed star with Satanic associations) on his palm and used a Polaroid camera to photograph his palm and the red welts that formed the star. He said he recited the following words over his mother's dead body: "Lord Satan thou I had stricken this woman from the earth, I have slain the womb from which I was born. I have ended her reign of desecration of my mind, she is no longer of me, yet only a simple serpent on a lower plane."[68]

After the murder, Jonathan partially burned and buried his notes, the photograph, the poem, and the clothes that he was wearing. When he was arrested two weeks after the homicide, he led police to the site where the charred evidence was buried. Jonathan's notes included two lists that he had drafted describing 11 steps in the plan to kill his mother and eight materials that he would need to execute the murder.[69]

Defense counsel planned for months to argue that Jonathan was legally insane at the time of the crime. Two mental health experts who examined Jonathan observed that the youth was extremely delusional and diagnosed him as paranoid schizophrenic. They concluded that the adolescent apparently heard voices commanding him to kill his mother at the time of the homicidal incident and appeared legally insane. Shortly before trial, however, the defense counsel entered a plea to murder in the first degree in accordance with his client's wishes. Jonathan, although clearly psychotic, had been found competent to stand trial (he knew the nature of the proceedings and was able to assist counsel in his own defense) and was therefore empowered to make his own decisions regarding legal strategies and pleas. According to the public defender who represented him, Jonathan did not want to put his family through the ordeal of a trial and preferred to plead guilty to first-degree murder in exchange for a life sentence. Neither the State of Florida nor the Cantero family was interested in seeking the death penalty, and the adolescent's plea was accepted.

In some instances, severely mentally ill parricide offenders are diagnosed as having a brief psychotic disorder, which can be brought on by overwhelming stress and exacerbated by excessive substance abuse. These individuals do not have a history of psychosis. However, they might have a history of depression, as in the case of Marcus Sanchez (pseudonym), a 17-year-old boy who appeared to have had a psychotic break when he killed his father. This youth was born to two drug-addicted parents. Marcus's mother reportedly stopped using intravenous drugs when Marcus was 3 or 4 years old. Marcus's father, unlike his mother, continued to use illegal drugs and to drink heavily throughout the boy's childhood and adolescence. Family members corroborated allegations of multiple forms of child maltreatment and of domestic violence between Marcus's parents.

Marcus had a long history of serious depression that began when he was 7 or 8 years old. It intensified when his father left his mother; Marcus was about 9 years old at that time. Marcus explained that "two forces were going against each other." He characterized it as the will to live and the wish to die struggling with each other. He acknowledged, "I hated my life." When asked what he hated about his life, Marcus said, "Everything." He related having to deal with the rules, hard times in the family, threats made by his mother that he would have to go back to his dad, and "just living." Marcus said, "It seemed better just to die." The "pain was always there." Marcus frequently thought about killing himself and had attempted suicide at least five times. He had intentionally hurt himself by using razor blades or burning himself about 20 times. He whipped himself or had others whip him. Marcus explained that the pain made him feel good. Records confirmed that Marcus had been in and out of counseling for years.

By the time Marcus was 15 years old, he was drinking heavily and using excessive amounts of drugs, particularly crystal methamphetamine, LSD, and marijuana. Family and friends recalled that Marcus seemed to have a lot of anger. He had episodes of acting out violently, such as punching walls, but he had not taken his anger out on people in the past.

Marcus's mother said that Marcus got into legal difficulties and became "a problem child" about two or three years prior to his arrest for killing his father. He was caught shoplifting on two occasions and was later expelled from school; "[f]rom there, it was downhill." She witnessed strange behavior from Marcus, which she believed was drug induced. He would not go to school and did not cooperate with home schooling. He worked for a short time and then quit. She acknowledged frequently threatening to send Marcus to live with his father as a way to control him. She recalled Marcus's saying that he hated it there and threatening to kill himself. On one or two occasions, she did send Marcus to his father's home because he was out of control. Marcus spent over a year there at one point. She thought everything was going well, but she later learned that Marcus was "ditching school" and was out of control there.

A few months before the homicide, Marcus was arrested for violation of curfew, possession of marijuana, and driving without a license. The judge who heard the case delivered a stern warning, imposed a fine, and gave permission for Marcus to leave the state to go live with his father. The hearing occurred a few weeks before the homicide. Marcus preferred living with his father to being locked up. He intended to go back to his father's home, work at his paternal uncle's auto body shop, go to school to get his driver's license, pay the fine, pay off the truck (co-owned by his father and the man's girlfriend), save some money, and then return to his home city and get an apartment there.

Mr. Sanchez was no longer physically abusive when Marcus went to live with him. According to witness accounts, the two got along reasonably well during the 10 days Marcus stayed with his dad, and they contemplated getting an apartment together. Marcus celebrated Father's Day by taking his dad out for several meals and spending the day with him. The two reportedly smoked marijuana a lot and got drunk, and they stayed that way as the days passed. Marcus recalled having fun with his dad during this period.

One day, in the early morning hours, Marcus, tormented by voices that commanded him to shoot, stood at his father's bedside with a loaded shotgun aimed at the man's head. He kept hearing a man's voice both inside and outside his head saying, "You have to do it." Marcus later said that the voice was "controlling me, controlling my body." Marcus had never heard the voice before. He described the experience as "scary" and said that he felt "uncontrollable." The voice was telling him to shoot his father. Marcus prayed to God to please not let this happen. As he tried to fend off the voices repeatedly telling him to kill his father, the gun went off. Mr. Sanchez's body jolted as the bullet lodged in his head. Marcus's ears were ringing and the whole room was "smokey." His father made no noise at all. Marcus believed his father was dead and thought he felt his father's spirit as he was walking out of the room.

At the time of my clinical evaluation, Marcus suffered from major depression of a recurrent and long-standing nature. His history of suicide attempts and of self-medicating himself was particularly alarming. Marcus clearly met the diagnostic criteria for PTSD. Marcus also had a substantiated history of poly-substance abuse and dependency with respect to marijuana, alcohol, crystal methamphetamine, and hallucinogens. Marcus's abuse of and dependence upon drugs exacerbated his depression and resulted in an increase in behavioral and cognitive disorganization. Long before the shooting, Marcus had lost the ability to perform the normal developmental tasks of adolescence. The results of testing administered by a consulting psychologist to Marcus a few weeks after the killing were consistent with that of an individual experiencing high levels of distress and with a severe mental disorder. The overall pattern in the testing was consistent with that of individuals whose thinking was disturbed, unreliable, and characterized by distortions of reality. The quality of Marcus's thinking appeared to have been impacted by his angry, pessimistic, and paranoid feelings.

Marcus pleaded guilty to second-degree murder. The court recognized that Marcus was mentally ill and needed treatment. Accordingly, the judge sentenced Marcus as an adult to a 16-year prison term for the murder and then suspended the sentence. He ordered Marcus to spend two years, at the expense of the State, at a long-term treatment facility located in a neighboring state, with the possibility of this commitment being extended until Marcus reached age 21. The judge also ordered Marcus to spend five years on probation after leaving the treatment facility, during which time Marcus was required to successfully complete three years in a residential treatment facility for the treatment of alcohol and drug abuse. The judge warned Marcus that if he failed to complete either treatment program, the court would send him to prison to serve the 16-year suspended sentence.

Some adult children who kill their parents, although mentally disturbed or overwhelmed at the time, do not have a severe and long-standing mental illness. These adult children, often in a caretaking role for parents with Alzheimer's or other debilitating diseases, have become overwrought by their parents' deteriorating health and the increasing demands placed upon them over the years.[70] They have killed their parent possibly while "under the influence of extreme mental or emotional disturbance." Although these acts are sometimes viewed as "mercy killings," they are clearly against the law.[71] In some cases, adult children appear not to be able to keep up with the increasing level of care that their infirm parents require and have neglected the parent's care, leading to the parent's death under circumstances that constitute criminal negligence.[72]

The Dangerously Antisocial Parricide Offender

This type of parricide offender is found among both adolescent and adult parricide offenders. Dangerously antisocial offspring kill parents for selfish reasons. For them, the parent is an obstacle blocking them from obtaining what they want.[73] For example, these individuals might kill a parent to get the parent's money, to take the family car, or to have more freedom. In one of my cases, for example, a 16-year-old girl appeared to have killed her wealthy parents because they disapproved of the young man whom she was dating. The young man, who was uninvolved in the murders, was a high school dropout with limited financial means. In two of my other recent cases, middle-aged sons were charged in separate incidents with killing their parents for pecuniary gain. Both men were reportedly in financial trouble at the time of the murders. Their parents, who had helped their sons in the past, had declined to provide additional monetary assistance prior to their deaths. Both men maintained their innocence and were convicted of two counts of premeditated murder in jury trials.

Dangerously antisocial parricide offenders usually have a long history of antisocial and criminal behavior. If these parricide offenders are under 18, they are likely to be diagnosed as having a *conduct disorder (CD)*. If they are 18 years of age or older, they are likely to be diagnosed as having *antisocial personality disorder (APD)*. Individuals diagnosed with these disorders have an established pattern of violating the rights of other people.[74] Some of these parricide offenders would also likely meet the diagnostic criteria associated with a *psychopath*, meaning that, in addition to having a history of antisocial behavior, they lack a sense of emotional connection to other people.[75] Psychopaths do not see themselves as responsible for the consequences of their behavior, are narcissistic, and lack empathy.

Individuals who are diagnosed as having CDs, APDs, or psychopathic personalities often appear to behave in an irrational manner, consistently demonstrating poor judgment and failing to learn from experience. Unlike those who are psychotic, however, these parricide offenders know what they are doing. Psychopaths, in particular, might come across as poised, even charming, largely because they are free of anxiety and guilt about their violation of norms and the rights of others. They are capable of only the shallowest of human emotions.[76]

At age 13, Cassie Sparkman (pseudonym) fit the profile of a dangerously antisocial child. When her attorney introduced me to her, she initially appeared to be a typical young teenage girl—youthful, vivacious, and chatty. She laughed frequently and easily; no sadness or tears were apparent during the four-and-a-half-hour evaluation. Cassie's upbeat persona seemed at odds with the demeanor one might expect from a girl who was recently charged with the first-degree murder of her stepmother Tanya and who was facing spending the rest of her natural life in prison if convicted.

At the time of her arrest, Cassie was living with her father. Her biological mother and father separated when Cassie was about 4 years old. She recalled seeing her mother four times over the next nine to 10 years. Her mother reportedly did not call to check in on Cassie or her younger brother. Cassie's father had a number of girlfriends over the years, some of whom lived with them for varying periods of time. Cassie's feelings toward them varied widely, from thinking of one as "fun and cool" to intensely hating another. Cassie did not like that her father's girlfriends all had children, too. Cassie felt that they were taking some of her father's attention away from her.

Cassie emphasized when I was introduced to her that she did not trust people, with the one exception of her one girlfriend. Cassie made it clear that people did not "mess with" her. The girl said that she got into 15 to 20 fights to protect others. She proudly acknowledged that she was a good fighter. "I have a heavy hand like my father," she said, meaning there was force behind her punches. Cassie was aware that she could intimidate other people because she was bigger than them and knew how to fight. "Everybody knew don't touch Cassie."

Cassie's school records indicated that Cassie presented significant behavioral problems at school. I counted 33 referrals in the academic year preceding Cassie's arrest for murder. Cassie was placed in an alternative school for five months because of behavioral problems. She had attended "regular school" for three days prior to being arrested for killing her stepmother. School records indicated that school personnel had difficulty reaching Cassie's father by phone. Sometimes Mr. Sparkman did not call back; other times, school staff and Mr. Sparkman apparently had difficulty connecting with each other. Cassie indicated that she intercepted some recorded phone messages that were intended for her father and erased them.

Most of Cassie's friends were reportedly older than her, ranging in age from 14 to 23. She found kids her age to be immature because they would do things like "fight over a guy." Her male friends "respected" her because, she said, "I could probably beat 'em up" and "they knew my dad. Everybody's scared of my dad, as far as my neighborhood because he's bigger than everybody."

Cassie indicated that she had had one previous contact with the law but had no convictions in juvenile court. She was charged with beating up a girl, but this charge apparently was dropped. Cassie admitted to breaking some windows with other kids. She denied any participation in robberies, theft, burglaries, or drug selling. Cassie stated that she had often thought about running away and did so twice. On one of these occasions, Cassie left and stayed with her boyfriend for about a week because she was very angry at her father's fiancée Tanya. "I had never seen daddy so serious about anyone before and I didn't like that." Cassie also resented that Tanya's two daughters, ages 8 and 9, were taking too much of her father's time.

Tanya and her children had been living with Cassie, her father, and her younger brother for about six months prior to the murder. Tanya and Mr. Sparkman had planned on getting married within the next several months. Cassie clearly regarded Tanya as her stepmother. The girl described Tanya as "OK," "not that bad," and "pretty nice." Cassie did not like, however, that Tanya "changed the rules." Her stepmother "was the one that did the discipline thing." Prior to that, "we could get away with [stuff] because daddy was never home." Tanya insisted that Cassie's father check in with Cassie's school, something Cassie maintained that he did not do before. Tanya wanted Cassie and her brother to ask permission before they took something to eat; Cassie was not used to that structure.

Cassie perceived that Tanya was trying to take over as her mother and also was taking her father away from her, which Cassie resented. Cassie maintained that she did not have hatred for Tanya. Rather, she had hatred for "my Uncle [who molested her], my daddy for not listening to me and letting somebody come in the house. I know that sounds stupid; he let someone come in there and take my place. I was mad about that. My mom for leaving; I should not have had hatred for her, but I did; it's natural I guess. All daddy's girlfriends were trying to be my momma, I had a momma, I didn't need another momma...*Daddy was the only one I had left and they was trying to take Daddy, too. That's my daddy. Even though I had a hatred for him too, I loved Daddy, I loved Daddy.*"

Cassie acknowledged that she conceived the idea to kill Tanya and orchestrated the event with her brother. There was no well-conceived plan to murder the victim. Cassie's account suggested that her behavior was largely impulsive and her planning short term, which was completely consistent with her low level of personality development. Cassie and her brother ambushed their stepmother as she sat doing a puzzle and fired multiple shots into her body until "she was not moving or anything."

Cassie did not think about her behavior as wrong when she initially thought about killing Tanya and during the murder; the girl was simply removing an obstacle that she perceived as negatively impacting her life. Cassie's idea to do away with the victim was indicative of a child's magical thinking: she and her brother would kill the victim and live happily ever after with their father. After the murder, Cassie initially panicked because she was concerned that her father would be mad about her getting the victim's blood all over the living room carpet. The girl also became concerned about getting blood on her sneakers because the blood could tie her to the crime.

When asked how she felt at the time of the evaluation, Cassie said, "I wished it would not have happened." Had she thought more about the consequences and known what would happen, she confided, "[I]t wouldn't be her. It would have been my uncle."

Cassie said that she had thought about the killing a great deal in response to her father's repeated questions about why she killed Tanya. Cassie said that she did not hate Tanya. "All of the hatred I had toward everybody and then her coming in—the little part she played in the whole thing just set it off because I had hatred for my uncle, hatred for my daddy because he won't listen to me, and all his girlfriends, and Mom and stuff, and she [Tanya] just happened [to be the one] ... That was what I was saying before—you get to the point when you can't take it no more."

Prior to her arrest, Cassie appeared to meet the diagnostic criteria for a behavioral disorder. School records and statements made by Cassie suggested that she met the criteria for *oppositional defiant disorder (ODD)*, which is "a pattern of negativistic, hostile, and defiant behavior lasting at least six months" that does not rise to the level of criminal behavior.[77] Cassie often lost her temper, argued with adults, and actively defied or refused to comply with adults' requests or rules. She was often touchy or easily annoyed by others, angry, resentful, spiteful, and vindictive.

ODD is the forerunner of CD. The girl appeared to be borderline with respect to meeting the *minimal* criteria for having CD. Remarks made by Cassie indicated that she often threatened or intimidated others and had initiated physical fights. In addition, she had run away from home on two occasions and had been truant from school at least twice. There were some data to suggest that she might have stolen items at school on at least one occasion.[78] It was clear at the time of the assessment that, without intervention, Cassie would develop CD, if she was not conduct-disordered already, and could easily continue on the path to a diagnosis of APD in adulthood. The three behavioral disorders can be placed along a continuum of defiance of authority and societal norms.

THE NEED FOR PSYCHOLOGICAL ASSESSMENT

The categories just described look clear-cut. In reality, cases sometimes contain facts that span categories and make rapid-fire classification prone to error. When youths are involved in parricide, assessment of the child by a mental health expert whose area of specialty includes children who commit violent acts is critical in order to determine whether the juvenile is really a dangerously antisocial youth. The case of Patty Smith (Chapter 9) illustrates this point. The media initially portrayed Patty as a youth who cold-bloodedly murdered her father because he took away the keys to her car. My in-depth examination of her, a detailed interview with her mother, and an extensive review of case-related materials led me to conclude that she was not a dangerously antisocial individual. Rather, she was a severely abused parricide offender who enlisted the help of her friends to kill her father because she felt there was no other way out.

The documentation of abuse and neglect, however, is not determinative in deciding the type of APO. Abuse and neglect are often found in the backgrounds of severely mentally ill or dangerously antisocial parricide offenders.[79] *The critical consideration in deciding the parricide type is the motivation for the killing.* It is important to note in particular that children who have been abused and neglected might adopt an antisocial way of responding to life as a means of psychic, if not physical, survival.

Cassie Sparkman is an excellent example of a girl whose history of child maltreatment led her to act out her anger and hatred toward others. Cassie's parents separated when she was a small child. Her mother moved more than 1000 miles away and had virtually no contact with Cassie over the years. In addition to the abandonment by her mother, Cassie's maternal grandmother, a White woman, rejected Cassie because her father was Black. Evidence suggested that Cassie's father was also emotionally unavailable to her; he did not give her clear messages that she was loved or help her with her problems. For example, my viewing of Mr. Sparkman's videotaped session with Cassie shortly after her arrest for murder showed that he did not comfort Cassie in any physical or emotional way during his visit. He sat down across the room from her. It was Cassie who approached him when he cried; it was she who attempted to comfort him.

In addition to emotional neglect by both parents, there were clear indications of physical neglect in that Cassie was not provided with adequate supervision, a safe place to live, and appropriate discipline by her father. In Cassie's words, prior to Tanya's arrival, she and her brother "could get away with [stuff] because daddy was never home." Despite repeated behavioral problems at school, Cassie was not taken for counseling, which is a form of medical neglect. There were allegations of physical and verbal abuse by Cassie's father and sexual abuse by an uncle, a convicted child molester, who periodically lived with them. Three reports were made to the state social services agency regarding the physical and sexual abuse, but the children recanted, so the allegations remained officially unfounded.

Cassie was deeply affected by the loss of several adults who were close to her over the years. These included her paternal grandfather, who died about four years prior to the homicide, and one of Mr. Sparkman's former girlfriends, who lived with them for four years. This woman took a real interest in Cassie and then left. At the time of the evaluation, Cassie had not grieved her grandfather's death or the loss of the woman who befriended her. In addition to these losses, Cassie had not dealt with the anger that she felt toward her mother for abandoning her and her maternal grandmother for rejecting her.

At the time of the murder, Cassie feared on a deep level that she might lose the one person who remained in her life—her father—to Tanya. The thought of losing her father preyed on her mind because she did not have the external and internal resources to understand that Tanya was not taking her father away. Unlike severely abused youth who kill parents, Cassie did not kill her stepmother to end abuse. Rather, Cassie masterminded the murder as a way to get rid of her stepmother because the girl perceived Tanya as a threat to her relationship with her father. The act, although a desperate one conceived by a youth with a significant history of childhood maltreatment, is unequivocally antisocial. Cassie Sparkman, at age 13, was a dangerous adolescent.

Cassie decided to plead guilty to second-degree murder. Had she gone to trial, there was a strong likelihood, given the facts in her case, that she would have been convicted of first-degree murder. If so convicted, she would have been sentenced to a mandatory sentence of life without parole under existing state law. Instead, she was sentenced to 18 years in prison, to be followed by lifetime probation.

WHEN DEEP-SEATED RAGE ERUPTS AND TURNS DEADLY

Although most cases of parricide appear to fit into one of the three categories, there are some exceptions. For example, I have found in a few cases that youths with poor impulse control have killed their parents when their deep-seated rage related to parental abuse and/or neglect was ignited by an external event. In some of these cases, alcohol and drug intoxication fueled the rage. Clinicians and lawyers need to look at the case before them closely in order to determine the dynamics that led to the homicidal behavior.

Karl Roberts (pseudonym) was 16 years old when he was charged with the attempted murder of his father, the first-degree murder of his father's fiancée Leslie, and armed burglary. Although a juvenile, under existing state law at the time, the boy was charged with capital murder and was facing death if convicted. Karl's murderous rampage appeared unintended. The dynamics that led him to kill were set in motion several years earlier. Karl was born to parents who drank excessively and smoked pot during his childhood.[80] Karl had a half-sister, Nora, who was two years older than him. The two siblings were close growing up. Their lives changed dramatically when Nora told her mother that her stepfather (Karl's father) had overtly sexually abused her (oral sex and digital penetration of vagina) at least 50 times when she was aged 10 to 15. Following Nora's disclosure, legal authorities were contacted and Mrs. Roberts separated from her husband.[81] Partly for financial reasons, the parents decided that Nora would live with her mother and Karl would stay with his father.

Karl was very upset that his father had sexually abused his sister and "hated him for what he did." Mrs. Roberts maintained that up until the parents' separation, Karl was "a very good kid." Corroborative data supported Karl's assertion that he became very rebellious when he went to live with his father. He got in trouble many times in school for skipping classes, smoking, and fighting. He was transferred to several alternative schools because of his behavior and stopped going to school in the eighth grade. Karl started smoking marijuana every day and experimented with other drugs. Collateral sources indicated that Karl ran away from home a few times and started to get into legal trouble after his parents separated. He had an extensive delinquency record that included 15 charges during a 13-month period.

Karl said that his father beat him up a couple of times after he went to live with his dad. Mr. Roberts soon learned that he could not control Karl and reportedly gave up. Information provided by Karl, his sister, and his mother suggested that physically abusive behavior by Mr. Roberts was not extensive. Karl and Nora indicated that when Mr. Roberts hit Karl, he had a reason to do so. There was some evidence that Mr. Roberts verbally and psychologically abused Karl on a few occasions. Karl denied that his father had sexually abused him.[82]

Co-defendant and witness accounts were consistent regarding the events that preceded the shooting. Karl and a few of his friends were talking during the afternoon about going to another state to live. They were thinking about leaving that night and realized that they needed money and a car to go. They decided to "rob a couple of houses" and steal a vehicle. Karl subsequently broke into a house while his friends stood guard outside. Karl took some jewelry, a .22 caliber gun, and a shotgun. He bought bullets for both firearms. After a few hours, Karl and his friends realized that none of them knew how to steal a car, and they went back to Karl's house. It was nighttime as the three boys sat around trying to figure out what to do next. At this point, one of them suggested that they take Karl's father's car. Karl's father and his fiancée were asleep in the father's bedroom.

Karl related that he had previously snuck into his father's room when the man was asleep to steal his cigarettes, so he figured he could pull it off. Karl entered the room where his father and Leslie were sleeping more than once. The first two times, his father woke up. The two exchanged some words about cigarettes, and Karl left the room. The third time Karl entered, he saw the dog sitting on the bed and immediately shut the door. At this point, Karl told the two boys that he was giving up. One of them suggested that Karl go back into the bedroom, kill them, and take the car.

Karl said that he told this kid that he could not kill his father and Leslie. This boy replied, "Remember what he did to your sister" (this statement was corroborated by the third boy). Karl's memory was blurry about what occurred at this point. He did not remember the third boy calling his name as he pivoted around with the gun and headed back to the bedroom door. In Karl's words, "The only thing I remember was the door opening—I think I kicked it open and there was flames coming from the gun. Then the next thing I remember I was on the other side of the room. That's when I pretty much came out of it. The gun just clicked, clicked, clicked, clicked, clicked, clicked. It was out of bullets."

Following the shooting, Karl grabbed the car keys and his father's wallet. He remembered his father asking him, "Why," but not his response. Karl recalled ripping the kitchen phone out of the wall, taking his father's car, and going to look for the two boys, who had left when the gunfire erupted. After picking them up, the three headed to another state. Within less than 24 hours after the shooting, their car was spotted by police. Karl's attempt to elude the police by driving at excessive speeds was not successful. He was subsequently arrested and extradited back to his home state to face murder and attempted murder charges.

Karl felt no remorse for shooting his father. He took some satisfaction from the fact that his father could barely move his right hand, which was his dominant hand. He bet that his father would never touch his sister again. In contrast to his feelings about his father, Karl felt badly that he had shot Leslie: "She was just an innocent bystander. She was there—she's never done nothing to me—at the wrong place, at the wrong time."

Although Karl met the diagnostic criteria for CD, Karl was not a dangerously antisocial parricide offender. He did not kill for a selfish, instrumental reason. Although his homicidal behavior was reactive to abuse, he was not a severely abused parricide offender either. He did not kill because he was in fear for his life. He did not kill in a desperate attempt to end the abuse of his sister, because the abuse was not ongoing. Rather, it appears that the recollection of his father's abuse of his sister at that moment in time unleashed the hatred and rage that Karl had been carrying toward his father for years.

Karl said that he smoked marijuana before and after the shooting. His later report that he had taken a large amount of speed before the shooting could not be verified. His account of the homicidal incident indicated that he was experiencing dissociation during the shooting. His accounts to me, his friends, the police, the detention deputy, and his mother all suggested that he was "on automatic pilot" when he turned around and kicked open the door to his father's bedroom. One of his friends described to police Karl's behavior prior to the shooting as "disturbed and confused." When asked in his deposition (sworn testimony) to describe the change in Karl, this same boy said, "He had no soul. He was just like staring…I was calling his name, like Karl, what's going on, and he kept staring."

Karl was clearly "under the influence of extreme mental or emotional disturbance" when he fired multiple shots at his father and his father's fiancée. He did not suffer from any severe mental illness, however, that caused him to take such violent action. Accordingly, he was not a severely mentally ill parricide offender. Karl pled guilty to the charges rather than risk being convicted of them at trial and sentenced to death. He was sentenced to life in prison.[83]

SOCIETAL REACTION

The media's portrayal of the murder of Richard Jahnke, Sr., in Wyoming by his teenage children, discussed earlier in this chapter, was sympathetic to the young killers. Richard and Deborah Jahnke became the prototype of the "severely abused child." The Jahnke case occurred a few years after the case of Terry Adams, the abused boy who killed both of his parents when his father attempted to impede his flight. *Time* magazine,[84] for example, headlined the Jahnke case by quoting a family friend: "It Made Terrible Sense." The conclusions reached in the article were sympathetic to the offenders rather than to the deceased victim. "Despite the coldly premeditated nature of the slaying, public sentiment in Cheyenne began shifting to the alleged killers as details about the Jahnke household emerged."[85]

Two weeks after Richard was convicted of the crime of voluntary manslaughter, a letter-writing campaign was initiated to influence the trial judge in his sentencing decision. Within less than three weeks, the Committee to Help Richard John Jahnke recorded more than 4000 letters urging leniency for Richard, and only one letter opposing it. The committee collected 10,000 signatures on petitions distributed locally and delivered scores of additional petitions that came from around the United States to the presiding jurist. While letters were pouring in to the committee on Richard's behalf, Deborah, in another court proceeding, was convicted of aiding and abetting voluntary manslaughter. Following the convictions of both adolescents, defense attorneys for both Richard and Deborah were similarly besieged with letters and phone calls urging leniency in sentencing.[86]

The letters did not have their desired effect, however. On March 18, 1983, Richard was sentenced to five to 15 years in prison; about six weeks later, on April 27, 1983, his sister was sentenced to three to eight years. While appeals were pending and the youths were on bond, a crew from *60 Minutes* arrived in Cheyenne, Wyoming, to investigate the story. On January 22, 1984, 14 months after this parricide occurred, the Jahnke case was the lead story on *60 Minutes*. An estimated 46 million viewers watched as the details of Richard's and Deborah's convictions were discussed. Correspondent Ed Bradley described the abuse that the adolescents had endured, the inability of Mrs. Jahnke to protect her children, and the failure of the state social service agency to investigate the child abuse report filed six months before the homicide occurred. Of the more than 1,000 letters written to the studio after the broadcast, only 10 objected to the sympathetic treatment of the Jahnke children's situation.[87]

When the convictions and sentences of the Jahnke teenagers were upheld by the Wyoming Supreme Court in separate appeals later that year, Wyoming Governor Ed Herschler commuted both sentences. Richard was ordered to be sent to a hospital for a few months for psychiatric evaluation and then placed in a juvenile facility until age 21. His sentence totaled three years, 13 days. Deborah's sentence was commuted to one year of probation to be preceded by one month of intensive psychiatric intervention. Thirty days later, Deborah enrolled as a freshman at the University of Wyoming.[88]

Some evidence suggests that the reaction of the judicial system to abused youths who kill their victimizing parents has also become more compassionate since the 1980s.[89] For example, Cornell, Staresina, and Benedek (1989) briefly described a case in which Fred, a 17-year-old boy who killed his father, was acquitted by reason of insanity. The authors concluded that "the jury's sympathetic reaction" to the youth who shot his father, "an alcoholic who was extremely brutal and tyrannical,"[90] as he was beating up the defendant's sister apparently influenced their verdict. The authors made the following observations in evaluating the jury's verdict[91]:

Fred did not suffer from schizophrenia or any similar mental disorder; he did not even profess amnesia for the offense or give any indication that he acted in a dissociated state. Moreover, Fred did not deny the intentional nature of his behavior or his awareness that his actions were wrong. However justifiable the offense might appear from some larger moral perspective, it is far from clear that the insanity statute represented the appropriate legal resolution.[92]

As public awareness of child abuse increases, arguments made by defense attorneys that abused children acted in self-defense when they killed their abusive parents are also winning more favor among jurors.[93] According to attorney Paul Mones, who has assisted in the defense of hundreds of APOs, juries in the United States over time have become more sympathetic to the plight of abused children.[94] A Los Angeles jury, for example, acquitted a 19-year-old male of the attempted murder of his father under an unusual set of circumstances.[95] According to court testimony, Johnny Junatanov made arrangements three times to have his father killed. The victim survived the first two attempts on his life. When Johnny was in the process of making arrangements for the third time to have his father killed, he was arrested by the undercover policeman he was seeking to hire as a hit man.

Johnny testified that he was desperate to kill his father. He explained to the jury that his father had beaten him, kept him in handcuffs, chained him since he was a child, and raped him three years earlier. A photograph and testimony by the boy's mother and grandmother and by the victim's employees corroborated the abuse.[96]

The Junatanov case was among the first cases in which adolescents were found not guilty of attempting to kill brutal parents on the grounds of self-defense when it did not appear that they were in imminent fear of death or severe bodily harm. Self-defense appears to be becoming a more viable argument, as is discussed in Chapter 7. Research has also suggested that laypeople's decisions to transfer juvenile parricide offenders to adult court and jury decisions to hold these youths fully accountable are likely to be affected by claims of abuse.[97]

In addition to jury verdicts, indications of a change in attitude and practice are noticeable in prosecutorial decisions, and even in actions taken by grand juries. One case considered as precedent setting involved 22-year-old Janet Reese, who killed her abusive father in Clearwater, Florida, in 1986. Although legally an adult, Janet was living with her younger brother at home with their father, who exercised strict control over Janet's activities. Janet's father divorced her mother, took custody of their two children, and moved away several years prior to the killing. Janet's mother died three years prior to the murder. Janet, who claimed that her father had been sexually abusing her since the first grade, shot her 42-year-old father after he came home for lunch and forced her to have sex. When grand jurors heard the circumstances, they refused the prosecutor's request to indict Janet for murder in the first degree and reduced the charge to manslaughter. The prosecutor's office subsequently advised Janet that the State would recommend probation if she pled guilty to manslaughter. Janet's defense attorney declined the plea bargain, maintaining that Janet would be acquitted by a jury if the case went to trial. The State eventually dropped all charges against Janet.[98]

Judges have, on occasion, clearly taken into account the effects of a history of abuse in handing down suspended sentences, keeping APOs in the juvenile justice system, sentencing them to youthful offender facilities rather than prison, giving them short prison sentences or probation, and even finding them not guilty.[99] In a 2006 case that attracted national attention, a trial judge in Alamogordo, New Mexico, noted that the situational factors that led 14-year-old Cody Posey to kill his father, stepmother, and 13-year-old stepsister influenced the court's decision to impose juvenile sanctions following his conviction rather than the life sentence that had been a possibility.[100] Cody was charged with three counts of first-degree (premeditated) murder in connection with the three murders. Evidence indicated that he shot the three victims and then buried them in a manure pile on the ranch that his father managed for veteran reporter Sam Donaldson.[101]

Cody told the police, and later testified, that shortly before the killings, as the boy was doing his morning chores, his father slapped him across the face and ordered him into the house. At that point, Cody retrieved a long gun from the barn and loaded it with six rounds of bullets. Thinking that the world would be better off without his father, Cody entered the house. Upon seeing his stepmother reading a book, he fired two shots into her head from a few feet away. As his father and stepsister ran into the house, Cody fired a single shot into his father's head. Cody then fired two more shots into the head of his stepsister so she would not tell on him.[102]

Cody tried to make the murder scene look like a burglary before fleeing the house. He threw the gun in a local river, washed up at a country store, and called his friends. He then spent the next two days playing and having fun with friends before the bodies were discovered. Shortly after being questioned by police, Cody confessed to the killings.[103]

The prosecutor argued that the killings were cold-blooded and premeditated. The defense maintained that the boy had "snapped" after years of abuse by both his father and stepmother. Cody's testimony, corroborated by more than 30 teachers, relatives, and friends, provided convincing evidence that Cody's father humiliated, beat, and isolated his son with the help of the boy's stepmother.[104] Jurors saw photographs of visible marks on Cody's buttocks that appeared after his father beat him with a board for getting bad grades in the second grade. The case was reported to authorities by Cody's mother but closed after authorities decided it was an isolated incident.[105] Cody testified that the night before the killings, his father burned him with a welding rod and a blowtorch after the boy refused to have sex with his stepmother. Although there were no witnesses to this event, Cody did have burn marks on his arms, and large amounts of pornography labeled "incest" were found on Cody's father's computer.[106] One of the defense psychologists who testified considered this event as the likely breaking point for Cody. She concluded that the defendant at this point was stressed beyond his capacity, filled with intense emotion, including fear, and saw no way out other than murder.[107]

Another defense psychologist testified that, for Cody, the fragile emotional state typical of adolescents was further compromised by the extensive abuse he endured from early childhood, several associated stress-related disorders, and signs of attention deficit hyperactivity disorder. The psychologist also said that Cody was deeply impacted by the tragic death of his mother, in a car accident, when he was 10 years old.[108] Cody had been living with his mother for a few months when the accident occurred. Cody's mother had remarried, recovered from a drug and alcohol problem, and gained custody of him after his father terminated his parental rights. When the accident occurred, Cody was riding in the car with his mother, and she died in his arms. After her death, Cody was sent to live with his abusive father.[109]

Both defense psychologists agreed that Cody's emotional condition at the time of the murders would have impaired his reasoning and affected his ability to control his behavior. However, similar to the prosecutor's expert, they acknowledged that Cody knew what he was doing when he shot the three victims and that he intended to kill them.[110]

Cody was convicted of voluntary murder for killing his father, second-degree murder for killing his stepmother, and first-degree murder for killing his stepsister.[111] The judge decided to sentence Cody to juvenile sanctions so that the youth could get treatment. The court found that Cody suffered from PTSD and depression at the time of the killings. In deciding upon the appropriate sanction, the judge noted that he had taken into consideration several factors, including the aggressive and willful nature of the crime, its seriousness, and the fact that a firearm was used. The judge decided not to impose a prison sentence because he did not believe that the prosecution had supported its argument that Cody had psychopathic traits and was not a suitable candidate for treatment: "The court is not convinced that the respondent has antisocial personality traits to the extent that would make him not amenable to treatment or rehabilitation."[112] The judge found evidence "that the situational nature of the violence makes it less likely that the respondent will pose a future danger to the public." The judge's ruling meant that state supervision of Cody would end at age 21 or sooner.[113] Cody was released from custody on his 21st birthday.[114]

SUMMARY AND CONCLUDING REMARKS

This chapter began with vignettes highlighting several parricide cases in order to demonstrate the variety of circumstances in which child, adolescent, and adult offenders have killed their parents. Terms pertinent to the killings of mothers, fathers, and families were defined. Discussion focused on why cases of offspring killing parents have garnered public attention and concern for centuries.

The incidence of parricide in the United States and in other countries was examined. Although rare, there is evidence of parents being slain by their children in nations across the globe. Statistical analyses of thousands of parricides occurring across more than 30 years indicated that most parents who are killed by their children in the United States are killed in single-victim incidents by adult sons acting alone. Parricides involving juvenile and female offenders and multiple victims, however, typically receive widespread news coverage.

This chapter highlighted the importance of the offender's age from developmental and legal perspectives. Thereafter, I discussed a typology of parricide offenders initially presented more than 20 years ago in my first book, *Why Kids Kill Parents*. The three types of parricide offenders originally proposed (the severely abused, the severely mentally ill, and the dangerously antisocial) have stood the test of time, as judged by cases referred to me for consultation or evaluation and by the use of this typology by other clinicians and researchers. Juvenile parricide offenders and APOs tend to fall into the "severely abused" and "dangerously antisocial" categories, and adult offenders into "severely mentally ill" and "dangerously antisocial." These three types have been illustrated through cases.

An in-depth assessment by a mental health professional is critical in determining the parricide offender type. This chapter has underscored that a history of abuse is not determinative in classifying a particular parricide offender. The most important consideration in deciding on the parricide offender type is the motivation that drove the juvenile or adult offender to kill his or her parent. This chapter noted that although most parricide offenders fit into one of the three categories, there are some exceptions. I have had several cases in which youths with poor impulse control have killed parents due to deep-seated rage that erupted into violence. Often, the homicidal rage was fueled by alcohol and/or drugs.

There is some evidence that the public has looked with compassion on severely abused adolescents who have killed parents in the past 30 years in the United States. In addition to jury verdicts, indications of a change in attitude and practice are noticeable in prosecutorial decisions, actions taken by grand juries, and sentences given by judges. In Chapter 2, the phenomenon of child maltreatment is discussed in depth because of its pivotal role in understanding why many APOs kill their parents.

2 Child Maltreatment and Parricide

Understanding the phenomenon of child maltreatment is critical in analyzing the dynamics leading to the killing of a parent. Research has clearly demonstrated that, with few exceptions, youths who commit murder, including those who kill parents, have endured significant trauma in their lives.[1] Many have been severely neglected and/or abused throughout their childhoods.[2]

Child abuse and neglect are defined by both federal and state laws. The Federal Child Abuse Prevention and Treatment Act (CAPTA) identified minimum standards that states must include in their statutory definition of child abuse.[3] CAPTA defines child abuse and neglect as "[a]ny recent act or failure to act on the part of a parent or caretaker, which results in death, serious physical or emotional harm, sexual abuse, or exploitation, or an act or failure to act which presents an imminent risk of serious harm."[4] Nearly all states provide definitions of child abuse and neglect in statutes and have provisions for the reporting of suspected child maltreatment to child protective agencies.[5]

In conceptualizing child maltreatment, as addressed in the CAPTA definition, the law distinguishes between crimes of commission and those of omission. Acts committed upon a child that are harmful are considered to constitute *abuse*; failure to act that results in harm to the child constitutes *neglect*. Not surprisingly, the focus in cases involving severely abused children is on the pervasive and extreme nature of the abuse and its threat to the child's physical and emotional well-being. In nearly all adolescent parricide cases, however, neglect accompanies abuse in one or more forms, making it difficult to separate the specific effects of each form of child maltreatment. Sexual and physical abuse are often specifically defined incidents. In contrast, neglect is often chronic, and it is more difficult to pinpoint.

In many cases, one type of child maltreatment leads to the other. A child who is physically or sexually abused by a parent, for example, becomes a victim of neglect if the parents fail to seek medical attention for resulting injuries or sexually transmitted diseases. I find it useful to distinguish among four types of abuse: physical, sexual, verbal, and psychological. Neglect can be categorized into three areas: physical, medical, and emotional. *Emotional incest*[6] frequently accompanies emotional neglect and often plays a role in parricide cases. Each of these specific types of child maltreatment is discussed and illustrated below.

PHYSICAL ABUSE

Physical abuse is generally defined as any "nonaccidental physical injury to the child."[7] I find it helpful to use a slightly broader definition. I define physical abuse as including inflicted physical injury or the attempt to inflict physical injury or pain that is indicative of the unresolved needs of the aggressor. This definition captures the dynamics of physical abuse by directing attention to both the victim and the offender.[8] It includes both cause and effect and can define physical violence perpetrated on the spouse as well as the child.[9]

The definition can be appropriately utilized when physical violence or force is used in obvious ways such as those first described by Murray Straus more than 30 years ago in the Conflict Tactics Scales (for example, threw something, pushed, grabbed, shoved, slapped or spanked, kicked, bit, hit with fist, hit or tried to hit with something, beat up, burned or scalded, threatened with gun or knife, or used gun or knife).[10] Straus's technique has been modified and used extensively in thousands of studies of family violence and is the most widely used instrument in measuring domestic violence.[11] Physical abuse can also be more subtle. Parents (almost always mothers) who simulate illness in their children or who intentionally make their children physically ill so that they may receive excessive medical attention are also physically abusing their children. These parents are initially seen as concerned parents and receive a great deal of attention from the medical community. This disorder, known as Munchausen syndrome by proxy, is frequently fatal for infants whose mothers are not correctly diagnosed and treated.[12]

Physical abuse by a parent might or might not be a reaction to the child's behavior. If the parent's behavior is not appropriate or proportional to anything the child has actually done, it is physically abusive. In some cases the offending parent attacks the child for no reason at all. The child might be simply watching television, walking through a room, or coming into the house when the abusive parent strikes. In other cases, the parent is clearly reacting to something the child has done. A parent might beat a 7-year-old for taking another child's toy, a 12-year-old for getting an unsatisfactory grade at school, or a 15-year-old for being disrespectful to his mother. In such cases the child often can identify the action that provoked the parental attack and might even mistakenly interpret the physical assault as deserved. If the parent's conduct does not actually cause injury or pain but could reasonably have been expected to have done so, the behavior is still physically abusive. Again, the criterion is that the parent's response to the child is inappropriate and out of proportion.

Physical Abuse in Adolescent Parricide Cases

Physical abuse is almost always a factor in cases in which severely abused children have killed fathers. In many cases of patricide, fathers have physically abused both their wives and their children for years prior to the homicide. The fathers' violence appeared to have been the result of their anger and dissatisfaction with their lives and marital circumstances. In some of these cases, the wives or common-law wives left their abusive spouses by divorcing them or fleeing, leaving the children with their fathers. When this separation occurred, the fathers typically continued to beat their adolescent children, sometimes even more frequently, claiming that the breakup was the children's fault. By blaming their children for their problems and seeking redress from them, these parents, like others who abuse their children, were denying their responsibility for life events.

Although none of the youths I evaluated were ever hospitalized as a result of physical abuse, most received injuries. For example, Patty Smith (Chapter 9) sustained a dislocated back after being severely kicked by her father. Peter Jones (Chapter 10) had bruises and welts on his back, legs, and arms from beatings inflicted upon him by his father. He was kicked; punched in the head, nose, mouth, and stomach; and led around by his hair. His father also threw things at him—once cutting him—and bent his thumb so far that the youth believed his thumb would break. Will Garrison (Chapter 7) also endured multiple forms of abuse. Will's father hit his son in the stomach with his fist, pushed him against the wall, choked him, hit him in the head with a wooden instrument, twisted his arm severely behind his back, and on several occasions bit him. Shortly before the killing, Will's father beat Will in an area where he had recently had surgery for a disc. The beating caused bleeding and necessitated more treatment, requiring significantly more healing time. In another patricide case, Scott Anders's (Chapters 7 and 8) father hit him "everywhere … stomach, face, and head." The beating was so severe that Scott's father would not allow him to go to school because he had "knots" on his head.

In addition to injuries and obvious attempts to hurt the children involved, these cases illustrate the pervasiveness of the threat of serious injury and even death. The fathers of Patty Smith, Peter Jones, and Scott Anders, for example, each threatened to kill their children. Patty Smith's father aimed a gun at her; Scott Anders's father propped a shotgun beside him on the night of the homicide after threatening to kill himself and his son. Terry Adams's father attempted to stab his son once, and another time he pulled a gun on him.

In cases in which adolescents have killed parents, particularly fathers, severe spouse abuse frequently also exists, often antedating the physical abuse of the child.[13] These adolescents' histories include the horror of witnessing extreme forms of violence as well as the terror of being a victim. The simultaneous experiencing of horror and terror might set the stage for parricide.

Individuals experience horror when they are witnesses to events that are so shocking that their minds cannot fully comprehend them. Though there might be no physical threat, the events are traumatizing to them and might stay lodged in their minds for years. Although fear might be an element of horror, the predominant feelings associated with horror are shock and dread. Individuals react with terror or experience intense fear when their own physical survival is threatened. With terror and horror, both body and mind are affected. Terror and horror immobilize the body and stun the mind.[14]

SEXUAL ABUSE

All states include sexual abuse in their child abuse definitions. Some states refer to different types of sexual abuse, whereas others define sexual abuse in general terms.

Most jurisdictions consider sexual exploitation of a child in their definitions of sexual abuse. Sexual exploitation of a child includes forcing or allowing a child to engage in child pornography or prostitution.[15]

I differentiate between two types of sexual abuse of children, overt and covert,[16] and forcible rape. Many years ago Nicholas Groth made a similar distinction between overt sexual abuse and rape by noting that sexual offenses against children can consist of acts of molestation or rape depending on the characteristics of the approach and the dynamics of the offender.[17] Table 2-1 illustrates the differences between the two types of sexual abuse.

Overt Sexual Abuse

Overt sexual abuse is the more readily identifiable of the two. It involves a physical form of offending. A parent who sexually fondles a child or who engages in vaginal intercourse, anal sex, or oral sex with a child has overtly sexually abused that child.

It is estimated that one in four girls and one in seven boys are overtly sexually abused before age 18.[18] Most of the offenders are known to the children; many of them are the children's parents or stepparents. Overt sexual abuse by a parent is a form of incest. When incest occurs between a parent and a child, the parent, regardless of the

Table 2-1 Overt and covert sexual abuse by parents

Overt Sexual Abuse	Covert Sexual Abuse
Physical form of offending	Exposing a child to sexual issues that are age inappropriate
"Hands-on" violation, direct contact	Raising the child in an environment that is sexually saturated and/or provocative
Parent fondles child	Parent masturbates in front of child
Parent engages in vaginal intercourse with child	Parent allows, encourages, or forces child to watch parent engage in sex with other parent or mate
Parent engages in anal sex with child	Parent shares pornography with child
Parent engages in oral sex with child	Parent routinely sleeps with adolescent child of opposite sex
Parent participates in or allows another adult or older adolescent to engage in sexual abuse of child	Parent forces or encourages child to commit prostitution or to engage in sexual performances or erotic dancing
	Other seductive behavior by parent toward child (e.g., a parent conversing in the bathroom with opposite-sex adolescent child as child showers, or a parent, while in a state of undress, visiting with child **might be** covertly sexually abusing the child)

Source: Reprinted with permission, K.M. Heide, *Why Kids Kill Parents* (Ohio State University Press; Sage, 1995).

circumstances, is *always* responsible. It does not matter whether the child appeared to be a "willing" participant. A child's consent to be sexually expressive with a parent is meaningless because of the differences in development and power between adult and child. A child who appears to consent to sexual behavior with a parent might be simply conceding to the parent's sexual demands in an unconscious effort to get his or her own needs for attention, affection, love, safety, and a sense of belonging met.

Covert Sexual Abuse

Covert sexual abuse involves exposing a child to sexual issues that are age inappropriate and raising the child in a sexually saturated or provocative environment.[19] Although direct sexual contact between parent and child does not occur, parental activities are sexually explicit.[20] A father who masturbates in front of his child or a mother who shares pornography with her son or daughter is abusing the child covertly. One teenage girl killed her father after enduring years of physical and sexual abuse and witnessing her father beat her mother. The girl was distressed by lewd valentines that her father sent her. One message, clearly covertly sexually abusive, said, "I would like your heart and I assume the rest of you will follow."[21]

Covert sexual abuse is typically very stressful for the child. It causes shame and confusion and might delay emotional development. The child generally knows that this activity is viewed as wrong, often within the family itself, and she or he knows, almost always, that it is condemned by the larger society.[22] The parent who covertly sexually abuses a child frequently conveys the implicit message that this activity is a secret between them because the other parent "simply won't understand."

A parent who frequently sleeps in the same bed with an adolescent child of the opposite sex is typically covertly sexually abusing that child.[23] It does not matter that no physical contact occurs between the parent and the child. Similarly, a parent who sits in the bathroom conversing with an opposite-sex adolescent as the youth showers or who visits with the child while purposely in a state of undress is also risking engaging in covert sexual abuse. The proximity of the opposite-sex parent in sexually provocative situations is sufficient to cause discomfort to a child who is going through puberty.[24] Adolescents know that it is unacceptable from the standpoint of society for them to fantasize about sexual involvement between them and their parents. Yet they are likely to feel very vulnerable because the closeness of the situations described suggests the possibility of increased sexual interaction, typically bringing fear and anxiety.

A parent who forces or encourages a daughter or son to engage in sexual performances or erotic dancing or to commit prostitution also abuses his or her offspring. It does not matter whether the child was willing—or even desired—to be in that setting.

Covert sexual abuse is potentially damaging to a child because of its frequently masked nature and the confusion these behaviors create.[25] It is often difficult for a child to realize that he or she has been victimized. Victims of covert sexual abuse tend to believe that the discomfort that they feel is somehow an indication of their "warped mind," that "there must be something wrong with them." As with overt sexual abuse, children typically believe that the abuse is their fault. Also, like overt sexual abuse, covert sexual abuse can result in lowered self-worth or self-esteem and can create confusion for the child about identity and personal boundaries.

Children's Reluctance to Report Sexual Abuse

Boys and girls who are overtly or covertly sexually abused frequently do not talk about it to others, even close friends, let alone school counselors, because of their shame and embarrassment. Although they might feel that sexual behavior with a parent is wrong, they are often forced to choose between believing themselves and believing adults who are important to them and who persuade them to engage in sexual behavior. These children might find it necessary to surrender their perceptions and give up control of themselves for psychological, and sometimes physical, survival.[26] In learning to concede to others' definitions of reality and to abdicate whatever power they might have had, these children often adopt an external locus of control; that is, they come to believe and accept that events in their lives are controlled by outside forces.[27]

In spite of the increased concern about sexual abuse in the United States, the problem is not clearly recognized. Children are commonly reluctant to talk about their victimization because they fear they will not be believed. Our society is uncomfortable with acknowledging the reality of sexual abuse. Some children remain silent because they think that it is their responsibility to take care of the offender or save the family unit from the dissolution that they have been told would result from disclosure. Even more sadly, some children, typically adolescents, resign themselves to the situation and make trade-offs with the abusing parent—in return for not reporting the parent to the authorities, these children accept privileges and material goods.

Forcible Rape

Overt sexual abuse is conceptually distinct from forcible rape. The characteristics of the two types of acts appear in Table 2-2. I use the term *overt sexual abuse* to describe sexual activities engaged in by a parent with a child that are often characterized by physical and emotional gentleness on the part of the parent. As noted by Groth in describing the dynamics involved in acts of molestation by pedophiles, the parent relates to the child sexually because of his or her inability to relate sexually and emotionally to a spouse or other age-appropriate mate.[28] The parent might be unable to relate to suitable sexual partners because his or her primary orientation is to children (the fixated pedophile) or because the individual is under a great deal of stress, loses control, or evinces poor judgment (the regressed pedophile). The parent's dysfunctional thinking leads him or her to look to the child rather than to an age-appropriate mate to fulfill needs for physical closeness and sexual expression.

The parent who engages in overt sexual abuse generally does not want to hurt the child physically or psychologically. Before attempting to have sexual intercourse with his child, a father might spend months, even years, engaging in a series of other sexual behaviors. Behaviors such as undressing each other, being naked in each other's presence, kissing, fondling, and having oral sex are often presented to the child as though they were a game. The father might take considerable time to stretch the opening of his young daughter's vagina so that it is able to accommodate his fully erect penis without causing her significant pain or injury. Although children generally experience tremendous guilt and shame when they realize that society condemns such intimacy between parents and children, the abusive parent typically did not intend to cause long-term trauma.[29]

Table 2-2 Overt sexual abuse distinguished from forcible rape

Overt Sexual Abuse	Forcible Rape
Often characterized by physical gentleness on the part of the parent	Characterized by brute force
Reflects parent's inadequacy	Reflects parent's rage
Parent looks to child to fulfill needs for nurturance, love, and intimacy	Parent selects child to vent anger and demonstrate power
Parent does not intend or desire to hurt child physically or psychologically	Parent intends and desires to hurt and control child
Child might not be fearful	Child is likely to be terrified

Source: Reprinted with permission, K.M. Heide, *Why Kids Kill Parents* (Ohio State University Press; Sage, 1995).

I reserve the term *forcible rape* for sexual encounters between parents and children in which the parent uses brute force to achieve ends far different from those generally sought by an incest offender. The father who sexually assaults his daughter or son because he is enraged or wants to demonstrate who is boss is no different from an "angry rapist" or "power rapist."[30] The sexual encounter serves to vent anger, demonstrate power, and humiliate the victim. Elements are present in a forcible rape that are often absent from a typical incest encounter. The child feels powerless to resist the attack and is momentarily terrified that she or he might not survive it. The parent-assailant does not select his daughter or son simply because of inadequacy in relationships with other adults; rather, he attacks in order to hurt and control.[31]

Sexual Abuse in Parricide Cases

Overt sexual abuse has been reported as a factor in several cases of girls who killed their fathers.[32] In these cases, the abuse had been long-standing, and the female adolescents and young adults took lethal action to end it. In three of my cases, the sexual encounters between the youths and their fathers paralleled the dynamics in forcible rape cases, wherein the perpetrator attacks his victim. Although the rapists in all three cases were fathers, one of the parricide offenders, Christine "Chrissy" Johnson (Chapter 4), killed her mother after Mrs. Johnson brushed aside the girl's torment and asked her to remain silent for the good of the family. Interestingly, one of the three adolescent parricide offenders who was sexually assaulted, Will Garrison (Chapter 7), was male.

VERBAL ABUSE

Verbal abuse consists of words spoken to a child, or remarks made in the child's presence about the child, that either are designed to damage the child's concept of self or would reasonably be expected to undermine a child's sense of competence and self-esteem. Swearing at a child can have a devastating effect on the child's sense of self. A father or a mother who calls a daughter a "slut" or "whore" is certainly risking undermining the girl's sense of self-esteem. Telling a child that he or she is "ugly,"

BAKER COLLEGE of CLINTON TWP LIBRARY

"stupid," "no good," or "good for nothing" is also obvious verbal abuse. The parent who remarks to another person in the presence of the child, "My daughter will never amount to anything," or "My son will die in the electric chair someday, wait and see," is attacking the child's self-concept.

Belittling remarks (for example, telling a 3-year-old child, "You're nothing but a baby," or an 8-year-old boy, "I thought you were man enough to do it; my mistake") can undermine a child's sense of competence. Statements that tear at the child's ego ("You wimp, you," "You'd forget your head if it weren't attached to you") can also damage the child's self-esteem. Parents who blame a child for their problems ("You're ruining my marriage," "If it weren't for you, we would be a lot better off financially," "It's your fault I didn't have a career; I had to stay home and raise you") are also likely to diminish the child's self-concept. Unfortunately, such comments are utilized by some parents to transfer their shame to the child[33] and to manipulate the child by making him or her feel badly.

Verbal abuse is common in parricide cases. For example, Mr. Garrison called Will a "sissy" and a "queer." He frequently cursed at him, calling him a "son of a bitch" and a "motherfucker." Mr. Sparkman called Cassie a "slut" and, in the presence of others, accused her of being sexually active when she was not. Mrs. Johnson called Chrissy a "shitty daughter" and a "bitch" many times and told Chrissy that no one could ever love her.

PSYCHOLOGICAL OR EMOTIONAL ABUSE

The terms *psychological abuse* and *verbal abuse*, although sometimes used interchangeably by both professionals and the public, are conceptually distinct. "Psychological abuse" is a far broader term than "verbal abuse," encompassing words and behaviors that undermine or would reasonably be expected to undermine a child's sense of self, competence, and safety in the world. Verbal abuse is just one type of psychological abuse. Almost all states include emotional or psychological abuse in their definitions of child abuse. Language typically used in these definitions includes "injury to the psychological capacity or emotional stability of the child as evidenced by an observable or substantial change in behavior, emotional response, or cognition," or as evidenced by "anxiety, depression, withdrawal, or aggressive behavior."[34]

Physical abuse and sexual abuse are also forms of psychological abuse when they are inflicted by a parent or guardian, because these acts represent a violation of trust. They destroy the child's sense of security in his or her home and impede the development of competence in interpersonal relationships.[35] If the child tells the nonoffending parent that he or she is being sexually abused by the other parent and is met with disbelief or indifference, as in the case of Christine Johnson, the child has been psychologically abused by both parents.

Psychologically abusive communications can be extraordinarily complex. These messages are particularly insidious because they often communicate to children that they are not valued for themselves or that they are unable to measure up to their parents' expectations regardless of what they do. Parents who constantly compare one child with a sibling to illustrate where the one falls short and does not measure up rather than accepting and valuing the differences in their children are undermining the child's self-esteem.

Parents who express dissatisfaction with a child's accomplishments regardless of the actual performance level, always demanding more, are also psychologically abusing the child. Take the case of a child who works extraordinarily hard to get a B– on a test and is greatly relieved, even pleased, by his performance. When he tells his mother, she says, "Why didn't you get a B?" For the next test, he works even harder and manages to get the B. He runs home with excitement to tell his mother that he got the B. She says, "Why didn't you get an A?" Eventually he gets the coveted A. Mom remarks at that point, "Was that the highest grade in the class?" "No," he tells her, "one of the kids in the class got an A+." She replies, "Why didn't you get the A+?"

Myriad behaviors can undermine a child's sense of self-esteem, competence, and security. Some acts parents commit are unquestionably cruel. One father, for example, strangled his child's pet as the boy watched. One mother called her son a "son of a bitch" and spat in his face when he brought his girlfriend home to meet her. Other acts seem designed to humiliate the child into complying with parental expectations that the child might be unable to meet. One woman whose son had a bedwetting problem decided that she would dissuade her son from wetting the bed at night by hanging out his urine-soaked sheets in the front yard to dry while the neighbors looked on.

Less dramatic psychologically abusive behaviors can also be very damaging to a child's sense of self. A parent who frequently wakes a child up in the middle of the night to accommodate the parent's needs (for example, Father wants the child to clean the garage, or Mother decides that she must vacuum the child's room at 3:00 A.M.) is communicating that the child's needs are not important.

Psychological abuse is pervasive in families in which parricide occurs. It consists not of one act, but of a series of hurtful actions that to the child might seem like "death by a thousand cuts." Psychological abuse was a primary factor that propelled sons and daughters to kill their mothers in several of my cases. They no longer could tolerate their mother's critical and often cruel behavior, which seemed unrelenting to them. For example, Chrissy Johnson had endured many psychologically abusive acts by her mother prior to her mother's indifference to the rape by her father. These included Chrissy's being prevented from seeing her godparents, who were very stable, good people and who had practically raised the girl from the time she was a baby to about age 12. Chrissy's boyfriend described her mother as "beyond mean." He said that Chrissy would get into trouble for everything around the house. "If the dogs peed on the carpet, it was Chrissy's fault. Everything was Chrissy's fault," as far as Mrs. Johnson was concerned.

PHYSICAL AND MEDICAL NEGLECT

Physical and medical neglect are relatively straightforward concepts. Parents are required by law to provide food, clothing, and a safe home environment for their children. In addition, they are expected to supervise their children adequately, set appropriate limits of behavior, and provide discipline when necessary. About half of the states include failure to educate children in accordance with state laws in their definition of neglect.[36] Parents who are unable or unwilling to perform these duties, despite being financially able to do so or having been offered other means that would allow them to do so, have clearly neglected their children's physical needs. Parents who cannot meet their children's physical needs because of financial hardship are still considered to have physically neglected their offspring when they fail to make other provisions to ensure that their children's needs are met.

Physical neglect need not be intentional. In adolescent parricide cases in which one parent, usually the father, is physically abusive, the nonabusive parent, usually the mother, must by law assume the responsibility of providing a safe environment. Her failure to provide a safe home for her children in these circumstances is rarely intended; her neglect is typically an unfortunate by-product of her inability to take care of herself and her offspring in a healthy and effective way.

Parents are also required by law in all states to provide health care for their children. Several states specifically indicate that parents have a legal duty to provide special medical treatment and mental health care needed by the child.[37] Many adolescents who kill parents are typically perceived by others as depressed and stressed for long periods before the killings. Parents who ignore their children's needs for medical care and treatment are guilty of neglect. Parents whose religious beliefs preclude certain types of medical treatment might not be considered neglectful of their children in some states when they choose not to seek medical attention; the state might, however, have provisions in its code allowing investigation and the ordering of medical services when the health of a child so requires.[38]

EMOTIONAL NEGLECT

Children have emotional needs as well as physical and medical needs. Research has established that meeting an infant's physical needs is not sufficient to ensure healthy physical development. Babies whose emotional needs are not met frequently do not gain weight and in some cases might actually die from a lack of human nurturing, also referred to as "maternal deprivation." This condition, known as nonorganic failure to thrive, is typically associated with two factors: inadequate feeding and a lack of bonding between the parents and the infant.[39]

Young children need to develop a healthy attachment to a consistent, nurturing caregiver. When children are nurtured, loved, and supported, they develop a sense of themselves as valuable individuals and learn to trust others. When emotional needs are not met, children are less likely to be able to engage in healthy and mutually satisfying relationships, and they are less prepared to master their school and neighborhood environments.[40]

Adolescent parricide offenders (APOs) are frequently victims of emotional neglect. Both the abusive and non-abusive parent, if there is one, are typically not emotionally available to their children. In case after case, abusive parents are described as failing to provide loving messages and gestures and as not listening to their children. In abusive families, the non-abusive parent often escapes either physically or psychologically. In many cases, the non-abusive parent leaves the children with the abusive spouse and moves elsewhere. By doing so, this parent becomes unable to protect the child and to provide ongoing emotional support. In cases in which the non-abusive parent remains in the home, that parent frequently copes with the stress caused by the abusive parent by "zoning out" through the use of alcohol or psychotropic drugs. Although this strategy might help the non-abusive parent cope with his or her situation, it often results in the emotional neglect of the child during a time of great need.

Emotional neglect was a primary reason that one 12-year-old boy killed his mother and his 9-year-old brother. Timmy Jackson (pseudonym) had initially intended to kill himself. Timmy decided, however, that before he took his own life, he would do "something nice" for his father and 9-year-old brother by killing his mother, whom he perceived as responsible for the unhappiness in the family.

Events did not follow the boy's expectations. Timmy's brother, Martin, arrived home before his mother. Martin's presence frustrated and panicked Timmy. He tried to persuade Martin to leave the house, but Martin would not go. Timmy eventually shot his brother in the head because he did not want Martin to see him shoot his mother and himself. When his mother arrived home, Timmy shot her in the head. "Scared" by the sight of the blood spattering and gushing from the wounds, the youth was unable to kill himself and called his father.

Mrs. Jackson's way of relating to Timmy and to her husband had hurt the boy deeply. Timmy perceived his mother as not wanting him, her older son; as hurting his father with her behavior; and as rarely being home. He interpreted being sent to daycare, survival camp, and military school as indications that she did not want him around, which made him feel "angry," "hurt," and "unwanted."

Timmy's reflections on his mother were without exception negative. Mrs. Jackson was depicted as overbearing, self-centered, materialistic, insensitive, nervous, lacking in willpower, demanding, unnecessarily restrictive of the boy's activities, and unaffectionate. Timmy stated that he could not talk to his mother because she did not like the things that he liked, such as clothes, pets, and leisure activities. Timmy thought, but was not sure, that the last time that his mother had hugged him was on his 12th birthday. The boy could not remember the last time that his mother had said that she loved him.

EMOTIONAL INCEST

Emotional incest occurs when a parent aligns with a child and relates to that child as though the child were his or her spouse.[41] Emotional incest is a common occurrence in cases of adolescents killing parents, particularly when the non-abusive parent has left the home or has withdrawn emotionally. In the absence of a spouse or age-appropriate mate, the abusive parent often expects the child to function like a surrogate partner, taking on the typical roles of a spouse and parent. The child might be expected to maintain the household (including cooking, cleaning, and raising younger siblings), nurture the parent, and act as the parent's confidant (e.g., discuss adult problems such as sexuality and relationships). In other cases, the non-abusive parent becomes increasingly dependent on an adolescent to the point that the youth feels compelled to serve as the parent's protector against the abusive parent.

Children might embrace this role because it seems to be the only way to receive parental attention, approval, acceptance, and love. In addition, they might feel a duty to help their younger siblings. Although on the surface the behavior of these youths often appears exemplary, it is not healthy. A parent's excessive dependence on a child is inappropriate because it typically creates enormous stress for the child and interrupts the natural developmental process. This type of neglect deprives the child of normal childhood experiences (such as participating in sports or extracurricular activities at school) and causes stress. Meeting expectations and assuming duties beyond their years is enormously stressful for children and adolescents. Children are ill-equipped to act as husbands or wives or, as so frequently occurs in dysfunctional families, to assume the role of parent and take care of their siblings and mother or father. When combined with other forms of abuse and neglect, the consequences can be devastating, with lifelong effects.

Emotional incest was one factor in the pathological family dynamics that led Peter Jones to kill his father. Peter functioned in many ways as a surrogate spouse and parent. Both his parents were receiving Social Security disability payments, had been diagnosed as having severe psychiatric illness, and were chemically dependent. Peter's father was an alcoholic who had been taking tranquilizers for about a year prior to the homicide. Mrs. Jones, who had a long history of stress-related ailments, had been taking painkillers and tranquilizers for years.

The medication that Mrs. Jones took would at times make her very drowsy and unable to discharge her parental responsibilities. Over the years, Peter increasingly cooked, cleaned, got himself and his younger brother off to school, and took care of his mother. He was a nurturing figure to his mother and felt a responsibility to protect her from his father. In many ways he acted more like a husband than a son. He had long been his mother's confidant and protector. Eventually, he became, in essence, her hero, by killing the man who had abused her for years. This pattern, as we will see in Chapter 10, endured throughout Peter's life.

PSYCHOLOGICAL AND BIOLOGICAL EFFECTS OF CHILDHOOD MALTREATMENT

Child neglect usually begins at an early age and can seriously impact development. Children who are emotionally neglected from an early age are at high risk of developing attachment disorders. The first two years, particularly the first six months, are a critical developmental period for children. The foundation for trusting others is learned during this period as a result of parents' or guardians' connecting with children and meeting their basic needs for food, physical comfort, and human contact. When the caregiver meets the baby's needs, the child develops a secure and healthy attachment that becomes the foundation for all future relationships.[42]

The absence of a consistent, nurturing caregiver who develops a relationship with the child and takes care of the child's needs is developmentally traumatic. Children whose emotional, physical, and medical needs are not met learn very early in life that they cannot rely on other people to respond to their needs or to soothe them. As a result, they do not trust others and might not form deep connections with other people, and they do not learn to regulate their emotions. These individuals might not develop empathy for other people. They are often filled with extreme rage and hatred. Their anger and pain are a direct result of their parents' failure to nurture and take care of them.

Like abused children, children who have been neglected frequently have disorganized, insecure attachments to their caregivers. Without this most basic relationship, these youths are unable to develop a healthy sense of themselves, and they often have difficulty relating to others throughout their lives. As a result of their early childhood experiences, many abused and neglected youths do not bond with others. These adolescents often lack attachments to teachers and conventional peers, as well as to parents. Consequently, they do not develop the self-concept, values, and empathy that foster self-control and could inhibit them from killing others. Studies indicate that neglect is more harmful to a child than abuse by itself. Prolonged neglect can set the foundation for explosive rage. On occasion, it can also lead to the development of the dangerously antisocial child.[43]

Brian Juniper (pseudonym), a 17-year-old youth from an upper middle class family, is an excellent example of a boy whose long history of attachment difficulties sparked homicidal rage. This case also illustrates that alcohol and drugs, when combined with unresolved anger, can provide the deadly nexus.

Brian was home from military school for the Christmas holidays when he was arrested for the attempted murder of his father and his stepmother. Brian was intoxicated on alcohol and drugs when he snuck into his father's house late at night, took a meat cleaver and a knife from the kitchen, and attacked his dad and stepmom in their bedroom. Brian said that he went into the house "to get his stuff" and armed himself in case he was confronted by his father.

Brian's statements indicated that he harbored a great deal of hatred and rage for his father. In contrast, he liked his stepmother, Julie, and felt badly that she had gotten hurt during his violent rampage. Brian's negative feelings toward his father were long-standing and reflective of the acute pain he had experienced since infancy as a result of several breaks in the bonding process. Brian's mother was a recovering addict when he was born. Reports indicated that Brian's father, Mr. Juniper, initially rejected his son and had very little contact with him during his infancy. Mr. Juniper also had a history of drug addiction and alcohol dependency and was a practicing alcoholic at the time of Brian's arrest.

Brian's biological parents never married or lived together. The boy lived with his mother until he was 2 years old. Records indicated that at that time, Brian's mother relapsed and abandoned him. At age 18, Brian had no memories of his mother and had never heard from her again.

Following his mother's departure, Brian lived with his father and was taken care of by babysitters. Records indicated that when Brian was about 3 years old, his father became engaged to a woman named Erin for about six months. Brian remembered Erin as a "very nice person" who cared about him. After the engagement was broken, Brian spent a lot of time in daycare. He did not hear from Erin until after his arrest for attempted murder.

When Brian was 6 years old, Mr. Juniper began living with a woman named Valerie, whom he subsequently married. Valerie was also a recovering addict. Brian and Valerie did not get along well during the six years that his father was with her. During this period, Brian did not see much of his father because Mr. Juniper worked long hours and had a significant commuting time to work. After the divorce, Brian rarely saw Valerie. Brian said that his father blamed him for their divorce.

Brian was sent to military school the following summer. Brian was 14 years old at the time. Brian remained at military school for the next 3.5 years. His contact with his father was reportedly limited to four home visits per year, one or two visits from his father at the school, one monthly phone call to his father, and one or two letters from his father monthly. Brian did not like military school and used alcohol and marijuana extensively to "calm" himself. He was caught using substances twice by school authorities and was disciplined.

During the summer preceding Brian's arrest for attempted murder, he was living at home. During this period, Mr. Juniper married Julie. Brian was seeing a counselor with whom he was discussing how to become independent or "emancipated" from his father. Brian said that, based on agreements reached with his father, he expected when he came home at Christmas that he would not return to military school in January. Instead, he would finish his last semester at the local high school, and his father would help him get emancipated by setting him up in an apartment. Brian wanted his own place because he "hated being around home." He and his father had not gotten along for years and argued frequently. Brian maintained that when he came home for the holidays, his father broke these promises, citing Brian's getting in trouble for using alcohol at school a short time before.

The boy acknowledged being very angry on the night of the attempted murder. Brian said that when he entered the house, he just wanted to get his belongings and leave, and he took the weapons with him "to intimidate, not to kill." Brian said that he went into his parents' bedroom because his father called him. He recalled his father yelling at him and an argument taking place. Brian said that he "lost it" and remembered little of the frenzied attack, during which his father and stepmother were both seriously wounded. Brian recalled taking his father's wallet, both sets of car keys, and the parents' cell phones and driving off in his stepmother's car. When asked during my evaluation whether he could see himself "losing it" again and hurting someone else, Brian replied no, explaining there was "nobody else I hated. Any voluntary relationship I would have [with my father] left a long time ago."

Brian's hatred and rage are understandable when viewed in terms of his childhood and adolescent history. The first abandonment by Brian's mother would be a traumatic loss to a child of 2 years old and a break in the bonding process. The trauma and the loss would be exacerbated for a small child by a second loss—in this case, Erin's departure. Breaks in the bonding process such as these would lead to difficulties trusting and forming attachment to others, and they could set up the foundation for rage and hatred.

During adolescence, Brian suffered repeated additional abandonment by parental figures. When Brian's father and his wife Valerie were divorced, Valerie did not maintain any meaningful contact with Brian. In addition, Brian was sent to military school within a year of the divorce. Brian said that his contact with his father was limited in terms of visits from his father, trips home, phone calls, and letters while he was in military school.

Adolescents need support from trusted adults as they move through this developmental period. Brian did not appear to have any adults available to him to help him process the difficulties of growing up, or to teach him how to resolve conflicts and deal with strong feelings. The message that Brian received as an adolescent would likely have been that he was not loved and valued, and that he was pretty much on his own. The repeated failure of the adults in Brian's life to parent him resulted in deep pain and anger.

Brian was particularly ill-equipped to resolve these feelings by himself. At the time of his arrest, Brian was functioning at a personality level that is normal for young children, but not for youths in their late adolescence. He did not see himself as accountable for his behavior and did not recognize that he had choices. Rather, he saw events as just happening rather than as a result of needs, feelings, and motives in himself and others. He had not reached a level of development at which he had incorporated a set of values that defined him and which, if violated, would cause him to feel badly. For example, Brian admitted that he had stolen money in the past from his father and stepmothers Valerie and Julie, but he then minimized his actions. He explained that he "didn't have any money" or "any allowance," and he objected to his father's making him work around the house to earn money. When asked about the $450 credit card charges that he had reportedly run up, Brian replied that it was "more like $300." He said that it was for food (pizza). He maintained that he did not steal the card; he photocopied it when his father gave it to him to use. He said that his father exaggerated the amount, implying that his actions were not as bad as it might seem.

Brian did not understand the complexity of other people. He was very restricted in terms of his awareness of his own feelings and was not capable of introspection. He was vulnerable to being overwhelmed by his feelings because he lacked insight. Brian used drugs and alcohol to self-medicate. At the time of the violent incident, he had a significant substance abuse history.

Brian's low maturity was atypical given the upper middle class nature of his environment. He lived in good neighborhoods and attended excellent schools. Arrested personality development is often a byproduct of stressful home conditions and the absence of supportive parental figures to help the child develop further.

The Role of Early Neglect in Subsequent Antisocial Behavior

The failure of parents to set limits and to impose appropriate discipline for misbehavior is also a form of neglect and can sow the seeds of death and destructiveness that will become evident years later. I have encountered several cases of adolescents who killed because they could not deal with the frustration they felt when their parents suddenly began setting limits after years of not doing so. The parents in these cases did not set limits for a variety of reasons. In some cases, they mistakenly expressed their love for their children by allowing the children to be in charge and were overindulgent. In other cases, parental discord and/or substance abuse consumed them and diverted attention away from their responsibility to set appropriate boundaries for their children. As a result, the children became accustomed to doing whatever they wanted whenever they liked.

The family dynamics that lead to the development of oppositional defiant disorder often begin with parental neglect early in the child's life. Children begin to learn societal rules, to obey authority, and to respect limits when they are between 2 and 5 years old. Parents' giving in to their children's demands might not seem that important when the child is 3 and wants cookies before dinner, or when the child is 5 and does not want to go to bed at the prescribed time. Unfortunately, the pattern becomes established and escalates over time. The problem is often recognized when youths are between ages 12 and 15 and are out of control, insisting that they are going to stay out until midnight and cursing at their parents for trying to "run their lives." Parents' efforts to set limits are typically ineffectual at this point.

Adolescents who lacked self-discipline as children and did not learn respect for authority in the home can easily cross the threshold from oppositional and defiant behavior to criminal behavior, including committing violent acts. Parents are by that time viewed as obstacles; their efforts to impede their children's goals are met with resentment, and often with contempt.[44] On rare occasions, these individuals become dangerously antisocial and intentionally murder their parents.

The failure of parents to set boundaries was clearly an important factor in understanding why two brothers, Brandon and Derek Hillsboro (pseudonyms), ages 15 and 17, joined by their 18-year-old cousin, Nathan, viciously stabbed and bludgeoned to death their father, mother, and only remaining sibling, an 11-year-old brother herein referred to as Eddie. My evaluation of the brothers, clinical interviews with family members, and review of extensive records revealed no evidence of parental abuse of any type.

The parents, however, were depicted as being "laid back" and very tolerant with respect to their sons' behavior as the boys were growing up. Available evidence suggested that Mr. and Mrs. Hillsboro were inconsistent about setting limits and imposing discipline. They tended to overlook misbehavior and talk to their sons rather than overtly sanction them. Sometimes they put the boys on restriction, but they had difficulty enforcing these punishments. Over time, the brothers became increasingly out of control. When Mr. and Mrs. Hillsboro tried to re-exert control, the brothers actively resisted and fought them.

Extensive records indicated that both boys had a long-standing history of acting-out behavior, defying parental authority, engaging in some delinquent acts, abuse of alcohol (primarily) and some drugs, and some participation in Satanic activities. At the time of the killings, the brothers were actively involved in a skinhead group known for propagating a hate-filled ideology, engaging in violent acts, and advocating anarchy. Mental health reports indicated that they had both been hospitalized previously for threatening and violent behavior directed against their parents. Records indicated that Brandon had threatened his mother with a hatchet when she tried to discipline him and that both boys had physically assaulted their father when he tried to exert some control. Both youths had been diagnosed prior to the murders as having conduct disorder.

The Hillsboro brothers had previously told mental health professionals and their friends that they were going to kill their parents. A few weeks before the familicide, Mrs. Hillsboro drafted a set of rules prohibiting Brandon and Derek from associating with individuals who were involved in drugs, alcohol, and neo-Nazism. This proclamation precluded the boys' continued association with their cousin Nathan, whom surviving relatives saw as a negative influence. At about the same time, Mr. and Mrs. Hillsboro went into the boys' room and threw out some of their Nazi materials. They took Derek's door off the hinges and left it that way. The murders occurred when the Hillsboro boys heard from another relative that their parents were investigating available channels to hospitalize them.[45]

My review of mental health records existing prior to the murders revealed no evidence that either Brandon or Derek suffered from psychosis, neurological impairment, or organic conditions. Mental health experts retained by the defense and others consulted by the prosecution found no evidence that either of the Hillsboro brothers had a psychotic process. Psychological testing done before and after the murders revealed that both boys had IQs in the normal range. Although I was not allowed as a prosecution expert to inquire about the murders in my clinical interviews with the defendants, my review of the defendants' videotaped confessions indicated that both boys had extensive recall of the events before, during, and after the triple murders. The extensiveness of their recall was inconsistent with their being in a dissociative state or severely intoxicated at the time of the homicides.

One might wonder why, if the boys were angry with their parents and murdered them for freedom, did they kill their little brother? Derek told police that his brother directed the killing of Eddie during the homicidal rampage; Brandon denied to police that he had done so. Information provided by Vicky, a paternal aunt who lived with the Hillsboro family for approximately 17 years, was helpful in this regard. The aunt said that she moved in shortly after Brandon was born and knew the boys during their whole lives. Shortly before the murders, however, this aunt moved out of the Hillsboro home at her brother's request because he feared for her safety.

Although she had never witnessed the older brothers threatening Eddie, she recalled that shortly before the murders, Eddie was frantic about finding a home for his dog because he did not want his dog to die. Eddie's fish and his crab had mysteriously died, and the boy attributed their deaths to his older brothers. Vicky cried as she related memories of the older brothers kicking this dog with their big steel-toed boots.

Vicky said that sometimes her brother and sister-in-law would ask her to take Eddie to her apartment if they knew there was going to be a confrontation. There were three or four times when the parents did not want Eddie to be at their home. Vicky took Eddie to her home to stay the Friday and Saturday nights before the murders. Vicky did not take Eddie the following night, when the murders occurred.

When asked whether Eddie had been afraid that something might happen, Vicky indicated that, in retrospect, he appeared to be. She recalled Eddie making a remark to her a night or two before the murders. Vicky and Eddie went to a small shopping mall where they saw Nathan and Derek quite unexpectedly. The older boys reportedly laughed and sneered at Vicky and Eddie. Vicky asked Eddie how his brothers were treating him. Eddie reportedly said, "You never know when you are going to die."

There were some indications in the records and in clinical interviews that the older brothers derived satisfaction from destroying things, inflicting pain, and scaring others. Did they take pleasure in terrorizing their younger brother? I noted that Screwdriver, a skinhead music group Brandon and Derek reported frequently listening to, had a song on their CD entitled "Time to Die." The song extols breaking rules and not letting anyone tell you what to do. The chorus talks about living life to the fullest: "It'll soon be time to die."

Biological Effects of Extreme Childhood Maltreatment

In addition to psychological effects, an adolescent who has suffered extreme, violent, and enduring trauma, referred to as Type III trauma,[46] is at risk of sustaining biological effects because early trauma adversely affects brain development. Early trauma also affects endocrine function. For example, early trauma recalibrates many components of the body's stress response system so that trauma survivors remain on constant alert in order to respond to real or perceived danger.[47] A few examples of the many biological effects of early trauma are presented in Table 2-3.[48]

The literature has repeatedly documented that children and adolescents who are not effectively treated for the long-term effects of early trauma typically struggle throughout their lives. Many of them develop post-traumatic stress disorder (PTSD). The three main diagnostic criteria of PTSD are (1) intrusive thoughts, images, sensory experiences, memories, and dreams; (2) avoidance of reminders of the traumatic event and/or emotional numbing; and (3) physiological hyperarousal.[49]

Long-term childhood maltreatment can lead to complex PTSD, a chronic form of PTSD. In complex PTSD, trauma survivors commonly experience additional symptoms, for example, depression and dissociation. They tend to be impulsive and aggressive toward themselves or others, and they might suffer from chronic feelings of shame and self-blame. Individuals with complex PTSD often have difficulty maintaining long-term relationships and might have only superficial connections with others.

Table 2-3 Biological effects of early trauma

What Can Happen	What It Means
Compromised right brain development	Affects right brain function: the right brain is dominant in processing information related to emotion, social interaction, and physiological states
Neural circuits connecting cortical and subcortical areas are modified	Can decrease the child's sense of self, lead to poor connections with other people, and affect the child's ability to understand other people's emotional experience, which affects the child's ability to develop empathy
Electroencephalogram (EEG) abnormalities	Associated with increased frequency of violence toward self or others
Abnormal concentrations of neurotransmitters	Affects mood, ability to inhibit inappropriate behavior
Limbic system (the emotional part of the brain) is not appropriately modulated	Its responses are exaggerated
Long-term changes in the sympathetic nervous system and endocrine response to stress	Faster, more intense response to stress

The limbic system in such individuals might remain on high alert, ready to react to danger, making the body physiologically hyperaroused.[50] These individuals typically have poor judgment and tend to be impulsive. Many of these individuals did not have an attentive, consistent, nurturing caregiver during their first year of life, and consequently they did not develop a secure attachment with another human being. They have difficulty trusting and developing and maintaining healthy relationships. They also have difficulty regulating their emotions.

Many adolescents with complex PTSD turn their anger inward and engage in self-harming behavior, including self-mutilation and self-defeating behavior. Some might act out impulsively and hurt others, but they might not be psychopathic.[51] Still others are psychopathic and might enjoy directing their rage toward hurting others. When alcohol and drugs are added to the equation, as they often are, the likelihood of poor decision making, impulsive behavior, and violent acting out by adolescents is greatly increased.[52]

Severe neglect and/or extreme abuse during early childhood can cause dissociation leading to fragmentation of the child's mind. Dissociation is a psychic response to overwhelming stress and hyperarousal. The child withdraws from the dangerous outside world and retreats into his or her internal world. With continued trauma, the internal world becomes progressively more complex, and the child's personality might split into several parts, each specialized to deal with some facet of the hostile environment. This condition is the dissociative disorder known as dissociative identity disorder (formerly known as multiple personality disorder). Sean Sellers, executed for killing his mother and stepfather at age 16, was diagnosed as suffering from multiple personality disorder (see Chapter 6).[53]

Legal and Moral Dilemmas in the 21st Century

Findings regarding the developmental neurophysiology of children subjected to severe and protracted abuse have important legal implications in how society deals with adolescent parricide offenders in the 21st century. Studies are increasingly linking extreme neglect and abuse with long-term changes in the nervous and endocrine systems. These changes affect cognitive, physiological, emotional, and social function. A growing body of research literature indicates that individuals with extensive trauma histories often have difficulty thinking logically and behaving prosocially and are thereby at higher risk of behaving violently than those without such histories.

Recent research findings also have indicated that neglect can have profound effects on children's development, including their ability to bond with others and feel empathy toward them, and to regulate and control strong emotions. These findings are best viewed in the context of recent research findings that have confirmed that the human brain is still developing through adolescence and is not fully developed until an individual is in his or her early to mid-20s.[54]

Advances in science are beginning to challenge fundamental notions of justice dating back thousands of years and might indeed pose a moral dilemma to society: Should these youths be deemed responsible for their behavior, as other killers who have had different childhood histories are, particularly if abuse and neglect have biologically compromised their ability to access higher cortical functions, regulate emotion, connect with other human beings, and respond adaptively to life's situations?[55] Issues relating to the defense of abused or "battered" children are discussed in Chapter 7.

SUMMARY AND CONCLUDING REMARKS

This chapter focused on specific types of child abuse and neglect, considering the often central role of child maltreatment in understanding the dynamics that lead to parricide. Four types of abuse (physical, sexual, verbal, and psychological) and three types of neglect (physical, emotional, and medical) were defined. These forms of childhood maltreatment were illustrated with examples from parricide cases. Emotional incest, a term used to describe the circumstance in which a parent inappropriately aligns with a child and relates to that child as his or her spouse, was also discussed in the context of offspring killing parents.

The psychological and biological effects of early and extreme childhood maltreatment, particularly child neglect, were explained with consideration of their significance in human development. Children whose emotional and physical needs are not met from an early age are at high risk of developing attachment disorders. Accordingly, they might not bond with other people and develop empathy for others. Often they have deep-seated anger and hatred, which can lead to explosive violence toward parents in later years.

The failure of parents to set and enforce appropriate limits for children from the time they are young children was also discussed in the context of neglect. Children who are not appropriately and consistently disciplined when they break rules or defy their parents do not learn frustration tolerance. These children are disadvantaged by their parents because they do not learn when they are young that they do not always get their way and the world does not revolve around them. Sadly, when parents do finally step in and attempt to set limits that should have been enforced years ago, these individuals, who might be juveniles or adults by this time, do not have the internal resources to deal with these boundaries. As a result, they might erupt with rage directed at their parents.

Research has shown that severe abuse and neglect compromise individuals' abilities to think logically, to calm themselves, and to respond adaptively, particularly in high-stress situations. In addition to psychological effects, children and adolescents who have experienced extreme, violent, and enduring trauma are at risk of suffering significant biological effects. This chapter discussed some of the biological effects of trauma with respect to brain development and endocrine function. The chapter concluded with a discussion of the legal and moral implications of research findings in the developmental neurophysiology of children in terms of offender accountability.

The professional literature on the characteristics of offenders and victims involved in patricide and matricide is reviewed in the next section of the book. Chapter 3 focuses on parricide in general. Chapters 4 and 5 examine matricides and patricides. Attention also is focused on the circumstances and motives that led to these killings.

3 Parricide: Basic Facts and Literature

- Blaine County, Idaho—A 16-year-old girl from an affluent family was arrested for shooting her parents to death. After an extensive investigation, police concluded that the girl acted alone.[1] The State argued that the girl killed her parents because they did not like her boyfriend and were taking steps to end the relationship. Although the girl proclaimed her innocence, she was tied directly to the murders by DNA. The girl was convicted of two counts of first-degree murder and sentenced to life without parole.[2]
- Chapel Hill, North Carolina—A 16-year-old boy from a prominent family was charged with first-degree murder for killing his father and mother. He told police that his father collapsed onto the kitchen floor after he fired the first shot but did not immediately die. As the father crawled toward the boy, the boy reloaded the gun and fired two more shots into his father's head at close range. Moments later, the youth left the kitchen and went to the master bedroom. He reloaded the gun and shot his mother in her shoulder and in her head. The youth wrapped the bodies in blankets and blocked the entrance to the master bedroom. On the weekend of the deaths, the adolescent attended his junior prom and invited friends back to the family home.[3] The boy told friends who commented on the bad smell in the home that meat had gone bad due to a broken refrigerator. The boy later checked into an upscale motel, where he was arrested about two weeks after the murders. The boy pled guilty to two counts of second-degree murder.[4] He was sentenced to a minimum of 20 years for killing his father and another 20 years for killing his mother.[5]
- Medicine Hat, Canada—A 12-year-old girl and her 23-year-old boyfriend were charged with three counts of first-degree murder in connection with the brutal stabbings of the girl's father, mother, and 8-year-old brother. E-mail evidence prior to the killings suggested that the girl was the mastermind behind the killings. The girl and her boyfriend were both convicted of multiple counts of murder.[6] The

girl, the youngest convicted killer in Canada, received the maximum sentence of 10 years.[7] Her boyfriend was sentenced to life without parole consideration for at least 25 years.[8]

- Swindon, Wiltshire, South West England—A 44-year-old man with a long history of mental illness was ruled unfit to plead to charges of killing his mother, age 76, and father, age 83. Nonetheless, he was found responsible by a jury for killing his parents. About four years prior to the killings, the man had moved in with his parents after being discharged from a psychiatric hospital. While in the community, the man was not monitored routinely by mental health professionals, and he stopped taking his medication. Following his conviction of the double murders, the man appeared in court via video link from a hospital where doctors had diagnosed him as having a delusional disorder. The judge ordered the man to be held indefinitely, noting that, despite repeated efforts by the family to get help, mental health agents had failed to intervene before this tragedy occurred.[9]

Parricide, as we have seen, is a rare event. The killing of parents is upsetting across the world, and killings perpetrated by females and young people are particularly disturbing and typically receive widespread news coverage. Parricides involving multiple offenders and multiple victims, such as those described above, also grab headlines and are particularly shocking.[10] In light of the interest in these particular parricides, this chapter and the two that follow on matricide and patricide incidents pay close attention to female-perpetrated parricide, youth involvement in parricide, and multiple-offender and multiple-victim parricides.

This chapter begins by setting the record straight about female and youth involvement in the killing of parents (parricide) and stepparents (stepparricide). Facts about parricides and stepparricides committed by multiple offenders and involving multiple victims are presented in general and in terms of female and youth involvement. Thereafter, the literature on parents killed is critiqued and reviewed. Virtually no studies have examined the phenomena of stepparents being killed.

This chapter focuses on parents killed as a general category rather than on specific victim types (mothers or fathers) for two fundamental reasons. First, as we shall see, many studies, if not most, discuss parricide victims and offenders in general rather than by specific parent types. Second, questions about incidence and about victim, offender, and case characteristics are often asked in terms of parents slain. For example, how many parents are killed each year? How many of those who kill parents are under age 18? How many parents are killed in multiple-victim situations? How often do those who kill parents act with accomplices? The following two chapters synthesize literature that has carefully examined offenders who killed specific parents (mothers or fathers).

FACTS ABOUT PARRICIDE AND STEPPARRICIDE

Much of what we know about parricide comes from the media and entertainment industry. I analyzed Federal Bureau of Investigation (FBI) arrest data in order to provide information on offenders involved in parricide and stepparricide incidents in 1976–2007.[11] Exact numbers regarding those involved in the killing of parents and stepparents[12] cannot be obtained because law enforcement agencies voluntarily submit arrest data to the FBI, and not all agencies participate in the reporting process.

The FBI's Supplementary Homicide Report (SHR) data sets allow national estimates to be made based on the information provided by participating police agencies.[13] In the analyses presented here and in the next two chapters, analyses are based on 32 years of police data and should be regarded as very good estimates and the best currently available.[14]

The analyses I have conducted are restricted to parricides and stepparricides in the United States because it, unlike other countries, has a national homicide data base that records information on victim type (mothers, fathers, stepmothers, and stepfathers) and makes the data accessible to researchers. When appropriate, I did statistical tests to determine whether certain findings (e.g., differences between two groups, such as juveniles and adults) were statistically significant, meaning that they did not occur by chance. These tests allow us to determine the likelihood or probability of there being no relationship between the variables (e.g., offender age and involvement in multiple-offender parricides). Researchers typically set the probability (p) at <.05, meaning that the likelihood that the differences occurred by chance is less than 5 out of 100. In most of the analyses I did, the tests determined that the likelihood of there being no relationship between the variables and the results being due to chance was less than 1 out of 1,000 (<.001). The statistical results are reported in the endnotes or tables when appropriate. Readers who are not interested in the statistical test results can ignore them.

Female-Perpetrated Parricide

Female-perpetrated parricide has been reported in the professional literature as particularly rare. Studies spanning more than 40 years have consistently concluded that when fathers and mothers are killed, their sons are typically the perpetrators.[15] In their review of the literature, d'Orbán and O'Connor[16] cited several studies indicating that the killings of mothers and/or fathers by daughters was very rare in England,[17] Scotland,[18] Finland,[19] France,[20] and Japan.[21]

Studies of parricide incidents in the United States have found that in the majority of cases, fathers and mothers are slain by sons. Nonetheless, the involvement of daughters in the killings of their parents is quite substantial. Over the period of 1976–2007, approximately 250 offenders were arrested each year for killing their parents in the United States.[22] Biological children who killed parents represented less than 2% of all offenders arrested for murder or non-negligent homicide.[23] As shown in Table 3-1, more than 80% of arrestees each year were males. Female involvement in parricide averaged approximately 15% (38 cases per year) over the considered time frame.[24] The percentage involvement of females in killing their parents was close to percentages reported in other studies.[25] Female involvement in killing biological parents does not appear to have been increasing over the past three decades.[26]

From 1976 to 2007, an estimated 58 offenders were arrested annually for killing stepparents.[27] Males constituted approximately three-quarters or more of arrestees each year. The percentage involvement of females arrested for killing stepparents also averaged approximately 15% (nine cases per year) over the same period. As depicted in Table 3-1, wide variation in stepdaughters' involvement in killing stepparents was apparent. Females made up varying percentages of all stepparricide arrests, from a low of 4.8% in 1995 to a high of 25.6% in 1998.[28] There was no evidence to suggest that females have become more involved in the killing of stepparents over time.[29]

Table 3-1 Estimated number and percentage of offenders arrested for killing parents and stepparents by gender; United States, 1976–2007*

Estimated Numbers and Percentages	Parricide Offenders Arrested			Stepparricide Offenders Arrested		
	Males	*Females*	*Total*	*Males*	*Females*	*Total*
Average per year	211	38	248	49	9	58
Average percentage over 32 years	85%	15%	100%	85%	15%	100%
Range (low to high) over 32 years (numbers/year)	160 (2007)–264 (1981)	27 (2001)–45 (1982)	193(2001 & 2007)–308 (1981)	24 (1996)–80 (1976)	2 (1995, 2004, 2006)–16 (1976)	30 (1996)–96 (1976)
Range (low to high) over 32 years (percent/year)	82.3% (1996)–88.4% (1980)	11.6% (1980)–17.7% (1996)	100%	74.4% (1998)–95.2% (1995)	4.8% (1995)–25.6% (1998)	100%
Total number	6768	1180	7948	1570	272	1842

*Supplementary Homicide Report offender data, all incidents, national estimates.

Approximately 80% of individuals arrested for killing parents in 1976–2007 were legally adults (over age 18). Males predominated among both juveniles (age 17 and under) and adults arrested for killing parents during the 32-period under review. The far greater representation of adults and males among parricide arrestees is consistent with other U.S. studies.[30]

Table 3-2 depicts the estimated number of sons and daughters arrested for killing parents from 1976 through 2007 by juvenile and adult status.[31] The estimated number of adults arrested for killing parents averaged 197 per year during this 32-year period. Adult daughters were the killers in 14% of these cases overall; the number of adult daughters arrested per year ranged from 20 to 33 and averaged 27. Adult sons were arrested in 86% of parricide incidents. The estimated number of adult male offspring arrested each year ranged from 143 to 213 and averaged 170.

The estimated number of parents killed by male and female juveniles was substantially lower than that of parents killed by adult offspring. The number of offenders under age 18 arrested for parricide ranged from 24 to 80 and averaged 49 per year. Girls under 18 constituted 19% of the parricide arrestees. Over the period examined, the number of girls arrested for killing parents ranged from two to 17 and averaged about nine per year. Males were arrested in 81% of parricides committed by juveniles. The estimated number of boys arrested for killing parents ranged from 14 to 69 and averaged 40 per year.

Although adults predominated among those arrested for killing stepparents, juveniles made up a higher percentage of those arrested for killing stepparents than for killing parents. More than 30% of those arrested for killing stepparents were under age 18, compared to about 20% of those arrested for killing parents. Males predominated among those arrested for killing stepparents among both juvenile and adult offenders. These findings are consistent with previous studies.[32]

As revealed in Table 3-3, the estimated numbers of adults and juveniles arrested per year for killing stepparents averaged 39 and 18, respectively. Girls under 18 composed 16% of juveniles arrested for stepparricide; their adult counterparts made up 14% of adults arrested for killing stepparents. Interestingly, in three of the 32 years, no female juveniles were arrested for killing stepparents in the United States.

Multiple-Offender Parricides

About 9% of parricide offenders were arrested with codefendants from 1976 to 2007 for killing one (7.9%) or more (0.9%) victims. Those who killed stepparents were significantly more likely to employ accomplices than those who killed parents. Nearly 14% of stepparricide offenders acted with others in killing one (13.3%) or more (0.6%) victims.[33]

As shown in Table 3-4, the estimated number of offenders arrested with others in killing parents averaged 22 per year.[34] Sons were arrested in approximately two-thirds of these cases. Approximately eight offenders were arrested with accomplices for killing stepparents per year. Nearly 80% of those arrested for killing stepparents were males.

Important age and gender differences were found in multiple-offender killings. Juveniles were significantly more likely than adults to use accomplices to kill parents

Table 3-2 Estimated number and percentage of juveniles and adults arrested for killing biological parents by gender; United States, 1976–2007*

Estimated Numbers and Percentages	Parricide Offenders Arrested					
	Under Age 18			Over Age 18		
	Males	Females	Total	Males	Females	Total
Average per year	40	9	49	170	27	197
Average percentage over 32 years	81%	19%	100%	86%	14%	100%
Range (low to high) over 32 years (numbers/year)	14 (2006)–69 (1978)	2 (1997)–17 (1976)	24 (2004)–80 (1976, 1978)	143 (2000)–213 (1981)	20 (1998)–33 (1982)	167 (1998)–244 (1981)
Range (low to high) over 32 years (percent/year)	53.8% (2006)–93.5% (1997)	6.5% (1997)–46.2% (2006)	100%	83.1% (1996)–89.6% (1988)	10.4% (1988)–16.9% (1996)	100%
Total number	1265	300	1565	5433	862	6295

*Supplementary Homicide Report offender data, all incidents, national estimates.

Table 3-3 Estimated number and percentage of juveniles and adults arrested for killing stepparents by gender; United States, 1976–2007*

| Estimated Numbers and Percentages | Stepparricide Offenders Arrested | | | | | |
| | Under Age 18 | | | Over Age 18 | | |
	Males	Females	Total	Males	Females	Total
Average per year	15	3	18	34	5	39
Average percentage over 32 years	84%	16%	100%	86%	14%	100%
Range (low to high) over 32 years (numbers/year)	2 (2003, 2006)–35 (1976)	0 (1995, 2004, 2006)–6 (1979, 1983, 1998)	2 (2006)–38 (1976)	19 (1996)–58 (1984)	0 (1991)–13 (1986)	24 (1996)–64 (1984)
Range (low to high) over 32 years (percent/year)	53.8% (1998)–100% (1995, 2004, 2006)	0% (1995, 2004, 2006)–46.3% (1998)	100%	73.5% (1986)–100% (1991)	0% (1991)–26.5% (1986)	100%
Total number	470	87	557	1091	171	1262

*Supplementary Homicide Report offender data, all incidents, national estimates.

Table 3-4 Estimated number and percentage of offenders arrested in multiple-offender situations for killing parents and stepparents by gender; United States, 1976–2007*

Estimated Numbers and Percentages	Parricide Offenders Arrested			Stepparricide Offenders Arrested		
	Males	*Females*	*Total*	*Males*	*Females*	*Total*
Average per year	15	7	22	6	2	8
Average percentage over 32 years	67%	33%	100%	79%	21%	100%
Range (low to high) over 32 years (numbers/year)	6 (1980, 2006) –23 (1988, 1992, 1998)	1 (1988, 1997) –15 (2005)	11 (1980)–33 (1998)	1 (1996, 2003, 2006)–15 (1987)	0 (1991, 1995, 1996, 2003, 2006)–5 (1992)	1 (1996, 2003, 2006)–18 (1987)
Range (low to high) over 32 years (percent/year)	40% (2006) –96% (1988)	4%(1988) _60% (2006)	100%	43%(1986)–100% (1991, 1995, 1996, 2003, 2006)	0 (1991, 1995, 1996, 2003, 2006)–57% (1986)	100%
Total number	467	234	701	197	51	248

*Supplementary Homicide Report offender data, multiple-offender incidents only, national estimates.

(18% vs. 7%),[35] but not stepparents (13% vs. 14%). Daughters were significantly more likely than sons to employ accomplices in the killings of parents, whether they were juvenile (36% vs. 14%)[36] or adult offenders (14% vs. 5%).[37] Females who killed stepparents were also significantly more likely than their male counterparts to enlist others to kill stepparents, whether they were under age 18 (21% vs. 12%)[38] or over age 18 (21% vs. 13%).[39]

Multiple-Victim Parricides

Precise data on multiple-victim parricides are difficult to obtain because of limitations in the FBI's SHR data base. It is not possible to determine in parricide incidents involving more than one victim who the other victims are. The relationship of the offender to the victim is linked to the first victim recorded by law enforcement. Accordingly, if a 17-year-old boy kills his father, mother, grandmother, and sister, the father will likely be coded with respect to the victim–offender relationship, the victim count will be four, and the homicide situation will be identified as involving multiple victims. Information pertaining to the other three victims cannot be accessed with the offender data base.[40] The same methodological limitation exists in the case of double parricides. For example, if a 25-year-old daughter kills her mother and another person, it is not possible with the current SHR offender data set to know whether the person killed with the offender's mother is the daughter's father, another family member, or an unrelated party.

Less than 8% of parricide offenders were arrested in 1976–2007 for killing multiple victims alone (6.9%) or with other offenders (0.9%). The percentage of stepparricide offenders involved in multiple victim killings alone (3.7%) or with codefendants (0.6%) was even smaller. The percentage involvement of juveniles paralleled that of adults in multiple-victim parricides (8.1% vs. 7.8%) and stepparricides (4.8% vs. 4.2%).

The data presented in Table 3-5 underscore the rarity of multiple-victim parricides or stepparricides, particularly among females. Fewer than 20 killings of biological parents each year involved multiple victims. The average number of multiple-victim killings involving stepparents, estimated at two to three per year, was likely far smaller than that involving biological parents for two reasons. First, there were fewer stepparents killed than parents during this period. Second, and more important, in multiple-victim situations, if a mother and stepfather were killed, the victim–offender relationship would likely have been identified as with the mother.

Offenders involved in multiple-victim killings involving parents or stepparents were overwhelmingly male. With respect to parents, males constituted 86% of juveniles arrested in multiple-victim killings and 89% of adults involved in such situations.[41] Regarding stepparents killed in multiple-victim killings, males made up 88% of juveniles arrested and 96% of adults arrested.[42]

Juvenile involvement in multiple-victim parricides was exceedingly rare. Over the 32-year period studied, an estimated 126 juvenile offenders (four per year) were arrested for killing biological parents in multiple-victim situations. It was estimated that another 26 juveniles (less than one per year) were involved in killing stepparents in multiple-victim homicides. Only three girls were identified as killing stepparents in multiple-victim homicides from 1996 to 2007.[43]

Table 3-5 Estimated number and percentage of offenders arrested for killing multiple victims in parricide and stepparricide incidents by gender; United States, 1976–2007*

Estimated Numbers and	Parricide Offenders Arrested			Stepparricide Offenders Arrested		
Percentages	Males	Females	Total	Males	Females	Total
Average per year	17	2	19	2	0	2
Average percentage over 32 years	88%	12%	100%	94%	6%	100%
Range (low to high) over 32 years (numbers/year)	9 (2002)–26 (1994)	0 (1996, 1997, 1998, 2001)–6 (1992, 2003)	10 (2001)–28 (1992)	0 (2007)–6 (1981)	0 (1976–1982, 1984 –2001, 2003–2004, 2006)–3 (1983)	0 (2007)–6 (1981, 2001)
Range (low to high) over 32 years[a] (percent/year)	70% (2003)–100% (1996, 1997, 1998, 2001)	0% (1996, 1997, 1998, 2001)–30% (2003)	100%	0% (2007)–100% (1976–1982, 1984–2001, 2003–2004, 2006)	0% (1976–1982, 1984–2001, 2003–2004, 2006–2007)–75% (1983)	100%
Total number	549	71	620	74	5	79

*Supplementary Homicide Report offender data, multiple-victim incidents only, national estimates.

[a] no offenders were arrested for killing stepparents in 2007.

Summary of Female Involvement and Multiple-Offender and Multiple-Victim Parricides

As we look back to our chapter opener, we see that adult males predominated in parricide and stepparricide incidents. Their involvement was even higher in multiple-victim killings involving parents and stepparents. However, as summarized in Table 3-6, a higher percentage of juveniles than of adults was involved in multiple-offender parricides. As the news clippings in the beginning of the chapter suggest,

Table 3-6 Synopsis of offenders arrested for killing parents and stepparents; United States, 1976–2007

	Parents	Stepparents
ALL INCIDENTS*		
• Estimated number per year	248	58
• Offender gender	85% male	85% male
• Juvenile offenders	81% male	84% male
• Adult offenders	86% male	86% male
MULTIPLE-OFFENDER (MO) INCIDENTS		
• Estimated number per year	22	8
• Offender gender	67% male	79% male
• Juvenile involvement	Higher percentage of juveniles involved in MO incidents than adults (18% vs. 7%)[a]	Juveniles and adults had about the same involvement in MO incidents (13% vs. 14%)
• Female juvenile involvement	Higher percentage of female juveniles involved in MO incidents than male juveniles (36% vs. 14%)[b]	Higher percentage of female juveniles involved in MO incidents than male juveniles (21% vs. 12%)[c]
• Female adult involvement	Higher percentage of female adults involved in MO incidents than male adults (14% vs. 5%)[d]	Higher percentage of female adults involved in MO incidents than male adults (21% vs. 13%)[e]
MULTIPLE-VICTIM INCIDENTS		
• Estimated number per year	20	2 to 3
• Offender gender	88% male	94% male
• Juvenile offenders	86% male	88% male
• Adult offenders	89% male	96% male

*Supplementary Homicide Report offender data, Single and multiple victims, single and multiple offenders; juveniles = under age 18.

[a] χ^2 (1, 7863) = 206.735, Phi = −.162, p < .001.

[b] χ^2 (1, 1564) = 82.558, Phi = .230, p < .001.

[c] χ^2 (1, 562) = 5.542, Phi = .099, p < .05.

[d] χ^2 (1, 6298) = 95.784, Phi = .123, p < .001.

[e] χ^2 (1, 1266) = 7.338, Phi = .076, p < .05.

girls often used accomplices in killings involving parents. In fact, the percentages of juvenile and adult females involved in multiple-offender situations involving both parents and stepparents were higher than those for their male counterparts.

LITERATURE REVIEW

This review[44] begins with a critique of the literature. After a discussion of problems in the literature, attention turns to three studies that used more sophisticated research designs to overcome the limitations of previous studies. These three studies analyzed matricide and patricide incidents in terms of male and female offenders.

A growing body of literature has examined adults who have committed matricide and patricide, and it has analyzed these offenders as separate groups. These studies are reviewed in the next two chapters, which focus on matricide and patricide offenders, respectively. In contrast to the adult literature, most of the research on youths who killed mothers and fathers has combined cases and analyzed them in terms of parricide offenders. Accordingly, results from studies of juvenile parricide offenders are summarized in this chapter. Case reports that focused specifically on juvenile matricide or patricide offenders are synthesized in the following two chapters.

The chapter then focuses on studies that have investigated double parricides and familicides. Special attention is given to female and juvenile involvement in multiple-victim parricides. The chapter concludes with a review of studies that compared samples of parricide offenders with other homicide offenders.

Methodological Issues in Parricide Literature

Examining the professional literature on matricide or patricide with the aim of comparing the motivations of different offender types (male adults, male juveniles, female adults, and female juveniles) is a difficult undertaking. The literature on matricide and patricide is not easily deciphered in terms of offender age and gender. Much of the parricide literature takes a broad approach to investigating the killing of parents by their offspring. Many of these studies use data that encompass all types of parricide and parricide offenders in the same report. That is, as is discussed below, samples often include both sons and daughters of varying age categories who killed or attempted to kill a variety of victim types (mothers, fathers, stepparents, adoptive parents, both parents, and parents along with other family members). In many of these reports, findings are not analyzed by victim gender or offender age and gender. In a recently published integrative review of the literature on schizophrenia and matricide, for example, the author did not analyze and discuss findings in terms of the age and gender of the offender.[45] Accordingly, it is not possible to draw conclusions from this study specifically with respect to a particular type of matricide offender, such as teenage daughters or adult sons who kill their mothers.

As summarized in Table 3-7, the literature on parricide suffers from several methodological problems.[46] Many studies and review articles combine cases of patricide and matricide and discuss their findings primarily in terms of parents killed by their children. This methodology has been used in studies involving both adult offenders[47] and juveniles who kill parents.[48] Combining matricide with patricide cases risks obscuring differences that might exist between the two victim groups. Research has indicated that differences in demographic and case variables between matricide and patricide

Table 3-7 Methodological problems in parricide literature*

- Combining patricide and matricide cases
- Combining cases of single parents killed with cases of both parents killed
- Combining cases of single parents killed with double parricides and familicides
- Combining cases of offenders who attempted to kill their parents with those who killed them
- Combining stepparents with biological parents killed
- Combining adoptive parents with biological parents killed
- Combining male and female parricide offenders
- Most studies focus on male parricide offenders
- Most studies focus on adult offenders
- Combining juvenile and adult parricide offenders
- Generalizing conclusions from hospitalized samples to the full population of parricide offenders

*Source: Heide & Frei, 2010.

offenders, victims, and incidents in the United States do exist.[49] In addition, there is evidence that psychiatric diagnoses, events leading up to the killing, and legal outcomes differed among patricide and matricide offenders.[50] Variations in the content of delusions and the age of illness onset between offspring who kill mothers and those who kill fathers have been reported.[51] Differences in motivational dynamics propelling the killings of mothers and fathers also have been suggested in the clinical literature.[52]

Some studies include in their analyses cases in which both parents are killed and cases in which a single parent is slain.[53] There are studies that include cases in which other relatives are killed, provided that there is at least one parent among the victims whom the offender killed[54] or attempted to kill.[55] The inclusion of double and multiple-victim parricide cases with single-victim cases is particularly suspect. The dynamics involved in these cases are quite likely to differ from those involved in cases in which an offspring kills one parent.[56] It is best to analyze these cases separately, as has been illustrated in the works of several investigators.[57]

Some studies include in their samples and subsequent analyses of parricide offenders individuals who attempted to kill their parents,[58] whereas others do not. The literature on homicide has established that often what distinguishes an attempted murder from a completed one is a chance factor, such as the marksmanship of the offender, the physical stamina of the victim, or the availability of medical care.[59] Thus, combining attempted murders with completed acts is defensible. However, some caution is advised, as comparative analyses of parricide and attempted cases have found some differences.[60]

Some studies include stepparents among their samples of parents slain.[61] The inclusion of stepparents, although common in the clinical literature, is not without risk. The motivational dynamics involved in killing a stepparent might differ from those involved in killing a biological parent, given that the relationships are fundamentally different.[62] In addition, differences in demographic and case variables between biological parents and stepparents slain have been found.[63] Including adoptive parents in parricide analyses[64] is questionable. Studies focusing on adoptees who kill their adoptive parents have suggested that the dynamics involved in these killings differ from those involved in the killings of biological parents.[65] One study proposed that a specific type of psychopathology, known as adopted child syndrome, exists in cases of adopted children who kill adoptive parents.[66]

Many studies combine both male and female offenders in their analyses of the killings of mothers and fathers. This methodological practice has been used in studies involving adult parricide offenders[67] and adolescents who kill parents.[68] Researchers have usually combined both genders in order to bolster the number of cases. The number of female parricide offenders in these studies is typically small and would not permit analysis by gender. Still, these studies risk obscuring gender differences.[69]

Many studies focus on males who kill parents. Although most of these focus on adult offenders,[70] some of them include both juvenile and adult subjects.[71] The inclusion of sample subjects without controlling for age is problematic. For example, research has revealed differences between juvenile and adult parricide offenders in terms of the weapons used to kill parents,[72] motivational dynamics behind the crime,[73] prevalence of psychotic diagnoses,[74] legal outcome,[75] threat assessment,[76] and birth order.[77]

Some studies that include both juvenile and adult offenders do discuss differences between these age groups, particularly as they apply to motivational dynamics. However, these studies do not differentiate between the type of victim (mother or father) and the gender of the offender. Rather, differences between juvenile and adult offenders are discussed in general without regard to victim gender.[78]

Some studies appropriately restrict their sample to adults only.[79] Samples from some of these studies, however, consist of hospitalized subjects.[80] The extent to which findings pertaining to subjects who are hospitalized for evaluation or found not guilty by reason of insanity are generalizable to the population of parricide offenders is not known; this point was made by a British scholar more than 30 years ago.[81] Hillbrand and colleagues extracted diagnostic information from seven studies published between 1966 and 1997 that focused on samples of parricide offenders.[82] They reported that 79% of the 237 offenders in their combined sample had been diagnosed with major psychopathology defined as schizophrenia spectrum diagnoses,[83] other psychotic disorders, or mood disorders. They concluded that pathology was likely over-diagnosed, as most parricide offenders were evaluated in forensic hospitals and diagnoses were made after the killings.[84]

Comparative Studies of Matricide and Patricide

This review of the literature found only three comparative studies of matricide and patricide events that examined the type of parricidal incident by gender of offenders. Diagnostic information was available in two of the studies. Researchers in the first study used coroners' records to identify 56 cases of parents killed by juvenile and adult offenders in Quebec, Canada, between 1990 and 2005.[85] Nine of these cases involved double parricides.

Approximately two-thirds of the 56 parricide offenders killed due to a psychiatric motive that resulted from depression or a psychotic illness. Two-thirds of the sample were found to have a psychotic disorder. Fourteen percent of the parricide offenders attempted suicide following the killings. This study found, consistent with previous literature, that parents were typically slain by adult sons; only four of 56 offenders were females. Three of the four female parricide offenders killed their mothers. Sons, in contrast, were more likely to kill their fathers; 36 of the 60 victims killed by sons were fathers. All nine of the double parricides were committed by sons.

The large number of male offenders permitted comparisons to be made between sons who killed mothers and those who killed fathers. Psychosis and/or psychotic delusions predominated in both patricides and matricides committed by sons. My analysis of the authors' data indicated similar Axis I findings for the 20 matricide and 27 patricide offenders for whom diagnoses were known. Nearly two-thirds of matricide and patricide offenders were diagnosed as having schizophrenia or psychosis (65% vs. 67%), and about 20% were diagnosed with depression (20% of matricide offenders vs. 18.5% of patricide offenders). Substance abuse/dependence was diagnosed for one matricide and two patricide offenders (5% vs. 7%).[86] Two matricide and two patricide offenders reportedly did not have an Axis I disorder (10% vs. 7%).

Two of the three female matricide cases were diagnosed with depression, and one was diagnosed with intoxication. Depression was diagnosed in the one patricide case committed by a daughter.

The second study focused on adult parricide offenders admitted to the only hospital for mentally disordered offenders in Zimbabwe from 1980 through 1990.[87] Information from hospital records was supplemented by information obtained from semi-structured interviews with patients and, when needed, contact with their families. Similar to the findings of the first comparative study, male parricide offenders predominated. The sample of 39 consisted of 34 men and five women, each of whom had killed one parent. The victims killed by men were fairly close in number—18 fathers and 16 mothers. In contrast, four of the five victims killed by women were mothers.

Not surprisingly, given that this sample consisted of hospitalized parricide offenders, the incidence of serious mental illness was high. Thirty-three (85%) parricide offenders were diagnosed as having schizophrenia/psychosis, five (13%) with epilepsy, and one (3%) with a personality disorder. Of the 16 sons who killed mothers, 12 were diagnosed as having schizophrenia/psychosis, three as having epilepsy, and one as having a personality disorder. Three of the four daughters who killed mothers were diagnosed as schizophrenic/psychotic, and the remaining one as epileptic. Seventeen of the 18 sons and the one daughter who killed fathers were diagnosed as having schizophrenia/psychosis; the remaining son was diagnosed with epilepsy.

The third comparative study used SHR data compiled over the 28-year period of 1976–2003 to examine gender differences in 2599 offenders who killed parents and stepparents in the United States.[88] Offenders aged 21 years and younger were included in the study. Consistent with past literature, boys outnumbered girls 7:1 in the killing of mothers. Several significant differences were found when results were analyzed by victim type. Girls who killed mothers tended to be younger than their male counterparts. Girls who killed mothers peaked in the mid-adolescent age category (14–17), whereas boys were in the late-adolescent age category (18 to 21). Although girls who killed fathers were significantly more likely than boys to be African-American, no significant racial differences were found between boys and girls who killed mothers. Contrary to the researchers' hypotheses, no significant differences were found in terms of offender gender in the selection of weapons used to kill mothers. Firearms were the most frequently selected weapon by both girls and boys.

Studies Involving Juvenile and Adolescent Parricide Offenders

The literature discussed below highlights primarily findings from studies of youths who typically ranged from 12 to 17 years of age. A few studies, however, included youths who were younger than 12, and some research efforts included adolescents in their late teens, that is, 18 or 19 years of age. In recognition of reporting practices in the professional literature, the terms "juvenile" and "adolescent" are treated as equivalent terms in the review that follows.

Several analyses of youths who killed parents included cases of both boys and girls in their discussion of the dynamics involved in the killings of parents.[89] Two studies that compared parricidal adolescents with other types of homicide offenders each had one girl in their respective samples of 10 and 11.[90] Most of the literature on juvenile and adolescent parricide offenders available in the English language consists of case studies or clinical reports involving primarily boys who killed biological fathers.[91] In these cases, youths were frequently portrayed as killing in response to long-standing abuse.

Heide identified 12 characteristics often found in cases of severely abused children, particularly boys, who kill parents, notably fathers.[92] These characteristics were extracted from many studies[93] and remain characteristic of young parricide offenders.[94] As listed in Table 3-8, these youths were raised in violent homes where parental brutality and cruelty toward the children, and often toward the spouses, were common. These young people were not successful in getting help from others or escaping the family situation by running away or attempting suicide. Over time, these adolescents experienced the home environment as increasingly intolerable and felt more helpless and trapped. Their inability to cope as stressors mounted led in some cases to a loss of control. As a group, these youths were not criminally sophisticated, having little or no prior criminal history. Guns were typically easily available in these homes. The parricide victims frequently had histories of substance abuse or dependence. Dissociation during the killing was commonly reported by these

Table 3-8 Common characteristics among severely abused parricide offenders*

Pattern of family violence

Youth's attempts to obtain help from other people fail

Youth's efforts to escape the family situation fail (e.g., running away, suicide attempts, suicidal thoughts)

Youth is isolated from other people

Home life becomes increasingly intolerable

Youth feels trapped and helpless

Youth loses control due to inability to cope

Youth has little or no criminal history

A gun is available

Victim (parent) is often a heavy user of alcohol and/or drugs

Evidence to suggest the offender is in a dissociative state in some cases

Parent's death is frequently perceived as a relief to the offender and to the surviving family members

*Source: Heide, 1992.

offenders. Adolescent parricide offenders (APOs) and their families often were initially relieved that the abusive parents were dead; often the APO felt no immediate remorse.

Recently, Buyuk and colleagues reported on their examination of archival data available from Specialization Boards of the Council of Forensic Medicine with respect to 39 boys and girls (ages 12–18) who killed 35 parents and four stepparents in single-victim incidents from 1994 to 2005 in Turkey.[95] This study is among the largest published studies of APOs. They found, consistent with Heide's typology and synthesis of the literature, that most parricide offenders were male, abuse was the most commonly identified motive in these cases, severe mental illness was rare, a previous criminal or antisocial history was uncommon, and firearms were the most utilized weapon. The board determined that the offenders in 35 of the 39 cases were fully responsible for their actions and referred them back to the court for trial and disposition. The board recommended that the four parricide offenders with psychiatric illnesses be sent to the hospital for treatment.[96]

Double Parricides Involving Adult Offenders

The limited literature on double parricides speaks to their rarity. Renowned forensic psychiatrist Manfred Guttmacher briefly described, in his book *The Mind of the Murderer*, a case of a 26- or 27-year-old psychotic man who killed his parents. The father was described as a very learned man who home-schooled his son and three daughters in order to prevent them "from being contaminated by the less godly children of the county."[97] The father imposed a strict code of behavior and, according to the son who later killed him, "lectured them incessantly about their deficiencies."[98] The mother was described by surviving offspring as subservient to her husband and largely uninvolved with them as a result of catering to her husband's whims. She reportedly wanted peace at any cost.

Family members recognized that the son was mentally ill a few months prior to the homicide. The father had become afraid of his son and was trying to get his son to see a psychiatrist. The son explained that he could not take the criticism anymore and had thought of killing his father about a week before taking action. He decided to kill his mother because she was sickly and he did not want her to suffer with the knowledge that he had killed his father. He plunged a bayonet into the chests of his father and mother while they slept.

Guttmacher diagnosed the son as paranoid schizophrenic. The young man was subsequently found not guilty by reason of insanity and was hospitalized. Guttmacher noted that the son expressed no remorse at any time. In addition, the psychiatrist reported that the sisters seemed very detached from the tragedy. Guttmacher diagnosed one of the sisters as clearly mentally ill; his account indicated that the behavior of the two other sisters was very odd.

In addition to Guttmacher's account, I located seven journal articles that reported on a total of 27 adults who killed two parents. All but one of these involved male offenders. Five of the seven articles consisted of clinical reports.[99] The remaining two were studies involving larger samples.[100] Although severe mental illness was commonly diagnosed in clinical reports, the larger samples of double-parricide offenders found a significant number of offenders to be more criminally motivated than psychiatrically impaired.

The first case report focused on a 22-year-old man[101]; the second clinical report provided information on two men, aged 29 and 35, who in separate incidents killed their parents.[102] Similar to Guttmacher's case, all three men in these clinical reports were diagnosed as suffering from paranoid schizophrenia, were found not guilty by reason of insanity, and were committed to mental hospitals. Sexually seductive behavior by the mother was noted in the first case report, but not in the other two cases. The men in the two remaining cases differed from the first man in that they had "an overprotective and domineering parent" and led "relatively dependent lives."[103]

A third clinical report, written in French, described a fourth case of double parricide committed by a 27-year-old man. Similar to the first three cases, this man was diagnosed as schizophrenic and had a history of previous psychiatric hospitalizations. He shot his parents with a hunting gun on Christmas day. He had a history of early school difficulties, employment problems, and violent behavior. After the review of two psychiatric assessments, in accordance with French law, mental illness was determined to be the reason for the man's violent acts; he was not prosecuted, and he was hospitalized in a unit for dangerously mentally ill patients.[104]

Two additional cases of adult males involved in double parricides were briefly described by forensic psychologist Gerard Cooke in a fourth clinical article on parricide.[105] Although both of these men suffered from serious mental illness, the diagnoses were different. The first, a 21-year-old, fit the profile described in the four case studies summarized above. He was also diagnosed as suffering from paranoid schizophrenia, found not guilty by reason of insanity, and sent to a state forensic mental hospital.

The second man, aged 23, had a long history of severe identity problems. He had difficulties in relationships with his parents and with women. After his second rejection by a woman, he developed "angry and morbid fantasies." The man told Cooke that he traveled to New York City with the intention of killing a stranger in order to gain "raw power" and to rid himself of his angry feelings before he killed a person close to him. After failing to find someone to murder in New York, he decided that he would kill his parents as a "political statement" about how "the system is screwed up" and anarchy should prevail. At the time of the killings, the man felt "despair, loneliness, and hatred." Killing his parents gave him feelings of "power, pride, and confidence" in his abilities.[106]

The forensic examiner opined that this man was guilty but mentally ill, because he knew his behavior was wrong but could not conform his conduct to the requirements of the law. During the pretrial period, the man decompensated and become catatonic. The court found that the man was incompetent to stand trial, and he was committed to a mental hospital for treatment. When his competency was restored, he was tried and found guilty but mentally ill by the court. The man was sentenced to prison and was periodically transferred to the state mental hospital when his mental health status deteriorated.[107]

The last clinical case to be discussed involved a 21-year-old man with a history of depression and difficulty adjusting to the army.[108] He was admitted twice to a psychiatric hospital, the second time following a serious suicide attempt. Prior to attempting suicide, he had considered killing a prostitute. During the man's hospitalization, Vereecken, the treating doctor, noted his psychotic condition and paranoid attitude. After some improvement, the patient was discharged from the hospital with the diagnosis "hebrephrenic deficiency with a serious affective neglect, stimulated by social frustration."[109] He moved into a boarding house, attended school on a scholarship, worked part time, dated a young woman, and participated in outpatient therapy with Vereecken.

The man did well for about three months before his life started to unravel. He experienced financial strain and social difficulties and blamed his parents. The treating clinician increased outpatient appointments amidst veiled threats by the patient that "bad consequences" were going to prevail for the patient, his girlfriend, his landlady, and Vereecken. The doctor, aware of the patient's "acute schizophrenic reaction," struggled against hospitalizing the man, hoping that he could stabilize the patient at the next appointment. Precisely at the time when he was due in the clinic for therapy, the patient stabbed his parents to death with a dagger. He subsequently told the police that he murdered two people. The patient was sentenced to 15 years in prison and "ordered to be detained during Her Majesty's pleasure after that period."[110] Vereecken noted that the murders were committed "in spite of rather than because of the treatment."[111]

Nine of the 56 parricide cases examined by Bourget and colleagues involved double parricides.[112] The researchers concluded that "severe psychopathology was prevalent in this group" and that most of them were "actively psychotic."[113] Six of the nine were diagnosed with schizophrenia, and one with depression. The remaining two expected to benefit monetarily from the killings. Five of the nine had attempted suicide, and three were successful.

In the largest study of double parricide to date, Weisman and colleagues retrospectively studied 11 cases referred for psychiatric evaluation in Southern California.[114] In 10 of these 11 cases, both parents died as a result of the attack. All parricide offenders were male. They ranged in age from 18 to 35 and averaged 25 years old. Ten of the 11 men were single. Researchers divided offenders into two groups (mentally ill vs. criminal) based on the ultimate disposition: four were sent to psychiatric hospital, and seven were confined in prison. Two cases were presented in order to illustrate the two subtypes.

The four confined in the psychiatric hospital all had diagnoses of schizophrenia that predated the killings. In contrast, of the seven sent to prison, one had a pre-offense diagnosis of schizophrenia, and two had diagnoses of substance disorder; four had no mental disorders. Personality disorders had been previously diagnosed in six of the seven prison subjects, compared to only one of the hospital subjects.

Diagnoses by forensic experts after the killings indicated that all four of the hospitalized subjects had psychotic disorders. One was never restored to competency and was civilly committed; the remaining three were reportedly found not guilty by reason of insanity.[115] Forensic expert diagnoses of prison subjects included two psychotic disorders, two mood disorders, and three personality disorders. Only one offender (prison sample) was intoxicated at the time of the killings. Sentencing information was provided for six of the seven offenders in the prison sample: One was sentenced to 12 years to life in prison, three were sentenced to life without parole, and two were sentenced to death.

Weisman and colleagues made several interesting observations. First, characteristics frequently encountered in murder cases, such as a history of juvenile violence, drug use, and family criminal backgrounds, were not found in double-parricide cases. Second, prior threats and assaults on the victims occurred in a majority of these cases. Third, no archival evidence of child maltreatment was found in case files to indicate that child abuse propelled the killings. The authors concluded, based on their sample of adults, that double parricides are primarily committed by sons due to serious mental illness or premeditated criminality.[116]

Adult-Female-Perpetrated Double Parricides

Double parricides involving female perpetrators are exceedingly rare.[117] Chamberlain discussed the dynamics behind the case of a 20-year-old woman who killed both parents.[118] The woman shot both her parents in the head and in the chest as they sat parked in their car. Afterward, she cut both their wrists and throats to make sure that they were dead. Psychotic symptoms were detected in the woman more than a year prior to the homicide, and she was referred for psychiatric care. There was some disagreement in diagnosis following the murders. In contrast to other mental health professionals who diagnosed the young woman as schizophrenic, Chamberlain believed that she was bipolar and committed the double parricide during "an acute manic episode marked by grandiose delusions and paranoid ideation."[119] The defendant was found not guilty by reason of insanity. Chamberlain followed her for a few years, during which she remained hospitalized.

Double Parricides Involving Adolescent Offenders

Juvenile involvement in parricides involving more than one victim is also very rare.[120] The literature contains only a few case reports of double parricides by adolescent perpetrators. Not surprisingly, almost all of these accounts involved sons who killed parents. Unlike the clinical reports on adults, those involving juveniles do not characterize these children as psychotic. Existing case reports typically depict these youths as severely abused, seriously depressed, and pushed beyond their limits of endurance.[121] However, cases of youths killing parents for antisocial reasons have been documented.

Two of the case studies profiled in a book by Reinhardt called *Nothing Left But Murder* involved double parricides.[122] One involved Lander, a 16-year-old boy who killed his mother and father, and the other involved Caron, a 16-year-old girl who killed her mother and stepfather.

Lander was "a fine boy" according to his neighbors and teachers.[123] He attended school regularly, got good grades, played sports well, and had musical talent. The boy was respected by his teachers and presented no behavioral problems at school. He was popular with his classmates and liked by their parents. He worked part time at a restaurant and made good money for a boy his age. His first brush with the law came when he was arrested for two counts of murder in connection with the shooting deaths of his parents.

Reinhardt described the events that led up to the killings. Lander was dating a girl named Christine. He was devastated when his mother suddenly changed her mind and told him that he could not use the car to take Christine to a dance. The boy sat in his bedroom trying to figure out a way to get his mother to change her mind. Suddenly he remembered that his father had a .22 caliber automatic rifle in his closet. Lander grabbed the rifle and went to the kitchen, where he pointed the rifle at his mother with the intention of scaring her. Lander maintained that she sneered at him and goaded him to shoot her. The boy shot his mother three times. Lander remembered being afraid when he saw his father rushing into the kitchen and immediately firing, killing him.

Lander recalled being engulfed by a terrible feeling after the killings. He knelt down alongside the bodies of his dead parents and prayed for them and for himself. For a while, he wondered whether the killings were perhaps a dream or a bizarre fantasy.

Soon after the killings, Lander told a neighbor that his parents had been called away on family matters. He took his younger brother to the neighbor's house and then returned to his parents' home. He dragged the bodies to the basement, where they would be out of sight. Suddenly, he remembered the school dance and drove the car to his girlfriend's house. It was too late to attend the dance, so he took Christine and her brother to a movie.

Lander kept the ruse of his parents being out of town going for two weeks. He told one of the senior men at his father's shop to run the business until his father returned. Lander stayed alternately with the neighbor, with a school friend, and at his parents' home. He buried his parents' bodies in a shallow grave in the backyard. During this time, he attended school, stopped at his father's shop, and went to church.

He confessed soon after police came to speak with him. Reinhardt's account suggested that the mother's sudden refusal to allow the boy to take the car to the dance was the precipitating event. Close reading of the account suggests that there was a long history of psychologically abusive treatment by the mother. For example, the mother did not like Lander's girlfriends. She called Christine "no good" and said that her whole family was "trash." She made fun of the boy's athletic and musical abilities. Lander did not believe that his mother really loved him. The boy recalled that his mother punched him in the stomach, locked him out of the house in the cold, and blamed him for everything that went wrong.

Accounts by Lander and others indicate that his mother had "nervous breakdowns" and was not mentally well. Neighbors and friends corroborated the mother's erratic and abusive treatment of Lander. One said, for example, that Lander's mother was very hard on him and was the cause of all his trouble. Another recalled that Lander could never count on anything because his mother was always changing her mind. Still another family friend wondered why the father, who thought highly of Lander, did not stand up for the boy, instead of always giving into his wife's whims.

The pre-sentence psychiatric report found no evidence of psychosis or hyperactivity. The record clearly indicated that Lander had been seriously depressed for a long time preceding the murders. Two of his close friends told Reinhardt that Lander appeared depressed for several days before the killings. He talked little and seemed to be in a "kind of stupor or daze." Lander was filled with remorse for the killings. Although he had dreams and fantasies of his mother dying prior to his murderous behavior, he found these thoughts abhorrent. He never intended to kill his mother, and he did not blame her for what happened. He pled guilty to two counts of second-degree murder and was sentenced to life in prison.[124]

Cooke briefly described a case of another 16-year-old boy who suddenly killed his parents. Those who knew the boy were shocked by his arrest.[125] This youth, similar to Lander, was depicted as a prosocial boy. Despite a learning disability, he was making progress in school, was on the swim team, and had a part-time job. He was regarded as a polite, quiet, and well-adjusted boy. Other than an occasional beer, he did not drink or use drugs.

The boy reportedly killed his parents after he received a failing grade on a test. The forensic examination indicated that the boy had become increasingly depressed during the two years preceding the killings. Testing revealed that he had "a poor self-image and felt inferior, insecure, and different from peers."[126] The boy felt pressured by his parents to get good grades so he could go to college. Although the evaluator did not see the parents' pressure as excessive, the boy increasingly felt "a sense of helplessness and futility due to the combination of his depression and learning disability."[127]

The boy was tried for two counts of murder. Although the boy was depressed, he did not meet the legal standard for insanity. After being advised by the judge that a murder conviction would mandate a life sentence, the jury found the boy not guilty by reason of insanity. The boy was remanded to a forensic mental hospital.[128]

Shelley Post, a former juvenile court social worker, described two cases of boys who killed two parents. She did not provide dispositions for these cases.[129] Stuart, age 15, shot and killed his father and stepmother. Close reading of Post's account indicates that Stuart and his younger sister Susan were physically neglected (deprived of food, not protected from harm), physically abused (severely beaten), and sexually abused (both children were made to watch the parents have intercourse, and there was seductive behavior by the stepmother toward Stuart). The parents were involved in domestic violence, which sometimes spilled over to their children.

Two years prior to the killings, Susan went to live with the children's mother. Stuart felt he had lost his only supporter. His attempts to get help from relatives and social services were unsuccessful. Five months before the killings, Stuart's stepmother gave birth to his half-sister. Stuart repeatedly saw his parents slap the baby and felt a responsibility to protect the infant. On the day of the killings, Stuart watched as the stepmother brutally beat his half-sister. Later that night, he shot his parents as they slept.

The second double parricide described by Post also involved a 15-year-old boy, Aaron, who had been subjected to years of abuse. Aaron was the oldest of five children. Although all of the children were reportedly abused, Aaron's siblings agreed that Aaron received the worst of the abuse. Aaron's grandfather witnessed Aaron's mother forcing another one of her sons to wrap Aaron's arms around a tree while she hit him repeatedly with a broomstick.

The parents also fought violently with each other. On one occasion, they even shot guns off at each other. Aaron was seen by his siblings as their protector, and they often went to him for help.

On the evening of the killings, Aaron's mother used a belt buckle to beat him. Aaron decided to escape and grabbed his shotgun to take with him. As he was leaving, his mother approached him armed with three pairs of scissors. Aaron shot her. When his father came rushing into the house, "yelling and cussing," Aaron shot his father, too. The boy was charged with two counts of first-degree murder.[130]

In contrast to these cases, Kashani and his colleagues reported two cases of boys who shot their parents to death because the parents would not allow them to use the family car.[131] They described one of these cases, involving a 16-year-old boy named Daniel. Daniel had a learning disability and did not like school. He used alcohol and a variety of drugs, which caused problems for him with his parents and resulted in his expulsion from school. Prior to the murders, the conflict between Daniel and his parents intensified. At one point, Daniel reported his parents to social services for abusing and neglecting him; however, the complaint was not substantiated.

"One of the major sources of parent-child conflict concerned Daniel's desire to drive,"[132] even though he did not have a driver's license. On the day of the killings, Daniel maintained that his parents reneged on their promise to let Daniel take the family car to attend a friend's birthday party. Daniel was "so outraged that he decided to murder his parents that night."[133] Daniel, who was under the influence of alcohol and drugs at that time, secured a revolver and a shotgun from the family barn. He shot his mother with the shotgun while she slept. He then fired multiple shots with the revolver at his father as the man entered the bedroom from the adjoining bathroom. After his father fell onto the floor, Daniel reloaded the revolver and continued to shoot.

Following the murders, Daniel drove the car to the party and later returned home. He took the car to school the next day, and he was arrested shortly thereafter. He was subsequently convicted of murdering both his parents. Kashani and colleagues noted that, although chaos and abuse existed in this home, the killings were not an act of self-defense. Rather, Daniel killed his parents to secure material gain.

Juvenile-Female-Perpetrated Involvement in Double Parricides

Girls are rarely involved in double parricides. However, cases of adolescent girls involved in the killing of both parents do exist. In four of the 16 cases identified by Marleau and colleagues in which females under 20 killed mothers, fathers were also killed.[134]

Reinhardt explained the factors that led Caron, a 16-year-old girl, to kill her mother and her stepfather as they lay sleeping.[135] Caron had never felt loved as a child. She deduced from events and her mother's answers to her questions that she was illegitimate. Corroborative data indicated that her parents were heavy drinkers and likely alcoholics. Caron's responsibilities included taking care of her five younger siblings while her parents drank in the tavern and then making sure her parents got safely home. Caron had an extensive array of chores to do that included stocking the feed on the farm, carrying heavy loads, toting bags of food, keeping up the household, and preparing breakfast. Caron was rarely allowed to participate in activities at school. Although her parents did not want her to date as a teen, they pushed her to see a 39-year-old man and to go off with him. Caron came to hate her parents.

Reinhardt's case report is replete with evidence that Caron was physically and emotionally neglected by her parents and subjected to both psychological and physical abuse by them. She became obsessed with the idea of killing her parents after her brother showed her how to load the shotgun. She got to the point where she felt that she could no longer endure living in that household with her parents and convinced herself that her younger siblings, whom she loved deeply, would be better off without their mother and father.

After the killings, Caron felt relief, not remorse. She experienced peace and happiness in the jail and was struck by the kindness of the sheriff's family and her clean and nice jail cell. The judge recognized that there were extenuating cases in Caron's case. However, he sentenced her to prison for 30 years because he believed that the punishment would deter other youths in similar or worse circumstances.[136]

Familicide

Familicide is the killing of more than one family member and is a type of mass murder.[137] As noted by psychiatrist Carl Malmquist more than 30 years ago, "familicides are rare catastrophes which occur unpredictably."[138] Destroying the family unit appears to be the killer's objective.[139] In addition to Malmquist's pioneering study of familicide, I located two clinical reports of familicides perpetrated by sons.[140] My review of the literature uncovered no cases of daughters killing three or more family members.

Malmquist's study involved eight cases in which male perpetrators killed multiple family members. Five of the mass murderers were fathers or grandfathers; only three killers were the victims' offspring. The three "children" were sons aged 14, 18, and 21; each of them killed both parents and at least one sibling.[141]

Little information is provided regarding the circumstances prior to the killings. The 14-year-old had difficulties dealing with his father's harsh demands for performance. The boy suffered from periods of severe depression and considered killing himself. "Instead, in a massive eruption of violence,"[142] he shot the five family members present, killing his parents and one brother and wounding two other brothers. The 18-year-old, consumed with feelings of being a failure and thoughts that he was being persecuted for not meeting his parents' demands, killed his parents and his sister. The 21-year-old was in a paranoid state when he beat his parents and brother to death with a baseball bat and then drove around the country trying to understand what had happened. He was the only one of the three sons whom Malmquist diagnosed as psychotic.

Malmquist maintained that the eight individuals involved in the familicides struggled for years with deflated self-esteem, grandiose aspirations, and bouts of depression. He concluded from his study of these cases that there was usually a precipitating event that sparked unresolved conflict that previous defenses could no longer contain. These individuals were narcissistic both before and after the killings. They described themselves as though they were observers of the destructive forces, "as much hopeless victims as those that had been killed."[143]

Psychologist Robert McCully wrote a detailed case study of an 18-year-old boy who killed his stepfather, mother, and 4-year-old half-brother on the night before Thanksgiving. The youth shot his stepfather and half-brother as the two sat together watching TV. He then fired at his mother as she came out of the bathroom and shot her another five times in the head. The boy reported that after the killings he heard "the laugh of Satan" and had "the most peaceful, restful night of my life."[144] The next day he went to his grandmother's house and wondered aloud with her why the family had not arrived to enjoy the holiday dinner. The police found the bodies later that day.

The adolescent appeared hostile and defiant at the funeral and was arrested shortly afterward. Despite the defense counsel's position that the youth was insane at the time of the multiple killings, the boy was convicted of the murders at trial and remanded to a psychiatric prison hospital.

The youth displayed no remorse. He told McCully that he would commit the murders now had he not done so already. He intended to recruit others in prison to engage in acts of destruction. He stated, "It doesn't matter how many lives it will take, I'll go down fighting and take as many of society as I can."[145]

McCully's description of the boy's life indicates that he was raised in an upper middle class family. His parents divorced when he was one year old, and he had little contact thereafter with his father. His mother remarried twice. The boy did not like his first stepfather. A nocturnal visit by his stepfather suggested the possibility of sexual abuse. Following this man's departure, the boy, age 12, slept in the same bed as his mother for a time.[146] When the boy was about 13, his mother remarried again. She had a baby with this man about two years later. The boy reportedly interpreted the birth of his half-brother as his mother rejecting him.

The boy had a history of engaging in antisocial behavior that dated back to the primary grades, when he began shoplifting toys. He started drinking in high school, cut school, and dropped out for a while. He became fascinated with Nazi philosophy, bought Nazi guns, and became an excellent marksman. He designed a suit after Napoleon's uniform in red and wore this outfit to his parents' funeral. He reportedly conspired with a girl to kill her father before his arrest for murder.

Evidence suggests that the boy was over-indulged by family members, particularly by his grandmother, with whom he lived periodically. She was unable to set boundaries for him, and he tormented her. He appeared to be obsessed with order and became enraged if his sense of perfectionism was disturbed.

McCully said that the boy was intellectually superior. Although not outwardly psychotic, the youth suffered from "borderline schizophrenia with a sociopathic understructure."[147] McCully did not believe that the boy was psychotic at the time of the killing. Although the boy was obsessed with Satanic imagery, none of the forensic examiners concluded that the boy killed his family because he believed that Satan ordered him to do so (hallucinatory command voices). The boy reportedly heard Satan laugh after he killed his family, and he had the presence of mind not to shoot himself. McCully concluded that the Satanic imagery empowered the subject to engage in acts of destructiveness. McCully clearly believed that this youth was a sociopath.[148]

Post briefly described a familicide by Paul, a 14-year-old boy.[149] The account of the dynamics behind this familicide differed greatly from the details recounted by McCully. Paul was the second youngest of eight children. Paul's father demanded that everyone work all the time. Post's account indicated that the father was physically abusive to all his children, but especially to Paul. Paul's father frequently hit the boy and used an electric "cattle prod" to punish him. Paul's siblings said that their father was particularly hard on Paul because the boy was the largest and strongest of the group. Paul's mother did not protect her children and had little interaction with Paul. Paul was afraid of his father and had considered running away and committing suicide to escape his father's wrath.

The threat of violence loomed large in this household. Paul's father frequently wore a handgun in a waist holster. At least a dozen guns were in the house. Paul recalled several incidents in which the brothers threatened one another with guns.

A couple of months prior to the killings, Paul's favorite brother left home. Paul and this brother had spent a lot of time with each other, often drinking together, in an attempt to deal with their problems. The tension Paul felt increased with his brother's departure and worsened when his father started calling Paul "animal" and put a sign on his door that read "Animal Den." One night Paul shot his parents, and when his brothers charged him in an ensuing scuffle, he shot them."[150] Paul was charged with first-degree murder of his mother, his father, and one of his brothers, and with felonious assault on two other brothers.[151]

Parricide Offenders versus Other Homicide Offenders

Two studies by Baxter and her colleagues[152] compared a group of mentally disordered offenders convicted of killing biological parents with a control group of offenders convicted of killing strangers. The two samples were generated from archival data of patients admitted consecutively to one of three high-security hospitals after killing biological parents or strangers in England and Wales over the 25-year period of 1972–1996. The parricide group consisted of 98 individuals involved in 57 matricides and 41 patricides. Six parricide offenders had killed both parents. The control group consisted of 159 offenders who had killed strangers. Of these 159, 20 had killed more than one victim. Males constituted 91% of the parricide offenders and 95% of the offenders who killed strangers. The mean (average) age at admission was 30.6 years for the parricide group and 31.4 for the group who had killed strangers.[153]

Several significant differences were found between the two offender groups. Parricide offenders, relative to killers of strangers, were more likely to suffer from schizophrenia (79% vs. 43%) but less likely to suffer from personality disorders (17% vs. 46%). Those who killed parents were less likely than those who killed strangers to have a history of juvenile delinquency (18% vs. 45%) or a previous criminal history (39% vs. 66%). Sexual components were more likely to be identified in crimes committed by those who killed strangers than by parricide offenders (23% vs. 0).

The researchers noted that previous attacks on the victim were identified in 40% of the parricide cases. In comparing offenders who killed mothers with those who killed fathers, they found no differences in the preponderance of schizophrenia as the diagnosis. Patricide and matricide offenders did not differ in terms of nondelinquent history or in child-rearing patterns to which they had been exposed.[154]

The second study by McCarthy and her colleagues is a companion study to the research project described above and included subjects from the original two samples. This study compared a group of 53 mentally disordered parricide offenders with 71 offenders who killed strangers on a number of outcome measures following their release from high-security care. Males made up 87% of the released parricide offenders and 93% of non-parricide offenders. The subjects in the released sample were similar to those in the initial sample in terms of diagnosis, criminal history, and the presence of a sexual component in the homicide.

These subjects were released under provisions of the Mental Health Act 1983 and were subject to close supervision during the follow-up period, which averaged six years. The researchers reported that at the end of follow-up, both groups had low levels of psychiatric symptoms. Both groups experienced difficulties in psychosocial adjustment. Those who killed parents and those who killed strangers found it hard to obtain full-time employment and to maintain regular relationships. Compared to those of the general population, the mortality rates in both groups were high.

The researchers noted several significant differences between the two groups. The parricide offenders, relative to the control group, committed fewer offenses. Parricide offenders averaged 2.3 offenses, compared to 9.8 offenses by those who killed strangers, during the follow-up period. Parricide offenders were less likely than those who killed strangers to be reconvicted of any crime during follow-up (8% vs. 15%) or to be sentenced to prison (3.8% vs. 11.3%) during this period.

Comparison of five-year recidivism rates of the two groups with statistics from the British Home Office indicated that the parricide offenders fared relatively well. Reconviction rates for grave offenses (i.e., homicide, serious wounding, serious sexual offenses, robbery, and arson) were 5.7% for the parricide group, 12.7% for the stranger-homicide group, and 4% for the Home Office analyses. Reconviction rates for standard list offenses for the five-year period were 1.9% for the parricide group, 14.1% for the stranger-homicide group, and 18% for the Home Office analyses.[155]

This chapter examined parents and stepparents killed alone or with other victims by biological children or stepchildren acting alone or with others. A series of vignettes highlighted actual cases involving juvenile and adult offenders involved in the killings of both parents in recent years. Special attention was focused on parricides involving youths under 18, females, multiple offenders, and multiple victims because of the enormous interest in these cases, despite their rarity.

Analyses of thousands of parricide cases in the United States over a 32-year period indicated that adult males predominated in parricide and stepparricide incidents. Their rate of involvement was even higher in multiple-victim killings involving parents and stepparents. A higher percentage of juveniles than of adults was involved in multiple-offender parricides. Girls who killed parents often had accomplices. In fact, the percentages of juvenile and adult females involved in multiple-offender situations involving both parents and stepparents were higher than those for their male counterparts.

Methodological problems in the literature were noted that sometimes make drawing firm conclusions about parricide victims, offenders, and incidents difficult. Three studies that used more sophisticated research designs and overcame the limitations of previous studies by analyzing matricide and patricide incidents in terms of male and female offenders were reviewed. Findings from studies of juveniles and adolescents involved in parricides were summarized. Most of the literature on young parricide offenders available in the English language consists of case studies or clinical reports involving primarily boys who killed biological fathers. These youths were typically portrayed as killing in response to long-standing abuse. Twelve characteristics extracted from many studies were discussed in the context of profiling cases and the circumstances behind these killings.

Research involving double parricides was synthesized. The limited research available on cases in which both parents were killed reflects the rarity of this type of parricide event. Most of the literature consists of case reports. With one exception, double parricides committed by adult offenders and reported in the professional literature were committed by sons. Most of these men were diagnosed as severely mentally ill, and many were found not to be criminally responsible. However, some were diagnosed as having personality disorders. In one study of 11 male double-parricide offenders, seven were convicted of their crimes and sent to prison.

There are also very few case reports of double parricides by adolescent perpetrators. With few exceptions, the perpetrators are boys. In contrast to their adult counterparts, juveniles who kill both parents are rarely seen as psychotic. These youths are typically depicted as severely abused and depressed individuals who can no longer endure the abuse.

The chapter also examined familicide, defined as parricidal events in which at least three family members are killed. I located only a handful of clinical reports on such killings, all of which were committed by sons. These reports varied in terms of the underlying dynamics involved.

This chapter concluded by discussing two studies that compared those who killed parents with those who killed strangers. These research efforts revealed important differences between the groups in terms of background and success after release. In the next chapter, facts and studies specifically relating to matricidal events are presented. In the chapter following that on matricidal events, information pertaining to patricidal events is covered.

4 Matricide: Basic Facts and Literature

- Tampa, Florida—Following a high-speed chase with police, a 15-year-old girl, her 19-year-old boyfriend, and another male teen were arrested for killing the girl's mother.[1] Trial testimony revealed that the girl's boyfriend injected the woman with a syringe filled with bleach and stabbed her in the neck while the girl reportedly held her down. The trio placed the mother's dead body in a garbage can and discarded it in the woods near the home of one of the boys.[2] Using the woman's car for wheels, the three partied for a few days in town, got tattoos, and took off on a cross-country road trip. As part of a plea deal to second-degree murder and a 25-year prison sentence, the male friend testified against the girl and her boyfriend. The boyfriend was convicted of first-degree murder and sentenced to death.[3] The girl was convicted of third-degree murder (death unintended while defendant engaged in another felony, grand theft auto) and sentenced to 15 years in prison.[4]
- San Jose, California—An 18-year-old boy killed his mother during a fight between the two. The mother, upset with the boy for skipping school the day before, broke a coat hanger over his back, threatened to tie him up, and followed him into the bathroom with a paring knife. A struggle ensued, the woman dropped the knife, and the boy picked it up. He swung the knife at his mother, cutting her jugular vein in the process. Prosecutors agreed to allow the adolescent to plead guilty to manslaughter because records indicated that the mother had verbally and physically abused the defendant, his older brother, and her estranged husband. The youth was sentenced to three years in prison.[5]
- Hunting Beach, California—A 32-year-old man pled not guilty by reason of insanity in connection with the killing of his mother. The man had been in and out of mental hospitals for most of his adult life. He told police that he killed his mother because he was advised to do so by a prophet. The man reportedly believed that his mother was a replica when he hit her with a barbell and stabbed her more than 70

times with a vegetable peeler and a pair of scissors. The jury rejected the defense's claim that the man was so mentally ill and delusional that he did not understand was he was doing. The man was convicted of first-degree murder and sentenced to 28 years to life in prison.[6]

- Albany, New York—Two sisters, ages 19 and 24, were taken into custody after their 42-year-old stepmother was found dead. Initial reports indicated that the stepmother was savagely attacked by her stepdaughters after she returned home from work and kicked their small dog.[7] The older sister was charged with murder, and the younger sister with hindering the prosecution of her older sister. The medical examiner testified that the victim received 112 wounds inflicted by three sharp knives and an open-end box wrench.[8] The jury rejected the defense's claim that the older sister lashed out in rage resulting from past trauma and multiple personalities and convicted her of second-degree murder.[9] She was sentenced to the maximum of 25 years to life in prison.[10] The younger sister was acquitted of covering up the murder.[11]

From the perspective of many, matricide is the most reprehensible of crimes. The killing of one's mother is often perceived as worse than the killing of a father because it involves the taking of the life of the person who gave that individual life. Regarding the cases described in the chapter opener, news clippings about the first case depicted the three teens who killed one mother as antisocial and merciless. The teen in the second case reportedly suffered long-standing abuse and struck back during a physical altercation that got tragically out of control. A third matricide offender had an extensive mental health history and appeared delusional when he killed his mother. The fourth case involved two young adult females who killed their stepmother. The cases raise questions about the involvement of juvenile (under age 18) and female offenders in the killing of mothers. Are offenders who kill their mothers and stepmothers likely to act alone or with others? When it comes to using accomplices, does the age and gender of the matricide offender matter? What is known regarding the motivations that drive juvenile and adult children to kill their mothers?

This chapter examines available knowledge on mothers slain. Readers who want to get a solid foundation on matricide victims and offenders will find this chapter very helpful. Acknowledging the lack of information available on stepmothers killed, this chapter includes some basic facts about the killings of stepmothers and compares statistical information for the two female victim types (mothers and stepmothers).

In this chapter, comparisons between mothers and fathers killed are avoided or kept to a minimum so as to help the reader grasp the essentials of female parricide victims. When studies have specifically contrasted matricide and patricide offenders, these differences are noted. The next chapter focuses in depth on fathers and stepfathers.[12]

I begin the chapter by presenting basic information about matricide and stepmatricide victims, offenders, and incidents. As in the previous chapter, these analyses were restricted to parricides in the United States because it, unlike other countries, has a national homicide data base that records information on specific victim types. I used arrests reported to the Federal Bureau of Investigation (FBI) by police agencies over the 32-year period of 1976–2007 to draw these statistical portraits.[13] When appropriate, I did statistical tests to determine whether certain differences were statistically significant, meaning that they did not occur by chance.[14]

After the discussion of the incidence of female parricide and the correlates of victims and offenders, I synthesize the literature on matricide. In my review, I found no in-depth cases of stepmothers killed.[15] This literature review focuses first on studies of adult or predominantly adult male matricide offenders, followed by studies of female parricide offenders that provided data on victim type, and then case studies of adult female matricide offenders. After the discussion of the adult literature, case studies of male and female adolescent matricide offenders are synthesized. The chapter concludes with a summary of important points about matricide.

BASIC FACTS ABOUT MATRICIDE AND STEPMATRICIDE

Matricide is a very rare event, constituting less than 1% of all U.S. homicides in which the victim–offender relationship is known. During the period of 1976–2007, 113 offenders were arrested on the average each year in connection with the killings of mothers. As depicted in Table 4-1, more than 80% of those arrested for killing mothers were male offenders.

Table 4-1 Synopsis of offenders arrested for killing mothers and stepmothers; United States, 1976–2007

	Mothers	*Stepmothers*
ALL INCIDENTS*		
• Estimated number per year	113 (18 juveniles, 95 adults)	7 (2 juveniles, 5 adults)
• Offender gender	83% male	86% male
• Juvenile offenders	77% male	84% male
• Adult offenders	84% male	87% male
MULTIPLE-OFFENDER (MO) INCIDENTS		
• Estimated number per year	10	1
• Offender gender	62% male	73% male
• Juvenile involvement	Higher percentage of juveniles involved in MO incidents than adults (22% vs. 6%)[a]	Higher percentage of adults than juveniles involved in MO incidents (16% vs. 12%) (not significant)
• Female juvenile involvement	Higher percentage of female juveniles involved in MO incidents than male juveniles (44% vs. 16%)[b]	Higher percentage of female juveniles involved in MO incidents than male juveniles (33% vs. 7%)[c]
• Female adult involvement	Higher percentage of female adults involved in MO incidents than male adults (13% vs. 5%)[d]	Higher percentage of female adults involved in MO incidents than male adults (22% vs. 15%) (not significant)

(continued)

Table 4-1 (Continued)

	Mothers	Stepmothers
MULTIPLE-VICTIM INCIDENTS		
• Estimated number per year	12	1
• Offender gender	89% male	94% male
• Juvenile offenders	86% male	92% male
• Adult offenders	89% male	96% male

*Supplementary Homicide Report offender data, single and multiple victims, single and multiple offenders, national estimates; juveniles = under age 18.

[a] Statistically significant [χ^2 (1, 3603) = 149.107, Phi =−.203, p < .001].

[b] Statistically significant [χ^2 (1, 565) = 45.579, Phi = .284, p < .001].

[c] Statistically significant [χ^2 (1, 73) = 7.368, Phi = .318, p < .001].

[d] Statistically significant [χ^2 (1, 3039) = 47.620, Phi = .125, p < .001].

Approximately 82% of matricide offenders acted alone when they killed their mothers. On the average, in the period studied, about 10 offenders were arrested each year for acting with codefendants to kill mothers. Interestingly, 38% of the offenders involved in these multiple-offender incidents were females. Juveniles were significantly more likely than adult offenders to use accomplices in killing mothers. Significantly higher percentages of both juvenile and adult females employed codefendants to kill mothers than their male counterparts.

About a dozen offenders each year were arrested for killing mothers and other victims during the same incident. Those arrested in multiple-victim situations were overwhelmingly male offenders.

Murders of stepmothers are even more rare events than those involving mothers. On the average, seven offenders were arrested per year for killing stepmothers. Similar to those who killed mothers, more than 80% of those arrested were males. A significantly higher percentage of girls under age 18 were involved in multiple-offender stepmatricides than boys. About one offender per year was arrested in multiple-victim homicides involving stepmothers.

Matricide Victims and Offenders

Given the construction of the FBI's national homicide data base, it is best to restrict analyses of the characteristics of victims and offenders to single-victim, single-offender incidents.[16] As shown in Table 4-2, about 98% of mothers killed were either White (72%) or Black (26%). Matricide victims killed by offenders acting alone ranged in age from 30 to 99 or older and averaged 60 years old.[17]

Not surprisingly, given the biological tie, the racial composition of matricide offenders was nearly identical to that of the victims.[18] Offenders who killed mothers in single-victim, single-offender incidents were male in 84% of cases. Matricide offenders ranged in age from 8 to 83 years of age and averaged 32 years old.[19]

As depicted in Table 4-3, about one out of seven matricide arrestees was under age 18. When adolescents through age 19 are included in the analysis, we see that

Table 4-2 Race of mothers and stepmothers killed in single-victim, single-offender incidents; United States, 1976–2007*

Race	Mother As Victim		Stepmother As Victim	
	Estimated Number	Estimated Percentage	Estimated Number	Estimated Percentage
White	2147	72.4%	114	75.5%
Black	765	25.8%	34	22.5%
Indian/Alaskan Native	13	0.4%	2	1.3%
Asian/Pacific Islander	42	1.4%	1	0.7%
TOTAL	2967	100%	151	100%

*Supplementary Homicide Report offender data, national estimates (not significant).

approximately 20% of matricide offenders were under age 20. When the age is extended through age 24, it is found that more than 35% of matricide offenders were juveniles, adolescents, or very young adults.

There is no evidence that the number of killings of mothers by youths under 18 is increasing. Indeed, the data indicate that both the number of matricides by juveniles and their proportionate involvement in all matricide arrests have significantly decreased over time. From 1976 to 1991, juveniles made up an estimated 14.8% of all matricide arrests; from 1992 to 2007, they made up an estimated 11.7%.[20]

In more than 60% of killings, matricide offenders selected guns (37%) or knives (29%). As shown in Table 4-4, in the remaining 38% of killings, they used a variety of methods, including blunt objects, personal weapons, strangulation, asphyxiation, or other means such as poison, drugs, explosives, pushing their victims out windows, or drowning. Important offender age differences were found in weapon selection.

Table 4-3 Age of matricide and stepmatricide offenders in single-victim, single-offender incidents; United States, 1976–2007*

Offender Age (Years)	Mother As Victim		Stepmother As Victim	
	Estimated Number	Estimated Percentage	Estimated Number	Estimated Percentage
Under 18	392	13.3%	51	33.3%
18–19	202	6.9%	17	11.1%
20–24	443	15.1%	30	19.6%
25–29	451	15.3%	15	9.8%
30–39	652	22.2%	19	12.4%
40–49	459	15.6%	9	5.9%
50–59	259	8.8%	7	4.6%
Over 60	85	2.9%	5	3.3%
Total	2943	100%	153	100%

*Supplementary Homicide Report offender data, national estimates.

χ^2 (7, 3096) = 70.06; Cramer's V = .150; p < .001.

Table 4-4 Weapons used to kill mothers and stepmothers in single-victim, single-offender incidents; United States, 1976–2007*

Weapon Used	Mother as Victim		Stepmother as Victim	
	Estimated Number	Estimated Percentage	Estimated Number	Estimated Percentage
Firearm/other guns	37	1.3%	3	2.0%
Handgun	605	21.3%	39	26.0%
Rifle/shotgun	408	14.4%	31	20.7%
Knife	831	29.3%	37	24.7%
Blunt object	383	13.5%	18	12.0%
Personal weapon (e.g., hands, feet)	338	11.9%	11	7.3%
Other (poison, drugs, pushed out window, drowning, explosives)	33	1.2%	0	—
Fire	60	2.1%	2	1.3%
Strangulation	90	3.2%	8	5.3%
Asphyxiation	53	1.9%	1	0.7%
Total	2838	100%	150	100%

*Supplementary Homicide Report offender data, national estimates (not significant).

Juvenile matricide offenders were significantly more likely than their adult counterparts to use firearms (59.8% vs. 33.4%).[21] Adults who killed mothers were significantly more likely than juvenile offenders to use knives (30.4% vs. 23.0%) or other weapons (36.2% vs. 17.2%).[22]

Stepmatricide Victims and Offenders

The racial distribution of stepmothers killed was very similar to that of mothers, with 98% either White (76%) or Black (22%), as shown in Table 4-2. Stepmothers were younger than mothers killed; they ranged in age from 23 to 91 and averaged 50 years old.[23]

Offenders who killed stepmothers were generally of the same race as the victim.[24] Offenders were male in 86% of the cases.[25] On the average, offenders who killed stepmothers were younger than those who killed biological mothers. Stepmatricide offenders ranged in age from 12 to 81 and averaged 25 years in age.[26]

Comparison of the offender age range categories in Table 4-3 reveals significant differences. One of three offenders who killed stepmothers, compared to one of seven who killed mothers, was under 18. Nearly 45% of stepmatricide offenders were under age 20, compared to less than 20% of matricide offenders. More than 64% of those who killed stepmothers, compared to about 35% of those who killed mothers, were under age 25.

The data do not indicate that juvenile involvement in stepmatricides has increased over time. Juveniles made up an estimated 37.1% of all arrests in cases in which stepmothers were killed in 1976–1991, compared to 28.6% of total arrests in 1992–2007.[27]

As shown in Table 4-4, offenders who killed stepmothers, relative to those who killed mothers, were significantly more likely to use guns (48.7% vs. 37.0%). Stepmatricide offenders were less likely than matricide offenders to use knives or an assortment of other methods to kill their victims.[28] Juveniles and adult offenders did not differ significantly from one another in the methods used to kill stepmothers. However, stepdaughters were significantly more likely than stepsons to use knives (45.0% vs. 21.4%). Stepsons, relative to their female counterparts, were significantly more likely to use guns (49.6% vs. 45.0%) and a variety of other methods (29% vs. 10%).[29]

LITERATURE REVIEW

As the discussion herein reveals, perusal of the available literature[30] indicates that several studies of adult matricide offenders exist. In-depth studies of juvenile or adolescent matricide offenders, in contrast, are few. Almost all of the research reported on matricide offenses involves male offenders. The literature on girls who kill mothers is sparse indeed. Special attention is given in this chapter to female matricide offenders, given the lack of research currently available with respect to this population and their fairly significant involvement in their killing of their mothers.

Studies of Adult or Predominantly Adult Matricide Offenders

Most of the literature on matricide involves killings by adult sons, as shown in Table 4-5. Several studies, however, include both juveniles and adults in their samples of matricide offenders. The studies that used mixed-age samples of offenders are presented in Table 4-6. Although most of the cohort studies and clinical reports indicate that adult matricide offenders were psychotic or otherwise seriously mentally ill, some offenders were found to be dangerously antisocial individuals with varying diagnoses, including a significant number with personality disorders.

Four cohort studies of adult male matricide offenders evaluated in forensic or hospitalized settings currently exist, with sample sizes ranging from 13 to 58.[31] Nearly all of the matricide offenders in these samples were single adult males. Schizophrenia was the most common diagnosis made among adult male matricide offenders in these cohort studies. The predominance of a schizophrenia diagnosis among adult male matricide offenders led one forensic investigator to refer to matricide as "the schizophrenic crime."[32] A minority of matricide offenders were diagnosed as having depression,[33] substance abuse psychosis or co-occurring alcoholism,[34] impulse disorders, and personality disorders (e.g., borderline, narcissistic, or antisocial personality disorder).[35] Although not considered causal, epilepsy and organic pathology were noted in a few sample subjects.[36]

Extensive histories of conflict-laden relationships between mothers and sons were typically apparent. Offenders in such cases often reported feeling that their mothers were either ambivalent toward them or excessively demanding and domineering.[37] Sexual elements were mentioned in some studies, with provocative behavior by the mother or incestuous impulses by the son suggested.[38] Homosexual interest, conflict, or behavior among adult male matricide offenders was also frequently observed.[39] Fathers were typically depicted as passive, uninvolved, or absent through death or marriage dissolution.[40] Extreme violence in matricidal incidents was common.[41]

Table 4-5 Adult matricide offenders (age 18 and over)*

Author(s)	Year of Publication	Country of Study	Number of Subjects, Sample, Design/Methods/Data Source	Offender Gender	
				Male	Female
Hill et al.	1943	England	Case study: male matricide offender, aged 20	✓	
Gonzalez Garcia	1947	Columbia	Case study: male matricide offender, aged 22	✓	
Guttmacher	1960	United States	Case study: female matricide offender, aged 38		✓
O'Connell	1963	England	Clinical analysis of 13 adult male matricide offenders, aged 19 to 40, in psychiatric setting	✓	
Oberdallhoff	1974	Germany	Case study: male matricide offender, aged 50	✓	
Tanay & Freeman	1976	United States	Case study: male matricide, aged 22	✓	
Green	1981	England	Clinical survey, 1960–1979: 58 male patients institutionalized in a psychiatric hospital (in 49 cases, mothers were only victims; in remaining cases, five fathers and eight other relatives were also killed); victims were 54 biological mothers, two adopted mothers, and two stepmothers. Matricide offenders were aged 18 to 51 at time of homicide.	✓	
Väisänen & Väisänen.	1983	Finland	Case study: female matricide offender, aged 22		✓
Campion et al.	1985	United States	Clinical evaluations: forensic sample of 15 men, aged 21 to 63, 1970–1982	✓	
Lipson	1986	United States	Case study: male matricide offender, aged 34	✓	

Singhal & Dutta	1992	England	Retrospective clinical survey: 16 schizophrenic males who committed matricide, aged 28 to 55	✓
			Control group used: 16 hospitalized chronically schizophrenic males who did not commit matricide, aged 28 to 55	
Meloy	1996	United States	Case study: male matricide offender, aged 33	✓
Silberstein	1998	Argentina	Review of parricide literature from a psychodynamic approach; case study: young adult male matricide offender	✓
Sugai	1999	Japan	Case study: male matricide offender, aged 25	✓
Livaditis et al.	2005	Greece	Forensic case study: male matricide offender, aged 43	✓
Dogan et al.	2010	Turkey	Case study: female matricide offender, aged 33	✓
Lauerma et al.	2010	Finland	Case study: male matricide offender, aged 20	✓
Aarab et al.	2012	Morocco	Case studies: male matricide offender, aged 46	✓
Abayomi	2012	Nigeria	Case studies: male matricide offender, aged 29; female matricide offender, aged 24	✓

*Includes studies on matricide and comparative studies on parricide that include matricide.

Table 4-6 Mixed samples of adult/juvenile matricide offenders*

Authors(s)	Year of Publication	Country of Study	Number of Subjects, Sample, Design/Methods/Data Sources	Offender Gender	
				Male	Female
McKnight et al.	1966	Canada	Clinical analysis of 12 matricide offenders, aged 15 to 39, in a psychiatric hospital	✓	
Gillies	1976	Scotland	Four hundred forensic evaluations (367 males and 33 females) between 1953 and 1974; six males, no females killed mothers (age of matricide offenders not reported)	✓	
d'Orban & O'Connor	1989	England	Seventeen women, aged 17 to 54, in prison or under medical care for killing a parent (14 matricide, three patricide)		✓
Kirschner	1992	United States	Case Studies (three cases): adult male adoptee, aged 44, killed mother; adolescent male adoptee, aged 18, killed both parents; adolescent male adoptee, aged 14, killed both parents	✓	
Clark	1993	Scotland	Retrospective/national study: all individuals in Scotland between 1957 and 1987 who were charged with the murder of their biological mother: 23 males and three females, aged 16 to 62	✓	✓
Fontaine & Guérard des Lauriers	1994	France	Case studies (three cases): juvenile female matricide offender, aged 15; adult male matricide offender, aged 21; adult male matricide offender, aged 45	✓	✓
Weisman & Sharma	1997	United States	Clinical archive study (retrospective, 1978–1996): 64 adjudicated adult cases, offenders aged 17 to 56: 40 male and five female parricide offenders; 16 male and three female attempted parricide offenders. Female offenders in both groups killed (n = 5) or attempted to kill (n = 3) only mothers. Forty-five parricide offenders: 23 matricide, 16 patricide, six parricide. Nineteen attempted parricide offenders: 11 attempted matricide, seven attempted patricide, one attempted parricide	✓	✓

Author	Year	Country	Description		
Holcomb	2000	Unknown	Synthesis of 25 case reports: 10 of 25 under age 18; three females, 22 males	✓	✓
Marleau et al.	2001	Multi-country	Thirty-eight cases of female adult and adolescent parricide offenders reported in the literature		✓
Bourget et al.	2007	Canada	Clinical archive study (retrospective, 1990–2005): comparative study between matricide and patricide. Fifty-six parricide offenders: 52 males, aged 14 to 58, 36 patricide and 24 matricide victims; four females, aged "late teens to 50s," one patricide and three matricide victims	✓	✓
Wick et al.	2008	Australia	Twenty-year retrospective review of matricide cases; 10 males and one female, aged 15 to 35	✓	✓
Liettu et al.	2009	Finland	Clinical archive study (retrospective, 1973–2004): 86 matricidal and 106 patricidal male offenders (single-victim only). Four matricidal and six patricidal offenders were under age 18. Study sample included 113 completed homicides, 48 attempted homicides, and 31 aggravated assaults.	✓	
Schug	2011	Several countries	Integrative review of 61 publications related to schizophrenia and matricide. Listing of case reports of matricide, descriptive studies involving matricide and schizophrenia, comparison studies involving schizophrenia and matricide, case studies not involving schizophrenia, and studies in which involvement of schizophrenia is unknown.	✓	✓

*Includes studies on matricide and comparative studies on parricide that include matricide.

Another study included both juveniles/adolescents and adults in its sample of 12 hospitalized matricide offenders; findings were not analyzed in this manuscript by age.[42] Results for this mixed sample were similar to those for adult matricide offender samples in terms of severe mental illness and the level of violence used. At the time of hospital admission, seven of these offenders had been found incompetent to stand trial, four were determined to be not guilty by reason of insanity, and one case had no formal disposition.

A more recent study, which also included juvenile and adult perpetrators, used autopsy files to identify 11 cases of matricide occurring from 1985 to 2004 in South Australia.[43] Ten of the 11 cases were committed by sons. One offender committed suicide following the killing. Of the remaining 10, seven were found not guilty by reason of insanity due to serious mental illness, and an eighth offender had charges reduced from murder to manslaughter due to mental impairment.

Caution is advised in generalizing to the population of adult matricide offenders from cohort studies of matricide offenders hospitalized for psychiatric evaluation following the killings. Additional factors, explanations, and motivations might be operative in cases of adult matricide offenders who are not hospitalized following the murders, as suggested in a recently published study in Finland. This study compared the mental disorders of males who killed or attempted to kill mothers and fathers, or who committed aggravated assault against their parents, in Finland over 30 years.[44] In Finland, unlike in many other countries, "practically all individuals charged with homicide and other severe violent offenses" are subject to extensive forensic evaluations.[45] Accordingly, subjects in this study were more likely to be representative of the population of parricide offenders than in other studies involving hospitalized defendants. Approximately 95% of the sample subjects were over 18.

The researchers used the words "matricidal" and "patricidal" in reference to offenders and incidents when referring to homicides, attempted homicides, and aggravated assaults in which parents were victims. A few of the 86 matricidal offenders (n = 4) and 106 patricidal offenders (n = 6) were under 18. Matricidal offenders were unlikely to be married or cohabiting. More than 90% had never been married (73%) or were divorced or widowed (19%). More than half (52%) had a previous history of psychiatric hospitalization. Nearly two-thirds (64%) were intoxicated at the time of the violent incident, and more than half had an alcohol/drug-related disorder (56%). In more than half (52%) of the incidents, the motive for the parricidal act was attributed to mental illness. Nearly half (47%) were diagnosed with a psychotic disorder, and many (45%) were also diagnosed with a personality disorder. In more than 80% of the matricidal incidents, offenders were found not guilty by reason of insanity (47%) or to have diminished responsibility (36%).[46]

The investigators found several significant differences between those involved in matricidal and patricidal violence. Relative to patricidal offenders, matricidal offenders were more likely to be older and to kill because of mental illness. They were more likely to be diagnosed as having a psychotic disorder, to be found not guilty by reason of insanity, and to be diagnosed as suffering from paranoid schizophrenia. Matricidal offenders were significantly less likely than patricidal offenders to be diagnosed as having a personality disorder. When analyses focused on only offenders who had killed or attempted to kill parents (leaving out aggravated assaults), the differences found between offenders who killed mothers and fathers remained and were more pronounced.[47]

Case reports of adult male matricide offenders also exist.[48] The majority of these case studies reported that men who committed lethal acts of violence against their mothers were seriously mentally ill and killed while in a mentally disordered state. These men were frequently described as considering the act of killing their mothers either as liberating and undertaken to maintain their masculinity or as protection against extreme emotions triggered by their mothers' behavior. Similar to cohort studies of matricidal men, the case studies generally depicted mothers and sons with long-term dysfunctional relationships that culminated in violence. Legal outcomes of these cases were briefly discussed, with many offenders receiving long prison sentences.

One recently published case study in the French language differed from previous clinical reports.[49] Aarab and colleagues described a case of a 46-year-old married man with two children who killed his mother. Unlike other case reports, this man had "a well-established socio-familial and professional life." At age 45, he presented with "a progressive installation of psychotic symptomatology." The man experienced auditory persecutory hallucinations, which abated after six months of "classical antipsychotic treatment." A year later, the man experienced a more severe episode. Auditory hallucinations directed him to kill his mother, believing that she was Satan. The man substantially improved following three months of treatment with antipsychotic medication. He was diagnosed with chronic hallucinatory psychosis, "considering the delayed start, the existence of rich hallucinatory persecuting elements with an absence of any dissociation."[50]

Although these case studies also depicted adult matricide offenders as suffering from mental illness, caution is advised in generalizing from clinical reports to the population of adult matricide offenders. A recent case report from Finland is instructive in this regard.

A man who strangled to death his mother when he was 20 years old subsequently strangled two other females, one a year later and the other six years later.[51] This matricide offender was known to be shy and "abnormally dependent" on his mother as a child. "Alcohol was used excessively" in the home, and the father was reportedly abusive.[52] However, there was no evidence of violence or sexual abuse involving the matricide offender or his one sibling during childhood. The matricide offender was a transvestite, possibly transsexual, who enjoyed sadomasochistic sexual behavior, including being strangled. The man reportedly had been drinking heavily prior to the three killings. Psychosis, brain abnormalities, defective intelligence, and dissociative disorders were ruled out. The man met the criteria for having an "asocial, narcissistic, and borderline personality disorder."[53] His score on the Psychopathy Checklist Revised put him in the severe psychopathy range.[54]

Matricide cases discussed in the literature on occasion cross age and gender categories. An article focusing on three matricide offenders, written in French, included two adult males and one female juvenile.[55] This article also indicates the diversity that exists among matricide offenders in terms of diagnosis. One of the adult offenders, age 21, and the 15-year-old girl were found to be seriously mentally disturbed and potentially treatable. The other male adult offender, age 45, was judged to be antisocial, not amenable to treatment, and more appropriately treated in the legal system than in the mental health arena.

The literature on adult daughters who kill their mothers is sparse relative to the literature available on parricide in general or on sons who kill mothers. Clark's study of matricide offenders in Scotland included all matricides that occurred from 1957 to 1987.[56] Three of the 26 offspring who killed their mothers were female. The low representation of females over the 30-year period indicates that women were significantly less likely than men to commit matricide in Scotland. Results were not analyzed by gender. Although psychosis was overrepresented in the sample of 26 offenders, Clark argued against viewing matricide as solely a schizophrenic crime. He emphasized the need for psychiatric assessment in these cases. Although 10 of the 26 offenders had suffered from severe mental illness (schizophrenia, psychotic depression, and hypomania), 16 did not have such diagnoses. Of these 16, four were diagnosed with alcohol dependence, and another five with personality disorders. The seven remaining matricide offenders were not diagnosed with a mental illness.

The 10 offenders diagnosed with severe mental illness all received hospital dispositions. Three of the four offenders with alcohol dependence, six of the seven with no diagnosis, and three of the five with personality disorders received prison sentences. Eight of the 12 sentenced to prison received life sentences. Clark (1993) noted that "where no explanation of behavior could be forwarded to the court, the individual was more likely to receive a life sentence."[57]

Studies of Females Who Killed Primarily Mothers

Parricide studies with large samples typically can say little about female matricide offenders because they tend to form a small percentage of the sample.[58] Bourget and colleagues briefly noted in a study of coroners' records generated over a 15-year period that only three of 24 mothers were killed by daughters. Two of the offenders, a girl in her late teens and a woman in her mid-30s, were psychotic or presented with psychotic symptoms. The third case involved a severely intoxicated woman who stabbed her elderly mother. All cases occurred in the home where the mother and daughter resided.[59] Weisman and Sharma noted that eight of the 64 offenders in their sample who killed or attempted to kill parents were daughters whose victims were mothers.[60] Other than the fact that most of these offenders were found not guilty by reason of insanity or incompetent to stand trial, no further information on these female matricide offenders was provided.

Only two studies that included more than a few cases of daughters killing mothers were located. Both of these noted that the motivation for the killing of parents varied depending on victim type and drew attention to the age of the offender. D'Orban and O'Connor focused on 17 women who committed 14 matricides and three patricides in England.[61] The matricide offenders ranged in age from 17 to 54 and averaged 40 years old; the three patricide offenders were ages 18, 20, and 26. Eleven of these sample subjects came from a female "remand prison" (detention facility), five from a special hospital, and one from a Regional Secure Hospital. Interestingly and importantly, five of these women had never been hospitalized. Had the sample been drawn exclusively from a hospital, nearly 30% of these cases would have been missed, a point noted by the investigators.

The researchers found that the social situation of these 17 women was characterized by extreme isolation. Only two of the subjects were married; 12 were single, and the remaining three women were divorced or widowed. Cases in which mothers were killed differed from those in which fathers were killed in terms of offender age, victim age, social situation, nature of the victim–offender relationship, and psychiatric history and diagnosis of the offender. Matricide offenders tended to be middle-aged women who killed their elderly mothers. Twelve of the 14 matricide offenders were living with their mothers at the time of the homicide. Their relationship with their mothers, with one exception, had been conflictual for years and was marked by extreme dependence on each other and underlying feelings of resentment and hostility.

All of the matricide offenders were diagnosed with psychiatric disorders. Eleven were diagnosed as suffering from a psychotic illness (six with schizophrenia and five with psychotic depression). Two were diagnosed with personality disorders, and one with alcohol dependence. Depression was observed as prominent in eight matricide offenders.

The three female patricide offenders, in contrast, were younger than the female matricide offenders. The patricide victims were correspondingly younger than the matricide victims (middle-aged rather than elderly). Only one daughter was living with her father at the time of the incident. Chronic conflict and abuse were suggested in all three patricide cases. One of the three women who killed their fathers was diagnosed as having an antisocial personality; the other two women were not viewed as having a psychiatric disorder.

Inappropriate sexual behavior by the father was reportedly involved in two of the three patricide cases. One of the patricide offenders reported that she had had sexual relations with her father since age 18 and reportedly killed him when he approached her in a drunken state to have sex. The second woman who killed her father stated that he had threatened her sexually and was excessively interested in her sexuality. In contrast, a sexual element was mentioned in only one of the 14 matricide cases. In that case, the woman, diagnosed as schizophrenic, "expressed delusional ideas about her mother having stolen her penis in childhood in order to satisfy herself sexually."[62]

All 17 parricide subjects were charged with murder. Only one was convicted of murder and sentenced to life imprisonment. Upon appeal, this individual was also determined to have diminished responsibility, and her sentence was substantially reduced. Of the remaining 16, three were determined to be incompetent to proceed, 11 were convicted of manslaughter on the basis of diminished responsibility, and two were convicted of ordinary manslaughter. Follow-up ranged from one to 15 years for sample subjects. Three of the women committed suicide. Only one woman committed another offense; this woman, who had been suffering from recurrent bouts of psychotic depression when she killed her mother, later killed her husband in a similar delusional state. She was again deemed to have diminished responsibility for her actions.

A review of the literature on female parricides by Marleau, Millaud, and Auclair, written in French, identified 38 cases of daughters who killed or, in five cases, attempted to kill one or more of their parents.[63] The authors analyzed these cases by victim type, age of offender, weapon used, and situational dynamics. Of the 38 cases, 22 involved mothers as the sole victim (16) or as among the victims (six). Sixteen of the matricide offenders in this sample of case reports were adolescents or young adults; only six of the incidents in which mothers were killed involved offenders age 20 or older. Marleau and colleagues concluded that the motivation for the killing of parents varied depending on the victim type and the age of the offender. They advised that females who murder parents should not be treated as a homogeneous category.

Case Studies of Adult Female Matricide Offenders

In contrast to the many case reports available on adult sons who killed mothers, only three case studies of adult females who killed mothers written in the English language and published in journals were located.[64] A fourth case was discussed by Guttmacher in his book published more than 50 years ago.[65] Two of the four cases involved women in their early 20s; the remaining two were in their 30s. One of the women clearly had a long-standing history of depression and substance abuse, largely a result of living in an abusive home situation. The other three women who killed their mothers were diagnosed with psychosis.

Väisänen and Väisänen presented a case study of Lisa, a 21- or 22-year-old daughter who killed her mother.[66] They described a home filled with violence and rancor. The parents were engaged in domestic violence, and there was apparently incestuous behavior between the father and the children, as well as among the siblings. The mother was described as physically, mentally, and verbally abusive toward her children. She reportedly tried to drown two of her children from her first marriage and later succeeded in killing her second husband, Lisa's father.

Lisa was tormented by her mother for years. Unable to get help as an adolescent, she attempted suicide later on, sought treatment briefly, and eventually ran away. When she returned home, she was drinking heavily and had obsessive thoughts that she would have to kill her mother or die herself. The matricide occurred on the one-year anniversary of Lisa's father's death. At the time of the killing, the young woman was drunk and had just been humiliated again by her mother. "In a flash thought that she would have to kill her mother," she stabbed her mother multiple times.[67]

Family and friends were not surprised by the killing. They expected that the mother would kill herself or kill Lisa because the mother had been saying farewell to friends and to her grandchildren prior to the killing. The authors viewed the murder as the daughter's acting as the agent of her mother's suicide. They noted that the family was relieved after the killing and intended to support the young woman during her prison sentence.[68]

The second case involved a 24-year-old single woman who suddenly hit her mother with a wooden pedestal during the course of a minor disagreement.[69] The woman had dropped out of high school, was unemployed, and living with her mother at the time of the homicide. She had a long history of mental illness dating back to childhood. She was diagnosed with paranoid schizophrenia and co-morbid complex-partial seizure disorder.[70]

The third case involved a 33-year-old Turkish daughter who killed her mother, decapitated her, and dismembered her body.[71] Evidence suggested that the woman had stabbed her mother 71 times. Most of the cuts were superficial; the five in the chest cavity, however, incapacitated the victim and were fatal. The woman was sitting on a bed a few feet from her deceased mother when the police entered the home that the two shared. The daughter told the police that "she had killed her mother because her mother always criticized and humiliated her."[72] The daughter had been diagnosed with schizophrenia and had been receiving treatment during the 15 years prior to the murder. She had always lived at home and was not working at the time of the killing. A psychiatric examination determined that the daughter killed as a result of her psychiatric illness. There was no history of previous violence between mother and daughter, substance abuse by either party, or maternal mental illness.[73]

The fourth case involved a 38-year-old psychotic woman who was living with her 60-year-old mother at the time of the incident. The woman initially had no memory of stabbing her mother in the heart with an ice pick, killing her, and subsequently stabbing and wounding her 10-year-old son. During a sodium pentothal interview given at the direction of Dr. Guttmacher, the woman recalled that she had believed that her mother and her son were having sexual intercourse. Moments before the stabbing, she heard a voice commanding her to kill her mother because of their sinful conduct.[74]

Case Studies of Male Adolescent Matricide Offenders

Frederic Wertham was the first mental health professional to take an in-depth look at adolescent parricide.[75] In his 1941 book, the psychiatrist described the case of 15-year-old Gino, who stabbed his mother 32 times, eventually killing her, after enduring years of abuse. Wertham found few clues with which to unravel the dynamics behind this homicide; there were only the murder itself, the manner of the murder, and Gino's behavior after it, "his first impulse had been to pacify and soothe the frightened children [his younger siblings]; and he had then gone voluntarily to the police with a confession."[76] Shortly after the killing, 31 neighbors who knew Gino in his daily life—"bakers, pastry-cooks, grocers, undertakers, florists, manual laborers"—signed a petition stating the following[77]:

We, the undersigned, affirm and declare that we know Gino very well, having had continuous contact with him, and therefore we can with full conscience state that he was a hard worker, scrupulously honest, of good and high moral feelings, of clean habits, and never associated with people of dubious character.

In his extensive analysis of why Gino killed his mother, Wertham used a primarily psychoanalytic approach.[78] After careful consideration, the psychiatrist rejected the possibility that Gino suffered from psychosis or had an antisocial personality. Although he did not explicitly identify Gino as a severely abused youth, the case analysis is replete with data indicative of various types of abuse (physical, covert sexual, and emotional) and neglect (physical and emotional neglect, emotional incest). Wertham's explanation that the matricide was the product of catathymic crisis, as defined below, is consistent with the portrait of a youth who had been pushed beyond his limits.

Catathymic crisis is a circumscribed mental disorder, psychologically determined, non-heredity-based, without physical manifestations, and not necessarily occurring in a psychopathic constitution. Its central manifestation consists in the development of the idea that a violent act—against another person or against oneself—is the only solution to a profound emotional conflict, the real nature of which remains below the threshold of the consciousness of the patient.[79]

The findings in relation to the cases involving matricide by juveniles/adolescents generally parallel the case studies of adult male matricide offenders discussed earlier in terms of family dynamics and psychological problems.[80] Dysfunctional families, dominating and verbally abusive mothers, and withdrawn, passive, or absent fathers were commonly identified in the case studies noted in Table 4-7. Boys involved in overly close and seductive relationships with their mothers were also noted in many of these cases.[81] An incestuous relationship that had been ongoing for several years was reported in the case of a 14-year-old boy who was experiencing a catathymic crisis when he killed his mother and then engaged in vaginal and anal necrophilia with her dead body.[82]

Table 4-7 Juvenile/adolescent matricide offenders

Authors(s)	Year of Publication	Country of Study	Number of Subjects, Sample, Design/Methods/Data Sources	Offender Gender Male	Female
Wertham	1941b	United States	Case study: 15-year-old male matricide offender	✓	
Schwade & Geiger	1953	United States	Case study: 13-year-old male matricide offender	✓	
Medlicott	1955	New Zealand	Case study: two female juveniles involved in matricide (one victim), aged 15 and 16		✓
Winfield & Ozturk	1959	United States	Case study: 13-year-old male matricide offender	✓	
Scherl & Mack	1966	United States	Case study (primarily): 14-year-old male matricide offender	✓	
Mohr & McKnight	1971	Canada	Case study (primarily): three male matricide offenders, aged 15 to 17	✓	
Sadoff	1971	United States	Case study: 17-year-old male matricide offender	✓	
Mack et al	1973	United States	Case studies (four cases): three male matricide offenders, aged 14 to 16; one female matricide offender, aged 16	✓	✓
Tanay	1973, 1976	United States	Case study: 15-year-old male matricide offender	✓	
Corder et al	1976	United States	Ten parricide offenders compared with 10 offenders who killed strangers and acquaintances/other relatives: nine boys and one girl killed parents (two matricides, six patricides, two double parricides); two of nine boys killed mothers	✓	
Russell	1984	United States	Case studies (four cases): four male matricide offenders, aged 15 to 16	✓	
Mouridsen & Tolstrup	1988	Denmark	Case study: 9-year-old male matricide offender	✓	
Heide	1992	United States	Case study: 12-year-old male matricide offender killed mother and brother	✓	
Dutton & Yamini	1995	Canada	Case study: 17-year-old male matricide offender	✓	
Schlesinger	1999	Unites States	Case study: 16-year-old male matricide offender	✓	
Lennings	2002	Australia	Case study: 14-year-old female matricide offender		✓
Slovenko	2003	United States	Commentary/review, legal case study: 15-year-old male matricide offender	✓	
Yoshikawa et al.	2006	Japan	Case study: male adolescent matricide offender (age not reported)	✓	
Heide & Solomon	2010	United States	Case study: matricide offender, aged 16		✓

Adolescent matricide offenders, however, are less likely than their adult counterparts to have long-standing histories of severe mental illness.[83] Holcomb examined 25 cases of matricide and found significant differences between younger (age 21 or less) and older (age 21 and older) offenders. Older matricide offenders were significantly more likely than their younger counterparts to have psychotic diagnoses and to be delusional at the time of the killing. Younger matricide offenders were significantly more likely to have been abused by their parents and to be free of overt signs of several mental illness.[84] Typically, the prognosis for youths who kill mothers in a psychotic state is better than that for adult matricide offenders.[85]

Russell's seminal study of 11 juvenile murderers of family members included boys who killed fathers (four cases), mothers (four cases), and siblings (three cases).[86] The four matricide offenders had histories of problematic relationships with their mothers, committed their offenses in response to an acute event in their lives in which the mother played a pivotal role, and had documented emotional difficulties. In sharp contrast to their adult counterparts, the teenagers involved in these crimes also had histories of maltreatment, including abuse and neglect. Mothers were depicted as critical, controlling, and unusually close to their sons. Fathers were reportedly cold, distant, punishing, and peripherally involved in the family.

These boys had run away from home and been returned to the care of their mothers even after seeking help from law enforcement, being monitored by social services, being diagnosed with severe personality disturbances, and having psychiatric care recommended. One of the four boys attempted suicide, two of the four boys had recommendations from mental health personnel to be removed from their homes, and one of the boys' mothers had been under psychiatric care after severely beating her son, yet none of these boys were permanently removed from their homes. Russell emphasized how dysfunctional parental relationships, internalized threatening circumstances, and intense conflict and provocation can lead to matricide. He argued that the response to these acts should focus on a therapeutic approach as opposed to a punitive one.[87]

In *Why Kids Kill Parents*, I highlighted the case of a 12-year-old boy who killed his mother.[88] As noted in Chapter 2, the boy's murderous behavior was propelled by psychological abuse and emotional neglect by his mother. Several other case studies of boys who killed biological mothers also depict the psychologically abusive nature of these relationships.[89]

A few clinical reports published in the 1950s suggested that biological factors might play a contributing role in matricide by adolescents. An abnormal electroencephalographic (EEG)pattern known as "14 and 6 per second positive spikes" was identified in two separate cases of 13-year-old boys who shot their mothers multiple times.[90] Although initially these patterns were considered evidence of epilepsy or other neurological conditions, they have since been determined to be normal variations with no clinical significance.[91] Close reading of these two case studies suggests family dysfunction in both homes. One of the mothers was depicted as physically and psychologically abusive,[92] and the other as psychologically abusive.[93]

One recent case study, however, suggested that an adolescent boy killed his mother largely due to biological factors.[94] This boy reportedly developed Asperger syndrome as a result of a brain tumor.[95] The surgery, radiation therapy, and the tumor severely damaged the youth's amygdala (the brain center associated with emotion). The boy acted violently toward his mother and tried to kill himself twice as he encountered difficulties with his mother during his adolescence. He eventually beat her to death.

The authors said that psychological tests and neuroimages suggested that the boy's violent behavior might have been caused by damage to the amygdala.[96]

In contrast to the adult matricide literature, killings by psychotic male juveniles have rarely been reported. Only two case reports were located. This first involved a 9-year-old boy who assembled a rifle, loaded it with ammunition stored at another location in his home, and, as he had planned, shot his mother multiple times from a hidden position. The boy also shot several objects in the home, including a picture of his mother. The forensic examiners found no evidence of violence in the home, physical abuse, or a disturbed parent–child relationship. The child was diagnosed as suffering from a schizophrenic disorder that likely developed in the years preceding the homicide. The record indicated that prior to killing his mother, the boy displayed a great deal of interest in guns and stories with "horrifying and destructive" themes. His complaints of being persecuted and beaten by his classmates were found to have no objective basis. Hallucinations that he reported included seeing a monster that threatened to kill him.[97]

The second case involved a 15-year-old boy, Robert, who stabbed his mother 24 times, causing her death, while on a visit with her to New Orleans.[98] The youth had been there previously and had associated with a group of Goth individuals. On this return trip, Robert visited again with his Goth friends and spent the night before the murder partying with them, drinking "untold amounts of liquor," and taking two hits of acid.[99] He stabbed his mother after she scolded him when he returned to the hotel room. Shortly thereafter, Robert slit his wrists and neck. He told an acquaintance who accompanied him to the hotel room that he was ending it all. He was sitting in a yoga position, bleeding, when the police arrived.

Robert was initially found not competent to stand trial. He was tried two years later for murder and pled not guilty by reason of insanity (NGRI). Trial testimony indicated that the youth had a long history of mental illness and was first hospitalized at age 6. Mental health professionals who treated him when he was between ages 11 and 13 reported that he had met the diagnostic criteria for schizophrenia and had shown evidence of organic brain damage as a child. They noted further that he was preoccupied with bizarre thoughts that included violent and destructive imagery. Accordingly, antipsychotic and antidepressant medications were prescribed for Robert. Mental health professionals who examined the youth after the murder and testified at trial diagnosed him as having paranoid schizophrenia and polysubstance abuse. Robert's father testified that he had allowed his son to go off his psychotropic medication before his trip to New Orleans and blamed himself for his wife's murder. The youth, although initially convicted, was subsequently found NGRI by the reviewing appellate court.[100]

Case Studies of Female Adolescent Matricide Offenders

In their synthesis of the literature on female parricide offenders mentioned above, Marleau, Millaud, and Auclair (2001) identified 16 cases in which female offenders 19 years of age or younger killed or, in four cases, attempted to kill mothers.[101] Many of the accounts mentioned in the literature reviewed were very brief,[102] and several others were not written in English, making them less accessible to those not fluent in other languages, particularly French and German.

In my review of the literature I found only five detailed case studies of girls who killed their mothers written in the English language.[103] Some of these cases have threads of mental illness and antisocial propensities; significant evidence of severe abuse appears present in three of the five cases. Medlicott discussed the motivational dynamics that led to the killing of a mother by the woman's 16-year-old daughter, Pauline, and her 15-year-old friend, Juliet, in New Zealand.[104] Medlicott attributed the killing to the infatuation that the two girls had with each other. Although the girls denied that they had a homosexual relationship, their writings provided convincing evidence that their relationship was indeed a sexual one.

Over time, the girls both developed a shared delusional belief system in which they saw themselves as geniuses with no equals. Although neither girl had a history of delinquent behavior prior to their meeting, their thoughts and writings became increasingly antisocial and violent over the nearly two-year course of their friendship. When it appeared that the girls would be geographically separated because Juliet's family was moving to another country, the girls became increasingly obsessed with doing whatever was necessary in order to stay together. With great excitement, they devised a plan to kill Pauline's mother, who was viewed as an obstacle preventing Pauline from moving away with Juliet's family because she disapproved of their relationship.[105]

Writings from Pauline's diary depicted the girls as very excited and exalted as they talked about the upcoming murder. Excerpts from the diaries indicated the girls had extreme mood swings ranging from euphoria to despair and seemed to require little sleep. They shared the same delusions, such as having an extra part of their brains that allowed them access to a special place called the "Fourth World," which they deemed "Paradise." Although the murder was premeditated, it was poorly planned, and the girls were quickly apprehended. Both confessed to their involvement in the killing.[106]

Medlicott and another defense expert believed that the girls suffered from "paranoia of the exalted type." Interviews with both girls clearly indicated that they knew the nature and quality of their act and that killing Pauline's mother was against the law and mores of the community. Accordingly, the jury did not find them insane and convicted them. Medlicott noted that the girls did not express remorse for the killing and seemed not to foresee the likely consequences that would result from their murderous behavior, which included separation from one another.[107]

The second in-depth analysis involved a 16-year-old girl named Nell, the only girl among four juvenile matricide offenders discussed in a book chapter by Mack, Scherl, and Macht.[108] Nell was one of six children and the only girl in "an upwardly mobile black family which placed considerable emphasis on social respectability and guarded itself against revealing inner conflict to the world."[109] The girl was reportedly a quiet and sullen youth. She shot her mother to death and later told police that she had intended to kill both her parents.

Similar to the situations of the three male matricide offenders, Nell's mother was depicted as "highly restrictive and critical."[110] Statements the girl made suggested that her mother physically and psychologically abused her. Mack and colleagues noted that, in contrast to their three male cases, Nell stated that she had never felt close to either parent and felt unloved since early childhood. Nell told her therapist that she felt that she had to kill someone. She wanted her mother dead because she hated her mother. She explained that if she had not killed her mother, no one would have realized that something was wrong with her.

The girl developed a paranoid psychotic state and experienced delusions and hallucinations. She was afraid her dead mother would return to earth to kill her. Although initially she maintained that her mother deserved to die, she later begged God for forgiveness so that she would not have to kill others or die herself. Unlike the three male matricide offenders, Nell did not show therapeutic improvement within several months of the killing. Three years after the killing, "Nell remained hospitalized in a deluded, paranoid, and child-like state, plagued with continuing homicidal and suicidal preoccupations."[111]

The third case involved a 17-year-old girl who stabbed her mother to death and reported no memory of the event. Kromm, Vasile, and Gutheil described an evaluative process designed to access the patient's personality and development through art therapy.[112] The girl was described upon admission to the hospital as "cooperative, controlled, distant, intelligent and articulate,"[113] and at times as having periods of dissociation. Testing indicated "a tightly controlled schizoid personality structure with marked narcissistic features, abnormal objects relations, and difficulty with impulse control."[114]

The girl lived with her mother as an only child for more than 16 years without any other significant relationships. Her parents divorced when she was an infant; she did not see her father again until she was 13 years old. The girl's mother was a successful businesswoman. The girl functioned in many ways as a surrogate spouse, cooking and cleaning, and serving as her mother's confidant. The evening before the killing, the woman came home drunk from a party, threw up, and was cleaned up by her daughter.

The girl had few friends of her own and socialized with her mother's friends. The girl aspired to go into a profession similar to her mother's. The consulting psychiatrist opined that "this close relationship was characterized by little depth of feeling as well as mutually shared and fragile ego boundaries in a symbiotic tie, in which murder may have been perceived as the only exit from an intolerable dependency."[115] The girl was subsequently found not guilty due to insanity at her trial for murder. She was treated and released from the hospital, and later committed suicide.

The fourth case involved a 14-year-old girl in Australia who fatally stabbed her mother while the two were cooking.[116] The killing was sudden and without explanation. The examining forensic psychologist found no evidence that the girl had been abused or witnessed domestic violence. Her drug and alcohol use was minimal. The examiner ruled out psychopathy or severe mental illness prior to the killing. He noted some "severe dissociative and pseudo-hallucinatory processes" after the homicide, but no signs of psychosis.[117] The girl reportedly embraced the Goth culture and had a rich fantasy life "that was more violent than her outward demeanor suggested" prior to the murder.[118] Prosecution was halted in this case; no reason was given. The girl expressed remorse and was haunted by visions of her deceased mother attempting to comfort her.

The fifth case was one of my own clinical accounts.[119] I was asked to evaluate Christine Johnson (pseudonym), aged 16, after she had been arrested and indicted as an adult for the first-degree murder of her mother. She was severely depressed when I met with her and cried throughout the evaluation. She was very remorseful as she related details of the struggle that resulted in her mother's death.

My evaluation of Chrissy convinced me that she was a severely abused child who dissociated under extreme stress. Chrissy's account of the events as they unfolded, coupled with scientific findings about the adolescent brain, provided convincing data that Chrissy, an untreated victim of post-traumatic stress disorder, was incapable of stopping to evaluate her behavior during the homicidal incident. As she repeatedly stabbed her mother, it was highly probable that Chrissy was not consciously processing what was occurring and did not know that her conduct was wrong. It appeared that her behavior was driven by her limbic system (the emotional center of the brain) rather than by the prefrontal cortex, with which people make rational decisions. The dynamics that led to her killing her mother were complex, as summarized in Box 4-1. They involved abuse and neglect by both her parents.

BOX 4-1 Christine Johnson, Aged 16: A Case of Matricide[122]

"Chrissy" was the older of two children born to Mr. and Mrs. Johnson. At the time when she stabbed her mother to death, Chrissy was a high school senior. She was an excellent student and was actively involved in school sports. Chrissy worked at her parents' company after school or sports practice. She had a small group of prosocial friends and was dating a boy who wanted to be "a cop." She was looking forward to graduating and going to college.

Chrissy's teachers were shocked by her arrest. She had no prior criminal involvement. The teen's grandparents, who played a significant role in raising her, particularly during her first 12 years, stood firmly by her side, as did her boyfriend and his family.

Chrissy was by all accounts "a daddy's girl." When she was 14, her father, who was a convicted sex offender, raped her. Chrissy told no one about the incident for more than a year. She rarely talked about her problems and thought about killing herself. Chrissy had a pattern of keeping her anger in rather than expressing it. She became sexual with several boys before she met her boyfriend Tony. She invested herself in school, work, sports, and her boyfriend in order to keep herself distracted from memories of the assault that haunted her.

One evening, as she stood with her mother admiring her younger sister Tanya, who was dancing at a dance studio, Chrissy felt that she needed to tell her mother about the assault in order to ensure that her sister was protected from a similar attack. Mrs. Johnson told Chrissy that they would talk about it later. As the three drove home from the dance studio, Mrs. Johnson quietly told Chrissy not to say anything further about the rape, as it would hurt the family. Her mother threatened Chrissy, telling her to keep her mouth shut or she would regret it.

Chrissy was distraught by her mother's reaction. Within a few minutes of getting home, Chrissy dressed up in her father's clothes, put a stocking over her face, and grabbed two knives from the kitchen. One she took with her, and the other she left on the dining room table as she moved toward her mother, who was washing clothes in another room. Chrissy planned to pretend that she was a robber and put the knife in front of her mother to scare her. Chrissy's fantasy was that her mother would not recognize Chrissy and would become scared. At that point, Chrissy intended to take off the stocking and tell her mother that she was strong and needed to be taken seriously. She expected her mother to recognize her strength and to agree to join her in protecting Tanya.

Events did not unfold as Chrissy had imagined. When Chrissy came up from behind and put a knife in front of her mother, the woman fought back. A violent encounter ensued as Mrs. Johnson tried to get control of the knife. At one point the two fell to the floor. Chrissy pushed the knife into her mother's neck. Scared, Chrissy got up and started to walk away.

(continued)

BOX 4-1 (Continued)

Chrissy's mom reportedly came after Chrissy with the knife, and the fight resumed. As the two struggled, Chrissy's mother let go of the knife. Mrs. Johnson told Chrissy she never loved her and did not want her as a daughter. Chrissy said, "I just stood up, and I stabbed her neck, and she just yelled, 'You, bitch.' And then I saw the other knife and I closed my eyes. And I just started going down. I do not know. I just kept doing it. I did not know what was going on. I just kept thinking about all the times that hurt and how she did not do anything about my dad—those times—and I wanted her, and I longed for her love, and she never gave it to me [client is sobbing.] And then I turned around, and my sister was there. And she looked at me, and I opened my eyes and I saw what had happened. [long pause] I freaked out. I saw the blood. [long pause] I was just, I could not catch my breath. So I went to the kitchen, and I got up [inaudible] and I called the police."

Chrissy's father made no attempt to speak to Chrissy at any time following her arrest. Chrissy's younger sister was removed from the home based on Chrissy's allegations of sexual assault.

Information provided by Chrissy and corroborated by others indicated that Chrissy was subjected to various forms of childhood maltreatment, including various forms of neglect (physical and emotional neglect and emotional incest) and abuse (physical, sexual, verbal, and psychological) by her parents. Chrissy was not provided with a safe place to live; she was sexually assaulted by her father. Chrissy was emotionally neglected by her mother, who failed to give her clear and genuine messages that she loved her. She saw her mother as giving her "the cold shoulder" and as not wanting to do anything with her.

Chrissy was expected to assume a lot of responsibilities around the house. These included cleaning the house and taking care of her sister. Chrissy indicated that her father talked to her about his personal problems, including his marital difficulties, his sexual relations with his wife, and his cheating on Chrissy's mother. In many ways, Chrissy was functioning as a surrogate spouse, which is a form of emotional incest, as discussed in Chapter 2.

Chrissy explained that her mother said things to her that made her feel badly. There were many examples of verbally abusive remarks. Chrissy said that her mother expressed dissatisfaction with her accomplishments, regardless of her actual performance level, which is a form of psychological abuse. Chrissy said her mother often did things that seemed cruel to her. She was sobbing when she said that her mother had again scratched her face during the killing. She described her mother as cold, and as showing no compassion toward her. She added, "I wanted to be loved; the more I put my heart out, the more it got ripped apart."

Chrissy had been physically abused (primarily hit and scratched) by her mother on many occasions. Chrissy had also witnessed violence between her parents. Her parents had been involved in several physical altercations. Records confirmed that Mrs. Johnson had been arrested for assaulting her husband with a knife about 10 years prior to the homicide. There was also a police report on domestic violence filed about four years prior to the killing.

BOX 4-1 (Continued)

99

Matricide: Basic Facts and Literature

Chrissy's statements are consistent with her being in a heightened state of arousal during the homicidal event. Chrissy was devastated by her mother's reaction to her disclosure of the rape by her father. Chrissy did not get the comfort and reassurance that she had expected and desperately needed. Mrs. Johnson's apparent dismissal of Chrissy's traumatic experience was more than Chrissy could handle, given what Chrissy experienced as years of trying to win her mother's love and approval. Mrs. Johnson's callous disregard of Chrissy's situation and her threatening remarks resulted in acute emotional distress for Chrissy. When Mrs. Johnson and the girls returned home, Chrissy's distress and inability to calm herself propelled the events that led to Mrs. Johnson's death a short time later.

Chrissy's "plan" to scare her mother shortly after they returned home was impulsive and poorly conceived. Her donning of her father's work clothes is significant because they were the same clothes that he reportedly wore when he sexually assaulted her. The girl's plan to scare her mother by dressing up like a robber suggests poor contact with reality at that point in time and a possible psychotic break. It is inconceivable that a girl of this level of intelligence, if in possession of her mental faculties, would think that if she put on her father's clothes and wore a stocking over her face, her mother would not recognize her when she brandished the knife.

Mrs. Johnson's fighting back added to Chrissy's acute level of stress, which had intensified to the point of dissociation. Chrissy's rendition clearly suggests that she was reacting to events as they spiraled out of control. She panicked and was terrified as her mother tried to defend herself. Chrissy believed that her mother was trying to kill her and believed that she was fighting for her life. At the same time, Chrissy was flooded with feelings from past hurts and perceived rejection by her mother, which exacerbated her stress and turmoil. Overwhelmed with feelings, Chrissy was not able to stop, think, deliberate, and make conscious decisions. She stabbed her mother multiple times.

Chrissy pled to an open count of murder. Three mental health professionals who evaluated her testified to the dynamics that led to the killing of her mother. A fourth mental health professional, an expert on risk assessment, calculated her risk of reoffending violently as exceptionally low. Her godfather and several teachers were among those who testified to her good character. The jurors were not sympathetic to her plight; they recommended a sentence of 40 years in prison. The judge followed their recommendation (Heide & Solomon, 2009).

SUMMARY AND CONCLUDING REMARKS

This chapter primarily focused on mothers killed by their biological children. Basic information on the characteristics of matricide victims and offenders in the United States over the period of 1976–2007 was provided. Given the very limited information available about stepmothers, analyses of stepmothers killed over the same period were also undertaken.

These analyses indicated that most female parricide victims were killed in single-victim, single-offender homicides. Multiple-victim and multiple-offender incidents were rare. However, as illustrated by the news stories presented at the beginning of the chapter, three findings with respect to multiple-offender situations emerged and are important. First, juveniles were significantly more likely than adults to be involved in multiple-offender incidents involving mothers. Second, female juveniles and female adults were significantly more likely to use accomplices in matricides than their male counterparts. Third, female juveniles were significantly more likely to act with codefendants in killing stepmothers than male juveniles.

Analyses focusing on single-victim, single-offender homicides revealed that mothers and stepmothers murdered were typically White (more than 70%), although a noticeable percentage were Black (between 22% and 26%). Stepmothers tended to be younger than mothers who were slain (50 vs. 60 years old).

Analyses indicated that sons and stepsons were the killers of mothers and stepmothers in more than 80% of cases. Killings by females, particularly in matricide situations, however, are worthy of note. About one out of every six mothers slain by biological children in 1976–2007 was killed by her daughter. During the same period, the proportion of mothers slain by female juveniles was even higher. Almost one of four mothers killed by juvenile offspring was killed by a daughter under 18.

Most mothers and stepmothers were killed by offspring over age 18. Offenders who killed stepmothers tended to be younger than those who killed mothers. The average age of stepmatricide offenders was 25, compared to 32 for matricide offenders. One of three offenders who killed stepmothers, compared to one of seven who killed mothers, was under 18.

Analyses indicated that offenders used a variety of methods to kill female parricide victims. Juvenile matricide offenders were significantly more likely to use firearms than their adult counterparts (60% vs. 33%). Offenders who killed stepmothers, relative to those who killed mothers, were significantly more likely to use guns (49% vs. 37%).

An extensive review of the literature revealed no detailed clinical studies focusing on stepmothers as victims. Studies and clinical reports on matricide offenders have concentrated largely on male offenders referred for psychiatric evaluation. My review of studies of adult or predominantly adult matricide offenders revealed that a high percentage of these offenders were found to be schizophrenic or otherwise seriously mentally ill.[120] Extensive histories of mental illness were common. Relationships between mothers and sons were typically conflictual and strained for years prior to the killings. Studies that have included nonhospitalized matricide offenders have found that not all offspring who kill mothers suffered from serious mental illness. Rather, some have been diagnosed with alcohol dependence; personality disorders, including antisocial personality disorder; or no mental illness at all.

The literature on adult daughters who kill their mothers is limited relative to studies involving sons. Similar to adult sons, adult daughters involved in matricide tended to be isolated and to have a history of dependent and ambivalent relationships with their mothers. Psychosis and depression were commonly diagnosed.

The literature on juveniles and adolescents who have killed mothers has concentrated largely on males. Case reports indicate that boys who kill mothers are less likely than their male adult counterparts to have histories of severe mental illness. They have typically had long histories of being abused by mothers.

Research efforts that specifically investigated mothers killed by daughters under age 18 are sparse. Only five in-depth case reports of female juveniles who killed mothers in single-victim incidents were located in the professional literature: (1) two adolescent girls who killed the mother of one of the girls in a case of folie à deux (shared psychosis); (2) a girl who killed her reportedly psychologically abusive mother, maintained that she intended to kill both parents and remained hospitalized for years in a psychotic state; (3) a girl who killed her mother, with whom she shared an excessively dependent relationship, had amnesia of the event, was found insane at trial, and later committed suicide; (4) a young adolescent who embraced the Goth culture and had a violent fantasy life who reportedly suddenly killed her mother for no apparent reason; and (5) a severely abused girl who killed her abusive mother after her mother refused to help and protect her when the girl told her mother that her father had raped her.[121]

Severe mental illness is evident in the first three cases. More research specifically focusing on girls who kill mothers is necessary in order to determine whether this particular group of young parricide offenders is more likely to suffer from severe mental illness than other juvenile parricide offenders. Abuse, including psychological abuse, is present in the cases of Nell, Chrissy, and the one reported by Kromm and colleagues. In at least one case, the daughter, Pauline, who acted with her friend to kill Pauline's mother, is presented as dangerously antisocial. In the case of Nell and the girl who identified with the Goth culture, antisocial themes are clearly present.

The next chapter concentrates on male parricide victims. Although the focus is mainly on fathers as victims, information pertaining to stepfathers is presented. Basic facts on killings involving fathers and stepfathers are presented, and the literature is synthesized.

5 Patricide: Basic Facts and Literature

- Pittsburgh, Pennsylvania—A 13-year-old girl was initially charged as an adult with criminal homicide after admitting that she had shot her father in the face with a 12-gauge shotgun while he lay in bed. The girl reportedly had been sexually molested by her father since she was 6 years old and had told a neighbor that she could not take it any longer. Neighbors stated that they knew the girl and her older brother were being abused. Child abuse reports had previously been filed with the state social services agencies. Police and court records indicated that there was a history of domestic violence in the home that had been ongoing for years. Two years before the killing, the girl's parents separated, with the father winning custody of two of the couple's three children. Arresting authorities described the home as deplorable and as reeking of animal waste. A health department report found major health code violations, including the lack of a bathroom sink or furnace, a leaking ceiling, holes in the walls, and a flea infestation from neglected animals including cats, dogs, and rabbits. The district attorney agreed to move the case to juvenile court after touring the girl's home. Following a negotiated plea, the girl pled guilty to a charge of involuntary manslaughter, the least serious degree of murder in Pennsylvania, and was adjudicated delinquent. She was placed on probation until age 21. Prosecutors agreed to expunge the girl's juvenile court record if she successfully completed probation.[1]
- Montezuma County, Colorado—A 20-year-old man initially pled not guilty by reason of insanity after he was charged with second-degree murder for killing and dismembering his father. The defendant told police that he shot his father in the back of the head after his father told him that he needed to get a sex change and become his wife and then raped him. The young man confessed that after he shot his father, he stabbed his dad 199 times with a knife and dismembered his body with an ax. He removed his father's hands, feet, and head and placed them in two

buckets. He then skinned his father's body and fed the man's flesh to coyotes. The defendant later pled guilty to manslaughter. The young man cried throughout the sentencing hearing as several friends and family members spoke on his behalf. The defendant's mother referred to her deceased husband as "a monster" and stated that her son was "a victim." The judge indicated that he took the sexual and mental abuse into account and imposed a sentence of three years in prison followed by 10 years of intensive supervision.[2]

- Bloomington, Illinois—A 20-year-old man was charged with first-degree murder after he called police to admit that he had hit his father multiple times with a baseball bat and stabbed him more than 40 times.[3] The defendant said that he feared his father was going to sexually assault him. He told police—and, later, mental health professionals who evaluated him—that he believed that God wanted him to kill his father and others who were "evil." The defendant subsequently entered a plea of not guilty by reason of insanity and asked for a bench trial (verdict rendered by the judge rather than a jury). He was examined by two psychiatrists retained by defense counsel and one psychiatrist hired by the prosecution. All three agreed that the defendant was delusional when he killed his father and that the young man's taking of LSD and marijuana had contributed to his mental state at that time. The two defense psychiatrists believed that the defendant's ingestion of LSD about a week before the killing triggered his psychotic behavior. Importantly, they maintained that he was at risk for a psychotic episode because of the extensive history of mental illness in his family. In contrast, the prosecution expert attributed the defendant's thinking and subsequent behavior to changes in brain chemistry caused directly by the LSD the defendant took a week prior to the killing and the marijuana he smoked hours before his violent rampage. The judge found the mental health testimony of the state's expert persuasive. The judge believed that although the defendant was "impaired" due to his drug use, he was still responsible. Accordingly, he rendered a judgment of "guilty, but mentally ill." The defendant cried throughout most of the sentencing hearing as family and friends asked the judge for leniency in his sentencing decision. The judge sentenced the young man to 27 years in prison, commenting that the victim's death underscored "the far-reaching and tragic consequences" of illegal drug use.[4]

- Tucson, Arizona—A 24-year-old man was charged with first-degree murder in connection with the brutal beating of his father. A family source indicated that the defendant "always was mad about something" and was "just crazy" when he used drugs, particularly methamphetamine. The defendant had had many brushes with the law, beginning at age 12 and extending into adulthood. The defendant reportedly had been kicked out of high school, had never held a regular job, and was a "self-proclaimed white supremacist." He had a history of prior domestic violence convictions and had recently been released from prison in connection with drug-related charges. The victim invited his son to live with him after he got out of prison because the defendant was drifting aimlessly and lacked direction. According to the defendant's cousin, the father was largely uninvolved in the defendant's upbringing, and the two had a strained relationship. The father apparently had drunk heavily in the past and had an extensive criminal history that included violent, property, drug, and DUI-related charges. The father reportedly was trying to change his life and wanted to help his son. The defendant arrived at his father's residence the day before the murder. On the day of the homicide, the two men were drinking at a gathering with family and friends when the defendant became bel-ligerent. The defendant was asked to leave the party, and the father went to check on his son shortly afterward. A few minutes later, the defendant returned alone. Waving his blood-covered hands in a triumphant way, the defendant reportedly said to a family friend that he had killed "his old man."[5] Trial testimony indicated that the victim was an alcoholic, had a history of domestic violence, and was prone to violent rages. The judge ruled at trial that there was not enough evidence to sup-port an intentional killing. Jurors rejected the defense's argument that the defen-dant acted in self-defense and returned a second-degree murder verdict.[6] Although the defendant faced a 22-year prison sentence, the judge sentenced him to 10 years, citing his abusive childhood and mental health issues.[7]

- Staten Island, New York—A 46-year-old man stabbed his 79-year-old father multiple times in the chest and neck, mortally wounding him. Neighbors were shocked by the killing, describing the victim as "a good man," "a family man," and "a great guy." Following the stabbing incident, the son drove 60 miles to the home of a childhood friend. There he doused himself and his car with gasoline, chained himself to the car's steering wheel, locked the doors, and ignited a fire. Police and firefighters arrived to find the car "engulfed in flames" and the man's body and vehicle charred beyond recognition. Family members stated that the son had mental health problems. The father, fearing for the safety of the family, had told his son that he needed to stay in a small tent in the backyard until he took his medication. A family friend confirmed that the son was very unruly when he was not on his medication.[8]

In the eyes of many, the killing of a father is an incomprehensible event. Fathers have been viewed historically as patriarchs and protectors of their wives and chil-dren. The horror evoked by this crime dates back thousands of years, as evidenced by plays such as *Oedipus Rex*. In the chapter opener, it is shown that news stories that try to make sense of patricide capture some of the frequent dynamics. These include youths pushed beyond their limits killing fathers who had severely abused them for years, mentally vulnerable youths who become delusional while using drugs and kill good fathers, antisocial young adults who cold-bloodedly murder their fathers in drunken brawls, and psychotic adults who kill their fathers as a result of a long-standing mental illness.

This chapter examines available knowledge on fathers slain and parallels the chapter on mothers killed by their children. Readers who want to get a solid foundation about what is known about patricide victims and offenders will find this chapter useful. Given the limited information available on stepfathers killed, this chapter includes some basic facts about the killings of stepfathers and compares the statistical informa-tion on the two male victim types (fathers and stepfathers).

This chapter is designed to help readers grasp the essentials regarding incidents involving male parricide victims. As in the preceding chapter on female parricide vic-tims, comparisons between mothers and fathers killed are avoided.[9] When studies have specifically contrasted matricide and patricide offenders, these differences are briefly noted.

I begin the chapter by presenting basic information about patricide and steppatri-cide victims, offenders, and incidents. As in the two preceding chapters, these analyses have been restricted to parricides in the United States and are based on arrest data reported to the Federal Bureau of Investigation over the 32-year period of 1976–2007.[10] When appropriate, I did statistical tests to determine whether certain differences were statistically significant, meaning that they did not occur by chance.[11]

After the discussion of the incidence of male parricide and the correlates of victims and offenders, I synthesize the literature on patricide. This literature review focuses first on studies of adult or predominantly adult male patricide offenders, followed by studies of females who killed fathers. After the discussion of the adult literature, case studies of male and female adolescent patricide offenders are synthesized. The chapter concludes with a summary of important points about patricide.

BASIC FACTS ABOUT PATRICIDE AND STEPPATRICIDE

Patricide is a very rare event, constituting less than 1% of all U.S. homicides in which the victim–offender relationship is known. During the period of 1976–2007, 133 offenders were arrested on the average each year in connection with the killings of fathers. As depicted in Table 5-1, 87% of those arrested for killing fathers were male offenders.

Approximately 91% of patricide offenders acted alone when they killed their fathers. On the average, in the period studied, about 12 offenders were arrested each year for acting with co-defendants to kill fathers. Interestingly, nearly 30% of the offenders involved in these multiple-offender incidents were females. Juveniles (under age 18) were significantly more likely than adult offenders to use accomplices in killing fathers. A significantly higher percentage of both juvenile and adult females employed code-fendants to kill fathers than did their male counterparts.

On the average, eight offenders each year were arrested for killing fathers and other victims during the same incident. Juvenile and adult offspring arrested in multiple-victim situations were overwhelmingly male offenders.

Murders of stepfathers are more rare than those involving fathers. On the average, 50 offenders were arrested per year for killing stepfathers in the period studied. Similar to those who killed fathers, more than 80% of those arrested were males. A significantly higher percentage of adult females were involved in multiple-offender steppatricides compared to adult males. About one offender per year was arrested in multiple-victim homicides involving stepfathers.

Patricide Victims and Offenders

Consistent with the preceding chapter, analyses of the characteristics of victims and offenders are restricted to single-victim, single-offender incidents.[12] As shown in Table 5-2, about 98% of fathers killed were either White (67%) or Black (32%). Patricide victims killed by offenders acting alone ranged in age from 30 to 99 or older and averaged 56 years old.[13]

Not surprisingly, given the biological relationship, the racial composition of patricide offenders was nearly identical to that of patricide victims.[14] Offenders who killed fathers in single-victim, single-offender incidents were male in 89% of cases. Patricide offenders ranged in age from 7 to 68 years of age and averaged 26 years old.[15]

As depicted in Table 5-3, more than one in five patricide arrestees were under age 18. When adolescents through age 19 are included in the analysis, one finds that nearly one-third of patricide offenders were under age 20. When the age is extended through

Table 5-1 Synopsis of offenders arrested for killing fathers and stepfathers; United States, 1976–2007

	Fathers	Stepfathers
ALL INCIDENTS*		
• Estimated number per year	133 (31 juveniles, 102 adults)	50 (15 juveniles, 35 adults)
• Offender gender	87% male	85% male
• Juvenile offenders	84% male	84% male
• Adult offenders	88% male	86% male
MULTIPLE-OFFENDER (MO) INCIDENTS		
• Estimated number per year	12	7
• Offender gender	71% male	79% male
• Juvenile involvement	Higher percentage of juveniles involved in MO incidents than adults (16% vs. 7%)[a]	Percentages of juveniles and adults involved in MO incidents both at 14% (not significant)
• Female juvenile involvement	Higher percentage of female juveniles involved in MO incidents than male juveniles (30% vs. 13%)[b]	Higher percentage of female juveniles involved in MO incidents than male juveniles (18% vs. 13%) (not significant)
• Female adult involvement	Higher percentage of female adults involved in MO incidents than male adults (16% vs. 6%)[c]	Higher percentage of female adults involved in MO incidents than male adults (20% vs. 13%)[d]
MULTIPLE-VICTIM INCIDENTS		
• Estimated number per year	8	1
• Offender gender	88% male	93% male
• Juvenile offenders	85% male	86% male
• Adult offenders	89% male	97% male

*Supplementary Homicide Report offender data, single and multiple victims, single and multiple offenders, national estimates; juveniles = under age 18.

[a]Statistically significant (χ^2 (1, 4261) = 78.565, Phi =−.136, p < .001).
[b]Statistically significant (χ^2 (1, 1000) = 32.164, Phi = .179, p < .001).
[c]Statistically significant (χ^2 (1, 3261) = 52.129, Phi = .126, p < .001).
[d]Statistically significant (χ^2 (1, 1122) = 6.828, Phi = .078, p < .01).

age 24, one sees that more than half of patricide offenders were juveniles, adolescents, or very young adults.

There is no evidence that the number of killings of fathers by youths under 18 is increasing. Indeed, the data indicate that both the number of patricides by juveniles and youths' proportionate involvement in all patricide arrests have significantly decreased

Table 5-2 Race of fathers and stepfathers killed in single-victim, single-offender incidents; United States, 1976–2007*

Race	Father as Victim		Stepfather as Victim	
	Estimated Number	Estimated Percentage	Estimated Number	Estimated Percentage
White	2457	66.7%	820	60.4%
Black	1162	31.5%	517	38.1%
Indian/Alaskan Native	31	0.8%	12	0.9%
Asian/Pacific Islander	36	1.0%	8	0.6%
TOTAL	3686	100%	1357	100%

*Supplementary Homicide Report offender data, national estimates. χ^2 (3, 5043) = 20.525, Cramer's V = .064, p < .001.

over time. From 1976 to 1991, juveniles constituted an estimated 24.3% of all patricide arrests; in 1992–2007, they made up an estimated 17.9%.[16] A consistent decrease in the percentage of all patricide arrestees who were under 18 is observable when the numbers are examined over eight-year periods. During the period of 1976–1983, juveniles comprised 26.0% (n = 316) of all patricide offenders; in 2000–2007, youths under 18 made up 14.7% (n = 94) of those arrested for killing their fathers.

In approximately 60% of killings, patricide offenders selected guns as their weapons of destruction. They used knives in 22% of the incidents. As shown in Table 5-4, blunt objects and personal weapons made up most of the remaining weapons used. Less than 3% of patricide offenders used fire, strangulation, asphyxiation, or other means (poison, drugs, defenestration, explosives, drowning) to kill their victims. Significant gender differences emerged among patricide offenders. Female patricide offenders, relative to their male counterparts, were more likely to use knives (29.1% vs. 21.2%). Males were more likely than females to use guns (60.0% vs. 57.4%) and other weapons (18.8% vs. 13.5%).[17]

Table 5-3 Age of patricide and steppatricide offenders in single-victim, single-offender incidents; United States, 1976–2007*

Offender Age (Years)	Father as Victim		Stepfather as Victim	
	Estimated Number	Estimated Percentage	Estimated Number	Estimated Percentage
Under 18	798	21.8%	411	30.4%
18–19	396	10.8%	180	13.3%
20–24	777	21.2%	317	23.4%
25–29	561	15.3%	171	12.6%
30–39	699	19.1%	186	13.7%
40–49	334	9.1%	65	4.8%
50–59	79	2.2%	24	1.8%
Over 60	22	0.6%	0	—
Total	3666	100%	1354	100%

*Supplementary Homicide Report offender data, national estimates. χ^2 (7, 5020) = 90.578, Cramer's V = .134, p < .001.

Table 5-4 Weapons used to kill fathers and stepfathers in single-victim, single-offender incidents; United States, 1976–2007*

Weapon Used	Father As Victim		Stepfather as Victim	
	Estimated Number	Estimated Percentage	Estimated Number	Estimated Percentage
Firearm/other guns	52	1.4%	21	1.6%
Handgun	1090	30.1%	432	32.3%
Rifle/shotgun	1017	28.1%	379	28.3%
Knife	799	22.1%	334	25.0%
Blunt object	295	8.2%	85	6.4%
Personal weapon (e.g., hands, feet)	278	7.7%	74	5.5%
Other (poison, drugs, pushed out window, drowning, explosives)	12	0.3%	4	0.3%
Fire	40	1.1%	3	0.2%
Strangulation	25	0.7%	4	0.3%
Asphyxiation	11	0.3%	2	0.1%
Total	3619	100%	1338	100%

*Supplementary Homicide Report offender data, national estimates. χ^2 (9, 4957) = 27.900, Cramer's V = .075, p < .05.

Important offender age differences were found with regard to weapon selection. Juvenile patricide offenders were significantly more likely than their adult counterparts to use firearms (79.4% vs. 54.1%).[18] Adults who killed fathers were significantly more likely than juvenile offenders to use knives (24.2% vs. 14.8%) or other weapons (21.7% vs. 5.8%).[19] Gender patterns held when examined within age categories, with sons more likely to use guns and other weapons, and daughters more likely to use knives.[20]

Steppatricide Victims and Offenders

As shown in Table 5-2, more than 98% of stepfathers killed were either White or Black. Significant racial differences were found between fathers and stepfathers killed. Noticeably, fathers were significantly more likely to be White than stepfathers (67% vs. 60%). Stepfathers were younger than fathers killed; they ranged in age from 20 to 89 and averaged 47 years old.[21]

Offenders who killed stepfathers were generally of the same race as the victim.[22] Offenders were male in 86% of the cases.[23] On the average, offenders who killed stepfathers were younger than those who killed biological fathers. Steppatricide offenders ranged in age from 8 to 58 and averaged 23 in age.[24]

Comparison of the offender range categories in Table 5-3 reveals significant differences. Approximately 30% of offenders who killed stepfathers, compared to 22% who killed fathers, were under 18. Nearly 44% of steppatricide offenders were under age 20, compared to less than 33% of patricide offenders. More than two-thirds (67%) of those who killed stepfathers, compared to about 54% of those who killed fathers, were under age 25.

The data do not indicate that juvenile involvement in steppatricides has increased over time. In fact, a significant decreasing trend is evident. Juveniles made up an estimated 34.5% of all arrests of stepfathers from 1976 to 1991, compared to 22.6% of total arrests from 1992 to 2007.[25] When examined over eight-year time periods, the percentage of arrestees under 18 who were arrested for killing stepfathers is seen to decrease from 35% (n = 177) in the earliest time frame (1976–1983) to 13.1% (n = 27) in the latest time frame (2000–2007).

As shown in Table 5-4, similar to patricide offenders, those who killed stepfathers were most likely to use guns (62.2%) or knives (25.0%). Steppatricide offenders were significantly less likely than patricide offenders to use other weapons (12.8% vs. 18.3%).[26] Gender differences were found among steppatricide offenders that mirrored those found with respect to patricide offenders. Female steppatricide offenders, relative to their male counterparts, were significantly more likely to use knives (41.8% vs. 22.3%). Males who killed their stepfathers, in contrast to females, were more likely to use guns (63.4% vs. 54.3%) and other weapons (14.4% vs. 3.8%).[27]

Gender patterns observed in weapon use held when the data were examined according to offender age. Juveniles who killed stepfathers were significantly more likely than adults to use guns (72.1% vs. 57.9%). In contrast, adults, relative to their younger counterparts, were significantly more likely to use knives (26.6% vs. 21.5%) and other weapons (15.6% vs. 6.4%).[28] Gender patterns held when the data were examined within age categories of steppatricide offenders, with stepsons more likely to use guns and other weapons and stepdaughters more likely to use knives.[29]

LITERATURE REVIEW

The literature on patricide is less extensive than that available on matricide. As the discussion will reveal, most research on patricide offenders consists of case studies. With the exception of a few reports, most studies have sample sizes of less than 20 cases. Similar to the literature on matricide, almost all of the research reported on patricide offenses involves male offenders. Importantly, the profile that emerges of the male patricide offender differs to some extent depending on whether sample subjects are hospital patients or defendants referred for forensic evaluation. As in the preceding chapter on matricide, special attention is given in this chapter to female patricide offenders, given the lack of previously published information on this population and their fairly significant involvement in the killing of their fathers.

Studies of Adult Male Patricide Offenders in Hospitalized Settings

I located two studies on adult patricide offenders (age 20 or older) in the professional literature that had sample sizes of 10 or more. Both of these studies involved male patricide offenders in hospital settings.

Cravens and his colleagues conducted one of the pioneering studies of patricide offenders.[30] They reviewed the records of 10 male patricide offenders referred for forensic evaluation from 1973 through 1983. They determined that all 10 had histories of past psychoses. Nine of the men were judged as having been delusional when they killed their father. In four of these cases, the sons "perceived their fathers as having posed threats of physical or psychological annihilation (or both) to them."[31] In the remaining five cases, the sons indicated that sexual conflict or threats to their masculinity were their primary reasons for killing their fathers. In the final case, the son killed his father during a drunken argument. Eight of the men were diagnosed with schizophrenia, one with schizophreniform disorder,[32] and one with alcohol abuse. The authors noted that nine of the 10 patricide offenders killed with excessive violence, nine had records of violent behavior, and nine had been unable to live independently.[33]

In the other study of male patricide offenders, Singhal and Dutta (1990) described the characteristics of 10 male patricide offenders admitted to three hospitals from court or prison because they were deemed amenable to treatment. Eight of these men were diagnosed with schizophrenia, and the remaining two with personality disorders. Brief case reports provided by the authors indicated that six of the patricide offenders, including the two diagnosed with personality disorders, were heavy drinkers. Seven of the psychotic patricide offenders and the two personality-disordered offenders described "cruel and unusual" relationships with their fathers. The authors "concluded that a bizarre relationship existed between the parent and the child in which the parent-victim mistreated the child excessively and pushed him to the point of explosive violence."[34] Comparisons between the parricide offenders and a control group of schizophrenic patients in the same age group indicated that the fathers of patricide offenders were significantly more punitive, depriving, and shaming than the fathers of nonpatricidal patients.[35]

Case Studies of Adult Male Patricide Offenders

Several case studies of adult patricide offenders written in the English language exist in addition to the two larger studies discussed above.[36] As noted in Table 5-5, most of these focus on sons in their 20s.[37] Seven of the eight male patricide offenders profiled in these reports were diagnosed or described as psychotic or as killing during a psychotic break with reality. Brutality by the father was identified in two of these reports and suggested in a third.[38]

The remaining study consisted of an extensive legal analysis of the case of a 20-year-old man, Robert Swift Willox, who was tried for killing his father in Scotland in 1929. This young man did not present as psychotic. Rather, the account was consistent with the behavior of an antisocial individual. The jury found the young man guilty, believing that he killed his father for money, and the Crown sentenced him to death. His sentence was subsequently commuted to life in prison by the Secretary of State for Scotland.[39]

Forensic Evaluations of Adolescent and Adult Male Parricide Offenders

The predominance of sons as the perpetrators in patricide cases is underscored in the results of forensic evaluations conducted by Gillies, a psychiatrist in Scotland, over a 21-year period, even when the sample is broadened to include juvenile and adolescent offenders.[40] Eight of the 400 murderers Gillies evaluated killed fathers; all were sons. In contrast to studies of hospitalized offenders, Gillies found that five of his eight patricide offenders were "normal" and killed their fathers during arguments. Of these, four were intoxicated at the time of the killing. Two of the three adjudged "abnormal" were youths involved in family homicides in which the fathers

Table 5-5 Adult patricide offenders (age 18 and over)*

Author(s)	Year of Publication	Country of Study	Number of Subjects, Sample Design/Methods/Data Sources	Offender Gender	
				Male	Female
Roughhead	1930	Scotland	Legal analysis/case study: 20-year-old male patricide offender	✓	
Moulun & Morgan	1967	United States	Case study: 20-year-old male psychotic patricide offender	✓	
Sadoff	1971	United States	Case study: 22-year-old male patricide offender killed during psychotic break	✓	
Lewis & Arsenian	1977	England	Case study: 25- or 26-year-old male psychotic patricide offender	✓	
Cravens et al.	1985	United States	Clinical archive study (retrospective, 1970–1983): 10 men, aged 20 to 40, charged with patricide and referred for psychiatric evaluation	✓	
Singhal & Dutta	1990	United Kingdom	Comparative study: 10 men charged with patricide (including two men charged with both patricide and matricide) compared to 10 schizophrenic patients (aged 20 to 40 years in both groups)	✓	
Funayama & Sagisaka	1988	Japan	Case study: 34-year-old female patricide offender		✓
Newhill	1991	United States	Case study: 19-year-old male psychotic patricide offender	✓	
Maloney (cited in Ewing, 2001)	1994	United States	Case study: male psychotic patricide offender in his late 20s	✓	
Lewis et al.	1998	United States	Case studies (two cases): 27-year-old male psychotic patricide offender and 68-year-old female patricide offender killed during psychotic break	✓	✓
Ewing	2001	United States	Case study: 20-year-old female patricide offender		✓
Yusuf & Nuhu	2010	Nigeria	Case studies: 25-year-old male patricide offender	✓	

*Includes studies on patricide and comparative studies on parricide that include matricide.

were among the victims slain. Brief descriptors suggested one youth who killed his "tyrannical parents" was abused; another who killed his father and two siblings was described as "psychopathic." The third patricide offender was characterized as a "middle-aged depressive" who "altruistically" killed his father because of his "delusion that the family business was bankrupt." See Table 5-6.

Weisman and Sharma examined the records of 64 offenders charged with the murder or attempted murder of a parent or both parents and referred for forensic evaluation in Southern California. They found that sons were the perpetrators in all incidents involving the killing of fathers (n = 16) and the attempted killing of fathers (n = 7). Male offspring were the killers or attempted killers in all cases involving both parents (n = 6 and 1, respectively). Their report suggests that sons who killed fathers were more likely to be sentenced to prison than those who killed mothers.[41]

A study of male parricide offenders conducted in Finland by Liettu and colleagues also found that most of the 106 patricidal offenders were not severely mentally ill. This study, discussed in the preceding chapter with respect to matricide offenders, reported on the results of routine evaluations of individuals charged with murder and serious violent offenses. In this case, sample subjects consisted of those who killed parents, attempted to kill them, or used aggravated violence against them. Patricidal offenders were unlikely to be married or cohabiting. More than 90% had never been married (76%) or were divorced or widowed (15%). Half had a previous history of psychiatric hospitalization. Seventy percent were intoxicated at the time of the violent incident, and 44% had an alcohol/drug-related disorder. In more than half of the incidents, the motive for the parricidal act was related to a drinking brawl (15%) or conflict resolution (39%).[42]

As noted in Chapter 4, matricide and patricide offenders differed in several respects. Relative to those who killed mothers or attempted to do so, offspring who killed or attempted to kill fathers (excluding aggravated assaults) were significantly less likely to be diagnosed with a psychotic disorder (24% vs. 47%) but more likely to be diagnosed as having a personality disorder (69% vs. 46%). Threats by the victim prior to the killing were significantly more common among patricide offenders than among matricide offenders. Offenders who killed fathers were significantly less likely to be found not guilty by reason of insanity than those who killed mothers (21% vs. 49%).[43]

Studies that Examined Females Who Killed Fathers

Parricide studies with large samples typically can say little about female parricide offenders. For example, only one of the patricide offenders identified from coroners' reports in Quebec over a 15-year period was female. The authors noted that she was a woman in her 50s who killed her elderly father by giving him a variety of intoxicating substances. She had been diagnosed with depression and had attempted suicide prior to the killing.[44]

Two studies, both mentioned in the preceding chapter on matricide, focused on female parricide offenders. Three of the 17 female parricide offenders identified by D'Orbán and O'Connor killed fathers.[45] As noted previously, this sample was not restricted to hospitalized patients and included 11 women from a detention center. The women who killed fathers differed in many ways from those who killed mothers.[46] Of particular note, in sharp contrast to matricide offenders, none of the female patricide offenders were diagnosed with schizophrenia or depression. One was diagnosed

Table 5-6 Mixed samples of adult/juvenile patricide offenders*

Authors(s)	Year of Publication	Country of Study	Number of Subjects, Sample, Design/Methods/Data Sources	Offender Gender	
				Male	Female
Gillies	1976	Scotland	400 forensic evaluations between 1953 and 1974; eight fathers killed by sons	✓	
d'Orban and O'Connor	1989	England	17 women, aged 17 to 54, in prison or under medical care for killing a parent (14 matricide, three patricide)		✓
Weisman & Sharma	1997	United States	Clinical archive study (retrospective, 1978–1996): 64 offenders adjudicated as adults, aged 17 to 56: 40 male and five female parricide offenders, 16 male and three female attempted parricide offenders. Only male offenders were involved in killings or attempted killings of fathers or double parricides. 45 parricide offenders: 23 matricide, 16 patricide, six parricide. 19 attempted parricide offenders: 11 attempted matricide, seven attempted patricide, one attempted parricide.	✓	
Marleau et al.	2001	Multi-country	38 cases of female adult and adolescent parricide offenders reported in the literature		✓
Bourget et al.	2007	Canada	Clinical archive study (retrospective, 1990–2005): Comparative study of matricide and patricide. 56 parricide offenders: 52 males, aged 14 to 58, killed 36 patricide and 24 matricide victims. Four females, aged "late teens to 50s," killed one patricide and three matricide victims.	✓	✓
Liettu et al.	2009	Finland	Clinical archive study (retrospective, 1973–2004): 86 matricidal and 106 patricidal offenders (single victim, male offenders only); four matricidal and six patricidal offenders were under age 18. Study sample included 113 completed homicides, 48 attempted homicides, and 31 aggravated assaults.	✓	

*Includes studies on patricide and comparative studies on parricide that include matricide.

with antisocial personality disorder; the other two had no psychiatric diagnoses. In all three patricide cases, chronic abuse and conflict were suggested. Reports of inappropriate sexual behavior by the father were present in two cases.[47]

In the second study, Marleau, Millaud, and Auclair reviewed the literature for accounts of females killing parents from 1940 through 2001. They identified 38 cases of daughters who killed or, in five cases, attempted to kill one or more of their parents.[48] As noted in the matricide chapter, the authors analyzed these cases according to victim type, age of offender, weapon used, and situational dynamics. Of the 38 cases, 20 involved fathers as the sole victim (13) or as among the victims (seven). Seventeen of the patricide offenders in this sample of case reports were adolescents or young adults; only three of the incidents in which fathers were killed involved offenders aged 20 or older.

Marleau and his colleagues advised that females who murder parents should not be treated as a homogeneous category, as the motivations for killing depended on the offender's age and the victim type. They noted that abuse was present in many situations involving adolescent patricide offenders. In the three cases of adults who killed fathers, the authors' brief notations suggested that one woman, aged 31, was severely mentally ill; a 20-year-old woman likely had been in a long-standing abusive relationship with her father; and another 20-year-old woman was dangerously antisocial.[49]

Case Studies of Adult Female Patricide Offenders

Consistent with Marleau and his colleagues, I found few case studies of adult females who killed fathers. In the three cases located, two of the women appeared antisocial; the third was clearly severely mentally ill at the time of the killing. Ewing described the case of a 20-year-old daughter who was convicted of soliciting her boyfriend and another male to kill her father and stepmother. Although the young woman denied that she had masterminded the killing, she did acknowledge during her court testimony that she stood to benefit financially from her father's death, had discussed killing her father with her boyfriend, and on one occasion had offered a friend $30,000 to kill her father.[50]

The second case, indeed a very unusual one, involved a 34-year-old housewife from Japan implicated in the killing of her father. This case also had an underlying antisocial element. When this woman was arrested for her father's death, she confessed to killing six newborn infants over an eight-year period. The woman was married and had four other children. Her husband frequently worked away from home and was unaware of her pregnancies. The authors suggested that the motive for all of the killings was economic. She stabbed her father and strangled him after the two quarreled about her taking care of him. The woman was indicted and convicted of killing her father and the last infant, and she was sentenced to eight years' imprisonment.[51]

The third case involved a 68-year-old widowed woman, Ms. J., who killed her elderly father.[52] The woman had previously taken care of her terminally ill husband and two sisters prior to her elderly father's coming to live with her. As her father's caretaking needs became greater, Ms. J. became less active in church and community affairs and no longer had time for socializing with her friends, her grown children, and her grandchildren.

Over time, Ms. J. became increasingly depressed by her caretaking duties and thought of killing herself. She started experiencing auditory hallucinations that told her it was her duty as a daughter to kill her father. Ms. J. talked about her depression to her family doctor, who decided against hospitalizing her. Within a few days, Ms. J. killed her father by smothering him with a pillow. She appeared to have killed her father during a psychotic break and was found not guilty by reason of insanity.

Case Studies of Primarily Male Adolescent Patricide Offenders

Since the early 1960s, more than a dozen studies have focused on juveniles or adolescents who killed primarily fathers. Three of these studies included cases in which stepfathers were killed.[53] As depicted in Table 5-7, most of these publications have focused on male adolescent patricide offenders. When girls have been included in the sample, conclusions typically have been drawn without respect to gender, largely because girls typically are involved in only one or two of the cases.[54] In almost all of these clinical studies or vignettes, the youths were depicted as prosocial children abused by their fathers and stepfathers and as without psychosis.[55] Two studies, however, diagnosed or described male children or adolescents as psychotic at the time of the killing.[56] One clinical report depicted a 17-year-old patricide offender as extensively involved in criminal activities, abusive toward his mother, and "psychopathic."[57]

As summarized in the literature review on adolescent parricide offenders in Chapter 3, most youths who killed fathers had been raised in violent homes where their fathers typically were physically and psychologically abusive toward the children and, often, their mothers. In some of these accounts, boys killed their fathers in order to protect their mothers, leading some clinicians to believe that the patricide was in some ways commissioned by the mother, although likely not in an overt (or even conscious) way.[58] Lack of protection by the mother, isolation of the family unit, and inability to get help from others were frequent factors noted in patricide cases. Adolescents' feelings of increasing helplessness as conditions in the home worsened and their inability to escape the family situation were also common elements in patricide cases.

Many studies have noted the easy availability of guns in these situations.[59] Analyses of parricide cases in the United States have found that youths under 18 were significantly more likely than adult offenders to use guns to kill fathers. Heide found that 82% of juveniles who killed fathers over the 10-year period of 1977–1986 used guns, compared to 60% of their adult counterparts.[60] The differences in these percentages held and remained significant when data were examined over the period of 1976–1999.[61]

One of the most impressive studies on adolescent parricide was published in the mid-1970s. Billie Corder and her colleagues compared a group of 10 parricide offenders with two control groups, each consisting of 10 youths, who killed strangers or acquaintances/other relatives.[62] These youths were charged with murder in the juvenile system and admitted to a regional forensic hospital during a 14-year period. The parricide group consisted of five boys and one girl who had killed fathers, two boys who killed mothers, and two boys who killed both parents. Parricide offenders differed significantly from one or both of the control groups on eight variables. Youths who killed parents had "fewer typical adolescent sexual outlets and social relationships (manifested by differences in dating patterns); fewer indications of poor impulse control or aggressive behavior; more indications of chronic physical abuse

Table 5-7 Juvenile/adolescent patricide offenders

Authors(s)	Year of Publication	Country of Study	Number of Subjects, Sample, Design/Methods/Data Sources	Offender	
				Male	Female
Sargent	1962	United States	Case studies (four cases): Two brothers, 7 and 8 years old, killed father Boy, aged 16, killed stepfather Boy, aged 15, killed mother's paramour Boy, aged 14, killed father	✓	
Reinhardt	1970	United States	Case study: 17-year-old boy killed father	✓	
Duncan & Duncan	1971	United States	Case studies (five cases): Girl, age 14, considered killing father (abandoned idea) Three brothers (aged 15, 13, and 10) killed father Boy, aged 18, killed father Boy, aged 15, killed stepmother Boy, aged 14, attempted to kill father and mother	✓	✓
Malmquist	1971	United States	Case study: 15-year-old boy killed stepfather	✓	
Anthony & Rizzo	1973	United States	Case studies (two cases): 15-year-old girl killed father 15-year-old girl attempted to kill father		✓
Tanay	1973, 1976	United States	Case studies (two cases): 14-year-old boy killed father 17-year-old boy killed father	✓	

(continued)

Table 5-7 (Continued)

Authors(s)	Year of Publication	Country of Study	Number of Subjects, Sample, Design/Methods/Data Sources	Offender Male	Offender Female
Corder et al	1976	United States	10 parricide offenders compared with 10 offenders who killed strangers and acquaintances/other relatives: Nine boys and one girl killed parents Two matricides, six patricides, two double parricides Two of nine boys killed mothers Youths were aged 13 to 18; average age was 16.6 years	✓	✓
Tucker & Cornwall	1977	United States	10-year-old boy attempted patricide	✓	
Post	1982	United States	15-year-old girl killed stepfather		✓
Russell	1984	United States	Case studies of four male patricide offenders	✓	
Mones	1985	United States	Seven case vignettes of teenage parricide offenders: Four boys killed fathers One girl killed father One boy killed mother, father, and two brothers One boy killed mother and stepbrother	✓	✓
MacDonald	1986	United States	Case study: 11-year-old boy killed father	✓	

			Cases		
Heide	1992	United States	Cases included the following, among others: Three boys killed fathers One girl killed father Two boys killed both parents One boy killed mother and brother	✓	✓
Dutton & Yamini	1995	Canada	Case study: 17-year-old boy killed stepfather	✓	
Malmquist	2010	United States	Six case vignettes: Three boys killed fathers Two boys killed mothers One boy killed stepfather	✓	

*Includes studies on patricide and comparative studies on parricide that include matricide.

by parents; more indications of overattachment to their mothers; more evidence of atypical sexual stimulation by parents; greater frequency of chronic abuse of a passive mother by the father; family patterns of absent fathers; and more instances of amnesia for the murder act."[63]

Case Studies of Female Adolescent Patricide Offenders

I located four case studies or vignettes of female adolescents who killed or attempted to kill their fathers written in English in the professional literature. I found one case of a girl who killed her common-law stepfather. Sexual abuse was evident in all of these cases, in addition to other types of abuse.[64] One of these cases is summarized below.

Psychiatrists Anthony and Rizzo presented the case of a 15-year-old girl who killed her father after enduring years of abuse.[65] The girl was one of five children raised in a poor family. From the time she was young, she was noticeably more nervous and aggressive than her four siblings. She "constantly" sought help from others "and spent a lot of time talking over her problems" with school counselors.[66]

The authors noted that the father's "aggressive and erotic activities were the main determinants of family transactions." He tyrannized the family in different ways depending on whether he was drunk or sober. He gave up drinking because of continual "visions" in which he saw himself killing his entire family.[67] He later became suspicious that the family was trying to kill him. The man beat his wife for years. He stopped six years prior to his murder following a drunken incident when he slapped his wife, pregnant at the time, in the stomach. His wife pulled a gun on him and threatened to kill him. From that day forward, the man never touched his wife physically or sexually. Instead, he focused his aggression and sexual needs on his children.

The father had intercourse with three of his four daughters and sodomized his son. He began having sex with each daughter as she reached puberty and discarded each for the younger victim next in line. Two of the daughters, including "the patient," became pregnant. The father aborted the first fetus with a TV antenna and drowned the second baby in the kitchen sink two hours after its birth. The mother helped bury the baby in a nearby field.

The father was "extremely strict about any extra-familial sexuality."[68] He was obsessed with his children's sexuality and warned the girls that he would kill them if they dated. When first married, the father had demanded sex from his wife three or four times per night and had extra-marital relations. When the father lost sexual interest in his wife, she was relieved because she was "usually very tired, and in fact, disgusted by sex."[69]

On the night of the murder, the girl and her siblings disobeyed their father by going to a drive-in movie. When he arrived at the location, he accused the girls of having sex with the men around them and took the girls home. The patient said that as she entered the house that night, she had a feeling that "something violent was going to happen so she went in and hid the guns," as she had done in the past when her father was violent, "so that nobody would find them." Shortly thereafter, as the girls began to argue with their father, he grabbed one of the sisters and started to strangle her. At that point, the patient retrieved one of the guns and told her father she would shoot him if he did not stop. Her father did not release his hold, and the girl shot him as her sister was "becoming cold and blue."[70]

The girl became extremely depressed after the killing. She maintained that she wanted to threaten her father but did not want to kill him. The examining psychiatrists diagnosed her as having a borderline personality, not as psychotic. They noted that she was immature and egocentric and had poor impulse control, a poor self-concept, and "a shaky sense of reality."[71] They noted that diagnostically she resembled her father in many ways.

The mother acknowledged the incest in the family, describing her deceased husband as "affectionate."[72] In addition to overt sexual abuse, covert sexual abuse was clearly evident. The mother showed the examiners a picture taken of herself and her husband having sex; the picture had been taken by one of her daughters.

SUMMARY AND CONCLUDING REMARKS

This chapter primarily focused on fathers killed by their biological children. Basic information on the characteristics of patricide victims and offenders in the United States over the period of 1976–2007 was provided. Given the very limited information available about stepfathers, analyses of stepfathers killed over the same period were also undertaken.

These analyses indicated that most male parricide victims were killed in single-victim, single-offender homicides. Multiple-victim and multiple-offender incidents were rare. Analyses focusing on single-victim, single-offender homicides revealed that fathers and stepfathers murdered were typically White (more than 60%), although a noticeable percentage were Black (between 32% and 38%). Stepfathers killed tended to be younger than fathers who were slain (47 vs. 56 years old).

Analyses indicated that sons and stepsons were the killers of fathers and stepfathers in more than 80% of cases. Killings by females of male parents and stepparents, however, are worthy of note. About one in eight fathers slain by biological children from 1976 to 2007 was killed by his daughter. The number drops to less than one in seven when the victims are stepfathers. During the same period, the proportion of fathers and stepfathers slain by female juveniles was even higher. Almost one of six cases of fathers and stepfathers killed by juvenile offspring involved daughters or stepdaughters under 18.

Most fathers and stepfathers were killed by children over age 18. Offenders who killed stepfathers tended to be younger than those who killed fathers. The average age of steppatricide offenders was 23, compared to 26 for patricide offenders. Thirty percent of offenders who killed stepfathers, compared to 22% of those who killed fathers, were under 18.

Analyses indicated that 60% of offenders used guns to kill male parricide victims. Juvenile offenders were significantly more likely than their adult counterparts to use firearms to kill fathers (79% vs. 54%) and stepfathers (72% vs. 58%).

Despite the greater incidence of fathers slain by their offspring, fewer patricide studies were located than matricide studies. Similar to the literature on matricide, studies and clinical reports on patricide offenders have concentrated largely on adult male offenders hospitalized or referred for psychiatric evaluation. Importantly, available studies, although few, indicate that diagnoses varied noticeably depending on the setting. Adult males who killed their fathers and were hospitalized typically had a history of psychosis and were psychotic at the time of the killing. In contrast, less than half of patricide offenders referred for forensic evaluations in a large clinical study were diagnosed as psychotic.[73] Moreover, more than two-thirds of the patricide offenders were diagnosed as having personality disorders. Notably, the existing literature reveals that although similarities exist between offspring who kill mothers and those who kill fathers, there are important differences between the two groups. One recent study found, for example, that relative to matricide offenders, those who killed fathers were significantly less likely to be found psychotic (24% vs. 47%) and not guilty by reason of insanity (21% vs. 49%).[74]

The literature on adult daughters who kill their fathers is even more limited than that available on sons. Interestingly, none of the three women who killed fathers in a sample of female parricide offenders was found to be psychotic or depressed. Two received no psychiatric diagnoses; one was diagnosed with antisocial personality disorder. Severe abuse was reported in all three cases; sexually inappropriate behavior was noted in two of them. Of the five case studies available,[75] two adult female patricide offenders appeared severely mentally ill, two antisocial, and one abused. Clearly, more research is needed in order to draw conclusions with respect to adult female patricide offenders.

Similar to the literature on matricide, available studies on juveniles and adolescents who killed fathers have concentrated largely on males. Case reports indicate that boys and girls who killed fathers were unlikely to have histories of severe mental illness, but they have typically had long histories of being victims and witnesses of abuse by their fathers. In the four studies or vignettes of girls who killed fathers, all of the girls reportedly were sexually abused by their fathers.

The next section of the book examines the legal issues involved in parricide. Chapter 6 focuses on the prosecution of parricide offenders. Chapter 7 examines defense strategies.

6 Prosecuting and Punishing Parricide Offenders

When a youth kills a parent, the legal system focuses on the same question that would be considered if the individual were an adult: Has a crime been committed? *Homicide* and *murder* are technically not equivalent terms. Homicide denotes the killing of another person and can sometimes be justified, as in the case of defending one's own life or the life of another. Under some circumstances, killing another human being, although clearly not justified, might be excusable, such as when the killer is a very young child or so severely mentally ill as to not comprehend his or her actions. Murder, in contrast, involves the unlawful taking of a human life and is a crime for which an individual, if convicted, will be punished.

Cases exist of very young children killing parents. In one of these cases, a 4-year-old child reportedly said to his mother after shooting his father, "Mommy, Mommy, I shot Daddy dead." When parricide offenders are age 10 and under, questions of legal culpability typically arise. Many states provide no minimum age for prosecution in juvenile court, allowing the juvenile court judge to determine jurisdiction depending on case law and the competency of the child.[1] Under Common Law, there was a conclusive presumption that children under the age of 7 lacked the capacity to form criminal intent.[2] However, one state, North Carolina, allows children as young as 6 years old to be prosecuted in juvenile court.[3]

Children involved in homicide might be prosecuted in either juvenile or adult criminal justice systems depending on state statutes. The 8-year-old Arizona boy arrested for killing his father and his father's friend (see Chapter 1) was initially charged with two counts of "premeditated" murder and faced prosecution in adult court. If convicted as charged, the boy would have faced life in prison. Four months after the double homicide, the boy pled guilty to one count of negligent homicide in connection with the death of his father's friend; the boy was not charged with killing his father. He was sentenced to residential treatment and intensive probation until age 18. This case is a good example of how the justice system handles cases involving very young parricide offenders.[4] In practice, young children are rarely held fully accountable for their actions when parents are the victims. These children are more likely to be referred to the mental health or social services systems for evaluation and treatment.

The prosecutor's office is likely to bring charges against juvenile parricide offenders aged 12 and older. Whether the prosecution will occur in a juvenile or adult court depends on state law and the circumstances of the case. I was recently consulted in an unusual parricide case. A 12-year-old boy was involved in killing his father and mother and critically injuring his younger brother and sister. The boy had no prior arrest history. He was a small-framed child who weighed 70 pounds when taken into police custody. He was known in his small community for his extensive involvement in church activities. Without exception, members of his family and church were shocked by the boy's arrest. In this particular state, a youth of age 12 could not be prosecuted as an adult without a transfer hearing. The district attorney (DA) in the jurisdiction retained me to assist the State in determining whether to keep the boy in juvenile court or seek to transfer him to the adult criminal justice system. The DA remarked that if the defendant were 25 years old, he would not care why the defendant was involved in such a terrible crime. However, in this case, given the boy's age, the DA felt compelled to understand the circumstances behind the youth's homicidal behavior before deciding on the right course of action.

After examining the facts of the case, the prosecutor might file charges ranging from first-degree murder to manslaughter. Determining whether the youth intended to take the life of another human being becomes the critical consideration in deciding whether first- or second-degree murder is an appropriate charge. The state attorney's office typically seeks to charge the adolescent with *murder in the first degree* if the parricide appears to be the result of a premeditated design to kill the parent, that is, if the youth intended to take the life of his or her mother or father. In many cases, abused adolescents kill their parents in non-confrontational situations (e.g., the parent is asleep or absorbed in a TV show and unaware of the child's presence) because they perceive that as being the only way that they can prevail in the situation.[5] In other cases, dangerously antisocial children confront their parents directly and kill them because their parents "get in the way," for example, of the child's taking the car and having fun. From a legal perspective, both of these situations could meet the legal requirements of first-degree murder.[6] In some states, the prosecutor might also file first-degree murder charges if the parent's death, although unintended, occurred while the son or daughter was involved in the commission of another felony, such as robbery.[7]

In nonfelony killings in which premeditation was lacking, the State might seek to charge the youth with *second-degree murder* if the youth behaved with callous disregard for human life. In such cases, the parent's death will have resulted from the adolescent's committing an act that was imminently dangerous to another human being. Second-degree murder charges are likely to be filed if the evidence does not establish that the killing of the victim was willful, deliberate, malicious, or intended.[8] For example, although he was initially charged with first-degree murder, the State allowed Evan Sutton (pseudonym) to plead guilty to second-degree murder. Evan reported that he had an argument with his father a few minutes before the shooting occurred. The boy remembered being angry and upset as he watched, from his bedroom balcony, his father leave the house, get into the truck, and prepare to drive away. Evan recalled getting two fully loaded guns and firing them from the balcony.[9] He was very confused as he related his memory of events surrounding the shooting and stated that he might have "snapped." He believed that he was firing the shots at the ground and maintained that he did not want to hurt anybody. When he saw his father fall forward in the truck, he called 911 and ran to help his father. Evan applied pressure to his father's gaping wound and began to administer CPR.[10] He screamed to his little sister to call 911 again when she appeared on the scene, and he waited for the police to arrive.

After examining the circumstances, the prosecution might conclude that murder in the first or second degree is not an appropriate charge and might consider filing less serious charges, such as manslaughter, or none at all if the killing appears *justifiable* (e.g., self-defense). Young killers often behave impulsively and maintain that they acted out of strong emotions due to previous actions by the victim. They maintain in these circumstances, often convincingly, that they never intended to kill the victim.

A homicide committed in response to adequate provocation traditionally has been defined as lacking "malice aforethought" (actual or implied intent to kill) and considered *voluntary manslaughter*. In order for voluntary manslaughter to be an appropriate charge, however, four elements of adequate provocation must be proven to exist. Criteria typically include both objective and subjective measures that pertain to the experiences of a reasonable person and the actual experiences of the defendant, respectively. The provocation must have caused the defendant to kill the victim, *and* it must have been such that it would have caused a reasonable person to lose control. In addition, the passage of time between the provocation and the homicide must not have been sufficient for the passions of a reasonable person to cool, *and* the defendant must not have cooled off during the time period between the provocation and the killing.[11]

Some situations that cause young killers to become enraged or distressed have not been recognized by the courts. Juvenile murderers have reported becoming very disturbed by something said to them (e.g., "Fuck you, asshole") or minor batteries (e.g., someone bumped or pushed them). They have felt "dissed" (disrespected) by these actions and compelled to redress the perceived affront. However, traditionally the courts have not considered words, no matter how vile or insulting, to constitute adequate provocation. Similarly, the courts generally have not viewed trivial blows, even if technically a battery, as qualifying as sufficient provocation to cause a reasonable person to engage in a killing frenzy.[12]

Evan reported escalating conflict between his father and him in the moments before the homicide. However, the facts did not support a manslaughter charge when viewed from the perspective of a reasonable person. Evan said that his father had been "barking orders" at him, had listened in on his phone call with his friend, and was angry that Evan had criticized his father to his friend. Evan said his father came into his room and might have hit him on the back of the head. The boy was upset by his father's actions toward him and was angry that his father was leaving the house to go back to work. These circumstances would not cause a reasonable person to be provoked to the point of losing control and killing another human being, particularly one who had left the scene.

The Model Penal Code suggests that a charge of murder should be reduced to manslaughter if the defendant was acting "under the influence of extreme mental or emotional disturbance for which there is reasonable explanation or excuse." The term "extreme disturbance" is similar to the concept of "adequate provocation."[13] Some courts have allowed cases of "imperfect" self-defense to be considered as voluntary manslaughter when defendants have provided evidence that they acted in self-defense but that their doing so was not reasonable under the circumstances.[14]

A killing has customarily been viewed as *involuntary manslaughter* if it occurred during the commission of an unlawful act not amounting to a felony or if it was the result of criminal negligence.[15] Some years ago, a youth who was driving recklessly was involved in a fatal car accident. The victim in the car he hit, who subsequently died, turned out to be his mother. Her appearance on this roadway was not anticipated, and her death was clearly not intended. Involuntary manslaughter charges could have been brought in this case.

TRANSFER TO ADULT COURT

Each of the 50 U.S. states and the District of Columbia has provisions to try juveniles in adult courts. Some states specifically mention murder when discussing transfer procedures in the state's juvenile code. In these states, the minimum age for exercise of criminal court jurisdiction in homicide cases is often lower than in other felony cases.[16]

Transfer mechanisms include judicial waiver, statutory exclusion from juvenile court jurisdiction, and prosecutorial discretion. Any or all of these transfer procedures might exist in a given state. Some states have provisions whereby the criminal court can impose juvenile sanctions instead of, or in addition to, adult sanctions or can transfer the case back to juvenile court for sentencing.[17] Since the mid-1990s, juveniles involved in murder have been typically prosecuted in adult court,[18] where they face long sentences, and under today's laws, can still be sentenced to life without parole.[19] Up until 2005, juvenile homicide offenders could be sentenced to death.[20]

Prior to the laws changing with respect to sentencing juvenile murderers to death and LWOP under *mandatory* sentencing structures, I evaluated four juveniles, three boys and one girl, who were facing the death penalty for killing parents. The girl was found guilty of second-degree murder at trial and thus was not eligible for the death penalty. The three boys pled guilty to first-degree murder in order to avoid the possibility of being sentenced to death at the time and were sentenced to life without parole under mandatory sentencing systems. Under the Supreme Court's decision in *Miller v. Alabama* handed down in June 2012, these individuals, along with more than 2000 others sentenced to LWOP under mandatory sentence systems, are entitled to new sentencing hearings where judges must consider the youth's character and life conditions, as well as the circumstances of the homicide.[21] Although none of the youths I evaluated received a death sentence, four cases do exist of defendants who killed their parents as juveniles being sentenced to death in recent times. These four cases are profiled below following a brief summary of the history of children under 18 being sentenced to death in the United States.[22]

Examining the four cases of juvenile parricide offenders sentenced to death provides a unique opportunity to look closely at cases judged as among the most egregious. It is a rare chance to see what the case materials revealed about these young killers in light of the currently available literature on juvenile parricide offenders. One could hypothesize that these youths would appear to be very different from parricide offenders often profiled in the news. Clearly, juries must have found that aggravating factors outweighed mitigating factors, and judges must have agreed with their findings. What might the underlying dynamics in these murders be?

There is currently no national data base that records the system processing of individuals arrested for murder. Although one can learn how many juveniles were arrested for killing parents, it is not possible to discern from any existing data base what percentage of these individuals were charged with first-degree murder, convicted as charged, and sentenced to death when it was constitutionally permissible. Available studies indicate that the imposition of death sentences is exceedingly rare in murder cases; less than 2% of arrests for intentional criminal homicide result in a sentence of death.[23]

Victor Streib, professor of law at Ohio Northern University, is the leading authority on juveniles sentenced to death in the United States.[24] One of the data bases he created and has maintained records the number of juveniles who were sentenced to death in the United States from 1973 until 2005, a period when juvenile murderers were eligible for capital punishment in many states.[25] In 1973, the death penalty was restored in many states to conform to the U.S. Supreme Court's guidelines in *Furman v. Georgia* (1972). A few years later, in *Gregg v. Georgia* (1976), the court held that the death penalty was not cruel and unusual punishment under the Eighth Amendment if the jury in the case had been provided with standards to guide their decision making, such as aggravating and mitigating factors, and their recommendation was subject to meaningful appellate review. Up until 1988, a murderer of any age could be sentenced to death. The case of *Thompson v. Oklahoma* (1988) was interpreted as prohibiting the execution of a youth under 16 years of age only in states where the minimum age of execution was not legislated. One year later, the court limited the application of the death penalty to juveniles 16 and older. The court held in *Stanford v. Kentucky* (1989) and its companion case *Wilkins v. Missouri* (1989) decided together that the Eighth Amendment did not prohibit sentencing convicted murderers to death for killings they committed while under the age of 18.

For many years the United States stood alone among Western industrialized nations in allowing the execution of individuals for murders that they committed as juveniles.[26] In 2005, the U.S. Supreme Court held in *Roper v. Simmons* that sentencing convicted murderers to death for killings they committed while under the age of 18 was unconstitutional under the Eighth Amendment. The court based its decision on the facts that juveniles, on the average, are not as developmentally mature as adults; that a national consensus appeared to be moving away from imposition of the death penalty in murder cases involving juvenile defendants; and that other countries did not permit defendants to be sentenced to death for murders they had committed as juveniles.[27]

Consultation with Dr. Streib indicated that only four (2%) of the 205 individuals sentenced to death from 1973 to 2005 for murders they had committed as juveniles killed parents. Those four juveniles were Sean Sellers, Frederick Lashley, Stephen McGilberry, and Mark Anthony Duke. Sellers and Lashley were executed. In contrast, Duke's and McGilberry's sentences were commuted to life in prison after the U.S. Supreme Court handed down its decision in *Roper v. Simmons*.

Extensive case-related materials were available on Sean Sellers, including his own personal writings about his life and reflections on his criminal behavior, which provided insight into his killing his parents. In Sellers's case, there is reason to believe that he was severely abused and mentally ill. However, his personal writings suggest that the abuse and mental illness, although likely contributors to his antisocial behavior and maladaptive coping strategies, were not the main factors propelling the murders. He appeared to be dangerously antisocial.

Materials on the other three cases consisted largely of court documents. The limited materials available on the backgrounds of these boys and the dynamics behind these murders make classifying these offenders into one of Heide's three types even more difficult than in the Sellers case. *An in-depth assessment of the youth is necessary in order for one to make a definitive determination of the adolescent parricide offender type.* Evaluating these individuals now is not possible, as two have been executed and the other two, whose sentences were commuted to life, are now grown men. Today, as individuals in their 30s, their reflections on their thoughts and behavior more than a decade earlier might be very different from their experiences at 16 years of age when they were involved in murder. The data that are on the record, however, provide some evidence that these three juvenile parricide offenders also might fit into the dangerously antisocial parricide offender type.

Sean Sellers

Sean Sellers was born on May 18, 1969, in California. His father was reportedly an alcoholic. When Sellers was 3 or 4 years old, his parents divorced. Shortly thereafter, his mother, Vonda, married Paul Bellofatto, a truck driver. From that point on, Sellers stayed with friends and relatives while his mother and stepfather traveled extensively. By the time he was 16, Sellers had moved more than 30 times.[28]

During Sellers's stays with his relatives, he was abused both physically and emotionally. It was during his early childhood that Sellers reportedly began experiencing the first signs of his later mental illness. By the time he was 6 or 7 years old, he had begun to hear voices in his head. He had also become increasingly paranoid. Frequent mood swings also characterized his adolescence, in which he went from a state of euphoria to being suicidally depressed.[29]

In his personal writings, Sellers stated that when he looked back on his life, he saw his turning point as occurring when he was 13. At that point in his life he became focused on four activities: he "played football, practiced Ninjutsu, collected comic books, and played Dungeons & Dragons (D & D)."[30] He and his family had moved to Colorado, where he was "really, really happy." When he was 15, however, his parents decided to move back to Oklahoma against his strong protests. After the move, Sellers's involvement in D & D and the occult increased exponentially, and he felt extremely angry at his parents for making him move. He also experienced heartbreak in the form of rejection by his girlfriend. It was then that he decided that he hated God, as "God had failed [him]."[31]

Sellers combined his new belief in Satanism with his prior love of Ninjutsu and D & D to form a group called the Elimination. By the age of 15, Sellers was practicing Satanic rites on a daily basis and had become increasingly obsessed with the theories behind good and evil. He performed acts of self-mutilation, drank blood, and took drugs. However, he felt that there was a "barrier" between him and the power he craved. He believed that barrier was that he had not yet committed murder.[32]

Sellers's first homicide took place after several discussions with his friends in the Elimination. This group performed rituals in order to invoke the power of Satan; to that end, the teens began to break biblical commandments, and finally only one remained: "Thou shall not murder."[33]

The group started talking about ways for them to break this commandment until "after a lust ritual with [Sellers's] second priest, Satan took over [their] actions."[34] On the night of September 8, 1985, Sellers and a friend drove to a convenience store at which the owner had previously insulted Sellers's friend's girlfriend and had refused to sell them beer. It was there that they killed Robert Paul Bower.

Sellers reported that after the killing, they walked out of the store and back to their car, where they "laughed as the evil delight of our action gripped us."[35] In the weeks following Bower's murder, Sellers became more involved in Satanic rituals and began consuming drugs frequently. Eventually the Elimination disbanded, but Sellers continued practicing rituals on his own. He wrote that his thoughts of that time in his life were that he was not happy and that the "blood, drugs, sex, hate, all of it had become boring."[36]

Sellers also recalled the effect that the killing had on his psyche[37]:

After that, I had killed someone. Sometimes I wanted to tell Dad so he'd be proud of my strength. He'd see me as strong, not weak. And sometimes I didn't even remember doing it. I didn't live under a constant awareness that I'd killed someone. Most of the time I didn't even know what I'd done. It was that blinking in my mind. The person who couldn't do it didn't know he did, then blink, the person who did do it, remembered. That's the best I can explain that. When I was that person, that murderer, I felt superior. I looked down on people with the secret knowledge that I had killed and was capable of killing them too. When I was not that person I was just a confused teenager, going to school, working, learning to drive, still full of anger, and counting the days when I'd be 18 so I could move OUT of that house.

Sellers recalled that he was very angry with his parents and life in general in the weeks preceding the double parricide. He described fights with his mother over a girl, Angel, whom he loved and his mother "hated." It all came to a head one afternoon when his mother told him, "You want to leave? Go. Pack your shit and get the fuck out!"[38] Sellers did leave that day, but that night his stepfather came and forced him to return to the house. Sellers stated that things grew increasingly worse from there[39]:

Mom ranted about Angel, we even got into a physical fight over her. It wasn't much of a fight. Mom wailed on me like she always did, but now I was bigger than her, and I just pushed her. All the while that blinking was getting worse in my mind. I couldn't get away. I couldn't move out. I decided to kill my mother. I bought some rat poison and put it in her coffee, but it didn't work, even when I served her 3 cups of it. But after that, blink! and everything was different. We argued, but I just wanted to leave, I didn't want to kill her. Then blink! and I'd be planning her death.

Sellers shot both of his parents to death on March 5, 1986. Sellers maintained that he could not remember what happened after that point and that his next clear memory was "of a jail cell two days later."[40] Years after the crime, Sellers said that he had started to regain some of his lost memories, and he revealed some of what had happened that night[41] (italics added for emphasis):

One night that blink happened and when I came home from work I was the cold murderer who had killed Robert Bower. I went to their room before they went to bed and took Dad's .44 revolver from the drawer beside the bed. I put it in my room and waited for them to go to bed. Dad talked to me about rebuilding the engine of my pickup together. When they were in bed I went to my room, did a ritual, dressed only in my black underwear, and then crept quietly into their room. There was nothing but cold hatred in me. There was some sense of, "Sean needs to be free and this will free him. This is the only way." That was not a conscious thought, just a sensation. It's like that was the motivation behind it. *I wasn't committing murder, I was removing an obstacle from my way. I was knocking down a door to a prison cage. All I felt, however, was coldness.* I put the gun close to Dad's head and fired, then immediately fired again at Mom's head. Her head raised up, neck craning backward, and I fired again. Then I laid the gun down in the hallway and went back to the room.

The public defender's main defense in Sellers's case was that he had been brain-washed by Satanism and D & D.[42] A defense psychologist testified that Sellers was not capable of forming the intent to commit first-degree murder for one of two reasons: (1) he did not know right from wrong and was therefore insane, or (2) he suffered from automatism and was "legally unconscious," meaning that he was unaware of what he was doing when he killed all three people.[43]

The jury was *not* given the option to find Sellers guilty of first-degree manslaughter if they doubted that he was able to form the intent necessary for murder. The judge limited the jury's possible options to two: find Sellers guilty of first-degree murder, or acquit him. The jury found Sellers guilty of first-degree murder. Following the verdict, the judge did not instruct the jury to consider Sellers's age at the time of the crime, 16, to be a mitigating circumstance in deciding whether to recommend a life or death sentence. Rather, the judge left it up to the jury to decide whether age should be considered a factor in the mitigation of death. On October 2, 1986, the jury, believing that Sellers represented a continuing danger to society, recommended that Sellers be executed.[44]

Dorothy Otnow Lewis, a psychiatrist renowned for her research with violent juveniles, including those on death row,[45] examined Sellers several months after he was sentenced to death. She diagnosed him as chronically psychotic, noting that he exhibited symptoms of paranoid schizophrenia and major mood disorder. Six years after the trial, Sellers was diagnosed as having multiple personality disorder, now known as dissociative identity disorder (DID), by three mental health professionals who performed several sophisticated tests and recognized that the voices and blackouts that Sellers reported experiencing as a child and as an adolescent were consistent with a DID diagnosis.[46] The experts concluded that one of the alter personalities likely did not know the difference between right and wrong. This alter likely had executive control of Sellers's body at the time of the murders.[47]

During the course of investigating Sellers's DID, it was discovered that Sellers had brain damage, which he sustained from head injuries as a child. Evidence from available sources at this time suggested that Sellers, in addition to having brain damage, might have suffered from several different disorders, including a psychotic disorder, DID, mood disorder, and substance abuse, and that such diagnoses might have been helpful to his case. One could argue that he also met the diagnostic criteria for conduct disorder.[48]

Based on this new information, Sellers petitioned for a new trial through the state and federal courts. When these avenues were denied, he unsuccessfully sought clemency from the parole board.[49] Sean's death sentence was carried out on February 5, 1999; he was the first person in 40 years to be executed for crimes committed while the offender was under the age of 17.[50]

Frederick Lashley

Little is known about Frederick Lashley's childhood before he was removed from the care of his father at the age of 2. Apparently, his mother had left him with his father, who severely abused him, and he stayed with his father until Janie Tracy (Lashley's cousin) took him in. Tracy essentially became Lashley's mother and provided for him in St. Louis, Missouri. She was physically disabled because of a neuromuscular problem and had had brain surgery that left a soft spot on her head.[51] This physical disability might have impaired her ability to supervise Lashley, as he was reported to have begun consuming alcohol at the age of 10. He also said that during his teens he was suicidally depressed.[52]

Tracy had gone to visit her sister hours before her murder on April 9, 1981. While she was gone, Lashley, 17, removed the bulb from the light socket on his cousin's front porch. He then entered the home, grabbed a cast-iron skillet from the kitchen, and waited inside for Tracy to return in order to rob her. Tracy returned home later that night. After discovering that the light was out, Tracy entered the darkened house, where Lashley proceeded to hit her on the head with the skillet so hard that the pan broke in two. Medical evidence also revealed that a knife was thrust through the soft spot on her head to pierce her brain. Following the killing, Lashley took his foster mother's car keys and $15 from her purse, locked the door, and drove off in her car. Slightly after midnight he was picked up by the police while still driving the stolen car.[53]

Lashley was high on phencyclidine (PCP), one of the dissociative drugs, at the time of the killing. These types of drugs "distort perceptions of sight and sound and produce feelings of detachment—dissociation—from the environment and self."[54] PCP has also been associated with paranoid delusions and violent behavior.[55] The defense attorney who represented him had no prior death penalty training; Lashley was his first capital case. After his conviction, Lashley tried to appeal his sentence based on the fact that he was a juvenile at the time of the crime, but the sentence was upheld. Twelve years later, on July 28, 1993, he was executed.[56]

Stephen McGilberry

Stephen McGilberry, 16, was living in Jackson County, Mississippi, with his mother, his stepfather, his stepsister, and her 3-year-old son when he brutally bludgeoned them to death with a bat on October 23, 1994.[57] Shortly before the murders, McGilberry's parents had revoked his driving privileges because he had received bad grades in school and lost his job. This punishment reportedly embarrassed McGilberry because he did not want his friends to see his mother driving him to school.[58] The plan to kill his family grew out of this sense of humiliation.

McGilberry's original plan was to steal his stepsister's car and drive it to New Orleans in order to sell it for cash or drugs. A week before the murders, McGilberry approached his friend Meyer Ashley with the idea of killing his family. They worked out a plan, but the Friday before it was to be carried out, Ashley decided not to go through with it. So McGilberry approached his other friend, Chris Johnson, 14, with the plan on Saturday.

That night, McGilberry had a dream of killing his family. When he woke, he went to Johnson's house, where they worked out the details of the plan.[59]

The two boys returned to McGilberry's house later that day. They decided to use utility knives to slit open the occupants' throats. However, the sleeping position of McGilberry's stepfather made this impossible. They then went to the garage, where they proceeded to smoke a cigarette and revise the plan. Johnson noticed a baseball bat in the garage and suggested that they use that to knock the family unconscious and then drop them over the pier. Because McGilberry's mother was awake, they decided to stash a few bats outside of McGilberry's bedroom window until everyone was asleep.[60]

Once everyone was asleep, the boys took the bats and split up. McGilberry was to kill his stepfather and stepsister, and Johnson was to kill McGilberry's mother and the stepsister's son. However, Johnson did not hit McGilberry's mother hard enough to kill her, so McGilberry went back and hit her again "because she was suffering." After the murders, the boys took some money and credit cards from the stepsister's purse and drove off in her car to a friend's house.[61]

Later that night, the stepsister's fiancé found the bodies and called the police. When they arrived, they realized that there was a missing member of the family and contacted McGilberry's friend so that he could tell McGilberry to come home. When McGilberry arrived on the scene, he was read his Miranda rights. He then waived his rights and proceeded to confess to all four murders. The jury convicted him of four capital murder charges and sentenced him to death.[62] Following the Supreme Court ruling in *Roper v. Simmons* (2005), McGilberry was released into the general prison population to serve a life sentence.

Mark Anthony Duke

Mark Anthony Duke was 16 when he cold-bloodedly murdered his father, his father's girlfriend, and her two daughters (aged 6 and 7) in their home in Shelby County, Alabama, on March 22, 1997.[63] Duke reportedly wanted to kill his father because his father refused to let Duke borrow the family's truck. After his father denied him access to the truck, Duke went to a friend's house to plan his father's murder with his friends. Duke decided that he also needed to kill his father's girlfriend and her two children in order to eliminate any witnesses.

Duke enlisted the help of his friends in planning how to carry out the killings and how to hide the evidence afterward.[64] Duke instructed the three boys on how to clean the prints off of two weapons, a .45 caliber gun and a .32 caliber gun. Duke and his friends returned to Duke's house, where he instructed his friends, Michael Ellison and David Collums, to meet Brandon Samra and him in the neighborhood behind the house.[65]

Then Duke and Samra entered the house, where the girlfriend, Dedra Hunt, was sitting on the couch with her two children. Duke had instructed Samra to kill Hunt while he killed his father and the two children. Because the father was nowhere in sight, the two boys went up to the master bedroom to look for him. When they did not find him, they returned to the kitchen, where they saw him sitting by the fireplace in the living room.[66]

As they planned, Duke went after his father and Samra after Hunt. Duke shot his father at close range but did not kill him. When his father started pleading for his life, Duke tried to fire another shot, but the gun was jammed, so Duke proceeded to stab and hit his father several times and then cleaned the gun out and shot him between the eyes. He reportedly told his father as he shot him that he would see him in hell.[67]

Meanwhile, Samra had shot Hunt in the head, but the bullet only knocked out some of her teeth. Hunt grabbed her children and ran upstairs in order to escape from Samra. Samra followed, but Hunt was able to lock herself and one of her children in the bathroom of the master bedroom. Samra was unable to pry the door open, so he waited until Duke was finished killing his father. When he arrived, Duke kicked a hole in the door and was able to unlock it. As they entered the bathroom, Duke shot Hunt, killing her instantly. He found the child hiding in the shower and proceeded to slice open her throat.[68]

The other child was found hiding under a bed in one of the upstairs bedrooms. When Duke tried to cut her throat as he had done to her sister, she struggled so hard that he was unable to accomplish the task. He asked Samra to help him, but Samra refused until Duke yelled at him. Then Duke held her down while Samra killed her. After the murders, Duke grabbed his father's wallet and left the house to dispose of the knives in a storm drain. Samra and Duke met up with the other two boys, who were waiting for them as they had planned. Duke warned the other boys that if any of them told, he would kill them as well.[69]

The boys washed up and threw their dirty clothes in a dumpster. In order to establish an alibi, they then went to a movie theater, but they did not stay for long; instead they went out to eat and play pool. The next morning Duke had the other boys come with him to ransack the house so it would look like a robbery. After rehearsing their alibi, they called the police. At their trial, both Samra and Duke were convicted of four charges of capital murder and sentenced to death.[70] Duke's sentence was commuted to life in prison following the *Roper v. Simmons* (2005) decision.

LIFE WITHOUT PAROLE FOR JUVENILE OFFENDERS

Recall that in 2005, the U.S. Supreme Court found that sentencing offenders to death for murders they committed as juveniles was unconstitutional. In May 2010, the U.S. Supreme Court held in *Graham v. Sullivan* that sentencing juveniles to life without parole (LWOP) in nonhomicide cases was also cruel and unusual punishment under the Eighth Amendment of the Constitution. The court's decision was based on factors similar to those relied upon in the *Roper* decision. The court noted that, although there was no national consensus emerging against LWOP, only 12 states had sentenced juvenile defendants to LWOP for nonhomicide cases, juvenile defendants were less culpable than their adult counterparts, and this sentencing practice had been rejected by all other countries. This ruling did not apply to cases in which juveniles were convicted of capital murder.

In 2012, the United States Supreme Court went a step further in recognizing the fundamental difference between juveniles and adults who commit murder. The Court held in *Miller v. Alabama* that it is unconstitutional under the Eighth Amendment's prohibition on "cruel and unusual punishment" to sentence a defendant convicted of a murder committed prior to age 18 to mandatory life without parole. This ruling struck down statutes in 29 states that permitted mandatory LWOP for juvenile murderers. The court reasoned that these sentencing structures "prevent the sentencer from considering youth and from assessing whether the law's harshest term of imprisonment proportionately punishes a juvenile offender. This contravenes *Graham*'s (and also

Roper's) foundational principle: that imposition of a State's most severe penalties on juvenile offenders cannot proceed as though they were not children."[71] The highest court was clear that the characteristics specific to juvenile murderers as individuals and as members of a class must be taken into account by the trial court judge:

Mandatory life without parole for a juvenile precludes consideration of his chronological age and its hallmark features—among them, immaturity, impetuosity, and failure to appreciate risks and consequences. It prevents taking into account the family and home environment that surrounds him—and from which he cannot usually extricate himself—no matter how brutal or dysfunctional. It neglects the circumstances of the homicide offense, including the extent of his participation in the conduct and the way familial and peer pressures may have affected him.... And finally, this mandatory punishment disregards the possibility of rehabilitation even when the circumstances most suggest it.[72]

I have had several cases of adolescent parricide offenders sentenced to LWOP. These youths are often portrayed as antisocial. Two brothers, aged 15 and 17, bludgeoned their father, mother, and younger brother to death (see Chapter 2). A 16-year-old boy shot his father and his father's fiancée; the father survived, but the man's fiancée did not (see Chapter 1). Another 16-year-old boy shot both of his parents to death (see Chapter 11). Not all youths sentenced to LWOP, however, appear antisocial. One case involving a 17-year-old boy, profiled below, struck a sympathetic chord in the hearts of many who knew him.

An Abused Boy Who Was Convicted of First-Degree Murder

John Eastbay (pseudonym) was considered by those who knew him as a good kid. When he killed his father, neighbors rallied behind him, raising money for his defense. Neighbors remembered how the boy took care of his mother when she was gravely ill with cancer and how he would rarely leave the house or yard.

John's mother died when he was 13. He never fully recovered from her death. John's mother was very involved in his life as he was growing up. She helped with his homework, watched him play, took him to school, and interacted with his friends. John deeply loved his mother and was very much affected by his father's insensitivity to his mother and to him during her long illness. John's father traveled overseas, where the man reportedly had a girlfriend, and was rarely home as the mother's condition worsened. John was deeply wounded when his father brought his fiancée to the mother's wake.[73] John was devastated when his father, soon after John's mother's death, moved his fiancée into their home and removed all pictures of his mother from display.

John endured years of abuse and neglect by his father, particularly after his mother died, almost all of which was corroborated by his deceased mother's family and his friends and their parents at his trial. Physical, medical, and emotional neglect were easily verified. Although John lived in a beautiful home in an upscale neighborhood, the boy was physically neglected after his mother died. He was not provided with adequate food or clothing by his father. John had to go to a fast food restaurant for food or get food from the restaurant where he worked because there was no food in the house. After buying him clothes once, John's father told him that he had to work for his clothes.

John felt safe when his mom was alive. Relatives verified that Mrs. Eastbay slept at John's door when he was a young child to protect him. She protected John from Mr. Eastbay's tirades and rages, such as when he would punch the walls. If Mr. Eastbay was mad, John's mother made sure that John was not present.

After his mother's death, John was not provided with adequate supervision. As an adolescent, John had his own hours and left whenever he wanted to leave. His father did not see that he attended school regularly and had no interest in meeting John's friends. In addition to physical neglect, Mr. Eastbay did not attend to John's medical needs. John had been placed on anti-depressant medication after threatening suicide on a few occasions. John's father stopped filling his son's prescription for anti-depressant medication and stopped making appointments needed to monitor John's depression.

In sharp contrast to his mother, John's father did not give him clear messages that he loved him. John never heard his father say, "I love you." He could not remember ever being hugged or kissed by his father. He did not remember ever seeing his father hug or kiss his mother. John's father did not take the time to really listen to him. One of John's aunts recalled that John's father never played ball with John and that she never observed any physical contact or affection from Mr. Eastbay toward John. It was apparent from various sources that John's father was uninvolved in John's life.

There was evidence of physical, psychological, and verbal abuse in John's case. On one occasion Mr. Eastbay's reported behavior was clearly abusive and grossly disproportionate as a form of discipline. About a year prior to the killing, John's father burned John with a cigarette when he caught John smoking. John had several visible burn marks. After his dad burned him, things changed for John. He began to fear that his father might seriously injure or kill him.

John saw the burns and his father's actions toward his mother as acts of cruelty. John's father reportedly expected him to act like an adult and told him, from the time when he was very little, that he was not allowed to cry. Mr. Eastbay compared John to other kids regarding his grades and expressed dissatisfaction with his accomplishments regardless of his actual performance level. John's aunt indicated that Mr. Eastbay often compared John to others in terms of his academic performance. John was very involved in sports. John's father drove him to his soccer games but then sat in the car and did not watch him play.

John's father often said things directly to John that made him feel bad, particularly after his mother died. Mr. Eastbay would tell John that he was an "idiot" or a "moron" because of his poor grades. John's aunt recalled Mr. Eastbay verbally abusing John by belittling him if he did not do well at sporting events.

The Homicidal Incident

John and another boy, Mike, were involved in the killing of Mr. Eastbay. Their testimony at trial as to what happened varied. Mike testified that the boys concocted a plan for Mike to shoot Mr. Eastbay. In furtherance of this plan, Mike took his rifle to the Eastbay residence, intending to wait inside alone for the victim to return home. Before Mr. Eastbay came home, however, Mike backed out, telling John over the phone that he could not shoot John's father.

Mike testified that at John's invitation, he returned hours later to John's house, bringing his rifle with him. According to Mike, the two boys again discussed shooting Mr. Eastbay. In the early morning hours, Mike walked out of the Eastbay home and rang the front doorbell. Mike's account suggested that the ringing of the doorbell was staged so that John could shoot his father as the man predictably left his bedroom and descended the staircase from the upstairs of the house to answer the doorbell.

John, in contrast, maintained that he had no intention of shooting his father. Rather, he took the rifle upon a dare from Mike to walk up the staircase with it. John maintained that he tried to get Mike's attention through the window to let Mike know that he had completed the dare so that Mike would not ring the doorbell. However, after the doorbell was rung, it was too late. John was on the landing as his father descended the staircase and saw him. John testified that at that moment, a confrontation ensued. John maintained that he was very scared that his father was going to hurt him and that he shot his father to protect himself and to get away from his father. John testified that he did not remember the number of times he fired the rifle (forensic evidence indicated that multiple shots were fired).

According to Mike, after the shooting, John ransacked the home and took his father's wallet and wristwatch to suggest that the victim had been killed by an intruder in a robbery. The two boys left the Eastbay home, went to another location, and changed clothes. Later, John returned to his home. He showered, got dressed in regular clothes, and called the police. John suggested to the police that his father had likely been shot by an intruder because he feared that the police would not believe that he had shot his father in self-defense. The two boys were taken into police custody soon afterward. Mike pled guilty to a reduced charge. John was charged as an adult with first-degree premeditated murder.

Trial and Conviction

The prosecutor believed that the defendant had enlisted the help of his friend Mike to kill his father and planned the murder in order to inherit his father's estate, which was valued at over $1 million. John pled not guilty and maintained that he had killed his father in self-defense. John's attorney asked the trial court to allow expert testimony on battered child syndrome (BCS) to help the jury understand the defendant's state of mind at the time of the killing. The attorney wanted to admit expert testimony on BCS in order to educate the jury about the devastating effects of Mr. Eastbay's emotional abuse on John and the possible effects that such abuse might have had on the boy's perception of fear.

BCS had not been recognized in the state in which the murder occurred. The trial judge held a hearing to determine whether this syndrome was generally accepted in the scientific community. In an attempt to persuade the judge of the relevance of BCS in John's case, defense counsel advised the court that many witnesses were available to testify that Mr. Eastbay was abusive toward John's mother and that Mr. Eastbay physically and emotionally neglected John and emotionally abused him. Counsel also offered to provide evidence, through witnesses, that Mr. Eastbay had an explosive temper, that John feared his father, and that the two had a tumultuous relationship. The court ruled that expert testimony could not be given on BCS in John's case on two grounds. The judge found that the doctors' testimony at the hearing did not establish that BCS had been generally accepted in the psychiatric and psychological communities. In addition, the court concluded that the evidence offered was insufficient to establish severe abuse in John's case.

The judge, however, did allow the defense to introduce evidence concerning the strained relationship that existed between father and son. Several witnesses testified that they had witnessed Mr. Eastbay berating his son, that John appeared to be afraid of his father, and, on one occasion, that John was suicidal. John testified that his father verbally abused him, was emotionally distant, had burned him with a cigarette, and had threatened him with a kitchen knife on one occasion.

The defendant testified that he was in fear for his life when he shot his father multiple times. The jury was not persuaded by John's claim of self-defense and found him guilty of first-degree premeditated murder. Under the applicable state law, he was sentenced to life without parole. The defendant appealed his conviction, arguing that expert testimony on BCS was erroneously excluded by the trial court. The appellate court affirmed the conviction, holding that the proffered testimony did not suggest the nature and severity of abuse required to allow use of this defense. The higher court cited appellate court decisions from other states that appeared to limit the defense to cases of substantial physical and/or sexual abuse. The state's highest court agreed with the appellate court that the proffered testimony did not meet the threshold of abuse required.

SUMMARY AND CONCLUDING REMARKS

This chapter began by discussing the charging decisions that prosecutors make when they consider the circumstances involved in parricide cases, particularly those involving child and adolescent offenders. Depending on the facts, prosecutors may charge youths who kill parents with murder in the first or second degree or with manslaughter. In cases of juvenile offenders, in many states it is at the prosecutor's discretion whether the case is retained in juvenile court or transferred to adult court. The forum used might have dramatic consequences for young killers. Juvenile and adolescent offenders who are convicted of killing their parents might face sentences calculated in months to life without parole depending on whether the case is handled in juvenile or adult court.

Up until 2005, juveniles could be convicted of capital murder and sentenced to death in the United States. During the period of 1973–2005, four adolescents were sentenced to death for killing parents when they were under age 18. Examination of available materials on these male youths indicated that these cases of parricide were particularly egregious. Although it is rarely possible to determine conclusively the adolescent parricide type without a comprehensive evaluation, facts present in these cases were consistent with the profile of the dangerously antisocial offender.

Up until 2012, sentencing structures that mandated LWOP for defendants convicted of first-degree murders that they committed as juveniles were constitutional in the United States. Under today's law, trial court judges are required to consider the youth's age, developmental and maturity factors, and other mitigating factors in their sentencing decision. Trial court judges now have the autonomy to look at the special circumstances that exist in cases involving juvenile murderers convicted of first-degree murder. Looking at the motivational dynamics that propelled the homicide is particularly important in cases of severely abused youths convicted of first-degree murder. Judges now have the authority to temper justice with mercy in their sentencing decisions when the background and life circumstances of the juvenile warrant it.

The next chapter discusses defense strategies in parricide cases. The legal and psychological underpinnings of the battered child syndrome are reviewed. Attention is focused on mental status defenses and on the doctrine of self-defense.

7 Defending Parricide Offenders

When a youth is arrested for the killing of a parent, similar to when the accused is an adult, psychological issues, as well as legal matters, immediately become important.[1] Attention typically focuses on the young killer's present mental status (competency), as well as his or her mental status at the time of the killing (sanity or capacity). In cases involving juvenile murderers, the defense attorney frequently seek the assistance of mental health professionals in evaluating the client's competency to stand trial and his or her sanity during the homicide.[2]

Which people can be designated as mental health professionals varies by state law. Individuals with advanced degrees in the social and behavioral sciences (e.g., psychologists, mental health counselors, social workers, marriage and family counselors, nurse practitioners) and psychiatrists (medical doctors with specialties in psychiatry) are generally recognized as mental health professionals.[3] Depending upon their credentials ("knowledge, skill, experience, training or education"[4]) and the case law and practices in the jurisdiction, these professionals might be "qualified" to testify in court as forensic experts and to render their opinions regarding the young killer's mental status at varying points in time.

A mental health professional with expertise in conducting forensic evaluations of youths charged with violent crimes can provide invaluable assistance to an attorney in understanding the youth and the factors contributing to his or her murderous behavior, as well as his or her mental state during the crime. Mental health experts are increasingly called upon by defense attorneys to testify about an adolescent's state of mind at the time of a killing. Consideration of the youth's mental status during the crime might persuade a judge or jury to excuse the defendant from whole or partial responsibility.[5] Indeed, as many commentators have noted, expert testimony might be the critical factor in helping jurors understand why an abused youth feared for his or her life at the time when the youth killed the parent.[6]

A thorough evaluation by a well-respected mental health professional might also assist the defense in other ways. Armed with a favorable report from a qualified forensic evaluator prior to trial, defense counsel might succeed in persuading the prosecution to dismiss or reduce the charges. In some of these cases, the defendant might be an adult, as in the case of Loretta Daniels (pseudonym). I was one of two defense experts retained to evaluate Loretta, a woman in her 30s who shot her father, a man in his mid-60s. After shooting her father, the woman shot herself. Fortunately, Loretta and her father survived, although both were seriously injured.

Within a few days of the woman's being released from the hospital to the jail, my colleague and I both conducted individual evaluations of the defendant. We did collateral interviews with Loretta's two daughters, her sister, her brother-in-law, and four individuals who had been friends with the defendant for many years. All depicted the woman as a good-valued and hard-working woman who loved her children more than life itself. They all described how for years the defendant had lovingly taken care of her father, who was disabled. There were extensive data corroborating that the woman had overcome severe childhood maltreatment and significant adult trauma. It was important to Loretta that she be a good mother, a good daughter, and a good friend. She dealt with life's adversities by refusing to dwell on the past and by moving forward. She was driven to provide a better life for her children than she had experienced.

Loretta had learned earlier on the day of the shooting that her father had sexually abused her daughter. When she confronted her father later that night, he made light of his behavior. Her father's cavalier dismissal of the sexual abuse of her daughter reopened the pain that Loretta had been avoiding for years. Loretta had also been sexually abused by her father as a child. She had blocked these events out of her life and did not think about them.

Loretta was flooded with feelings as she thought about her daughter being sexually abused by her father, a man whom she loved and had grown to trust. She felt betrayed by her father and guilty that she had not protected her daughter. At the time of the shooting, the defendant, an untreated victim of severe trauma, was overwhelmed with feelings and was unable to think clearly and to process events as they were unfolding. Loretta's account suggested that the stress that she was experiencing was so extreme that she dissociated. In this state, given the intensity of her feelings, it was highly unlikely that Loretta could access the higher cortical processes of the brain associated with thinking, deliberation, and judgment and formulate the intent to hurt her father and to take her own life. Rather, it is likely that her behavior was driven by the limbic system, the emotional part of the brain, as discussed in Chapter 2. In the minutes preceding the shooting, Loretta reacted to the feelings that engulfed her—pain, confusion, anger, and despair.

My colleague and I both concluded that the defendant did not represent a danger to herself or others. We noted that she had no prior history of violent acting out. Loretta had a mental disorder, post-traumatic stress disorder, which could be treated in the community. She was amenable to treatment, and treatment was available in the community. The victim of the shooting, Loretta's father, was arrested for sexually abusing Loretta's daughter, his granddaughter, and charged with capital sexual battery, given the child's age at the time of the alleged molestation. The father reportedly admitted his guilt. Given the circumstances, the State decided not to charge Loretta.[7]

At the very least, a solid mental health report can persuade the prosecutor to forgo seeking the death penalty in cases involving defendants who were 18 or older at the time of the killing. In cases of minors, it might persuade the State to retain a juvenile parricide offender in juvenile court rather than transfer him or her to adult court.[8]

Testimony by mental health experts can also be enormously valuable at sentencing. In a capital case, defense counsel may use findings from the examiner's assessment to convince the court to choose a sentence other than death if the defendant is convicted of premeditated murder. The examiner's conclusions might also have a positive impact in terms of reducing the sentence length when defendants are convicted of first-degree murder in jurisdictions in which mandatory life sentences without parole are not automatically imposed or when defendants are convicted of second-degree murder or manslaughter. State statutes pertinent to the death penalty and felony sentences often contain specific mitigators, such as those shown in Box 7-1, that mental health professionals have the expertise to address. The mental health expert who has completed an in-depth evaluation could also testify to nonstatutory mitigators that might be relevant in understanding the parricide offender's involvement in the murder. These factors might include factors pertinent to the experiences of a battered child, such as the effects of being a victim of severe child maltreatment or of witnessing domestic violence. Other relevant testimony might include whether the defendant appears genuinely remorseful, is amenable to treatment, or is presently dangerous and likely to constitute a continuing threat to society. It is not unusual in a complex parricide case for several mental health experts to be involved.

BOX 7-1 Mitigating Circumstances

Circumstances under which a departure from the lowest permissible sentence is reasonably justified include, but are not limited to, the following:

- The capacity of the defendant to appreciate the criminal nature of the conduct or to conform that conduct to the requirements of the law was substantially impaired.
- The defendant requires specialized treatment for a mental disorder that is unrelated to substance abuse or addiction or for a physical disability, and the defendant is amenable to treatment.
- The victim was an initiator, willing participant, aggressor, or provoker of the incident.
- The offense was committed in an unsophisticated manner and was an isolated incident for which the defendant has shown remorse.
- At the time of the offense the defendant was too young to appreciate the consequences of the offense.

Source: Excerpted from Florida Statutes 921.0026 (2012).

COMPETENCY AND DEFENSE STRATEGIES DISTINGUISHED

Juveniles who are transferred to the adult criminal justice system, like their adult counterparts, must be competent to stand trial. Many states have recognized the right of youths who are retained in juvenile court to be competent to stand trial in recognition that adjudication in juvenile court can be punitive and can result in negative consequences.[9] In adult court and in those states that recognize the competency rights of juveniles charged with delinquent acts, it is important that the adolescent understand the nature of the proceedings, that is, that he or she is being tried for allegedly participating in a murder. The juvenile murderer must be capable of comprehending that, if convicted, he or she could be confined for many years, possibly even for life, depending on which court retains jurisdiction and the laws of the state. The youth must be able to provide information to his or her attorney so that counsel can prepare a legal defense. The offender must also be capable of maintaining appropriate behavior in court.[10] The competency of the 8-year-old Arizona boy who killed his father and the father's friend was clearly an issue in that case.[11]

Issues of competency can be raised at any point in the proceedings and can include other matters prior to trial. These may include competency to plead guilty, to refuse an insanity defense, to waive the right to counsel, and to confess.[12] For example, the attorney might question whether the youth was competent to waive his or her Miranda rights when the youth confessed to the police. Did the adolescent actually understand when arrested that he or she did not have to give a statement to police and that any statements made would be used against him or her?

Scott Anders, a 15-year-old boy who killed his father, said that the police "had really messed me up that night for something I totally misunderstood, which I thought I understood at the time but I misunderstood it." He explained that when he confessed, he thought anything that he said could be used *for* or against him. Not talking, he thought, would be akin to an admission of guilt.[13]

Initially, facts in the case suggested that the boy shot his father in self-defense. After the boy talked to the police, however, the police arrested Scott for murder. Mr. Anders had a history of physically abusing his wives/girlfriends and Scott. Following the departure of his second wife, the man became increasingly depressed and used drugs more frequently. In the month preceding the shooting, Mr. Anders blamed Scott for his wife's leaving him and threatened to kill himself and his son on several occasions. On the night of the homicide, Scott and his father argued. The boy ran out of the house, something that he had never done before. He "hauled ass" because his father was angry and he was scared. When he returned home a little later, Scott noticed immediately that "the shotgun was sitting there beside" his father, who was smoking a joint. Mr. Anders said, "You shouldn't of done that. I'm gonna have to beat your ass." Scott's response was almost instantaneous: "I just grabbed the gun and shot it."

When asked, Scott said that he did not know what was going on in his mind at the time of the shooting; he just reacted. He explained to the police, and later to me, that he fired a second shot after his father fell on the floor: "Well, I thought he was still alive and I thought he was suffering, and he raised me up when I used to go hunting and you shoot a bird or something, he raised me up, don't let nothing suffer. And I felt bad 'cause he was suffering, you know." The boy's firing of the second shot, although clearly an empathic reaction, led the prosecutor to conclude that the killing was a premeditated act and to charge Scott as an adult with first-degree murder.[14]

Issues of competency can be revisited during the trial if the defendant does not appear to be functioning adequately. In addition, many states have provisions such that if the defendant appears to decompensate after he or she is convicted, he or she can be evaluated for competency prior to the sentence being imposed or during its imposition, whichever applies. In these states, if the defendant or inmate is determined to be incompetent, provisions are to be made for treatment prior to sentencing or during the sentence, depending upon the circumstances operative in the case.[15] The

U.S. Supreme Court has held that a defendant sentenced to death must be competent at the time of execution.[16] However, as discussed in Chapter 6, since the U.S. Supreme Court's decision in *Roper v. Simmons*, juveniles cannot be sentenced to death.[17]

Typically, both the State and the defense will be interested in what was going on in the mind of the parricide offender at the time of the murder, as well as in his or her present state of mind. The young killer's perceptions, intention, and mental status at the time of the offense might have dramatic consequences, depending on the specific facts of the case. Looking at the total spectrum, in-depth analysis of the adolescent murderer and his or her actions at the time of the killing might mean the difference between the youth being sentenced to life without parole or set free.

If there is substantial evidence that the youth killed the victim or was otherwise involved in the homicidal incident, defense counsel will typically consider exploring defense strategies based on the youth's mental status or competency at the time of the offense. Defenses available might vary by state law, and might be different even within the same jurisdiction, depending upon whether the young killer is tried in a juvenile or adult forum.[18] In adolescent parricide cases, defense counsel will typically investigate two avenues of defense when charges are filed by the prosecutor: self-defense and insanity. Self-defense results in the acquittal of the defendant when successfully litigated during a murder trial. From the standpoint of society, the defendant's lethal act is considered justified under the externally defined circumstances. The defendant is not deemed culpable or blameworthy for the actions that resulted in the death of the victim because of the attendant circumstances.

Self-defense is based on the *law of justification* and needs to be distinguished from the concept of an excuse. Excuses consider the subjective characteristics of defendants at the time at which they engaged in acts that are criminal. This subject is discussed at length later in the chapter; in brief, excuses can be complete, such as insanity or automatism, or partial, such as diminished capacity or voluntary intoxication. *Complete excuses* allow defendants to be totally exonerated for their actions, but at the same time these defendants' unlawful actions are condemned. *Partial excuses* allow defendants to be held accountable for their unlawful behavior, although to a lesser extent than would otherwise be the case. Partial excuses reduce the degree of the criminal offense or the punishment rendered in consideration of the defendants' subjective or mental state at the time of the criminal events. Partial excuses, for example, might lead to a reduction in the degree of the killing from murder in the first degree to second-degree murder or manslaughter, based on evidence presented at trial that indicated that the defendant was in a state wherein he or she could not form the intent needed to constitute premeditated murder. Partial excuses might also serve as mitigating factors at sentencing, resulting in a judge imposing a less severe sentence than statutorily possible.[19]

SELF-DEFENSE[20]

Generally, a person may lawfully use deadly physical force against another in self-defense only when under the *reasonable belief* that the other is threatening him or her with imminent death or serious bodily injury and that such force is necessary to prevent the infliction of such harm.[21] In most jurisdictions, an honest belief on the part of the defendant that he or she was in imminent danger is not sufficient to constitute self-defense, although some evidence exists that this concept might be changing.[22] In addition to a subjective standard (the defendant's belief), the doctrine of self-defense typically has an objective standard that requires that the appearance of danger must have been so real that a *reasonable person*, faced with the same circumstances, would have entertained essentially the same beliefs.[23] Typically states have defined the "reasonable person" standard in the context of a man "possessing the intelligence, educational background, level of prudence, and temperament of an average person."[24] In other words, the law requires that a reasonable person would also have believed at the time that (1) death or serious bodily injury at the hand of the victim was about to happen, and (2) that the use of deadly physical force was necessary in order to avoid the harm.

Some jurisdictions require that in order for a defendant to claim self-defense, he or she must have exhausted all possible avenues of retreat before responding to force with force. In jurisdictions that impose a duty to retreat, an exception is often made to permit the defendant to stand one's ground and use force when threatened with imminent harm in situations in which one is attacked in one's home.[25] When both the assailant and the victim share the same residence, however, society's expectations have historically appeared to be different, particularly in cases of women who killed their abusive partners.[26] "In cases in which the battered woman kills her abuser, the burden of proof falls on the woman to show why she could not leave the relationship, even though legally she need only demonstrate that she was in danger and was legitimately standing her ground in her own home."[27]

The majority of jurisdictions do not impose strict requirements of retreat before a person can use deadly physical force in self-defense. However, evidence that the defendant could have safely retreated is relevant in determining whether the use of deadly force was reasonably necessary.[28] Accordingly, convincing a judge or a jury that an adolescent acted in self-defense when he or she killed the parent is difficult unless (1) the youth slew the parent when the parent was attacking the youth and (2) the possibility of the adolescent parricide offender (APO) retreating at that particular moment in time without sustaining serious injury or death seemed extremely remote.[29]

The doctrine of self-defense as formulated almost a thousand years ago was designed to address combat situations between men. It did not take into consideration differences in physical size and strength between men and women[30] and between parents, particularly fathers, and their children.[31] In addition, the doctrine did not address circumstances related to psychological injury and the perception that important aspects of one's self are being severely damaged, and possibly irreparably destroyed, by another individual.

A compelling argument has been made that the doctrine of self-defense should be broadened to include psychological self-defense.[32] Children and adolescents who have been severely abused, similar to battered wives, might believe, based on their experiences, that they are in danger of being severely beaten or killed in the near future if they do not take lethal action when it is possible.[33] Abused adolescents who do not believe their physical survival is threatened might feel compelled to aggress against the abusive parent because they perceive that their psychological survival is at stake. Perceiving that they are unable to engage in physical battle as an equal with the abusive parent, these adolescents often strike when the abusive parent is physically defenseless (e.g., passed out from drinking).[34] Defense lawyers argued self-defense in the case of Lyle and Eric Menendez, two brothers who joined forces to kill their wealthy parents as Mr. and Mrs. Menendez sat watching TV and eating ice cream in the family den in 1989. The jurors were not swayed by their defense[35] (see Box 7-2).

BOX 7-2 Self-Defense or Premeditated Murder?

When adolescents kill their mothers and fathers, severe mental illness is typically ruled out. The question frequently becomes, was the adolescent "a severely abused child" or was he or she "a psychopath"? This question is the one that appeared to polarize the nation, including the juries, in the 1993 trial and 1996 retrial of Lyle and Eric Menendez, who at the ages of 21 and 18, respectively, killed their parents, Jose and Kitty Menendez. The defense argued that "the boys" were abused by both parents. Defense attorneys contended that the brothers killed their mother and father because they feared that their parents were going to kill them for threatening to reveal the sexual abuse within the family. The prosecution argued that the abuse was a fiction. The State maintained that the "young men" were dangerously antisocial—they plotted to kill to inherit their parents' $14 million estate because they feared that they were going to be disinherited.

I did not evaluate Lyle or Eric Menendez and have no direct knowledge of the veracity of Eric and Lyle's statements about the nature and extent of the alleged child maltreatment. However, my opinion was repeatedly sought by mental health professionals, lawyers, the media, students, and the general public. The question was almost always framed like this: "Do you think those guys were really abused, or do you think that they did it for the money?"

Evidence was presented at the Menendez trials that, *if true*, would indicate that Lyle and Eric Menendez were victims of several different types of abuse and neglect as defined in Chapter 2. Trial testimony suggested that Eric and Lyle Menendez were overtly sexually abused and raped by their father and covertly and overtly sexually abused by their mother. Reported accounts suggested that they had, in addition, been physically, verbally, and psychologically abused by both parents. Statements made at trial further suggested that the Menendez boys had been emotionally neglected by both parents. Testimony also suggested that they had been physically neglected by their mother, who allegedly failed to protect them from their father's alleged sexual abuse and rape.

However, even if these statements were in fact true, the verification of child maltreatment does not necessarily uncover the underlying motivation for the double homicides. The Menendez brothers could have been both "battered children" and "psychopathic." The two categories are not, as the opposing lawyers in the Menendez case seemed to argue, mutually exclusive. Some children raised in abusive homes become "conduct disordered." In fact, as discussed in Chapter 1, the development of "antisocial personality disorder" is often rooted in early and pervasive childhood maltreatment. Evidence indicates that histories of childhood abuse and neglect are often found in those diagnosed as psychopathic. Put another way, the Menendez brothers could have been abused and still have killed their parents for the money.

The critical question in the Menendez case is, as in any parricide, *what propelled the homicides?* Individuals who are severely abused often have mixed feelings about their abusive parents. These feelings might include fear, anger, hatred, hurt, betrayal, and a desire for revenge, as well as love. If Lyle and Eric Menendez killed Jose and Kitty Menendez out of hatred and rage stemming from years of severe abuse, that motivation is clinically significant, but it is not self-defense.

(continued)

BOX 7-2 (Continued)

It is interesting to note that the behavior of Lyle and Eric Menendez after the homicides was markedly different from the behavior typically shown by severely abused adolescents who kill their parents to end the abuse (the first of my three types). The Menendez brothers concocted an elaborate alibi and maintained their innocence for several years after the murders. They acknowledged their involvement in the killings only after it was determined that statements they had made to their psychologist about their role in the murders would be admissible at trial. Shortly before the trial, it was publicly disclosed that the Menendez brothers had been abused—information that neither had at any time disclosed to their therapist. The psychologist testified that when Lyle and Eric were discussing the killings with him, they did not indicate that they had been abused and feared for their lives. In contrast, severely abused adolescents who kill their parents to end the abuse are typically apprehended shortly after the killing and admit their involvement soon after their arrest.

Individuals whom I have classified as *severely abused parricide offenders* have a number of characteristics that the Menendez brothers do not appear to share. For example, prior to the killings, these youths have typically attempted to get help from others and have tried to escape the family situation. Severely abused parricide offenders who kill to end the abuse do not report seeing psychotherapists on a regular basis from whom they withhold information about the abuse that they had endured for years. Severely abused youths who report feeling trapped and perceive no other way out of the family situation do not have the freedom to leave their homes for extended periods. Unlike Lyle Menendez, they do not have opportunities to attend a major university 3,000 miles from their parents' home. They are not allowed to play tennis for weeks in Europe, as Eric Menendez did.

These discrepancies and others that appear in the case do not rule out the possibility that Lyle and Eric Menendez were severely abused individuals who killed because they believed they were about to be killed by their parents. However, they raise questions that need to be asked in order for one to understand the motivation that propelled the killings of Jose and Kitty Menendez. Clearly, the jury verdict in the second trial indicated that jurors did not believe that "the boys" were in fear for their lives when they ambushed and repeatedly shot their parents. The jury convicted the brothers of two counts of first-degree murder and found that two aggravating circumstances applied: multiple murder and lying in wait for their victims. In a separate hearing, held weeks later, the jury declined to recommend that Lyle and Eric be sentenced to death. Instead, they recommended that the two men be sentenced to life in prison without parole.

Battered Child Syndrome

The term "battered child syndrome" first appeared in the *Journal of the American Medical Association* approximately 50 years ago as a diagnosis for physical abuse.[36] Since the 1980s, this term has increasingly been recognized as encompassing both psychological and physical effects of prolonged child abuse.[37] Mental health professionals, researchers, and legal scholars have been quick to point out the similarities between battered child syndrome (BCS) and battered spouse syndrome.[38] Battered woman's syndrome (BWS) is used as a "shorthand reference to the body of scientific and clinical literature that forms the basis for much expert testimony in domestic violence cases."[39] In her book *The Battered Woman*,[40] Lenore Walker identified three phases that typify the "cycle of violence" of abusive relationships. "The pattern is characterized by a series of stages with differing engagement, coercion, and physical aggression" that vary in severity, intensity, and duration across battering relationships.[41] These phases include (1) tension-building, (2) acute-battering, and (3) contrite-loving stages.

The cycle of violence provides the backbone of the psychological construct of "learned helplessness."[42] This psychological theory "describes what happens when a person loses the ability to predict what actions will produce a particular outcome. Because the battered woman tries to protect herself and her family as best she can, those with learned helplessness choose only those actions that have a high probability of being successful."[43] As the battering intensifies and persists, the victim might perceive that there is no escape and that survival of the abuse is her first priority.

Parallels between BWS and BCS clearly exist, although they are not necessarily equivalent processes.[44] Battered spouses display hypervigilance and observe danger signals that others might overlook.[45] Similarly, battered children often develop permanent emotional sensitivities that make them react differently than normal people would under the same circumstances.[46] Like abused women, these abused children cultivate awareness of subtle cues of behavior that might indicate imminent danger, and they prepare to defend themselves with little notice.[47]

The admissibility of expert testimony on a defendant's state of mind at the time of a killing has been greatly impacted by state and legislative acceptance of battered spouse syndrome defenses. As noted by psychologist and lawyer Charles Patrick Ewing, "virtually all legal commentators and courts now agree" that testimony pertaining to BWS should be allowed in murder trials involving abused women who kill their alleged batterers.[48] Since the mid-1970s, "the criminal justice system has come to recognize that abuse of women by men is a widespread societal problem .... [I]n most situations, the women are psychologically trapped in their abusive relationships. In spite of the numerous protective and counseling resources available, because they have been abused on a consistent basis over an extended period of time, the women in this situation often feel that they will never be safe from their abusers ...." They come to believe that "killing their abusers is their only viable means of escape."[49]

In a comprehensive trend analysis of 238 state and 31 federal case holdings and 12 state statutes, a National Institute of Justice special report found that "while much variation remains, expert testimony on battering and its effects is admissible or has been admitted without discussion in each of the 50 states plus the District of Columbia."[50] The report noted that 90% of states have accepted expert testimony in cases of traditional self-defense, that is, when a woman kills her abuser during a physical confrontation. In addition, and importantly, the analysis demonstrated that a substantial number of states have also allowed expert testimony for nontraditional (e.g., nonconfrontational) killings, such as when a woman hires a killer or attacks her abuser while he is sleeping.[51] Nearly 70% of the states have also held that expert testimony is pertinent in explaining the defendant's state of mind at the time of the charged crime.

Legislative Responses to Battered Children Who Kill Parents

Although states have been receptive to the plight of battered women, legislators have been much more hesitant to adopt statutes allowing the admission of battering evidence in parricide cases involving abuse. It appears that only eight of the 50 states in the United States specifically have legislation that pertains even broadly to BCS (see Box 7-3).

Three additional states have had BCS extended to them through rulings in courts. As a result of the Ohio Supreme Court's decision in *State v. Nemeth*, Ohio Evidence Rule 702 has case notes stating that expert testimony on BCS is admissible when it is relevant, "beyond the ken" or knowledge of the ordinary person, and reliable.[52] A Washington statute states that, per the Washington Supreme Court's decision in *State v. Janes*, BCS evidence is admissible to help prove self-defense if relevant to the case.[53] An Arizona appellate court found that BCS evidence was sufficient to establish that the defendant's heated passion, which was caused by provocation by the victim, justified a manslaughter conviction rather than a conviction for murder in the case of a girl who shot her mother in the back of her head as she slept.[54]

BOX 7-3 Statutes Allowing Evidence of Domestic Violence and Abuse, Expert Testimony

Kentucky allows

- "any evidence presented by the defendant to establish the existence of a prior act or acts of domestic violence and abuse" committed by the victim to establish the use of physical force in self-protection (Baldwin's Kentucky Revised Statutes Annotated M.G.L.A. 233 § 23F (2010), KRS Section 503.050, current through 2009 legislation).

Louisiana allows

- the use of expert testimony regarding the victim's character in the context of self-defense to shed light on the use of physical force in cases in which the defendant and the victim live in "a familial or intimate relationship," which includes parent and child, as well as husband and wife (Baldwin, citing La. Code Evid. Ann. art. 404A(2)(a) (1994). Current law through 2009; see *State v. Gachot*, 609 So. 2d 269, LA Court of Appeals, 3rd Circuit, 1992; reconsideration denied, *State v. Gachot*, 620 So. 2d 830, LA Supreme Court, 1993).

Massachusetts allows, in support of self-defense,

- "evidence that the defendant is or has been the victim of acts of physical, sexual or psychological harm or abuse" in criminal cases involving the use of force against another in which the issue is self-defense or the defense of another party (Baldwin, 2001, p. 128; M.G.L.A. 233 § 23F [2010]), and
- "evidence by expert testimony regarding the common pattern in abusive relationships; the nature and effects of physical, sexual or psychological abuse and typical responses thereto, including how those effects relate to the perception of

the imminent nature of the threat of death or serious bodily harm; the relevant facts and circumstances which form the basis for such opinion; and evidence whether the defendant displayed characteristics common to victims of abuse" (M.G.L.A. 233 § 23F [2010]).

Nevada allows, in the context of excusing from criminal liability or of self-defense,

- "evidence of domestic violence and expert testimony concerning the effect of domestic violence, including, without limitation, the effect of physical, emotional or mental abuse, on the beliefs, behavior and perception of the alleged victim of the domestic violence" (Nevada Rev. Stat. 48.061 [2009]).

Oklahoma Code of Criminal Procedure stipulates,

- "In an action in a court of this state, if a party offers evidence of domestic abuse, testimony of an expert witness concerning the effects of such domestic abuse on the beliefs, behavior and perception of the person being abused shall be admissible as evidence" (Okla. Stat. Ann. Tit. 22 Sect. 40.7 [2006]).

Texas allows, in prosecutions for murder, if the defendant raises justification as a defense,

- "relevant evidence that the defendant had been the victim of acts of family violence committed by the deceased" in order "to establish the defendant's reasonable belief that use of force or deadly force was immediately necessary" (Vernon's Ann. Texas CCP Art. 38.36 (b)(1) [2009]), and
- "relevant expert testimony regarding the condition of the mind of the defendant at the time of the offense, including those relevant facts and circumstances relating to family violence that are the basis of the expert's opinion" (Vernon's Ann. Texas CCP Art. 38.36 (b)(2) [2009]).

Utah allows, when using force in the context of self-defense, that

- "[i]n determining imminence or reasonableness … the trier of fact may consider, but is not limited to, any of the following factors:(a) the nature of the danger;(b) the immediacy of the danger;(c) the probability that the unlawful force would result in death or serious bodily injury;(d) the other's prior violent acts or violent propensities; and(e) any patterns of abuse or violence in the parties' relationship" (Utah Crim. Code 76–2-402(5) [2010]).

California allows, as noted by the court in *State v. Nemeth* (1998), p. 214,

- testimony on the "physical, emotional, or mental effects upon the beliefs, perceptions, or behavior of victims of domestic violence" as defined in Cal. Fam. Code 6211 and Cal. Evid. Code 1107 (2009).
- Domestic violence is defined under this Family Code section as abuse perpetrated against " a child of a party" and "any person related by consanguinity or affinity within the second degree." This definition encompasses parental abuse of children (West's Ann. Cal. Fam. Code 6211[e, f])(West, 2012).

Some state statutes preclude the use of this defense with children as a justification for homicide. For example, Wyoming[55] has statutory provisions for expert testimony on BWS that do not statutorily apply to cases of battered children. In cases in which battered spouses or children do have statutory provisions, it is frequently difficult to get their state of mind presented into evidence if the court does not find sufficient cause of imminent danger in proximity to the homicide event. Missouri, for example, provides that "evidence that the actor [is] suffering from the battered spouse syndrome shall be admissible upon the issue of whether the actor lawfully acted in self-defense or defense of another."[56] Another "crucial determination of whether a battering episode and commission of a homicide are reasonably proximate in time—makes the provisions of [the Missouri statute] difficult to invoke in a nonconfrontational situation."[57]

The Missouri statute is one example of how states have presented numerous challenges in terms of the way parricide offenders may use a self-defense justification for their actions. "Since state law remains inconsistent, or altogether silent on the issue, the state of a defendant's residence determines what kind of justice he receives. In most states, 'justice' is achieved without the introduction of battered child syndrome."[58] Statutes such as those in Box 7-3 leave no doubt that evidence consistent with BCS does not in and of itself establish a claim of self-defense.

Judicial Responses to Battered Children Who Kill Parents

It appears from an extensive review of case law that the highest courts in only four states have recognized BCS. Interestingly, only two of these four states indicated that evidence of BCS should have been admitted by the trial court based on the records before them. In 1993, the Washington Supreme Court in *State v. Janes*[59] recognized BCS in the context of a self-defense justification in a murder case. The court reached this conclusion only after analogizing BCS to battered wife syndrome.[60] The Washington court "ruled that it was reversible error to exclude evidence of battered child syndrome, since admission of expert testimony on the syndrome would 'aid the jury in evaluating the manner in which a battered child perceived the imminence of danger and his or her tendency to use deadly force to repel that danger.' "[61]

Advocates of using a justification defense in parricide cases such as this one hoped that the courts would begin to be more open to accepting expert testimony of BCS, just as states had done for battered spouse syndrome. In the two decades following the landmark decision in *Janes*, however, few other state courts have held that testimony regarding BCS should be admissible in a murder case because it might be relevant to the mental status of the offender at the time of the killing. In 1998, the Ohio Supreme Court in *State v. Nemeth* [62]upheld an appellate court decision overturning a murder conviction based on the trial court's decision to exclude psychological testimony related to BCS in the case of a man who killed his mother. The high court noted that even though the defense is not an independent defense in Ohio, it was an error to disallow expert testimony on the syndrome in support of a claim of self-defense or in terms of mitigating the degree of the offense.[63]

In the 2003 case of *Smullen v. State*, the Court of Special Appeals in Maryland recognized BCS as a legal defense and vacated the murder convictions of a teenager who killed his father because the court had not allowed expert testimony on this syndrome.[64] Judge Hollander wrote in the 2–1 majority opinion that the court was "satisfied that Battered Child Syndrome is, generally, the functional equivalent of Battered Spouse

Syndrome. Further, even without legislative authorization, such evidence may be relevant to the state of mind in a parricide case."[65] The court acknowledged that abused children might indeed suffer more trauma than adults and, therefore, are entitled to the protection of the defense. Judge Hollander noted that "we cannot articulate any sensible reason why such evidence would be relevant and admissible when the battered person is a spouse, but irrelevant and inadmissible if the battered person is a child."[66]

Upon appeal, the Court of Appeals of Maryland reversed the lower appellate court decision, reinstating the murder conviction of the defendant.[67] The higher court agreed that battered spouse syndrome, as recognized by state statute, applied to battered children. However, the higher court stated that the trial court did not err in refusing to allow testimony on BCS in this case because the defense had not presented relevant evidence that indicated that the defendant was in fact a battered child. The higher court compared the testimony of "random and undefined acts of abuse perpetrated at undefined times in the past, none of which apparently caused serious physical injury, or required any medical attention, or attracted the notice of anyone in a position to notice them" in the Smullen case with the corroborated testimony of extensive records of abuse in other cases in which BCS had been successfully litigated, specifically citing the *Janes* and *Nemeth* cases.[68]

In 2005, the Minnesota Supreme Court held in *State v. MacLennan*[69] that expert testimony on BCS, similar to expert testimony on BWS, should be admissible if the evidence is relevant because it might help explain "a phenomenon not within the understanding of an ordinary person."[70] The court ruled that the yardstick with which to determine the admissibility of BCS was the Minnesota Rules of Evidence 702, not the Frye-Mack test used by the trial court.[71] The court indicated that "relevant evidence that helps explain the characteristics possessed by children who have been battered and outlines the probable responses to traumatic events would be allowed."[72] Experts would not be allowed to testify to the "ultimate fact that the particular defendant suffers from battered child syndrome," because that fact is one to be determined by the jury.[73] After determining that the trial court erred by applying the wrong test, the Minnesota Supreme Court noted that the trial court properly excluded the proffered expert testimony because, although it established "a tense relationship" between the defendant and his father, it did not "give rise to battered child syndrome."[74] The court held that the defense had not met the threshold requirement of showing that the defendant was physically or sexually abused and cited *Smullen*, *Janes*, and *Nemeth* decisions in support. The failure of the defense to establish "both the physiological and psychological effects of a prolonged pattern of physical, emotional, and sexual abuse" in order to support expert testimony on BCS was also noted by the Tennessee Court of Appeals in the 2004 case of *State v. Dunham*.[75]

From 2005 to 2011, no other cases involving BCS were decided by the highest appellate courts. A 2006 intermediate appellate court decision in California, however, is worthy of note. The court held in the case of *People v. Jason Victor Bautista* that the trial court erred in relying on the Kelly-Frye test to exclude expert testimony on BCS.[76] The appellate court noted that the California Supreme Court had never used this test in the case of medical testimony, even when offered by a psychiatrist and considered as "esoteric" or to refer to an illness not formally recognized in the diagnostic manual of the American Psychiatric Association. The court concluded, however, that denial of testimony about BCS did not deprive the defendant of a chance to present a defense and resulted only in some evidence not being presented. Based on the court record, the court did not believe that a different conclusion would have been reached by the jurors had the testimony on BCS been allowed, and it affirmed Bautista's conviction.[77]

BCS was formally addressed by one appellate court in juvenile proceedings. In 1994, an intermediate Arizona appellate court recognized that BCS, which had initially been described in medical terms and accepted as admissible evidence, had been broadened to include psychological effects suffered by abused children.[78] In this case, although the juvenile court allowed testimony on BCS to support a claim that a 12-year-old girl killed her mother in self-defense, the court found the girl guilty of manslaughter. The appellate court affirmed the defendant's conviction for manslaughter, agreeing with the trial court that the record supported a conviction of manslaughter because the girl killed her mother in a "sustained heat of passion" and as "a result of adequate provocation."[79]

Legislation Enacted and Judicial Decisions Relevant to Battered Person Syndrome

It appears that only Georgia[80] has enacted specific legislation that allows courts to consider the effects of *battered person syndrome* in a larger context. As noted above, other states have taken a broader approach and have statutorily allowed for the admissibility of abuse and its effects. West Virginia has enacted legislation requiring magistrates and family court judges to complete a minimum of three hours of training each year on "domestic violence which shall include training on the psychology of domestic violence, the battered wife and child syndromes," and other related matters.[81]

Battered person syndrome is considered by the state of Georgia to be an analogous, gender-neutral form of BWS. Both syndromes comprise a collection of behavioral and psychological characteristics that specifically include symptoms of post-traumatic stress disorder and learned helplessness. They describe the long-term effects that prolonged and repetitive patterns of physical and emotional abuse cause in the victim.[82]

Many experts, including attorney Paul Mones, who has represented hundreds of youths charged with killing their parents, believe it is necessary to introduce testimony on battered person syndrome at trial in order for the jury to understand the defendant's state of mind at the time of the killing.[83] As the Georgia Supreme Court in *Chester v. State*[84] observed,[85]

[It is] unfair to hold a battered individual to the same standard as a typical reasonably prudent person, when at the time she uses defensive force, she may be existing in a dissociative state unsure of when the next attack upon her may begin and is unable to discern between her present and past realities.

Battered person syndrome is the means by which a defendant introduces the existence of "a mental state necessary for the defense of justification although the actual threat of harm did not immediately precede the homicide."[86] It is used by defense attorneys to help juries understand the state of mind and behaviors of abused people. The situation in which this syndrome typically comes into play is one in which a woman is charged with the murder of her spouse or intimate partner and is claiming that she acted in self-defense. If she has proof that she was battered, then expert testimony on battered person syndrome can be admitted as evidence. This evidence must demonstrate that she acted upon a reasonable belief of imminent danger to her, even though the killing occurred during a nonconfrontational situation.[87]

It appears that Georgia is the only state to clearly set forth the elements necessary in order for a defendant to use evidence of being battered by the victim to establish a defense of justification in a prosecution for murder or manslaughter.[88] Section 16–3-2 of the state's statutory code states that evidence of battered person syndrome can be brought before the jury for the limited purpose of illustrating that the defendant reasonably believed that the use of deadly force was immediately necessary in order to defend oneself; it is not a defense in itself. This statute was enacted in response to the landmark case of *Smith v. State*,[89] in which a wife shot her abusive husband after an argument. Vernita Smith was convicted of manslaughter after the trial court denied defense counsel's motion to provide instructions to jurors on battered person syndrome. The conviction was eventually reversed by the Georgia Supreme Court and set precedents concerning the proper use of this syndrome.

Although this statute specifically references BWS but not battered person syndrome, it recognizes the latter as analogous. Therefore, this statute is cited extensively in Georgia case law concerning battered person syndrome as evidence of justifiable homicide committed in self-defense. A subsection (d) was added to this statute[90] that states that the defendant may offer the following:

(1) Relevant evidence that the defendant had been the victim of acts of family violence or child abuse committed by the deceased, and (2) Relevant expert testimony regarding the condition of the mind of the defendant at the time of the offense, including those relevant facts and circumstances relating to the family violence or child abuse that are the basis of the expert's opinion.

When battered person syndrome is advanced by the defendant as evidentiary support for a claim of justifiable homicide by self-defense, it is necessary that the defendant request that specific instructions be given to the jury to explain to them the relevance of such evidence.[91]

The Georgia Supreme Court's decision in *Smith v. State* proved useful, shortly after it was decided, in the case of James Freeman, who, without immediate provocation, shot to death his stepfather and his stepfather's friend. At his initial trial, Freeman was denied the use of battered person syndrome, despite his claims of continual abuse at the hands of his stepfather. Freeman was convicted on both counts of murder. While Freeman's case was on appeal, *Smith v. State* was decided, which directly influenced the appellant decision in *State v. Freeman*.[92] The *Freeman* ruling reversed the conviction for the murder of Freeman's stepfather, holding that the denial of the use of battered person syndrome was an error on the part of the lower court. Freeman could not, however, use that as a defense in the murder of his stepfather's friend because there was no evidence that the man had a history of abusing Freeman.[93]

In order for battered person syndrome to be allowed into evidence, the accused must be able to establish a prima facie case of self-defense. Furthermore, there has to be documented evidence of the abuse, whether physical or emotional, and expert testimony on the validity of the syndrome and its symptoms. Several cases were barred from using the defense because they failed to provide adequate documentation; to wit, the defendant could not prove a history of abuse or a personal or intimate relationship with the alleged abuser. Other cases have failed because battered person syndrome

(BPS) was improperly introduced as a defense in itself. When BPS is successfully introduced but fails to sway the jury, fault most commonly lies with the court's exclusion of expert testimony or the court's failure to provide the jury with specific instructions about its application.

Observations and Conclusion

BCS shares many similarities with BWS and its name variants, battered spouse syndrome and battered wife syndrome. BCS differs from BWS in a very fundamental way: *unlike BWS, BCS has not been widely recognized in case law or state statutes.* Given that abused children would appear to be more vulnerable and even less culpable than their adult female counterparts, as others have rightly pointed out, it is puzzling that legislators and judges have been slow to enact legislation and court precedents that would bring relief to abused youths who kill their parents. Box 7-4 presents seven explanations for the reluctance of legislative bodies and courts to be proactive in recognizing BCS as a defense.

BOX 7-4 Seven Reasons for the Reluctance of Legislative Bodies and Courts to Recognize Battered Child Syndrome

(1) Fear that the existence of this defense will result in more parricides, as many of these killings do not occur during confrontations

(2) Other available legal alternatives, such as factors in mitigation introduced at sentencing, are deemed more appropriate

(3) The belief that the rare occurrence of parents being slain by youths does not necessitate recognition of a special syndrome

(4) The reality that the most egregious cases of abused children killing their parents will be accommodated by the legal system in terms of reduced charges or decisions not to prosecute

(5) Information available on the most appropriate and best cases is lacking because many of these cases are not litigated in the lower courts; rather, they are handled through dropped charges, retention in the juvenile justice system, pleas to lesser charges, truncated sentences, and probation dispositions

(6) Executive clemency is believed to be a safety valve

(7) Because of the rarity of this event, a significant lobby group has not emerged to advocate for youths involved in parricide

Source: Heide, K. M., Boots, D., Alldredge, C., Donerly, B., & White, J. R. (2005). Battered Child Syndrome: An Overview of Case Law and Legislation. *Criminal Law Bulletin, 41(3)*, 219–239.

In light of the similarities between BWS and BCS, a compelling argument recently has been made that expert testimony about the psychological effects endured by all victims of severe domestic violence should be incorporated into a new term called "domestic abuse syndrome" and admitted as relevant to a self-defense plea when children or adult victims of domestic violence kill their abusers.[94] Another argument has been made that the "accumulated sense of humiliation and shame" experienced by abused adolescents might constitute grounds for a defense based on duress. As discussed by psychiatrist Carl Malmquist, "continuing threats and humiliation lead the adolescent to believe that death is imminent and the only way to avoid it is to engage in criminal behavior that, in a literal sense, violates criminal law. Duress can be seen as the reason that an adolescent ultimately overcomes his moral controls and engages in homicidal behavior."[95]

Even when courts have allowed testimony regarding BCS, however, available evidence suggests that use of the defense rarely leads to exoneration of the defendant. Instead parricide offenders are usually convicted of second-degree murder or manslaughter, largely because of the nonconfrontational nature of parricide killings by adolescent offenders. In such cases, BCS can serve as an appropriate foundation for mitigation of the child's culpability "within the framework of excuse, which focuses on the unique characteristics and circumstances of the individual defendant."[96] Expert testimony at trial might be helpful in persuading a jury that under the attendant circumstances, the parricide offender was so emotionally overwrought that he or she did not have the capacity to form the intent required to commit first-degree murder. Accordingly, testimony relevant to the offender's diminished capacity might result in a conviction of second-degree murder. Alternatively, a mental health expert might testify that the defendant was so provoked by the victim's conduct that he or she was operating under "extreme emotional disturbance" when he or she killed the abusive parent, possibly resulting in a manslaughter rather than a murder conviction.[97] Mental status defenses might also become relevant at this juncture. The failure to call a mental health expert to testify in abuse cases can have serious consequences, as illustrated in the case of Will Garrison below.

GOVERNOR GRANTS CLEMENCY TO ABUSED SON

Will Garrison (pseudonym), age 16, was charged with the first-degree murder of his father. Will testified that he killed his father in self-defense. The court restricted testimony by witnesses about prior acts of abuse by the victim. The jury rejected the defendant's self-defense argument and convicted him of second-degree murder.

The judge would not allow any evidence to be presented at sentencing regarding the "prior bad acts or character of the victim." Will was sentenced to prison for 20 years, with a three-year mandatory sentence for use of a firearm, to be followed by 10 years of probation. Appeals of legal issues at trial and of his sentence were not successful.

I was appointed by the governor to evaluate Will when he applied for clemency about three years after his conviction. I was asked to limit my evaluation to the following two questions:

(1) Is there substantial evidence to indicate that Will was abused by his father?
(2) If such evidence exists, might this abuse have significantly affected Will's judgment as to the subject offense?

The governor's office, the parole commission, the clemency administration, and the state's attorney's office were all very cooperative in getting materials to me for review. These included the complete trial transcript, police reports, the medical examiner's report, transcripts of police interviews of key witnesses, and a pre-trial psychological evaluation of Will by Dr. Monahan. I also reviewed school records; letters from Will's teachers, neighbors, and former employer; correspondence from family members to Will after the homicide; and correspondence from family members to the parole board.

I spent approximately six hours evaluating Will in prison. In addition, I had separate clinical interviews with Will's mother, the three living siblings of the deceased, and the deceased's nephew, Johnny.[98] I also met with Will's former girlfriend Carol Clark and her parents. These eight individuals were all cooperative and willingly answered questions about Will and the Garrison family. It was apparent from their cracked voices and the tears in their eyes that each of them cared deeply and felt it was his or her moral obligation to render assistance.

With Will's permission, I consulted with the defense attorney, Mr. Eddings, about his strategy at trial. In addition, I spoke with Will's prison classification officer and with a supervisor at a national drugstore where Will had sought employment in order to verify information that would give me independent measures of the credibility of some of Will's statements.

Profiles of Mr. and Mrs. Garrison and their only child Will emerged from clinical interviews with Will, his family and the Clarks, and a review of the materials on file. Mrs. Garrison was a quiet and shy woman. Like her son Will, the evidence indicated that she was relatively passive. Statements from the deceased's siblings and nephew (hereafter referred to as the deceased's family) indicated that they had gotten along with Mrs. Garrison in the past and considered her a nice person prior to the shooting. The deceased was by all accounts a jolly man, a man who loved to joke, to play, and to have fun. He worked hard at two and sometimes three jobs and provided well for his family. There was persuasive evidence from the deceased's family, as well as from Mrs. Garrison and Will, that Mr. Garrison had been a heavy drinker, quit, and then went back to drinking, though apparently not as heavily. In addition, there was strong evidence that Mr. Garrison would not let people push him around; if challenged, he would not back down. He took pride in being "macho."

Will was a quiet and well-mannered boy. He interacted in a respectful way with adults and his peers and sought their approval. Will had just completed the 10th grade and was barely passing when he was arrested. From all accounts (including the review of school records and letters from his teachers), he was not a youth who got in trouble at school often and had never been suspended or expelled. Will rarely challenged adults. Family members could remember only two times when Will had "acted mean." These incidents occurred when Will was age 4 and 16, respectively, and appeared to have been isolated incidents. The youth's pattern was unquestionably to withdraw and to isolate. He preferred to be with his mother and actively avoided his father.

Evidence indicated that Will did not drink alcohol or use illicit drugs, including marijuana. He was a good worker and a valued employee. Will stated that he had not engaged in illegal activities, such as shoplifting, stealing, robbing, and burglarizing homes, because these things were wrong. Official records indicate that he had no prior record as a juvenile or as an adult.

Question 1: Was Will Garrison Abused?

There was substantial evidence that Will was physically, verbally, and psychologically abused. There was also some evidence of covert sexual abuse by the father.[99] My conclusions were based on my clinical interviews with Will and his mother and corroborating evidence obtained from his girlfriend, Carol, and her father. Statements made by Mr. Garrison's nephew about Will's father calling his son a sissy, expelling gas as he sat on Will's face, and resorting to violence on occasion also lent additional weight. Sworn testimony at trial by those whom I interviewed, and also by Will's maternal grandfather and the next door neighbors, Mr. and Mrs. Alldredge, was persuasive in light of statements made to me. School records indicating that Will had been observed grabbing the genitals of other children suggested the possibility of inappropriate sexual behavior occurring at home. Box 7-5 contains examples of abuse that were corroborated.

BOX 7-5 *Corroborated* Abuse and Neglect in Will Garrison's Case

Physical Neglect

- Not provided with a safe place to live

Emotional Neglect

- Father did not give clear messages that he loved son

Verbal Abuse

- Father belittled son (told son he was worthless, called him a "sissy," "queer," "faggot", and "idiot")
- Father cursed at son (called him " motherfucker," "son of a bitch," "asshole")

Psychological Abuse

- Father often belittled son and questioned his manhood (e.g., father hit son, age 14 or 15, with lawn mower blade after son had difficulty changing blade and said that he should have known better—if he wanted a man, he should have gotten one)
- Father threw son to the ground on multiple occasions and expelled gas on him (father thought this behavior was funny and performed it in front of others)
- Father would not tolerate son's crying after father hurt him (father would get mad, said "Men don't cry," threatened to give son something to cry about)
- Son could not do anything right or to his father's satisfaction
- When son was little, father would pull son's pants down in front of others and comment on his "little dick"
- Son witnessed father physically abusing mother (son did not intervene because of "fear of Dad")

(continued)

BOX 7-5 (Continued)

- Son, as a young child, inadvertently witnessed his mother in distress as a man had sex with her while his father watched (son did not understand what was occurring; mother said that boy's father made her have sex with other men as father watched)

Physical Abuse

- Father hurt or attempted to hurt son on many occasions because father was angry
- Father punched son in stomach and hit him with fist multiple times
- Father grabbed son by the hair more than 20 times
- Father slapped son in harsh or humiliating way more than 20 times
- Father bit son on his hands many times when boy was younger (boy experienced as painful; father said he was "playing")
- Father slapped son around (boy experienced as painful; father said he was "playing")
- Father beat son on his bare buttocks when son was younger
- Father choked son on a few occasions
- Son sustained bruises across his back area, in his stomach area, and across his chest
- Father beat son in an area where son had just had surgery for a disc (son had to go back to doctor for treatment of injury; injury had not healed at the time of the homicide and was treated while son was in jail)
- Father struck out at son when he had done nothing at all to deserve it
- Father's discipline was out of proportion to misdeeds by son (in mother's words, "The way he whipped him with a belt. It wasn't a whipping; it was a beating. I mean, he's left bruises on and welts on him [son]. And then as he [son] grew older, hitting him with a fist, choking him, and stuff like that.")

Covert Sexual Abuse

- Father showed son pictures of his mother naked and sitting on the toilet seat (father thought it was "funny")

Mistreatment of Will's Mother Witnessed by Him

- Mother was verbally abused by Will's father
- Mother was physically abused by Will's father
- Mother was sexually abused by Will's father (husband made her have sex with other men while he watched; Will saw mother in distress with a man on top of her as young boy but did not understand the situation)

There was also substantial evidence that the deceased's relationship with Will's mother was abusive and that Will was a witness to emotional abuse and physical violence. This conclusion was based on statements made to me by Will, Will's mother, and the deceased's sister; sworn trial testimony made by the Alldredges; and a written statement from a retired social worker contained in the parole commission's confidential case analysis. Substantial evidence existed that Will was emotionally neglected by both of his parents because of their turbulent relationship. Will was physically neglected by his mother, who failed, because of her own psychological difficulties, to protect Will from emotional and physical harm from his father.

Question 2: Might This Abuse Have Significantly Affected Will's Judgment When He Killed His Father?

The facts in this case suggested that Will's judgment was affected by the abuse he endured. His abuse history, when combined with his restricted personality development, impacted how he perceived the events during the day of the homicide and what behavioral choices he thought were available to him. Will's personality development was arrested when he was very young because his environment provided more stressors than he could successfully accommodate. His perceptions of himself and others were very limited and remained those of a much younger child. He did not understand his own feelings and needs or those of others. He was taught respect, and he learned to be passive in relationships with others. He gravitated toward adults who were nice to him and had strong, dependent relationships with his mother and his paternal aunt. The evidence was clear from all accounts that Will restricted his contact with his father. He typically was successful in avoiding his father by going to his room.

On the day of the homicide, Will had retreated to his room. His father came to speak to him, and a fight ensued. According to Will's accounts to me and at trial, he had been beaten by his father two or three times that day and was fearful that his father might resume the beating. His statement that he got the gun in an attempt to make his father get out of the way is consistent with his personality development. Low-maturity subjects look for formulas to get what they want.[100] They are impulsive. Those who adopt a behavioral response style of conforming to those who are more powerful, as Will did, tend to withdraw psychologically or physically. Will's statement that when he got the gun what was uppermost in his mind was "to get out of the house" because he had received the worst beating in his life was convincing, given his typical response pattern.

There was some disagreement between what Will allegedly told the police and his paternal aunt and what he said to Dr. Monahan, his testimony at trial, and his statements to me. The important area of disagreement was whether Will called his father back into the house on the pretense that his father had a phone call and then shot him, or whether his father suddenly appeared after Will hung up the phone, as Will had told Dr. Monahan and me and had testified at trial.

I related to the governor and the clemency board that I did not know which version was the correct one. However, Will's personality development and typical response pattern and his fear of his father strongly suggested that he would have been more likely to shoot his father upon suddenly seeing him than to seek him out actively for confrontation. Once the confrontation began, it was highly likely that Will would have been flooded with anxiety and terrified in light of his father's alleged remarks that he would kill him when he got a hold of him, as well as previous threats that his father had made in the past about what would happen if Will ever struck out at him.

Will's Statements about the Shooting

Will seemed certain that his father had beaten him at three discrete times right before the shooting. "I remember him leaving three times, I remember words each time, but as far as what happened when exactly each time, it's kind of blurry; everything in the order of the three meetings, it's sort of, I don't remember exactly." His rendition follows.

Will was in his bedroom when his father came in and confronted him about missing class. Will told his father that he wasn't skipping school. His father called him a liar, cussed at him, and began hitting him with an object in the back of the head. (Will didn't know what it was when the beating first began; later he saw that it was his father's pocket knife.) Will's father was standing right next to Will when he hit him, and Will fell on the floor, holding onto the bed. His father started jumping on him, but then the phone rang, and his father left to answer the phone. (Will did not know who had called.)

Will stayed in his bedroom, and his father came back. Mr. Garrison resumed beating Will. "He had the knife and he was hitting me all on the back of the head and he got my face down and he was grinding me down in the back of the head. Then he said, 'I'd better leave before I hurt you' and he left." Will explained further: "But all during this time, before he left, he was grinding it. First, when he came in, he came in that time, and I was up on the bed. He got me and slung me across the wall, and brought me down, and started grinding the knife in back of my head." His father told Will, "We'll finish this conversation later."

Will did not know where his father went. He might have been outside smoking. The phone rang repeatedly. Will answered the phone. The female caller, whom he recognized as his father's girlfriend, mistook Will for his father. Will told her that he was not Mr. Garrison, and she hung up. Mr. Garrison appeared suddenly and asked who had called. Will said, "Johnny." He did not know why he lied about the caller's identity; it was the first thing that came out. Will returned to his room. Mr. Garrison called Johnny and started to sound "hostile" on the phone. He came into Will's room and said, "Why are you always lying?" Mr. Garrison called Will names and began beating Will again with the knife. Then his father left again. Will did not know where he went.

At this point, Will got the gun. He was not sure whether he loaded the gun or not (because of things he heard at trial), although he believed he did: "It seems like I got a shell from the bottom drawer." The gun was his father's. Will did not remember leaving the room; he was pretty sure that he retrieved the gun from his closet. He remembered going down the hallway and seeing his father come from the living room. Will met his father between the kitchen and the living room. "I got the gun and I was gonna leave, so I got the gun, and here he comes. He's like, 'What's going on?' I told him, 'I'm leaving,' and he told me, he'd kill me before I left. And he came at me, and I shot him. So he went back in the living room [Mr. Garrison fell into the chair]. And I just dropped, dropped down. And I got back up, and he's coming at me. He's telling me, he's gonna kill me." While Mr. Garrison was coming at Will, Mr. Garrison was reportedly "cussing."

Will said that he hit his father with the butt of the gun about three or four times by swinging the gun back and forth rapidly like a baseball bat while his father was standing directly in front of him. Will said that he hit his father on the left side and back of the head, and his dad "finally went down." He fell into trays over by the table and then fell on the floor. "And he's still getting up—he's on all fours and as I'm leaving, I put the gun down. And he calls me, and he tells me, to cut off the stove." Will ran right by his father to get to the stove and turn it off. Will was certain that he did not hit his father when he was lying down. He had no memory of his father asking him to call an ambulance. He locked the doors and drove off.

When asked what he was thinking when he got the gun, Will said, "[T]o get out of the house … because I had just received the worst beating of my life." When asked what made it the worst beating, he replied, "It was just so different—many times, the knife, the grinding, and all that—he was losing it." Will knew that his father was mad. When asked what he was feeling, Will replied, "[S]cared." "He said one time he was coming back. I didn't know if he was coming back again or not, so I figured he ain't gonna mess with me. If I've got a gun, he's gonna let me leave." Will estimated that his father was about five to seven feet away when he shot his dad.

When asked whether he had ever been concerned before that his father would hurt him and cause injury, Will said yes. He said that the day of the homicide was different because "he was so angry and violent that day." Will remembered feeling some anger that day and acknowledged that it was possible that he had taken all that he could. When asked what was uppermost in his mind when he got the firearm that day, he said without hesitation, "[T]o leave." When asked if his father had backed down or gotten out of his way, would the shooting still have occurred, Will said, "I don't know. I don't think I would have. I can't say." He explained, "I feel that it had to happen like that. But I feel I was in a situation where it might have been me that was dead, you know. He would have hurt me or killed me that day 'cuz it was not like the rest of days; he would have hurt me or killed me that day. I'm not sorry because he put me through a lot. I loved him, but it had to happen … because he came at me. If I wouldn't have shot him then, after I put the gun on him, he would have hurt me then."

Will was not engaged in hand-to-hand combat with his father during the homicidal event. When asked whether he had sustained any injuries from the beating, Will stated that he had some cuts, abrasions on his forehead and behind his left ear, and "the whole back of my head was knotted up" (swollen from the beating). He assumed his elbow was swollen from his father's twisting his arm around. His jaw also became swollen after his father slammed him onto the ground and he fell face forward.

Will did not remember driving to his girlfriend's house, which was about five miles away. He remembered telling Carol that his father had been beating him and that he shot his father. Will called his mother while Carol called her father.

Carol cried as she told me about Will coming to her house after the shooting. He had a cut on his forehead and blood on his hand. When she asked him what had happened, he told her that he had shot his father and he started to cry. At first he would not talk; he kept walking back and forth. Will told Carol, " 'He came after me. He hit me. I don't know what happened. He kept hitting me and he wouldn't stop.' Then he shot him and he didn't go into anything else." Will told Carol that he was sorry that he shot his father and that he did not want his dad to die.

Mr. Clark told me that when he first saw Will, he could not believe it. "He [Will] looked like somebody put him through a meat grinder. His whole face was beat. His head was cut and bleeding. I couldn't believe that somebody could do that to somebody. Work 'em over like that. It looked like his jaw was broken; it was all swollen. His eyes had welts all around 'em. He was bleeding from the scalp in two places." Mr. Clark also remembered seeing lacerations on Will's scalp, two of them up by his forehead, and discoloration on his ear.

Mr. Clark asked Will who had hurt him, and Will said his father had. Will told Mr. Clark that he had shot his father, and he started to cry. Mr. Clark remembered Will as being upset and angry. Will understood when Mr. Clark told him that he would have to go with the police. Will told Mr. Clark that he had had no choice; his father would not let him out of his house. Mr. Clark asked Will what had provoked this incident. Will said it was over a report card.

Mr. Clark got Will a cold washcloth and ice for his jaw and "got him cleaned up a bit" while they were waiting for the police. Mr. Clark asked the police to get Will immediate medical attention. Will remembered riding to the police station. He did not know why he told the police that his father did not beat him. He thought that maybe he was protecting his father.

When asked whether he was concerned about the possibility that he would be involved in another violent solution, Will said, "It was the situation. It was 16 years. That day—some people say '16 years and I popped.' It's that, but it's not just that. That day he beat me, he beat me, and like I said, it was the worst beating I ever received. You know, it was me or him that day, and I believe that."

Self-Defense and the Role of the Mental Health Professional

I was asked specifically by the governor not to address the question of self-defense because this question had been put before the jury and rejected. It is important to note, however, that the jury might have reached a different decision in evaluating Will if they had been provided with testimony from a mental health professional explaining the dynamics in homes where physical and emotional violence occur and the effects of such violence on family members. Testimony about the adaptations made by both women and children who are abused might have helped the jury. Mrs. Garrison's statements to me about why she stayed and her general demeanor were consistent with the literature on battered women.

No mental health professional was called by the defense to testify at trial. In reading the trial transcript, I noted that the defense attorney argued in the opening arguments that Will was an abused child who killed his father in self-defense. He provided examples of conduct that were indicative of various types of abuse (physical, sexual, spousal, verbal, and psychological) and emotional neglect. He did not explicitly name and identify these types of child maltreatment then or during the trial.

Both Will and his mother said that Dr. Monahan, the psychologist who evaluated Will, was expected to be a key witness at trial. This doctor's report was provided to me. I noted that the statements that Will made to Dr. Monahan about his father's behavior toward him and his mother and the circumstances leading up the shooting were consistent with those he made to me. Dr. Monahan concluded that Will had been "physically and psychologically abused throughout much of his life." He opined that "the destructive behavior towards his father was largely defensive."

Mr. Eddings, Will's lawyer, explained to me that he thought Will's case had been going very well and was strong when he rested the case. He was hesitant to call Dr. Monahan because he believed it would necessitate continuing the trial while the State appointed its own expert to examine Will. Mr. Eddings believed that Dr. Monahan had written an "excellent report" and would have been a very strong witness. He was concerned, however, that Dr. Monahan might have been "too cosmopolitan" for a jury in a rural community.[101] Dr. Eddings said that if he could do the trial over, he would call Dr. Monahan.

I also asked Mr. Eddings about his brief closing argument, in which he focused on the jury instructions rather than returning to the points he had set out to prove in his opening argument (i.e., that the defendant was an abused child who killed in self-defense). He explained that he intentionally made his closing argument brief, so as to limit the State in terms of the areas it could address in its rebuttal. Mr. Eddings was concerned that the State was saving the bulk of its argument for use after the defense had finished. Mr. Eddings stated that during the voir dire (a transcript that I did not have), he asked potential jurors to pay particular attention to their oath. He was thinking that an appeal to jurors drawn from a Bible Belt area to uphold their oath would be helpful to Will's case.

Governor and Cabinet Grant Clemency

Based on a full review of the case, including new information that surfaced after the trial and my report, the governor issued an executive order conditionally commuting Will's sentence. Will's time in prison was reduced by 11 years, and the Department of Corrections (DOC) was instructed to place Will in a work release setting for 18 months in order to facilitate his re-entry into society. While Will was in work release, the DOC was to ensure that he received "evaluation and psychotherapy relating to his family history." Will's time in work release and his return to society are discussed in Chapter 14.

THE INSANITY DEFENSE AND OTHER MENTAL STATUS DEFENSES

The insanity defense is one of several defenses that focus on the defendant's state of mind at the time of the killing. It is currently recognized in federal courts and in 45 of the 50 states in the United States. Five states (Idaho, Montana, Utah, Kansas, and North Dakota) abolished their insanity defense laws through legislative action.[102] Numerous tests have been formulated by courts over the years to guide judges and jurors in deciding whether defendants should be acquitted because they were insane at the time of the crime. These tests require that the defendant had at the time of the crime a sufficient mental impairment that compromised his or her ability to the extent that he or she met the legal standard of insanity in the jurisdiction.[103] The mental impairment requirement is typically used in the context of mental illness or mental retardation. However, it also might be met in some cases of involuntary intoxication. Jurisdictions that allow involuntary intoxication to be used in an insanity defense typically require that the defendant's long-term intoxication led to a permanent impairment, such as organic brain disease, that so negatively impacted the defendant's abilities that he or she met the legal standard of insanity.[104]

Essentially, insanity tests can be grouped into three broad categories according to their primary focus: defects in cognition (understanding), defects in volition (ability to control behavior), and defects in mental or emotional processes or behavioral controls.[105] Table 7-1 compares the legal standards of five insanity tests.

Table 7-1 Comparison of the various insanity defenses

Test	Legal Standard
M'Naghten	"Didn't know what he was doing or didn't know it was wrong"
Irresistible impulse	"Could not control his conduct"
Durham	"The criminal act was caused by his mental illness"
Brawner-ALI	"Lacks substantial capacity to appreciate the wrongfulness of his conduct or to control it"
Present federal standard	"Lacks capacity to appreciate the wrongfulness of his conduct"

Adapted from Morris, N. (1986). Insanity Defense, *National Institute of Justice Crime File Study Guide.* U.S. Department of Justice, National Institute of Justice/National Criminal Justice References Service, Rockville, MD.

The procedures required in order to raise the defense are not uniform across jurisdictions. The defendant who asserts this defense has *the initial burden of going forward with the evidence* suggesting that he or she was insane at the time of the crime, because a presumption of sanity exists in all jurisdictions. After the defendant has raised the issue, jurisdictions vary regarding the party that has *the ultimate burden of proof.* Since John Hinckley was acquitted in 1982 of the attempted assassination of President Reagan, however, states in the United States have increasingly required defendants to prove their insanity by means of clear and convincing evidence.[106]

Despite the attention the insanity defense receives, it is seldom used and rarely successful.[107] The insanity defense is more likely to be utilized in cases of adult parricide offenders than with their adolescent counterparts. As discussed in the preceding chapters, adults who kill parents are more likely to be seriously mentally ill than adolescents. Not guilty by reason of insanity (NGRI) judgments are not uncommon in cases of adults who have longstanding mental illnesses and are psychotic at the time of the killing. Occasionally, adolescent parricide offenders are acquitted on the basis of insanity, as in the case of Peter Jones, discussed in Chapter 10.

When the defense is successful, the defendant is hardly ever set free. Instead, he or she is almost always committed to a mental hospital pursuant to state or federal statute for assessment as to his or her present psychological condition.[108] State statutes vary with respect to the procedures required in order to commit a person found NGRI. In most states and in the federal system, the trial court or some other judicial body retains jurisdiction over insanity acquittees after they have been committed to a mental hospital. Release is usually contingent upon the former defendant's proving to the court by the weight required that his or her confinement is no longer appropriate with respect to mental illness and/or dangerousness under the governing statute.[109]

Other Mental Status at the Time of the Offense Defenses

Automatism, a defense recognized more in the United Kingdom and in Canada than in the United States, is a clinical concept used to denote "unconscious involuntary behavior over which the defendant has no control."[110] Unlike the insanity defense, this defense does not require the existence of a mental disease or defect. When successfully litigated at trial, the automatism defense excuses the defendant from criminal responsibility. The rationale for acquitting the accused is that if the defendant did not have conscious control of his or her body at the time of the offense, then no act has occurred that is sufficient to impose criminal liability.[111]

Although the automatism defense seems applicable, it has not been used frequently in U.S. cases in which it would seem likely to be successful, such as those of defendants diagnosed with dissociative disorders, including dissociative identity disorder, formerly known as multiple personality disorder. An argument could be made that conduct engaged in by a defendant in a dissociative state is "involuntary" and no longer under the conscious control of that individual. However, U.S. defendants who maintain that they were in a dissociative state are more likely to use an insanity defense than an automatism defense. These defendants are likely to be convicted because jurors tend to reject insanity defenses based on claims of "temporary insanity."[112]

The concept of automatism is more frequently utilized in cases involving unconscious behavior by a defendant that appears to be caused by external factors such as concussions or other head injuries, medical administration of drugs, hypoglycemia, shock created by bullet wounds, or involuntary ingestion of drugs or alcohol. Other classic examples of automatism include epilepsy and sleepwalking.[113]

Other defenses, when successfully pled, might not completely exonerate the adolescent parricide offender for his or her conduct. However, they might reduce the grade of the offense or lead to mitigation of the punishment in consideration that the APO, although partially responsible for his or her conduct, should not be held fully accountable. Diminished capacity and voluntary intoxication are examples of defenses of this type.

Not all jurisdictions recognize the concept of diminished capacity. Many states, however, do allow evidence pertaining to the defendant's mental disease or defect to be admissible at trial to show that the offender lacked the capacity to form the requisite mental state to commit the crime. Typically, these jurisdictions restrict testimony about diminished capacity to specific intent crimes, such as murder.[114]

The voluntary use (or abuse) of alcohol or other drugs might arouse passions, lower inhibition, or cloud reason and judgment. However, voluntary intoxication does not excuse a defendant from responsibility for the commission of a criminal act and therefore lead to his or her acquittal. In many jurisdictions, however, voluntary intoxication is recognized in the context of negating a specific intent if required by the crime charged.[115] Evidence presented by a medical or mental health professional that an APO was so intoxicated at the time of the crime that he or she was incapable of forming the specific mental state required (e.g., premeditation) might be introduced to show that the youth did not commit that particular crime (e.g., murder in the first degree). Accordingly, the defendant might be convicted of a lesser included charge (e.g., second-degree murder).

SUMMARY AND CONCLUDING REMARKS

This chapter examined defense strategies often used in parricide cases. The discussion highlighted the importance of the early involvement of mental health professionals (MHPs) in helping defense lawyers understand the dynamics that lead sons or daughters to kill their parents. MHPs with extensive experience in criminal cases are trained to evaluate the defendant's mental status at the time of the crime. In addition, they can play a central role in determining the offender's competency to stand trial and to waive Miranda rights if the parricide offender gave a statement to police at the time of the arrest. A favorable evaluation by a forensic examiner can result in several positive outcomes, including reduction or dismissal of the charges, a reduced sentence, and, in the case of adult defendants, the State's withdrawal of a possible death sentence in cases of first-degree murder.

Given the focus of the book, defense strategies were explored that are often used in parricide cases involving adolescent defendants. The law of self-defense was explained, with special attention given to battered child syndrome (BCS), given its relevance to youths who kill their abusive parents. Parallels between battered woman's syndrome (BWS) and BCS were examined. Judicial and legislative responses to battered children who kill parents were reviewed. In addition, legislation enacted and judicial decisions relevant to battered person syndrome (BPS) were discussed so that readers would be aware that in recent years, some states have taken a broader approach and have statutorily allowed the admissibility of abuse and its effects. The synthesis of statutory and case law revealed, however, that despite their similarities, BCS, unlike BWS, has not been widely recognized.

Clemency, although rare, can provide a safety valve for adolescent parricide offenders who were not permitted to introduce evidence of BCS during their trial. The court's exclusion of testimony by an MHP can seriously impact the ability of jurors to understand the defendant's mindset at the time of the killing. One case in which a battered child was granted clemency illustrated how central the role of the MHP can be in evaluating issues related to the defendant's culpability.

The chapter concluded with a review of other mental health status defenses, most notably the insanity defense. Adult parricide offenders are more likely to be found not guilty by reason of insanity (NGRI) than adolescents. NGRI judgments are more common among adult parricide offenders than younger parricide offenders because adults who kill parents are more likely than their adolescent counterparts to have a documented history of severe mental illness and to be delusional at the time of the killing.

The next chapter discusses the importance of a thorough clinical assessment in understanding why an individual kills his or her parent. This discussion lays the foundation for the clinical case studies that follow. These cases focus on youths whom I evaluated who fit the profiles of the severely abused child, the severely mentally ill child, and the dangerously antisocial child. A case study is also presented that shows how drugs and anger can lead to lethal violence.

PART TWO

CASE STUDIES

8 Forensic Assessment of Parricide Offenders

Understanding why a particular youth killed a parent involves knowledge of the adolescent, his or her family, and the home environment. Clinical interviews with defendants are a critical source of information. The semi-structured interview that I conduct typically lasts five to eight hours and includes some testing. It is designed to assess the level of personality development of each adolescent parricide offender. Its format also permits the exploration of the youth's perceptions of the killing, processing through the justice system, and sentencing. In addition, the interview examines other areas of importance related to the youth's social history, including family relationships, school, work, friends, dating and sexual history, drug and alcohol involvement, activities, group and gang involvement, music/movie/videogame preferences, physical and mental health history, self-perceptions and values, coping skills and affectivity, prior delinquent activity, and future orientation.

Each interview provides extensive data on the adolescents' perceptions of themselves, others, and the world around them, as well as on their characteristic ways of responding to events. The information provided by adolescent parricide offenders (APOs) across myriad content areas makes it possible for one to understand them, evaluate the plausibility of the youths' statements about the killings, unravel the dynamics behind the murders, and make recommendations regarding the disposition of their cases.

Attorneys are often present when I first meet with defendants. At the beginning of the interview, I stress the importance of being honest and forthcoming. I explain that for me, it is like putting a puzzle together. Things that they might see as unimportant or "bad" might be just the pieces of the puzzle that put it all together. Defense attorneys typically join me in emphasizing to their clients that their credibility is critical, even in cases when I am evaluating the defendant at the request of the prosecutor. My experience is that most defendants are generally honest. In cases in which they minimize their involvement, it is frequently a reflection of their personality development, as discussed below.

Given the high stakes defendants face in homicide cases, however, corroboration is essential. It is important that a mental health professional verify data obtained from the APO during the clinical interview. Collateral sources of information are often invaluable aids in verifying information, evaluating competing theories, determining the credibility of the youth, and coming to a conclusion regarding the motivation behind the homicide. Sources include police reports, offender statements to law enforcement officers and defense counsel, autopsies, and witness depositions, as well as the offender's previous medical and mental health records, school records, and previous social services investigations.

Valuable corroborative sources often include clinical interviews with family members, friends, and neighbors and, on occasion, consultations with professionals who have had previous or ongoing contact with the youth. These might include mental health practitioners, school teachers, social services staff, or law enforcement personnel. In addition, psychological and neuropsychological testing of the defendant can provide important corroborative data and should be administered by forensic psychologists or other qualified mental health professionals to every adolescent charged with homicide. On occasion, a neurological assessment by a neurologist also might be indicated.[1]

I usually spend 30 to 50 hours when I evaluate an adolescent charged with homicide. This time includes that spent reviewing pertinent case materials, preferably before meeting the youth; conducting a clinical evaluation of the defendant; doing collateral interviews with family members and other pertinent parties; consulting with attorneys and, on occasion, other experts; analyzing and synthesizing clinical and test data; addressing the motivational dynamics behind the crime; and preparing a detailed report.

My reports are very comprehensive (often 30 pages or more) and contain the foundation for my conclusions. Table 8-1 contains the index of a report I recently completed. The case studies presented in Chapters 9–13 are based on forensic reports prepared for defense counsel. Readers who are interested in more detailed information about the specific components of my assessments of homicide offenders are directed to Chapter 4 of *Young Killers.*[2]

The Importance of a Thorough Assessment by a Mental Health Professional

Thorough assessment in each case involving an APO is critical regardless of the factual situation. It should not be abbreviated when severe abuse is apparent, because, as we have seen, severe abuse is often found in the backgrounds of dangerously antisocial individuals. Severe childhood maltreatment, for example, has been noted in the backgrounds of many destructive individuals, including Charles Manson[3] and several serial killers.[4] I refer to these individuals as nihilistic killers because they seem to enjoy acts of destructiveness.[5]

Interestingly, the first victims of some serial killers were family members. Henry Lee Lucas, for example, was arrested for killing his mother when he was 23 years old.[6] After serving 14 years in prison and in a mental hospital, he was released and claimed to have spent the next several years killing hundreds of people across the United States with his accomplice Ottis Toole.[7] Edmund Kemper, whose last victims included his mother, killed his grandparents when he was 15 years old. Soon after being released from a psychiatric hospital, he abducted and killed six college women.[8]

TABLE 8-1 Sample index of one of Dr. Heide's forensic evaluations

KATHLEEN M. HEIDE, Ph.D.

Center for Mental Health Education,

Assessment and Therapy

806 W. DeLeon Street, Tampa, Florida 33606

phone 813–250–0224   fax 813–225–2577

ASSESSMENT OF PARRICIDE OFFENDER—PRIVILEGED AND CONFIDENTIAL

CASE:	State Public Defender
DATE OF BIRTH:	XXXXXXXXXXXX
DATE OF OFFENSE:	XXXXXXXXXXXX
AGE/ OFFENSE:	16 years 1 month
DATE OF EVALUATION:	XXXXXXXXXXXX
AGE/EVALUATION:	16 years 7 months
DATE OF REPORT:	XXXXXXXXXXXX
EXAMINER:	Kathleen M. Heide, Ph.D.
REPORT PREPARED FOR:	XXXXXXXXXXXXX

INDEX TO REPORT

Another word of caution is needed regarding youths who meet the diagnostic criteria for a conduct disorder. This diagnosis should not be taken as dispositive proof that an adolescent is dangerously antisocial. Some youths who are abused act out their distress and might break the law. The important consideration is what motivated the youth to kill. If the youth is basically prosocial and killed because he or she was terrified or desperate to end unrelenting abuse, past minor legal transgressions (e.g., shoplifting, burglary) can be addressed in treatment. It is quite likely in these cases that minor delinquent acts were maladaptive coping strategies adopted by the youth in order to deal with internal distress.

In contrast, youths who are conduct-disordered *and* seem to lack concern for others should be examined closely. Determination of whether the youth scores high on indicators of psychopathy, particularly factor 1, is essential. Factor 1 assesses affective and interpersonal components of a person's personality.[9] The prognosis for an APO, for example, who seems to be manipulative, to lie easily, to be callous, and to lack empathy for others should be considered guarded, as this individual has characteristics that suggest he might be a danger to society.

It is important to note in addition that a diagnosis of psychosis in and of itself is insufficiently explanatory when attempting to understand the youth and his motivation for killing a family member. At the very least, some determination must be made about whether the severely mentally ill parricide offender's communications, the content of his or her delusions and hallucinations, and/or his or her behavior are indicative of an individual who has embraced an antisocial lifestyle, such as the case described by McCully in Chapter 3. It is critically important to determine whether the youth's destructive acts are rooted in his character. Identification of a psychopathic structure could serve as a warning signal that a particular youth poses an increased risk to society. Youths with psychopathic or nihilistic traits warrant incapacitation, whether in a mental hospital or in a correctional facility, unless and until this motivational pattern is eradicated.

THE NIHILISTIC KILLER

In every evaluation, I am on the alert for individuals whose acts of destruction appear to be rooted in their character. Known as nihilistic killers, these murderers represent a grave risk to society. They are individuals who intend to kill and who derive pleasure from watching others suffer.[10] This pattern categorizes the adult serial murderer, who kills many victims over time for no apparent reason other than satisfaction and release of tension.[11]

In the course of the 30 years over which I have been evaluating adolescents charged with murder, I have encountered a few adolescents who fit this nihilistic pattern; they truly seemed to enjoy telling me about their murderous activities. These youths were typically charged with killing strangers. These adolescents laughed heartily as they recounted the homicidal events and said that they experienced the victim's dying gestures as "funny." My clinical experiences with young killers have indicated that the best source of data in uncovering this destructive pattern, however, was not typically the adolescents' descriptions of their homicidal activities. Many youths were understandably guarded in their accounts of the murders. As a result of the depth of my clinical interviews and the broad array of topics explored, unguarded remarks were sometimes made about seemingly "innocuous" material, and these provided invaluable data regarding sadistic and destructive character traits. These content areas included girlfriends, pets, activities, careers, and movie and music preferences.[12]

Youths with nihilistic traits would often become animated as they related incidents in which they scared others by catching them off guard, intimidated others through their persona, beat others badly, and destroyed other living things, such as dogs, cats, and lizards. Calvin, an adolescent who was responsible for multiple killings, said that he would like to be a mortician when he got older because he found death "funny sometimes and just interesting." He recalled really enjoying a movie in which people died from doing "stupid things," such as bungee jumping. The idea of being a mortician was appealing to Calvin because, he explained, they make a lot of money, people are always dying, and he has always been fascinated by death. Calvin took delight in talking about violent music and was heavily into "gangsta rap." When asked, he easily described each of the rap singers/groups to which he reported listening. Spice 1 was about "killing a lot of people." MC8 was about "killing, making money, fucking whores, and shooting." 8Ball & MJG rapped about "a lot of robbing." Scarface and Geto Boys sang about "killing." When asked why he killed a clerk, who offered no resistance, soon after entering a convenience store, Calvin responded with the lyrics of one of the songs. He replied that he had gotten "trigga happy."

The question of whether an APO enjoyed acts of destructiveness was a concern in the case of Daniel Culbreath (Chapter 12). It was also one I faced in the case of Scott Anders (Chapter 7). Recall that Scott Anders, at age 15, killed his father. Initially, facts suggested that Scott killed his father in self-defense. He was charged with first-degree murder after telling police that he fired the second shot, as his father lay on the floor dying, to end his dad's suffering. Scott's statements were consistent with earlier remarks he had made about killing animals for food. In addition, his confession left doubt as to whether he consciously planned to kill his father when he fired the second shot, because it appeared that he experienced dissociation during the homicidal incident.

Notwithstanding these data, I was concerned because Scott had been arrested previously for threatening a girl with whom he had run away and had been charged with attempted rape. When asked, Scott admitted to me that he had been "talking about raping her, cutting her pants off, slashing her with a razor blade." He explained that he was angry because she had gotten him into trouble and he had "a lot of pressure" on him at the time. Scott maintained that he did not touch the girl and would not have carried out this behavior because he wasn't "that kind of person." Scott said that this incident was the only time that he scared anybody, and he felt sorry about it because "it wasn't the right thing to do" and "it was stupid."

In light of the boy's previous episode of violent behavior, it was particularly important to ascertain whether Scott might have nihilistic traits. What clearly emerged across various content areas were indications of life-enhancing qualities rather than destructive forces. One theme that Scott mentioned several times was the importance of love to him in his current and future relationships. Scott did not approve of scaring people, another indicator that he did not derive pleasure from exercising sadistic control over others. The dialogue about kindness quoted below occurred toward the end of the clinical evaluation. It provided convincing evidence, when examined in light of material presented throughout the entire four-and-a-half-hour period, that Scott was not a nihilistic killer.[13]

Heide: How would you treat girls?

Scott: Oh, I treat 'em nicely.

Heide: Would you? What does nicely mean?

Scott: I'd treat 'em like a regular human bein'. Treat 'em kind, you know. Everybody needs to be kind. Damn sure wouldn't call her nothin'. I wouldn't hit 'em.

Heide: OK. Why is kindness so important?

Scott: 'Cause everybody likes kindness.

Heide: OK.

Scott: Life is supposed to be kindness.

Heide: Um hmmm.

Scott: Animals, you know.

Heide: Sorry?

Scott: You know little animals, you know?

Heide: Yeah.

Scott: They kind. You could be an animal, you know. We are animals.

Heide: Yeah.

Scott: Really, we are.

Heide: OK.

Scott: You know, we can make people go out there and kill rats and stuff like that. But what if you was a rat? You want somebody tryin' killin' you? You know, rats gotta live. He gotta eat.

Heide: Uh hmmm.

Scott: And they gotta raise little babies.

Heide: Yeah. OK.

Scott: It's stupid to call it a rat, but, you know, look at it—look at it that way, you know. Everybody say, "Ah, you're crazy. A rat's a rat. Kill 'em." I ain't gonna kill no rat.

Heide: Yeah. I think that makes sense to me.

Scott: This is the way I feel about it.

Heide: Uh, that's good.

Scott: Now here I'm telling somebody I feel sorry for all the rats and everybody, and I already killed somebody myself.

Heide: OK.

Scott: Can't bring him back so what can I do? Nothin' I can do. Only thing I can do is try to live right. Start all over.

PERSONALITY ASSESSMENT

An assessment of the adolescent's personality or ego development is as essential as obtaining a complete social history. Personality assessment reveals how an individual makes sense of the world. In addition to providing insight into the meaning of behavior, knowing the youth's personality level can help in determining the credibility of his or her statements. It is also critical when evaluating issues related to the likelihood of continued criminal behavior and in charting treatment strategies.[14]

In addition to standardized personality tests, such as the Minnesota Multiphasic Personality Inventory (MMPI 2)or the Personality Assessment Inventory(PAI),[15] several frameworks with which to measure personality or ego development currently exist.[16] The youths whose stories are told in the clinical sections were classified according to Interpersonal Level of Maturity Theory (I-Level). This theory of personality development originated with a group of psychology students in Berkeley, California, in the early 1950s. It has its underpinnings in child development, psychoanalytic theory, Lewinian theory, phenomenological theory, and social perception.[17] Over the past 50 years, it has been widely researched and used with both juvenile and adult offender populations for treatment and management purposes.[18]

I-Level classifies people into one of seven categories according to how complexly they perceive themselves, others, and their environment. The theory postulates that individuals progress from level 1 to higher levels as they resolve problems encountered at the respective levels. Very few individuals, if any, reach the ideal of social maturity associated with the highest level, 7. If the developing child is presented with a very stressful or threatening experience, he or she might resist change and make desperate attempts to remain at his or her existing level of development because it appears safer than advancing to the next level.[19]

In maintaining that individuals are accountable for their actions, the criminal justice system assumes that defendants are at level 4 or higher. The maturity levels that have been found in offender populations range from level 2 to level 5.[20] In a population of more than 1,000 delinquents ranging in age from 11 to 19 years, 95% were classified as perceiving at level 3 (31%) or level 4 (64%).[21] Among the adolescent murderers whom I have assessed, about 40% to 45% perceive at level 3, and about 50% perceive at level 4. Very few are at level 5.[22] Salient dimensions of these four levels are depicted in Table 8-2 and discussed briefly below.[23]

Most people will advance to at least level 3, which is considered normal development for toddlers and prepubescent children. Research has indicted that by 14 years of age, 66% to 75% of youths will have moved beyond this level.[24] Adolescents older than

Table 8-2 Salient dimensions of I-levels 2 through 5

Level	Dimensions
2	Typical of very young children.
	Others are viewed in terms of whether or not others give them what they want.
	Do not know how to predict or influence the behavior of others.
3	Typical of young children.
	They know that their behaviors affect the responses they get from others.
	They see people in stereotypic ways and as objects to be manipulated.
	They look for simple formulas to get others to give them what they want.
	Their planning is short-term.
4	Typical of youths by the time they enter their teenage years.
	They have a set of internalized values.
	They see themselves as accountable for their behavior.
	They are aware that they have choices.
	They tend to be rigid about codes of correct behavior.
	They are aware of feelings and motives in themselves and others.
	They can enter into a reciprocal relationship with another.
	They are capable of feeling remorse.
	They are often concerned with their own uniqueness.
5	Not typical in offender populations.
	They continue to see themselves as accountable for their behavior.
	They are less rigid in their lives and less judgmental towards others.
	They can understand viewpoints different from their own.
	They can truly empathize with people whose lives are different from their own.
	They can play different roles (e.g., mother, employer, sorority sister, graduate student), but may experience role conflict.

Source: Heide, 1999. Reprinted with permission from Sage Publications.

age 14 who perceive at level 3 are more likely to get into legal trouble than are higher maturity adolescents in the same age range.[25]

Persons classified at level 3 are primarily concerned with identifying who the powerful people are in any given situation. They do not yet appreciate that other people have needs and feelings different from their own. Instead, they see others in stereotypic ways. These individuals try to get their needs met by figuring out what formulas to use to get what they want from others. They might conform to the demands of whoever has the power at the moment or attempt to control others through attack or intimidation. They frequently deny that they have strong feelings about things or deep emotional involvements. They do not feel guilty or perceive a need to make amends for their misbehavior because they typically perceive that they have not done anything wrong. They basically see others as objects to be manipulated.[26]

Individuals who advance to level 4 incorporate the values of "the big people," typically their parents and teachers, and want to be like them. Unlike individuals at earlier stages, they are able to evaluate their behavior and others' actions in relation to an internalized set of standards. They have some perception of how their needs and those of others influence their behavior. They can empathize with people whom they perceive as like themselves. They recognize that they have choices and might experience guilt when they fail to behave according to their values. Those who perceive at this level want to make something of themselves and to be recognized by those they admire for their ideals or interests, their potentialities or accomplishments. Individuals at this level have the ability to make long-range plans and to delay their response to immediate stimuli. They are capable of entering into a reciprocal relationship with another person whose needs, feelings, ideals, or standards of behavior are similar to their own.[27]

Persons at level 5 are increasingly aware of different ways of behaviorally coping with events. They begin to distinguish roles for themselves and others that are appropriate for different occasions. Although individuals at this level might wonder which of the roles is "the real me" on occasion, they are aware of continuity in their own and others' lives. Individuals classified at level 5 are able to appreciate people who are different from them and to understand what they do and how they feel. They are capable of empathizing with others, including people different from them, because they can compare their impressions of events and activities with those of others.[28]

CLINICAL PORTRAITS OF YOUTHS WHO KILL PARENTS

Case studies of APOs are presented in the next five chapters. These include clinical portraits of youths who were diagnosed as severely abused, severely mentally ill, or dangerously antisocial. I also discuss one case in which drugs ignited deep-seated anger to the point of homicidal explosion.

The first two cases are representative of the first type of parricide offender, the *severely abused parricide offender*. Patty Smith, a low maturity offender, killed her father in a desperate move to end abuse. Peter Jones, a high maturity offender, killed his father because he was terrified that his father was going to kill him. Although the prognosis was better for Peter, follow-up data indicated that Patty made a successful adjustment to society, whereas Peter did not. The reasons for the success of Patty and the failure of Peter are identified in these chapters.

The third case, that of James Holt, involves a high maturity offender who was recognized by the court as a *severely mentally ill parricide offender* after his conviction for the murders of his mother and father. Despite this judicial finding, the judge ordered that the youth be sentenced to adult prison for life. Although treatment was ordered by the court, the department of corrections did not provide it. This young man was a very bright and talented individual at the time of his conviction, and has remained so. For nearly three decades, he has steadfastly maintained his innocence with respect to the deaths of his parents. James could have been helped if effective and meaningful intervention had been provided. From the perspective of James, ironically, he became "the outlaw" the criminal justice and correctional staff had destined him to be.

Daniel Culbreath, another low maturity youth, is the subject of the fourth case study presented. When Daniel's parents were found murdered, his friends knew immediately who was responsible. Daniel repeatedly had talked about killing his parents. Daniel derived a sense of pleasure from and felt empowered by his parricidal thoughts. He fit the profile of the *dangerously antisocial parricide offender* at the time of the evaluation. When I met with him years later, he seemed less of a risk, although I would rate his prognosis at the time of the follow-up interview as guarded.

The last subject, Ben Simpson, is another low maturity youth. Ben is representative of several youths I have evaluated who aggressed against their parents when their parents started to enforce limits on the adolescents' behavior. As we shall see in the next section, in Ben's case, unlike in the four cases highlighted above, there was no evidence of parental abuse. Ben was over-indulged by his parents. As a result, he did not have the frustration tolerance needed in order to cope when his parents finally started setting boundaries. His anger, when fueled by alcohol and drug intoxication, led to an explosion of homicidal rage that left his father dead and his mother seriously injured.

Before moving to these clinical chapters, readers are reminded that several cases of male APOs are presented in preceding chapters. Two cases of girls who killed parents also have been presented. These included Cassie Sparkman, who killed her stepmother (Chapter 1), and Christine Johnson, who killed her mother (Chapter 3.) Cassie fit the profile of a *dangerously antisocial parricide offender*; Chrissy was categorized as a *severely abused parricide offender*.

Case Studies in Perspective

The clinical case history approach has some limitations as a research method.[29] The studies are typically retrospective. Therefore, the data on which interpretations are based might be inaccurate. This potential limitation can be resolved to some extent by relying on primary sources, corroborative data, and collateral sources, as I have done in my evaluations.

Another potential drawback is that each case history is unique and cannot be replicated. It is unknown to what extent the findings in a particular case study can be generalized to others in the population. For example, in the case histories of the two adolescents classified as severely abused parricide offenders, severe child maltreatment was documented, but to what extent severe abuse and neglect exists in the histories of adolescents who do not kill their parents is unknown because not all cases of child maltreatment are reported. In addition, available data do not classify reported cases by degree of severity. As a result, causation cannot be determined with this method. The case study method investigates only individuals who have a particular problem or fall into a particular category and does not focus on those who do not.[30]

The clinical case study, however, has several advantages. It involves studying actual people with real issues or difficulties and, unlike laboratory experiments, is not contrived or artificial. In addition, the clinical case history can investigate phenomena that are so rare that, as in the case of individuals who kill their parents, it is unlikely that they could be studied ethically or practically using any other standard method of research. Clinical case studies are often instrumental in generating hypotheses about the causes of particular problems and in suggesting solutions. On occasion, case studies can also be helpful in providing confirming or disconfirming evidence with regard to a prevailing hypothesis.[31] As illustrated in this book, they can help elucidate pathways to homicide by identifying parricide offender types.

Table 8-3 lists characteristics of different parricide offender types based on individuals I have evaluated, cases on which I have consulted, and my knowledge of the literature. The first column contains criteria *required* in order to make the parricide offender type designation. The second column, similar to *DSM-IV*, includes criteria that are *frequently associated* with this type but are not considered essential to making the classification.[32] The third column contains criteria that *might be* present. Note that the crossover in some associated and possible features (columns 2 and 3) is similar to the reporting features in *DSM-IV*. As in any heuristic classification system, additional empirical verification is needed and desired.

Table 8-3 Characteristics of parricide offender types

Parricide Offender Type	Features		
	Essential/ Required	*Associated/ Frequent*	*Possibly Present*
SEVERELY ABUSED			
Killed out of terror and/or desperation	X		
Killed to protect self or others	X		
Intentional killing			X
Long-standing history of severe abuse (physical, sexual, verbal, psychological)	X		
Neglect present (physical, medical, emotional)		X	
Emotional incest		X	
Victim was drinker and/or substance abuser		X	
Adolescent was isolated/had few outlets		X	
Attempts to get help failed		X	
Attempts to run away		X	
Suicidal thoughts and/or attempts prior to killing		X	

(continued)

Table 8-3 (Continued)

Parricide Offender Type	Features		
	Essential/ Required	Associated/ Frequent	Possibly Present
Family situation became increasingly intolerable		X	
Adolescent feels trapped		X	
Inability to cope led to loss of control		X	
Criminally unsophisticated		X	
Dissociation during homicide		X	
Victim's death initially perceived as a relief		X	
Post-traumatic stress disorder diagnosis		X	
Depression diagnosis		X	
Conduct disorder diagnosis			X
SEVERELY MENTALLY ILL			
Defendant is severely mentally ill	X		
Diagnosis of schizophrenia or other disorder along schizophrenic spectrum		X	
Delusions or hallucinations		X	
Bizarre behavior		X	
Killed as a result of mental illness	X		
Intentional killing			X
Significant history of mental illness		X	
History of severe abuse (physical, sexual, verbal, psychological)			X
Neglect present (physical, medical, emotional)			X
Emotional incest			X
Victim was drinker and/or substance abuser			X
Dissociation during homicide			X
Intoxicated during homicide			X
Post-parricide suicidal behavior		X	
DANGEROUSLY ANTISOCIAL			
Killed to serve selfish purpose	X		
Intentional killing	X		
History of defiant behavior	X		
History of antisocial behavior		X	
Buying spree after killing		X	
History of severe abuse (physical, sexual, verbal, psychological)			X

(continued)

Table 8-3 (Continued)

Parricide Offender Type	Features		
	Essential/ Required	Associated/ Frequent	Possibly Present
Neglect present (physical, medical, emotional)		X	
Emotional incest			X
Over-indulgent or lax parents		X	
Victim was drinker and/or substance abuser			X
Conduct disorder diagnosis		X	
Antisocial personality disorder diagnosis		X	
Psychopath diagnosis			X
Nihilistic killer			X
POSSIBLE ADDITIONAL PARRICIDE OFFENDER TYPE			
Killed out of rage	X		
Intoxicated during homicide		X	
History of antisocial behavior			X
Poor impulse control		X	
Dissociation during homicide			X
Diagnosis of conduct disorder			X
Diagnosis of antisocial personality disorder			X

SUMMARY AND CONCLUDING REMARKS

This chapter discussed the importance of a thorough evaluation by a mental health professional of individuals charged with killing a parent. Areas I explore in a clinical interview were noted. The need for corroborative sources was emphasized, and necessary components of an evaluation were identified. These included an assessment of the individual's level of personality development. The main tenets and levels of a personality theory used widely in the classification of offenders, Interpersonal Level of Maturity Theory, were presented. This theory is very helpful when one is attempting to understand the dynamics that led an individual to engage in violence, determine the credibility of the person's statements, and chart appropriate intervention strategies. Discussion focused on the importance of identifying an individual whose destructiveness is characterologically based; this individual was referred to as the nihilistic killer.

The advantages and disadvantages of case studies were summarized in this chapter. The value of evaluating many parricide offenders is that patterns become discernible and clinical types are identifiable, as presented in Chapter 1. Clinical portraits of five adolescents who killed parents are presented in the next five chapters. Four of these case studies involve boys; the remaining case involves a female adolescent parricide offender who killed her father.

9 Patty Smith
No Way Out but Murder

Patricia Smith, a 17-year-old White girl from a middle-class background, was arrested about 32 hours after killing her father. Police charged her with first-degree murder. Within 24 hours police also arrested four of Patty's friends, ages 17 and 18, and charged them with being accessories after the fact. Three—Mary, Tom, and Jim— were charged with disposing of evidence and withholding knowledge of the crime; the fourth, Joe, was accused of lying to police to provide an alibi for Patty.

Investigation by the police and statements made by Patty and her codefendants yielded the following sequence of events. Patty was having difficulty with her father. At one point the idea of killing him occurred as a possible solution, and she asked her friends, "Who would be stupid enough to shoot my father?" Mary said that she would, and Tom and Jim offered to dispose of the body and other evidence.

Mary stayed over at Patty's home and, in the middle of the night, as planned, went into the victim's bedroom with a handgun, only to emerge a few minutes later to tell Patty that she could not shoot the victim. Patty said that she would do it herself, but her first attempt was unsuccessful because the handgun jammed. She quickly secured another handgun and shot the victim in the head at about 4:00 A.M. on Saturday morning as he lay sleeping.

After the shooting, the girls went to Tom's trailer and then to a park in search of other friends. There they located Jim, Joe, and another youth, Curtis, and invited these boys back to Patty's house to verify that the victim was actually dead. After observing the body, Curtis and Joe wanted to go back to the park. While Patty was driving them back, Jim and Mary remained behind, showered, and had sex in Patty's bedroom while Mr. Smith lay dead in his bedroom.

When Patty returned (it was still morning), Jim fixed pizza and drinks for the three of them, and Patty made three phone calls. She told her father's secretary, Joy, that she had gotten in a fight with her father and he had left. Patty asked Joy to handle the payroll and said she would come by the office later to pick up her car and her driver's license, which her father had taken away from her recently as a disciplinary measure. Patty called the real estate agent who was handling the sale listing of her house next because Patty did not want the house to be shown. Finally, she called her mother, who had been divorced from Mr. Smith for several years and lived about a thousand miles away. Patty told her mother that her father had left following a fight with her and that she was "O.K." Jim also assured Mrs. Smith that he would take care of Patty.

The three retrieved the house key from the realty company and then went to Tom's trailer. Tom accompanied Patty, Mary, and Jim to Mr. Smith's office. Within a few minutes the four drove off in Mr. Smith's two cars. The youths gassed up the cars and spent Saturday afternoon picking up or checking on friends and driving around. They returned to Patty's neighborhood to discover that it was swarming with police. As evening passed into night, Patty took refuge in Tom's trailer, leaving only to drop Mary and another girl off at a party. When Mary returned, Jim advised Patty to take the back roads out of the neighborhood and to go to a nearby city. He gave her the phone number of a pay phone on the corner and told her when to call in. Jim and Tom disposed of Mr. Smith's wallet, the murder weapon, and the empty casings.

Patty and Mary checked into a motel in the city and made a series of phone calls to friends between 11:00 P.M. and 3:00 A.M., when they went to bed. The following morning, the girls ordered room service, and Patty made a few more calls to friends to see what was happening back home. Patty was talking on the phone when the police knocked on the door.

The grand jury indicted Patty as an adult on first-degree murder charges. Two months after the indictment, the assistant state attorney prosecuting the case announced the State's intention to seek the death penalty. (Executing juveniles was constitutional in the United States at that time.) About three and a half months after the five youths were arrested, the state prosecutor filed new charges of conspiracy to commit first-degree murder against Mary. Previously Mary had faced a maximum sentence of five years for being an accessory after the fact, with state guidelines calling for a "non-state prison" penalty, but she now faced a maximum of 35 years including prison time. At the same time that the State was upgrading her charges, the three boys, who had also been formally charged as accessories to the murder, were given the opportunity to testify in Patty Smith's murder trial in exchange for one- to three-year probation terms to be decided by the judge after the trial. The boys accepted the State's proposal. One month before Patty's trial, Mary agreed to testify against her in return for the State's recommending that she serve only one year of prison time. I was retained by defense counsel as a confidential defense expert to evaluate the defendant's mental status at the time of the shooting and to investigate the motivational dynamics behind the killing.

THE CLINICAL EVALUATION

The assessment of Patty Smith was based on clinical interviews with the defendant and her mother, plus a review of hundreds of pages of pertinent materials. My seven-hour interview of the adolescent occurred over the course of two consecutive evenings. It was almost five months after the homicide when I interviewed Patty in private in the adult women's jail. Within a week of examining Patty, I spent five hours interviewing her mother.

Before speaking with Patty, I studied numerous police incident reports and supplemental investigation reports containing police interviews with the codefendants and 35 other individuals. These 35 people included Patty's friends and classmates and a few of their parents, relatives of Mr. and Mrs. Smith, Mr. Smith's employees, staff at the realty company, one of Mr. Smith's former girlfriends, service personnel who had contact with the youths after the homicide, the newspaper delivery girl, bank personnel, an employee of the diet center where Patty was enrolled, a man who had recently sold Mr. Smith a camper, two neighbors, and a psychic who advised Mr. Smith about financial affairs.

In addition to police reports, I examined statements Patty had made to jail deputies and defense counsel staff and defense notes from interviews with six of Patty's relatives, two of her classmates, and two former neighbors. I also perused her medical records, the psychological self-report data collected by the weight management center, and a report of a child abuse incident dated approximately one year before the homicide.

Prior to the trial, I was able to review photographs and correspondence between Patty and her mother dating from both before and after the homicide; correspondence between Mr. and Mrs. Smith; and defense counsel notes from interviews with six individuals who had worked for Mr. Smith. Before drawing final conclusions and making recommendations, I reviewed Patty's high school records, Mrs. Smith's medical records, and depositions from Patty's four codefendants.

BEHAVIORAL OBSERVATIONS

Patty was about 5'6" tall and somewhere between 50 pounds (her estimate) and 100 pounds overweight and had a severe case of acne at the time of the assessment interview. She had a speech impediment that made her a little difficult to understand at times and which appeared to cause her mild discomfort. The girl's answers to questions showed that her long-term and short-term memory processes were good. There was no evidence of hallucinations or delusions.

Patty was alert throughout the two evenings and took the interview seriously. Her concentration was generally good. She was, however, occasionally distracted by passersby, voices outside, ants crawling on her towel, and the need to call her mother. Patty gave the impression that interviews by her attorney, a psychologist, and myself were an imposition.

Patty appeared fairly relaxed throughout the interviews. Rapport was easily and quickly established, and she related in a warm and trusting way. Her eye contact was typically very good, and her mood generally was good throughout the interviews. At times, however, she seemed angry, particularly when describing her father and her home situation.

Patty made some attempt to answer every question that was asked. She was reluctant to discuss abuse by her father at length, and her discomfort increased when questions focused on determining whether she had been sexually abused.

PERSONALITY DEVELOPMENT

Patty perceived at I-level 3, which is relatively low on the continuum of personality development. Her low level of development was a critical factor in understanding her motivation in this case. Patty thought very concretely and in terms of external dimensions, such as places, events, and surface characteristics. Her self-definition was restricted, and her self-esteem low. She was relatively unaware of the role that such internal dimensions as needs, feelings, and motives played in her life and in the lives of others. She had little motivation to integrate, interpret, or resolve information about herself and others and was unable to empathize with others. Patty was not capable of long-term planning.

Patty did not see herself as really responsible for her behavior. She had not internalized a set of values that she could use to evaluate her behavior. Because she did not see herself as having choices, she did not typically feel guilt or remorse for her behavior. She was essentially concerned with power fields, viewing herself and others in relation to who had power, and searching for rules, formulas, and techniques that she could use to get what she wanted. For example, she saw her father as a very powerful man. She believed that he had an "in" with the police and could influence other people and institutions in the community.

Among level 3 individuals, there are three behavioral subtypes.[1] Patty's behavioral response was that of the *passive conformist* (*Cfm*). She saw herself as inferior to others and had a high need for social approval. She tended to overestimate the power of others, conforming to people who made explicit demands of her. Patty described herself in conventional, socially desirable terms and saw her involvement in antisocial behavior as the result of peer pressure, not as acceptable behavior. She was responsive to adults and authority figures and wanted to do right. The range of her emotions was restricted to anger, sadness, hurt, and fear; the relationship of her emotions to her behavior was minimized.

RELEVANT SOCIAL HISTORY

The following information was reported by the defendant. I obtained the additional information and corroborative data reported later in this chapter from Patty's mother.

Family Constellation

Patty was the only child born to John Smith and his second wife, Theresa Baxter Smith. Mr. Smith had five children from his first marriage. Patty's half-siblings (one brother and four sisters) ranged in age from about 33 to 37 at the time of the patricide. Patty was not close to any of them and had very negative feelings for all except the youngest, Joan, who apparently made some effort to keep in touch with Patty before the homicide.

When Patty was a young child, her half-brother, Harold, lived with her and her parents. She described Harold as just like her father: physically and psychologically abusive to her mother. Patty believed that all her half-siblings were aware of the spouse abuse.

Patty's memory for dates was fuzzy. She described living in the Midwest until she moved to the South. She thought that her parents might have separated when she was in the sixth grade (she was about 11 or 12) and gotten divorced when she was in the seventh grade (12 or 13). She remembered that her father went to another state for about two months and that he moved out in order to establish a residence with Judith Thompson, a woman he met while away. After Mr. Smith moved out, Patty lived with her mother in the Smiths' beautiful home with a pool until Mr. Smith stopped paying the mortgage, at which point they moved to "a poor apartment." They remained there until the summer between Patty's eighth and ninth grade years, when Mrs. Smith moved to one of the Mid-Atlantic states. Patty spent about a month of that summer with Mr. Smith, returned to her mother's residence to get her belongings, and moved back south to live with her father and his girlfriend.

Patty explained that she decided to leave her mother's residence because her mother had already had open-heart surgery once and was "due to have a second one with no chance of coming out of it." She moved in with her father to give her mother more time to live. Patty said, "In your mind and different people talking to you, raising a teenager would give her too much trouble, too much stress, maybe you could add more time to her life."

Patty remained with her father for about two and a half years before she killed him. Judith Thompson left Mr. Smith about 16 months before the homicide. Although Patty and Judith did not get along, her home life got worse when Judith left. Patty had to do the cooking, and Mr. Smith blamed Patty for Judith's leaving and "took it out on [her]." Patty reported that her father sexually assaulted her, drank more, and got more into one-night stands with women after Judith's departure.

Despite her father's abuse, Patty did not return to her mother because he had threatened to kill them both if she did. She had not even told her mother about the abuse because she believed her father's claim that such news would kill the sickly woman. She also worried that her mother might not believe her.

School History

Patty liked school and her teachers and had experienced problems with only a few. When Patty was in the tenth and eleventh grades, almost all her teachers were male, and she claimed that she could learn better from them because they were stricter. She said she got along fine with "the other kids."

Patty reported that her grades were B's and A's "if I tried" and tended to go down when there were problems at home. She claimed that she got F's in physical education because she did everything to get out of it. She did not like wearing shorts because she had bruises on her legs. She did not tell the defense attorney appointed to represent her after the killing "the truth" about her reason for avoiding physical education because she found it hard to talk to him; the tone of his voice made her think he did not believe her at times.

Patty's statements suggested extensive extracurricular involvement. She was the basketball manager for both the junior varsity and the varsity teams for both boys and girls. As the basketball manager, she had two assistant managers working with her. In addition, Patty was the head track manager, with 10 assistant managers below her. Her four codefendants were all assistant managers.

Patty noted that before eleventh grade she was rarely in trouble. She was suspended for three days in ninth grade for forging her teacher's name on a pass and in tenth grade for skipping school. In eleventh grade she stopped going to homeroom and regularly skipped her astronomy class.

Work History

Patty worked for about three months at her father's water treatment plant. As a phone solicitor, she worked from after school until about 9:00 P.M. and received minimum wage and a bonus when she "sold" a free water test. The work was unpleasant because her father would bring their personal life into the office. He would not allow her to work at another job; it was "his office or nothing."

Alcohol and Drug Involvement

Patty stated that she did not drink often, "maybe twice a year," and had never been drunk. She was about 14 or 15 when she first tried alcohol, at a party she gave in her mother's absence. She denied any drug usage.

Friends

Throughout the interview, Patty defined scores of people as her friends and did not discriminate between friends and acquaintances. She saw her codefendants Mary, Tom, and Jim as the "wrong crowd." When Patty started hanging around with them in eleventh grade, she started skipping school and getting into trouble. Patty described Jim and Mary as leaders; Tom also was a leader, but "in some cases, he can be a follower." She saw herself and Joe as followers. According to Patty, Jim was lying when he said that the whole murder plan was done according to her commands.

Activities

Patty enjoyed art and had acquired some skill in oil painting, particularly in painting animals and nature scenes. She liked going to the mall, watching sunsets on the beach, going for a drive, sitting and talking (especially with Jim), managing and coaching the basketball and track teams, watching soap operas, playing video games, and going to the movies with her friends. Action-packed movies and books in particular interested her. Her interest in romance books waned after her incarceration.

Patty had played the organ when she was younger. She enjoyed listening to music, including heavy metal, soft rock, and country. She did not feel that the lyrics had any negative effect on her. In heavy rock, artists were "really singing about life, about what goes on in the world, what drugs can do to you, having boyfriends and breaking up."

Sexual History

Patty claimed sex was something she could take or leave. Sex was "something you enjoy…you and him have a commitment, he cares about you and you care about him, a small commitment." She reported first having sexual intercourse when she was in eighth grade, with "a guy I liked." She explained that "you're curious the first time." She reported having had sexual intercourse with about 12 partners, but only one before her father began sexually assaulting her.

Patty told me that she had not received formal instruction about sex. She learned about sex from her friends. She did not use birth control but claimed the boys used "rubbers." She stated that she had never been pregnant. Although Patty stated that all of her sexual encounters except those with her father were "consensual," at least one involved a person who was considerably older than her. This man, who was in his 20s, was the chaperone at her 15th and 16th birthday parties and her best friend's brother.

Self-Perception

Patty described herself as someone who "can help people," is "good to be friends with," and "can hand out advice to those who need it." When asked to discuss the things that she really liked about herself, Patty said, "I'm easygoing, have a good spirit…you can come to me and tell me your problems." The girl suggested that her mother might have confided her problems to her. She named three people, none of them codefendants, to whom she could open up. When asked what she did not like about herself, Patty said, "I don't like that I am a follower" because that's how "you get yourself in trouble" and "sometimes you have to take the lead in your life." She also said, "I'm scared to speak my opinion, to say what I think is right," because she was afraid of losing people.

Physical and Mental Health History

Patty had relatively good health. She had trouble with her ears and a back injury, both documented. She sustained the back injury when her father kicked her.

Patty had a history of depression. She said that she contemplated suicide before the homicide and had once attempted suicide by taking an over-the-counter drug to induce sleeping.

Prior Delinquent History

Patty had never been arrested before the homicide. She had run away on five or six occasions but had always been caught and returned to her father. The girl recalled getting into trouble and being "grounded" by her father for "doing do-nuts" in the car on the beach with Jim and damaging the motor mount on her car. The girl also acknowledged truancy and attempted forgery of her father's checks.

Adjustment in Jail

Patty was not afraid of the inmates and considered most of the guards her friends. Patty's mother shared my belief that she seemed relatively happy inside the facility.

At one point, however, while in jail, Patty tried to kill herself with an office staple. She did not pose a serious suicidal risk at the time of the assessment interview. Patty believed that her suicide would kill her mother, about whom she cared deeply. It seemed likely at the time of the evaluation that if correctional staff continued to give her some attention and be supportive, her half-hearted gestures toward self-destruction would cease.

Future Orientation

Patty had wanted to pursue art as a career. At the time of the evaluation, however, she had become increasingly interested in counseling as an occupation and dreamed of opening up a residential counseling center for abused kids in California. She intended to get her GED, take college courses, and major in counseling so she could have her "place on the beach where teenagers (under 17, problem people) can sit out with their friends," with an "art shop on the side."

Patty did not see herself getting married because it seemed to her that "all of them end up in hurt" and divorce. She did wish to have children and wanted a girl and a boy. She believed that she would be a "pretty good parent" because of what she had gone through. She would raise her children differently from the way she had been raised, making sure that they had guidelines.

CLINICAL INTERVIEW WITH PATTY'S MOTHER

Mrs. Smith, whom I interviewed six days after my assessment interview with Patty, was on antidepressant medication. She was very alert and cooperative throughout the interview. Her good memory was helpful in reconstructing some of Patty's history. She appeared fairly at ease and in control of herself, although she did smoke about seven or eight cigarettes and cried twice.

Before interviewing Mrs. Smith, I doubted the extent of Patty's alleged victimization and her depiction of her father. After talking to the girl's mother, virtually no doubt remained in my mind that Patty's allegations were truthful. Mrs. Smith remained in an abusive relationship with Mr. Smith for 17 years before she divorced him. Her statements corroborated Patty's stories that Mrs. Smith was a victim of physical, verbal, sexual, and psychological abuse. Mrs. Smith described her former husband as follows:

[John] was a very violent man, a very physical man, verbally very abusive, he used every filthy word that was known. . . . Every other word was "Fuck," you were a "whore," you were a "tramp," you were a "slut," every other word, "F you". . . . Also with his hands, I have been beat up several times, more times than I care to remember, last time, probably the worst, I was black and blue from knee to hip, he damaged my sciatic nerve, I went and had shots . . . until I couldn't have any more, so I could walk.

Mr. Smith had pulled a gun on her "I don't know how many times. He always went for a gun, very easy, very quick, he cocked it and only shot at me once." She sustained injuries after Mr. Smith kicked her because "I didn't get a pair of shoes out of the closet fast enough." On another occasion, her former husband had backed his car up against hers in order to prevent her escape and appeared intent on killing her.

[John] backed me up in a corner. He had already slit my hand with the keys to the car, laughing because he had backed me in. He cut my hand open with the car keys, he literally sliced it up. He backed me in a corner with a knife above my head and he was coming down with it. I came up with my knee and I kneed him. He did back off. Patty at the time was out on the street screaming for help.

Mrs. Smith spoke at length of the difficulty of placating her former husband. She explained, for example, that Mr. Smith wanted his supper on time, but that she never knew when that would be. "If he came in, and it wasn't ready, you got it. If it was, and he wanted to relax with a drink, then he was upset too."

Some data indicated that Mr. Smith might have been an alcoholic who had long periods of sobriety interspersed with periods of heavy drinking. When he drank, he "always drank pretty regular to the point of getting drunk" and would get "very mean." She recalled his making a "funny statement" after his common-law wife Judith left: "You don't think I could ever be an alcoholic?" Mrs. Smith thought that Mr. Smith might have used tranquilizers from the time of their separation, approximately four years before his death. Sedatives were found in the body.

Mrs. Smith's description of her former husband was consistent with the depiction of the narcissist formulated by Alexander Lowen, a psychiatrist and psychoanalyst by training.[2] The narcissist is absorbed with his image and invests himself in maintaining an image rather than being who he is. Mrs. Smith made the following observation about her husband: "[John] did everything for looks. Big house, nice furniture, nice cars, boat, if he never went out on the boat—fact was, it was for show—this is what he was and, you close those doors, he was a terrific salesman, he was good at selling himself until you got to know him."

The narcissist denies his feelings and puts an exaggerated emphasis on winning. The denial of feeling gives the narcissist the license to do whatever he desires because of his insensitivity to others' rights and needs. By exercising power and control over others and situations, the narcissist protects himself from sadness and fear, which make him feel particularly vulnerable. Mrs. Smith described her former husband as "a very strong man over weak people, not strong people." She said her husband kept her isolated from others to ensure his dominance and her dependence. He always carried both a gun and a knife on his person. She saw him as a coward because he would not fistfight someone unless it was somebody that he could beat. "If [John] drank, he wanted sex. He would then demand it. I used to try and get him, like, to pass out. I'd watch TV or I would stay out in the family room. One night he slammed the TV off. 'This is my house, my TV, and you'll go to bed when I say so.'…It was more like I submitted."

Lowen identified five types of narcissists. Mrs. Smith's description of Mr. Smith placed him as a psychopath who sometimes slipped over into the paranoid personality—the two furthest points along the continuum of narcissism.[3] The psychopath considers himself superior to others and often expresses contempt for them. His lack of feeling toward others is extreme, and he has a tendency to act out antisocially. His ability to manipulate people is keen; his ability to tolerate frustration is minimal. The paranoid personality distrusts others and is suspicious of them, often believing that others are conspiring against him.

Mr. Smith's obsession with controlling others extended to his employees. If he could not control an employee, he did not want that worker around. "If you worked for him, he wanted you around 24 hours a day. He cross-checked on people. He would spend all evening calling [his employees to check up on them]."

Mrs. Smith was terrified of her husband from the early days of their marriage. Her methods of coping were endurance and the use of tranquilizers. Sometimes she fled from her husband, taking Patty with her if she could get to the child, and stayed at her sister's house.

Mrs. Smith had had a serious heart problem since childhood. Medical records confirmed the gravity of her illness and the limitations it imposed on her. When Patty was about 6 years old, Mrs. Smith had her first open-heart surgery. After returning home for four weeks, the woman was hospitalized again with hepatitis. At that time her husband was barred from the room, according to Mrs. Smith, because she had attempted to swallow "a bunch of Valium because he wouldn't leave me alone." A few weeks before the homicide, Mrs. Smith was again hospitalized for open-heart surgery; her prognosis was uncertain at that time.

The home environment was so stressful during the marriage that at one point Mrs. Smith had "a mental breakdown" and had to be hospitalized for a short period. She used Valium extensively from the time Patty was 6 until she was 13. Mrs. Smith's addiction to Valium made her unresponsive to Patty's emotional needs. She said Patty's third- and fifth-grade teachers had thought that Patty was an unloved and unwanted child. After meeting Mrs. Smith, these teachers did not understand what was going on, because it was apparent to them that Mrs. Smith did want and love her little girl. What these teachers didn't know was that "I was not there when I was on Valium." Thus, Patty was raised by one, if not two, parents who were chemically dependent.

Mrs. Smith had been aware of her husband's emotional abuse of their daughter. She described it as constant. "He took something you cared about and then destroyed it." Mr. Smith had bought Patty a phone and a radio; one night he got angry and smashed them. The verbal abuse is clear from this statement: "If anybody was around, it was 'This is my baby girl' and 'I am proud of her.' As soon as they walked out the door, he would switch, 'you pig,' 'you fat slob,' 'you slut,' and 'fuck,' every other word."

Patty's mother had also seen some of the physical altercations between father and daughter. She described an incident that occurred a few months before the homicide in which Mr. Smith became angry because a car hose had sprung a leak and "raised a wrench as if he were going to hit her [Patty]." Although he did not actually hit the girl with the wrench, "he did slap her with both hands and hard."

Mrs. Smith said that she knew a complaint about physical abuse had been made to the state social services agency. The woman remarked, as her daughter had previously, that Mr. Smith always made friends with the sheriff or local police authorities and "made you look like an idiot" if you said anything against him.

Mrs. Smith had no trouble believing that her former husband could have sexually assaulted their daughter in order to punish Patty and, even more so, punish Mrs. Smith "because he couldn't control me anymore." Patty's description of the circumstances leading up to her father's raping her vaginally and anally sounded to Mrs. Smith like her husband's style. Mrs. Smith portrayed her husband as a promiscuous man who hated women. Other remarks she made convinced me that Mr. Smith was capable of committing the acts that his daughter alleged. Mrs. Smith said that Mr. Smith made love "to" her rather than with her and used explicit and degrading language when performing sexually. He was obsessed with anal sex, interested in sexual instruments such as vibrators and dildos, and absorbed in pornography.

Mrs. Smith said that Mr. Smith did not adequately meet Patty's material needs. She bought all of Patty's clothes because Mr. Smith would not. Even though her former husband and her daughter lived in an expensive home and Patty had her own car at 16, Mrs. Smith maintained that Patty had very little and was not "a rich kid" at all.

Mrs. Smith was unaware of the extent of the abuse inflicted on her daughter because Patty did not talk about it. It seemed to Mrs. Smith that Patty had come to assume the chores of a wife in the Smith household in recent years—cooking, buying groceries, and so on. When she visited during the holiday season, approximately two months before the homicide, Mrs. Smith felt an eeriness in the house; Patty and Mr. Smith would not stay in the same room.

Mrs. Smith's relationship with Patty was good when Patty was young, but it deteriorated during the years when her Valium usage was high. As a teenager, Patty adopted a protective stance toward her mother. Mrs. Smith said that Mr. Smith would not allow Patty to come live with her and used their child to maintain control over her. Patty told her mother about two months before the homicide that she intended to leave home as soon as she turned 18, an event that was only eight months away.

Mrs. Smith did not believe that her daughter was the mastermind behind this crime and had some question as to who really shot Mr. Smith. Patty's mother was perplexed by the fact that her former husband did not wake up during the incident, because she knew him to be a very light sleeper.

Mrs. Smith was supportive of Patty. After the homicide, she made arrangements to relocate to the city where her daughter was incarcerated pending trial. She talked with Patty daily and visited weekly. Her willingness to testify was never in question, and she saw her testimony as critical. Mrs. Smith said that she was recovering from open-heart surgery despite the homicide, but she expressed concern that because of the stress she might not survive the trial.

MOTIVATIONAL DYNAMICS BEHIND THE HOMICIDE

In this homicide we again see an abused child who has been pushed beyond her limits. The involvement of one friend as a coconspirator and three others as accessories makes the case of Patty Smith different. Patty's behavior, though at first shocking, is understandable in the context of this adolescent's level of personality development and the deteriorating conditions in the home environment.

Patty's Environment

From the time Patty was born, her life was both horrifying and terrifying.[4] Patty's recollections, corroborated by her mother, show that she had been exposed to a broad array of psychopathology. She had seen the physical, verbal, and psychological abuse of her mother by her father and half-brother and other extreme forms of violence; she herself had been a victim of physical, verbal, and psychological abuse, and of forcible rape perpetrated by her father. Her father's possible alcoholism and her mother's drug addiction and debilitating illness made Patty the victim of emotional neglect and emotional incest as well. Physical neglect was also present because of the mother's failure to protect Patty from her abusive former husband.

Physical and Psychological Abuse of Mrs. Smith

Patty remarked that from the time of her earliest memories she had seen "Dad kicking Mom, Dad hitting Mom, Dad throwing glass at Mom, Dad shooting at Mom." Her half-brother, Mr. Smith's only son, had also physically abused her mother: "What I lived through, either my brother would start a fight with my mom, start hitting her and all. My dad would finish, and my brother would go to his room, shut the door, turn the stereo on so he couldn't hear, or my dad would start and my brother would join in and they both would finish on my mom."

When asked how she felt when her father was beating her mother, Patty replied, "Helpless, because I knew I couldn't do anything." The girl believed that if she went into the room where her mother was being assaulted and tried to help her, she would also be beaten.

Patty witnessed other episodes of extreme violence. Mr. Smith's business building was firebombed and burned to the ground. According to Mrs. Smith, an investigation suggested that the arsonists "were more after the man than they were the business," and Patty was put on restrictions at school for her protection.

Physical Abuse of Patty

Patty had been physically "abused on and off most of my life." If Mr. Smith's common-law wife was late, she said, he would beat his daughter up, "start slapping me around. Start kicking, hitting."

Patty had lived in fear ever since she could remember because her father carried a gun or had one nearby 24 hours a day. "It makes you scared. Scared if you do something really wrong; any time he can just whip the gun out and shoot you." He pulled the gun out on her once.

Patty felt that there was nothing she could do when her father verbally abused her or accused her falsely. If she protested, "All I would get was a backhand across the mouth or a fist in the mouth or end up getting things worse 'cause I knew what was coming," referring to physical abuse and sexual attack. Her friends witnessed some of the physical abuse, as did her mother.

On one occasion Patty reported her father's physical abuse to the state social services agency. Her remarks indicate her loss of faith in the ability of the system to help her and in her own ability to escape the situation.

I went to [the agency] once and that time all I had was a cut over my eye, and they said there was no evidence. But I found out later that before [the agency] worker talked to me, she had talked to my dad, even before she saw and talked to me, she talked to my dad. As soon as I walked in, she sat me down and she goes, "There is no evidence" and she goes, "You have to go back with your dad." And she said, "By the way, your dad will be here to pick you up after school." And I was really scared, if I went and tried to find help that would always get back to Dad, and Dad would always be free. He would always be able to find me and I would just end up going back to him, and it would end up being worse than it ever had been. Every time I ran away he always found me. And every time I ran away it wasn't ten minutes after he found out that I was gone, there was always an APB [all points bulletin broadcast by law enforcement to other agencies] out on my car. I have like, five or six runaways on my juvenile record.

Patty ran away more when she got her car, but her father always found her. When asked where she ran away to, the youth said that she usually went to a friend's house because she really did not know where else to go: "I couldn't go to my mom's. He said if I ever went back up to Mom's, he would kill me and Mom both, and Dad is the type of guy to do it."

Verbal and Additional Psychological Abuse of Patty

Instances of Mr. Smith's verbally abusive remarks abounded. In addition to cursing her, Patty said her father would say things "that would tear down your confidence, tear you down, make you feel like you weren't worth doing anything." Mr. Smith told her that she was nothing but "fat and sloppy," that all she did was lie around on the couch and eat chocolates. "He told me I was sleeping with everybody in my class and how I was nothing but a whore, a slut, and all that." The girl said that her father would tear down her friends, insisting that they were only using her. He would also belittle her paintings. Once he scoffed at a painting that she did, telling her it looked like something a little child had done, and he threw it in the trash.

Patty as a Victim of Incest/Forcible Rape

Patty was reluctant to talk about sexual assaults by her father. The first assault that she discussed occurred when she was 14 and living with Mr. Smith and his common-law wife, Judith. Her father became angry because she had been on the phone too long, an argument ensued, and the two wound up fighting in Patty's bedroom.

Patty: He pushed me down on the bed, and he kept on saying it's all my
        fault for everything that's been happening, the divorce with Mom and
        all. Sometimes I would think it was my fault. Sometimes I would.
        Then he kept on saying it was my fault that the way Mom was, she's
        taking so much Valium and all. He kept on saying he'd have to teach
        me a lesson, so I won't be destroying people's lives anymore. And
        he pushed me down on the bed, and I was wearing jeans, I kept
        on asking what he was doing, he said, "I'm going to give you your
        punishment for breaking up our marriage, and trying to ruin my life"
        and all that. And I just looked up at him, kept on trying...every time I
        tried to fight him off, he kept on hitting me and slapping me. And the
        next thing I knew, he had my pants off, even with me fighting him.
        And it seems like even if I was going to fight with him, it wouldn't do
        any good. It got worse if I kept fighting. And the next thing, he didn't
        have his pants on, and he just had sex. He kept on hitting me and
        repeating, "This is your punishment."

Heide: How long did the whole thing last?

Patty: I don't know, I didn't keep track of it.

Heide: At that point, aside from thinking, how could he do this to his own daughter
        [a statement that Patty had made in reference to the sexual assaults during
        the assessment interview the evening before], is there anything else that went
        through your mind?

Patty: I was real scared and didn't know what to do. I just laid there after he got done,
        he left, and I just laid there on the bed crying.

Heide: And then what did you do?

Patty: I stayed in my room almost all of the night, didn't come out for dinner, didn't
        come out for anything. Then he came in, him and Judith came in, and was
        lovey-dovey like nothing happened.

Heide: To you?

Patty: Yeah.

Heide: Did he tell you not to tell anybody?

Patty: Yeah. He said that, if I ever told anybody what was going on, that he
        would kill me, and if I went to Mom, that he would make sure Mom
        got killed.

Patty reported that the sexual assaults did not happen often at first but occurred more frequently after Judith left because Mr. Smith blamed Patty for Judith's leaving. It seemed to Patty that at some point Mr. Smith began raping her "once a week or something like that." Patty indicated that intercourse with her father, unlike sex with her boyfriends, hurt. She stated that her father had anal intercourse with her three or four times, and that these acts were "really painful."

He wanted dinner on the table as soon as he walked in the door, he could walk in any time, and I almost had supper ready, couple of minutes until it was done, he came in, and he was mad that I didn't have supper on the table. We got into a big argument, and he started hitting me and all. I had a pair of handcuffs. He had a couple of like leather straps and all he had kept in his bedroom [Mr. Smith had a box in which he kept sexual paraphernalia]. And we were fighting, fought and fought, an hour yelling back and forth, he kept on slapping me, and I kept fighting him that night, kept hitting him back, telling him to leave me alone. I guess because I was fighting him, I really got it bad. He pushed me in my bedroom...he put the handcuffs on my hand so I couldn't move, and he had my feet strapped down to the bed to the end of the bedpost. He ripped my shirt off. He took my pants down and he had sex with, intercourse, and he kept on saying, "This is your punishment, this is what you get for not having dinner on the table when I come into the house." And I kept on hitting him and he goes, "Well, since you're going to fight me this time, I guess I'll have to make your punishment worse." And he undid my hands, handcuffs, and so he flipped me over, I was twisted. I was lying on my stomach halfway and my back halfway. My feet were still strapped, and he put my hands back up on the bed, and he bent my feet, and the next thing, I felt real sharp pain and having anal [inter]course. I kept on trying to kick him, but my feet were not doing it because they were strapped. I kept on trying to buck him off, nothing would, nothing would get him off. So I finally gave up. I decided that if I quit fighting, then I wouldn't get it so bad.

The Chemically Dependent Family System

Patty's mother was chemically dependent and emotionally unavailable to her from the time Patty was about 6. Both Patty and Mrs. Smith characterized Mrs. Smith as a "zombie" during the seven years she was addicted to Valium. "She [Mrs. Smith] would sit there and watch TV and that was it. She would fix dinner, but you couldn't talk to her." With Mr. Smith, the evidence of a problem with alcohol, and perhaps later with tranquilizers, as discussed earlier, though not definitive, was strongly suggestive.

Changes in the Environment before the Homicide

When Mr. Smith's common-law wife left his house, approximately 16 months before the homicide, conditions went from bad to worse. Patty's father had kept a tight rein on Judith, as he had on his former wife. Patty explained that when Judith left, Mr. Smith tightened his hold on her.

It was like she [Judith] was all there was in his life. There was no outside activity and that was what he expected from me. Just go to school and come straight home and that was it, have no friends or anything else because that's what he had. When she took off, they had a fight one night, and she took off while he went to go calm down, and I couldn't hardly go to school during the first three months she was gone. He didn't want me out of his sight. He didn't want me to have friends over or call anybody. He was calling the house every ten minutes. And he really got bad after she left. He really got worse after she left, more than I have ever seen him.

The Environment at the Time of the Homicide

At the time of the homicide, Patty's mother had just had open-heart surgery and was recuperating far away. Before the surgery, there was considerable doubt as to whether Mrs. Smith would survive or how far she would recover. Although Patty made several efforts to secure help from others, each one failed. Her attempt to get help from the state agency was unsuccessful, and her claim that she had received no help from a weight counselor to whom she reported sexual abuse was verified. Two of Mr. Smith's employees indicated that Patty had told them of incidents of covert sexual abuse and they had done nothing to help her. Patty had told these two women that Mr. Smith used to converse with her in the bathroom while she was in the shower and had once made her watch while a woman performed fellatio on him.

Patty's efforts to escape the family situation had also failed. Her attempts to run away had been futile, her attempts at suicide half-hearted. With Judith's departure, she became increasingly desperate and isolated. In the week before the homicide, her feelings of isolation intensified when Mr. Smith took her car away as a punishment for misbehavior. The car symbolized temporary freedom from an increasingly intolerable environment. Her father was calling her repeatedly at home, met her at the bus, and made it clear that her friends were not welcome at their house.

Patty: Even now [five months after the killing] I tried to think what I could have done. I tried running away, but I always got caught. I always got brought back.

Heide: Yeah.

Patty: I saw what he did to Judith after Judith left, the harassment...and I knew, at that time, I couldn't talk to Mom, if I did talk to Mom, he had to hear what I was saying.

Heide: How would he hear?

Patty: He would pick up the phone and listen on the other end.

Heide: O.K. Did you ever think of going to a pay phone or at your friend's house and calling your mom?[5]

Patty: Well, toward the end I didn't have my car. He was picking me up. He was watching me to make sure I got on the school bus in the morning. He was picking me up after school, after track practice because I got out two hours early, and I usually just messed around the school and helped out my teachers, or helped out the basketball coach until track practice started.

Heide: Yeah.

Patty: And then I went to track practice, and track practice got over, he picked me up. Then I was there at the office with him or I was at home with him. I wasn't out of [his] sight.

Making Sense of Murder

Of critical importance, given Patty's personality development, was the fact that her friends were willing to support the idea of patricide. When Patty asked her friends, "half-joking, half-serious," "Who would be stupid enough to kill my father?" she was desperate. There seemed no other way out but murder. If her friends had laughed and told her to forget such "a stupid idea," she probably would have.

On the basis of Patty's 45-minute description of the homicide, there was indeed a plan, although a poorly conceived one, to kill Mr. Smith. Guns were readily available; Mr. Smith was a gun enthusiast and had many firearms throughout the home. Much was left to happenstance, as was consistent with Patty's level of personality development. The homicide appeared to be almost farcical. Patty had given no thought, for example, to disposal of the body—she figured "the boys would do it." She had no plans to get away and had not thought about getting caught. She figured that she would just "let the house go" and live in her car, taking some food from the house for her and her dog, until she could save up some money to get a place for her and her friend Mary.

When Mary, who had agreed to shoot Mr. Smith, "chickened out," Patty was flooded with anxiety. She seemed to feel a need to go through with the plan out of desperation, "to end the hurt," and also to get the social approval that she so badly wanted from her friends. As she stood in her father's bedroom the second time, after an aborted first attempt to kill him with a malfunctioning gun, she reported flashbacks of what he had done to her and to her mother and pulled the trigger, shooting him in the head.

I stood there for seven minutes, cause he didn't get shot until 4:07...and I thought what he did to Mom, I thought of all the trouble he caused me, pain he has put me through, and actually I don't remember pulling the trigger. I just remember the shot firing and the sound that he made. I don't remember my hand pulling the trigger. All I remember, what I was thinking and the time on the clock.

Defendant's Sanity at the Time of the Crime

Patty remembered pulling the trigger on the gun that jammed, but not on the one that actually killed her father. Although the escalating stress might have in fact produced a dissociative reaction, the facts did not suggest that she was insane at the time of the homicide under the state standard, the M'Naghten test. The attempt to shoot the first time was the critical factor in determining Patty's mental state at the time of the incident. She intended to kill her father, clearly knew what she was doing, and, from all available evidence, knew that this conduct was against the law.

Patty suffered from post-traumatic stress disorder (PTSD) due to events preceding the murder and the shooting itself. Interviews with Patty and her mother provided a consistent picture of the victim, Mr. Smith, and of the home environment. There was clear evidence corroborated by Patty's mother to indicate that Patty had witnessed events to which no one, and especially no child, should be exposed: physical and psychological abuse of her mother and other forms of extreme violence. Patty's and her mother's statements described a child who had been a victim of physical, verbal, and psychological abuse by her father and emotional neglect by both parents. Her statements about sexual victimization were credible. They were consistent with reports from other sexual assault victims, with the portrait Mrs. Smith painted of her former husband, and with others' reports about him. Patty's sexual victimization could be more appropriately characterized as brutal rape than as sexual abuse, as distinguished in Chapter 2.

Patty seemed to be overwhelmed by life and survived for years by passively conforming to whoever had power. She perceived herself as helpless to control her life.

At the same time, she viewed her friends, whose approval she desperately sought, as the "ones who call the shots." That Patty's friends were willing to entertain the idea of killing her father was crucial to Patty's going through with it. Patty fit the profile of the most commonly encountered adolescent parricide offender, the severely abused child. Her low level of personality development made her even less able to handle the psychopathological home environment than individuals at higher levels of personality development.

Patty said that she experienced "nightmares" and "flashbacks" that were "real painful" after the killing. She explained at the time of my initial evaluation that "it's like I have to relive…relive all of it. It's not like, he's not really dead." Still, she expressed relief as she recounted the desperation that drove her to murder. Patty said, "Well, I feel relieved that he's gone, because I don't have to worry, and Mom don't have to worry. 'Cause Mom was real worried about my living down there with him. And then again, the fact that he was my dad, that he bring me in the world, this disappointment…he destroyed most of the love I had for him."

CASE PROCESSING AND DISPOSITION

There was no question about who killed Mr. Smith. Patty's guilt or innocence rested on one point: Was the 17-year-old a dangerously antisocial youth, as the State argued, or was she a severely abused child—a victim herself—who killed out of desperation in an attempt to ensure her psychological, and perhaps physical, survival, as the defense contended?

The State attempted to portray the adolescent as a psychopathic youth who killed her father because he disciplined her for getting bad grades, skipping school, and other misbehavior. In the words of the prosecutor, Patty was "a vicious, mean, spoiled young woman" who murdered her father in cold blood because he kept her on a tight rein and took her car away as a punishment. Patty's codefendants all testified against her. In recounting the events following the homicide, Tom, Jim, and Joe suggested that Patty was untroubled by having killed her father. Jim indicated that Patty seemed amused as she related the details of the killing.

Mary testified that when Patty had asked her whether she would sleep over at the Smith household and really kill Patty's father as he slept, she replied "Yeah, whatever." Mary testified further that Patty said that she could live with Patty in the Smith home after Mr. Smith was dead. According to Mary, Patty had promised to give her an unspecified amount of money and some rock concert tickets for killing Mr. Smith. On the night of the homicide, Mary dressed herself in black, entered Mr. Smith's bedroom, stayed there for about a minute, and pointed a gun at him for at least 15 seconds. She then left the bedroom, claiming that she was just playing out the final segments of a joke and had never intended to kill Mr. Smith. Upon re-entering the living room, Mary told Patty that she could not carry out the plan. Patty said then that she would have to do it herself.

The defense contended that Patty was a child trapped in an intolerable home situation, where she suffered continuous "mental, physical and sexual abuse" from her father. The public defender argued that Patty killed her father because "he was slowly killing her" and she could find no other way out. Defense counsel buttressed its position by calling former employees of Mr. Smith, his former in-laws, the defendant, and two mental health experts. Several of Mr. Smith's employees described him as an employer who publicly berated his workers and never seemed to be satisfied by their job performance and efforts. The victim's former father-in-law and his former wife painted a picture of Mr. Smith as a violent and abusive man. They recounted specific incidents of Mr. Smith's violence against family members. Mrs. Smith vividly portrayed her former marriage as one filled from the beginning with fear, threats, and physical and mental abuse. She testified that Mr. Smith always carried a gun and usually kept brass knuckles and a switchblade knife nearby.

Patty Smith testified about the physical and mental abuse and sexual assaults to which her father had subjected her. She explained that classmates who testified were unaware of the physical abuse because she wore long-sleeved shirts and long skirts to hide any marks. She told the jurors about the two occasions when she sought help to no avail and reported that she had tried to run away on several occasions, but her father always found her. Her attempt at suicide failed, she stated, because she failed to take enough pills to kill herself. The defendant related the events on the night of the homicide in a detached way, admitting to the jurors that she came to see killing her father as the only way out.

The other mental health expert who examined the defendant, a psychologist, shared my opinion that Patty was sane and suffering from PTSD because of the conditions in which she had been raised. I testified about the abuse and neglect that had existed in the Smith household for years, explaining each of the areas of victimization discussed in this chapter. The wide array of materials made available to me proved to be invaluable in substantiating that Mr. Smith was a person who had used sex as an instrument of power and who could have sexually assaulted his own daughter. Statements made by former employers to defense counsel revealed that Mr. Smith used sexual remarks and demands to intimidate them at work. Mr. Smith fit the profile of an extremely narcissistic individual whose behavioral style most closely resembled that of a psychopath. Such an individual, I testified, would be capable of raping his daughter.

My testimony also focused on how conditions in the household worsened after Mr. Smith's common-law wife left. The pivotal role played by Patty's friends in bringing her to the point where she stood with a loaded gun pointed at her father's head as he lay sleeping, believing that there was no other way out, was explained to the jury. Evidence that Mr. Smith's continued abuse, committed verbally, psychologically, physically, and sexually, might have caused Patty to be in a chronic state of fear and to believe that he was capable of killing her at any time was presented to the jury.

The jury deliberated for more than 10 hours before finding Patty Smith guilty of murder in the second degree. The jury's selection of this verdict appeared to have been a compromise. This verdict precluded Patty's being sentenced to either death in the electric chair or life imprisonment with a mandatory 25-year sentence to be served before parole eligibility, which were the penalties at the time for defendants convicted of first-degree murder. The defense had hoped that the jury would return a verdict of excusable homicide or manslaughter, believing it unlikely that jurors would conclude that Patty acted in self-defense.

Sentencing guidelines called for a 12- to 17-year period of incarceration for an individual convicted of second-degree murder who did not have a significant prior record. The prosecution asked the judge to impose a 30-year sentence, arguing that aggravating factors in the case warranted a longer term. During the sentencing hearing, the prosecutor attempted to read into the record portions of the adolescent's diary that detailed her sexual encounters with two boys and a pamphlet of Patty's that apparently showed various sexual positions, but he was not allowed to do so by the court. Based on comments that the assistant state attorney made to the press prior to attempting to introduce these materials in court, it appeared that he believed promiscuous behavior to be evidence against being a victim of sexual abuse. The fact that sexually abused children frequently act out sexually is well known among those who work with this population.[6] This fact was specifically noted during the trial by the other mental health expert when he mentioned the characteristics of the abused child. Patty's sexual history was also discussed at length in my report.

The defense asked the judge to suspend the prison sentence and order confinement in a facility that offered intensive psychiatric treatment. I testified at this hearing that Patty was not a criminally sophisticated youth. She needed a structured environment where she could get psychiatric help. If Patty were sentenced to adult prison or a youthful-offender facility, she would encounter more criminally oriented individuals, homosexual play, and "familying," a process in which woman set up make-believe families, sometimes including sexual affiliations, in order to survive the physical and emotional deprivations of imprisonment.[7] Because of Patty's personality development, she would be at considerable risk of detrimental influences from more hardened inmates. Despite her size and age, Patty was still a little girl who craved attention and wanted to be liked. Her desires clearly affected her judgment.

Patty needed intensive therapy in three main areas. First, in-depth psychological intervention was needed to help her deal with the trauma she had experienced. She needed to confront feelings of rage, betrayal, abandonment, and powerlessness safely and rebuild her self-concept. Second, therapy was also necessary to help Patty develop healthier, more mature coping techniques. In addition to discussing Patty's passive way of responding to others, I advised the court that the adolescent had signs of an eating disorder, underscoring that an addictive pattern was already in place and could be life threatening if not checked. Finally, Patty needed professional help to facilitate more mature ways of perceiving. Counseling could help Patty see herself as responsible for her behavior, increase her awareness of feelings and their relation to her behavior, and foster empathy. I recommended placement in one of three psychiatric hospitals instead of prison because each had programs that could benefit Patty.

The court sentenced Patty Smith to 17 years in the women's prison, noting that a life had been taken. In pronouncing sentence, the judge commented that, independent of the mental health testimony, the court believed that Patty had a problem and needed treatment. He strongly urged the state corrections authorities to put Patty in a facility where she could receive some counseling, stating on the record that he was aware that there was little in the way of treatment available in prison. He specifically noted that it was a "great failing in our system" that people who need help do not get it in the prison environment. He expressed dismay that our society did not recognize this fact and that the legislature had not seen fit to change this state of affairs.

FOLLOW-UP DATA

Patty served approximately one-third of her 17-year sentence.[8] I saw Patty three times during the six and a half years that she was in prison. In addition, Patty wrote many letters to me while she was incarcerated. Mrs. Smith also wrote and called a few times over the years to update me on Patty's situation. I visited Patty almost 18 years after the murder; she had been living in the community for approximately 10 years. After our visit, Patty touched base with me occasionally by phone or e-mail over the years. She made significant strides in adulthood.

Clinical Interviews with Patty in Prison

Patty adjusted well during her early years in prison. Initially, she lost about 50 pounds, looked good, and seemed happy in prison. She had a "whole family." Her "mom" was an 18-year-old woman who was serving a 15-year sentence for murder. Her "dad" was "like a dad I never had…she's older, 23–24, she's serving 16 years, she was gay on the street." Patty met her "brother" in county jail: "She's not like a female to me, she plays more of a dominant role." She had four uncles and four aunts, and a grandma who was a "nut, she's crazy, my mom's mom." Patty said, "They help out a lot."

For the first couple of years, Patty was invested in learning what she could. She completed her GED and finished courses in graphics, computers, and nursing aid. She had jobs in the warehouse, on the grounds, and in the library. She said that in the first nine months, she got eight disciplinary reports for breaking rules and lost gain time. After two years, staying out of trouble was still difficult, but she had found a formula to help her. "All what I do is go to work and stay at work all day. Then I go to the dorm at night and stay on my bed.…All the stuff I learn in here can help me when I get out of here. So I try to learn all what I can while I'm in here. And when I do have spare time I crochet. I learned how to crochet about a month ago.…As long as I keep my hands busy, I keep my mouth shut. And if I keep my mouth shut, I stay out of trouble which is what I am doing."

After almost four years of incarceration, Patty's attitude and mood had changed. She was unhappy and angry that she was still incarcerated and felt that she was being treated unjustly. Prison "family" members had been released, and she decided it was better for her to stay by herself. She decided to take a dorm job and stop pursuing further training because learning more did not seem to help her and she did not like having people over her. She spent her days hanging out in the dorm and did not even go outside for exercise. She said she rarely visited the prison psychologist (although she liked this doctor), never attended any support group meetings, and was never contacted by the local rape crisis counselor who had agreed to see her. She had more than gained back the weight she lost and had little interest in her health or appearance.

With the exception of Patty's mother, family members and friends did not keep in touch with Patty. Patty's mother accepted weekly telephone calls from Patty; she lived a thousand miles away and had become too ill to visit Patty in her later years in prison.

Clinical Interviews with Patty and Her Mother 17 Years after the Murder

I saw Patty and her mother 10 years after Patty's release from prison. Mrs. Smith encouraged Patty to speak with me and facilitated a dinner meeting for the three of us. I also met privately with Mrs. Smith for a few hours prior to our meeting.

At the time of our meeting, Patty was 35 years old. She presented as a large woman, at least 100 pounds overweight. Patty had a hard time losing weight and was considering weight loss surgery. She had injured her ankle and was walking on crutches. Patty was pleasant and polite. She seemed young and awkward, much like the adolescent I had evaluated 17 years earlier in jail. Patty answered each of my questions with a few words. She was clearly more engaged with her mother than with me. Patty related to her mother in a very warm and devoted way.

When Patty was released from prison, she initially went to stay with her mother, who lived about a thousand miles from where Patty had been incarcerated. Patty had few relationships following her release from prison. She initially became close to an older woman and spent time with her. Later she became involved with a man, with whom she moved away. This man "put her down" and treated her poorly. Patty ended the relationship and moved back to where her mother and grandmother were living about four or five years prior to my visit. At the time of my follow-up interview, Patty was living alone in a trailer and did not have any plans to get married or have a family. She had two cats and took great pleasure in taking care of them.

Upon her re-entry into the community, Patty worked hard, often holding two jobs at a time, and she had been employed at several jobs. Some job applications inquired about prior criminal history; others did not. Patty answered truthfully about her criminal past when specifically asked on her job applications. She had worked as a troubleshooter for three years for a five-star hotel in a major Southeastern city. In this capacity, she handled bookings and complaints from across the county. This company did not inquire about her arrest or conviction history when she was hired. Patty was dismissed from this job when management subsequently checked criminal histories on all their employees.

When Patty returned to her mother's community, she had trouble finding work because unemployment was high, and she was out of work for about a year. At the time of the follow-up interview, Patty had been working full time as a manager at the YMCA for more than a year. Prior to becoming a full-time employee, Patty had worked part-time there. She liked the structure of going to work and made her job a priority. Her mother said that Patty "goes out of her way for people."

Patty had no further trouble with the law. She maintained that she made up her mind that she was not going back to prison. Patty did not go to college following her release from prison. She did see a psychiatrist for a short time and then got a full-time job. She never discussed the sexual abuse with her mother.

Patty drank very little, explaining that she did not care for it, and did not use drugs. She said that she often spent her leisure time with her mother and occasionally went out to eat or to see a movie with a co-worker.

Mrs. Smith related that she was very proud of Patty's accomplishments. She attributed a large part of Patty's successful adjustment to the support that Patty had received from herself and Patty's maternal grandmother. Mrs. Smith indicated to me privately that she was living on "borrowed time." She had had three open-heart surgeries and a brain aneurysm. Mrs. Smith was very worried about what would happen to Patty after she was gone. She said that she wanted to live for many more years so she could be there for Patty.

Phone and E-mail Contact with Patty after our Visit

Patty worried greatly about her mother's health. She e-mailed me a couple of years after our visit and wrote that she was planning to take her mother to Florida for a vacation. She wanted to visit the theme parks with her mother and expressed concern about her mother's stamina. She had hoped to connect with me on the visit, but their schedule did not permit it. They had a great time, and Patty was very happy about their trip.

A few years after I saw Patty, she had bariatric surgery and was presented with concerns she had not experienced before. She told me that men were noticing her and expressing interest in her. Although she was 37 years old, Patty had done very little dating in her lifetime and was apprehensive about men. She met a man named Bob who seemed to genuinely care for her. Patty found it hard to trust Bob. She said she felt that she was pushing him away and she did not know why.

Mrs. Smith told me that she liked Bob and she thought he was a good person. Patty and Bob got engaged. At age 40, Patty was looking forward to getting married.

Patty called me when her mother died. She was very upset, having lost her "rock." We talked about how much her mother had loved her and the difference that she had made in Patty's life. Her mother had "hung on" despite her precarious health for years longer than anyone expected. Patty believed that her mother finally felt that she could "let go" now that Patty was with Bob. She was certain that her mother would continue to watch over her.

CASE COMMENTARY

Ten of the 12 characteristics commonly found in cases of severely abused children who kill their parents were clearly present in this case. These include a pattern of family violence in the Smith home, Patty's inability to get help or escape the family situation, and the increasing isolation the youth felt as her freedom was restricted. Patty felt increasingly helpless to deal with her home situation as her father's violence toward her escalated to an intolerable level, including sexual assault.

Patty was not a criminally sophisticated youth. She felt trapped and was desperately seeking a way to end the abuse inflicted by her father. Both of the girl's parents had used alcohol or drugs to deal with their problems, and neither had modeled good communication and effective coping strategies when Patty was growing up. The easy availability of multiple firearms and the encouragement of friends made killing Mr. Smith seem like *the solution to her problem—the way to end her torment.* After the killing, Patty remembered feeling relieved. She remarked, "It was like a big rock was being lifted off my shoulders."

Prognosis

It has now been more than 25 years since Patty killed her father. The prognosis in her case is very good. Patty has been out in the community for more than 18 years and has not engaged in any criminal, antisocial, or violent behavior. She rarely drinks and does not use drugs.

Patty lived independently for years. She has a strong work ethic and embraces the structure of a job. Patty walked away from an abusive relationship. Years later, she entered into what appears to be a healthy relationship with a good man.

Patty's success is largely due to her decision not to go back to prison and the strong structural support that she received from her mother and maternal grandmother.

Her mother's worry about Patty's making her way in the world was a reasonable one; Patty's support system was largely family-based for many years.

Patty married Bob shortly after her mother's death. At the time this book was completed, she and her husband were expecting their first child. Hopefully, her relationship with Bob will continue to be a supportive one and give her the strength to carry on now that her mother is gone.

10 Peter Jones
Repeating the Past

Peter Jones, a 17-year-old white male from a lower-middle-class background, was arrested within five hours of killing his father. He shot his father twice in the back of the neck and once just behind the ear with a .22 caliber rifle as the man sat watching television in the middle of the night. Peter told a law enforcement officer when he was arrested that his father had threatened to kill him the evening of the shooting. Peter said that for years his father had beaten him and his mother. Shortly after Peter's arrest, Mrs. Jones corroborated her son's statements about the father having repeatedly beaten them both.

In the state in which this homicide occurred, charges of first-degree murder could be brought only by the grand jury; in this case, it refused to do so. The prosecutor was forced to reduce the charge to second-degree murder. I was retained by defense counsel as a confidential defense expert to evaluate the defendant's mental status at the time of the shooting and to investigate the motivational dynamics behind the killing.

THE CLINICAL EVALUATION

My assessment of Peter is based on a six-hour clinical interview and a review of numerous case materials. The interview was conducted in private in the adult county jail without interruption and was tape recorded with Peter's consent.

Before evaluating Peter, I reviewed his medical records, a psychiatric evaluation done three months after the homicide, news articles reporting the homicide, and Peter's handwritten responses to a reporter's questions. Additional materials reviewed prior to trial included the autopsy report, the police incident and arrest reports, and eight supplementary reports prepared by the police during their investigation. I also had the opportunity to review four statements made to the police by Paul, an 18-year-old unemployed boarder at the Jones home; a sworn statement made to police by the friend to whom Peter fled after the homicide; and eight depositions by four law enforcement officers, three neighbors, and the boarder. Finally I perused two statements Peter prepared for defense counsel describing the homicide; public defender investigative reports summarizing interviews with three relatives, two neighbors, and the boarder; and reports prepared by two other court-appointed mental health professionals. Prior to finalizing my conclusions, I met for several hours with Mrs. Jones. Her statements strongly corroborated those made by the defendant.

BEHAVIORAL OBSERVATIONS

Peter was alert and cooperative throughout the clinical evaluation. His responses to questions indicated that he was actively processing them. He did not refuse to answer questions even when they caused him discomfort or pain.

Peter did not appear to be at all manipulative during the interview. His responses to hundreds of questions and his behavior during the interview strongly suggested that he was being as truthful and accurate as possible. The youth's answers revealed that he was able to handle conceptual material and to consider alternative ways of responding to a particular question. Responses to some questions suggested that he might have an auditory processing problem and might be dyslexic. I noted that Peter might be learning disabled and recommended that he be evaluated by a special education professional.

Peter appeared fairly at ease during the interview. His eye contact was excellent, but he was rarely animated. His mood was somber, and he seemed depressed. A couple of times during the interview, he was near tears. His depression seemed to be in part occasioned by the homicide. Peter appeared, however, to have been chronically depressed for years because of his home environment.

PERSONALITY DEVELOPMENT

Peter perceived at I-level 5, which is very high on the continuum of personality development and rarely found among offender populations. He was able to look for and understand the reasons for his and others' behavior. The youth had a set of values against which he judged his and others' actions. He felt accountable for his conduct and could feel remorse when his actions hurt others or he failed to abide by his values.

Even more important, Peter was able to appreciate and respond to others as individuals. He could understand fairly easily what others were feeling. Peter could also view interpersonal situations from the perspective of several others' needs and motives. The youth was aware of assuming a variety of roles (son, parent, boyfriend) and was receptive to change. At the same time, he was able to see his own behavior and that of others as possessing continuity.

Peter had a lot of anxiety and pain that went back to early childhood. As is typical of individuals who adopt a neurotic pattern of coping, one of the behavioral response styles identified among level 4 and 5 lawbreakers, Peter did not attempt to resolve the anxieties and pressures that caused him discomfort. Those classified as having a neurotic behavior response either ruminate excessively about their problems (*neurotic anxious—Nx* subtype) or avoid thinking about them (*neurotic acting-out—Na* subtype).[1] Peter fit the Na subtype. He kept a strong front, took on responsibilities that were far too stressful for an adolescent, and just kept going. As a result, he suffered from severe anxiety that manifested in physical as well as psychological ways. His way of dealing with events was self-defeating. Peter's killing of his father and his criminal behavior several months after his trial and many years later was directly related to his neurotic pattern of coping.

RELEVANT SOCIAL HISTORY

The following information was largely obtained from the defendant. I received additional information and corroborative data from the defendant's mother and medical records.

Family Constellation

Peter was the older of two boys born to Mr. and Mrs. Jones. Medical records from six years before the homicide stated that there was "a deep-seated family problem between the parents," who had separated on four or five occasions. In addition, the family doctor recorded that Mr. Jones was addicted to alcohol and that continuous problems existed between the father and Peter.

A psychiatrist who had treated both parents described them as having "severe psychiatric illness." When asked to examine Peter at his parents' request approximately 20 months before the homicide, the psychiatrist noted that Mr. Jones had a "severe mood disturbance," was "very tense and irritable," and had been "quite physically abusive" throughout Peter's childhood. According to Mrs. Jones, her husband had also been diagnosed as schizophrenic. Statements made by Peter and Mrs. Jones suggested that other relatives suffered from mental illness. One of the individuals mentioned, the victim's brother, was staying at the Jones residence when Mr. Jones was killed.

At the time of the homicide, both parents were living on Social Security disability payments. The victim, 38, had worked as a corrections officer for about five years but had been unable to work for the two years before his death, apparently because of mental illness. Mrs. Jones, also 38 at the time of the tragedy, had not been able to work for more than five years because she suffered from Crohn's disease, an intestinal disorder aggravated by stress. During the 17 years of their marriage, the Joneses moved frequently; Peter estimated that the family had moved eight or nine times in less than 10 years.

Peter described his mother as a nice person, soft-spoken, sensitive, and caring, with a sense of humor. He chronicled her long history of psychophysiological ailments and suffering with compassion. He explained how he had increasingly come to assume family and household chores as a result of her illness and the heavy dosage of Valium that she took for years to stay calm. The youth said that his father was an alcoholic, had "smoked dope" when he was younger, and had been taking Valium for about a year. Mr. Jones was physically abusive to him and his mother, but not to his younger brother, Patrick, whom Peter protected. Peter felt that Mr. Jones did not trust him and acted "mean" toward him and others.

Patrick was almost seven years younger than the defendant. Peter described his brother, who was 11 at the time of the homicide, as smart for his age, funny, and a typical little boy who wanted to have fun. When asked about his feelings toward Patrick, Peter stated without hesitation that he loved his brother and would do anything for his brother and his mother. He was upset that Patrick had told his mother that if he had been Peter, he would also have killed Mr. Jones. This remark really hurt Peter; it was not "a natural thought for an 11-year-old … to think of killing somebody."

School History

Peter dropped out of school in the 10th grade and was attending night school at the time of the homicide. He had failed the fifth and 10th grades and believed that his failures were due to three primary factors. First, reading and writing were very hard for him, and he had trouble keeping up with what the teachers were saying. Second, as he got older, he became increasingly frustrated with the way his father treated his mother and stopped caring about school. Third, because his mother was continually ill and sometimes even hospitalized, Peter did all the household chores, including cooking, cleaning, and taking care of his younger brother.

Peter stated that he had never gotten into any real trouble at school and had been in only a couple of fights. He did not get close to any teachers because his workload at home left him no time to stay after school to talk to them. He expressed his intention of getting his high school equivalency diploma.

Work History

Peter had a job at a fast-food restaurant for nine months while he was still in high school. He got along well with his coworkers and with his boss. He worked overtime, was fast, and did what he was told, including cleaning up, closing the store, and helping the boss with the paperwork. Peter quit when he asked for a raise and the boss gave him an additional 10 cents an hour; he thought that he deserved more.

Alcohol and Drug Involvement

Despite an arrest for driving under the influence, Peter did not appear to be a heavy user of alcohol. He drank a couple of beers occasionally with his girlfriend, but he did not drink to get drunk. He had tried marijuana twice but did not like the feeling it gave him. When asked, he denied using other illicit drugs.

Friends

Peter's peers were not involved in delinquent activities. He described his best friend, John, as a "caring person" who would not hurt anyone or anything. Boys who were athletic and who liked to do "fun things" were the kind of youths Peter sought as friends.

Activities

Peter liked to play pool and to take his girlfriend out alone or with his best friend and the friend's girlfriend. He enjoyed sports, including football, track, tennis, weightlifting, racquetball, and swimming. He was on the track and football teams in junior high and remained on the football team in high school.

Sexual History

Peter told me that he had a girlfriend, Becky, whom he genuinely loved and with whom he hoped to be reunited. He liked her because they communicated well. Both of them had to work hard in school, and they had fun together. The youth was pleased that she acted like "a lady" because he didn't like girls who "cussed" or "drank a lot." For Peter, sex was an act of love and not something he would engage in with just anyone.

Self-Perception

Peter described himself, after a long pause, as a person who thought of other people and their feelings and who worried about what other people thought of him. He saw himself as outgoing, athletic, and someone who liked to do things and have fun. He suggested rather shyly that he was a nice person. When asked whether there was anything that he might like to change about himself, he mentioned his study habits. He remarked that he needed to push himself more; if he did not push, he would quit when he "got down."

Physical and Mental Health History

Peter, who stood about 5'11" and weighed less than 155 pounds at the time of the assessment interview, described his health as "pretty good." While in jail, however, he lost quite a bit of weight because of his dislike for the food and his depressed state. Medical records supported statements that he had a history of a hearing (auditory processing) problem, enuresis (bedwetting) at age 11, and recurrent migraine headaches.

The doctor who treated Peter at age 11 for his "nerves" recorded his diagnostic impression as "childhood anxiety and depression syndrome manifested by enuresis, attention problems in school and psychosomatic complaints including muscular tension headaches." He prescribed antidepressant and analgesic medications for the boy. When these medications did not prove effective within three weeks, he added a beta blocker commonly used to prevent migraine headaches. Six weeks after the initial consultation, the doctor noted, "[T]he boy continues to be in an environment full of stress and continues to complain of headaches." At this point, the doctor prescribed an anticonvulsant in addition to the beta blocker. Six weeks later the doctor recorded that he had spent "a considerable amount of time" talking to Mrs. Jones about the stressful nature of the environment and "advising strongly a consultation with a family counselor." The doctor prescribed the same medication and told the family to return "when they had been for at least one month under counseling."

The next entry in the chart was dated two and a half years later. Mrs. Jones called to report that Peter, now almost 14, was experiencing headaches and chest pains. The doctor prescribed antihistamine and narcotic analgesic medications. Six months later, Peter's mother requested these medications again. She was instructed to make an appointment because the patient had not been seen for three years. Mrs. Jones brought Peter in for his last visit to this doctor a few weeks later.

In the last entry in the chart, made almost three years before the homicide, the doctor noted that Peter had had no significant recurrence of headaches since he started taking antihistamines. His anxiety and depression had improved. The doctor renewed the medication and asked Peter to return in six months. Peter told me that he took "the medicine for my nerves ... on and off until about the sixth grade."

Prior Delinquent History

Peter's involvement with the police was fairly minimal. In the fifth grade he was picked up when he and two of his friends attempted to run away. Three years later the police were called because Peter was in a fistfight with another boy who had called Peter's girlfriend a name and threatened to slap her. Peter was sent to "opportunity school," a school for youths with disciplinary problems, for several weeks as a result of this incident. His third police contact involved an arrest at age 15 for driving under the influence. According to him, he had been drinking with two of his friends when four older boys came up and tried to rob them. When one of the older boys pulled a knife on Peter, he got into a truck, which he did not know how to drive, and hit two cars. Peter was held in a detention center for a few days, put on house arrest, and ordered to pay $2,000 in damages.

Adjustment in Jail

Peter found jail very unclean and crowded. He did not feel that he could trust the inmates or the correction officers. The boy commented sadly that he had never been in an environment "where the inmates throw shit at the officers." The behavior of the juveniles was "aggravating" to him. He had had things stolen from him and had been jumped on and beaten up. Whereas he had never really had to fight at school, he had to be ready to fight in jail. When asked about the incidence of sexual assault in jail, Peter talked about sexual activity that he had witnessed. He said, "I ain't never seen anything like that." His voice quivered and he started to cry.

Values and Future Orientation

Peter was not a criminally sophisticated youth; his values were very conventional. What he wanted most in life was to have a wife and a family and enough money to give them what they needed and wanted. Although he had been exposed to an excessive amount of violence, he did not approve of violence except under extreme circumstances. The youth suggested that he would fight, for example, if his life were threatened or if another man tried to assault him sexually. In less extreme cases— for example, if his home were broken into or his car vandalized—Peter said that he would "call the cops" rather than take the law into his own hands.

Peter showed no signs of nihilistic traits. What emerged clearly across various content areas were indications of life-enhancing qualities rather than destructive forces. Peter had no need or desire to control people. His accounts of his relationships with others and his fondness for dogs and cats showed that he had no interest in destructive acts or sadistic control.

MOTIVATIONAL DYNAMICS BEHIND THE HOMICIDE

This homicide represents the most common type of adolescent parricide: the abused child who has been pushed beyond his or her limits. Peter had been living in a very stressful home situation for years. He became even more vulnerable as the stressors in his environment increased, particularly during the 30 days before he shot his father. At the time of the parricide, Peter was in a dissociative state, unaware that he was killing his father.

Peter's Environment

Peter was raised in a home with an alcoholic father. His life was both horrifying and terrifying. His recollections of his life before the homicide indicated that he had witnessed spouse abuse, other extreme forms of physical violence, and verbal abuse. He was himself a victim of physical and verbal abuse, physical and emotional neglect, and emotional incest. This high-stress environment was a major contributing factor to the psychopathology.

Physical and Verbal Abuse of Mrs. Jones

From when he was a little boy, Peter recalled seeing his father beat his mother's head and bang it on the floor. He could remember being "so little I can't do nothing about it." Up until Peter was about 10, Mr. Jones would beat his wife "all the time." Peter's mother was afraid of her husband, but "she couldn't say anything or he would bad-mouth her." Peter gave these examples of remarks his father made to his mother: "You don't know nothing, bitch" and "Shut the fuck up."

The physical violence directed at his mother occurred "every day for a long time." "She left him [her husband] so many times," but Mr. Jones would come back and get her, promising to reform. The father then would be all right for a couple of weeks. Eventually, however, he would hit his wife again and threaten that it would be worse the next time. Mr. Jones would tell his wife that if she left, he would kill her.

When asked, Peter named several people who had seen the spouse abuse (all of his father's brothers and his mother's two sisters). He stated that neighbors knew (they heard the arguments) and that he had on occasion summoned John, "a big guy who lived down the street," to help when his father was beating his mother. The police, however, were never called. Peter was too scared to call them; his father had "yanked the phone off the wall" when his mother tried.[2]

Peter remembered seeing many violent acts at a very young age. In one incident his father was in a bedroom in the boy's maternal grandparents' home beating his mother. The father came out and began beating his wife's sister. Peter's grandfather asked Mr. Jones what he thought he was doing, and Mr. Jones hit the boy's grandmother, breaking her ribs. Mr. Jones then reentered the bedroom and shut the door. The grandfather shot at him through the door. The bullet grazed Mr. Jones in the mouth, with a great deal of blood spewing in the process. Peter stated that during this incident, "I was going crazy … I was young." He said that he could still see the incident in his mind.

Physical Abuse of Peter

Data regarding Peter's physical abuse abounded. Peter was never hospitalized for any of his injuries, but he had sustained bruises and welts on his back, legs, and arms from beatings given to him by his father, who would on occasion use "a switch—a stick," which would "sometimes draw blood." His father would sometimes "bust [his] lips" and punch him in the nose, mouth, and stomach. In addition, the man kicked Peter, punched him in the head, and grabbed him by his hair to move him around. His father threw glasses at him and hit him on the leg with a fruit bowl, cutting his ankle. "He tried to ram my head into a wall, stuff like that, punching me and every-thing, and my mom would try to get him to stop."

When asked whether he was ever afraid of being more than hit, Peter said yes, just within the last year. At that point the boy had started standing up to his father. He made it clear that he had respect for his father and would try to push his father away rather than strike back.

When questioned about whether he had ever worried about being maimed or dis-figured, Peter told how his father had bent his thumb back until he thought it would break and he was on the floor. When asked what was going through his mind at that moment, Peter replied, "Fear … he was going to hurt me." The following interchange depicts the extent of this fear.

HEIDE: What is the worst thing you thought he might do? Feared he might do?

PETER: Try to kill me. Because he is a big man.

HEIDE: How big?

PETER: 6'3", 250 [pounds].

HEIDE: That is a big man. What is your own size?

PETER: 155, 5'11". That is now, I was smaller then.

HEIDE: What made you think that?

PETER: Because of what he would say. "Keep pushing me [Peter], because I'll lose my cool and I'm going to do something to you … I'd be scared … like kill you."

HEIDE: Did you think he might do it?

PETER: Yeah, the way he acted, yeah. I'd run from him; he'd corner me.

As Peter got older he began to fear that his father would kill him. When he was 14 or 15, his father would say, "You think you are a man" and go on to say "mean" things. When he was 16 and 17, his father actually threatened him. "Last couple of times we left him, he was coming at me, he'd be beating my mom. I'd say, 'You want to kill me, you kill me.' 'All right, I will' and he started coming at me." On the night of the homi-cide, his father threatened him. "Either he was going to kill me or I was going to kill him. That's what it came down to, I guess."

Verbal Abuse and Covert Sexual Abuse of Peter

Mr. Jones would "cuss," "put down," and say unkind things to his son. Psychologically abusive statements made by Mr. Jones included "You ain't worth shit," "You're stupid, just like your damn mother," and "You're nothing but a sorry son of a bitch."

Although Peter said that his father called him "pussy," he denied any overt sexual abuse. When I asked him about indicators of covert sexual abuse (e.g., exposure to pornography, taunting with sexual comments or intimations regarding girlfriends by father), his answers were generally negative. Some inappropriateness regarding sexu-ality concerned "off the wall stuff" that Mr. Jones said when drunk. For example, "If you brought a girl into the house, he wouldn't care." Peter suggested only one other indicator of possibly covert sexual abuse: his father's walking around the house in his underwear. This behavior clearly embarrassed the boy: "I didn't think it was right. Put some clothes on."

Physical and Emotional Neglect and Emotional Incest

Peter was not allowed to be a child. Like other children raised in an alcoholic family system,[3] from early childhood on Peter was largely on his own. Mrs. Jones's deteriorating physical condition and her addiction to tranquilizers made her unable to give her son a safe environment and provide for his emotional needs. In many ways Peter assumed a parental role. He cooked, cleaned, got himself and his brother off to school, and took care of his mother.

Peter deeply loved and cared for his mother. He worried about her while he was in jail and unable to help her. He had been a very nurturing figure to her, far more like a husband than a son. Peter had been his mother's confidant and protector for years.

Although Peter's behavior throughout the years might have seemed exemplary, it was not healthy. His mother's dependence on him was a form of emotional incest. Mrs. Jones treated Peter more like a spouse than her son. In addition, she did not protect Peter. Instead, her own psychopathology resulted in her physically neglecting her children, and she allowed a highly stressful situation to be perpetuated.

Changes in the Environment before the Homicide

Living in a household with two chemically dependent parents was enormously stressful for Peter. His father would suddenly turn on him. "He would change. You wouldn't know if you could say anything. He could explode at any time like a bomb. That's what we were scared about." In this environment Peter became hypervigilant and numbed his feelings, characteristics of those with post-traumatic stress disorder (PTSD).

When she [his mother] was at home this last year, he'd start, he'd be off ... we'd all be in the kitchen ... he has said it ["I'll kill you"] in front of my mom, but when he says this, I block everything out. I really don't know who's in the room. It's like I keep my mind on him. 'Cause I watch him. He makes a move. I'm gone. That's just the way it is.

Mr. Jones stopped drinking about a year before the homicide in response to his wife's threats to leave him. From that time on, Mr. Jones took Valium daily to keep himself calm. During the month before the homicide, circumstances deteriorated even further, causing additional stress for Peter. Mrs. Jones was again hospitalized and unable to buffer the situation. Peter did not think he would have killed his father if his mother had been home. The youth said, "She could talk him out of stuff. Why don't you [father] just sit down and talk to him [son]?" During the mother's absence, Mr. Jones resumed drinking. Peter reported a difference in Mr. Jones's behavior.

The medicine would have no effect. The beer kept it out. He'd be like his old self, he would start on us, want to get violent ... you'd say something wrong and that's it, he'd jump on you, "What did you say?" He had a hearing problem, too. Before you could tell him, "You [are] hearing me wrong," he'd say "I know what I heard." You can't tell him he's wrong.

Mr. Jones argued more with his son during the last month because "he was worried about my mom, he didn't like her to be away." At the same time as he was experiencing difficulties with his father, Peter was increasingly frustrated with the young boarder, Paul. Peter believed Paul was not trying to get a job: "He was living off us. We argued a lot." Peter had assumed a parental role toward Paul as well, getting him up for work when he was employed, washing his clothes, and so on.

Peter had two major disappointments in the month before the homicide. His girlfriend, Becky, who was his first and only significant girl, broke up with him: "She started liking this other guy." Peter took this loss very hard. When asked how he felt, the boy replied, "I cried. I felt like she was all I had."

The second disappointment involved the sudden and mysterious disappearance of a cat Peter loved. Peter was told by his uncle George (not a very reliable person by the youth's account) that his father was responsible. Although his father denied it, Peter believed Mr. Jones was responsible. In earlier years Peter had had two dogs, both of whom also vanished. He suspected that his father might have had something to do with their disappearances.

The Night of the Homicide

Peter told me that he did not remember "a lot of things" that happened on the night of the homicide. He remembered "bits and pieces of that night. I remember some things of what I did. I remember doing it. I don't know if it's in order." His recollection of events had "hurt me for a long time. When I remember it, it would seem intentionally I did it."

Paul and Peter's uncle George said that Mr. Jones had hit Peter a couple of times while they were in the kitchen because the boy did not have dinner ready on time, and Peter accepted their report. Peter remembered that his uncle and Paul left and that he ran out the door while saying, "Fuck you, asshole" to his father. He also remembered that his father went into the house and got something, which Peter assumed was car keys, and drove off. Peter surmised that his father thought that he had gone to a friend's house and perhaps intended to go get him.

At this point Peter went back into the house and entered his father's bedroom, where he got a rifle and three bullets. After that he went to his own bedroom and loaded the rifle. About that time, his father pulled up. Peter recalled putting the rifle under his bed before taking flight. "He was coming in the door and I was running out of my bedroom door and he started to chase after me and I ran out the back door and ran around the house. He hollered, 'You have to come in some time!'"

Peter saw his father sit down "in front of the window, in front of the chair and TV." As he crawled though a window, Peter felt very afraid that his father would catch him. His father had sometimes booby-trapped windows so he could tell if Peter had reentered the house. Peter "vaguely" remembered a board falling as he came in his bedroom door and feared his father had heard the noise.

I was looking constantly at my bedroom door to see if it was going to open. And I just grabbed the gun and snuck out my bedroom window and when I went to the front window, he was sitting there. And that's when I aimed the gun up to his head and I just kept thinking about all the things he's done to my mom and me and Patrick, and

I was tired of this. Then it's like I blacked out, I just remember, it seemed like my eyes closed, like I closed my eyes, and then the gunshots woke me up, it seems like, I thought I only shot him one time, I thought I shot him one time. I never found out until the police told me that I shot him three times. Then I ran back into the house after I dropped the gun and I saw what I did, and I was shocked. I didn't think I had done that. In a way I didn't want to, you know, and I seen the blood coming down all over him and everything, and I was hugging him and telling him not to be dead, you know, and I got Paul. I told him to call the cops and the ambulance. I forgot about my little brother. Paul said to get out of here and hide the gun. I left and went to John's [his friend]. I told John and his mom. I don't remember if I went to sleep or anything. Then I remembered my little brother. I was going to the house to get him. Before I got there, the police stopped me.

When asked how much time had elapsed between his father leaving and the shooting, Peter's confusion was apparent: "I don't know. I was like crazy. I couldn't say. It seems like it happened so fast. I don't even know how it got so late. I can't remember anything. That's all I can remember." Peter reported having flashes go through his mind at the time of the homicide:

Things I remember, pictures of him hitting my mom, hitting me. It was like I blacked out. Like I was thinking of then [those times in the past], I guess, that I did that. It was like I pointed the gun, that was it. Flashes going through my mind. My brother tells me he said that he [the father] had to have really scared me ... to really have got at me in order to make me do that. Because before I would just leave, run away until he calmed down, you know, and come back.

Paul and others had said that Peter had been talking to them that day "like I was freaked out, talking about leaving," apparently because he was scared of his father. His mother said his suitcase had been found packed. "I must have tried to have left and my dad caught me—I don't know. I try to remember. It's like a black in there." Peter mentioned that his friend John had also said that Peter had been "acting weird a couple of days. Different."

"All that week," Peter said, "he was really bad on me ... that's why I think I was really planning on leaving." He tried to call his "aunt" Joan (really a cousin), who lived about 300 miles away, because he thought that he could go there.

Peter was pushed to his breaking point after years of living in an environment fraught with stress. At the time of the homicide, the boy believed his life was in imminent danger. Peter's belief that he could be killed by his father was reasonable in view of past beatings and the threats his father made that night and earlier. Given Peter's apparent intention to leave the home and the thwarting of his efforts, his feeling of being trapped would have been reinforced.

The boy's claim that he blacked out and still has gaps in memory is credible. In addition to being terrified by his father, Peter was horrified by the memories that flashed before him as he stood holding the gun. He was overcome by the terror and horror that he experienced. The adolescent's report that he closed his eyes, lost consciousness temporarily ("blacked out"), and in essence was unaware of his conduct when he fired the gun is consistent with reports of other adolescent parricide cases.

CASE PROCESSING AND DISPOSITION

At Peter's trial, the defense presented numerous witnesses, including Peter's relatives and neighbors, who graphically corroborated the extensive physical and psychological abuse Mr. Jones had inflicted on Peter and Mrs. Jones for years. In the opinion of all four mental health experts who examined the youth, the boy was legally insane at the time of the crime under the prevailing state standard, the M'Naghten test. I testified that the stress in the home in which the boy was raised was similar to that experienced by soldiers in combat and that the boy's hypervigilant behavior and flight into attack were consistent with a diagnosis of PTSD. The cumulative effect of the abuse and its escalation during the month before the homicide conspired with the events of the evening to push the youth over the edge. All the experts agreed that the boy was in a dissociative state at the time of the crime; he was both reexperiencing episodes of past trauma and terrified by the events that took place on the evening of the homicide. In addition, as noted earlier, Peter had a documented history of suffering from excessive anxiety and worry for several years and had been diagnosed with generalized anxiety disorder.[4]

After resting its case, the defense made a motion for a judgment of acquittal, arguing that the State had introduced no evidence to rebut the position that the boy was legally insane when he shot his father. Even some of the State's witnesses supported the defense's contention that the boy was legally insane at the time of the crime. The motion was, however, denied at first. Closing arguments were presented, and the case went to a six-person jury. After more than a day's deliberation, the jury stated it was hopelessly deadlocked and could not reach a verdict.

The defense renewed its motion for a judgment of acquittal after a mistrial was declared. This time the judge granted the motion, and Peter was found not guilty by reason of insanity.

Three of the mental health experts who had testified at the trial were again subpoenaed to testify at the disposition hearing two weeks later. We agreed that Peter needed in-depth psychotherapy in order to resolve the long-standing trauma to which he had been exposed and that a brief period of hospitalization would help him to make the transition from jail back to the community. I testified at this hearing that Peter's successful adjustment in the community would depend on the whole family's undergoing treatment. The most important criterion for success was that the mental health professional be knowledgeable about the dynamics and treatment of alcoholic family systems. The deep-seated problems that Peter, his brother, and his mother had developed from living with Mr. Jones did not end with the man's death; unless they were addressed, the family pathology would continue. I recommended that, in addition to intensive psychotherapy, all three attend community support meetings in self-help—Al-Anon for Mrs. Jones and Peter, Alateen for Patrick, and Adult Children of Alcoholics for Peter.

The judge ordered Peter to be transferred to a local hospital to undergo at least two weeks of psychotherapy before release. She accepted defense counsel's plan to have Peter treated by the psychiatrist who had seen him on two occasions and who had treated Peter's parents.

Peter was hospitalized for one month. In a follow-up letter written to the court at defense counsel's request, I stressed the need for Peter to participate in therapy that would facilitate the release of his emotions. Conflict with his mother was to be expected, and Peter's unresolved anger toward her had to be safely discharged.

About three months after Peter's release, he was arrested and charged with four armed robberies of convenience stores. In statements made to the press, Peter said that he had committed the robberies because he needed money to give to his mother. Details provided to me by defense counsel indicated that Peter's treatment program had failed to address the deep-seated family pathology. In the absence of meaningful psychotherapeutic intervention, it was not surprising that, as stress in the family intensified, Peter's conduct took an antisocial course in a series of desperate attempts to solve escalating financial problems at home.

Five factors were primarily responsible for Peter's failure to make a successful adjustment to society: (1) the lack of change in the home environment, (2) the effect of drugs on Peter, (3) mounting financial concerns, (4) the lack of meaningful treatment and failure to coordinate treatment services, and (5) the lack of therapeutic intervention when the family situation had reached crisis proportions.

During the three months when Peter lived in the community, there was no change in the problems that existed in the home environment. He and his mother argued frequently. He would leave his mother's home, usually retreating to his cousin's home. When Mrs. Jones thought Peter was upset, she would give him some of her Valium to calm down.

Within a week of Peter's return to his home, the defendant's 20- or 21-year-old cousin moved in. Peter drank beer and smoked marijuana almost daily with this cousin for about two or three months prior to his rearrest. Alcohol and drugs allowed him to escape from the pressure he felt his mother exerted on him and the problems of reentry into society. The drugs he took made him even more likely to behave maladaptively. The adolescent explained that he was "different" on drugs and that he would get even more depressed when he thought about the family's problems.

Financial concerns mounted. Peter had difficulty getting a job because of the notoriety of his case. His efforts to secure work on a daily basis through the labor force were partly successful, and he earned $26 per day. He felt compelled to quit, however, after three days, when he received a traffic ticket for driving without a license. He did not have the money to pay for the ticket and for a license, and he could not rely on his mother for transportation.

During this period, Mrs. Jones was also very worried about finances. She told Peter that she could not pay for needed car repairs and was afraid that they would be evicted because she was $100 behind in the rent. Peter asked her to explore different payment arrangements, but she was too obsessed with their financial problems to take the necessary action. His mother told him, "I can't do anything. You live here, too."

Family problems were escalating, but there was no meaningful treatment and no coordination of services. Only one family counseling session took place in the three-month period between Peter's discharge from the hospital and his rearrest. This session, conducted by Dr. Broker, a psychiatrist, and his wife, ended in an argument between Peter and his mother. Following this session, Peter was seen only by the psychiatrist's wife, who lacked appropriate credentials. Peter's younger brother was not seen again. When I visited Peter, he told me that he saw Mrs. Broker weekly and that she knew he was drinking, smoking marijuana, and using cocaine with his cousin, but she took no action. He also told me that the social services worker in his case was aware that he was using drugs to cope with his problems.

In the month preceding the robberies, tension in the Jones home came to a head. Mrs. Jones packed up Peter's belongings, and he went to stay with his cousin. The day after he left, the state social services worker met Peter at his vocational school and told him that he was in violation of a court order. Peter had to return home until a court date could be set to reevaluate his residence. Despite the crisis, there was little that the state worker could do. The psychiatrist and his wife were out of town for two weeks and had made no therapeutic provisions for the Jones family. The judge who had presided in the case was also unavailable.

Stressors in the home environment bore heavily on the adolescent. Peter knew that the family needed money, and he eventually came to see robbery as a way to get it. About a month before the four robberies, he saw his cousin rob a convenience store by threatening the clerk with a crowbar. Peter remarked that, although he was unaware of his cousin's intentions when they entered the store, he was surprised at how easy it was to commit a successful robbery. When Peter committed the robberies, he had reached the point where he "didn't care anymore."

By the time Peter appeared before the trial judge at the hearing scheduled to discuss a change in residence, he had four new charges pending for armed robbery. Peter committed the robberies two days after he appeared in court before another judge for his traffic ticket and was apprised of the fines that he had to pay.

When he committed the robberies, Peter stated that he was feeling "really foggy" due to the ingestion of alcohol and some Valium that his mother had given him. He had used a crowbar to rob two stores and a brick to rob two others in a two-day period. The youth told me that although he had no recollection of two of the four robberies, when the police showed him photographs taken at the scene, he realized that he must have committed all of them.

Each robbery count was handled individually. Peter was found guilty of armed robbery by one jury and convicted of a lesser charge by another. He pleaded guilty to lesser charges on the other two counts of armed robbery. Sentencing guidelines indicated that a seven- to nine-year prison term was appropriate.

At the sentencing hearing, an assistant state attorney argued that Peter be sentenced to a nine-year prison term to be followed by 15 years' probation. Defense counsel summed up the problems Peter had had in obtaining help following his original acquittal. The boy's lawyer then asked the judge to sentence the defendant to probation with two stipulations: (1) Peter would live and work in a community restitution center in a major city located about 40 miles from his home, and (2) he would undergo intensive psychotherapy with a therapist who was familiar with the treatment needs of this type of youth.

The judge, who also presided over Peter's murder trial, found merit in the defense's contention of mitigating factors. She imposed a four-year prison term to be followed by six years of probation.

Given credit for time served in jail and the accumulation of gain time in prison, Peter served seven months in adult prison.[5] Defense counsel's plan was not implemented upon his release. Peter did not relocate and had difficulty obtaining employment in the community in which he had been raised. Arrangements he made to live with a roommate did not work out satisfactorily, and he was not allowed to live with his mother. Peter's probation officer confirmed that Peter had been offered no meaningful therapeutic help. The probation officer was seeking alternative housing and trying to implement a treatment program for Peter when he absconded. Within 10 months after Peter's release from prison, a warrant for his arrest was sworn.

Some years later I heard informally that Peter's probation matter had been straightened out and that he was living in another state. He was reportedly in a stable relationship with a woman, and together they had a baby girl.

About 14 years after Peter's trial and acquittal, I received a phone call that left me speechless. Peter had been arrested for allegedly killing two people: a man and a woman. Internet news clippings were sketchy. Reports said that Peter and a female co-defendant had allegedly killed two people with whom they were involved in a check-kiting scheme. The victims had been shot, stabbed, and bludgeoned. Claims were made that Peter and his co-defendant took items from the house and money from the male victim's pockets.

Seventeen months after Peter's arrest, his attorney contacted me. He advised me that Peter had been charged with two counts of premeditated murder and was facing the death penalty if convicted. Despite my offer to evaluate Peter pro bono, Peter's attorney did not follow through on getting records to me and arranging for me to evaluate his client. I did consult over the phone with a psychologist who resided in Peter's state and who was appointed to evaluate Peter. Both of us expressed frustration about Peter's attorney's failure to return phone calls and his "dropping the ball" as far as our involvement was concerned. The psychologist expressed concerns about Peter's credibility. I sent records, including the doctors' reports, from the trial in which Peter was charged with killing his father to this psychologist. Other than that, I was not much assistance, as I had no records regarding the double homicides or Peter's statements regarding this incident to the police, defense counsel, or the psychologist.

The Long Winding Road Back to Murder

Peter was convicted of two counts of first-degree murder and two counts of aggravated robbery. He was subsequently sentenced to life in prison. Within a month of Peter's conviction, I met with him for about two hours in jail. It had been almost 17 years since I had last seen him. The boy I remembered was now 35 years old. He seemed "shell-shocked." He remembered me and was oriented to the situation. He was very talkative, perhaps somewhat hyper. I noted that he remained very co-dependent with his mother.[6]

About a year later I met with Peter in prison for approximately four hours. Peter was very pleasant and engaged in our meeting. He was again very talkative. His eye contact and his sense of humor were both good. He made reference to his mother repeatedly throughout the interview. Between these two visits, I was able to piece together what had transpired in the intervening years.

I asked Peter to start with his being sentenced to prison for the armed robberies and the report that he had absconded within less than a year of subsequently being released from prison. Peter said that he had no formal counseling during the seven months when he was in prison. He completed his GED, attended Narcotics Anonymous and Alcoholics Anonymous meetings, and took a course on communication skills. He got one disciplinary report for fighting. Peter explained that he left the state after he was released from prison because his probation officer had erroneously maintained that he had a much longer period of probation than he had been given. He fled to the state where his cousin lived and to which his mother and brother Patrick had relocated.

In this neighboring state, he met Rita, had a baby with this young woman, got a job, and was doing well when the authorities arrested him for absconding. He was transported back to his home state, where he spent 90 days in jail waiting for his hearing. The lawyer who represented him at his trial for killing his father assisted him at the hearing.

The judge was impressed that Peter had worked for nearly a year and a half, had stayed out of trouble, and had a family, including a year-old daughter. The judge agreed to transfer probation to the neighboring state. Peter was ordered to serve one year on probation; there were more than 20 stipulations, including drug and mental health treatment and a requirement that Peter not live with his mother.

The probation officer in the receiving state reportedly told Peter that she was not going to worry about the stipulations. He was told to stay out of trouble and to not use alcohol or drugs. Counseling was waived.

Peter successfully completed probation and did well for about six years. He maintained continuous employment. Peter, his common-law wife Rita, and his daughter lived in the same home with his mother and brother. Peter and Rita argued frequently. His life began to unravel when he learned that Rita had had an affair with his boss. He was devastated when she ran off with this man. Peter overdosed on drugs and was hospitalized. Later Rita decided she was a lesbian. She reportedly used Peter's past history in an attempt to keep him from seeing their daughter.

About this time Peter started hanging out with another young woman, Claire, whose father was a drug dealer. Peter started doing "coke and meth" with Claire. The two had been living together and using drugs for about six months when Peter went to jail on a burglary charge. When Peter was released, he lived off and on with Claire. He continued to use drugs during the next four years until he was arrested again for passing a bad check in order to buy drugs.

Peter was sentenced to 30 days in jail and 28 days of treatment, followed by time in a halfway house and then a year of intensive supervision. He successfully completed his sentence and was trying to straighten out.

Peter maintained involvement with people he had met in the halfway house after he completed his sentence. Two of these people, Dennis and Tina, who later would become the murder victims, were mixed up with others in a check-kiting scam whereby they would cash worthless checks. Peter was invited to participate by making the worthless checks. Peter rationalized that by producing these checks, he was not doing anything "really wrong" and he was making money.

The situation was complicated by the fact that Peter's mother interacted with these individuals. Dennis and Tina were intimately involved and living together. Peter reported that Dennis physically abused Tina and that Tina confided in Mrs. Jones, seeking her counsel and support. Peter objected to the way Dennis treated Tina and did not want his mother involved in their relationship. About three or four days before the killings, Peter reportedly told Dennis to keep Tina away from his mother.

Things reportedly came to a crisis when Peter learned that his mother had gotten involved in the check-kiting scheme. Peter was angry that Dennis and Tina had gotten his mother involved. Peter explained that his mother was likely sedated when she cashed two stolen checks and not really cognizant of what she was doing. In addition, Mrs. Jones told Peter she felt threatened by Dennis and did not want him around anymore. Peter decided to go with Erin, another individual involved in the check-kiting scheme, to Dennis and Tina's home to tell them both to stay away from his mother.

Peter reported that while he was at the victims' home, things took an ugly turn. Dennis picked up a club that had a putty knife screwed into the top of it and tried to hit Peter. Peter blocked the club, getting cut in the hand in the process, and took the club from Dennis. Peter explained that he was there to protect his mother and had to defend himself in the meantime.

They had involved my mother. That's when the whole thing went, that I went over there about to stop the issue. And then, one thing led to another. There was mention about the police being called and that's when everything had broke out. And the girl [Erin] had the gun, you know, I mean that's what I'm saying. Yeah, and I had a knife, but it was that individual's knife [Dennis's] in their own club. Things that was used to [be in the past] just snapped out—that's what I'm saying. From, with my past, that's why I'm very protective of my mother .... When something comes to my mother, what me and her's got that bond, what we've been through with, and they, you just dealing with another violent issue, person, you feel that your life's in danger, you're gonna react in another, just another mode.

Peter related that he and Dennis got into a fight, and Erin shot him. Peter characterized it as "a snapping point." He was adamant that he "was not going intentionally over there to do no harm to those people. It was, like I said, with my mom being involved and, when I found out, and then I went over there."

Peter recognized how much he was impacted by the abuse he and his mother had endured. He said, "And that I would go to a point, because that's just the truth, I would go to a point, I would kill somebody over my mother if it come down to protecting my mother, and on that issue. But I did do the right thing is what I thought. What are you supposed to do? I went over there and talked to the individuals when I found out they involved my mom."

When I asked Peter how the incident turned violent, he immediately tied it back to the incident involving his father.

Well, it was just like, it was just like, like when I told you before, about with my dad, but it wasn't that I went and blacked out and seen other things. It was like I just had this, like tunnel vision come over me, like I felt like when you're watching a movie. It just felt like I was watching someone else. Everything was real slow motion, and I felt just real emotion—intense on me, feeling on me. I just didn't feel it was me in other words. I felt something else, but I was just watching everything, and when I started talking to him, then I seen him get an attitude. When he got an attitude, that's when I started feeling really nervous and just real, started shaking, you know? And scared, and then, that's when, like I said, he had that club and he started. Erin was arguing with the girl, and that's when he ended up saying, "Don't come in my house disrespecting," and things like that. And then that's when all I said was, "Look, all I know is, I done told y'all not to involve my mom in y'all's personal business." And I get real irate. Like I can stay calm with you right now, but in there, in that situation ... trying to explain it and talk, and not understand it, and watching to see how this guy was gonna react, you know? And already knowing, or hearing about, how he was, or things that he had been involved in. I was more or less scared that I needed to do something. You know, put myself, my foot down because they already went and crossed the line with me, involving my mom.

Peter commented as he described what had happened that he was jumpy, "real nervous." He explained that he has difficulty communicating with people, especially if he feels that there is going to be a confrontation.

And that's where I have an issue of dealing with the problems of communication at times with people like that, especially if I feel that there's going to be a confrontation, and then I get upset because I don't know how they're gonna react. And I definitely don't want to deal with a confrontation because then bodily harm or whatever just takes me into another level, mode of the past, abuse with Dad, or anything. You get into a fight—you want to avoid it at all costs if [you] can. I just try to do that to where, but yet when I try to explain an issue and somebody gets in an argumental state, I don't know how to deal with that, to where I do get nervous or jumpy, a defense mode in other words, feeling that I have to defend myself, more than I do, know how to just, "O.K. let's just do this or that." I can try that, but then when somebody starts getting argumentative, loud, then I get in another level that I get real nervous, and I start thinking, "O.K. man," and then duh-duh-duh-duh, and I'm twisted up or whatever. But then when it was Mom, I was trying to stand my ground because I thought I was right. And I was just telling them that it involved Mom, about the hospital, the beating on Tina and stuff, and then they go and now get her involved in the checks, and I says, "Enough's enough." I said, "Y'all just need to stay away." I said, "Or the law, the cops will be called." That's when he got real—[and said] "What?," you know? And then I seen like that look on his eyes, and then that's when, like I said, he picked up that club.

Peter explained that he hyperextended Dennis's arm and grabbed him by the throat in self-defense. At that point, he started getting "tunnel vision. It was like black." Peter said that he started thinking about things Dennis had done in the past, including coming to his apartment with a knife in his back pocket, looking for a young man whom Dennis had "ripped off" in the past. Peter did not want to get involved in their business and did not like Dennis's threatening posture. As Peter thought of these things, he hit Dennis with the club. As the two fought, Dennis "kicked and busted up the dining room table."

Peter reported difficulty remembering the events that transpired. He has pieced some of it together from what others have told him. "When I went over there that night, that's where I know only what people was saying they remember, makes me remember, okay, yeah, that lines up with what I remember here and there." From what Peter remembered, Erin grabbed one of the table legs and hit Tina with it. Dennis reportedly later took a knife from his pocket, and Peter grabbed it. He remembered hearing shots fired and thought that his co-defendant Erin shot both of them.

Peter's entire trial lasted two days. No defense witnesses were called. Peter was sentenced to life plus 20 years. Erin reportedly pled out to facilitation, meaning that she had something to do with the two murders but was not the one who caused them. She was sentenced to 25 years in prison with a 30% reduction for good behavior. After Peter was convicted, his attorney asked whether he would be willing to testify against Erin if the State would drop his conviction from first-degree murder to second-degree. Peter's answer was very telling: "I don't know if I could do that because she probably saved our lives, her having the gun, you know?"

Peter's resolve to protect his mother runs throughout both interviews. She had not fared well during the intervening years. She had lost a lot of weight, was "in and out of the hospital for nerves," and was on antidepressants. She retained fluids, which made her ill, and had had breast implants that made her sick. Her memory was declining, and she had been on disability for a long time. Her condition reminded him of the past, as she would lie on the couch and sleep.

Peter related that a couple of months prior to the double homicide, he had insisted that his mother leave his brother's residence and move in with him because Patrick, a heavy drinker, was taking her money. Peter said that he had to "watch out for her" as she was recovering from surgery, drains from breast implants, and colon cancer. He said, "Mom is just Mom. You know, Mom—dumbfounded to the world, gullible, I guess. Naive, being that's how Mom is. Mom has not been out here, running around in society. Me and my brother and her is all she's either lived with since all that back there with Dad. And we've all just stayed with each other, lived with each other."

Peter gave a statement to police about his involvement in the homicidal incident after they threatened to arrest Mrs. Jones if he did not talk to them. Peter said, "It wasn't a whole true statement that I gave them because I nullified everything about my mother in it." He wanted "to make sure there was nothing about her, because there was nothing said about her with the checks and those people."

Oddly, on the day of the incident, Peter had started regular probation after finishing intensive supervision. At his first probation visit, he tested positive for drugs. Peter explained that he had been partying with his friends for "that whole week." He "celebrated" his completing house arrest by drinking and using drugs, including marijuana, methamphetamine, and cocaine. The probation officer decided to give him a second chance. From Peter's perspective, things were going well for him. He had his own place, a bank account for the first time in his life, and "a good job." He was getting along with his daughter's mother and was going to see his daughter. He had his mother staying with him. He was interested in having a relationship with a woman and starting a new life. He called Marcia, a woman with whom he had broken up about three weeks previously, and asked her to come pick him up. Marcia used to "do meth" with Peter but had quit and encouraged Peter to do the same.

It was reportedly during the period when Marcia and Peter had been separated that Peter got involved with Erin, who would later become his co-defendant in the double homicide. As Peter waited for Marcia to come to his apartment on the day of the murders, there was a knock on the door. Erin appeared. Erin wanted Peter to accompany her to Dennis and Tina's apartment so that they could confront them about the checks. Peter said that Erin wanted "to fight, to do something" to them, but that he did not want to go because his mother had given him some medication and he had been sleeping. Peter tried to make excuses, but eventually he went. Before doing so, he "downed a 40 ounce beer," explaining he was "feeling nervous about confronting these individuals anyhow."

Peter expressed remorse for the killing. He wished the killings had not happened and stated that the deaths could have been avoided. Although he said that Dennis in particular had a checkered and violent past, Peter did not judge either of the victims.

So I understand I'm hearing bad things about them, but also they probably had a bad past just like I did too, but it was the way they wanted to choose to react. I didn't choose to react to people. I chose to react on another emotion of the reaction that I feel being reacted at me. I thought that they was bad people, and I thought that I was doing the right thing for my mother … who had been through a lot of things. And I reacted, overreacted in another bad way that then resulted in two deaths of people that probably could have been prevented.

Peter admitted this tragedy could have been avoided if he had "stood up and said 'no more' to these individuals, of saying, 'No, I don't want this in my house. I don't want this around me 'cause I am trying to change.'" Peter explained further,

I allowed myself and my mom and us to be involved into a situation there and, over just thinking, just because it was some easy money that I know somebody, that they propositioned me with that, nothing else was going to occur from it. That's where all my focus was, not over the overall picture, being one dimensional, I guess. That's where my bad, that's where my fault's at. I was just not thinking it over, comprehending everything at once.

Peter expressed concern for his daughter, approximately age 15, when I met with him the second time post-conviction. He saw her about three or four years prior to our visit. He still hears from his mother and talks to her on the phone occasionally. Peter has not heard from his brother.

Peter has kept in touch with me since his conviction of the two murders. His appeals for a new trial were denied. More than six years after his conviction, I was subpoenaed for a hearing on ineffective assistance of counsel by a new lawyer who was handling this petition. I testified at the hearing about my willingness to evaluate Peter pro bono following his arrest and his trial lawyer's failure to follow up with me despite repeated attempts to contact him. I also told the court about my evaluation of Peter during his first trial, diagnoses given by the mental health professionals involved, and the pathology in the Jones family, including Peter's relationship with his mother. During the hearing, the judge who presided over the original trial asked me questions related to my testimony. The questions struck me as appropriate and as designed to clarify information I provided.

During my testimony, Peter asked to speak. After the judge denied his request, Peter muttered something and challenged the judge. The judge warned Peter to stop or he would find him in contempt. Peter persisted, and the judge found him in contempt, sentenced him to 10 days, and had him removed from the courtroom.

The judge allowed me to continue with my testimony. When asked, I acknowledged that my knowledge of Peter's role in the double homicide was based solely on the defendant's report and that I was unaware that Peter had allegedly stabbed one of the victims multiple times. The judge commented that Peter's memory seemed "selective" and implied that his account might be self-serving. The judge postponed the hearing to a later date so as to allow Peter to testify. Given the circumstances, I was unable to meet with Peter at the conclusion of the hearing.

About six weeks later, Peter wrote to thank me for traveling and testifying at his hearing. He explained that he spoke out because he thought that the judge was being argumentative and disrespectful to me. He apologized for his outburst. "I let my emotions get the best of me."

Several months later, Peter wrote to advise me that his post-conviction motion had been denied by the trial court judge. The court did not find that errors made by

Peter's attorney met the legal threshold to establish ineffective assistance of counsel. Accordingly, he was denied a new trial. At the time this book was completed, Peter was waiting for an appellate court to review the trial court's decision.

CASE COMMENTARY

At least three parallels appear to exist between the first and second homicidal incidents: (1) Peter's overall mental health, (2) Peter's mental status at the times of the killings, and (3) the continuing family pathology. It is almost as though Peter has been frozen in time. During my two post-conviction meetings with Peter, he reported symptoms consistent with earlier diagnoses of generalized anxiety disorder and PTSD. He said that he still has trouble "dealing with confrontations," gets very nervous, feels very anxious, and watches people very closely to see how they are acting. He acknowledged having a "rapid thought pattern" that gets excessive and leads to his talking faster. He said that when he gets anxious, he feels badly, tries to hold the feelings in, and then blows up. He reported feeling panicky and threatened on occasion. He would be on "red alert," feeling like he had to defend himself. Although he denied nightmares or flashbacks from the past, he indicated that he gets triggered by events that remind him of his father's abuse of his mother. He tries to calm himself through meditation. His rendition of the homicidal event clearly suggested that he dissociated during the heated interchange.

Peter received no individual treatment aimed at helping him resolve issues related to the past. Treatment appeared limited to group treatment at the halfway house and attendance at drug and alcohol support meetings. As Peter grew into manhood, he continued to take care of his mother and to protect her. Despite probation stipulations to the contrary, Peter lived with his mother. Even at the time of our post-conviction meetings, Peter was convinced that his role was to protect and defend his mother. More than 20 years after the killing of his father, characteristic of the Na behavioral subtype, Peter was still behaving in the self-defeating way he had behaved in as an adolescent.

Peter's statements to me suggest that when Peter went to the victims' home to tell Tina and Dennis to stay away from his mother, he was in a high arousal state. He had been using drugs, including cocaine and methamphetamine, for a week. Peter said that "meth" made him more agitated and amplified his "paranoia." Shortly before leaving his home, Peter said that he had taken sleep medication and consumed a 40 ounce beer. As events unfolded at the victims' house, Peter apparently grew more and more anxious. The confrontation with Dennis reminded him of past altercations with his father, making it difficult for Peter to stay focused. Peter's account suggests that he again perceived himself as being in a life and death situation and likely felt fear, possibly to the point of terror, and anger, possibly to the point of rage. It is unlikely that at that point Peter could stop, think, and make conscious decisions. Rather, it appears that his actions were driven by the limbic system. This is consistent with reports that Peter repeatedly stabbed one of the victims and possibly bludgeoned one or both with the dining room table leg.

It is possible that Peter's statements to me, as the judge suggested, were an effort on his part to avoid taking complete responsibility for his actions and to delude himself. Despite his brushes with the law, Peter does not see himself as a criminal or embrace a criminal lifestyle. He related that he wanted to lead a good life and had thought, just hours before the killings, that he was on the right path for doing so.

Regardless of what interpretation one prefers, one conclusion can be stated with complete certainty: the ending of Peter's story is tragic. Following his acquittal for killing his father on the grounds of insanity, Peter was a high-functioning and prosocial youth. With treatment, he stood a chance of leading a good life and making a contribution to society. Instead, denied treatment, he continued to stay enmeshed in an unhealthy relationship with his mother. He coped with anxiety and difficulties in the same way his father and mother did: he self-medicated. Unlike his parents, however, he used illicit drugs and embarked on illegal activities to support his habit. Peter's decision to remain involved with known criminals and to get involved in a check-kiting scheme was a poor one; it ultimately led to the deaths of two people and to Peter's likely spending the rest of his life in prison.

11 James Holt
The Making of a Murderer

I met James Holt, a White Hispanic boy, in jail under an unusual set of circumstances about a year after he was charged as an adult with the killings of his parents. I was not asked to do an evaluation of the 16-year-old defendant. Rather, the prosecutor and defense attorney involved in the case thought I might benefit professionally from meeting James, given the nature of my research on juvenile homicide offenders. The invitation was extended to me as a professional courtesy while I was visiting their area of the country. I was not asked to provide any feedback on the meeting, and did not do so.

James was accused of shooting his parents multiple times while they were asleep. The facts established that, after being called to the house in the middle of the night by James's mother, police arrived to find the boy's father dead and the mother mortally wounded. Prior to her death, Mrs. Holt scribbled a note and told police that James was the person responsible for the shootings. James was arrested within hours of the shooting. James adamantly denied to legal authorities and to his defense counsel that he had killed his parents.

The juvenile court found probable cause that James was involved in the murders and held a hearing to determine whether the boy should be retained in juvenile court for the proceedings. After four days of testimony, the court determined that James was mentally ill and that no appropriate treatment facilities were available for treating him in the juvenile system.[1] Accordingly, the judge ordered that James be prosecuted as an adult.

I met with James in detention while he was awaiting his trial in adult court. He presented as bright and cocky. He was not concerned about his upcoming trial. He maintained that he would not be convicted because the State could not prove its case—he had not committed the murders. In contrast to his prediction, James was convicted of two counts of first-degree murder. He was sentenced to two consecutive sentences of life in prison plus an additional 16 years. The court ordered at sentencing that "[t]he defendant be confined in a facility or facilities providing an intensive psychotherapeutic treatment program for the defendant's specific psychological problems" within the state department of corrections.

About 14 years after first meeting James, I received a call from a defense attorney asking me to evaluate his client, a man in his early 30s who had killed an inmate in prison while he was serving a life sentence in prison. The attorney sought my expertise because his client had killed his parents at age 16. As the attorney gave a brief sketch of the case, I recognized that the inmate being discussed was James. At this juncture, James was charged with first-degree murder and was facing the death penalty if convicted. I was asked to evaluate the defendant with respect to the motivational dynamics behind the killing of the prison inmate and to address factors in mitigation of imposition of the death sentence.

THE CLINICAL EVALUATION

My assessment of James Holt is based on an eight-hour clinical interview conducted with him and my review of more than 1,000 pages of materials relevant to James's childhood, the murder of his parents, the murder of the inmate, and his experiences in prison. Documents included school records, news clippings regarding the murders of the parents, police reports, corrections files, and prison mental health records. I met for several hours with an elderly married couple, Mr. and Mrs. Morrison, who were former neighbors of the Holt family. James considered them "surrogate grandparents." They had known James since he was 6 years old and had kept in touch with him over the years through frequent letters and visits to prison. They shared with me letters James had written to them, sketches he had drawn, and figurines he had made during his incarceration.

I also spoke to the Morrison's adult daughter, Susan Frazier, on the phone. Mrs. Frazier's son played with James while they lived in the same neighborhood and after they moved. I also consulted with a nationally known forensic psychologist who evaluated James after he killed the inmate.

BEHAVIORAL OBSERVATIONS

James was 32 years old when I met with him the second time. James indicated that he had recently been prescribed Elavil for depression and had been taking it for about a week prior to the evaluation. He was alert and cooperative during the eight-hour period over which we met in the public defender's office.

Soon after we started the assessment, James volunteered that he was being honest and that he initially experienced his thoughts as racing. He seemed to enjoy the interaction and was very reflective throughout the assessment. He listened intently to hundreds of questions and maintained excellent concentration and generally good eye contact. He was noticeably bright, articulate, and polite. His mood was serious for the most part, which was appropriate given the content of the evaluation, as well as reflective of his depressed state.

The defendant's answers clearly indicated that he was oriented in time and space and that his short-term and his long-term memories were intact. He said that he remembered meeting me many years ago when he was awaiting trial in connection with the killings of his parents. There were no data to suggest that he was responding to private sensory experiences (hallucinations). There was some evidence of grandiosity in James's thinking, although he did not appear to have a systematic delusional network in place. For example, he maintained that when he was age 2 or 3 he observed his parents' parenting skills deteriorating, that he was babysitting at age 4, that he read when he was 2 years old, and that at the time of his parents' murders, when he was 16, he was well on his way to Hollywood for a career in special effects. James had features of a personality disorder with schizoid, schizotypal, and narcissistic traits.[2]

PERSONALITY DEVEOPMENT

When I met with James in connection with the killing of the inmate, he perceived at level 4 and would be considered a high-maturity individual. He recognized that he was accountable for his behavior, had an internalized value system, and was capable of experiencing remorse. He was able to identify his feelings and discuss them in some depth. He was aware of the role that needs and motives played in his behavior and, to some extent, in the behavior of others. Typical of others at this stage of development, James was capable of working in furtherance of a goal. In his case, he invested 10 years of his life post-incarceration in filing habeas corpus petitions supporting his position that he was wrongfully convicted of the murder of his parents. When these papers were lost during a prison transfer to another state, hereinafter called Badstate, James was devastated.

James's behavioral response style seemed to be a composite of the *neurotic acting-out* (*Na*) subject and the *cultural identifier* (*CI*) at the time of the evaluation.[3] Individuals who adopt a neurotic behavioral pattern generally feel anxious and conflicted because of unresolved issues, guilt, and feelings of inadequacy dating back to childhood. Deep down inside, they have a poor self-image and feel unworthy. Individuals with an Na pattern act out their difficulties rather than try to resolve them. They often adopt a tough exterior, project an air of independence and superiority, and challenge others either behaviorally or verbally. For them, criminal behavior has a private meaning and is often a reaction to an accumulation of stress. During his incarceration, James seemed to have maintained some of the characteristics of the Na pattern. For example, he repeatedly challenged correctional authorities, which in some respects was self-defeating, as it might have played a role in their decisions to transfer him to many prisons.

At the same time, James's thinking and his behavior were affected by his 15 years in prison. His statements suggested that he had taken on some of the values and responses of other inmates. James, as is characteristic of those who adopt a CI behavior response style, had adopted at least some nonconventional values and defended these values as right courses of action.

RELEVANT SOCIAL HISTORY

The following information was largely reported by the defendant. Corroborative data are included when available.

Family Constellation

James was the oldest of three children born to his parents. His sister and brother were four and 10 years younger than James, respectively. James characterized his early years as happy and reported having his needs met. He remembered his parents and siblings as warm and loving. He indicated that he had a very close relationship with his brother and raised him. He recalled having pets. James said that after he reached age 6, his family life became poor and his parents seemed like strangers.

James described his parents before and after they became Jehovah's Witnesses (JW). Mr. and Mrs. Holt reportedly became JW when James was about 5 or 6 years old. Before becoming a JW, Mrs. Holt, in James's eyes, was very caring, involved, and warm. She was a teacher, a housewife, and person of average intelligence. After joining JW, she changed completely. She yelled, hated everybody, was stressed out all the time, and was a "stranger to me." He remembered her as a terrible mother who stopped vacationing and family trips. Sometimes, he would see a glimmer of his old mother.

James's father was reportedly in Korea during James's early years. Prior to joining JW, Mr. Holt was quiet, nice, and of average intelligence. He was warm and hugged James. After joining JW, he yelled and left the house "all the time," threatened to have affairs, teased his wife, and forgot he had children. Neither parent drank or abused drugs. James depicted his parents as neglectful and possibly abusive in his later childhood. They were more interested in religious activities than their children. They did not give the children gifts and did not attend parent–teacher conferences.

James indicated that he had not seen his sister in more than 10 years. He had contact with her through phone calls and letters. James's relationship with his brother had faded over the years as a result of James's being transferred to out-of-state prisons.

James's uncle and aunt had had little contact with James since his conviction more than 13 years prior to my evaluation. James's uncle reportedly believed that James was guilty of the murders of his parents and that he was "possessed, crazy, or hired someone." This uncle got custody of James's siblings, and his wife resented it. James's uncle's wife reportedly thought James was "demonic" and "evil." James's relatives were devout Catholics and believed in evil. "Some thought I was possessed; I was a total anomaly." James said that he had been "extremely unusual from childhood." He had an interest in monsters, which concerned his family. James made masks, which signified to them "evil in the purest form." It was "reality to them, not movies." James related that after they joined JW, his parents believed in possession and demons.

Self-Reported Child Maltreatment

James's responses suggested that after his parents joined JW, he was physically, medically, and emotionally neglected. James indicated that "taking care of the kids was secondary" to religion. James reportedly was not provided with adequate food, a safe place to live, and adequate supervision as a child. He stated that his parents left his younger sister with him to babysit when he was 4. James maintained that neither his father nor mother often gave him clear messages that they loved him or took the time to genuinely listen to him after they joined JW.

There was some indication of verbally, psychologically, and physically abusive behavior. James said that his parents complained about everything (e.g., friends, clothes), yelled when stressed, cursed at him, and blamed him for their marital and financial problems. James maintained that his parents were resentful of his accomplishments and felt inferior to him. He recalled them being mean to each other and arguing frequently in front of others. They reportedly teased him about his eyesight and his skinniness.

James reported a few instances of physically abusive behavior. He recalled a parent throwing something at him once, as well as being pushed by his dad and slapped by his mom. He said that he was spanked, although rarely. He recalled his father verbally threatening to use a gun against him. He remembered both parents striking out at him toward the end, although it was infrequent. When asked whether the discipline given by his parents ever seemed out of proportion to what he actually did, he said no, because he "never did anything wrong."

James denied that he had been covertly or overtly sexually abused by his parents.[4] James said his parents had each threatened to hurt each other physically but had not actually assaulted each other; they were more into "emotionally scarring" each other. James indicated that he had been emotionally abused by his teachers prior to being incarcerated.

Coping Strategies

James indicated that he participated in about the same level of activities after school as other kids. He had fewer friends and got in less trouble in school and with the law than other kids his age. Prior to his arrest, he talked to his grandparents, relatives, and some friends about problems in his home. Talking helped a little bit because others provided opportunities to James that his parents were not providing. James rarely thought about running away and never did so.

James denied having blank spells or periods of missing time that he could not remember. However, there was some evidence that James experienced dissociation. He indicated that since age 18, and including the six months prior to this evaluation, he had found himself in an unfamiliar place, not sure how he had gotten there. He indicated that he had felt disoriented a few times. The disorientation was temporary. He said that it was a shock to realize that he was in prison. He felt "detached from my own body." This experience reportedly happened two or three times per year.

James denied that he turned to drugs, alcohol, or food as a way to feel better while growing up. He denied acts of self-mutilation. Prior to age 18, James reportedly never thought about killing himself. Since age 18, he had sometimes thought about it. After his habeas corpus papers were lost, he often thought about killing himself. He said that he refrained from killing himself because of his curiosity, his desire to help his friend and later co-defendant Paul, and his internal drive to succeed. James indicated that he thought about suicide during the six months preceding the assessment "very often, every hour." James maintained that he had never attempted to kill himself.

James minimized or denied having parricidal ideation prior to the murder of his parents. He said he joked about killing his parents but was not serious. He said that he might have fantasized about teachers dying during the school day, but not seriously. James maintained that the idea of actually killing someone never entered his mind when he was growing up. James related that he watched movies and TV to get distracted as a way to cope with difficulties at home. He said that he could get lost in fantasy, and that helped him.

School History

James said that his grades in elementary school were above average, and they were mixed in high school. They were not good in later years because he had a lot of absences and did not do his homework. He was absent as a young child because he had bronchitis and pneumonia a number of times over the years. Later, he missed school because of his "career." School records indicated that James missed at least 27 days in the two quarters preceding his arrest. Newspaper accounts indicated that he had dropped out of school about seven weeks prior to the murders.

James stated that he was in special education classes for gifted children from the beginning because he had a high IQ. School records indicated that James's IQ was in the above-average range of intelligence. His verbal and performance scores placed him in the 93rd and 97th percentiles, respectively. Several measures of James's intellectual abilities as a child, however, suggested a possible learning disability. Records indicate that James was placed in special education one day per week.

James denied being in special education due to an inability to do math. He said he found school work "boring and easy" and depicted math as "too boring to tolerate." He indicated that he was not a disciplinary problem in school and had never been suspended.

Hand-written remarks by Mrs. Holt dating from when James was in the sixth grade suggested a sensitive child trying hard to please others in order to gain praise. James's mother wrote that James "needs a lot of attention," is "very sensitive to criticism by teachers," "doesn't like to be teased," "is a perfectionist," and "strives to gain praise." Mrs. Holt also observed that James "has a lot of responsibility with smaller brother and sister." Mrs. Holt opined that James "has too much responsibility." James's mother apparently found her son to be difficult because she stated that she "would like his attitude and behavior to improve." Mrs. Holt also noted when James was in the sixth grade that controlling others was important to him. She related that James had a "few chosen friends that he can control" and that his playmates "have to be under his control."

Friends

James recalled that his family moved around frequently until he was about 9 years old. He recalled nine moves. He maintained that he could make friends easily and got along with people. When asked, he said that he liked friends who were intelligent, nice, motivated, creative, or talented and who had common sense. He claimed to have a few friendships that had lasted several years. After his arrest, friends abandoned him over time.

Sexual History

James stated that at the time of his arrest for killing his parents, he had more girlfriends than guy friends but was dating no one special. He reportedly began dating at age 14 and dated about a dozen girls, never having a bad relationship or experience. His girlfriends were "all special." His longest relationship lasted about one year. He was "not promiscuous."

James told me about Charlotte, a person whose existence could not be corroborated by defense counsel. James said that he met Charlotte, one of the two people closest to him in his life, when he was 14 years old. In that same year, she reportedly died in a car accident. James related that he immersed himself in special effects and did not openly grieve her death. He indicated that he thinks about his past girlfriends and tries to keep the past in the foreground. He lost contact with everybody as a result of out-of-state prison transfers and is lonely. He reportedly had relationships with three women over the years while in prison. He denied homosexual interest or activity.

Activities as a Child

James recalled being an active child. He liked track, fishing, bike riding, rollerblading, hiking, and camping. He liked animals his whole life and considered being a paleontologist. He would not let school interfere with his life, which included playing with friends, toys, and the snow.

James participated in the Boy Scouts for about a year. He also was involved in after-school clubs, including "Olympics of the Mind," and videotapings. He made home movies with space ships and science fiction themes.

Maskmaking and Special Effects Activities

James indicated that he had a special effects career that began when he was in his early teens. He recalled that he started making masks and doing makeup when he was about 14. At about age 15, he was selling some of his creations and advertising in magazines. He was "ahead of his time" with respect to special effects.

James's maskmaking was influenced by horror movies, such as *Halloween, Friday the 13th*, and *American Werewolf in London*; Dungeons and Dragons, which he played a few times; and videogames in arcades. He described depicting skeletons, half-eaten corpses, lizard people, and monsters. James made masks mostly for Halloween and for local events and festivals. He hired friends to help him with sculpting, makeup, carpentry, metal working, feathers, and hair. His creations were experimental and versatile; he created a "glorified puppet."

Friends and girlfriends were admiring. His parents were not supportive at first but later encouraged him. His parents reportedly objected to anything that looked scary, but not the special effects per se. When James was about 13 years old, his parents packed up his room and took his masks and "everything else." His parents had just seen *Halloween* and depicted James's work as "evil." An aunt who lived in a distant state also supposedly thought his artwork was evil. When his parents got out of JW, they were purportedly less worried. Some family members were reportedly admiring of James's special effects until after his arrest; then his work became "demonized." James said that his art was not restricted to horror; he had a wide range, including mermaids and Barbie.

Music and Movie Preferences

James reported liking a wide variety of music. His preferences regarding movies were more restricted. James liked the *Alien* movies, *Star Wars*, *Jaws*, and the *Psycho* movie made after his incarceration. He enjoyed *Silence of the Lambs* and felt an affinity with Hannibal Lector in terms of the "petty indignities" of incarceration, not Lector's cruelty. James also liked *The Simpsons, Beetlejuice* (a cartoon about ghosts), and *101 Dalmatians*. His favorites were horror movies, cartoons, and romance films such as *Titanic* and the 1968 version of *Romeo and Juliet*. James explained that movies sometimes brought out his feelings. He could relate to tragedy; he felt sadness, for example, when Leonardo DiCaprio's character died in *Titanic*.

Prior Delinquent History

Despite some evidence to the contrary, James maintained that he grew up in an upper-middle-class area with no criminals. He denied any involvement in drugs or alcohol while growing up. He had never been arrested prior to killing his parents. He acknowledged some petty vandalism and shoplifting once or twice as a youth.

James denied any affiliation with gangs at any point in his life. James also denied being involved in a Satanic cult, maintaining that assertions to this effect were based on his liking of monster movies and the link between Satanism and monster movies being made and perpetuated. He said that some people thought he had an "evil aura" and that there was "something off about me" that had been with him his entire life.

Self-Perception

When asked to describe himself, James replied there were three versions: (1) pre-incarceration, (2) before his habeas corpus papers were lost as a result of his prison transfer, and (3) the present (at the time of the evaluation). He differentiated among the James created by the media, the "real" James, and the interactive James in prison. He saw himself as multi-faceted. He described himself as sensitive and caring. However, since his habeas corpus papers were lost, he had been angry all the time, which was new for him. He indicated that he was talented and used to be intelligent and creative. He would be a good parent and husband because he was a good son and a good babysitter. He said that he loved animals. He could envision himself hurting someone who was guilty. At the time of the evaluation, James perceived himself as loyal and self-sacrificing. He related that he felt "emotionally arrested," lonely, and suicidal.

When asked what he liked best about himself, James said that he had integrity, was a "true person," and was free of hypocrisy. He tried to be loyal and to speak up for what he believed in. When asked what he would like to change about himself, James said his situation, his circumstances, his age, his appearance, and his eyesight. He indicated that he was judgmental and narcissistic. He was concerned about his receding hairline and opined that stress affected him physically.

When asked whether there was anything he regretted, James said initially, "Not enjoying little things more." He then added, "Not my actions, I regret … my inaction. Not being able to live up to my potential. Getting caught" for the killing of the prison inmate.

When asked about mistakes, James related that he should have "acted more like a kid when I was a kid." He added that he should not have cooperated with the police when his parents were killed and apparently should have killed himself. He had no regrets about losing touch with his family over the years because he had tried very hard to maintain contact.

When asked what he felt guilty about, James replied, "Relatively minor stuff." He said that there were people to whom he should have been nicer rather than overreacting. He felt guilty for not being there for his siblings. He felt guilt for the effect that his killing of the prison inmate had on people like his "surrogate grandmother," Mrs. Morrison.

James stated that time had stood still for him while he had been incarcerated. He said that he still felt young and thought of himself as a boy rather than a man. He related that he had a good memory and depicted himself as an "observer all the time." He maintained that all the information comes in. "I see too much. I don't forget it. I overanalyze it. I hold it in." James said that his awareness had become "more of a curse than a blessing."

James related that news stayed with him emotionally. Tragedy stayed with him, such as a story about a missing child. He explained that stories about kids, old people, the helpless, and animals bother him. His outlook reflected the worst-case scenario. James said that he was "nihilistic" and "negative." James indicated that he had become stronger since being incarcerated. He indicated that he had lived his whole life vicariously through the media.

Feelings

James makes distinctions among his feelings. His remarks indicated that he had a great deal of anger, of which he was aware. He maintained that he had been angry since his habeas corpus papers were lost. James acknowledged a pattern of internalizing his anger, which dated back to his youth. James said that his anger had hurt him more than it had others. He controls his anger by trying to resolve it logically; if he cannot, it festers inside.

James reportedly has been depressed since being locked up, and the depression has intensified since his habeas corpus papers were lost. James related that before he was incarcerated, he could control his environment and actively resolve problems. If he could not resolve a problem, he would ruminate about it. At the time of the evaluation, he felt a sense of complete hopelessness.

James indicated that he felt "extreme loneliness" in prison. James said that he could not relate to anyone in prison. He expressed disdain for the guards, who have jobs rather than careers, and he viewed the inmates, unlike him, as sociopaths.

Religious Affiliation

James stated that he was exposed to Catholicism early on. He never believed in God, even as a child, because he was "not a magical thinker." He saw religion as "ritual." As he got older, he saw more and more hypocrisy. During the evaluation, he expressed hatred toward religion.

Mental Health History

James said that he had never been to counseling prior to his arrest. From his perspective, he had no problems prior to his incarceration.

James opined that he might be "manic depressive." He explained that at times he was "almost giddy" and was elated for no reason (this behavior has been post-incarceration).

He felt that his symptoms matched his understanding of the illness. He related that he required little sleep—about three or fours hours per night—but that his need for sleep had varied over the past five or six years. James maintained that his sleep was troubled. When asked what was the longest period during which he had stayed up, James said 48 hours. He sees himself as grandiose on occasion, but then he goes back to his "normal depressed feelings." He said that he was always irritable in the prison environment.

Physical Health History

James recalled having bronchitis and pneumonia as a child. [School records confirmed these illnesses and also indicated a history of dental problems.] He had no broken bones and was never hospitalized as a child. James recalled himself as being healthy. His vision deteriorated after he was incarcerated, and he has experienced headaches since a prison transfer about three years ago.

Future Orientation

Prior to his arrest, James indicated that he had a special effects career and was planning to go to California, where he expected to make money writing scripts and directing. He expected to get married and have kids. He wanted to help missing children because he always had a soft spot for kids. He recalled babysitting for his siblings and other kids in the neighborhood. It upset him when kids were hurt.

If he had been successful regarding his habeas corpus, he had wanted to get a quieter job away from people so that he could heal. If released someday, he would like to work with animals and be "around real people." When asked whether he was "dangerous," James said, "Only to guilty people who deserve it." He does not know whether he will kill again, saying it depends on "a certain combination of factors; suicide is more likely."

LIFE IN PRISON

James said that prior to killing the inmate, he received virtually no treatment in prison. My review of hundreds of pages of his correctional file revealed several references to James's need for treatment that went unaddressed. Soon after James arrived in prison, for example, a prison psychologist characterized James as an "angry, rebellious individual" who "may be unpredictable, impulsive, and odd in appearance and behavior." He recognized James as inadequate and weak, "egocentric," and "grandiose." The psychologist recommended "intensive psychotherapy in a structured environment to deal specifically with issues relating to anger, grandiosity, and feelings of inferiority." His directives were not followed.

By my count, James was transferred 12 times prior to the prison murder. Three of the prisons were in different states. In contrast, since the murder, both he and his co-defendant had been housed in a special pod supervised by the mental health program.

Jobs and Grievances

While in prison, James had some jobs. He worked mostly in education. He later worked in the snack shop, selling sandwiches and running the cash register.

James maintained that he had been mistreated by the guards and wardens in "every way—physically, verbally, emotionally, and financially." James indicated that he fought the system when he felt his rights were being violated. He reportedly filed about 200 grievances regarding property, food, medical care, mental health care, recreation, and abusive guards. Matters were "always an injustice to me." James stated that he won some of his grievances. He maintained that the institutions "hated" his filing grievances.

James said that 100 of these grievances occurred after he was transferred to Badstate prison, where conditions were deplorable. At this facility, he was housed in a 12-man cell. He and other inmates were allowed no radios, no TV, and no property. They were restricted to their cells; there was no recreation. Cells were dirty and had roaches and rats in them. The lights were always on. The facility was noisy. As a result, James related, the inmates were sleep deprived. He recalled being in a "constant state of stress and alertness." It was at this facility that James lost all his possessions, including his habeas corpus materials. [Information about the poor conditions in out-of-state prisons was corroborated by one of his lawyers.]

Contact with Outsiders While in Prison

James said that he was close to both sets of grandparents growing up. After James's arrest for the murder of his parents, James's grandparents were supportive but not proactive. When asked, James replied that "dozens of people" kept in touch with him prior to the trial related to his parents' deaths. After the trial, some family and friends communicated with him when he was confined in his home state. With each transfer out of state, he increasingly lost touch with family and friends. He reported feeling "more detached" and "starved for affection." After he killed the inmate, James was sent to the state's maximum-security facility and lost contact with more people.

At the time of the evaluation, three of his four grandparents had died. His paternal grandmother was the only one left. She visited him when she was able to do so; her last visit occurred three or four years prior to the evaluation. James reportedly attended his maternal grandmother's funeral. He said that he did not cry, adding, "I don't express emotion." He explained that his lack of emotional expression dated back to childhood. He was aware of feeling emotions, but he did not show them.

James related that Mr. and Mrs. Morrison, his surrogate grandparents, had been involved in his life since he had been their neighbor. They visited him once per month when the prison was close by. He depicted them as gentle and insightful people in their 80s who were active for their age. Mrs. Morrison has consistently written to James over the years.

James opined that the Morrisons kept in touch with him because they were close before he was incarcerated and because James had helped their grandson, who was four years younger than James. James indicated that they saw that he had a lot of potential and "may realize I'm innocent" of the murder of his parents. According to James, the Morrisons have an intellect similar to his. Their continued involvement in James's life meant a lot to him and was a positive force. James indicated that he felt closer to the Morrisons than to his blood relatives.

INTERVIEW WITH MRS. MORRISON

Mrs. Morrison retired after a 30-year career as a teacher. She had fond memories of James playing with her grandson Justin when the two were boys. James taught Justin how to take pictures and make robots and figures. Their friendship continued for many years.

Mrs. Morrison described James as "a very nice, quiet, polite boy" who was "immaculately clean." She remembered him as always being frail and slight. He was a sickly child who had colds, flu, pneumonia, bronchitis, and "frequent sick spells." He was confined to bed on a number of occasions because of sickness. Mrs. Morrison did not see James as an angry child. He had a few friends and a girl whom he liked. She remembered that James's cat disappeared on Halloween and that he felt badly. She recalled that James was not interested in guns or violence and was opposed to alcohol and drugs.

Mrs. Morrison indicated that she did not know James's parents well. She remembered James's mother as very polite. They appeared to be a normal family. She remembered that the parents became JW for a while and that the children were not allowed to go to parties.

Mrs. Morrison and her family were shocked by James's arrest for killing his parents. Her grandson said that James could not have done it, but that if he did he was "not in his right mind." Mrs. Morrison said her daughter Suzie recalled James as "a wonderful boy." She reportedly believed that any trouble was a result of his parents' involvement in the JW.

Mrs. Morrison recalled that Halloween was James's favorite holiday. He made "fabulous masks" and monsters. His figures were "gruesome." James had big ambition; he wanted to build sets for movies. Mrs. Morrison saw James as an "extremely talented" and "very bright" child who was "a pretty normal kid." She had heard that on one occasion, James's parents threw out his drawings and the things he was making. However, she recalled Mrs. Holt being proud of the haunted house her son made for the school carnival and her saying, "My James made this." Mrs. Morrison never thought of James's creations as "evil" and stated that there was "nothing evil about him." Mrs. Morrison consistently kept in touch with James during his incarceration. When he was confined in his home state, she visited him three or four times per year. Mrs. Morrison's sister, who had been an artist and was deceased at the time of the evaluation, also visited him a few times. Mrs. Morrison indicated that James had been pretty much the same over the years. She characterized his letters as cheerful, for the most part. However, she noted that he complained about the treatment he received in the out-of-state prisons. James told her that when he killed the inmate, he was trying to help his friend who had been molested.

To her knowledge, James had been "abandoned" by his family. He indicated in a letter to her that he had talked with his siblings when his maternal grandmother died, a few months prior to my evaluation.

INTERVIEW WITH SUZIE FRAZIER, MRS. MORRISON'S DAUGHTER

Mrs. Frazier recalled James as a very creative boy who made movies and did things normal kids do. He was a sweet and frail child who was not much bigger than her son, although James was four years older. He looked weak and was sickly. She remembered that he had pneumonia three times in one year and missed a lot of school.

Mrs. Frazier recalled that because of their religion, the Holts did not celebrate any holidays, except Halloween. They were very strict parents. She remembered normal interactions between the parents and their children. She recalled Mr. Holt as being a very nice, good-looking, and very macho man who worked on his car. She wondered what it was like for Mr. Holt to have a weak son.

Mrs. Frazier said that when Mr. Holt lost his job, the Holts moved to a rough and crime-ridden area where gangs were prevalent. James, aged 15 at the time, lived for a while with his paternal grandmother and then went to live with his parents. She felt that it would have been very hard for "a nerdy-looking kid" to go to school in that area. She characterized James as "defenseless."

She, her husband, and her son were all shocked by James's arrest for the murder of his parents. They believed that he had to have been "out of his mind." Mrs. Frazier thought that living in that "horrible stressful place" "pushed him over the edge."

JAMES'S HOMICIDAL BEHAVIOR

Correctional records indicated that James generally behaved well in prison. Early in his institutional career, he was placed in the honors dorm. James attended school for years and received "good time" (time taken off of his sentence for good behavior in prison).[5] Records also revealed that prior to killing an inmate named Larry, James had committed only one minor infraction, early in his institutionalization—he refused to obey a lawful order (he did not go to work as instructed).

Events Leading Up to the Prison Murder

James described himself as a "model inmate" prior to his being transferred to a prison in Badstate about a year and a half before his killing the inmate. He had goals, among the most important of which was preparing his legal materials for a habeas corpus filing. In Badstate, James said that he "lost everything that defined me as a person." James characterized his trip and experience in Badstate as "abusive." He has been "filled since with negative emotion, anger, hatred, pain."

Upon being returned to Homestate, James was reportedly housed in a pod with sex offenders and informants. The man James eventually murdered, Larry, a convicted child molester, was assigned to this pod. James maintained that he tried to ignore sex offenders. He said, "I was judgmental, but not actively so."

James maintained that prior to killing Larry, he had been experiencing a great deal of stress. He told the prison warden that he did not want to be housed with child molesters, needed eye surgery because his retinas were detaching, and wanted psychological treatment. When he heard that some inmates were going to be transferred again to out-of-state prisons, James wrote to the governor that these transfers were going to make people violent. He informed multiple people in key roles in person or through letters that he needed to talk to someone and should not be transferred. These people included the prison warden and assistant warden; the prison psychologist and caseworkers; and his classification officer, teachers, and work supervisors. James maintained that all of these people were aware that Badstate had been a terrible experience for him. In addition, he said that being transferred in itself was stressful. His repeated requests to see a psychologist after returning from Badstate were ignored.

James believed that the prison staff had lied to him about the possibility of getting treatment. In addition, he had "really bad headaches." Classification reportedly recommended that James have a CAT scan about a year after he started complaining. At the time of the evaluation, about two and a half years later, James still had not had a CAT scan. He did have eye surgery on both eyes following the prison murder.

The Prison Murder

Despite his pleas, James was on the list of inmates to be transferred. On the night of the homicide, James reportedly was packing in his friend Paul's room in preparation for the pending transfer. Other people were present, but James did not remember who they were.

James related that at this time Paul mentioned that he had given some of his belongings to Larry. Paul also told James that Larry had exposed himself to Paul on an earlier occasion. James said that this revelation was "the straw that broke the camel's back." James characterized Paul as having been shocked and disgusted, as freaking out, and as not being able to defend himself. James stated that he had "a nurturing instinct" toward Paul and felt protective of him because Paul had allegedly been raped before in prison. Paul was young, reminded James of his brother, and was one of James's few friends. James claimed that his response was immediate.

James recalled the murder of Larry as though he were detached from the act of killing the victim. He said that he watched himself killing the victim. Although he knows that he killed the victim, he said that he has no actual memory of it. He reportedly felt no pleasure in killing the victim.

James stated that he did not remember being in Larry's cell. His friends reportedly came and got him. He said that he was "on automatic, on autopilot, in a fugue." Time was distorted to him. He remembered his friends trying to help him. James indicated that the murder and what happened afterward were "a blur."

Investigative reports indicated that James repeatedly stabbed Larry while his codefendant Paul restrained the victim and other inmates stood guard. James maintained that Paul was not involved in killing Larry, despite Paul's statements to the contrary. James said that Paul only participated in the clean-up. James opined that Paul said that he participated in the killing because it would have been "unbearable" for him to admit to being flashed and raped; it was better for him to say that he was involved in the murder so that he could save face. James related that he wanted Paul to be exonerated and be aware that James took full responsibility for the murder. When asked, James denied that he deliberately killed Larry in order to avoid being transferred. He also denied that he had considered hurting correctional staff in order to avoid the pending transfer prior to the murder.

At the time of the evaluation, James stated that he expected to be convicted of first-degree murder and wanted to be sentenced to death. He said that after losing all of the materials that he had spent 10 years compiling, he no longer had the opportunity to pursue habeas corpus in federal court, because the filing period was almost up. Since losing his materials, James related that he had given up and had become less inhibited, getting in more fights than previously.

James's Feelings toward the Inmate He Killed

James's feelings regarding the murder of Larry were inconsistent. On the one hand, he said that he had some guilt about killing the victim because the man was still "a person." James thought of the victim's family and how they must feel given their loss.

On the other hand, James saw the killing of Larry as "for justice" because Larry was a convicted child molester. James related that Larry had been in a wheelchair because he had been shot by a parent whose child he molested. Larry reportedly had raped again in prison and was going to be released in about a month when James killed him. James stated that the victim had been boasting about kids he had molested in the past and how he was going to go after the girl he had molested.

James said that he was a "vigilante rather than a sociopath." James said that Larry had been dating James's cousin. James maintained that "pedophiles never change" and that he could have "stopped hundreds of molestations." James related that for years, everyone had been saying he was a murderer. Now, he said, it was true—"a self-fulfilling prophecy."

James's Involvement in the Murders of His Parents

James continued to deny any involvement in the murder of his parents. When asked, he said that he was convicted because of the dying declaration of his mother, who identified him as the killer. In addition, he did not present well on the witness stand. James recalled testifying for three days. He said that he came across as "emotionally detached" and as "a zombie" because it did not bother him that his parents were dead.

When asked, James denied that he could have blacked out and committed the murders. He maintained that his mother blamed him for religious reasons. He said that his parents, although they did the best that they could, were not equipped to deal with a gifted child.

More than 15 years after the murders, James continued to present as completely disconnected from his parents. He seemed to express contempt toward them. Testimony at James's trial for the murder of his parents, observations of James's uncle, and James's diaries indicated that James harbored very strong negative feelings toward his parents prior to their murders. These feelings clearly had not abated.

The Habeas Corpus Petition

The hope that he would be eventually exonerated for the killing of his parents kept James going for many years in prison. He indicated that he had three grounds for appeal: (1) prosecutorial misconduct (the prosecutor concealed important evidence, and the police were corrupt), (2) ineffective assistance of counsel (the public defenders who handled the case had never tried an adult murder case or one with such high publicity), and (3) the fact that there was no physical evidence that tied him to the crime.

James said that he worked on his case for more than 10 years. The habeas corpus was "the culmination of a decade of work." James characterized his loss as "the greatest travesty of justice" because his federal avenues of appeal were cut off. He indicated that he felt hopeless because the state avenues were subject to corruption.

Motivational Dynamics behind the Prison Killing

The killing of Larry appeared to be a reaction to an accumulation of stressors James faced over the years in prison. In particular, James's loss of his habeas corpus materials, representing 10 years of work and his perceived ticket to freedom, was devastating to him. It likely reawakened in him feelings similar to those occasioned when his parents seized his collection of masks and special effects when he was a boy. James perceived his transfer to a more restrictive facility as another loss. At that point, having felt hopeless for a long time, it was possible that James felt that he had little or nothing to lose by killing the victim. Co-defendants' statements, if true, suggested in addition that James thought that the murder might result in the halting of the pending transfers, so there might have been a gain as a result of his actions.

The frenzied nature of the attack, however, did not suggest an orchestrated plan to kill Larry. Records indicated that the victim was stabbed more than 200 times. The overkill suggested intense rage; the evidence left tying James to the crime suggested that the murder was "disorganized," which is consistent with a psychotic process. James's statement and the nature of the attack suggested that at the time of the killing, James was "under the influence of extreme mental or emotional disturbance," and they clearly left doubt as to the extent to which James could control his behavior at the time when he was stabbing Larry.

Although James admitted killing Larry, he did not see himself as a criminal like the other inmates. He depicted the other inmates as "sociopaths" who were still committing crimes. James maintained that he was not a sociopath; rather, he was similar to a police officer or a soldier. In his words, James killed the victim "for justice."

Although James did not see himself as a criminal or "a sociopath," he seemed to have taken on values of the inmates whose culture he had lived in for the past 15 years. James maintained that his ethical sense, for example, was very strong. He differentiated between what is legal and what is ethical, meaning "the spirit of the law." He believed in a "sense of community" and "instant justice." "Rehabilitate or kill 'em; warehousing is not a solution. Prison solves nothing."

James related that "stealing, robbing, and wife beating" were wrong. In his eyes, however, the criminal justice system was corrupt and unfair. Although James maintained at one point that he did not premeditate the killing of Larry, he said at another point that he killed Larry because he was a child molester. James related that he knew that Larry was going to molest others when he was released. James maintained that he was the only one who could do something because the victim was getting out in a month and James was getting transferred.

James acknowledged that he had "a vengeful side" and was essentially playing the roles of judge, jury, and executioner. He maintained that there was a difference with respect to wrongdoing. He claimed that he was aware of several individuals who had been sexually abused and he could feel their pain, even though he denied being sexually abused.

CONSULTATION WITH FORENSIC PSYCHOLOGIST

Dr. Mitchell related that he had talked to James's maternal aunt. She stated that her mother (James's maternal grandmother) was schizophrenic and that both of James's parents were immature. The aunt indicated that James's mother thought of her son as demonic and was psychologically abusive.

Dr. Mitchell also diagnosed James as having a personality disorder with schizoid, schizotypal, and narcissistic features. He noted that his behavioral mode was on the continuum of schizophrenia. Dr. Mitchell's testing documented a split in brain functioning between affect and intellect. The cause was neurologically based. Testing indicated that the right and left sides of the brain had a weak connection. Dr. Mitchell also noted that James attended 12 different schools prior to the homicide. As a result, his oddness was not as easily detected, although some high school teachers apparently did comment that he was a little strange.

Dr. Mitchell commented that the area in which James lived as an adolescent would have been a hard environment for a frail, arrogant kid. Dr. Mitchell thought, as did I, that James had a poor self-concept and that his grandiosity was a defense.

Dr. Mitchell reached a similar conclusion with respect to the motivational dynamics behind the homicide. He agreed that the murder of Larry was indicative of rage and dissociation, but not homosexual rage. He agreed that the loss of the habeas corpus materials was similar to the loss that James experienced when his parents discarded his drawings and masks.

Dr. Mitchell and I both had questions regarding whether the killing of Larry might have been premeditated. However, Dr. Mitchell was convinced that James had had psychotic breaks when he killed Larry and when he killed his parents as a result of the enormous stress that he was experiencing at those times. Although I tended to agree with Dr. Mitchell, I was less certain because of the statements that James had made to me justifying his actions and statements that he purportedly made to other inmates prior to the killing. Dr. Mitchell and I agreed that James was amenable to treatment and that he had had no treatment prior to the second killing.

TRIAL AND SENTENCING

At a jury trial, James was convicted of first-degree murder, conspiracy, and tampering with evidence. I did not testify at James's trial or sentencing hearing. Defense attorneys were concerned that statements contained in my report about the murder could be potentially harmful to James. Rather than testify, I was asked to disclose only the 19 mitigating factors I had found (see Table 11-1) to another defense expert, who subsequently testified along with Dr. Mitchell at the sentencing hearing. Eight of these mitigating factors pertained to James's childhood and made him more vulnerable to breakdown and maladaptive behavior than children without these difficulties. Seven additional factors in mitigation pertained to James's experiences in prison, and one specifically to the murder of Larry. The remaining three factors related to James's amenability to treatment. The jurors returned a recommendation for a life sentence, which the judge imposed.

James's co-defendant, Paul, waived his right to a jury trial in exchange for the State's agreeing not to seek the death penalty. Paul was subsequently convicted of the same charges as James at a bench trial. He was also sentenced to life for the killing of Larry.

FOLLOW-UP DATA

I conducted a follow-up interview with James five years after evaluating him in connection with the killing of the inmate. This meeting was my third meeting with James over a period spanning more than 20 years. Recall that I met with James for the first time when he was an adolescent facing trial for the murder of his parents, and the second time when he was aged 32 and charged with killing a prison inmate.

TABLE 11-1 Factors in mitigation of a death sentence

Mitigators	Explanation
Mitigating Factors Pertaining to Childhood	
(1) James had significant physical problems.	Stressor; increased his vulnerability to maladaptive behavior, isolation from peers, and breakdown.
(2) James appeared to have been learning-disabled.	Stressor for a child, especially one with a high IQ. Learning disability has a strong biological component, suggesting James had more intrinsic vulnerabilities than other children.
(3) James's attitudinal and behavioral difficulties as a child were not treated.	Medical neglect—Mrs. Holt expressed concern to school about her son's traits and behaviors; school teachers noted James's oddness; Mrs. Holt reportedly told criminal justice personnel, neighbors, and her daughter that she was worried that James might harm the family. Nevertheless, James never received counseling prior to the murders of his parents.
(4) James had excessive demands placed upon him by his parents with respect to his siblings.	Stressor; Mrs. Holt said James had "too much responsibility" placed on him. He was expected to act more like an adult than a child.
(5) James's interest in the macabre was not appropriately addressed by his parents.	Warning signal unheeded, medical neglect. James was fascinated with themes of death and dying and other macabre themes. James should have been psychologically evaluated, because an intense interest in nihilistic themes can be an indication of rage, intense hatred, or fantasies of hurting and killing others. Parents were inconsistent in their reactions to James's art work and at times were psychologically abusive, characterizing his artistic creations as evil and demonic and later destroying them.
(6) James experienced difficulties adjusting to the relocation of James's family to a low-income and crime-ridden area.	External stressor; James was ill prepared to cope in a violent and tough environment. Living in this environment would have combined with James's intrinsic vulnerabilities, leaving him more vulnerable to maladaptive behavior.
(7) James's apparent detachment from, hatred of, and contempt for his parents as he got older were clear indications that something was terribly wrong.	James's hatred toward his parents, his fascination with death and destructiveness, and his desire to control are indicative of a child with severe bonding breaks. Youths who develop attachment disorders have not had their basic needs met as young children. They typically have been abused and neglected. James depicted his parents as having been neglectful and psychologically abusive during his childhood.

Table 11-1 (Continued)

Mitigators	Explanation
(8) James was found to be mentally ill by the juvenile court at the transfer hearing and by the trial judge at sentencing for the deaths of his parents.	There is some evidence that James might have suffered a psychotic break or dissociative episode due to the accumulation of stressors and his genetic vulnerability. On several occasions, he had been diagnosed as having a personality disorder. Pre-existing personality disorders can predispose a person to a brief psychotic break, particularly if stressors are intense.

Mitigating Factors Pertaining to Experiences in Prison

Mitigators	Explanation
(9) Court's order that James be treated was not followed.	Institutional and medical neglect; correctional records indicate that James received virtually no treatment prior to the murder of the inmate.
(10) Department of Corrections staff themselves noted a need for treatment early in James's incarceration, which went unheeded.	Institutional and medical neglect; correctional records document that staff requests were not acted upon.
(11) James requested psychological help in the months preceding his killing the inmate.	Institutional and medical neglect; correctional records document that James's requests, made to numerous correctional staff, were ignored.
(12) Correctional records indicate that James was generally a good management inmate.	Correctional records document that James was not a behavioral problem.
(13) James was transferred multiple times, including to prisons in several states, which he found very stressful. The murder happened on the eve of a transfer to a new prison, the conditions of which were perceived as substantially less favorable.	Internal and external stressors; James was negatively affected by being sent to out-of-state facilities during the preceding two years. These locations were also more restrictive and reduced his opportunities for visitation because of their distance from friends and relatives.
(14) James was severely traumatized by the loss of habeas corpus materials that occurred as a result of an out-of-state transfer.	Major stressor; James "lost everything that defined me as a person." He had spent 10 years compiling materials in support of his position that he was wrongfully convicted of his parents' death. In addition to these materials, James lost all his creative writings and drawings, letters from his family and the Morrisons, and addresses of correspondents.

(*continued*)

Mitigators	Explanation
(15) James suffered several significant losses in prison.	Three of his four grandparents died, contact with siblings became minimal to non-existent, and with few exceptions, friends abandoned him.

Mitigating Factor Pertaining to the Killing of the Inmate

(16) Evidence of dissociation and possible decompensation.	Possible psychotic break or dissociative episode fueled by long-standing and immediate anger, despair since the loss of habeas corpus materials, and the stress of the pending transfer.

Mitigating Factors Relating to Amenability to Treatment

(17) James was amenable to treatment when he was sentenced to prison for the murder of his parents.	There was no coordinated treatment plan, and no significant treatment was provided.
(18) James has made progress in therapy since it has been provided (about 18 months) and remains amenable to treatment at the present time.	Department of Corrections records indicate that after the prison murder, a coordinated treatment plan was put in place, and that James was participating consistently and appropriately and making measurable treatment gains.
(19) James's personality development was a good prognostic indicator.	The inmate murder was clearly tied to issues and behaviors that were long-standing and were not therapeutically addressed in prison. Individuals with James's level of development and behavioral response style are capable of changing with significant psychotherapeutic intervention.

At the time of our third meeting, James was 38 years old and was housed in another out-of-state prison about 1,500 miles from his home state.

James was pleasant and engaged during the four hours of our meeting. He was very reflective about his life in prison and self-revealing. He appeared honest, although his statements seemed, in places, reflective of an idealized self rather than his real self. There was some evidence of grandiosity in his thinking. He was eager to share his thoughts about the experiences of juveniles in adult prisons. James did not seem anxious. His eye contact was very good. He presented as somber and sad and met the diagnostic criteria for major depression and a personality disorder with schizoid, schizotypal, and narcissistic features.

I noted that James seemed to have grown in terms of personality development and seemed to be perceiving at level 5. James was able to see things from different perspectives. He was aware of patterns in his life and how he had changed over time. Remarks he made suggested that he was capable of empathizing with others. For example, he felt badly for Mr. and Mrs. Morrison after he killed the prison inmate because he knew that he had disappointed them and "how that must make them feel." He explained that the Morrisons believed in him, and for him "to do something really bad" made it hard for them, because they would wonder what had happened to James to lead him to kill someone. He speculated that "there might be some small level of guilt" on their part even though "there's nothing that they could have done" to prevent it.

Murder of the Inmate

James maintained that his killing of Larry "wasn't a premeditated or intentional act"; he was defending his friend Paul. He said that the State's theory that he killed Larry in an attempt to avoid being transferred was not true.

James said that he did not like the way his attorneys defended him with respect to the inmate murder case. Although James understood that his attorneys in the second murder case were trying to save his life, he felt that their strategy "sabotaged" his first case. He explained that his attorneys were trying to show the jurors that James had a history of acting violently during blackouts, so that they would believe that he had blacked out again when he killed the inmate. He recognized that if the jurors believed that James was mentally impaired during the killing of the inmate, they would be more likely to recommend a life sentence, knowing that James already had two life sentences for killing his parents and would never be released.

James felt that his lawyers let him down in their "ideological fight against the death penalty." James stated with fervor, "I didn't care about the second case; my first case was the important one, that's the one I am innocent of." He complained that he did not have the resources to prove his innocence in connection with killing his parents, and after three murder convictions, "no one believes me, it's like everything I say is in doubt."

Murder of His Parents

James has always maintained that he did not kill his parents and had nothing to do with their murders. He never wished that they would die. He said that there was "no animosity" between him and his parents.

James conceded that his mother's dying declaration that he attacked her and his father was very damaging evidence. He explained, "It's my belief that no matter who did it, she would have said it was me … because I was possessed, I could look like anyone, or that whoever she saw looked like me, or that she couldn't see who did it because it was dark and she wasn't wearing her glasses." He stated that his parents were not prepared for a gifted child, "someone who was born an atheist and had these creative impulses." Although James recalled his parents encouraging him with his career, he felt that they could not relate to him, as he was different from all his other relatives.

James explained that, at age 38, he hated his parents because he had been incarcerated for 21 years. James insisted that at the time of their deaths, however, "there was no hatred. I wasn't abused. I mean, I've been neglected, minimal. And, I was 16, if things were bad enough, I could have run away or whatever." James was angry that surviving family members thought that he was involved in his parents' murders. "They're superstitious. They think, well, he was possessed. They also believed in demon possession and that complicated my case a great deal."

James said, with bitterness, that if he had taken a plea bargain, he would have been released years ago. "If you're innocent you actually get burned worse and, if you are guilty, they [prosecutors] actually help you." James is hoping that DNA can exonerate him (the necessary technology did not exist when he was convicted).

Prison System

James maintained that the prison system misrepresented the behavior of inmates when they transferred them. Prison officials reportedly sent information to the new prison that could not be used in court and which they knew was not true. However, James said that "no one is going to refute it, and that makes it more difficult for the prisoner that arrives there because he has, you know, all of this baggage following him that isn't true."

James related that he did O.K. in prison for many years. When the transfers began, that "totally destabilized" him "mentally." In James's words, "There's a surreal aspect to my existence that, like I have so many prison numbers, I don't even know where I am anymore …. I'm getting worse and worse as time goes on, very, very bad."

At the time of the follow-up interview, James was convinced that the prosecutors and corrections system were involved in a cover-up with respect to his case. He believed that they intentionally warded off his legal actions for more than 20 years because they knew there was "something to uncover, there's people to be held accountable, people who will lose their jobs, lawsuits to be uncovered. And I think I've caused a lot of problems for a lot of people, and they don't want that. They are saying, well, instead, let's stress him out. Let him get in trouble in prison, let him get a death penalty, let him kill himself, ship him out until he just dies or something, and that way, no one's ever going to know anything."

I told James that I had encountered difficulty locating him, as his name no longer appeared in the state department of corrections inmate locator system. I found him by contacting one of his attorneys from the second trial. James said that he had been confined in about 50 facilities in nine different states during his 21 years of imprisonment. James stated that about a year after his conviction for killing the inmate, consent decrees mandating minimal conditions for prisoners were abolished and mental health programs were cancelled in his state.

James was convinced that officials in the department of corrections did "everything in their power" to make things worse for him. He said that he was transferred 25 times in one state alone, was put in "supermax" facilities, was given increased punishments, and had his possessions stolen. At one point, a judge reportedly barred Homestate from sending him back to this new state, stating that the treatment given James violated a prior court order and was cruel and unusual punishment. Homestate then reportedly left James in supermax to punish him by making him ineligible for group therapy or counseling. He reportedly had stayed there or in slightly less restrictive quarters for several years preceding my meeting with him. He was moved from supermax to maximum security after his attorney from the second case intervened for him.

James claimed that he had become "a great risk for all kinds of awful things" because of the conditions under which he had lived. James indicated that, although it might sound "kind of dumb," he had "always been a pretty nice person … despite being charged with these various murders, and being guilty of the last one." Although he did not see himself as a violent person or murderer by definition, he admitted that prison had had a negative impact on him. James's words are unsettling, as they show the destructive impact that years of imprisonment have had on him.

I try to avoid things, I mean I don't like confronts, I don't like fights. I don't like seeing other people have fights. And yet, as time is going on, especially since [Badstate], I can see myself getting more aggressive, more violent, more homicidal. You know, I hate to say it, but it's true. *Every day it's just, there's only two things on my mind: suicide, homicide, suicide, homicide.* And I try real hard to fight that because I don't want to. I've always told myself, I'm not going to be that way, you know. I'm [pause] ... I'm being totally honest with you because I know it will help your research. I've always been more of a vigilante where I think murder is just [when] applied in certain situations. I know most people don't, but I do. The thing is, serial killers and all those other people who kill surrogates, they kill for fun, and they have personal motivations for murder. And me, I'm not reaching that point yet, but I'm reaching the point where it wouldn't bother me to kill indiscriminately like, well, if I can't get this governor, then I would get someone in his place. So I'm starting to think about surrogates now. And before, I would never have considered that. I would never harm an innocent, and now, I'm getting so bad, eventually I probably will want to.

James tied his killing of the inmate to his wrongful conviction of his parents' murders and his years of living in prison.

I'm becoming a murderer, I'm becoming everything they told me I would .... When I came to prison, the whole world told me, and my family told me, that I'm a murderer, and I'm a parent killer, matricide, patricide, and all this. And now, I've actually become what they always said I would. You know, prison changed me. I mean, I know I can't shift my own blame, but I know I wouldn't have killed [Larry] ... if I hadn't been harassed, if I hadn't been transferred around. So I'm not going to minimize my personal responsibility in the matter, but I am going to say that there is no way that this would have happened if it wasn't for the correctional system and what the system itself has done to me. In my prison experience, prison makes you like what I was told—you're predator or prey.

James explained further that he did not see himself as a predator, but that he could be "a bit aggressive." He stated that had been involved in "a lot of violent episodes" in order to help juveniles for which he had never been caught. He saw his killing of Larry as having a deterrent effect with respect to rapes in prison. He described himself as "a necessary evil in the prison .... If I'm given the choice between letting a kid get raped, or killing a guy, I'm always going to side with the child or the young man."

James denied that he had been victimized by other inmates or had been in protective custody. When asked, he acknowledged that he was short, thin, wore glasses, and would seem like someone who would be victimized by others. He suggested a number of reasons that other inmates have left him alone: some might have thought he was "crazy" because he was convicted of killing his parents, or some might know that he has weapons and is willing to use them. Given that those explanations would not explain why he had not been victimized out of state where others did not know of his reputation, James concluded that inmates did not "mess with" him because he did not "mess with them," and because "there must be an aura or light about me that people just say, you know, there's something wrong here." James characterized it as "a tangible attitude maybe, or presence that a person puts out that other people can read on, especially in prison, apparently. I think it's because they're familiar with that kind of way of being, so they see it in other people, might be special."

James reflected that it was "a small miracle" that he had "gone 21 years without doing drugs, smoking, drinking, tattoos, homosexuality." He characterized himself as "a nonconformist." He expressed disappointment in himself for killing Larry because he "shouldn't have taken it that far." He felt badly that he had "played into their hands" and recognized that he could have helped his friend Paul without killing Larry. Overall, however, James felt that he had "done a good job from preventing" himself from becoming "either institutionalized or becoming a criminal."

James attributed his success in prison to his "strength of will." He said that he had been "born an atheist" and questioned everything from an early age, "instead of accepting it." He explained that most children are taught from an early age to accept authority, and that "actually works against them because they believe in adults" and become "vulnerable to adults." Unlike him, most people do not question authority and are "followers."

James said that he experienced intense loneliness in prison despite the fact that he was "never alone. It's like my worst nightmare. I'm around everybody I hate most in this entire world; [I am] constantly and horribly lonely." He had had many acquaintances in prison, but few friends. He defined "friends" as people he respected, enjoyed being with, admired, and cared about. They have to use their minds, care about him, and share his "sense of ethics." James indicated, "I'm not going to be friends with someone in a gang, someone who rapes, someone who is always using drugs. I can tolerate some drug use, but not an addict."

As a result of his transfers and close custody status, James has had difficulty maintaining friendships. His activities have been restricted. When he has been able to, he has worked and participated in college courses and vocational programs. When restricted, he has watched TV and listened to the radio. He used to do "a lot of writing" but has had difficulty concentrating in recent years as a result of all the transfers. He has continued drawing cartoon figures and has become interested in mythology. His mind has remained creative. When we talked he was "still creating movies, stories, visualizing hobbies ... reliving the past, reading books"—in his words, "My research, my studies, my goals. I still behave as though I will get out."

James told me with sadness that "at the end of the day" he was still in prison and apparently never getting out.

My past is erased. I have no future. My present is a hell. So yeah, that's about, yeah, literally every hour of every day, I like say, like a mantra in my mind, "I wish I was dead, I wish I was dead." So, really, it's just a living hell. One of the reasons that I don't commit suicide is because my enemies would be happy. It would be closure for them. I'll never prove my innocence from my first case, they will be like—that we won .... And as far as my purpose for living, I guess, another reason that I don't commit suicide is because I usually have a friend I'm trying to help. Like I have a good friend that I've met here in this facility and, if I'm gone, he's at risk of being preyed on by people. But, while I'm here, at least he has one person in the world who will kill for him or die for him. Who will take extreme measures no one else will.

James related that one of his attorneys from his prison trial had maintained contact with him and helped him over the years. He described her as "a decent human being." He said that there was little that could be done in his case because he already had three life sentences and was "a political hot potato." The state department of corrections "hates him" and is "so entrenched in local politics" that "it scares a lot of people off who otherwise might help me, like prisoner advocate groups." At the time of the follow-up evaluation, James was intending to seek habeas corpus relief with respect to the murder of his parents, repeated transfers, and the police having broken his leg during an out-of-state prison transfer.

James's Desire to Help Juvenile Inmates

James indicated that he had had extensive experience with juveniles in prison. He believed very strongly that most could be rehabilitated. He thought it was "just monstrous" that juveniles, particularly first offenders, were sentenced to life without parole. He noted the irony in the fact that "true sociopaths," whom he speculated probably made up 75% of the prison population, "get out again and again and again."

James related that he had made it a point to help younger inmates who were "going to be raped or coerced or robbed." He noted that most inmates would not step in to help juveniles and said that sending a juvenile to prison was one of "the most horrible things you could do" to that person. James commented that predators seek out boys who are young, quiet, and pretty. James would teach them about grooming techniques used by predators, such as bribes, force, drugs, or offers of protection, so they could avoid them. "There is no limit to the sick games that the inmates play to victimize young men and it is not always sexual." James explained that he had felt "sympathy" toward these young offenders since he was first incarcerated.

James indicated that many things could be done to help juveniles in prison. He stressed that first offenders should always be separated from habitual offenders and that juveniles should be separated from adults and from anybody who has a history of sexual perversion. James recommended that cameras be added for inmates' protection and that outside parties come into prisons. James reiterated that juveniles needed to be protected, particularly from sexual assault, because when young males are raped, "their minds gone, they become criminal, and it destroys their life, they never recover." James noted that "drugs are very common in prison and juveniles are very susceptible to them."

James also advised that prisons should provide opportunities for male offenders to interact with women "so they start developing normal ways of relating with them." He explained that when inmates who have been incarcerated for years "see someone our age, we would think of our mothers or aunts" rather than a possibly appropriate dating partner. He suggested that inmates be allowed pornographic material to promote "a healthy outlook." From James's perspective, "there is no such thing as a consensual homosexual relationship in prison," and such relationships are destructive for juveniles in terms of their identity.

James suggested that warehousing those sentenced to life without parole is akin to torturing those individuals "for the rest of their lives" and is immoral, particularly for juvenile homicide offenders (see Box 14-2). James suggested that the prison system takes away all hope for lifers and then expects them to accept their situation and conform. In James's words,

It's sick. But what kind of life—is that any better than what these criminals are doing? No, they [prison officials] are consciously destroying lives knowingly. And they're getting revenge basically. They're no different than what I did to [Larry], you know. But they think, it's okay to execute people, they think it's okay to send to prison for life, now, and they're going to be raped, so whatever. I don't see how that's any different except they have the authority to commit these acts and I don't. And their motives are even less pure than mine, because it's their job or for profit, for political gain, or to be tough on crime .... And again, I'm not trying to say what I did is okay.

James decried inmates' victimizing each other: "It's like prison is not bad enough, we have to prey on each other." He has always tried to tell juveniles, "Look, it should be us against the administration, not us against each other."

James's Health

James described his health as having been generally good over the years, with the exception of his eyesight. He has had no dental care in prison. He stopped exercising because he had no interest in being healthy. He described himself as being "too tense and too depressed" and as wanting to die. He tried several antidepressants but discontinued them because they had side effects or made him "extremely hostile." He has always found it difficult to express emotion.

Contact with Outside World

Other than his attorney from his second trial, James has no contact with people from the outside. He has not heard from his siblings in years. His grandparents died or became too ill to visit him. The Morrisons, who were the closest to him, had both died since I had last met with James.

CASE COMMENTARY

As I conclude this chapter, it has been more than 25 years since I first met James. Over the years James has sent me many letters and personal writings. His commentaries on prison are provocative, and his short stories are creative. James has shared his insights after reading my books and academic journal articles, which I sent to him upon his request. He has thoughtfully sent me announcements about books and news clippings related to juveniles and homicides. His drawings reflect remarkable talent.

In his letters, James has shared observations about parricide cases in the news, such as those involving school shooters. He has continued to advocate that adolescent parricide offenders should be retained in the juvenile justice system and treated. He has maintained that most juvenile homicide offenders can be rehabilitated and that more should be done by society to prevent violence by young people.

James has experienced "crippling depression" that has affected his concentration and creativity over the years. It has been very hard for him to accept that he was sentenced to the longest prison sentence given to any adolescent parricide offender in his state and now has a third life sentence that makes any chance of release exceedingly unlikely. He noted that conditions in prison have become worse because of the country's economic situation. Despite his personal circumstances and the external conditions, James said that he has worked and taken college courses in prison when he has had the opportunity to do so. He has recently begun to write again.

James has continued to maintain his innocence with regard to the deaths of his parents. He wrote with disappointment in one letter that Paul's appeal (his co-defendant in the prison inmate murder) was denied. James felt badly that Paul, who would have been released from prison had he not been convicted of the prison murder, was now serving a life sentence. John admitted that he minimized the involvement of Paul in the killing of the inmate at the time of his trial because he was trying to help Paul by taking the blame. James explained that Paul was originally sent to prison as an adolescent in connection with the shooting of his parents, who survived and testified against him. James was very critical of prison officials who put Paul in a housing unit with predatory inmates and gang members. James held them responsible for Paul's being raped and subsequently involved in a murder.

James maintains that corrections officials have assaulted both James and his codefendant, psychologically tortured them, and exiled them to other states. James has continually maintained that he has been subjected to "hostile vendettas by D.A.'s and prison officials." James listed 29 facilities in nine states in which he had been confined during a 22-year period. My review of prison records and consultation with an out-of-state corrections official corroborated multiple transfers within and outside James's home state. From James's perspective, the prison transfers have been "always very costly and destructive."

James's case fills me with such sadness. He is a very intelligent and talented individual. I wonder what he could have become had he been treated when he was a teenager by skilled mental health professionals as ordered by the trial judge. Department of Corrections files indicated that when coordinated and effective treatment was provided to James following his murder of the inmate—more than 10 years after his conviction for the killing of his parents—he participated consistently and appropriately in individual therapy, group life skills, and substance abuse groups. Records verified that at that point in time, James was capable of processing painful and difficult material verbally. He recognized that he had been consumed with anger, resentment, and bitterness for years and had a negative self-concept. He displayed insight into the source of his problems and showed progress regarding finding alternatives to acting out his anger. In a progress report filed two years after the murder of the inmate, staff noted that James was "responsible, accepts staff direction," demonstrated "increased impulse control and improved regulation of emotion," and "verbally communicates his needs in an appropriate manner." *One can only wonder what gains James might have made had treatment begun when he was sentenced, more than a dozen years before the murder of the inmate, and had it been allowed to continue.*

There is no doubt in my mind (and in the minds of his attorneys) that James does not believe he was involved in his parents' murders, despite his having been found guilty by a jury trial. At the time I followed up with James, I met briefly with the attorney who has kept in touch with James for many years. She related that James has consistently maintained his innocence with respect to these convictions. In his defense, physical evidence tying him to the crime, such as blood, fingerprints, and gunshot residue, was lacking. However, jurors found the State's case compelling. Evidence persuading the jury of James's guilt included his mother's dying declaration and his sister's testimony that she heard their mother say James shot them. Testimony from James's uncle, sister, and police suggested that Mrs. Holt feared that James was going to hurt the family prior to the shooting. Testimony that James's parents had thrown away his artistic creations that depicted macabre themes provided a motive. James's uncle testified that James looked down on his parents and expressed contempt for them prior to the murders. Evidence indicating that the doors were locked apparently ruled out the defense's theory of an intruder, even if jurors were inclined to consider defense counsel's assertion that Mrs. Holt falsely implicated James because of her belief that he was possessed by demons.

Assuming that James did kill his parents, one might wonder how he could be so strongly convinced of his non-involvement. A plausible explanation is that he killed them during a psychotic break or dissociative episode. Evidence on the record suggested a genetic vulnerability to psychoticism, which, when combined with external stressors, such as his parents' possible religious fanaticism and his moving to a tough neighborhood in his teen years, could have resulted in an acute psychotic break.[6] Alternatively, he might have dissociated in response to intense external stressors at the time of the killings. If this were the case, he might not remember what happened. If either of these events occurred, it would indeed be plausible that he would not remember the killings because in an adult prison environment James had to remain on "red alert" to survive. Had James been treated by mental health professionals in a therapeutic setting following his conviction, it is possible that he would have been able to recover traumatic memories, including the murder of his parents, and work through them, reducing the risk of his being violent in the future.

In his book, *Severe Personality-Disordered Defendants and the Insanity Plea in the United States*, forensic psychiatrist George Palermo recently noted that neuroimaging studies of the brains of offenders with severe personality disorders (borderline, paranoid, schizoid, schizotypal, and antisocial) show similarities with the neuroimaging studies of the brains of psychotic persons. These studies suggest that under internal or external stressors personality-disordered offenders might easily decompensate into psychotic behavior. Palermo has argued that offenders with "severe personality aberrations (inclusive of some temporary state of psychosis)" should be allowed to enter a plea of not guilty by reason of insanity or diminished capacity if it can be shown that they offended while decompensated into a brief psychotic episode.[7]

This case has elements that apply to all three types of parricide offenders. However, in classifying this case, the most important consideration is what propelled James to kill his parents, if he indeed did so. There is some suggestion of childhood maltreatment. James did not view his parents as abusive. However, their throwing out James's artistic creations would clearly constitute psychological abuse. James suggested that he was expected to take on too much responsibility for his siblings, which was corroborated by the mother's handwritten notes in school records. I would not classify James as a "severely abused" parricide offender because there is no persuasive evidence that James killed his parents because he was desperate to end the abuse or terrified of them and saw no other way out.

James's interest in nihilistic and macabre themes suggests an antisocial aspect to James's core personality.[8] As noted earlier, these interests should have been considered as a possible warning signal that James was angry and disturbed. His behavior might have been an indication of an attachment disorder. It is possible that Mrs. Holt did not bond with James when he was an infant, which could have set the foundation for hatred and rage. Although I see James as dangerous, I would not classify him as a "dangerously antisocial" parricide offender because there is no evidence to suggest that James killed his parents to serve a selfish, instrumental purpose, such as getting more freedom.

Based on the available facts, I would classify James as a "severely mentally ill" offender. Evidence suggests that he killed his parents as a result of mental illness. His denial of his involvement for more than 20 years is consistent with a psychotic break or dissociative episode. He was found mentally ill by the juvenile court prior to his transfer to the adult criminal justice system for trial. His killing of the inmate in prison occurred during a period of acute stress and might also have occurred during a psychotic break or dissociative episode. Clearly he was acting under "extreme mental and emotional disturbance" when he stabbed Larry more than 200 times.

Is James dangerous? Yes, according to both society and James himself. James recognizes that he has become dangerous over the years. He explained the process: "You lose faith in the system and you become cynical and jaded. And of course, that turns to hatred. And then you add the loneliness and the depression—you either become a very deranged individual, a very self-destructive one, or a very dangerous one, and I'm all of them." James opined that an inmate's misery increases in proportion to his intelligence. "If you are a mindless follower, you're just a sheep, you don't know you're being shorned." From James's perspective, he has become "more maladjusted as the years have gone on."

Is James antisocial? This question is more complicated than that related to his dangerousness. James has a strong code of morality. Some of his values are conventional, whereas others are clearly not. He described his purpose as helping juvenile offenders. He indicated that his violent striking out is in the service of good. He did not see himself as "a sociopath." In fact, he maintained that if he became a sociopath, he would kill himself because he would not be able to live with himself if he hurt someone innocent. In his words, "But if they're guilty, it doesn't bother me. For me it's an individual act of vengeance."

12 Daniel Culbreath
Fantasy Becomes Reality

Daniel Culbreath, aged 20, lived with his parents in a lovely home set on a hill facing the pounding waves of the sea. His parents were well known and respected residents on this picturesque British island. When his parents did not report to work one morning, their employers knew something was wrong and called the police to investigate. Within hours of their bodies being found at the Culbreath home, Daniel was arrested.

Legal authorities were confident they had the killer. While Daniel was being interviewed, three of Daniel's friends told police that he had talked repeatedly about killing his parents. Daniel was subsequently charged with two counts of first-degree murder.

Shortly after his arrest, Daniel mentally decompensated and was hospitalized. Daniel spent two months in a mental hospital prior to doctors concluding that he could be safely transferred to jail. I was retained by the Crown to assist defense counsel as a confidential defense expert. I was asked to evaluate the defendant with respect to his mental state at the time of the murders and to address the motivational dynamics behind the killings.

THE CLINICAL EVALUATION

My assessment of Daniel Culbreath was based on a six-and-a-half-hour evaluation conducted in jail about nine months after his arrest. Extensive case-related materials I examined included police reports, crime scene photos, investigative materials, and a videotape and transcript of the defendant's confession. I reviewed statements from 11 young people who told police that Daniel had talked to them about killing someone or murdering his own parents prior to the murders. I examined school and medical/hospital records, as well as newspaper clippings. I conducted individual phone interviews with Daniel's girlfriend, her mother, and Daniel's friend

Ralph. I also consulted with a well-respected forensic psychiatrist who had evaluated Daniel.

BEHAVIORAL OBSERVATIONS

Daniel, a White male, was 21 years 9 months old when I met him. The defendant had a medium build, was about 6'1" tall, and weighed about 215 pounds. He had a few scars sustained from several sporting injuries, but no tattoos. Daniel reported that he was not on psychotropic medication.

Daniel was socially skilled and appropriate. Prior to lighting a cigarette, he asked whether his smoking would bother me and made an effort to blow the smoke in a direction away from us.

Daniel was alert and cooperative, and his eye contact was generally very good. He listened intently to hundreds of questions and maintained good concentration. Daniel could grasp the meaning of most questions with apparent ease. However, his answers were often restricted by his level of personality development. The young man's responses indicated that he was oriented in time and space and that his short-term and, for the most part, long-term memories were intact.

There were no data to suggest that Daniel was responding to private sensory experiences (hallucinations) or that he had delusional beliefs or a delusional network in place. Daniel indicated that he had experienced his dead mother talking to him on a number of occasions when he was in the hospital, but not since then. In these episodes, his mother was reportedly telling him that he was smoking too much, watching too much TV, or lying around too much. At the time of my evaluation, Daniel was coherent and appeared to be handling stress reasonably well.

Daniel's responses to questions and his behavior generally suggested that he was trying to be truthful. Daniel initially seemed somewhat formal and distant, but as the interview progressed, he relaxed more. He moved around frequently in his seat, which seemed to be more indicative of his general way of behaving than reactive to the clinical assessment situation. His mood was depressed and generally serious, and his affect was restricted.

Daniel presented as much younger than his chronological age. His way of relating, particularly when examined in the context of his personality development, was more typical of a child to young adolescent than someone in his early adult years. He came across as compliant and as wanting to make a good impression.

Daniel's demeanor changed noticeably while we were discussing the homicidal event. His eyes were downcast and his body appeared pulled down and inward. His arms encircled his stomach area as if he were holding himself together. Tears flowed down his face as he described seeing his parents after the shooting. He appeared haunted as he recalled the vivid images of his deceased parents after shooting them. His crying and loss of composure appeared genuine.

PERSONALITY DEVELOPMENT

Daniel's personality development is relatively low. In Interpersonal Level of Maturity Theory, he would be classified as primarily perceiving at level 3. Daniel, as is typical of those who perceive at level 3, was very much concerned with power relations. He was interested in knowing who had the power in a situation so he could adapt accordingly. Daniel operated primarily on the basis of formulas that provided the structure that he wanted and needed in order to get by in life. He characterized jail, for example, as a "totally different society." Daniel maintained that one has to know how to behave in jail or it could be a very bad situation. He learned how to function successfully in the jail from one of the older men who lived on his "range." This man, who had spent more than 20 years locked up, helped Daniel learn what to expect should he go to the penitentiary. The defendant explained that certain words were trigger words in this environment. There were "rules you go by," such as that "you don't ask questions. If someone who is doing something wants you to know, they will tell you." Other rules included the following: "You don't whistle. If you have cutlery, you don't bang it together because it sounds like keys."

Daniel indicated that there was "a well-defined line" between the staff and the inmates. He characterized it as an "us versus them" situation. Daniel stressed the importance of "connections" in this world; if an inmate upset another inmate who was known and respected by others, there could be serious ramifications.

Daniel thought rather concretely and tended to see the world in black and white dimensions. His perceptions of others were deficient and stereotypic. For example, he described his friend Ellen as someone who "should have been a flower child." He indicated she was into "the green issue and things like that."

Daniel was relatively incapable of thinking in terms of needs, feelings, and motives in himself or others. Although he could provide some indication of how he was feeling when asked, his awareness of his feeling states and his ability to discuss them in depth were limited. The defendant was not typically introspective. Instead, he tended to be event oriented (for example, "This happened, then this happened, then this happened … I did this, then I did that, then I did that").

The defendant had not reached the developmental stage at which he could empathize with others. Daniel related an incident when his mother suggested he should "see somebody" after a commercial plane had crashed nearby. His mother was concerned because the accident did not bother him. Daniel said that "230 people or something died when the plane went down." He did not have any feelings about the incident because "I didn't know any of them."

As is characteristic of those who perceive at level 3, the defendant's ability to plan prior to the arrest seemed to be limited typically to short-term events, and his behavioral responses appeared impulsive and non-evaluative. Daniel had not reached the stage of development at which he had internalized a value system by which he judged himself. He did not perceive that he had choices in a situation. He did not typically feel badly inside when he did something that was morally and/or legally wrong. He did not evaluate his behavior against a conventional standard of behavior and experience guilt. For example, as will be discussed subsequently, he repeatedly took pleasure in the thought of killing other people, including his parents. He did not feel badly about selling his parents' alcohol or stealing things when the opportunity arose.

Among those who perceive at level 3, three behavioral subtypes have been empirically identified. Daniel's behavioral response style was characteristic of the *level 3 passive conformist (Cfm).*[1] Individuals who adopt this mode of relating see themselves as fairly conventional people. At the time of the assessment interview, Daniel did not regard himself as "a criminal" or "a gangster." He indicated that prior to his being arrested, the thought of committing crimes with other kids and "living in the fast lane" did not appeal to him. Even though he smoked marijuana frequently, Daniel said that he never thought of it as bad. He acknowledged that he drove drunk but rationalized that he drove mostly at night when there were fewer people on the road. He was proud that he had devised a way to drive with double vision.

Consistent with other passive conformists, Daniel indicated that he did not have very good feelings about himself and desperately wanted the approval of others. When asked whose approval he desired, Daniel said, "Anybody's." He wanted the approval of adults as well as of people his own age.

Daniel admitted that sometimes he would con people who did something offensive to him or con those he did not like. Daniel maintained that his primary way of operating, however, was to conform to others' wishes. He never felt that he fit in with any group of young people, so he floated from one group to another and "would go along with the crowd." He explained, "I'm too paranoid to lead the crowd, because I'd always be worried the crowd's not going to follow me. That's why I adapted into whatever group I was with. People used to tell me, you know, 'Daniel, we don't understand you. When you are with the skaters, you are this way, and when you are with the hicks, you talk just like them,' you know. I used to talk, used different slangs and everything, and I wasn't even thinking about it at that point in time. I had just gotten so used to trying to fit in with them."

RELEVANT SOCIAL HISTORY

The following information was largely reported by Daniel. Information related to Daniel's parents' lineage, his extensive alcohol and drug usage, and his school history was verified through collateral sources.

Family Constellation

Daniel's parents were both born in England but relocated to the island where Daniel was born. About a year and a half after Daniel's birth, their daughter Anne was born.

Daniel's father was a government-employed professional. Daniel described his father, after a long pause, as "quite … uh … righteous—always on the straight and narrow, always paying their bills, stuff like that." Daniel saw himself as different from his father in that "I never had his drive."

Daniel's mother was a primary school teacher. When asked what his mother was like, Daniel paused again for a long time and then said, "She was obsessive about cleaning the house … uh … she couldn't drive." He clarified his statement to mean his mother could not drive as well as he did.

Daniel did not see any ways in which he was similar to either of his parents. He characterized them as "perfectionistic." He had difficulty recalling good times with them. Daniel said that he rarely felt comfortable at home. When asked what things were like growing up, Daniel indicated that there had been "a lot of fights." From his standpoint, "They were always criticizing me." When he spent money, his parents reportedly maintained that it was not justified. Daniel recalled that his parents took an interest in his schoolwork, but he felt that they were always pushing him to do better. He reported that he had to do chores for them, such as mow the lawn.

Daniel characterized his relationship with his father as having "a lot of friction." He related they could not work together and got into a lot of arguments. He perceived that his mother was "always going on about school work" and jobs after school.

Daniel believed his parents treated his sister differently than they treated him. He indicated, however, that Anne got better grades and described her as "Goody Two-Shoes." He said that his parents might have seen him as a disruptive influence on Anne. He believed that Anne always did the right thing and would tell his parents when he did something wrong.

Daniel mentioned a few times that he never had any privacy at home. His mother listened to his phone conversations and went through some of his belongings in his room. He resented the fact that she bought his clothes for him. He maintained that he had to wear old clothes because his mother thought they were still good enough to wear, whereas his mother and Anne frequently bought new clothing. Daniel indicated that he was not allowed to close his door properly because his parents wanted access to his room.

Daniel described his parents as inconsistent in applying discipline. One parent might be adamant about one thing, whereas the other parent was adamant about something else. As a result, consequences for his shortcomings were not always forthcoming. Sometimes Daniel indicated that one parent would intercede on his behalf.

Daniel indicated that his father did most of the disciplining. He recalled an incident in which his parents were fighting in their bedroom. His father reportedly came into his room naked and told Daniel to get out of the house, telling him they did not need him to be there.

Daniel stated that he was kicked out of the house three or four times. He recalled the first incident as occurring about two years prior to the murders. His parents said he was not working hard enough and was not doing his share around the house. Daniel went to stay with his friend Ralph. Daniel went back to his parents' house after his mother secured a job for him and suggested that financially it made sense for him to move back home.

Financial matters were a source of conflict for Daniel and his parents. Daniel initially was paying rent to his parents while living at home. Then his parents reportedly took his paycheck and gave him an allowance. He complained that without money, his parents had control over what he could do. When they signed for a loan on his car, Daniel perceived them as garnishing his check for the car loan.

The second time Daniel was kicked out was eight or nine months prior to the killings. He was spending a lot of time with his friend Nolan. Daniel had just received $2,000 from a car insurance settlement. Daniel's father told Daniel to give the money to him. Daniel wanted to give his father only half of the money. He reportedly stayed with Nolan for three or four days before going to stay with his friend Ralph. Daniel spent the $2,000 from the insurance settlement on alcohol and drugs within a few days.

Daniel stayed with Ralph for about a month but did not feel comfortable there. Daniel said that he asked his parents whether he could come home. He went back about seven months prior to the murders and remained there. Daniel was apparently receiving unemployment checks during this period.

Daniel stated that the other times he had been thrown out of the house, he was away for very short periods. He had some belongings packed. However, his parents would say that he did not have to go, so he remained in their home.

Daniel recalled that a few years prior to the murders, his mother and sister went to England for a period of time. In recalling this time, Daniel said with veiled anger that while his mother was in England, he was making the payments on her car and taking care of it. This car was "supposed to be mine." When his mother returned, Daniel had to give the car back to her.

Daniel said he spent as little time as possible at home when his parents were there. When his parents were not home, he could "get high" and watch whatever he wanted on television. If his parents were home, he could smoke cigarettes but not marijuana.

Daniel related that all of his relatives lived in England. He indicated that he did not know his family over in England because he had infrequent contact with his grandparents and could not remember when he saw them last. Daniel's family traveled to England every second or third year to visit relatives. His parents stopped taking him when he was about 15 because he did not spend time with his family. "Maybe they thought that was wrong because I didn't get to see them much, but they didn't mean anything to me," he explained.

School History

Daniel reported that he attended one local elementary school and one high school. He recalled his grades in elementary and high school as mixed. Available school records confirmed grade fluctuation and grades often in the average and below-average ranges.

Daniel reported that he got in trouble "quite frequently" in elementary school. He got in physical fights with the other kids and verbal fights with the teachers. Daniel characterized his behavior in elementary school as "generally being bad." He recalled an incident in elementary school when the teacher said, in front of his peers, that he was "rude, vulgar, immature, and a disgrace to my family." What bothered Daniel was that the teacher said it with "absolute conviction." Daniel recalled that he started crying because it was "quite embarrassing." Afterward he "clammed up."

Daniel's behavior reportedly improved in high school, and he got in less trouble than other youths. Daniel said his parents told him not to hit back, so he stopped. He maintained that the only person he ever hurt after this point was himself (e.g., he punched a hole in the wall).

Daniel was enrolled in French immersion classes in high school. He took 90% of his classes in French. His marks dropped during grades 7 to 12. He explained that he really did not care at this point and said he did not try because he was afraid that he might fail. He acknowledged that marijuana might have contributed to the decline in his grades. He also admitted he skipped school, missing 88 or more days during his senior year. Daniel indicated that he was never left back, suspended, or expelled.

Daniel took two years off before going to community college. Daniel indicated that he was taking an "electro mechanical" course at the time when he was arrested. He said that he did not want to take a technical course of study, but his parents wanted him to complete this program because his sister's boyfriend was enrolled in it and it would give him a trade.

Daniel agreed to take the course because the federal government was paying for it. He admitted he often did not attend. Daniel said he would drive four people to the college every day. He used the money they paid him to buy "dope." He would go to the mall or home, get high, and return later to pick these individuals up from school.

Work History

Daniel said he started working at the age of 12 mowing lawns and stayed in the landscape business until he was about 18. After that he worked at a shellfish company for more than a year. Initially he did menial jobs; later he was commissioned to drive long distances to buy shellfish. Daniel indicated that he worked hard at first but then became bored. He would frequently call in sick. "That's why I ended up quitting— being let go. I was never clear on what happened." Daniel stopped working at the shellfish company about eight or nine months prior to the shootings.

Daniel indicated that he got along with his boss and drank with him. He recalled an incident when he was so drunk that he almost passed out while he was driving. He almost drove off the side of the road. The next day his co-workers came to his house to get him because he was so drunk that he was unresponsive to the telephone.

Daniel was unemployed for several months. Then his father got him a job working at a private construction company as a surveyor's assistant. He characterized it as a fairly easy job. Daniel quit the job to attend community college.

Difficulties Fitting In

Daniel confided that when he was growing up, he felt other kids generally treated him as an outcast. He related four painful incidents when he perceived other youths as having rejected him. In each of these cases, he felt there was nothing he could do to redress the affront and to gain acceptance.

Daniel described an incident when he had rocks thrown at him by other kids. He said that he became friends with a boy who had been considered an outcast. This boy then became friends with another boy Daniel knew. One day these two boys were biking in the area. They stopped and put their bikes on the wharf and started throwing rocks at Daniel while he was swimming in the water. Daniel was 11 or 12 at the time. Daniel recalled that he laughed and said, "Hey, guys, stop throwing rocks at me." He said his parents had instilled in him the belief that he was not supposed to hit them. Daniel found this experience "humiliating."

Daniel recalled that he frequently got teased in junior high school. He related that the area in which he lived had no boys with whom he could play, so he would wrestle with his sister in the front yard. Kids who observed him wrestling with Anne taunted him by saying that he was having sex with his sister. Daniel told them to "fuck off." Daniel indicated that when people gave him a hard time, he would "back down."

In another incident Daniel asked one of the boys to call him so they could do something. The boy never called. The next day when Daniel said something to the boy, the boy replied he had called Daniel from his front porch. It was apparent to Daniel that the boy was mocking him. Daniel said, "They didn't like me. I never fit in with those kids."

He related a story about this boy and others intentionally locking him out of another boy's house. Daniel began walking away from this house after his repeated attempts to gain entry were ignored. The boys came down the road in a car and beeped the horn at him. He felt they were making fun of him.

Friends

Daniel did not see himself as picking his friends; rather, he became friends with people who smoked, drank, and hung out with him. Daniel indicated that he had been very close with Nolan for several years. They spent a lot of time drinking and going to nude bars. He also felt close to a girl, Alicia, although he did not have a sexual relationship with her.

At the time of the assessment, Daniel considered his girlfriend Cary, her brother Steven, and Ralph as his primary friends. He explained he hung out with other groups because he was always worried that one of the kids from his past would tell others about him and that they would tease him.

Daniel indicated that Ralph in particular had been a good friend. Daniel met Ralph when he was about 14 or 15 years old. They would joke around, criticize one another, play cards, and watch movies together. He recalled smoking dope, drinking alcohol, dropping acid, and getting take-out food with Ralph. Ralph had let Daniel borrow his car and stay with him a few times when Daniel was kicked out of the Culbreath home.

Sexual History

Daniel acknowledged having had about eight to 10 sexual relationships. He indicated that he had not had any really satisfying relationships and that his longest relationship lasted perhaps a year. Daniel said that his relationships with girlfriends would last about two weeks because he did not feel comfortable around the girls and would eventually become bored with them.

Daniel described his current girlfriend, Cary, as "the first person that ever listened to me and told me I wasn't being foolish or silly." He stated that he spent a lot of time with Cary and that they took acid together. When asked how Cary responded to his arrest, Daniel indicated that she blamed herself, believing that she should have said something to him when he was talking about killing his parents. He told her not to blame herself and that there was nothing she could have done because "none of us expected this to happen."

Daniel did not see sex as a big thing for him prior to his arrest, although it was "great if I got it." Daniel indicated that for quite some time, he was more interested in drinking than having sex.

Daniel admitted that he had had sex with a male friend, describing it as "different" and "very, very strange." He said he was kind of torn, wondering whether it really mattered that he had had sex with a man and whether he liked the experience or not. He concluded that "it wasn't bad" [meaning unpleasant], and he did not think much more about it.

Activities

Daniel played soccer and hockey. He indicated that he had fun by hanging out with his friends and partying. Daniel reportedly would go to the city to get drunk and enjoyed visiting dealers and bootleggers. He related that "driving around was a big thing after I got my car."

Prior to being incarcerated, Daniel read extensively. He recalled that he had won an award at school for reading the most books in his class. Daniel indicated that he liked reading because he could make everything look the way he wanted it to be. He preferred science-fiction books. He particularly enjoyed *The Lord of the Rings* because there were "a lot of heavy descriptions." Daniel described the book as being "part of a fantasy series where different animals and warlocks are on a quest to destroy evil." In the story, evil is overcome by means of swords, arrows, and magic.

Music/Movies

Daniel enjoyed music. He said he listened to everything from Bach to Rob Zombie (founder of the heavy metal band White Zombie). He particularly liked heavy metal music, and he did not care for gangster rap music. Daniel said he was most likely to play alternative music in his car. He liked recording artists who sang about being an outcast and being lonely.

Daniel stated that he enjoyed watching movies. He was particularly fond of comedies and action-type films. When asked, he recalled that he had watched the film *Natural Born Killers* about six or seven times. He indicated that he had rented this film on several occasions because he was "drunk and missed parts of it." Daniel mentioned that he did not like horror movies because he was not allowed to watch them as a child or growing up and never got into them.

Alcohol Involvement

Daniel indicated that he began drinking when he was about 15. For a while, Daniel believed that he was an alcoholic. He indicated that when he was 19 and 20, he drank very heavily. Daniel admitted that when he was drinking daily, or almost daily, he used to joke around a lot and do a lot of driving. Drinking was the driving force for him. He said that at one time he was drinking a flat (24 beers) every night.

Daniel recalled an occasion when he spent $200 on alcohol in 90 minutes or less with his friend Steve and another guy at a bar. They then took 12 beers for the ride home. He indicated that he could hardly walk but was driving very well when they noticed a police car. He reported that they out-raced the police car and eluded detection.

Daniel indicated that, in addition to beer, he drank rum "quite frequently." He estimated that he would drink at least two times a week and would consume "a 40 ouncer" of rum. Daniel explained that his drinking was not done to be social—"I was always drinking to get plastered."

Daniel's heavy drinking ended about 10 months prior to the shootings. He indicated that he got back into smoking marijuana and added that he always preferred smoking to drinking. Daniel indicated that his parents thought he had a problem with drinking.

Symptoms Daniel reported confirmed that he had a severe substance abuse problem and was likely dependent on alcohol for a period. When asked what it was like when he decreased or stopped his drinking, Daniel indicated that it was "rough." He would "slip back" on occasion for a weekend. However, he added that he was smoking so much marijuana that he really did not need a drink very often.

Drug Involvement

Daniel reported that he first smoked marijuana at age 16. He indicated that he smoked marijuana regularly when he started hanging out with Steven. Daniel said that he smoked every day of the week during the two-and-a-half-year period before he was arrested, unless marijuana was not available. He indicated that after a while, the effect of his smoking marijuana would just make him feel normal. On a typical day he would "smoke four joints upwards to no limit, depending on how much there was."

Daniel indicated that he had used other drugs. Daniel stated that he had tried amphetamines ("speed") about a dozen or so times about a year before the shootings. Daniel reported using Valium on only one occasion—the night of the incident. He said he took the Valium after the shooting because he could not sleep. He reported keeping Valium in his car in case somebody tripped out on acid.

Daniel reported very limited use of narcotics. He said he had been given morphine for pain when he broke his nose. He also indicated that he had obtained morphine while in jail, used it for about three days, and enjoyed it.

Daniel indicated fairly extensive use of LSD about a year prior to the shootings. He stated that he took it almost every day for about two months. He said he used it mainly by himself but recalled also taking it with Cary (this was confirmed by Cary). He claimed he liked the experience and never had a bad trip. However, he had suicidal thoughts that were quite intense while on acid. He reported having flashbacks of instances when people were talking to him.

Daniel maintained that he had lied to the police after being arrested when he said that he had not taken acid for a long time. He told me he had taken acid within a week prior to the homicides. His lawyer told him that his drug test was positive for Valium and marijuana, which was consistent with his statements to me and my review of hospital records.

Daniel indicated that he also had used mushrooms on about five occasions. The last time he had taken mushrooms was more than a year prior to the shootings. He reported that he had a vague memory of having sniffed gasoline on one occasion. Daniel had been smoking cigarettes regularly since he was about age 16. Prior to his arrest and while in jail, he smoked less than a pack per day.

Daniel reported frequently using alcohol and marijuana together. He had on occasion consumed alcohol or marijuana with acid. However, he found that the other drugs did not enhance the acid experience. He was apt to take more acid if he wanted to improve or intensify the high.

When asked, Daniel admitted that he thought he might have a problem with marijuana. He reported that he would go to the drug dealers after work to give them an advance and wound up being obligated to them financially. When asked whether his parents ever confronted him about his drug usage, Daniel indicated that they did, but he always lied about it. He said that his parents would argue about it and that he would just sit there. (Ralph indicated that Daniel's drug abuse was extensive.)

Physical Health History

Daniel described his health as good. He did not recall ever having been hospitalized. When asked, Daniel suggested he might have lost consciousness in two of the car accidents in which he had been involved (one in a company truck and the other with a friend) for a very brief time.

Daniel related sustaining several injuries. He showed me scars on his hands that were the result of his father accidentally skating over his hand. This injury was a significant one because the tendon reportedly had been cut and required some time to heal. Daniel mentioned having another scar on his leg from skating. Daniel said that he broke his nose four times in sports injuries. He also sustained some scars from a fall. Several stitches were needed to heal the injury.

Daniel also indicated that he had had two cysts removed from his forehead. These were apparently hereditary. He related being very self-conscious and taking the liberty to have them removed for cosmetic reasons. Daniel also said that he had a scar on his back where he had had a cyst removed.

Mental Health History

Initially, Daniel indicated that he had never seen a counselor at school. He then related having seen a counselor briefly after his friend committed suicide. He said this friend, David, "was going through a suicide thing" and "managed to get it done." Daniel explained that his friend always said that he was going to commit suicide, and it got to the point at which "you just told him, 'go ahead,' [be]cause you knew he was never going to do it. It was just his way of getting attention." Daniel said that when he learned that his friend had killed himself, it bothered him, but "not to the extent that I thought it would."

Daniel recalled that after his arrest he had been given medication to suppress thoughts of the murders and to relieve anxiety. Daniel admitted he had considered killing himself since his arrest. However, he realized that it would not accomplish anything because it would not change the past. Daniel indicated that when he was arrested he was put in an "anti-suicide suit." When he arrived at the jail, he was put in an isolation room with a camera and subsequently transported to the hospital.

Daniel indicated that he spent approximately two months in the hospital, and he does not remember most of the first week. He said he did not see most of the staff because he looked downward to avoid making eye contact. Daniel recalled spending seven or eight weeks in the hospital and seeing a few of his friends before being transferred to jail.

Religious Affiliation

Daniel's parents were Anglicans. Daniel indicated that he did not go to church if he could help it. He was forced to go to Sunday school for a time, but he stopped as soon as he could. He considered religion "a bit of a joke." He explained that priests are supposed to be such good people, but, with all their wealth, "you don't see them helping people."

Daniel explained that "you can't prove God's existence," and he was reluctant to take God's existence on faith. Daniel did not believe in God as the Bible describes Him. However, he believed there was something more advanced than us.

Self-Perception

When asked to describe himself, Daniel paused for a long time before replying, "I don't know." He then added, "I like to party, I try to be good to my friends. I am not really trustworthy." Daniel explained that he tended to embellish stories, particularly with people he did not know, because he felt that what he had to say was not special or good enough.

When asked what things he liked best about himself, Daniel responded without hesitation, "My ability to drive." When asked what he would like to change about himself, he said, "My insecurity around large numbers of people; not trying, just doing enough to get by." When asked how come he did just enough to get by, Daniel indicated that he "never had any ambition to do anything."

Feelings and Responses to Situations

Prior to his arrest, Daniel reported feeling depressed "over the weirdest things," such as what he was doing or where he was going with his life. Daniel said, "There were a lot of times when I was out there that I almost shot myself." He said it would be the easiest way out. He did not think anyone would miss him that much. He recalled how he used to think about his funeral—he envisioned about a dozen people being there, if he was lucky. Daniel indicated that he had on occasion cried when his parents got into fights, but he tried not to cry because he did not want to cry.

At the time of my evaluation, Daniel had a great deal of anger inside him. His answers on 15 of 23 statements measuring anger were indicative of someone who was experiencing considerable anger and who kept it in rather than dealing with it directly. For example, Daniel said, "I still get angry when I think of the bad things people did to me in the past."

Prior Delinquent and Criminal History

Daniel had not been arrested as a juvenile or an adult prior to his arrest for killing his parents. He acknowledged being stopped by the police and given warnings on two occasions for minor traffic infractions and littering.

Daniel admitted involvement in illegal activities for which he was not caught. He indicated that he had repeatedly driven while drunk. "No matter how drunk, how stoned, how much acid I was on, I always drove." He admitted driving recklessly when he was in his own car. In contrast, he said that if he was driving someone else's car, he was very cautious. Daniel maintained that he drove "smarter" when he was "messed up" because he was trying to avoid detection. He knew that if he was going to "play around" when he was high, he needed to do so in a safer area. He described "doing donuts" (riding around in tight circles) in the car and "patching out to leave rubber" as activities that he enjoyed. Daniel was proud of having a car with a lot of power.

Daniel reported being involved in three accidents. Two of the three were related to heavy drinking. The remaining one occurred while he was driving a company truck and before he had time to get high on marijuana.

Daniel indicated that he had sold drugs in high school. He stopped selling because he found that it was "a pain in the butt." Other kids were hustling him to get drugs, apparently when they did not have the money to pay for them.

Daniel denied involvement in burglaries. However, he admitted he had gone into abandoned houses to look around and see what was there. Once inside, he and his friends would sometimes "smoke dope" and drink.

Daniel acknowledged that he had taken things from other people without confrontation. He described it as "just sneakily" taking things when the opportunity arose. For example, "If I was really hard up for cash and there was money lying around somebody's house, I would just take it." He recalled an incident when a car had rolled into a ditch. Daniel and his friends agreed to help. At Daniel's suggestion, they took "CDs and a knife and things like that" from the car. Daniel initially denied stealing cars. He did acknowledge taking his parents' car when they were not at home and without their permission.

Adjustment in Jail

Daniel had been in jail for about seven months when I met with him. He indicated that he got along fine with the guards at the jail and at the hospital. Daniel had not been subjected to physical or sexual violence or threats. He had not had any belongings taken from him and had not been intimidated by other inmates.

Daniel expressed some fear about going to the penitentiary because he was afraid he "might slip up and be stabbed." He had been told that the penitentiary was a highly volatile area and a much more dangerous place than jail.

Daniel indicated that on a typical day, he got up at noon for lunch and took a shower. He might go to the "rec room" in the afternoon. He mainly sat around, watched TV, and played cards and occasionally a game of chess. Daniel said that he also read a lot. He described a broad range of books including *Crime and Punishment* by Dostoyevsky, *The Canterbury Tales* by Chaucer, and books by Robert Ludlum (American author of thriller novels) as materials he had read since being incarcerated.

Daniel reported that his sister had visited him twice and had written to him once since the shootings. He described his last visit with his sister, which was a month or two prior to our meeting, as "rough." Daniel said that he felt that she would like to see him die and that he could see in her eyes that nothing was going to change her feelings. He indicated that his maternal aunt was supposed to be coming to see him. He had had no contact from his father's side of the family since his arrest.

Daniel stated that the only people who had visited him regularly were Cary and Steven Bradley and their mother. He indicated that Ralph had sent him money and called him every weekend since he had been incarcerated. Nolan had come to visit him only once since his arrest.

Future Orientation

Daniel indicated that he did not think about the future. He acknowledged that there has to be something out there that he could enjoy, or at least tolerate, for 20 years or so. Daniel related that, if at some point he is released, he would like to get reacquainted with his family, especially his sister. He said that although they were never really close, he would like to tell her what happened and let her know that he is sorry.

SELF-REPORTED CHILD MALTREATMENT

Daniel's responses did not suggest that he had been physically or medically neglected or that he had been a victim of emotional incest. The data did not suggest any significant physical or sexual abuse.

Daniel's responses raised the possibility that he might have been emotionally neglected and that his parents might have been verbally and psychologically abusive on occasion. Data provided by Mrs. Bradley were somewhat corroborative in this regard. However, the parental behaviors reported herein and by Mrs. Bradley (see the discussion of her interview later in this chapter) were hard to evaluate, given Daniel's history of behavioral problems. It was possible that remarks that Daniel interpreted as critical were warranted, given Daniel's lack of interest in school, repeated lying, abuse of drugs and alcohol, and apparent promiscuity.

Physical and Medical Neglect

Daniel indicated that he had always been provided with adequate food, clothing, and a safe place to live. It appeared that he had been adequately supervised as a child and a young adolescent, but not as he advanced into his later adolescent years. To the extent they could, his parents saw to it that he attended school regularly. Once Daniel had a car, his school attendance was difficult to monitor.

Daniel's parents saw to it that his medical needs were adequately met. They did not prepare him to deal with sexual development, however, according to Daniel.

Emotional Neglect

Daniel supposed that his mother often gave him clear messages that she loved him. He indicated, however, that he was "not into" this type of behavior. He did not feel that his mother often took time to genuinely listen to him; rather, he felt she criticized him. Daniel indicated that his father often did not give him clear messages that he loved him when he was younger because his father worked late and Daniel would be in bed when his father returned home. He recalled his father giving him "a hug now and then" when he was older. Daniel said, however, that his father did not often listen to him.

Verbal Abuse

Daniel indicated that his parents often said things that made him feel badly. For example, his parents threatened to ship him off to a private school because of his behavior. His parents reportedly said he always took the hard road rather than doing things right. They also allegedly said that he was acting stupid but they thought that he was smart, although perhaps they were wrong. Daniel indicated that his parents often said things to him that he felt were belittling. For example, they said that he was lazy and that he did not care about anybody. They also accused him of not doing enough for them.

Daniel related that negative comments were made to him when he was in trouble or whenever the situation warranted it. He estimated that remarks like these were made by his parents "maybe 10 to 20 times per year."

Psychological Abuse

Daniel indicated that his parents often compared him with his sister. However, in the examples Daniel gave, it appeared that he was the one who was doing the comparing. He would ask, for example, why his parents let Anne, when she was age 16 or 17, have her boyfriend over to sleep when they would not allow him to do the same with a girlfriend at age 20. Daniel expressed some resentment toward Anne who, unlike him, was allowed to close her bedroom door. In addition, she could spend her money on items she wanted.

Daniel indicated that his parents, particularly his father, often expressed dissatisfaction with his accomplishments regardless of his actual performance level. Daniel explained that his father had been his hockey coach for a number of years. Daniel hated when his dad was his coach because his father, reportedly, would repeatedly find fault with his performance.

When asked whether his parents ever did anything that embarrassed him in front of others, Daniel provided one example. He reported that on two or three occasions, his mother had been sunbathing on the front deck when he and his friends came home. She reportedly did not have the top of her bathing suit on, exposing her breasts at least momentarily. When asked whether his parents often did things that communicated to Daniel that his needs were not important, he said "Yes" but could provide only one example, namely, he was not allowed to have a phone in his bedroom.

Physical Abuse

Daniel reported that his father hurt him physically because his dad was very angry a couple of times. He recalled his father slapping him and shaking him between two and five times. He reported that his father had pushed or shoved him a couple of times. Daniel recalled his father slapping him "twice maybe," and his mother perhaps as many as three or four times. Daniel also recalled his father spanking him in a harsh and humiliating way. Daniel indicated that the spankings occurred quite frequently when he was younger. He recalled his father breaking a spoon on his buttocks on one occasion and hitting him with a belt once or twice. From Daniel's perspective, neither Mr. nor Mrs. Culbreath ever struck out at him physically when he had done nothing at all to warrant it. Although Daniel saw the discipline given to him by his parents as out of proportion to what he actually did, "it always seems like that when it's you."

Daniel indicated that he had to stay when his parents verbally fought with him. He usually would not say anything to his parents; typically he would just nod his head. He recalled his parents making him stick out his tongue so they could put mustard powder on it. This punishment "burned quite a lot." He had to sit on a chair in the living room for about an hour as punishment; he recalled the last time as occurring before junior high.

Spouse/Sibling Abuse

To Daniel's knowledge, there was no physical violence or threats between his parents or toward his sister Anne. Daniel indicated that his parents treated Anne differently, acknowledging that this was partly due to the fact that she did not do things "wrong."

Sexual Abuse and Boundary Violations

Daniel denied having been overtly sexually abused. There were no absolute indicators of covert sexual abuse.[2] However, there were a few indications that the boundaries in this family were somewhat loose, causing Daniel to feel some sense of discomfort. For example, he indicated that there were no restrictions on the use of the bathroom when other family members were using it. He said that his parents and his sister were allowed to walk in on him when he was in the bathroom, including when he was in the bathtub. He recalled being embarrassed on one occasion when he was in the tub and had an erection because his father came in to use the toilet and observed Daniel's condition. Daniel indicated that after a while Anne started locking the door of the bathroom, something that he was not allowed to do.

Daniel also indicated that his parents often questioned him about friends or about dates in a manner that showed that they did not trust him. He believed that, from his parents' perspective, his life should have been an open book. He felt that his parents were very invasive. Daniel related not wanting to tell his parents anything "because I got criticized about whatever I told them."

Daniel said, with resentment, that his mother read his letters and listened to his phone conversations. He believed that his parents pried into his affairs only and respected Anne's privacy. Daniel indicated that, in contrast to his sister, he was not allowed to lock his bedroom door or properly close it.

Chemical Dependency and Family Dysfunction

Daniel indicated that as far as he knew, neither of his parents had a problem with alcohol or illicit drugs. He recalled no occasion when either of his parents used mood-altering drugs. He recalled, however, that his mother had "a breakdown" when he was about age 18. He recalled her lying on her bed, staring out the window and refusing to talk to anyone for about two or three days. As far as he could remember, she spoke to a counselor but was not hospitalized.

Coping Mechanisms

Daniel displayed little insight into the extent of the family problems. When asked how he coped with things growing up, he reported that he just "clammed up." He did not talk to other family members about the problems in his home. Daniel reported that he did talk to some of his friends about these problems once he got older and when he was kicked out of the house. He indicated that when he talked to others, no one helped him, and it did not do him good just to talk.

Daniel recalled turning to alcohol and drugs to forget. He indicated that getting high was his primary way of feeling better, although on occasion he did hurt himself on purpose. He reported that when he was very upset on one occasion, he broke his hand by punching a wall. He also recalled another incident when he was upset in which he shot his hand with a pellet gun. On both occasions, he felt better after hurting himself. He also recalled cutting his arm with a pencil sharpener on a few occasions. Daniel indicated that prior to his arrest, he sometimes thought about killing himself. He recalled being home alone one weekend and feeling down because he could not reach anyone. He said, "I sat with a gun for a half an hour or so." Then the phone rang. The caller's invitation to do something with him ended the suicidal ideation for the time.

Daniel reported that he thought about running away when he was younger. He recalled actually preparing to leave three or four times. He was never away long because his parents came after him right away.

Daniel indicated that there were large parts of his childhood after age 5 that he could not remember. Daniel reported having some blank spells or missing time; however, these episodes appear to be tied to his ingestion of alcohol or drugs.

INTERVIEW WITH MRS. BRADLEY

Daniel's girlfriend's mother, Mrs. Bradley, spoke freely about dynamics in the Culbreath family and appeared to have insight into Daniel. She knew both of Daniel's parents. She described the Culbreath family as a "typically British family." They were "the picture-perfect family."

Mrs. Bradley indicated that the community reaction to the homicides was very negative toward Daniel. She said Daniel had a car and a computer. He had "a good life in many respects," but there were conditions placed on it.

Mrs. Bradley described Daniel's sister Anne as "the perfect good one" and Daniel as "the bad one." She indicated that Anne was very connected to her parents and that Daniel was very resentful of Anne.

Mrs. Bradley said that Daniel's parents were very strict and had high standards. From her perspective, Daniel never felt adequate. She described Mr. and Mrs. Culbreath as "very exacting." She felt that Mr. Culbreath pushed Daniel when it came to hockey and was verbally abusive, constantly putting Daniel down.

Mrs. Bradley related that Daniel was very resentful of his father. She described Mr. Culbreath as very nice to everyone else but mean to Daniel when he was coaching him with respect to hockey. Mr. Culbreath reportedly pushed Daniel to do better, calling him names and shaming him in front of others for his performance.

Mrs. Bradley indicated that Daniel liked his mother. It appeared to her that Mrs. Culbreath cared about her son. However, Mrs. Culbreath said things in front of others that Mrs. Bradley felt were not appropriate. Daniel never reacted to criticism. He came across as very well behaved. She felt, however, that he had a great deal of resentment in him.

Mrs. Bradley knew Mrs. Culbreath better than Mr. Culbreath and described her as strict, "bossy," and "really cold." Mrs. Bradley said most of her relationship with Daniel's mother consisted of "superficial talk." She never felt she could talk to Mrs. Culbreath about "anything deep."

Mrs. Bradley described a special meal that Daniel and her daughter, Cary, had prepared for the Culbreath family. When Mrs. Culbreath arrived home, she said that she wanted to sunbathe and was not interested in sitting down with them for dinner. After declining to join them at the table, Mrs. Culbreath would not let Daniel and Cary take their dinners into the living room to eat.

Mrs. Bradley did not believe that the homicides were about money because Daniel did "a horrible job" in committing the murders. She believed it was "something much more deep." Mrs. Bradley believed that fantasy played a role in the murders. She did not see Daniel as having a firm grip on reality. Mrs. Bradley had read some of Daniel's poems. She said these poems, which were written shortly before the incident, were about being possessed.

Mrs. Bradley indicated that her children, Cary and Steven, and their friend Alicia all liked Daniel's parents. She said the children felt guilty because they treated Daniel's remarks about how he was going to kill his parents as "a big game." They did not understand "how vulnerable he was." She said that "they goaded him terribly."

Mrs. Bradley believed that Daniel had attention deficit hyperactivity disorder (ADHD) because he had difficulty concentrating in school, was good with games and computers, and appeared hyperactive. She indicated that he could not sit still, that he was "always running, always moving."

Mrs. Bradley described Daniel as "a well-mannered boy." She indicated that although "he knew how to be with people," he came across as "never fitting anywhere." Mrs. Bradley saw Daniel as having "a lot of potential." He was smart and had good writing abilities. Initially she liked him, but she did not trust him. She said that Daniel had a tendency to lie and manipulate, but that was not his general style. She indicated that he had to defend himself because he never felt good enough; he could never measure up.

Mrs. Bradley was concerned that Daniel would not get therapy in prison. She described him as "a chameleon," indicating that, to his detriment, he had the ability to adapt to the prison environment. Mrs. Bradley indicated that Daniel liked order and opined that he would be good in the army because he responded well to structure.

Mrs. Bradley did not feel unsafe with Daniel. She said he was "never ever violent." She did recall an incident, however, when her daughter was very upset because Daniel and his friends ran over a fox and returned later to take pictures of the dead animal.

INTERVIEW WITH GIRLFRIEND CARY BRADLEY

Cary estimated that she had dated Daniel for about eight or nine months prior to his arrest. She indicated that Daniel had lots of girlfriends, whom he tended to keep for about two weeks, and many superficial friends. She related that the guys did not like him because he "took things." Cary said Daniel frequently lied about stupid things, such as the amount of drugs he had. She said, "He lied when it was not necessary." She described him as "a good bullshitter." She maintained, however, that he did not lie to close friends.

Cary indicated that Daniel was not nice to some people, especially people he considered "insipid, pathetic, or losers." Cary said he would put these people down, but he would do it behind their backs. He did not confront others.

Cary indicated that she had observed Daniel with his parents on a number of occasions. Daniel and his parents seemed to get along, but there were many things that his parents did not know. She said Daniel "was trying so hard to please them" when he was with them. She added that he would change his voice and put on a British accent when he was around them. "He was always pretending, so they would be pleased with him."

Cary indicated that she had had extensive contact with Daniel's parents. She described Daniel's mother as "very controlling, but she was nice." She related the incident when Daniel, Cary, and Daniel's father made dinner and set the table and Mrs. Culbreath would not join them because she had other plans. Cary said that Mrs. Culbreath was "worried about her house, that she liked her house orderly." Cary added, however, that she did some "very sweet and nice, little things."

Cary recalled an incident when Daniel's mother called Cary's house because she could not find the remote control for the VCR. Daniel had to leave and go home to find the remote control. Cary related that Daniel never "mouthed off" at his mother. He was "very well mannered." Cary indicated that she did not observe either his mother or his father directly criticizing Daniel.

Cary indicated that she really liked Daniel's dad. She described him as a "very nice, kind of funny," and "really sweet kind of guy." She thought Daniel and his father got along very well. Cary said she and her friends found it humorous when Daniel talked about killing his parents; she related that her friend Alicia would make fun of him. She insisted that no one believed Daniel was serious. When Daniel told her he had shot his parents, Cary indicated that she did not believe him because it seemed impossible for him to do something like that. She did not see him as violent. However, she recalled the incident mentioned by her mother when Daniel intentionally ran over a fox and returned to the scene afterward to photograph it.

Cary described Daniel as "very, very upset" after the shooting. He appeared "all freaked out." She recalled him as being "red and sweaty" and "very shocked and scared" when he told Cary, Steven, and Ellen that he had shot his parents.

INTERVIEW WITH FRIEND RALPH

Ralph indicated that he had known Daniel for about seven or eight years. Ralph said he and Daniel stayed in touch through visits and weekly phone calls after Ralph moved away, a couple of years prior to the shootings.

Ralph characterized Daniel as his best friend and considered him trustworthy. He claimed that Daniel never mentioned anything to him about hurting or killing others. Ralph indicated that although Daniel was an aggressive hockey player, he was not a violent person. Ralph indicated that Daniel had never struck any of his girlfriends or hit any guys back. Daniel reportedly never picked fights and would walk away from them.

Ralph confirmed that Daniel liked action movies and those with explosions and guns. He liked comedies and James Cameron films[3] (*Titanic*, *Aliens*). Ralph indicated that Daniel had indeed watched *Natural Born Killers* at least a couple of times.

Ralph indicated that he disliked Mr. and Mrs. Culbreath. Daniel's relationships with his parents seemed "tense and strained" to Ralph. Ralph felt that Daniel's father was manipulative. He related that Daniel moved out on two occasions. His parents called Daniel, and he returned home.

Ralph characterized Anne as "the perfect child." Daniel had a problem measuring up to his sister. Ralph said Daniel would be different around his parents; he would speak differently and put on a British accent. From Ralph's perspective, Daniel could not relax around his parents and desperately wanted their approval.

Ralph maintained that he was completely surprised by the shooting. He described Daniel two days after the arrest as "completely a mess." Daniel was crying and "walking around like a zombie." He said the shooting behavior clearly was not Daniel Culbreath as he knew him.

MOTIVATIONAL DYNAMICS BEHIND THE HOMICIDE

Daniel's statements to me were consistent with those he made to the police. His eye contact and his body posture were also similar to that observed on the videotaped confession. It appeared that recalling the homicidal scene—specifically, the sight of his parents lifeless and bleeding—was very painful for Daniel and caused him extreme anguish.

Parricidal Ideation

Daniel admitted that when he was growing up he thought about killing his parents. He dreamed, and even fantasized during the day, about killing his parents. He admitted he sometimes was afraid that he might wind up killing his parents.

When asked, Daniel recalled the thought of killing someone as first occurring to him when he was working for the shellfish company. One day while he was driving, he heard a news report on his car radio that a murder had happened somewhere. He began thinking, "I wonder what it would be like to kill somebody." At that time he was driving on a deserted stretch of road and noticed a house and nothing else in the vicinity. He wondered what would happen if he came back at 3:00 in the morning and went in—what it would be like to kill somebody. He mentioned this thought to his friend Nolan, who asked Daniel what he meant. Daniel reportedly never talked to him about it again.

Daniel related thinking about killing someone "on and off" for more than a year prior to the murders. He began thinking about killing someone particularly when he was "drunk or stoned." He remembered that he got into a fight one night with his parents and went out the next night. He was telling somebody about the fight, and, although he did not tell this person then, the thought of what it would be like to kill his parents occurred to him at that time. Daniel began thinking of this action as a possibility. Later, he mentioned the thought of killing his parents to others, and they thought it was "funny."

Daniel recalled that whenever he got into a fight with his parents, "that's what ran through my mind, you know. And that was my way of getting them. They'd be sitting there yelling at me and I'd be sitting there listening and I'd be thinking, 'Yeah, I was thinking about killing you last night.'" Daniel recalled that "it got to the point where it was a joke with a lot of people, and I'd get in situations where it would be brought up by somebody else. Oh yeah, oh yeah, I'd talk about it and stuff."

Daniel indicated that he did not know why he repeatedly talked about killing. He did not know whether he was trying to shock other people. "It got to the point where I was thinking about it a lot, you know, whenever I'd get mad at them [parents] or whatever." When asked, he replied that he had parricidal thoughts "three, four, five times a week."

Daniel reportedly told approximately 50 people about his thoughts of killing people. He indicated having told different things to different people. He asked some what it would be like to kill someone. If he knew people well, he would talk to them about killing his parents. Daniel related having talked about killing with people from all walks of life and noticed that people reacted differently. Daniel related how some people thought his homicidal or parricidal thoughts were "sick." Others, however, indicated that they, too, had thought about it. Some just laughed. Daniel indicated that some of his talking about killing might have been for attention.

Daniel told people he knew on various occasions that he had a new plan for killing his parents. At times he said he scared himself by saying that he would "do it tonight" and asking them to help. He maintained that "a lot of people took it like a weird twisted joke."

Daniel denied being serious about killing his parents. However, he indicated that "it always made me feel better when I was angry." For him, the parricidal thoughts were a way to get back at them. He envisioned himself saying to his parents, "If you knew what was running through my mind right now, you wouldn't be saying that to me, that I'm dumb, whatever."

Daniel admitted that he had told others that he stood to inherit a lot of money if he killed his parents and that he had talked about how he would do it. "I'd break into the house, make it look like a robbery, take electronics, you know. Told people the gun is not registered, so nobody has to know it was there." Daniel indicated that there was no serial number and that it was an old rifle. He maintained that "lots of people" thought it was a good idea. He said, "Jokingly—obviously—some people offered to help: 'You give me some of the money, I'll help you.'" He maintained that "it was a sick, running gag."

At the time of the clinical interview, Daniel insisted he did not know how much his parents were worth. He had specified different amounts to different people. He suspected his parents had an insurance policy but claimed he did not know for sure.

Daniel strongly denied having made the decision to kill his parents a few days before the shootings so he could spend time with his friends and girlfriend Cary. He said, "Any references to killing my parents would have been just talk—only this time it happened."

The Shootings

When asked how the fantasy wound up playing out, Daniel said he did not know. He repeatedly maintained that "it was never supposed to happen." Daniel appeared quite upset as he related the incident, and his behavior suggested he was reliving the scenario. When asked what he was thinking about as he sat there with me, Daniel replied, "My dad—with his head lying over the side. He still had his glasses on with all this stuff dripping on the floor."

Daniel related the events leading up to the shootings. That day his mother called him at Cary's house to return home to cook steaks. Daniel indicated that he had been "high all day" on marijuana and did not want to go home when his mother called. He said that he had had plans to go camping with Allan that night and wanted to visit with Cary before he left.

Daniel denied thinking about killing his parents when he was on his way to their home on the night of the shooting. His remarks indicated, however, that he was angry as he drove home. He acknowledged, "I was pissed because they called me. I kinda looked dumb because I am 20 and my parents are calling me and saying, 'You have to come home and have supper,' you know, it's like when you are 8 years old or whatever, and you are out playing in the yard with your friends, and your mum comes out and says, 'Supper time,' and you go running in to eat supper."

When he arrived home, Daniel and his parents got into an argument. Daniel's anger intensified:

And when I got home, that's when it started. They were mad at me for spending so much time away from home; [they said] how I only came home after they are asleep, [that] I'm not doing my share of stuff around the house, how I am lazy, how a smart boy should be able to figure this out for himself. You know, they always thought I was smart, but maybe I'm not, maybe they were wrong. Obviously they were wrong, they said, because "Look at you. Obviously we were wrong, because you never learn."

Daniel indicated that his father was in a bad mood because he had an ingrown toenail and his foot was really bothering him. "Dad was shaking me and stuff and saying 'You always take the hard road, you never take the easy road. We tried to show you the easy road.'" Daniel said that his father was shaking him and that he felt "like a fucking little kid." He recalled, "I just stood there and took it, and never said nothing. And then I just went to the bathroom. I was in hard shape. I was really pissed at them. I took the gun out of the closet. I walked out. I shot Dad twice, and then I shot Mom."

When asked what was going on as he was relating this incident, Daniel said, crying, "I don't like seeing them the way I last saw them. They tell me that Dad never saw it coming, but Mom did though. She screamed [defendant is crying]—she screamed when I shot Dad." Daniel was crying as he visualized what had occurred. He accepted a tissue to wipe his tears and confirmed that it was his mother's screaming that really bothered him.

Daniel indicated that *he was really angry while he was shooting his parents*. He told me that he did not understand why he did it. It puzzled him that he could have gone that long without hurting anybody and then suddenly killed his parents that day. When asked what he was planning to do when he went to his parents' house, he said, "To cook supper and get out of there." He wanted to get back to Steven and Cary's house to visit before meeting up with some of the kids from the community college. He intended to buy some dope and go to the campsite. He insisted, "It wasn't supposed to happen. I was supposed to get out of there."

Daniel said that he should have left when the argument began or stayed away altogether that evening. "There are so many times I wish I hadn't gone home that day. [I wish] that I had said, 'No, I'm not going home to cook the supper. I don't want to come home.'" Daniel was convinced the murders would not have occurred if he had moved out of the house after he graduated from high school. If he had taken a job and stayed at an apartment, his parents would not have called him and expected him for supper.

When asked what he was thinking in the bathroom, Daniel said he did not remember. He said, "I was mad, really mad. I had enough time to walk in the door, turn the barbecue on, [long pause] then it started." He recalled his father shoving him and then letting him go. He indicated that he could have walked out the door and that he did not know why he went to the bathroom. He said that maybe it was to get the gun. Daniel remembered closing the bathroom door and getting the rifle from the bathroom closet. He said that the gun was loaded. Daniel remembered opening the door and coming out of the bathroom. He recalled looking at his father, who was sitting in a chair in the dining room, soaking his foot. Daniel remembered raising the rifle: "I just remember bringing it up and shooting." Daniel did not look to see whether he had his target in his sight.

Daniel recalled that he shot twice. When asked how come he fired the second shot, Daniel replied, "I didn't think he was dead … he started this gurgling noise in his throat, disgusting. There was this dripping noise, and all that stuff dripping on the floor. It sounded like somebody had spilled milk." Daniel thought that this was his father's brains spilling out. He then continued: "And I heard Mom, and I turned around and I shot her." He remembered that his mother screamed and just stood there. He stated, "I just pivoted, I just turned and shot" her. He continued: "She just crumbled; she just dropped. Like one minute she was standing there; another minute she was on the floor; and there was all this blood behind her. And I started screaming. I was just screaming."

When asked why he was screaming, Daniel said that he was "mad" at them because he "didn't want to be stupid."

Behavior Following the Killings

Daniel said that he left the scene quickly. He took the gun, locked the doors so nobody else would find them, and got in his car. He disposed of the gun and then went to Cary and Steven's house. He repeated at least three times that he had to tell someone. He told Steven, Cary, and Ellen—the first people he saw. He seemed conflicted, both wanting to tell someone and not wanting to tell anyone.

Daniel took a cold shower because he was sweating and he was hot. To his knowledge, there was no blood on his clothing. After showering, Daniel reportedly sat on the couch and drank a shot of rum. He related that he asked Steven to say he never left, because he wanted to believe this was the case and also to establish an alibi. He said the event did not seem real to him at all. He was trying not to think about what he had done and was telling himself that maybe he had not really left and the shootings had not happened.

Daniel explained that going camping as he had originally planned reinforced his thought that maybe the murders had never occurred. He said the guys were talking about normal things like girls and cars, and he seemed to fit right in.

Daniel recalled smoking two or three grams of marijuana that night. He also said he had a couple of drinks. He said he had difficulty sleeping and took a Valium that he had in the car.

When he woke up the next day, he said, "It just seemed so damn normal." He ate breakfast, rolled up some dope, and smoked a joint. Daniel was driving Allan home and hoping that maybe the murders had never happened when he saw the roadblock and said he "knew somebody found them."

Daniel in Police Custody

The police took Daniel to the police station and put him in an interrogation room. He related initially telling the police just about everything he had done, except the part about going home and committing the murders. Daniel said that the police left him in the interrogation room for a while. He recalled calling "Legal Aid." A man came over and told him to wait for his lawyer before speaking to the police.

Daniel recalled that he was given a warning at the beginning of the interrogation. Daniel knew his rights (the same as Miranda warnings) and recited them to me. He repeatedly asked to speak to his attorney. He eventually told police what had happened after his requests to see his lawyer "over, and over, and over" were ignored and police questioning continued. Daniel was subsequently charged with two counts of first-degree murder.

The Effect of the Killings on Daniel

Daniel's statements indicated that at the time of my evaluation, he was being tormented by thoughts and images of the murders. He said that when he was trying to go to sleep, thoughts about his parents sometimes kept appearing in his mind.

Sometimes these thoughts would wake him up or keep him up. Daniel indicated that he had nightmares and thought about "how useless my life was; how totally unexplainable what I did was; why I did it." Sometimes he saw images of his parents after the shooting happened. He related that when he saw these images of the murder scene, it was because something triggered it, such as a snippet of a song. The flashbacks were as if he was watching the murder happen in a video; he knew the events were not real.

Daniel reported that these flashbacks occurred a lot in the hospital but less since he had been in jail. Daniel indicated that he had been "smoking dope" since being in jail,[4] explaining that "the marijuana dulls it for awhile." He was able "when high" to play cards, and he could laugh and joke with the other inmates. The scenes of the murder did not come back to him when he had been under the influence of marijuana. He tried actively not to think about the shooting. Daniel indicated that he had difficulty concentrating on and off, in addition to falling or staying asleep. He reported that he was nervous and often jumpy and felt depressed when he thought of his current situation.

Daniel's Current Feelings about Killing His Parents

When asked how he felt about what happened that day, Daniel replied, "Dead." He explained, "I miss them a lot sometimes, but sometimes I just don't feel anything, anything at all. Happy, sad, angry." He said that sometimes he had felt numb before the incident, but not really to the extent that he felt it at the time of my evaluation. He said, "I don't give a flying rat's ass about anything anymore." Making it clear, he said, "I don't care what happens to me."

When asked whether he missed his parents, Daniel replied, "Sometimes. Not very often." He added, "Sometimes I'm not sure if I'm missing them or if I'm feeling bad for what I did. I don't know." When asked what he would say if he could speak to his parents right now, he said, "I'm sorry." When asked for what, he said, "For killing them; [long pause] for not making something out of my life, for just being me."

When asked what he would say to his sister if he could speak to her, he replied, "I'd apologize. I'd say, 'I'm sorry for taking your parents away and I hope you can do more with your life than I did with mine.' There's nothing I can say that is going to change the way that she feels or what happened. Sometimes I really wish that wasn't the case."

Daniel's Perception of Himself and His Situation

Daniel did not see himself as "a tough guy," and he did not believe that anyone else would perceive him in such a light. Daniel did not see himself as getting into trouble again because he wanted to try to "live right." He was aware that he faced a possible sentence of 25 years to life. He realized that, if sentenced as a dangerous offender, he could do life unless the parole board decided some day that it was safe for him to be released.

Daniel did not see himself as a dangerous person. He explained, "I never got mad at anybody. I never hit anybody. I am afraid of confrontation in here because, if somebody comes after me, I'm gonna back down—you can't do that in here, but I cannot not [sic] do it."

Daniel said he wanted to get help. He believed he must need it "because most normal people don't do what I do, or did." He related wishing he could have talked more when he was in the hospital, but he was not supposed to talk about his case. He was surprised that the people in the hospital were generally really nice to him, given what he did.

EVALUATION OF FORENSIC ISSUES RAISED

Daniel was competent to stand trial. The consulting forensic psychiatrist and I agreed that Daniel was sane under his country's legal code, which used the M'Naghten Test of Insanity. Daniel's rendition to me indicated that Daniel knew the nature and quality of his act during the homicidal event. He had excellent recall of the events during the killings, as well as events leading up to and following the murders. Daniel knew that he was engaged in the shooting of his parents and said that he fired the second shot at his father in order to cause his death. Daniel was aware, when he heard his mother scream and pivoted around, that he was raising the gun toward her to shoot her.

Daniel's behavior after the killings indicated that he knew his actions were wrong. He specifically said that he locked the door so that no one would find the bodies. He stated that when he realized that he had the rifle, he knew he had to dispose of it and went to a place where he thought its discovery would be unlikely. He admitted that he asked Steven to state that he had never left the Bradley residence in order to establish an alibi. He knew that was also wishful thinking on his part.

I had some doubt as to whether these murders were planned and deliberate. Although Daniel repeatedly talked about killing his parents, events did not unfold in a methodical way. Daniel did not carry out basic acts he had said he would do in an attempt to avoid detection, such as the taking of electronics to make it look like a robbery.

Offenders who perceive at level 3 typically do not plan events, especially in the long-term sense. Instead, they generally act impulsively and without much deliberation. Daniel's fantasizing about killing his parents and repeatedly talking about this act made this idea easily accessible to him.

It appears based on multiple sources that talking about killing his parents brought Daniel attention from his friends, none of whom apparently took him seriously. Cary was a prime example in this regard. In her interview with the police, she indicated that Daniel said to her on the day before the killing that he would kill his parents the next day and make sure that it did not interfere with his plans for the weekend. Cary told the police and me that she played along with him because she never believed that Daniel would murder his parents.

Daniel repeatedly stated that he never intended to carry through on his statements to kill his parents. He indicated that the idea to kill his parents routinely popped into his mind when they were arguing with him. The idea brought him some sense of empowerment when he perceived his parents as being critical of him. According to Daniel, this idea to kill his parents often appeared when he was angry over what they were saying to him and he felt unable to defend himself. The idea of killing his parents was consistent with a child's fantasy of getting back at his parents without having a solid appreciation of the consequences of his actions. As discussed earlier (Chapter 2), research has indicated that the part of the brain associated with critical thinking and deliberation (the prefrontal cortex) is not fully developed until age 23 to 25.

Daniel acknowledged that he was angry about being called home on the evening of the murders. If an argument ensued soon after Daniel's arrival, as he reported, he was likely to have become even angrier. His statements about how he was feeling immediately prior to the shooting suggest that he might have been enraged, particularly if his father shook him, as Daniel consistently maintained. His statements suggested he was responding from the limbic system (the emotional part) of the brain as he argued with his parents. If Daniel suffered from ADHD (discussed below), he would have been at even higher risk of behaving impulsively. Individuals with ADHD have difficulty deliberating and tend to react rapidly to stimuli. In a low-maturity individual who has ADHD, the steps between having an idea and acting on it are even more likely to get short-circuited, impeding conscious deliberation of the response.

The Voluntariness of the Confession

After I had viewed the videotape and read the transcript of Daniel's confession, it did not appear to me that Daniel was in a mental framework to voluntarily consent to talk to the police following his arrest. Daniel declined to speak to the police and made references to wanting to speak to his lawyer eight times. Despite Daniel's statements that he did not desire to speak with the police, two detectives kept talking to him. Police tactics were manipulative and psychologically coercive. One detective, for example, was hard on him; the other presented as his "buddy." The defendant's body language was consistent with someone who has been worn down. A low-maturity individual who was frightened by his arrest could hardly be expected to believe that he had the power to decline to speak to the police after his repeated attempts to cease questioning were completely ignored by the interrogators.

DIAGNOSTIC IMPRESSIONS

When I evaluated Daniel, he met the diagnostic criteria for major depression and post-traumatic stress disorder (PTSD). The PTSD seemed to be a reaction to the scene of his parents being killed rather than earlier traumas sustained as a child. In addition, he had a history of abusing alcohol and cannabis and appeared to have periods when he was chemically dependent with respect to both of these drugs. Data provided were not sufficient for me to determine whether Daniel had ADHD as a child and adolescent and, if so, whether he continues to have this disorder as a young adult.

There was clearly a history of antisocial behavior dating back to childhood. David met the diagnostic criteria for conduct disorder (CD): he initiated fights as a child, engaged in vandalism, broke into houses, stole items without confrontation, was truant, and lied to his parents. There was also evidence that he met the threshold requirement to be diagnosed as having antisocial personality disorder.

CD, as we have seen, is the precursor to antisocial personality disorder (APD) (see Chapters 1 and 2). Data provided by Daniel suggested that "a pervasive pattern of disregard for the rights of others occurring since age 15" might have been in place prior to his arrest for killing his parents. He manifested at least four of the seven diagnostic criteria for APD; only three are needed in order to establish the diagnosis. Daniel repeatedly drove while intoxicated, despite having two accidents while high, indicating a failure to conform to social norms with respect to lawful behaviors, as well as evincing a reckless disregard for the safety of himself and others. Daniel was deceitful, repeatedly lied to his parents, and "embellished" stories, apparently to gain favor with others. He repeatedly missed school despite being paid by the government to attend, demonstrating consistent irresponsibility, because he was enrolled to learn a trade. Daniel evinced no remorse for any antisocial behavior predating the murder of his parents. This illegal conduct included stealing from others, destroying others' property, and subjecting others' to physical danger.

Daniel had a number of psychopathic traits. These included shallow affect, pathological lying, callousness and lack of empathy, sexual promiscuity, impulsivity, irresponsibility, failure to accept responsibility, and juvenile delinquency.[5] There was also evidence that Daniel derived satisfaction from fantasies and acts of destructiveness. These included his parricidal and homicidal thoughts, watching the film *Natural Born Killers* on several occasions, and allegedly intentionally running over a fox and returning later to photograph it. These were unfavorable prognostic indicators.

There were a few favorable prognostic indicators, however. Oddly enough, killing his parents was a traumatic event for Daniel. He seemed remorseful for killing them and sorry for the effect that his behavior has had on his sister. I advised counsel that Daniel appeared receptive to treatment at the time of my evaluation and seemed reachable. In Daniel's case, treatment was critically needed in order to help him find healthy and socially acceptable ways to deal with conflict and to feel effective as a human being. Without treatment, the prognosis for this individual seemed poor.

CASE DISPOSITION

This case concluded unexpectedly within a few months of my completing my evaluation. I received a letter from Daniel's defense counsel advising that pursuant to a search warrant, the police had seized Daniel's hospital records and reviewed them with the prosecutor. As a result of information contained in Daniel's medical records, the prosecution had indicated that it intended to call nine caregivers from the mental hospital to testify against Daniel at his trial.

The defense attorney immediately moved to halt the use of these materials by arguing that the search warrant was invalid and the use of private medical information by the police was illegal. At this same hearing, defense counsel also argued that Daniel's confession was illegally obtained after he was denied access to counsel following his arrest. The court agreed with defense counsel and ruled that the search warrant was invalid and that Daniel's medical rights were violated. Although the court directed that the prosecutor could not call the hospital witnesses, the court did not rule that the prosecutor could not use the knowledge gained from the illegally seized records if Daniel decided to testify.

The court also agreed with defense counsel that Daniel's constitutional rights had been violated by police when they denied him access to counsel after his arrest. However, the court was not prepared to exclude Daniel's statement to the police or any of the derivative evidence that went with it. The defense attorney told me that, given that the illegally acquired information could be used, the prosecutor was unwilling to consider any reduction in the charge or penalty for Daniel.[6] As a result of these court decisions, Daniel indicated that he desired to terminate the proceedings so as to spare his extended family any further hardship. Daniel pled guilty to two counts of first-degree murder and was sentenced to life imprisonment with parole consideration after 25 years.

FOLLOW-UP INTERVIEW

I met with Daniel six years after my initial evaluation. He was 27 years old and housed in a medium-security prison. He was personable and interested in participating in the interview. He presented as calm and content. His eye contact was good.

I noted that Daniel had advanced in personality development from level 3 to a low level 4. As is characteristic of those who perceive at level 4, Daniel displayed some insight into his behavior. He expressed concern about others and felt badly for the hurt that he had caused his surviving family members.

Daniel said he had seen his sister three times since the murders: once while he was in the mental hospital, another time in jail, and the most recent time, when he was in prison. He found her last visit "difficult." Daniel explained that it was "hard" because in prison he did not have to confront things. "I can think about them, but in the sense that you think about a chapter in a book that you just read. Whereas with her, I'm actually sort of, not just facing her, but the reality of what I did and who I am."

Daniel stated that only one other family member, his maternal grandmother, had visited him in prison. He experienced her visit as also very hard. In his words, "As soon as I saw her, I just felt like this lump in my chest and, I'll be honest with you, I started crying." He was amazed that she would give him a hug. Similar to his sister, his grandmother wanted to know why he killed his parents. Daniel said that he had no explanation.

Daniel maintained that every single day he wished that he "could go back and stop that [the murders] from happening," even if he had to spend the rest of his life in prison. He stated, "I regret it with every fiber of my being …. Aside from being the most insane thing, it was like, it was a combination of all the dumb ass things I've ever done in my life, but like a million times worse."

The Dynamics behind the Murders of His Parents

I proposed to Daniel three possible theories regarding his involvement in the murders: (1) His talking about killing his parents began as a fantasy but took on a life of its own. As friends encouraged him, the course was set, and Daniel was carried away as events unfolded. Not following through on "his plans" became less and less of an option. (2) The police were correct in their theory that the murders were planned for financial gain and freedom. Daniel had told his friends he stood to gain a large inheritance and offered them compensation to help. (3) The idea of killing his parents popped into Daniel's mind, was rehearsed in conversations with friends, was fantasized about during arguments with his parents, and exploded into reality when he erupted into rage. Without a moment's hesitation, Daniel said, "The third one."

Daniel confided that when he got into arguments with his parents and was "steaming mad," he took pleasure in thinking about how his parents would react if they knew of the homicidal thoughts he entertained regarding them. He talked to many people about killing someone because, he said, it made him feel "special." Daniel said that he did not want to go home the day of the murders. He insisted that if he had not returned home when summoned by his parents, the murders would not have occurred. When asked, Daniel maintained that there had indeed been a confrontation and his father had shoved him immediately prior to the shootings. However, he explained that the rage he felt was not totally due to his parents. His remarks suggested he experienced shame and self-hatred.

I wasn't so much very, very angry solely with them, or directly with them. It was more I was so frustrated with where my life was, or where it wasn't at that point in time because I saw community college as the bottom of the barrel. I felt like a failure going to community college 'cause it's community college. Growing up in a sort of predominately middle-class sort of area and growing up, you just sort of expected to go to university. You know, university is where you're supposed to go. And going to community college is like for—I don't want to say "dummies," because it's not. But for people who are looking for a trade as opposed to, you know, what university offers, I guess .... I just felt like a failure going to community college, I did. I felt worthless.

Daniel seemed pained and puzzled as he explained that he had "absolutely no ambition for anything growing up," including sports and school. He said he never applied himself, even though he believed he had the ability. His lack of interest predated his "smoking weed or drinking." "The only thing" Daniel worried about was how other people perceived him, "as opposed to the reality." He acknowledged at the time of the follow-up interview that he was still concerned with how others saw him, but "to a lesser degree." Daniel recognized that he spent his time trying to figure out what to say or do to fit in with one person versus another rather than trying to find his real self.

Life in Prison

Following his conviction, Daniel spent time in only two prisons: the reception center and the prison where he was confined when I met with him. He described prison conditions in his country as "a little more relaxed" than he imagined they were in the United States based on things he had seen on TV. He said that after work hours, inmates were allowed to wear their own clothes. He was housed in a one-man cell where he had a TV, stereo, small refrigerator, and toilet. He preferred his living situation to a two-man cell because, even though he had less room, "there is enough room in there that it gives you that personal space, like if I am having a day where I don't really want to talk to anybody, I can go in there and lock the door. And if someone wants to talk to me, they can come and knock on the door, and if I want to answer, I answer, and if I don't, I don't." He opined that there was less violence in prisons in his country, relative to the United States, because inmates know that they have "a lot more to lose" if they act out.

Despite these comforts, Daniel acknowledged that prison had been an adjustment for him. He had to learn how "to deal with a wide variety of personalities," some of whom were "overly aggressive." He admitted that at the time of his conviction, he was not criminally sophisticated. He saw himself as fortunate to have learned how to survive in prison from other inmates, particularly from "lifers," whom he considered essentially "peer counselors." He related only one incident in which he was physically assaulted. In the process of defending himself, he pushed the aggressor out of his cell, and he was put in segregation (solitary confinement) as a result. He denied being sexually assaulted or threatened in prison. He reportedly got in trouble for getting tattoos. At the time of the follow-up evaluation, Daniel noted that it had been three years since he had spent time in segregation, and his security rating had been adjusted to indicate that he was less of a risk.

Daniel said that, with the exception of his first few days, he had not really felt fear in prison. He explained that "doing a life sentence here carries a little more respect" than a five-year sentence. "Like, cause, I'm doing a life sentence. So the guy looking at me is gonna say, well, geez, if I come after him, right, well then, you know, he has nothing to lose. Well, he's got no parole to lose or anything like that. So if I come after him with a shank or something, and he gets it off me, then, I know, I'm dead."

Daniel maintained that he got along pretty well with the other inmates. He tried to "judge everybody on their own merits." He related that over the years he had learned how to interact better with other guys, an area in which he felt inept and inferior. He found that most of the guards were "actually quite easy-going," and he had not had problems with any of them.

At the time of the follow-up, Daniel said that he worked out several days a week by lifting weights and playing hockey. He had held several jobs during his confinement; these included working in the laundry, being a helper in the canteen, cleaning the common area while in segregation, and cleaning tables. Daniel did not participate in any vocational programs because he was not interested in those available, such as welding or woodworking. He had not participated in educational programs because he would have to pay for correspondence courses and he had no money. He had no interest in attending religious services. He remained an avid reader and used the prison library. At the time of our meeting, Daniel reportedly was reading *The Iliad* and was hoping to read *The Odyssey.*

Daniel declined several opportunities for counseling because he did not trust the mental health staff. However, Daniel did participate in testing and several therapy sessions after prison staff agreed not to ask any questions related to his family. Participation would help him qualify for visits from his friend Ralph. He recently had considered participating in counseling because he had been told that he might then become eligible for higher paying jobs in the prison.

Daniel related that he would do his job, go through the day, and sometimes shut out the outside world for days. During these periods, he felt tired and lonely. He would tell himself that what has happened has happened and "there's nothing I can do about it. It really serves no purpose." Sometimes he would then work out. He said that he tried to make the best of what he had and to "be nice to people and get along with people."

Daniel implied that he had smoked marijuana or hashish on many occasions since being incarcerated. He had tried other drugs and alcohol made in prison but did not care for them. He indicated that the guards overlooked when the inmates smoked marijuana because it tended to mellow the inmates out. At the time of our meeting, Daniel no longer felt that he had a problem with alcohol or drugs. He had not participated in Alcoholics Anonymous in prison because he did not feel the need to do so.

When asked how he thought he had adjusted in prison, Daniel replied, "I think, unfortunately, quite well." He had accepted that prison life "sucks" and that he had to "adjust to this kind of life" because he could not change it. The pain he felt is clear from the following statement: "There's the worst guy here, and his mother is still coming to see him. Or, you know, something like that. And I think about what I did, and you know, it's not fun." He reported having flashbacks of the murder, but far fewer than in the past. He had become increasingly able to control the images of the homicides when they appeared in his mind.

Daniel's health had been good during his years in prison. The dental staff told Daniel that he had been grinding his teeth during his sleep and had "the wear on my teeth of a 40-year-old man." He indicated that he was no longer on antidepressant medication. He stated, however, that there were days when he was not sure whether he experienced depression or self-pity, or whether there was "much of a difference between the two." When asked, Daniel said the hardest thing about being in prison was "just the limitations … like on everything, I guess really, the portions on the meal line … just having to be here." He expressed doubts about whether he was "mature enough to survive socially and physically" in prison.

Daniel suggested that over the years he had lost track of events "outside the walls" and had become institutionalized. Only two of his friends from the past had kept in contact with him. Nora, a former girlfriend, started writing to him several years ago. His close friend Ralph had spoken to him regularly on the phone and visited him once or twice yearly. Daniel said that Ralph had provided "a lot of support" for him over the 14 years they had known each other. Daniel had been able to get approved "trailer visits" with Ralph, whereby he and Ralph had been authorized to spend a couple of days together alone visiting on the prison property, cooking their own food and watching TV. Contact with these friends has given Daniel hope. In his words, "They still care about you and believe that one day you'll be alright again."

CASE COMMENTARY

Daniel's attorney asked me whether Daniel possibly had experienced a catathymic crisis and, if so, whether this disorder could be used to bolster a defense arguing that Daniel lacked full or partial responsibility for killing his mother and father. I replied that Daniel's thoughts about killing his parents did not meet the diagnostic criteria. Features of this pathological condition include the emergence of a violent idea, initially considered abhorrent, after a precipitating traumatic event. Thoughts of putting the violent plan into action become so extreme that the person finds it increasingly difficult to refrain from committing the act. Over time, the person's thinking becomes delusional, rigid, and illogical. Eventually the individual commits the violent act and then experiences relief from the tension that has consumed him or her.[7] In Daniel's case, the idea of committing the violent act brought him pleasure rather than distress. He denied that his thoughts of killing his parents led him to construct a plan to free himself from an uncontrolled violent obsession.

At the time of my original evaluation, Daniel appeared to fit the profile of the *dangerously antisocial parricide offender*. Although he maintained that he did not intend his parents' deaths when he opened fire, he did acknowledge repeatedly thinking about killing them. His statements indicated that parricidal thoughts brought him pleasure and a sense of empowerment. When Daniel fantasized that about killing his parents, he saw himself as exerting power and winning the battle against them. In addition, he said that he enjoyed talking about killing people in general and gauging their reactions.

In my follow-up evaluation six years later, I noted that Daniel had advanced slightly in personality development from level 3 to a low level 4. Oddly enough, killing his parents appeared to have pushed him developmentally forward. As is characteristic of those who perceive at level 4, Daniel seemed to more fully comprehend the hurt his behavior caused than he had when I first met him. He was now at a point in his development at which he was able to take responsibility for the murders and understand the dynamics behind the crime.

Daniel realized that the rage that led to the murders was strongly related to his pervasive feelings of self-hatred and shame. Deep down inside, Daniel felt like a complete failure prior to the shootings because he did not measure up in his parents' eyes or in his own. Unlike his sister, he had a lifetime of poor choices with tragic results. Sadly, six years after I first met with him, Daniel still had a poor self-concept and was still struggling to find himself. His self-esteem remained low.

Daniel's statement that he had adjusted to prison "unfortunately quite well" seemed both accurate and insightful. He appeared content when I met with him. He accepted the structure of confinement and had made a life for himself in prison with the comforts he had in his cell.

Daniel did not seem interested in "making something" of himself. Although his concerns about opening up to mental health staff in prison might be justified, it is unlikely that Daniel will resolve his conflicts without professional help. Daniel's growth in terms of personality development over the years suggests that he has the potential to understand and resolve the interpersonal conflicts that led him to make bad decisions, abuse drugs, engage in antisocial behavior, and behave violently. With intensive treatment by skilled clinicians, it is possible that Daniel could develop a healthier self-image and learn to deal effectively with conflict.

If Daniel does not resolve his past issues and develop further in terms of coping strategies, communication ability, and vocational skills, the prognosis for a successful adaptation to the community is not good. If Daniel is released while still feeling inept and inferior, will he again resort to destructive fantasies as a way to empower himself and gain mastery over events? Could these fantasies then set the foundation for another violent explosion? Acts of malignant aggression are often committed by individuals who feel condemned to ineffectiveness.[8]

13 Ben Simpson
An Over-Induldged Child

At about 1:50 on a Thursday morning, Ben Simpson, age 18, called 911 to request that an ambulance be dispatched to his parents' home. He advised that his parents had been shot. When asked by the dispatcher, Ben said that he did not know who shot them and then said he had to hang up because he had "other things to do right now." Moments later, another call came into the call center from Mrs. Simpson, advising that she and her husband had both been shot by their son, Ben, who had fled the scene in his father's truck.

Police units arrived at the Simpson home within a few minutes of receiving the 911 calls. Both victims were conscious and identified their son as the shooter.[1] Mr. and Mrs. Simpson, both seriously injured, were transported to a local hospital.

While police were investigating the shooting at the Simpson home, an officer on patrol spotted the truck and called for back-up. As the officers pursued the suspect's truck, it picked up speed. Shortly thereafter, the driver lost control of the vehicle and crashed. Deputies with guns drawn converged on the truck. Ben exited the truck as instructed and was arrested. A .12 gauge shotgun was found in the front seat of the vehicle, along with a bag containing numerous rounds of ammunition. One of the arresting officers noted in his report that Ben spoke in a slurred fashion and appeared intoxicated. This officer also noticed that when they arrived at headquarters, Ben staggered and at one point slipped on the stairs.

Shortly after his arrest, Ben gave a statement to police. He said he had an argument with his parents over a vehicle that had been "trashed" in the mud flats a couple of days before. He left his parents house at about noon on Wednesday and returned right before the shooting. His parents were asleep in the master bedroom when Ben arrived. Ben told police that he went to his bedroom, retrieved his shotgun from his closet, loaded it, and returned to his parents' bedroom with the intent of killing them. He fired two or three shots, striking both parents. He then called 911 and left in the truck.

When asked why he took the shotgun and ammunition, Ben said that he was going to look for the people who had trashed his vehicle and shoot them. Ben denied that he was under the influence of alcohol or drugs when detectives questioned him.

Mr. Simpson died of multiple gunshot wounds within a few days. Mrs. Simpson survived; her recovery took a few months. Ben was subsequently charged with capital murder in connection with the death of his father and with attempted first-degree murder with respect to his mother. He mentally decompensated in jail and was put on suicide watch for several weeks. I was retained by defense counsel to evaluate the defendant with respect to his mental status at the time of the shooting and to address factors in mitigation.

THE CLINICAL EVALUATION

My assessment of Ben Simpson is based on a five-hour evaluation conducted in jail two years after his arrest. Prior to meeting with Ben, I reviewed police reports, the 911 call, the autopsy report, the audiotaped and transcribed confession made by Ben, and jail mental health records. I also read individual statements and depositions made by five of Ben's friends who were at a party with him before the shooting. I conducted a two-hour interview with Ben's mother. I spoke briefly with her current husband, Mr. Kennedy, who married Ben's mother after Ben's father died. I also interviewed Ben's maternal grandparents and several others who knew Ben well. These included two friends of Ben's maternal grandmother who had known Ben and the family for many years, a friend of Ben's father who worked with Ben on archery and traveled with them to archery tournaments, Ben's third-grade teacher, and Ben's best friend since childhood, Jim. These interviews ranged in length from a half-hour to an hour.

BEHAVIORAL OBSERVATIONS

At the time of the clinical assessment, Ben, a White male, was 20 years 6 months old. He was 6'2" tall and weighed about 230 pounds. Ben reported that he was not on psychotropic medication.

Ben was alert and cooperative during the evaluation. His eye contact was generally good. He presented as personable, polite, gentle, and placid. His demeanor was more that of a "big boy" than of a young man of college age.

Ben listened intently to hundreds of questions and did not refuse to answer anything asked of him. He appeared to be of low to average intelligence.[2] His answers were often restricted because of his level of personality development, rather than his withholding of information. His responses to questions and his behavior during the interview suggested that he was trying to be truthful. He did not come across as manipulative.

The youth's answers clearly indicated that he was oriented in time and space and that his short-term and, for the most part, long-term memories were intact. He had little memory of events surrounding the homicidal incident. There were no data to suggest that he was responding to private sensory experiences (hallucinations) or that he had delusional beliefs or a delusional network in place. Ben did not appear to be depressed. Although his affect was fairly restricted, he smiled and laughed at several points during the assessment.

Ben's personality development was low. In Interpersonal Level of Maturity Theory, the youth would be classified as perceiving at level 3. As is characteristic of individuals at this level, Ben thought rather concretely and tended to see the world in black and white dimensions. His perceptions of others were deficient and stereotypic. For example, he saw all Black people and guards as the same. He described himself, his friends, his girlfriend, and one of his employers as "alright" without elaboration or distinction.

Ben was not introspective. When asked what he liked best about himself, for example, Ben said he had "no idea." He smiled broadly and added, "I just like me, I guess." When asked whether there was anything about himself that he would like to change, Ben said that he was "a little bit lazy." He would "like to be more motivated and more strong." He did not know why he was lazy, that was "just the way I am." When asked how he was similar to his mother, Ben stated that he did not know. He volunteered, "I don't look at myself like that. I don't examine myself."

Ben had not internalized a value system by which he judged himself. He had not reached a stage of development at which he saw himself as accountable for his behavior and felt badly when he did something that was wrong. Rather, he operated on the basis of formulas that provided the structure he wanted and needed in order to get by in life. His ability to plan prior to the arrest seemed to be limited typically to short-term events, and his behavioral responses appeared impulsive and non-evaluative. For example, Ben said that he had "a bad habit of taking vehicles out to the woods and wrecking them." He stated that about four cars "died out there." He recalled with pleasure how he would "sink 'em; not on purpose—except for one." It was "fun, a blast." Ben explained that the last car, his mother's Lincoln, got stuck in the mud. It was his friend's idea "to do an insurance job and make it look like it was stolen," so he went along with it.

Ben perceived that he was in trouble with respect to the shooting because of his ingestion of drugs. He had difficulty experiencing genuine remorse for his criminal behavior because he did not fully understand what he had done to his family. He had not reached a stage of development at which he could truly empathize with others. Ben was relatively incapable of thinking in terms of needs, feelings, and motives. Although he could provide some indication of how he and others were feeling when asked, his awareness of feeling states and his ability to discuss them in depth were limited. Ben was able to say that it had been hard for his mother to lose a husband and have her son in jail. When asked how come his mother was supportive of him, Ben replied, "I don't know why. She's Mom, I guess. She knows it was me … but not me."

Ben's behavioral response style was characteristic of the *level 3 passive conformist*.[3] The youth saw himself as a person who got along with others, including both adults and peers. He had a tendency to go along with others as a way to fit in and get approval. For example, he said that when he was housed in the mental health wing, he smeared "poop" because the other inmates did it and he wanted "to be like everybody."

Ben indicated that he tried to avoid getting into trouble. Family and adults who knew him well did not see him as a behavioral or discipline problem, or as an angry or explosive individual. Ben engaged in activities without thinking of the consequences. For example, he took his cars out to the woods and "went mudding" without thinking that his actions would likely destroy these cars. Ben did not see himself as a criminal, even though he had engaged in other delinquent acts and had been charged with murder. He genuinely appeared to see his involvement in the homicide as the result of external forces—particularly drugs—and not as acceptable behavior. He came across as relatively open to listening to authority figures.

RELEVANT SOCIAL HISTORY

This section summarizes material reported by Ben. Information he gave about his family, school, friends, and activities was corroborated by his mother. His drug and alcohol usage was corroborated by his best friend.

Family Constellation

Ben was the only child born to his parents. He described his mother as "alright, a Christian, on the religious end of the family." He indicated that "she is always there; she's Mom." When asked how he was different from his mother, Ben replied, "I like hunting and fishing and outdoor stuff. She likes the mall."

Ben characterized his father as "cool." They enjoyed doing the same things, such as hunting and archery. Ben saw himself as a lot like his father and "more like him than anybody else." He talked with his father more and had more of a relationship with his father than his mother. Ben said his father was helpful to him.

Ben said that his mother did not drink or use drugs of any type. He indicated that his father drank when Ben was younger and then pretty much quit, drinking a few beers a year. Ben's father did not use drugs. Ben maintained that there were "a lot of drunks in the family" on both sides and identified them by name.

Ben had not heard from his father's relatives since his arrest and indicated that he had had little contact with them growing up. His contact with his mother's brothers was limited to a few times per year.

Ben related that when he was younger, he was spanked with a rod by both parents. Corporal punishment stopped as he got older. He smiled as he tried to recall how his parents disciplined him when he got older. He said, "Something had to happen. I just don't remember what" they did when it came to discipline.

School History

Ben related dropping out of school in the seventh grade, when he was about 12 or 13 years of age, because he did not like school. He had attended a private Christian school up until the sixth grade and then was enrolled in public school after his parents went bankrupt. Ben indicated that his grades deteriorated in public school, and he repeated the sixth grade. Ben disliked public school because he did not like the teachers or the kids. He maintained that he could do the work but did not do anything. He was not enrolled in special education classes but claimed to have been in some advanced classes.

Ben was never suspended or expelled from any school. Although he "mouthed off once in a while," he was not a behavioral problem and did not get detentions very often. After he dropped out, Ben was home schooled by his mother for a year or two.

Ben attended vocational technical school when he was 17 and 18 years old. He wanted to learn auto mechanics. He liked the course and had attended for about three-quarters of the year when he was arrested. Ben related being unable to do "the book work and the reading"; he learned by doing and seeing. He recalled that when he was in regular school, he had trouble focusing. He did not remember being hyperactive.

Work History

Ben worked at a number of jobs. Most of these jobs (for example, apartment maintenance, pizza delivery, McDonald's, appliance delivery) lasted from a week to a month or two. Two of them, however, were held for significant periods of time. Ben helped his father with electrical work "off and on for a couple of years." He also worked for "a couple of years" learning gunsmithing (changing and making parts for guns).

Friends

Ben indicated that Jim was his "only real friend." Ben had known Jim for about 10 or 12 years; they lived in the same neighborhood. Ben liked guys who enjoyed doing the same things as he did; he did not like kids who got into trouble.

Sexual History

Ben had only one real girlfriend, Lila. He dated her for about two or three months. She was "halfway decent." They broke up about 10 months prior to the homicide. Ben indicated, when asked, that sex was not a big thing for him prior to his arrest. He had had sex with only Lila. He liked girls who were "rednecks"[4] and enjoyed doing the things he liked to do.

Activities

Ben liked to go out to the woods, build a bonfire, and relax. He described himself as "an addict" when it came to the woods, to "being out there." He would go into the woods "almost every day" by himself or with others. Ben felt peaceful, whether he was high or not, when he was in the woods. He liked to go swimming and "go mudding." He used to enjoy going fishing and hunting but had not engaged in these activities in the year or two prior to his arrest.

Gang Involvement and Tattoos

Ben denied any involvement in gangs, Satanic cults, or skinhead groups. He indicated that he was bald-headed because he was lazy, had had head lice when he was in school, and found short hair easy to take care of and comfortable. Ben had no tattoos because he was "not into pain."

Music/TV/Movies

Ben liked country music. He liked the music more than the words. He was not a fan of "heavy metal" or "gangsta rap."

Ben had no favorite TV shows. He watched sitcoms and whatever was on. He liked adventure movies. He could not think of a movie he really liked or watched repeatedly.

Alcohol Involvement

Ben stated that he started drinking at age 16. He drank weekly and sometimes daily, sometimes alone and sometimes with other adolescents. He typically drank beer, but he also drank hard liquor (Jack Daniels) about once a week. During the six months prior to his arrest, Ben drank daily with Jim and some other kids. He would drink "a 12-pack" after work, "sometimes more, sometimes less," and would get "a nice buzz." When he was buzzed, he would be "laid back, sit around, and hang loose." He would be mellow and not get into fights. Sometimes he got "trashed" and would be "stumbling."

Ben did not see himself as having a problem with alcohol, and no one suggested to him that he might have a problem as far as he could remember. His mother reportedly knew that Ben drank, but not the degree of his alcohol consumption.

Drug Involvement

Ben indicated that he had used marijuana, cocaine, acid, and mushrooms on a number of occasions, as discussed below. He tried huffing some carbon dioxide cartridges a few times, but he stopped because he was afraid it would kill him. Ben related having tried pills a few days before the shooting and said, "This is where it landed me."

Ben said he smoked weed daily from the time that he was 16 or 17 years old. He smoked between a quarter- and a half-ounce per day, frequently in "blunts." He felt "laid back, tired, mellow" when he was high on marijuana.

Ben used LSD on about 20 to 25 occasions over a period of one to one and a half years. He would sometimes take four or five hits at a time. The most that he ever took at one time was 10 hits. When on acid, Ben felt "alright." He was happy; he would laugh and "see stuff." He never had a bad trip and still experienced flashbacks on occasion.

Ben also reported using mushrooms on a few occasions. He liked mushrooms better than acid. He recalled on one occasion being "messed up severely—laughing, happy, trashed, couldn't drive home."

Ben used powder cocaine about 10 or 12 times when dating Lila. The first time he smoked it with marijuana; after that he snorted it. Ben related that coke was "alright," but he "liked weed better." Ben stated that he had not used cocaine for probably a couple of months before the homicide.

Ben said that he bought 20 Xanax bars before he was arrested. Although he had intended to sell them, he used them himself. He remembered that when he was at a friend's apartment, he took two of these pills soon after he got them and then drank a liqueur known as Avalanche. Ben reported taking more Xanax, but he did not remember how many or over what period of time. He learned from reading depositions that his usage of Xanax occurred over two or three days.

Ben acknowledged using two or more mind-altering substances at one time. He used marijuana and cocaine; alcohol and marijuana; and acid, marijuana, and alcohol.

Ben smoked about two to two and a half packs of cigarettes daily prior to getting arrested. He started smoking at age 16 "on a dare" and continued.

Physical Health History

Ben described his health as "pretty good" prior to his incarceration. He reported never having been hospitalized overnight and had no memory of losing consciousness. He recalled having stitches when younger for cuts on his foot, leg, and toe. While in jail, Ben had a number of ailments, including being infected with lice.

Mental Health History

Ben said that he had never had counseling or been on psychotropic medication prior to his arrest. He had no history of psychiatric hospitalizations.

Ben indicated that he was feeling "alright" at the time of the clinical evaluation. He related that he had seen a jail psychologist more than 20 times but did not remember the content of their discussions during his sessions. Ben reported that he still had fleeting thoughts of killing himself but did not know why. He indicated that psychotropic medication was prescribed for him in jail for depression for about a week. [Mental health records verified that it was discontinued after about a week.] The defendant was stockpiling pills, reportedly to kill himself. Ben said he was put "butt naked" in a cold cell while he was under suicide watch. Consequently, he stopped telling jail personnel about his suicidal thoughts.

Religious Affiliation

Ben indicated that he was Christian. He did not attend church on a regular basis while growing up. He had been reading the Bible since being incarcerated and had found it a source of comfort and peace.

Feelings/Coping Strategies/Responses to Situations

Ben thought that his family had about the same amount of problems as other families. He felt that he coped "alright" with things at home when he was growing up. He sometimes talked to friends about problems in his home, but not to relatives, teachers, clergy, or school counselors.

Ben did not report being angered by many things or erupting with anger when he was growing up. He said that he would get angry with himself when he felt he had lost control of his emotions. He got depressed when things did not go well. He reported turning "very often" to alcohol, drugs, food, and taking cars into the woods as ways to feel better.

Ben said that there were large parts of his childhood after age 5 that he could not remember and attributed this to having a bad memory. He reportedly never had blank spells or periods of missing time that he could not remember (unrelated to alcohol or drugs). He recalled thinking about running away once, doing so, and being gone for about a week because of a conflict with a friend. He often thought about killing himself but never attempted to do so.

Prior Juvenile Delinquent and Criminal History

Ben had no prior arrests as a juvenile or an adult. He recalled that he had racked up "a lot" of speeding tickets because he liked to go fast. He also received one ticket for reckless driving in connection with drag racing. Ben experienced racing and going 100 mph as fun. He volunteered, "I don't think of the consequences until it happens and then it's shit."

Ben stole alcohol on a few occasions. He shoplifted the alcohol and on at least one occasion simply walked out of the store carrying it. He never used or threatened violence in order to obtain alcohol.

Adjustment in Jail

Ben had been incarcerated for two years when I evaluated him. For much of his stay, he was housed in the mental health wing. Ben was housed in general population in an open bay area at the time of my evaluation. He indicated that he had been threatened physically and sexually and had about $40 to $50 in belongings taken from him. He did not perceive his size as an advantage. He had been involved in three or four fights. He received only one disciplinary report (DR) for fighting; his involvement in the other fights was reportedly viewed as necessary to defend himself.

Ben did not have any friends in jail. He did not like the guards because he had had a number of negative experiences with them (for example, they didn't feed him, or they threatened him) and felt they had betrayed him. He characterized his jail experience as congruent with an expression he had heard, "being among the living dead."

Mrs. Kennedy had been visiting Ben four times weekly after she recovered from the wounds he had inflicted. Ben had asked his mother to stop visiting him a few months prior to my evaluation because it was "getting too much for me" and "killing me mentally" that he could not leave jail. At the time of the evaluation, Ben was calling his mother weekly to biweekly.

Future Orientation

Ben said that if this matter were favorably resolved, he would not go home because his mother and grandmother had been through a lot. He had some business ideas, but nothing definite or solid. He would like to get married and have kids because "it would be nice to have someone you can count on." He stated that he would not get in trouble again because he did not want to go back to jail. He did not see himself as dangerous because the jail psychologist had told him that 80% of murderers did not kill again.

SYNOPSIS OF CONSULTATIONS WITH FAMILY AND FRIENDS

I designed the clinical interviews with family members and friends to examine areas that surfaced in my clinical evaluation of Ben or in my review of materials provided by defense counsel. These areas included information pertinent to their reactions to Ben's arrest, his personality and overall behavior, descriptions of his mother and father, Ben's feelings toward his parents, school experiences, alcohol and drug involvement, behavior shortly before the homicide, and behavior after his arrest in jail. The eight people with whom I spoke each had had extensive contact with Ben and his parents. All individuals were pleasant and cooperative and seemed honest and direct.

Family's and Friends' Reactions to Ben's Arrest

All eight individuals were shocked at Ben's involvement in the shooting. None could imagine any rational reason to explain why Ben shot his parents. Those who had a theory regarding his involvement believed that he was compelled to violence by the drugs he consumed in the days and hours preceding the shooting.

Ben's Personality and Overall Behavior

Ben's mother described Ben as "a very gentle person" who had "a sweet spirit about him." She said that she had had "no real trouble with him" and that he was "a good kid" who was "pretty obedient." She depicted him as a "complacent child" who was "never rebellious" and rarely disrespectful to either of his parents. Ben did not raise his voice and never cursed at his parents.

Ben's mother recalled that Ben did not stay angry long. He was "not pouty, not broody." She remembered only one incident, about a year prior to the shooting, when Ben seemed very angry and insisted he had to leave. She had been in the process of helping him sell his car and asked him to wait, but he seemed unable to calm down, and he left. He was gone for a week.

Ben's maternal grandmother described Ben as a "perfectly normal child" who was "very loving." As an adolescent, he gave monosyllabic answers and was not a verbal child. Ben's grandmother had heard that Ben, like his father, had a temper. She recalled that he did not verbalize his feelings well and believed that he tried to suppress his anger. Ben's grandparents both commented that they had never observed Ben being disrespectful to his parents. Ben's grandmother said that her daughter had never indicated that Ben was acting out or behaving badly.

Ms. C, one of the grandmother's friends, recalled Ben as "always mannerable, very respectful, obedient, and compliant." Ben was "a big kid" who was somewhat "awkward." She had never known him to be violent. He would hug her when he met her and always went out of his way to speak to her. When her son died, Ben sent her a sympathy card with a personal note from jail, which had been a great source of comfort to her.

Ms. M, another of the grandmother's friends, described Ben as a quiet kid who would talk and answer questions. He was "a typical kid." He was very polite and never disrespectful. He was "not a sullen or arrogant kid." Ms. M recalled Ben as a "pretty easy going kid." She had never observed him having any violent outbursts. She said that Ben spent a great deal of time around his grandmother, whom she described as "a great role model."

Ben's third-grade teacher remembered him as a "happy-go-lucky kid." He was pleasant, respectful, compliant, even tempered, funny, and well liked. She did not recall him getting upset or "flying off the handle." Ben did not like school; he liked to play. He would do his schoolwork when she sat down with him. This teacher recalled worrying about what would happen to Ben when he got to the fourth and fifth grades, when children were expected to work independently.

Mr. D, a friend of Ben's father, characterized Ben as "a typical teenager, a good kid, who played around too much." Mr. D recalled that Ben "listened good" when his father "told him to stop" and was "never mean or nasty with his parents." Ben was "a good kid who wound up doing a stupid thing."

Ben's stepfather saw Ben as "mellow, not a tough kid." Ben did not come across to him as a confrontational individual.

Ben's friend, Jim, depicted Ben as "laid back, an outdoorsman, and shy." He was not a tough kid. Ben was "a good friend" who was there for him and never betrayed him. Ben had a temper; he made threats and "would run his mouth." Jim remembered only one time when Ben "went ballistic"; Ben wanted to take off, and Mrs. Simpson would not let him. Jim knew of only one fight in which Ben had been involved. Jim said that Ben had gotten speeding tickets because he liked to drive fast, have fun, and be "playing around and it got out of hand."

Ben was seen by those who knew him as having low to moderate self-esteem. Although he could sometimes take the lead, the general consensus was that Ben was a follower. In his mother's words, he was "easily swayed."

Ben's Mother and Father

Ben's parents were depicted as loving and devoted parents who were interested and involved in what Ben liked to do. Ben's father fished and hunted with Ben. When Ben showed ability in archery, his parents encouraged him to develop his skills. Both parents learned archery so that all three of them could participate in competitions. Ben's father was very proud of Ben's ability. Both parents were supportive of Ben. Ben's mother was viewed as a good mother and a very caring person who took the time to home-school Ben.

Ben's grandmother characterized her daughter as more of the disciplinarian in the family. Ben's mother indicated that she and Mr. Simpson had gone through several stages of discipline that included spanking Ben with a rod for about a month, discussions, and groundings. She reflected, "Thinking back, we were very inconsistent." Ben's mother said that Ben's father had a "strong personality, a presence"—he could look at Ben, and that would be all it took to set Ben straight. Ben and his father had "a very good relationship." Ben's mother explained that Ben's dad "would rarely discipline him"; instead, he would talk to Ben.

Ben's grandmother and mother both said that Ben's father saw the "mudding" as a phase that Ben was going through. Ben's father rationalized Ben's behavior in the context that Ben was not using drugs or robbing people like other kids his age. Ben's parents figured that Ben was acting somewhat responsibly by going into the woods, drinking there, and not driving.

After Ben "trashed" a couple of cars in the woods, Ben's parents specifically told him not to take the Lincoln into the woods. Later, when they learned from police that this car had been destroyed, Ben denied involvement. Ben's mother said she did not believe Ben; his father, however, did believe him. Ben's mother related that she was "mad" about the "trashed" Lincoln; Ben's father was more "disgusted." His father's stance was, however, that if this were the worst thing their son did—wrecked a few cars—then it wasn't so bad. Mr. Simpson decided to let Ben feel the natural consequences that followed from Ben's behavior, such as being without a car to drive to work. Ben's mother reflected that this event was the "first time we let him [Ben] feel the full consequences" of his behavior.

Mrs. Simpson explained that Ben grew up with a father who tried to work things out with his son. As long as Ben told his parents the truth, the message was that things would be O.K. Mr. Simpson "could always fix things. He could always make it right."

Ben's friend Jim described Ben's mother as "a cool, nice lady" and Ben's father as "a nice guy." They were "average parents—interested and involved." Jim felt that they were both strict and over-concerned, that "any little thing they would punish him for."

Ben's Feelings toward His Parents

Ben's grandmother indicated that Ben loved his parents. Ben's mother related that Ben and his father had a very close relationship. Mr. D recalled that Ben got along very well with both parents and that their home life appeared "all good." Jim said that Ben loved his parents.

Ben's School Experiences

Ben's mother said that Ben did not like school. In public school, Ben knew the material and did the homework, but he did not turn it in. He repeated the sixth grade in public school. He worked with his mother when she home-schooled him.

Ben's mother and his third-grade teacher agreed that Ben met the criteria for attention deficit disorder after I reviewed the *DSM-IV* criteria with them. Both recalled that Ben could do the work but did not seem to stay focused on completing assignments on his own. Ben's teacher recalled that Ben had difficulty writing and agreed, after looking at his test results from years ago, that testing for a learning disability would have been appropriate.

Ben's grandmother, mother, and teacher agreed that Ben was never a troublemaker. He would sit and do nothing. He was kind of timid, "a big kid" who was not a bully or a fighter.

Ben's Alcohol and Drug Involvement

Ben's mother and Mr. D did not see any evidence that Ben was heavily into drugs. Ben had told his parents he had tried marijuana but did not like it. They believed he did not use drugs. His parents were aware that he drank alcohol to some extent.

Ben spent a lot of time with Mr. D up until six months preceding the shooting. Mr. D was sure that he would have been aware of it if Ben had been drinking or using drugs when they were together. Mr. D's 18-year-old son, Sam, told his father Ben was not using drugs when they were hanging out together during the archery competitions.

Jim said that Ben was using drugs more heavily a few months before the shooting and had been using drugs around the time of the homicide. Ben smoked marijuana a few times per week or more. Ben used Xanax pills during the two weeks preceding the shooting. He had used these pills more heavily a couple of days before the shooting. Jim recalled Ben taking eight or ten pills at a time. Jim knew that these drugs affected memory because he had used them as well. Jim stated that Ben drank alcohol a couple of times weekly, more to be social than to get drunk.

Ben's Behavior Shortly before the Homicide

Mrs. Simpson related two incidents when Ben behaved oddly within less than 24 hours of the shooting. Both occurred on Wednesday, two days after the "trashing" of the Lincoln. [Police notified Ben's parents regarding the car on Monday at about 4:00 or 5:00 A.M.] Mrs. Simpson remembered Jim coming to pick up Ben early in the afternoon. Ben came out with a gun, saying that he and Jim were going to find out who "trashed" the Lincoln. Ben's mother told Ben that the police would find out who the people were and that he should put the gun away. Ben put the gun back as instructed.

On the Wednesday night before the Thursday early morning shooting, Ben's mother observed Ben urinating on the driveway. She yelled at Ben and told her husband what she had observed. Ben's father said he would handle it. She related that, as a direct result of the "trashing" of the car, Ben had lost his job because he had no car to use. Mr. Simpson assured Ben that things would work out. His last words to Ben, said a few hours before the shooting, were "I love you, Bud."

Jim said that Ben had a short temper and that Ben felt he had a lot of problems prior to the shooting. He characterized Ben's perceived problems as "family-related" and as involving the loss of use of a car and his difficulty in getting another job. Jim said that Ben's father had reportedly told Ben's employer a few days before that Ben would have to resign because he no longer had transportation to work.

Jim recalled that Ben looked angry on the night (a few hours) preceding the shooting. Jim thought it was probably the angriest that he had ever seen Ben. Ben was angry about being accused of "trashing" the car. Ben adamantly denied being involved in the "trashing" of the Lincoln. Jim mistakenly believed Ben because, he said, Ben did not normally lie.

Jim related that he and Ben had gone to a party a few hours before the shooting. Jim recalled that Ben said he had taken two Xanax before the party. Then Ben left to buy more. After he returned, Ben had two beers, became loud, and was "way too messed up"—he was stumbling and losing his balance. Ben knocked over the coffee table and dropped beer. His perception was off. When he was asked to leave, Ben got confrontational. He argued outside with two or three people who had arrived later. He was mad, yelling on the way home and "cussing a lot about the kids he had an argument with and his parents." Jim said Ben's being loud, being confrontational, and "cussing" were out of character for him. Jim recalled that Ben got out of Jim's truck, walked in front of it, fell down, got up, and then went inside the house. It was after midnight.

Jim recalled that Ben had said that night that he was going to kill his parents. Jim did not believe him; he thought Ben was "just running his mouth." Jim recalled that Ben had said "hundreds of times" that he wanted to kill his parents because of conflicts over "stupid stuff—staying out too late, getting in trouble at school."

Ben's Behavior in Jail after His Arrest

Jim saw Ben in jail on the Saturday after the shooting. Ben cried as he told Jim, "They say I shot my parents." The only thing Ben remembered with respect to the incident was "when he wrecked the truck [after the shooting], lying under it; the police arresting him."

Ben's grandmother described Ben as "downcast and morose" in jail. He did not talk much. He told her that if he had committed the crime, he deserved to die. She believed he could not take a plea because he could not admit to himself that he shot his parents.

Ben's mother said that Ben had been very upset in jail. He had sent her letters telling her how sorry he was. She was not sure whether he felt badly about what he did or about the mess he found himself in.

EVIDENCE OF CHILDHOOD MALTREATMENT AND FAMILY DYSFUNCTION

No evidence provided by Ben, his mother, his grandparents, or family friends suggested that Ben was sexually, verbally, or psychologically abused by either parent. Although both parents used a rod to spank Ben when necessary when he was a boy, neither Ben nor his mother characterized the spankings as excessive, disproportionate, or humiliating.

Data from several sources indicated that Ben's emotional and basic physical needs were met throughout his growing-up period. About nine years prior to the shooting, Ben's parents declared bankruptcy. The family had to move, and Ben was taken out of private school to go to public school. Although times were difficult for a couple of years, Ben's grandmother and mother insisted that Ben never went without.

As Ben advanced into his later adolescent years, it appeared that Ben's parents did not supervise him adequately and did not set appropriate limits for him, which is a form of physical neglect. Information provided by Ben and his mother indicated that Ben was not subjected to consistent discipline. The lack of limits was particularly evident with respect to the way Mr. and Mrs. Simpson dealt with Ben's destruction of two or three cars. The parents' failure to address Ben's disinterest and difficulties in school and his apparent disregard for property was puzzling. Some question of medical neglect also could be raised with respect to the parents or the school for their not referring Ben for mental health assessment and treatment.

Family Members' History of Mental Illness and Chemical Dependency

Ben's paternal grandfather was reportedly hospitalized for some type of mental illness. Other than that, no other relatives reportedly suffered from mental illness. Alcoholism and heavy drinking appeared to be common on both sides of Ben's family.

Ben's father reportedly drank to excess early in his marriage to Ben's mother. Ben's maternal grandfather recalled two episodes when Mr. Simpson behaved in a violent manner: Mr. Simpson slugged one of his wife's relatives at a wedding reception, and he put his fist through the wall of his house. Mr. Simpson stopped drinking when Ben was about 3 years old.

Evidence of Family Dysfunction

Ben's grandparents and mother related that Ben's father stopped talking to his wife's father and two brothers when Ben was about 5 years old. The period of silence had been going on for about 15 years at the time of Mr. Simpson's death. These three seemed unaware of what had caused the rift between Mr. Simpson and Ben's mother's family, although it appeared to have been related to the maternal grandfather's firing Mr. Simpson. Ben's mother indicated that her husband felt betrayed by her family but said they never talked about it.

Ben's father refused to join in holiday celebrations with his wife's family. As a result, Ben's mother and Ben went to see Mrs. Simpson's relatives without Ben's father on Christmas. Mr. Simpson was reportedly also estranged from his own family for many years.

MOTIVATIONAL DYNAMICS BEHIND THE HOMICIDE

Ben maintained that he had no memory of shooting his parents. The account he gave to me was completely different from the full confession he gave to police within a few hours of the shooting. Ben's recollections of events surrounding the shooting and the "trashing" of the Lincoln, as well as his reflections and feelings regarding the shooting and death of his father, are recapped below; my conclusions follow.

Ben's Recollection of Events Surrounding the Shooting

Ben indicated that his last memory was being at a girl's apartment with three other kids. He stated that it was either Monday or Tuesday night, not a few hours before the homicide. He recalled that he had intended to get marijuana to sell but wound up getting Xanax instead. Ben recalled that two other kids came after the four of them were already there. Then he and one of these kids left to buy more Xanax.

Ben remembered buying 20 Xanax tablets and going back to the girl's apartment. He said that he took two or three Xanax and then drank Avalanche. He and three of these kids then went to a Mobile gas station.

Ben maintained that he had no memory from this point in time until his waking up in jail after he was arrested. When asked, Ben indicated that he had no memory of speaking to the police. He maintained that no memory of the events had returned to him during the two years since the shooting. When asked, Ben stated that he has read the depositions or statements given by five of his friends. He has also read some police reports. Ben listened to the recorded statement he gave to the police within hours of his arrest for the shooting of his parents. He said that the voice did not sound like him.

Ben stated that he apparently had an argument with his mother at about 8:00 P.M. the night before the early morning shooting. Ben had no memory of this argument. Jim, who was present, said that the argument was over the "trashed" Lincoln. Ben's mother, in contrast, maintained that the two had words because she had seen Ben "taking a leak in the driveway."

The Relevance of the "Trashed" Lincoln

Ben blamed the drugs for the shootings. He maintained that at the time of the shooting, he and his parents were no longer upset about the "trashed" car. He acknowledged that his parents were "pissed off" right after it happened because this car was the second one he had "trashed" in the mud. He maintained, however, that they had cooled off by the time of the incident.

Ben said his parents told him they were not going to replace his car and that from then on, he had to walk. Ben maintained that he did not remember his parents saying that they were going to prosecute anyone whose fingerprints were on it. He smiled broadly as he stated he was not worried about being prosecuted because naturally his fingerprints would be on his mother's car. When asked, he indicated that four kids were involved with him in the "trashing" of his mother's Lincoln and named them. He said that a statement to police from another kid backed his story.

When asked whether Ben had any feelings about "trashing" the car, he replied, "It got me half-way here." Ben said that he probably would not have gotten the Xanax if they had not "trashed" the car.

Ben's Reflections and Feelings about the Shooting

When asked whether he had any feelings about the homicide, Ben said it was "weird," adding that he had no memory of the shooting and that it was hard for him to believe. Ben denied having any memory of expressing parricidal thoughts in the hours immediately preceding the shooting. He laughed as he recalled saying that he had wanted to kill his parents perhaps as many as 20 times. He explained that "he was mad at them" and "talking shit." He maintained that he was essentially blowing off steam and that "everybody does it."

Ben was aware that his case did not look good. He maintained that what happened was "not my decision anymore," and he was resigned to whatever happened. He said "going home" would be the right outcome from his perspective. He believed a suspended sentence would be fair. If released, he would use his freedom to help kids. He predicted that there would be more parents killed in the next few years because of "drugs and no discipline."

When asked what he would say if he could talk openly to the jurors, Ben replied, "It is something that happened. You can't do anything about it. It could happen to anyone." Ben recognized that he had hurt a lot of people. He believed drugs were 100% responsible for the shooting.

When asked how he felt about the killing of his father and the wounding of his mother, Ben said he was "pretty much at peace with it. Can't do anything about it. Some days are better than others." He stated that he had felt this way for perhaps as long as a year and had received help from God and one or two inmates in dealing with it.

Ben said it took a long time for him to get over his father's death. He experienced the horror of seeing the photo of his father after he was shot. He replayed that image in his mind. He had trouble remembering what his father used to look like.

Prior Parricidal Ideation

Ben denied ever thinking seriously about killing his parents prior to the shooting. When asked, he said he had never dreamed or fantasized about killing either of them. While growing up, he was never afraid that he would kill his parents. Ben indicated that there were four, five, or six firearms in the home because Ben and his father hunted. Ben said of the firearms, "More of them were mine than his."

Dr. Heide's Conclusions Regarding the Homicidal Incident

Ben's lack of memory of events appeared to be the result of a blackout due to the ingestion of drugs in the hours preceding the shooting rather than malingering (feigning memory loss in order to avoid responsibility). Evidence supporting this conclusion came from statements Ben made to his best friend and to jail personnel soon after being incarcerated. It was unlikely that Ben would have been able to fabricate this story on his own soon after being placed in jail. It was also unlikely that he would have had the emotional strength to stick to this version had it not been true. At the time of my evaluation, he was a low-maturity adolescent, likely to be overwhelmed by being incarcerated, which jail records confirmed. In addition, he was criminally unsophisticated and unlikely to be knowledgeable of psychiatric disorders.

Ben was crying as he told Jim, within a few days of his arrest, that he had no memory of shooting his parents. Jail mental health records verified that Ben reported having no memory of the shooting when initially incarcerated. The psychiatric screening a couple of days after the shooting indicated that Ben's remote memory was "impaired" and that Ben "states [he] doesn't remember the last few days." An entry a few days later read that Ben took 9 or 10 Xanax tablets two days prior to his arrest and approximately 5 the night of his arrest. "Xanax caused him to black out and not remember events."

There was substantial evidence from five of Ben's friends to suggest that he was intoxicated when he shot his parents. Jim's account to me and statements made about Ben's behavior by his friends in their depositions were consistent with Ben being intoxicated shortly before the shooting. Two of Ben's friends stated in their depositions that Ben had taken three Xanax bars and had drunk beer in their presence a few hours before the shooting. Another friend told police that he had seen Ben take Xanax pills and drink beer, and that Ben was stumbling and appeared to be under the influence when he left the party. The deputy who arrested Ben, apparently within less than a half-hour after the shooting, noted in his report, "This subject appeared to have been intoxicated by the way he spoke in a slurred fashion."

Additional evidence of intoxication came from my listening to Ben's statements to the police. *A very different impression was obtained by listening to the taped confession than by simply reading it.* When I read the confession, Ben sounded cold, callous, and angry. In contrast, when I listened to the confession, Ben came across as drugged and/ or mentally dull.

Ben's statements to the police from 5:33 to 5:40 A.M. (about three hours after the shooting) suggested that in addition to being intoxicated, he was enraged with his parents when he shot them. When asked why he went into his parents' bedroom with the shotgun, Ben replied, "Because I was pissed and planned on killing both of them." Although Ben's words to the police suggest that he might have formulated the intent to kill his parents, his account of events three and a half hours after the shooting is a little suspect. Did Ben actually formulate the intent to kill two parents he loved at 1:50 A.M.? Or was this an attempt of a low-maturity youth to come up with an explanation for behavior that made little or no rational sense? Behaving impulsively was characteristic of Ben and consistent with his personality development; behaving violently, in contrast, was not characteristic of Ben's personality or behavioral history.

DIAGNOSTIC IMPRESSIONS

At the time of the assessment, Ben did not appear clinically depressed. Jail records indicated that he had had symptoms of major depression while incarcerated, which appeared to be situationally induced. These symptoms were in partial remission when I evaluated Ben.

Ben had a history of substance abuse, particularly with respect to alcohol and marijuana. He had taken a drug that he believed to have been Xanax in excessive quantities within the few days and hours prior to the homicide.

There was no evidence of psychosis at the time of the clinical evaluation or upon Ben's admission to the jail. Ben's aberrant behavior after the "trashing" of the Lincoln and extending to the killing of his parents, however, seemed consistent with an irrational and delusional thought process. His behavior raised the possibility that he might have had a brief psychotic episode occasioned by feeling—for the first time—the full effect of the consequences of his behavior. Alternatively, it also raised the possibility that Ben might have been experiencing a manic episode that had begun prior to the destruction of the car. Ben's denial of his own involvement in the trashing of the Lincoln was extreme. He was so convincing in his denial that his father and friend Jim believed him. In addition, statements made by Ben's mother indicated that Ben apparently became delusional to the point that he armed himself with a firearm and was going out to find those who destroyed his mother's car prior to shooting his parents. After the killing, Ben told police he had the bag of shells and the shotgun "because I was going to look for someone, whoever trashed my car."

Review of *DSM-IV* criteria with Ben's mother and third-grade teacher indicated that Ben met the diagnostic criteria for attention deficit disorder. Ben's statements, a review of school records, a consultation with his third-grade teacher, and neuropsychological testing indicated that Ben was learning disabled.[5] A subsequent evaluation by a neurologist suggested that Ben had minimal brain dysfunction.

CASE DISPOSITION

I advised defense counsel that there was persuasive evidence that Ben was angry and intoxicated when he shot his parents. In light of his personality development and behavioral history, I questioned whether he had the capacity to formulate the intent to kill his parents at the time of the shooting. In my clinical opinion, this question remained open notwithstanding Ben's statements to the police three and a half hours after the shooting that he had intended to kill his parents. I identified 12 factors in mitigation in Ben's case (see Table 13-1).

Ben decided to take a plea offer rather than risk being convicted of first-degree murder and possibly sentenced to death. He pled guilty to second-degree murder in connection with the death of his father and second-degree attempted murder with respect to the shooting of his mother. He was sentenced to 45 and 30 years in prison for the two crimes, respectively. The sentences were ordered to run concurrently.

FOLLOW-UP INTERVIEW WITH BEN

I met with Ben five years after my initial evaluation. He was 26 years old. At 6'3" tall and 210 pounds, he had the build of a mature man. Despite his size and age, Ben struck me as about 15 years old. He was pleasant and engaging. I saw no evidence of growth in his personality development since I had last seen him. Ben's perceptions and his behavior were characteristic of a young teenager rather than a man in his mid-20s. He was not on psychotropic medication when I met with him.

Table 13-1 Factors in mitigation of a death sentence

Mitigators	Explanation
(1) The defendant had no significant prior criminal history.	Ben had no prior juvenile delinquent or adult criminal history and no history of violent acting-out.
(2) The capital felony was committed while the defendant was under the influence of extreme mental or emotional disturbance.	Jim indicated that Ben looked angry on the night (a few hours) preceding the shooting. Jim said it was probably the angriest that he had ever seen Ben. When Ben was asked to leave the party, Ben got confrontational. He argued outside with two or three people who had arrived later. He was mad, yelling on the way home and "cussing a lot about the kids he had an argument with and his parents." Ben's being loud, being confrontational, and cussing were out of character for him.
(3) The capacity of the defendant to appreciate the criminality of his conduct or to conform his conduct to the requirements of the law was substantially impaired.	Ben's statements to the police indicated that at the time of the offense, the youth knew what he was doing (M'Naghten test). It was clear from Ben's remarks made subsequently to me and to others, however, that he had no emotional appreciation at the time of the shooting of the consequences of his behavior. He had no emotional appreciation of the effect that killing his father and attempting to kill his mother would have on him and his family. In addition, given his intoxicated condition, enraged state, and personality development, it was unlikely that he could have conformed his behavior to the requirements of the law; he simply reacted to the torrent of feelings within him. It was unlikely that, under these circumstances, Ben could stop, think about his behavior and its likely consequences, and refrain from doing the act.
(4) The age of the defendant at the time of the crime.	Ben was 18 at the time of the shooting. Adolescents' maturity, ability to cope, and life experiences are typically less than those of adults.

Table 13-1 (Continued)

Mitigators	Explanation
(5) Ben was intoxicated at the time of the shooting.	Ben's emotional state, perception, judgment, behavior, and ability to think rationally, make conscious decisions, and control his behavior were further affected by his intoxicated state.
(6) Ben had attention deficit disorder and was learning disabled.	Ben had difficulties focusing and processing information. His ability to focus, discern relevant information, and make a rational decision in an emotionally charged and intoxicated state was more compromised than that of an individual without such neurological impairments.
(7) Ben did not have a criminal self-concept, did not characteristically behave violently, and was not part of a violent subculture.	Unlike many adolescents involved in homicidal behavior, Ben did not see himself as a criminal. He did not have a history of responding violently to interpersonal conflicts. He was not a member of a gang or group that endorsed violence.
(8) Ben was amenable to treatment and prosocial influence.	Ben's behavioral response style (*passive conformist subtype*) indicated that he was open to adults and authority figures and liked to please others. He was cooperative, complacent, and compliant and wanted to stay out of trouble.
(9) Ben was over-indulged and subjected to inconsistent discipline by his parents.	Ben's parents did not set definite boundaries and limits for Ben. His mother indicated that the first time Ben felt the full consequences of his behavior was after he destroyed two or three cars and his parents said that they would not get him another vehicle. As a result of the lack of limits, Ben did not learn frustration tolerance. As his mother explained, Ben's father always knew how to fix things. His parents also cleaned up Ben's messes. He did not have the internal resources to deal with disappointment and to handle stress.
(10) Ben's difficulties were long-standing, and no meaningful intervention occurred.	There were indicators that Ben needed counseling. He had difficulty focusing in school and did very poorly from the fourth to seventh grades, at which point he dropped out. He also acted irresponsibly. Destroying cars evinces a callous disregard for his parents' property.

(continued)

Table 13-1 (Continued)

Mitigators	Explanation
(11) There was evidence of chemical dependency on both sides of Ben's family and family dysfunction in his immediate family.	Ben's family was positive for alcohol addiction on both maternal and paternal sides. Ben's father abused alcohol when Ben was young and stopped communicating for 15 years with his wife's relatives. Chemically dependent families have difficulties communicating and functioning. Individuals in these families learn not to trust, not to talk, and not to feel. Ben would have been affected by these dysfunctional patterns.
(12) Ben had the support of his family.	Ben's mother, a victim of the shooting, supported her son. In addition, his maternal grandparents and several friends of Ben and of his family believed Ben's behavior on the night of the shooting was uncharacteristic of him and propelled by his ingestion of drugs.

Life in Prison

Ben said he had been in five institutions since beginning his prison sentence nearly five years earlier.[6] After a few months, Ben had started getting into trouble. He received many DRs for offenses such as refusal to work, disobeying orders, disrespect, contraband (cigarettes), and count violation.[7] He received a DR for arson; Ben explained that he had piled a couple of mattresses together and set them on fire in his cell in an effort to get the prison officials to fix the heaters because he was cold. He also received "lots of" corrective consultations (written warnings) for minor infractions, such as not shaving, being on the wrong cell block wing, and not having his shirt tucked in.

As a result of his misbehavior, Ben was transferred to at least two close management (CM) facilities, where his movement was severely restricted. In addition, he spent many months in disciplinary confinement (DC). In DC, inmates were not allowed visits or phone calls. Ben said he liked being by himself. While in DC, he read the Bible, received mail from his family, and wrote. He noted, "It's just subtract and relax, and ride through it."

Despite his difficulties, Ben indicated that he had adjusted "pretty good." Over the years, he had learned to think about "what the reaction's going to be to the action, and that kind of slows" Ben "down a little bit." Sometimes, however, he would get into "little funks" and just react without thinking.

Ben thought the "worst thing" in prison was the "lack of friends." He experienced becoming more aggravated than depressed in prison. He maintained that "it's just a question of when," rather than if, "you're going to bug out." Ben explained that there was "no vacation"—no getting away from the stress.

Ben has had no counseling in prison. He "tried to stay away from the psychs." He attended Alcoholics Anonymous on occasion, but it was not available in CM.

Ben participated in one vocational program, auto body, while in prison. He said he was bumped from other vocational programs because of his sentence length. Ben has had primarily maintenance jobs. He did not like working on inside grounds, refused to work, and was sent to CM as a result. At the time of the follow-up interview, Ben was working in a water treatment plant in prison and felt that he was learning something.

Ben has not experienced prison as violent. He said it is "more like mental-head games type they play." Ben explained that he "played" to an extent because he was "surrounded" by it. He would "end up that way, like playing like sex games, and stuff like that, goofing up, you know."[8] He said eventually an inmate had to say or do something, or the situation would escalate. An inmate needed to be prepared to fight. It did not matter whether the inmate won; it mattered that he stood up for himself. Ben related that taking another inmate's belongings was serious because inmates did not have much. Theft was "like a death sentence thing." The victim retaliated by catching the thief when he "ain't paying no attention." Ben has resolved difficulties, "some diplomatically and some violently basically, you know. Nothing crazy or nothing like that."

Ben said that alcohol and drugs were available in prison. He did not like the alcohol the inmates made; it was "rotgut stuff." He smoked marijuana "every now and then." He got a DR for dirty urine once and had to do time in DC.

Ben's mother, stepfather, and maternal grandparents have visited him at least monthly since he has been in prison. He has talked to his mother every night, except when he was in CM. His childhood friend Jim has remained in touch through phone calls.

At the time of the follow-up interview, Ben expressed fear about being released from prison. He confided that he had never lived on his own; "I would have to have Mom, you know, to help me basically."

Ben was concerned that he had become "institutionalized" during the seven years he had spent in jail and prison. He was afraid he would not know what to do in society. He said, "I've learned more about, as far as crime and stuff like that, than education." Ben related that he had learned "all kinds of stuff from stealing cars to cooking dope and selling dope. All that. Credit card scams. It's like a college for criminals basically. Because there's nothing to do, but set around and talk about 'old war stories' or what not. And how you did stuff and how you got caught, and how to do it differently, whatever."

Ben worried that the longer he stayed in prison, the more he would become like the "criminals" with whom he has lived. He said, "Even in my outlook, I used to be a lot more passive and stuff. And the longer I've been here, the more aggressive I get for some reason, you know. And I don't know how to stop, you know, basically."

Ben's Reflections about His Childhood

In recalling his childhood, Ben said that he stopped attending school and was home-schooled because he was not doing well, disliked reading, and "kept going downhill." Ben talked openly about his mischievous behavior when he was a boy. He mentioned stealing cigarettes and setting newspapers and cardboard boxes on fire. He said his dad would discipline him by giving him "a good whipping with a rod, wooden spoon" until he was about 13 or 14. After that, when he misbehaved, his parents did "nothing really." He recalled how he had liked "mudding" with cars and said he would probably still enjoy doing it.

Looking back, Ben stated that he had had a good childhood. He said, "I had good parents. Usually anywhere Dad went, he took me with him, like fishing and hunting, and all that stuff." Dad had done fun things with him "ever since I was a little tadpole."

Ben's Reflections about the Shooting

Ben had very little memory of the shooting at the time of the follow-up interview. He strongly denied that the crime was premeditated and said that any remarks he had made about killing his parents were uttered because he was venting or trying to be funny. When asked what his current feelings about the homicide were, Ben said, "I would much rather have Dad back and none of this would have happened, but now I just go from here." As is characteristic of low maturity individuals, Ben had no idea how the homicide could have been prevented. He said, "If I had never did drugs, maybe, but outside of that," he saw no other way. Similarly, he saw no way to caution others to avoid similar tragedies. He explained that people do not see things as happening to them "until they hit that wall themselves, and by then, it's too late."

FOLLOW-UP INTERVIEW WITH BEN'S MOM, MRS. SIMPSON KENNEDY

I met with Ben's mother in her home for about two hours several months after the follow-up meeting with Ben. She and her current husband, Mr. Kennedy, have a beautiful house overlooking a small lake in a gated community. Mrs. Kennedy's love for her son was apparent throughout the interview. Her remarks reflected empathy for Ben's situation and compassion for other inmates who have made mistakes.

Mrs. Kennedy's Current Relationship with Ben

Ben's mom said that her loving feelings toward Ben had grown stronger over the years. She never had "any unforgiveness toward him." She added, "I mean, I love him more than myself. I would give my life. He is my life. I love him. I mean, I love him so much." Ben's imprisonment has "deepened" Mrs. Kennedy's love for him. Tears welled up in her eyes as she said, "It breaks my heart to see him, what his life is now." Mrs. Kennedy stated that Ben loved his dad and he loved her. As Mr. Kennedy told her, Ben's homicidal behavior was "just a stupid, stupid thing."

Mrs. Kennedy related that she, Mr. Kennedy, and her parents visited Ben monthly. They used to visit Ben more often when he was incarcerated in a prison closer to their home. Ben calls his mother every day, and "sometimes two, three times a day" on weekends. She was pleased that Ben's friend Jim had stayed in touch with him by phone.

Mrs. Kennedy's Reflections Regarding the Shooting

Over the years, Mrs. Kennedy has thought many times about the shooting that killed her first husband and seriously wounded her. She confessed that she sometimes wondered what she and Ben's dad did wrong. Mrs. Kennedy said, "And part of me thinks that, maybe, you know, that maybe we didn't discipline him enough because he was just, you know, did he run so rampant with this or think that he was owed so much? You know, whatever was going on in his mind, although he never said any of those things. My question myself is—where did I miss this, and why didn't I see this? Because people have said to me, 'Didn't you know, he was on drugs?' No. I didn't, honestly."

When asked, Mrs. Kennedy said she and Ben's dad over-indulged Ben "probably to a fault." She explained, "Like in things of, matters of taking care of things, we took care of them. And to the point that maybe we should have let him take care of some of his own things, and we didn't." Mrs. Kennedy said that she knew Ben was immature as a teenager, but she did not give his immaturity much concern because she knew boys matured more slowly than girls.

Ben's Time in Prison

Mrs. Kennedy has not seen much change in Ben during the time that he has been incarcerated. She said she still sees him as "a good kid" with "a great sense of humor." However, she observed that Ben is "still immature for his age. You know, he's 26, but he's not 26."

Mrs. Kennedy related that Ben got into trouble frequently during his first few years in prison. She explained that he had difficulty obeying the rules because he thought they were "stupid." In her opinion, Ben was not challenging authority; rather, he did not think about the consequences and engaged in "dumb things" or "kids' stuff," such as smoking in an unauthorized area. As a result, Ben spent about three years in solitary confinement. At the time of our interview, Mrs. Kennedy indicated that her son seemed to be more adjusted to prison life and to think more about consequences before acting.

One of Mrs. Kennedy's biggest concerns when I met with her was that Ben "does nothing all day. He just lays around all day." Ben told her that he spends much of his time "hanging out" and reading because, even when he has had a job, little was required. He admitted that he has become "so lazy" that he does not want to do any work.

Mrs. Kennedy recalled that Ben finished his GED in prison. However, there were no provisions for more advanced learning. Ben's mom has tried to motivate Ben to take an interest in a profession so that he has something that he enjoys doing and could do when he is released. Because of his long sentence, it took Ben nearly five years to get into a program that he liked (auto body). At the time of our interview, Ben was learning plumbing.

Ben's mom related Ben had had no counseling in prison. Mrs. Kennedy said it troubled her that Ben has not had anyone with whom he could talk about the shooting and the death of his father. She recalled that when Ben used to bring up the shooting with her, she would start crying, so he stopped discussing it. She said with anguish in her voice that Ben did not have the time to grieve his father's death and to work through the fact that he was the person responsible. Mrs. Kennedy was concerned that Ben had had no treatment for his drug problem while he had been in prison and was worried that he would get back into drugs when released.

Mrs. Kennedy's Reflections Regarding Ben's Release from Prison

Mrs. Kennedy said that her second husband, Mr. Kennedy, had been very supportive of Ben over the years. They have no concerns about Ben acting violently if he is released back into the community in the near future. Ben's mom strongly believes, based on research she has done, that the drugs Ben ingested (Xanax) were responsible for his violent behavior.[9] Ben's mom explained, "He never ever gave us any indication that he was violent. I mean he never raised a hand to me. He never pushed me. He never even threatened, he had never gotten in my face, he never did anything that would [indicate violence]. Because, that's other things that people would say to me, 'Were you ever afraid of him?' Never. Not for a second. You know, like I said, because he never did anything that would make me afraid of him."

Mrs. and Mr. Kennedy were exploring the possibility of an appeal at the time of my follow-up interview. They were hoping Ben would not have to serve the 45-year sentence imposed. Ben's mother believed that her son's immaturity should be taken into consideration, as well as his intoxicated state at the time of the shooting. She said that "Ben was 14 mentally and emotionally .... Does he deserve to lose his life for that? Or give up three quarters of his life because he made a really bad choice, a really bad, made a really bad mistake? I think except for the grace of God, there goes anyone of us."

Mrs. Kennedy related she and Ben were advised before Ben entered a plea that intoxication could not be used as a defense against the charges because of recent changes in the law restricting its use.[10] Without the use of drugs as a defense, it appeared that Ben was "just a spoiled brat kid that wasn't getting his own way and decided he was going to shoot his parents."

Mrs. Kennedy maintained that a 45-year sentence was "ridiculous" when you could give inmates "an education, give them the help they need, give them mental help or whatever kind of help at such a low cost" relative to the cost of keeping them in prison for decades. She argued that after providing services, the system should "send them on their way. And get them out [of prison]. Then they would be contributing to the tax base." Warehousing them "doesn't make any common, good common sense at all." She believed that it was foolish "to let people leave prison in the same state that they came in, and expect a different result." If inmates' problems and needs are not being addressed, there is no way that they can go back to society and succeed.[11]

Ben's mother is hopeful that Ben will be released while she is young enough that they can enjoy each other. She wants him to get out so "he can still have a life, and have a family, and have a normal, you know, have somewhat of a normal life." Mrs. Kennedy lamented the way society treats offenders. "Our society has gotten so tired of, you know, violence of criminals and stuff like that, that we do have such a thing of 'lock 'em up and throw away the key.' And then, they do get out. But [society believes] 'you still can't be any good.' I think it's just a societal thing. No, these people are just like you and me. And they've made some mistakes. And if we educate them, if we could give them skills to walk out of that prison to put them back into society, and then hire them, so that they don't have that ... stigma to them."

Mrs. Kennedy believes that we have become a selfish society. She maintained that if people were not so caught up in their own worlds, they could impact others positively by doing small things. "It's the simple things that do change somebody else's life and make an impact on them." Ben's mother reflected that when individuals are behind bars, "it's almost like they're not human." People don't have to think about inmates and being nice to them. She noted further that conditions in prison are "demeaning and degrading." She asked, "How do you think that you can treat people this way and expect a different outcome, expect to treat them that way, and then not be afraid for your life?"

CASE COMMENTARY

Ben's case is a very important one because it does not fit into one of the three basic types of parricide offenders. He does not fit the profile of the *severely abused child* because there was no evidence of abuse. In fact, the evidence is strong and persuasive that Ben's parents greatly loved him and spent time with him. I was very moved when I interviewed Mrs. Kennedy seven years after the shooting in which she almost died; her love for Ben was genuine and unconditional.

Ben did not fit the profile of the *dangerously antisocial child*. There is no evidence that he decided to kill his parents because he perceived them as obstacles in his way. In fact, after he shot his parents, Ben called 911 when his father told him to do so.

Ben did not fit the profile of the *mentally ill child*. Ben had no history of serious mental disorders such as depression, bipolar disorder, or psychosis. There were some data, however, to suggest that he might have been delusional in the few days preceding the homicide. Recall that Ben convinced his father and best friend that others trashed the Lincoln and maintained that he was going to hunt down the transgressors. As suggested above, having to face the consequences of his misbehavior for the first time appeared to generate *fear to the point of panic* and *anger to the point of rage* within Ben. A low-maturity youth, Ben was overwhelmed by the intensity of his feelings and did not have the inner resources to calm himself down. His ingesting excessive quantities of Xanax and alcohol further reduced the limited ability that he had to evaluate his behavior. In his intoxicated state, Ben's ability to access higher cortical functions of the brain would have been very low. The limbic system of the brain was likely in charge when he opened fire on his parents and then fled the scene. Under these circumstances, the shooting was impulsive.[12]

As we can see, many factors came together for this "perfect storm" to cause death and destruction. One early contributing factor was Ben's parents' failure to set consistent limits for Ben. Unquestionably out of love, they over-indulged their son and tried to right his wrongs. As a result, Ben did not grow up. At 18, he had not learned how to tolerate frustration and solve his problems. The shooting likely would not have occurred if Ben had not become severely intoxicated and returned home in his delusional and enraged state. The ready availability of firearms made it all the more difficult for this youth to resist the impulse to react violently.

My follow-up interview with Ben underscores the deleterious effects of prison for adolescent parricide offenders. Although Ben was a low-maturity individual when he was convicted, the prognosis in his case was favorable because he was prosocial, open to authority figures, and receptive to treatment. In prison, as is typically the case, Ben received no treatment. He was confined with other offenders whose development had been arrested. Given the institutional needs of prison, he was not encouraged to take responsibility and to grow; rather, he was told what to do and punished for noncompliance. At age 25, Ben remained the young and immature boy I had met years earlier.

PART THREE
SOCIETY'S RESPONSE

14 Treating Severely Abused Parricide Offenders

with Eldra Solomon, Ph.D.

Adults who kill parents, as we have discussed, are typically severely mentally ill or antisocial. Outcomes in these cases are usually fairly straightforward. Adult parricide offenders who kill their parents while in a delusional state typically have a long-standing documented mental illness. They often are found not guilty by reason of insanity and are likely to be sent to a mental hospital where they will remain for years. Those who are antisocial typically are convicted and sentenced to long prison sentences. In some cases, adult parricide offenders who are convicted of premeditated murder are sentenced to death.[1]

Adolescents, in contrast to their adult counterparts, are rarely psychotic. They typically have extensive histories of neglect and/or abuse. Child maltreatment is also often found in the histories of antisocial parricide offenders. Youths found to be operating according to antisocial motives will typically receive long prison sentences. Those adjudged to be acting out of terror or desperation to end the abuse, referred to as the severely abused parricide offender type, although rarely exonerated, might be convicted of a lesser offense and shown some mercy by the court.

In light of these dynamics, this chapter devotes special attention to the treatment of the severely abused parricide offender type. This type is the most common among adolescents who kill their parents and is the type with the most favorable prognosis. It is our hope that social service agency providers and state attorneys, as well as defense attorneys and judges, will acquaint themselves with the issues discussed in this chapter. Understanding these issues will facilitate their making sound recommendations regarding the treatment and disposition of adolescent parricide offenders. Guidance counselors, teachers, and other school personnel are encouraged to become familiar with this material because it might help them make appropriate referrals in cases of child mistreatment that have not resulted in homicide. Students and general readers also might find treatment issues and strategies of interest. Before turning our focus to issues related to the adolescent parricide offender, however, we provide available information on the treatment of the severely mentally ill parricide offender, most likely to be an adult.

THE LITERATURE ON THE SEVERELY MENTALLY ILL PARRICIDE OFFENDER

The severely mentally ill parricide offender is likely to be diagnosed as suffering from psychosis, often schizophrenia or schizoaffective disorder; a paranoid disorder; major depressive disorder with psychotic features; or bipolar disorder with psychotic features. As illustrated in the literature review and case studies, psychotic individuals have lost touch with reality. Their personalities are typically severely disorganized, their perceptions distorted, and their communications often rambling and incoherent. They might experience hallucinations and bizarre delusions. Individuals with psychotic disorders often do not understand that they are mentally ill and might behave bizarrely, even violently, because of their belief systems or sensory experiences.

Severely mentally ill offenders frequently need to be hospitalized until their mental disorder has been stabilized. Psychotropic medications are often helpful in reducing psychotic symptoms, including hallucinations and delusions. Psychotic parricide offenders need to be monitored closely, as they are at high risk for suicide. As noted recently by Hillbrand, "most who commit parricide are not chronically dangerous mentally ill individuals but rather mentally ill men and women who have committed an act of desperation and who are at greater risk of killing themselves than of harming others."[2]

Several studies have noted that a fairly large percentage of parricide offenders kill themselves or attempt to do so following the murders of their parents.[3] Although these studies sometimes include a few parricide offenders under age 18, most are adults with diagnoses of mental illness.[4] An examination of coroners' files in Quebec, Canada, for the period from 1990 to 2005 revealed that 17% of the 37 parricide offenders killed or attempted to kill themselves following the murders.[5] A study in Finland that followed up on parricide offenders three to 24 years after the killing found that one-third of those who died during this period committed suicide. Six percent of the 99 matricide offenders and 8% of the 113 patricide offenders committed suicide during the follow-up period.[6] Consistent with other studies, the suicide rate of parricide offenders exceeded the rate in the general population. Notably, the age at which matricide offenders killed themselves was significantly younger than that of patricide offenders, suggesting that matricide offenders are at higher risk for self-harm than patricide offenders.[7]

An archival study of newspaper accounts of parricide from 1851 through 1899 revealed that postparricide suicides are not a new phenomenon. Offenders in 8% of parricide incidents in the second half of the 19th century committed or attempted suicide following the murder of their parents. Those who engaged in postparricide suicidal behavior were equally likely to kill mothers and fathers.[8]

The literature contains very little on the treatment of mentally ill parricide offenders. Akuffo and colleagues described the successful treatment of a 46-year-old man who killed his alcoholic and domineering mother during an argument.[9] The man presented with psychosis, mental deficiency, and evidence of temporal lobe epilepsy. He had a history of seizures beginning at age 7 and had been hospitalized on more than 20 occasions prior to the murder. Shortly before the killing, the man's father, who had performed a peacekeeping role, died. Arrangements were underway to move the son to a supervised living situation, given the volatile nature of the mother–son relationship, when the homicide occurred. The man was remanded on a charge of manslaughter to a psychiatric hospital for assessment and treatment.

The authors noted that the man's psychotic symptoms improved with medication and he was easily managed. After three years of treatment, he was free of psychotic symptoms, evaluated as not dangerous, and moved to a community-based hospital for the mentally handicapped. During the next 10 years, he made steady progress to the point that he was able to live with a female companion in semi-independent housing near the hospital, hold a full-time job, and travel as needed on his own. He availed himself of the support of community nurses and saw a psychiatrist monthly. Although he occasionally relapsed into delusions, these abated when his medication was adjusted. The man's epilepsy was generally controlled with medication. The authors concluded that "intensive multidisciplinary treatment and rehabilitation" enabled this man to live successfully in the community. They hoped that this case would "serve as a model of encouragement for similar cases."[10]

Hillbrand and Young reported on the successful group psychotherapy experiences of a cohort of hospitalized adult parricide offenders whom they have described as "a particularly treatment-refractory set of psychologically tortured and severely isolated individuals."[11] Prior to the group's inception, the authors noted that these parricide offenders seemed to have given up. "They appeared profoundly dysphoric, socially isolated, and minimally involved in treatment."[12] The group, known as the Genesis group, is based on the assumption that only parricide offenders can comprehend the existential experience of having killed their parents. The major therapeutic goals include helping parricide offenders tolerate the emotions related to the crime, distance themselves emotionally from their killings, and stop equating themselves with the killings. The focus is on parricide offenders' coming to understand the dynamics behind their killings and the role that their illness (usually schizophrenia) played while accepting responsibility for their actions. In the process of redefining themselves as individuals who have committed terrible acts, as opposed to terrible people, group members identify suitable ways "to lead the remainder of their lives in a meaningful, dignified manner" and to find "some limited self-forgiveness."[13]

The Genesis group has been effective largely because members who have been in the group for long periods have made strides in treatment, serve as role models for new members, and give others hope that recovery is possible.[14] The authors stressed that hope is essential in order for forensic patients to progress through the stages of recovery. They noted further that participation in the Genesis group, which has been in existence for more than 10 years, has enabled many of its original members to leave the maximum-security hospital and lead more independent lives.[15]

Gabison-Hermann and colleagues reported on the progress of 29 parricide offenders hospitalized in France. Nearly 80% of these patients were diagnosed with paranoid schizophrenia. Seven years after the killings, 71% were still involuntarily hospitalized. Of these, 59% were working or involved in therapeutic activities. The authors concluded that the results indicated "relatively good psychosocial functioning" considering the crime's seriousness, and they called for studies with follow-up periods of 15 to 20 years.[16]

THE LITERATURE ON TREATING JUVENILE AND ADOLESCENT HOMICIDE OFFENDERS

In consideration of the fact that youths who kill parents are a subset of juvenile and adolescent homicide offenders, we initially review the literature on the treatment of youthful murderers. This literature is pertinent to the treatment of two of the parricide types commonly encountered among juvenile and adolescent populations: the severely abused parricide offender and the dangerously antisocial parricide offender. In many respects, the literature on treating violent juvenile offenders is more relevant to the dangerously antisocial parricide offender. The parricide offender who kills to end abuse, as we have seen, rarely has an extensive delinquent history, and typically requires different treatment than the chronically aggressive delinquent.[17] Following this review, we discuss the treatment of young parricide offenders, particularly those with histories of severe abuse and neglect.

Despite the fact that many, if not most, young killers will be released back into society, few receive any type of mental health treatment following the homicide. In fact, the likelihood of juvenile murderers' receiving intensive psychiatric intervention appears to diminish as they enter adolescence.[18] The literature on treating adolescent murderers, including parricide offenders, is sparse and dated.[19] Several reports and reviews focused on the treatment of serious young violent offenders, including juvenile homicide offenders, in the mid- to late 1990s.[20] Few scholarly publications have focused on the treatment of juveniles who have committed homicide or serious violence since 2000.[21]

The extent to which the cases of juvenile murderers presented in the literature are representative of the population of young killers is unknown. In addition, the interventions used are often not based on established therapeutic principles or empirically documented successes.[22] Programs are also frequently not tailored to the type of juvenile murderer.

Very young children who kill are commonly hospitalized, whereas psychiatric hospitalization is rarely used for adolescent murderers. Adolescents are more likely to be hospitalized if they appear psychotic, remain homicidal, or need intensive psychopharmacological management.[23] Inpatient treatment can be particularly helpful in stabilizing the youth, redirecting the rage that drives his homicidal impulses, and reducing his internal conflict.[24] In addition, it can provide an optimal setting for evaluating the youth, assessing his potential for continued violent behavior, and understanding the family system of which he is a member.[25]

Unlike the homicidal child, who is typically viewed as psychologically disturbed,[26] the adolescent killer is often regarded as impulsive or antisocial and is likely to be institutionalized in a facility for juvenile delinquents or adult criminals.[27] Confinement in an adult prison, although common in the United States, is ill advised, as treatment is unlikely to be provided.[28] Research has indicated that nearly 60% of juvenile homicide offenders who were released after serving time in adult prisons in Florida recidivated; most of these failed within three years of their return to society.[29] Studies that followed up on serious juvenile offenders retained in the juvenile justice system found that they were less likely to reoffend, less likely to commit a serious offense, and went longer before reoffending than comparable youths who had been transferred to the adult criminal justice system.[30]

Long-term commitments in the juvenile justice system, however, are not the solution. A study published in 2011 that followed up on 1,354 serious juvenile offenders aged 14 to 18 years for seven years found that "longer stays in juvenile facilities did not reduce offending."[31] The investigators concluded that "incarceration may not be the most appropriate or effective option, even for many of the most serious offenders," who could be successfully supervised and treated in the community.[32]

The importance of treating juvenile offenders is underscored by research that has conclusively demonstrated that many treatment programs do work,[33] particularly if they match youths' risks, criminogenic needs, and responsivity to treatment.[34] Moreover, studies have shown that juveniles who commit serious crimes, including homicide, can be effectively treated and that intervention can reduce recidivism[35] and be cost-effective.[36] For example, sophisticated analyses of 200 programs that treated serious juvenile delinquents found an overall 12% decrease in recidivism relative to controls. Researchers estimated that the use of the most effective treatment programs could reduce recidivism for non-institutionalized and institutionalized juvenile delinquents by 40% and 35%, respectively.

The most effective treatment for non-institutionalized juvenile offenders included individual counseling, interpersonal skills training, behavioral programs, and the use of multiple services. The most effective programs for institutionalized delinquents included interpersonal skills training, teaching family homes, behavioral programs, community residential programs, and the provision of multiple services.[37] Programs involving family, particularly multisystemic therapy, repeatedly have been shown to be effective in improving family and individual functioning and in reducing recidivism by young offenders.[38]

Reduction in recidivism rates could be significantly enhanced if developmentally appropriate and intensive treatment were provided to youth targeted as most at risk of acting violently. These programs should be based on actuarial testing, particularly in geographical areas with high homicide rates.[39]

A recent study evaluating the cost effectiveness of an intensive treatment program for severe and violent delinquents with high psychopathy scores and extensive violent histories found that the benefits of treatment outweighed the costs by a margin of 7 to 1.[40] Relative to the control group, treated youths were less likely to reoffend or to commit serious offenses if they did reoffend. The authors noted that this study adds to a growing body of "empirical research that had consistently found a cost-benefit for more treatment-focused services over harsher or more security-focused sanctions for serious and violent youth."[41]

In *Young Killers*, psychologist Eldra Solomon and I recommended and discussed 12 components in the treatment of juvenile homicide offenders.[42] Our treatment recommendations were based on the pioneering work of psychologist Vicki Agee, who identified 11 of these components while treating juveniles in correctional settings. She selected these elements based on her review of the literature,[43] as well as on more than 20 years of clinical experience with residential treatment programs for juvenile delinquents, many of whom committed violent crime and were characterized as emotionally disturbed.[44] These components included (1) effective and extensive assessment using a variety of data sources; (2) comprehensive cognitive behavioral programming or restructuring; (3) prosocial skills training; (4) positive peer communities; (5) anger management; (6) empathy training; (7) clear, firm, and consistent discipline; (8) drug and alcohol abuse counseling and education; (9) transition, including family counseling when appropriate; (10) intensive and extended aftercare; and (11) medication when necessary.

We added another component to Agee's list: (12) educational and vocational programs and other activities that promote prosocial opportunities for success. Since the publication of *Young Killers,* Eldra Solomon and I have added a 13th treatment component: (13) resolve traumatic experiences with a focus on learning to calm the body, regulate emotion, and develop cognitive skills aimed at prosocial decision making.

These components are especially well suited to antisocial youths who kill their parents in order to achieve a selfish instrumental objective and to youths with low frustration tolerance who kill out of rage, often fueled by drugs and alcohol. They also apply to some extent to severely abused children and adolescents who kill their parents to end abuse. These strategies are consistent with the therapeutic recommendations discussed by psychiatrist Susan Bailey, who evaluated and treated young homicide offenders in England.[45] They are in agreement with the conclusions drawn by researchers who evaluated the effectiveness of treatment programs specifically targeting violent juvenile delinquents[46] and serious delinquents.[47] They include the four critical facets of successful programs: highly structured interventions, linking cognitive components to specific skills, family involvement, and comprehensive interventions addressing multiple risk factors across different contexts.[48] The 13 treatment components are ideally suited to identifying youths' strengths as a way to reduce risks associated with continued antisocial behavior, and they can be effectively tailored to offender gender.[49]

TREATMENT PROGRAMS FROM THE PERSPECTIVES OF A VICTIM AND AN OFFENDER

Interestingly, Mrs. Kennedy, Ben Simpson's mother (Chapter 13), stressed the need for treatment programs when I met with her about seven years after the shooting that claimed her husband's life and nearly took her own (see Box 14-1). She emphasized the value of encouraging young offenders to become more educated so that they could grow personally and support themselves when released. Her comments are timely, given the cost cutting in educational, vocational, and therapeutic programs in correctional facilities across the United States in recent years. Her argument that prisons need to provide the means for inmates to develop themselves while they are serving their sentences is made more feasible in some respects in the age of the Internet and on-line degree programs.

Box 14-1 A Survivor's Reflections on What Offenders Need

Mrs. Kennedy, whose son Ben Simpson killed his father and attempted to kill her (Chapter 13), commented that the prisons "don't have enough jobs for everybody to do to keep busy, so all the more reason for education and to do things. Make them sit in a class for four hours a day …. That's just a simple solution because then so many people would come out of prison without the problems they went in with."

Mrs. Kennedy identified ways to cut costs, such as sharing materials or taking advantage of on-line education. She would like to see prisons implement programs to help inmates learn trades such as electrical work or plumbing. If offenders are incarcerated for a long time, they could get a college education or "go all the way to a PhD."

Box 14-1 (Continued)

Mrs. Kennedy posed a question: "[If] you have no education, what are you going to do for money?" She added, "If they at least had a good education, it would give them at least some kind of a leg up because—you know what?—even if you couldn't get employed, then [you could] go make your own business."

Mrs. Kennedy suggested that prisons give aptitude tests and help inmates identify work they might like. Big benefits could follow from teaching inmates what "they would love to do. I'm a serious believer in, if that's where you're supposed to be, and that's the love of your life, that the money doesn't matter so much. You know, because, you know, you get some kind of fulfillment out of what you're doing. And everybody has something in your life that, that they get fulfillment out of what they are doing .... It's not a matter of getting them educated so they can go out and make a lot of money .... It's a matter of making money, so they can make a living for themselves ... helping them find their niche."

James Holt (Chapter 11) also advocated strongly for treatment for young offenders. James expressed concern that juvenile offenders do not have an identity when they come to prison and can be molded negatively by racial stereotypes and gangs. He observed that most juvenile offenders lack goals. He maintained that juveniles need "a sense of where they are going in their life. They need to know they have the option of, not a job, a career."

James stressed that prisons need to do more than offer vocational and GED programs; they need to provide "individualized" programming to give juveniles hope. James advocated for youthful offender programs, recognizing that some juveniles are at risk from other youths, particularly gang members who are "very violent people."

From James's perspective, programs need to be available to all inmates in order to decrease recidivism. He noted with disapproval that those with life sentences are often excluded from program participation.[50] James suggested that juveniles be able "to tend dogs and cats and groom animals" because "being around animals has a wonderful effect on prisoners and juveniles in particular." Outsiders need to come into the prison so juveniles can interact with healthy individuals. They need to have opportunities to keep up with current events and technological advances. James advised that "the poverty angle definitely has to be looked at with juveniles because they are being denied opportunity that other inmates have as simple as a medical prescription." In addition, juveniles without family and financial support are "more susceptible to victimization" in prison.

THE LITERATURE ON TREATMENT OF ADOLESCENT PARRICIDE OFFENDERS

In the preceding section, we highlighted the literature on therapeutic interventions with juvenile homicide offenders. Now, we turn to a review of studies that have discussed treating youths who have killed parents. Only five studies of adolescent parricide offenders (APOs) have addressed treatment issues, which is not surprising given the relatively small number of APOs among homicide offenders.[51] The treatment of young parricide offenders suffers from the same problems as the general literature on juvenile homicide and violent juvenile delinquents.[52] Most of the treatment results are based on clinical case reports of a few cases referred to the author for evaluation and/or treatment.

Sargent advised that children who acted out the unconscious wishes of one parent by killing the other need to be advised of the role that the surviving parent played in encouraging the youth to kill. He advocated family therapy if reunification of the child with the family is desired.[53] Scherl and Mack described the post-homicidal symptoms and behavior of one adolescent matricide offender and noted that he was not receptive to beginning treatment until almost two years after the homicide. After a year and a half of therapy, they noted that, although the prognosis was guarded, the youth seemed able to control his impulsive acting out and to consider the consequences of his behavior.[54] Details of treatment were not provided. Duncan and Duncan maintained that the APO must be institutionalized until he or she can regain self-control. They stressed that external structure must be provided by non-punitive staff who refuse to validate the offender's justification for his violent acts.[55]

Russell recommended that youths who kill family members be confined for one to two years in a secure juvenile facility that functions as a therapeutic milieu. He cautioned, however, that treatment is particularly difficult because these youths have deficiencies in their emotional and personality development, which are further impacted by the commission of the crime. He recommended that the youths be given much emotional support while being confronted with reality.[56]

Although their work was not specifically geared to the treatment of APOs, Kromm and her colleagues discussed the use of occupational therapy in the treatment of a 17-year-old girl who killed her mother. The authors reported that conventional therapy had not been successful because of the girl's defenses and concerns with "maintaining outward appearances."[57] Art therapy enabled the clinicians to gain insight into the patient's personality, to understand her relationships with others, and to access her cognitive and functional abilities. The patient was subsequently found not guilty by reason of insanity, treated, and released. She later committed suicide.[58]

EFFECTIVE TREATMENT FOR THE SEVERELY ABUSED APO

This discussion of treatment is based on the literature, on outcome research related to current treatment programs, on our assessments of APOs, and on effective intervention with hundreds of survivors of severe child maltreatment, many of whom reported that they entertained homicidal thoughts and made plans to kill their parents. We hope it will serve as a guide to mental health professionals who encounter parricide offenders, as well as other adolescent offenders, who have been severely neglected and/or abused. So that pronouns will not be an issue of confusion, the APO has been designated as male, and the therapist female, in the following discussion.

As should be clear from earlier chapters, most APOs have experienced a lifetime of dysfunctional parenting. They have an extensive history of trauma, including neglect and abuse. Understanding the extent of trauma and its effects is critically important in forensic assessment and in treating offenders.[59]

Empirical studies, as well as a great deal of clinical data, have demonstrated that when children are neglected and/or subjected to repeated abuse, they experience traumatic stress, which compromises development. Traumatic stress interferes with the development of neural circuits connecting critical areas of the brain. These neural circuits are essential for normal physiological, cognitive, psychological, emotional, and social development. For example, some of these neural circuits are critical for making logical, thoughtful decisions; others, for regulating emotion. Other effects of neglectful, inadequate, and abusive parenting include a poor and sometimes fragmented self-concept; low self-esteem; distorted thinking; an inability to understand or express emotions; and self-defeating, destructive, and impulsive behavior.

Many children who are neglected and/or abused develop post-traumatic stress disorder (PTSD).[60] Traumatic stress can also result in complex PTSD, as discussed in Chapter 2. Clearly, treatment must address these issues.

Many APOs can be successfully treated and eventually returned to society to lead productive lives. Therapeutic intervention is critical for reclaiming the individual parricide offender as a productive member of society and for protecting the public. However, both the juvenile justice and adult justice systems have long overlooked the fact that juvenile homicide offenders require extensive services in the form of assessment and treatment.

We focus here on two major aspects of treatment and the issues that accompany them. First, the APO's current crisis must be addressed. The youth must deal with the homicide and its aftermath with respect to himself and other family survivors. Second, treatment must focus on teaching the youth the skills he needs to cope more effectively with ongoing life events. Intervention must help the youth to resolve the traumatic experiences and their effects that propelled the violence. The youth's history of victimization in the home must be unraveled and resolved.

Addressing the Immediate Crisis

As with adult offenders, society's first response to parricide in cases of children and adolescents is a legal one. Determination of the young person's guilt or innocence might take a year or longer. However, immediate decisions must be made by legal professionals, hopefully with the input of mental health professionals, regarding the placement of the APO. During this period, the youth is typically incarcerated in a juvenile detention center or, if charged as an adult, in a juvenile wing in an adult jail.

Treatment typically begins months later, after the youth's conviction (or [rare] exoneration). Meaningful therapeutic intervention actually should begin immediately following the tragedy. Although the biological and psychological effects of trauma are not always obvious, they are present both immediately and after many years.[61] The homicide itself is an extremely traumatic experience that might result in symptoms of PTSD. The killing might also trigger memories of earlier trauma.

The extreme stress of the events leading up to the homicide and the killing itself might cause the APO to dissociate during and/or after the parricidal event. He might not immediately remember the homicide itself. The APO might need his attorney and a mental health professional to help him orient to his immediate circumstances, that is, to talk about where he is and what is going to happen next.

Daniel Culbreath, who killed both parents (Chapter 12), remembered years later the compassionate care given to him by the nurses at the hospital following his arrest. He credited them with helping him move forward.

They were fantastic with me …. They never showed any disdain toward me or any resentment or anger or anything like that. They were, they seemed genuinely concerned about my well-being and, I think, that was really important to me … they didn't judge me before, just because, I—"Look, this guy just murdered his parents," you know. "Oh, my God!" They were more concerned about my well-being than what I'd done, I guess, is the best way to put it. And I really appreciate them for that ... they made a huge difference in me.

Long-Term Placement

Before sentencing, available long-term placements must be identified and assessed. Whenever possible, the APO should not be incarcerated in a prison, because prison psychological services are rarely adequate to deal with the depth of his problems. Institutional programs emphasize behavioral control and conformity to the institutional regime as a measure of progress and success, rather than individualized and specialized treatment of the youthful offenders.

Myers has argued persuasively for the development of a "corrective emotional experience" for a subgroup of juvenile murderers who have killed as a result of interpersonal conflict (Cornell, Benedek, and Benedek's conflict group) as opposed to furtherance of another crime (Cornell, Benedek, and Benedek's crime group).[62] This subgroup consists "primarily of youths with some degree of psychological problems (e.g., adjustment disorders, depression), disturbed family functioning, and concomitant stressful life events."[63]

Myers recommended placement of these youths in a "therapeutically designed institution" staffed by sincerely interested, empathic, and supportive adults who would function as "prosocial role models" and set appropriate behavioral limits. The program should be tailored to ensure that each youth receives quality mental health care and educational and vocational programs that are consistent with his ability.[64] The outcome literature has indicated that troubled adolescents placed in residential and inpatient treatment show positive behavioral changes and increases in adaptive family and social functioning.[65] Evidence, largely from case reports, indicates further that the long-term outcomes of criminally unsophisticated youths who were involved in what appear to be isolated acts of violence, often involving intense interpersonal conflict with the victim, including family members, have been favorable when treatment has been provided.[66]

Consistent with the recommendations made by Myers and by Benedek, Cornell, and Staresina,[67] we suggest that the APO be placed in a structured therapeutic environment for a period of stabilization. This environment might be a psychiatric hospital or clinic specializing in child abuse or dysfunctional family dynamics, or a group treatment home with professional mental health staff.

Forensic Evaluation

Hopefully, a mental health professional will become involved immediately following the homicide and will begin the process of forensic evaluation. Ideally the mental health professional will remain involved throughout the process. A thorough forensic evaluation includes assessing the level of personality development and obtaining as complete a psychosocial history as possible.

As discussed in Chapter 8, assessing the youth's level of personality development provides critical information about how the youth perceives himself and his relation to others and to outside events. This information is important in understanding the dynamics that led to the parricide. In general, the higher the level of personality development, the better the prognosis. Knowing the client's level of personality development is also very important in charting realistic and effective treatment goals and objectives.[68]

Treatment strategies often need to be structured differently for low- versus high-maturity youths. High-maturity adolescents typically experience remorse for wrongdoing. In parricide cases, however, the remorse might not be immediate. The initial feeling after the parent's death might be relief. The therapist must help the youth to deal with the reality that the parent is dead. The parent's death, even if excusable under the law, is still a loss. The parricide offender needs to grieve the loss of the parent and acknowledge the sadness he might feel about their relationship not having been the positive one he likely desired. He must come to terms with the fact that, regardless of the legal outcome, his life and the lives of other family members have been forever altered by the lethal actions he took.

Sometimes the remorse occurs soon after the killing. For example, one severely abused boy who bludgeoned his mother to death said, at the end of his confession to police, that he realized that he had killed the person who loved him most in the world. A young psychotic adult with a history of severe child maltreatment sobbed uncontrollably when the police arrested him for killing his mother. Both of these parricide offenders cried when I evaluated them months after the killings.

Low-maturity youths, by definition, lack awareness of feelings and do not see themselves as responsible for their behavior. I have had several cases of youths who blamed drugs for homicidal behavior directed at their parents. Abuse was not necessarily a factor in these cases. Failure of parents to set appropriate limits with these children as they were growing up, however, was typically present. One of my recent cases involved a girl whose boyfriend killed her father. The girl blamed her boyfriend even though the two had discussed the killing beforehand and she had let him in her house with knowledge of what probably would happen to her father. Later, she felt very badly about the fact that her "father was gone," meaning dead. Before low-maturity individuals can feel genuine remorse for their crimes and empathy for the victims and their families, they must come to see themselves as accountable for their actions and realize that they had choices available to them when they committed the homicides or participated in these parricidal events.

Understanding the family history and dynamics is also essential. As discussed in Chapter 8, among the many areas we explore are family relationships; school experience; work; friends; dating and sexual history; drug and alcohol involvement; medical and mental health history; activities; music, movie, and video game habits and preferences; coping strategies; prior delinquent activity; values; and future orientation. The client's psychosocial history is of paramount importance in reexamining the past, dealing with the present, and projecting the future. The evaluation process includes reviewing school records, medical and treatment records, and any social services or juvenile court records, in addition to police reports related to the homicide. It is also important to interview family members, teachers, friends, and other individuals with knowledge of the defendant and his family in order to corroborate information.

Need for Immediate Treatment

Delay in addressing the issues that led to the homicide can be dangerous. Because these youths are rarely criminally sophisticated, they often have a hard time adjusting to incarceration. Depression is likely to be exacerbated by confinement. The possibility that the youth might attempt suicide under these conditions must be seriously considered.[69] Cases of youths killing themselves following the killing of their parents have been reported in the literature.[70]

Therapeutic Approaches

Many APOs have complex PTSD as a result of their traumatic childhood experiences. As we have seen, individuals with this disorder suffer from a combination of cognitive and physiological symptoms, including anxiety, hyperarousal, and depression. Most therapies, including cognitive-behavioral therapy (CBT), focus almost exclusively on cognitive processing. The client is taught to use cognitive strategies to manage or inhibit disturbing thoughts and feelings in order to decrease problem behaviors. For example, CBT helps clients understand how their traumatic experiences have affected them and teaches them to challenge and change their irrational beliefs. This approach helps clients gain insight into their thoughts and behavior. Many survivors learn to identify stimuli that trigger them and understand why they respond in maladaptive ways. They might learn to manage disturbing feelings.

The problem is that CBT alone does not assist the client in processing the traumatic memories or in resolving the client's emotions and physiological hyperarousal. Consequently, the client continues to be triggered by stimuli that remind him of his traumatic experiences. The client might continue to respond maladaptively. Even with years of therapy, immediate responses to triggering stimuli tend to be physiological rather than logical. In treating trauma survivors, CBT is helpful and effective, but not sufficient.

Biologically informed psychotherapy resolves memories of the traumatic experience and addresses the physiological effects of trauma, and it seeks to reverse these changes.[71] Clients learn how to calm their bodies. This approach helps clients reconnect with their bodies and with their feelings. Clients learn to tolerate intense feelings and to release emotion in appropriate ways. They learn to calm their physiology.

Several treatment approaches have been developed that consider the biological aspects of trauma recovery. Eye movement desensitization and reprocessing (EMDR), an evidence-based treatment for trauma, is an effective combination of body-focused treatment and CBT.[72] EMDR helps trauma survivors access and process traumatic memories so that they can be brought to an adaptive resolution.[73] Other treatment strategies, including art therapy, have been effectively used with serious juvenile offenders.[74]

Recently published studies by Zagar and his colleagues provide strong evidence that meaningful assessment and effective intervention must consider biological as well as psychological factors. Research over the past 20 years has underscored the importance of biological effects on human development. We now know that the brain does not fully mature until 22 to 25 years of age. Furthermore, the prefrontal cortex, the part of the brain responsible for critical thinking and sound judgment, is the last part of the brain to mature. Consequently, an adolescent, under the best of conditions, is not fully capable of making thoughtful, adaptive decisions.[75] When the effects of compromised neural development resulting from early abuse and neglect are added to the equation, it is clear that the APO is at a serious biological disadvantage. In some cases, the APO will need several years of treatment before his return home can be considered.

The Capital and Serious Violent Offender Treatment Program

The Capital and Serious Violent Offender Treatment Program (C&SVOTP) at Giddings State School in Giddings, Texas, has shown remarkable promise in treating serious violent offenders. This intensive 24-week or longer residential treatment program targets emotional, social, and cognitive developmental processes, as well as psychological issues. The program facilitates emotional regulation, appropriate expression of thoughts and feelings, and the development of empathy.[76]

The C&SVOTP follows a significant preparatory regimen of treatment. Juveniles who are incarcerated for murder (including parricide) or other serious violent offenses, such as armed robbery or kidnapping, are selected for this program depending on their earlier progress at Giddings. The program utilizes an intense group process that consists of three major components. Each youth first tells his life story, then tells the story of his crime, and later learns about relapse prevention.

The juveniles are required to participate in psychodramatic role-plays that help them break through the walls they have built around their feelings. Group members begin to form attachments to one another as each of them takes a turn acting out his personal story. Next, each youth plays himself, the offender, when he tells his crime story. In a later psychodrama, he takes the victim's role in the crime reenactment. After these youths learn to feel compassion for themselves, they start to develop empathy for their victims and for others in general. The program overview states: "The connection between emotion and cognitions enables youth to develop remorse and personal accountability for their life choices. Cognitive restructuring, the replacement of delinquent rationalizations with prosocial attitudes, is more successful when reconnected to underlying emotions."[77] Participation in C&SVOTP decreased the probability of being reincarcerated for any offense by 55% and for a felony offense by 43%.[78]

The C&SVOTP is an excellent example of a program that offers an alternative to sentencing juvenile homicide offenders to adult prison. Programs with demonstrated track records in rehabilitating youths who have acted violently provide a realistic option for judges to consider. As the U.S. Supreme Court made clear in its 2012 holding striking down mandatory life sentences without parole for defendants convicted for murders they committed as juveniles,[79] psychological, biological, and sociological factors that define the lives of youths are important factors to consider at sentencing. James Holt, who was sentenced to life (Chapter 11), has made a compelling case against sentencing juveniles to life. His essay is reprinted, with permission, in Box 16-1.

SUMMARY AND CONCLUDING REMARKS

Very little has been written about treating parricide offenders. This chapter began by reviewing the available treatment literature with respect to the severely mentally ill parricide offender, who is likely to be an adult offender. Thereafter, the literature on the treatment of juvenile homicide offenders (JHOs) in general and then on juvenile/adolescent parricide offenders in particular was synthesized. The literature on JHOs is particularly pertinent to parricide offenders with histories of acting-out behavior, who might be diagnosed with conduct disorder and even classified as dangerously antisocial parricide offenders. This literature is also relevant to the treatment of the severely abused parricide offender. More recent and methodologically sophisticated studies have shown promise in treating serious and violent juvenile offenders, including those who have committed homicide.

The literature on the treatment of children and adolescents who kill parents is sparse. These studies tend to describe the interventions used with the severely abused parricide offender type. After reviewing these clinical reports, psychologist Eldra Solomon and I discussed the treatment needed for severely abused parricide offenders. Our recommendations are based on evidence-based treatment, our assessments of parricide offenders, and on effective intervention with hundreds of survivors of childhood trauma, many of whom entertained parricidal thoughts.

Effective treatment for adolescents who have killed parents is vital. As we have seen, given the home environments in which many APOs were raised, they are often victims as well as offenders. Treatment must initially focus on helping the youth deal with the killing and its effect on him and other family members. While they are confined by the state, it makes sense to help these individuals resolve their traumatic pasts, develop more effective coping skills, and learn to express feelings in a more appropriate way. Resolving the underlying trauma can help these youths to learn to make logical decisions and behave more adaptively.

Examination by a mental health professional soon after the arrest is recommended from a therapeutic standpoint. Placement in a secure therapeutic environment is preferred to incarceration in a juvenile detention center or adult jail. Continued involvement by clinical staff is important. APOs are typically traumatized by the killing and might decompensate further in jail. Treatment can lessen the risk of these youths' committing suicide. In light of the psychological and physiological effects of trauma, we recommend that treatment strategies combine body-focused approaches, such as EMDR, with cognitive-behavioral strategies.

The authors invite other therapists who deal with this population to join us in empirically testing the treatment methods described in this chapter. The conclusion of Benedek, Cornell, and Staresina, following their review of the literature on the treatment of adolescent homicide offenders, remains true today, more than 20 years later: "The appropriate psychiatric/psychological treatment of the homicidal adolescent is a critical area that leaves much room for further research …. Treatment planning for the violent juvenile is only in an experimental stage."[80]

In the next chapter, I report on what happened years later to 11 APOs I evaluated. All of these youths were incarcerated in adult prisons. Some were released and reincarcerated; others were still in prison at the time of the follow-up interviews.

15 Follow-Up Studies of Adolescent Parricide Offenders

Past studies, although few, have suggested that the prognosis for a successful reintegration into society for adolescent parricide offenders (APOs) has been generally good. Duncan and Duncan noted that in four cases in which follow-up data were available, APOs had not committed further crimes during the 10-year period following their release.[1] They drew the following conclusion: "It appears that in cases where the murderer is sane, where the victim is the original hated parent and not a surrogate, and where immediate apprehension and control are established, then the chances that the offender will kill again are minimal."[2] Long-term follow-up data on three APOs (over 10 years in one case) provided by Tanay indicated that each made a successful adjustment when released to the community.[3]

Corder and her colleagues' analysis of follow-up data, which averaged four and a half years after the offenses, revealed that adolescents who killed their parents "adjusted well outside prison with minimum psychiatric intervention and treatment."[4] Only one of the 10 parricide offenders remained incarcerated. In contrast, 19 of the 20 youths who had killed strangers, acquaintances, and relatives other than parents were still incarcerated.[5] Limited (time unspecified) follow-up data on two APOs provided by Post indicated that they made successful adjustments upon release into the community; neither had been rearrested.[6]

Follow-up data provided by Schlesinger on an unusual matricide case committed by a 16-year-old boy was also positive.[7] The boy strangled his mother, with whom he had had an incestuous relationship for many years. After her death, he had vaginal and anal sex with her. After serving two years in prison for manslaughter, he participated in psychotherapy for two and a half years and was able to make a successful adjustment. He worked part time and attended college. A 10-year follow-up indicated that this matricide offender had finished college, had secured a job in his chosen field, had a steady girlfriend, "and apparently has had no severe long-term problems stemming from his experiences as an adolescent."[8]

Past follow-up studies of APOs have also indicated that relationships with surviving family members are frequently maintained.[9] Corder and her colleagues noted, for example, that all eight of the APOs for whom follow-up data were available had been accepted by their families; seven maintained frequent contact, and four returned home to live with them.[10]

Not all follow-up data on APOs are positive, however. Scherl and Mack provided nearly four years of follow-up information on a boy who killed his mother.[11] The boy was diagnosed as having "a character disorder, mixed type, with conversion and dissociative symptoms."[12] After the killing, the boy developed a number of neurotic and transient psychotic symptoms. He reported images, nightmares, and hallucinations in which he saw his mother. He was transferred to a hospital setting where he established with several female patients "a pattern not unlike that which he had existed with his mother. He involved himself quickly in intense relationships with these girls, and then was unable to control the sexual and aggressive behavior which was stimulated thereby."[13]

Although the boy made some progress in therapy over the three-year period, the authors described his prognosis as guarded, concerned that the youth would reconstitute the relationship that he had had with his mother with a girlfriend, "with possibly disastrous results."[14] At the time of their report, the boy, then 18.5 years old, had been on parole for four months. He had resisted urges to get into trouble in order to avoid returning to the institution. He was attending school, living in a group home, and seeing his therapist weekly. Scherl and Mack noted, "[H]e longs for a girl or wife to take care of him, and became attached briefly to an older woman whom he drove away through the urgency of his demands."[15]

Mack, Scherl, and Mack provided follow-up data on the case of Nell, a 16-year-old girl who killed her mother. This case, discussed in Chapter 4, involved the only female among the four adolescent matricide offenders evaluated by the author team. In contrast to her male counterparts, who "made a form of clinical recovery within months of the crime," three years after the killing, "Nell remained hospitalized in a deluded, paranoid, and child-like stance, plagued with continuing homicidal and suicidal preoccupations."[16]

Russell provided long-term follow-up data on two APOs (nine years in one case, more than 10 in the second). One APO had made a successful adjustment; the other was violently explosive and "wonders if he isn't going to get someone to kill him just as he killed his father; or will he kill himself first?"[17]

Reinhardt followed up on Leith, a 17-year-old male patricide offender who did kill again. Although the youth stated that he killed his father because his dad was mean to his mother and to him, he did not meet the profile of the severely abused parricide offender.[18] Leith had a long history of lawbreaking beginning when he was a young child and was described as "a hardened criminal before he was twelve."[19] Prior to her husband's murder, the boy's mother told the police that her son had threatened to kill his father, but law enforcement took no action. The youth spent five years in a reformatory in connection with the murder of his father. In the eight-year period following his release, Leith was arrested 17 times for "prowling, breaking and entering, attempted robbery, and for making vicious threats against people he didn't like and who got in his way."[20] He and an accomplice robbed an elderly man and killed him. Leith was distraught at age 30 when he was sentenced to life in prison and complained bitterly that he had been treated unfairly because he was "an ex-con" and had killed his "old man."[21]

Anthony recounted a case of a 13-year-old male patricide offender who also murdered again.[22] The boy was "the only son of a well-to-do, well-adjusted family in which both parents behaved with conventional morality toward the children."[23] Prior to the killing, the youth had attempted suicide and tried to run away. He said he killed his father because he was afraid that he would be beaten for not doing well in school. Follow-up data revealed that as a young man, he later killed his mistress "after a somewhat bizarre interchange with her husband."[24] He was convicted, sentenced to prison, and later "transferred to a mental hospital because of his violent paranoid tendencies."[25] He subsequently committed suicide, 18 years after killing his father. The reporting clinician opined that, although psychosis played a role in the second killing, public opinion that judged him harshly for killing his father likely played a role in exacerbating his delusional mental state.

FOLLOW-UP ON A SAMPLE OF DR. HEIDE'S PARRICIDE CASES

I was able to follow up on 11 parricide cases I had evaluated.[26] Five of these cases are presented in the clinical chapters; the remaining six are discussed in Chapters 1, 2, 6, and 7. At the time of their initial evaluation, these youths were diagnosed as followed: severely abused (n = 4), dangerously antisocial (n = 3), severely mentally ill (n = 2), and drugs/anger (n = 2). Nine were males. At the time of the murders, the offenders ranged in age from 13 to 20 years old. Their mean and median ages when the homicides occurred were both 17 years old.[27] Five were 17 when they killed their parents. With the exception of Peter Jones, who had been found insane and sent to a psychiatric hospital for a short time, the parricide offenders had been incarcerated in adult prison following their convictions of the murder of their parents. Recall from Chapter 10 that Peter Jones was sentenced to prison in connection with strong-arm robberies he committed to help support his mother several months after his release from the mental hospital.

The time from the crime to my follow-up interview averaged 12 years[28] and ranged from seven to 21 years. At follow-up, sample subjects ranged in age from 21 years to 37 years. Their average (mean) age was 29.5 years old.[29] At the time of follow-up, six were still incarcerated in connection with the murder of their parents. Five of these six had killed or attempted to kill more than one victim. Each of the five who had been released after serving time in prison had killed fathers. Of these five, three were back in confinement when I conducted follow-up interviews with them.

The semi-structured interviews I conducted with the 11 parricide offenders generally lasted two to three hours. I inquired about their experiences in prison, their post-release experiences when applicable, their reflections regarding the killings, and suggestions regarding treatment and prevention. Across the content areas investigated, four findings stood out: these offenders had little treatment, as a group they did not fare well in prison, those released had difficulty adjusting, and for the most part little growth in maturity was observed.

Experiences in Prison

With respect to their experiences in treatment, the parricide offenders reported receiving very little treatment, even when treatment had been specifically ordered by the judge, as it was in at least six cases.[30] Educational programs in prison were limited to GED. A few offenders took correspondence courses, usually related to the Bible, if they had funds to pay for it. Although there was interest in on-line college courses, prison security did not allow offenders to participate. There were select vocational programs available in prison. Although most of the parricide offenders participated, some programs were closed to those with long sentences. Most offenders reported having jobs in prison. Some offenders reported participating in programs such as Alcoholics Anonymous, life skills, and work release.

The difficulties that the offenders experienced in prison varied widely. Most claimed that they held their own. There was also wide variation in the disciplinary infractions incurred in prison. Some APOs received none, whereas others accumulated many over the years. Prison records indicated, for example, that Karl Roberts, whose story was highlighted in Chapter 1, accrued 26 charges and was put in disciplinary confinement at least 14 separate times in his first 10 years of confinement in prison.[31] Cassie Sparkman, also highlighted in Chapter 1, related that she was repeatedly in trouble during her first five years in prison, accruing over 29 disciplinary reports; as a result, she spent a large amount of her time in disciplinary confinement. Overall, few of the parricide offenders adjusted well in prison. Importantly, good adjustment in prison did not predict post-release success or maturity, as in the case of Will Garrison profiled in Chapter 7 and discussed below.

There was wide variation regarding the offenders' contact with surviving family members. After years of confinement, some had little or no contact with family, whereas others received continuing support. For the most part, offenders had very little contact with friends or dating partners whom they knew prior to killing their parents. Only two of the 11 had biological children; one was conceived while an offender was out of prison, before he was sent back for a technical violation of probation.

Parricide Offenders Released

Four of the five parricide offenders released fit the profile of the severely abused parricide offender; the remaining one was classified as severely mentally ill. Of the five released, only one had committed no further crimes. As shown in Table 15-1, four were rearrested. One was returned to prison for a technical violation after serving nine months on probation. A second was arrested on drug-related charges after serving eight months on parole. A third was sent back to prison following his conviction of burglary of a store and grand theft; he had served 13 months on probation before reoffending. The fourth had been out of prison for more than 12 years before he was rearrested in connection with killing two people. He was

Table 15-1 Follow-up on released adolescent parricide offenders

Type	Offender	Victim	Convicted	Sentenced	Years Served	Outcome
Severely abused	Girl, 17, Patty Smith	Father	Second-degree murder	17 years	6.5	nearly 20 years crime-free
Severely abused	Boy, 16, Will Garrison	Father	Second-degree murder	20 years, commuted by governor	About 6	New crime within 13 months
Severely abused	Boy, 17, Evan Sutton	Father	Second-degree murder	15 years	6.33 (with 2 years' jail time)	New crime within 8 months
Severely abused	Boy, 17, Peter Jones	Father	Not guilty by reason of insanity, committed to hospital for about a month	Sentenced to 4 years on robbery charges (occurred within 3 months of release from hospital)	About 1 (for robberies)	Rearrested about 6 years after robbery convictions; arrested later for double murder
Severely mentally ill	Boy, 17, Marcus Sanchez	Father	Second-degree murder	16 years suspended, 2 years treatment, 6 years probation	3 (4 with jail time)	Violation of probation within 9 months

subsequently convicted of two counts of second-degree murder and sentenced to life in prison.

Parricide Offenders Not Released

Of the six parricide offenders who had not been released, three fit the profile of the dangerously antisocial parricide offender, and one was classified as severely mentally ill. Drugs and anger played critical roles in the remaining two cases. As depicted in Table 15-2, the adjustment of four of these offenders in prison was poor, based on their disciplinary records. One of these offenders killed an inmate in prison. The adjustment of one of the two remaining offenders characterized as dangerously antisocial appeared excellent; that of the other was fair to good.

Recidivism Regarding Murder

As noted above, follow-up data indicated that two of the 11 parricide offenders killed again. These findings are surprising in two regards. First, the literature, although limited, suggests that juvenile homicide offenders rarely kill again. Two follow-up studies on juvenile homicide offenders in the United States and another in the Netherlands found that few released offenders killed again.[32] Second, it is often reported in the literature on APOs that they are prosocial youth who represent little threat to society.[33] One of these, Peter Jones, was considered at the time of his trial to be "a good risk" offender. As the clinical chapter illustrated, although treatment was court ordered, Peter did not get it and did not resolve the issues he had with his mother. Years later, as we have seen, he killed two people, ostensibly for the same reason he killed his father—he felt it was his obligation to protect his mother. The second homicidal event was a clear case of "history repeating itself."

The second repeat killer, unlike Peter Jones, was a high-risk offender. James Holt likely killed his parents in a psychotic state. Although ordered to receive treatment, he received none in prison. As chronicled in his case study, his years in prison intensified his rage and hatred. In his mind, James Holt became what the system designated him as—"a murderer."

Growth in Maturity

For the most part, despite the passage of time, little change was observable in the maturity level of the parricide offenders. Despite their chronological age, most seemed developmentally "very young." As discussed in Chapter 8 with respect to Interpersonal Level of Maturity Theory, individuals advance in maturity as they resolve interpersonal problems in their lives. If conditions for growth are unfavorable, some individuals get stuck and do not advance to higher levels. Table 15-3 briefly recaps the salient dimensions of low- and high-maturity subjects.

In general, high-maturity individuals are better risk offenders than lower maturity offenders. However, high-maturity offenders who have adopted a neurotic pattern of coping with long-standing pain, anger, and anxiety from childhood might continue to behave in self-defeating ways if these underlying issues are not addressed in treatment.[34] Marcus Sanchez (Chapter 1), for example, failed to tell his probation officer

Table 15-2 Follow-up on adolescent parricide offenders not released

Type	Offender	Victim	Convicted	Sentenced	Served (Time From Crime To Follow-Up)	Prison Adjustment
Severely mentally ill	Boy, 16, James Holt	Father and mother	First-degree murder, 2 counts	Life	21 years	Poor; killed inmate
Dangerously antisocial	Boy, 20, Daniel Culbreath	Father and mother	First-degree murder, 2 counts	Life	7 years	Fair to good
Dangerously antisocial	Boy, 17, Brandon Hillsboro	Father, mother, brother	First-degree murder, 1 count	Life	9 years	Excellent
Dangerously antisocial	Girl, 13, Cassie Sparkman	Stepmother	Second-degree murder	18 years	7 years	Poor
Other—drugs/anger/ abuse reactive	Boy, 16, Karl Roberts	Father and his fiancée	Attempted first-degree murder and first-degree murder	Life	12 years	Poor
Other—drugs/anger/ over-indulged	Boy, 18, Ben Simpson	Father and mother	Second-degree murder and attempted second-degree murder	45 years	7 years	Poor

Table 15-3 Characteristics of low- and high-maturity individuals

Low-Maturity Individuals (I-level 3)	High-Maturity Individuals (I-Levels 4 and 5)
• Do not see themselves as accountable for their behavior	• See themselves as accountable for their behavior
• Are concerned with figuring out who has the power in the situation	• Have an internalized value system that guides their behavior
• Look for formulas to get what they want	• Recognize that they have choices
• Do not feel badly when they do wrong; feel badly when they get caught and incur negative consequences	• Are capable of feeling genuine remorse when they do wrong
• No real insight into their own behavior (typical of young children)	• Are aware of feelings, needs, and motives in themselves
• Relate to others more in terms of stereotypes and do not really understand people	• Can empathize with others to varying degrees

he was leaving the state to see his pregnant girlfriend, an action he could have taken without penalty if he had asked for permission, as he had done several times previously. When I talked with Marcus after he was re-confined for this technical violation, however, he recognized the stupidity of his behavior. He had become more reflective on his life and accepted responsibility for violating the conditions of probation and the consequences that followed. He seemed committed to making the best of his life while incarcerated and reportedly was not using drugs or alcohol. He was involved in a committed relationship with a young woman he had known prior to his arrest and was excited about being a father to their baby girl, who was then about 1.5 years old. By all accounts, Marcus's girlfriend was a stable and responsible person and a devoted mother. Although I am often skeptical of jailhouse conversions, Marcus's religious conversion seemed to help him.

Among lower maturity individuals, some offenders are better risks than others assuming of course that structure is provided to them and that their treatment needs are addressed. Those who conform to whomever they think has power because they seek approval from others and want to be liked ("passive conformists") are better risk offenders from a therapeutic standpoint than those who conform to delinquent peers ("cultural conformists"). Both of these low-maturity subtypes pose less risk than offenders who are strictly out for themselves and counteractive to power ("antisocial manipulators"). The third low-maturity subtype is adept at conning and intimidating. When these techniques fail, he might resort to attacking others if the conditions are favorable.[35]

As depicted in Table 15-4, nine of the 11 offenders seemed "frozen in time." They either did not advance in personality growth or maturity or continued to behave in self-defeating ways. Interestingly, James Holt observed over the course of his 20 years in prison (see Chapter 11) that APOs suffered from "arrested development" as a result of being imprisoned (see Box 15-1). After six years in prison, Cassie Sparkman (Chapter 1), for example, did not see any way that the killing of her stepmother could have been prevented. She felt that it was "destined to happen" and believed that there was "a

Table 15-4 Adjustment and maturity of adolescent parricide offenders

Type	Offender	Maturity/Subtype	Victim	Prison Adjustment	Release Experience	Maturity Growth
Severely abused	Girl, 17, Patty Smith	Low, passive conformist	Father	Uneven, fair to good	Good	No
Severely abused	Boy, 16, Will Garrison	Low, passive conformist	Father	Excellent	Poor, convicted of burglary	No
Dangerously antisocial	Boy, 20, Daniel Culbreath	Low, passive conformist	Father and mother	Fair to good	Not released	Yes
Other—drugs/anger/over-indulged	Boy, 18, Ben Simpson	Low, passive conformist	Father and mother	Poor	Not released	No
Dangerously antisocial	Girl, 13, Cassie Sparkman	Low, counteractive to power	Stepmother	Poor	Not released	No
Dangerously antisocial	Boy, 17, Brandon Hillsboro	Low, counteractive to power	Father, mother, brother	Excellent	Not released	Yes
Other—drugs/anger/reactive to abuse	Boy, 16, Karl Roberts	Low, counteractive to power	Father and his fiancée	Poor	Not released	No
Severely abused	Boy, 17, Peter Jones	High, neurotic	Father	Excellent (confined re: robberies)	Fair initially; rearrested a few times, 2 murder convictions	No
Severely abused	Boy, 17, Evan Sutton	High, neurotic	Father	Poor	Fair initially; arrested on drug charges	Yes, with caveat*
Severely mentally ill (abuse history)	Boy, 17, Marcus Sanchez	High, neurotic	Father	Uneven, fair to good	Fair initially; parole violation	Yes, with caveat*
Severely mentally ill	Boy, 16, James Holt	High, neurotic	Father and mother	Poor; killed inmate in prison	Not released	Yes, with caveat*

*Growth in perceptions, but behavior still reflected an Na pattern.

time for everything." She confided that she probably should have killed the uncle who sexually abused her and "would have felt better" being in prison.

Interestingly, two of the parricide offenders who seemed to advance developmentally were both low-maturity youths who fit in the dangerously antisocial category at the time when they committed the crime. Daniel Culbreath's insights into the reasons for his homicidal behavior and his recognition of the hurt he caused are discussed in his case study (Chapter 12). Significant changes were also apparent when I spoke with Brandon Hillsboro (Chapter 2) nearly 10 years after the triple family killings.[36]

The boy I experienced years prior as angry, defiant, and cocky had softened. Brandon Hillsboro no longer took pride in his ability to intimidate others. The tattoos that he took pleasure in showing me during my initial evaluation had become a source of discomfort for him. These included an Aryan man on his right shoulder, a Swastika on the right side of his neck, and a white power design that spanned his chest. Brandon also had the word "Berzerker" prominently displayed on his forehead; he told me in our initial meeting that this was an old Viking term that meant that men would "get drunk, harder, become frenzied." Brandon related during our follow-up interview that he wanted to have the two most visible tattoos removed (the Swastika and "Berzerker") and was pursuing options within the prison system to do so. He explained that the tattoos fit with the person he was at age 17 and reflected his poor self-esteem, his "impulsiveness," and his "need to belong." He had not completely renounced Hitler, however, at the time of the follow-up interview. Brandon still saw Hitler as a great orator and as a charismatic leader. However, he noted that Hitler had the wrong ideas.

Years later, Brandon's perceptions seemed more characteristic of a person perceiving at I-level 4 than at I-Level 3. Brandon related that he had matured over the years. He believed that he had overcome problems in the past, had developed a work ethic, and was determined to better himself. He recognized that when he was younger, he was not mature enough to look beyond himself for solutions. He got into trouble as "a way to get attention."

Brandon appeared to feel badly when he recalled the killings. He indicated that he had a few beers and got into an argument, and "events spiraled out of control." If he could talk to his parents, he would tell his mother, "I wish it hadn't happened." He would tell his father, "I wish we had been closer." Brandon felt the worst about the killing of his younger brother, Eddie. His face became flushed as he said his younger brother "got caught up in the middle of it."

Brandon believed the murders could have been prevented because there were "other solutions." He felt that if he had been nicer to other people, they would have helped him. There were people willing to take him in. He explained that he could have gone his way, and his parents could have gone theirs. He commented, "I didn't have the life skills to handle it."

Brandon related that he acted out initially when he was confined in his first prison. He recognized at the second prison that the officers treated him with respect, and he decided to behave accordingly. Since my follow-up visit more than seven years ago, Brandon has sent me occasional letters. It appears from his letters that he has stayed out of trouble and has remained positive. He has been in contact with several family members, including his brother Derek. He has been watching court cases involving juvenile offenders with keen interest, hoping that one day his sentence will be commuted from life without parole to time served, and he will have a second chance.

Box 15-1 An Inmate's Observations of Adolescent Parricide Offenders

James Holt (Chapter 11) said that during his 20 years of being confined, he had met about 12 kids who admitted they killed their parents. Although he acknowledged that some were "just greedy and selfish sociopaths," most were "abused in some manner." James noted that "they tended to be a lot different" than other inmates. James found that almost all of them were of average intelligence, "not your traditional animal abusers," polite, hard working, and motivated to do things. He contrasted them with the average inmate who "just wants to get high. He just wants to gamble, have sex, lie in his bunk." In James's opinion, most parricide offenders were abused, and "their situation drove them to do that" rather than their being "criminally motivated." He noted that although juvenile parricide offenders technically are "murderers," they are not "criminals"; they almost always have no prior offense history.

"They don't know about bank robberies. They don't know about selling drugs. They don't really have street smarts. The ones I've met are almost always your middle-class suburban, the last people you would have expected to be in prison. And these parricides, all of them, adjust very poorly to prison. All of the ones I've met, they've all had problems—most of them, because of their looks and their age, of course. And some of them, they have, there's another phenomenon that has happened to all of us, and that is arrested development. I mean, none of us have matured, mentally and emotionally—we are still little kids. Even though I'm 37, I still think and act like a teenager, like adolescence, like I'm stuck in that kind of mindset. And all of them, you know, I communicate with them when I am able to. And the ones that I've met within prison say the same thing—they say, "I feel like a teenager, and I'm never going to grow up." And if they don't get out of prison, of course, they can't. If they get out of prison, who knows?"

James indicated that he had made it a point to help these juveniles because they have "potential." He noted that some of them received long sentences, but most of them were eventually released. In James's experience, all of the parricide offenders regretted killing their parents. He maintained that "even when the parents seemed to deserve it, they regretted it. It made them feel bad, so they can be rehabilitated."

The lack of developmental growth applied to both low- and high-maturity offenders. What went wrong? Several factors appear to be involved. Lack of treatment, lack of social support, and lack of aftercare services were primary reasons that even good risk offenders failed.

EVAN SUTTON—WHEN CORE ISSUES REMAIN UNADDRESSED

Evan Sutton, whose case was briefly mentioned in Chapter 6, is an excellent example of a promising youth who failed when released because the underlying issues that led to his violent behavior were not addressed in prison. Evan was the oldest of three children born to immigrant parents. His father was a successful surgeon from South America, and his mother was a nurse from the British Isles.

Evan was "the perfect son" in many respects. At the time when he killed his father,[37] Evan was a senior in high school studying for his final exams and was within days of graduation. His record of achievement was impressive: he was a straight-A student with a full scholarship to the premier state university, served as president of the student council, played football, lifted weights, and participated in his high school mock trial events. In addition, he worked about 35 hours per week at two jobs and spent weekends training with the National Guard. Although he had tried alcohol and marijuana, he did not care to use either substance.

Evan's recollections of his home life prior to the homicide, corroborated by his mother, provided convincing evidence that Evan had been physically and emotionally neglected by both parents. He was a victim of emotional incest, the process wherein a parent (in this case the father) treats the child more as a surrogate spouse than as a child. Evan was also physically, verbally, and psychologically abused by his father. In addition to being a victim himself, he was a witness to verbally and physically abusive acts committed by his father against his mother, and to some extent against his brother. Corroborative data regarding Dr. Sutton's verbally abusive behavior toward Evan and toward women in general, plus his lack of parental involvement with his sons, was provided by several staff who worked with Dr. Sutton at the hospital.

Evan's mother described Dr. Sutton as an "explosive" man and as "a perfectionist" who blamed everyone else for his problems. At the time of his death, they had been divorced for about four years. Her answers confirmed that she had been physically assaulted by Dr. Sutton and verbally and psychologically abused by him throughout their marriage. Evan's mother indicated that she and Evan were "the scapegoats" in the Sutton family and that they sustained more abuse than the two younger children. She described the verbal and psychological abuse inflicted by Dr. Sutton as an "everyday" occurrence for her and Evan. She related an incident when Dr. Sutton came to her house and attempted to strangle her. Had Evan not intervened by shooting a gun in the air, she believed Dr. Sutton would have killed her. Evan's mother indicated that she had been estranged from Evan and her other son for more than three years prior to the homicide, largely as a result of the boys' negative attitudes toward her, which were inculcated by their father.

When asked what the worst thing he feared his father might do was, Evan did not consider the possible escalation of the repeated physical violence to which he had been subjected for years. Instead, he said that he feared most that his father would "stop loving me and leave us."

Evan experienced the *mental abuse* as worse than the physical abuse because of the feelings he had toward his father. *During my clinical assessment, Evan said on at least four occasions that he loved his father.* "I loved my dad and I believe he was a good man. He was a good doctor and I know he didn't do any of these things intentionally … he was doing it and trying to motivate me, but he used to compare me to lots of people in an uncomfortable light. I could never be good enough …." Evan was adamant that "it was impossible to live up to his standards." Throughout his father's life and even after his death, Evan was consumed with the desire to make something of himself so that his father would be proud of him.

Evan recognized that he had a poor self-concept. He described himself as shy. Despite being a nice-looking young man, he felt ugly, unattractive, and unlovable. It bothered him that he had never had a girlfriend. He related feeling very badly a few weeks before the homicide when a girl he took to the high school prom went off with another boy at the event. While in jail awaiting trial, a 33-year-old woman took an excessive interest in him. Despite the age difference, Evan saw her as a girlfriend. He explained, "She loves *me. Me.* I never really felt loved before, by my mom, by my dad. The only one I really feel love from was my brother and sister; we were so close, there was no choice."

Prior to the shooting, Evan had been in legal trouble only one time. He got into an argument with his mother's new husband. During the altercation, he hit his stepfather and his mother. He was arrested, processed in juvenile court, and sentenced to probation and community service. When I met with her, Evan's mother recognized that Evan had been in a great deal of pain for many years and needed "deep therapy."

Evan pled guilty to second-degree murder. Several mental health professionals, including myself, testified at the sentencing hearing that this youth had a history of major depression and remained clinically depressed. Some experts thought he should be diagnosed as having bipolar disorder, believing that Evan had had at least one manic episode, as well as a history of depression.[38] Members of Dr. Sutton's family and several people from the community spoke on the boy's behalf. The judge sentenced Evan to 10 years in prison.

I conducted a follow-up interview five years after the sentencing hearing. At the time of our first follow-up meeting, Evan was 24 years old and on parole. I asked him about his experiences in prison and on parole. I met with Evan for a second time about 18 months later after learning that he had been rearrested and was in jail.

Evan's Experiences in Prison

Evan spent two years in jail prior to his conviction. He was initially sent to one prison for classification. During the next four years, Evan served time in four other prisons. Evan characterized his prison time as "tough." He explained that, unlike other inmates who grew up expecting to go to prison, he was "not a thug' and did not fit in. Evan related that when an inmate first comes into the prison system, the choices that he makes are very important and will follow him through his incarceration.

Evan spent 18 months at the second facility. He spent nine months of this time in "lockdown." At this facility, he befriended a male inmate, who was a drag queen, named Reena. Evan referred to Reena as "she" and confided that he had his first sexual experience with her. Reena was serving a long sentence for murder. At Reena's invitation, Evan became "her man" and fought to protect her. Evan said that as a result of this "choice," he was branded "a fag," a label that followed him.

Evan was transferred to a third facility, where he spent seven months. During this time, he learned computer repair and took some college courses. He was placed in an "old man" pod and felt vulnerable, given his youth. He got into trouble there for refusing to identify an inmate who was involved in questionable activity. He explained that being "a snitch" is condemned and not tolerated by inmates. He was put in lockdown for two months and transferred to the state maximum security prison.

Evan spent 14 months in lockdown in this fourth facility. He spent his time reading and watching TV in his cell.[39] He was let out for 15 minutes to shower each day. Despite regulations, inmates did not go out to the recreation area every day. As a result, Evan gained about 50 pounds.

Evan was sent to a fifth prison from which he was paroled. There he was placed in a gang unit, a hard place for him because he had never been a gang member. Evan was happy in this prison because Reena was subsequently transferred there. When prison authorities decided to transfer Evan to a lower security unit, he refused to go because he did not want to leave Reena. Evan was subsequently injured in a fight with guards, sent to the hospital, and placed in lockup for six weeks. He said that when he would visit with Reena on the prison grounds, the inmates would throw rocks at them. Evan asked the prison psychologist to help by transferring them to the same unit. The transfer did not occur, and the harassment by the inmates continued.

Evan related that violence was an everyday occurrence in prison. He had been beaten up many times. Reportedly, he was stabbed once, although the wound was superficial. Evan did not request protective custody because that is negatively viewed in prison and would have "marked" him. He was subjected to repeated indignities because he was publicly identified as a "homo." Inmates would show him their genitals, attempt to grab him, and touch him.

Evan said that, although there was a treatment plan, he was not sent to the facility agreed upon at his sentencing hearing. He did participate in weekly therapy when he was not in lockdown. In one prison, Evan was in a therapeutic community where he had group therapy, anger management, and alcohol and substance abuse counseling. When he was in lockdown in the maximum-security prison, he read many self-help books. Evan took psychotropic medication for a couple of years in prison, but he stopped taking it because he did not feel that he needed it.

While in prison, Evan took whatever courses were offered, including computer repair courses, college math classes, and a few businesses courses. He worked at various jobs in the kitchen and the library and was a teacher's aide. Evan did not see these jobs as giving him any skills. He felt that prison did little more than "warehouse people."

Evan's mother visited him a couple of times while he was in prison. He occasionally spoke on the phone to his brother and one cousin, and to two women who kept in touch with him. After serving about four years in prison, Evan was released on parole to serve his remaining two years. He was ordered to spend the first eight months on intensified supervised parole (ISP), under which conditions were more stringent. He was required to report to his parole officer twice weekly and to attend individual therapy, anger management, and substance abuse group sessions weekly. It was expected that after eight months on ISP, he would be required to report less.

Evan's First Few Months on Parole

Evan had served four of eight months on ISP and was age 24 when I conducted my first follow-up interview with him. He said that he had not been on psychotropic medication for the past three years and felt fine without it. Evan did not see himself as suffering from depression or bipolar disorder. He maintained that when he was sad, it was appropriate, and that he did not have manic-like episodes. He saw himself as more in control of his emotions than in the past. He drank socially but did not use drugs.

Evan had his own apartment and was working full time as a roofer. He was taking 21 credits in community college, getting A's, and working for an associate degree in welding. He wanted to be a plastic surgeon but did not know whether he would be allowed to be a doctor, given his criminal history.

Evan had frequent contact with his younger brother, who helped him get settled when he was paroled. Evan talked to his mother weekly. He had some ambivalent feelings toward her because he felt she had abused him. Although he had strong positive feelings toward his younger sister, he had little contact with her, reportedly as a result of geographical distance and his mother's over-protectiveness.

Evan stated that he had had two girlfriends since his release. One hurt him badly by leading him on and then becoming sexual with another man in his presence. The incident reminded him of his high school prom, when his date went off with another boy. Evan recognized the similarities between the two incidents.

Evan related he allowed a homeless girl to stay with him. He intimated that the two of them had had a sexual relationship. He asked her to leave because he felt that she was taking advantage of him. It was hard for him to take this action, but he believed he needed to do so.

Evan's Personality Development and Reflections at First Follow-Up

In the five years since I had seen Evan, he had grown in terms of personality development and was perceiving at or close to I-level 5. He was able to view issues from different perspectives and to truly empathize with others. He mentioned his father several times and was deeply remorseful.

Evan related that he loved his dad and missed him. He said several times that his father's death was his fault. "Every day I live with it." Although he saw his father as very abusive and as responsible for the low self-esteem that he had as a youth, Evan believed his father did not want to hurt him. Evan indicated that his father wanted him to be a success but did not know how to parent and communicate effectively.

Evan said that he tried so hard growing up. He told me that all he did in high school—his grades, school activities, jobs, National Guard—did not seem to matter after he committed the crime. Evan hated that he might be judged for the rest of his life on the basis of his actions during "20 to 30 seconds" of his life. He felt thrown away and believed that he should have received more treatment in the juvenile justice system. He maintained that "people can change." He wanted to help someone and for his life to have a purpose.

Evan stated that "it was a great disservice to send me to prison." At the same time, he recognized some positive aspects of prison and named them. For example, Evan could identify with more people. He had had to develop parts of his personality that he would otherwise not have developed. He had had to dig deep inside and find the strength to get through this experience.

Ironically, Evan noted that the path he had traveled led to the results his father wanted. He maintained that he now had "the fiber and inner fortitude" and felt good about himself. He was proud that he survived in prison "against all odds" and that prison did not change him (meaning in a negative way). He explained that he did not get into protective custody, become a "snitch" or "a catcher" (the receiver in a homosexual relationship), lose his morals, get tattoos, or join a gang. He saw his crime as an "abomination." He was committed to making the best out of prison through "my choices and actions." He saw himself as a good communicator, an "outside-of-the-box thinker," and "the author of my destiny."

Evan spoke very openly during our meeting. Seven years after the shooting, Evan still harbored a great deal of pain from the past. I noted that his way of relating to the past (Neurotic Acting-Out [Na] behavioral subtype) might still be operating. He wanted so much to be successful and in control. Although he maintained a strong front, he felt a great deal of distress regarding his life, Reena, and his relationship to women and his family. Evan assured me that he would successfully complete parole, as he was determined to do so.

Dr. Heide's Second Follow-Up Visit after Evan's Arrest

Three months after my follow-up visit, Evan was arrested on drug-related charges. At that point, he had been on parole less than eight months. When I visited him in jail about 10 months after his arrest, Evan explained the circumstances behind his arrest. His arrest was the result of his romantic involvement with "a girl" named Marsha.

Evan described Marsha as a beautiful woman who worked as a stripper. He was flattered and surprised when she flirted with him. Evan quickly developed strong feelings for her and her 6-year-old son. Evan was pleased when the boy started to call him Dad, and he loved the child as a son. When Marsha and her son were kicked out of their apartment, Evan invited them to live with him "temporarily." Reportedly, he initially was unaware that Marsha had criminal convictions for drug-related offenses, used cocaine, and sold drugs. When he discussed these activities with her, Marsha told Evan to stay out of her business. Evan said that he told her she needed to stop using drugs and maintained that "she at least cut down a lot." When asked, Evan acknowledged that he recognized the risk of living with a felon who was involved in criminal activity. He knew that Marsha was not going to change and that the only way "to really avoid the situation was to leave her," but he did not want to break up with her. He related that he loved her and even bought her a ring. Evan said that some of the happiest moments of his life were with Marsha because he "just felt loved."

Evan put himself at additional risk prior to his arrest by buying a firearm to protect Marsha.[40] Evan explained that before Marsha moved in, he had allowed Henry, a parolee whom he knew from prison, to stay with him. When Evan learned that Henry "was on the run," sold methamphetamine, and was a heavy user, Evan wanted him out. Evan was relieved when Henry left his apartment because he had observed at times that Henry was delusional, paranoid, and dangerous because of his drug use. He was afraid, based on remarks made by others, that Henry might come over to steal drugs from Marsha, so he purchased a gun illegally.

One evening, parole agents and police officers barged into Evan's apartment, without a search warrant, given Evan's parole status. They observed drugs in plain view and arrested both Marsha and Evan. Marsha reportedly had drugs in her pocket. Although Evan maintained that he had no involvement in drug selling, he had a list of client names and dollar amounts in his pocket. He was subsequently charged and faced 19.5 years if convicted.

Evan related that jail time gets easier when one has done a lot of time. He said that after seven years of being locked up, jail was "almost like a second home." He was starting to wonder whether he had become institutionalized. Evan stated that, compared to the outside, being in jail seemed easy. He opined, "And that's not good. I mean, if it becomes easy for people to do time, then it becomes a lot easier for them to come back, you know?" Evan laughed as he said, "I can truthfully tell you, I am more of a criminal now, than when I first went in." He explained that "your moral compass" changes. "The first thing that's brainwashed into a person … never tell nobody, I mean, never, you know. And, now, that's just one of the little things, and there's plenty of other things."

Evan said that people in jail had made reference to his relationship with Reena. Evan kept in touch with Reena until he became involved with Marsha. Evan maintained that he would not get in another relationship like the one he had with Reena if he were returned to prison. He related that in the past he had been vulnerable and lonely, and he admitted he "just needed somebody." In his words, "I went to prison a virgin …. I really just wanted somebody to care about me." Evan stated that if he gets out this time, he wants to focus on himself.

Evan felt really badly about his arrest because he let his brother down and also let himself down. Although he had been laid off from his job, he was still going to college full time and had a future ahead of him at the time of his arrest on drug charges. Evan recognized that he "should've just set better boundaries" and not been with Marsha.

In the year since I had last seen Evan, his contact with his mother had lessened, and he harbored ambivalent feelings toward her. He admitted that he missed his father a great deal. Evan said, "It was always in my mind, you know, the person that would've helped me the most is gone, you know?" Evan had hoped that he would have gotten out of prison and done very well. He recognized that his story "seems just as common as all the other people that are charged with crimes and fail."

Case Commentary

Evan was a young man with great potential. Throughout our three meetings, Evan's pain was apparent. He never felt loved by either parent. He told me when I first met him that he had been abandoned by his mother and was a disappointment to his father. His tremendous need to be loved and validated led him into relationships that were not good for him. While in jail awaiting trial, Evan became emotionally involved with a woman 15 years older than him. In prison, he entered into his first sexual relationship with a drag queen who sought his protection. After being paroled, he allowed a convicted felon to live with him and deal drugs out of his apartment because she was "beautiful" and "loved" him. He had strong feelings toward these individuals and was hurt deeply by them.

Evan exercised poor judgment in these relationships because of his core belief that he was unlovable and the deep and abiding pain he had experienced since childhood. Evan confided that he had never felt "accepted fully." He felt like the "odd man out" in high school and in prison.

These cognitions, feelings, and ways of responding were not addressed in treatment, leaving him vulnerable to people who professed loving feelings toward him. Evan had trouble setting boundaries with others who used him for their own purposes because he did not have a strong sense of himself. His difficulty maintaining boundaries was not addressed when he was on ISP, and during that period, the monitoring of his living arrangements was lax. The inadequate aftercare created the conditions that ultimately led to Evan's violation of probation and re-arrest.

WILL GARRISON—THE NEED FOR AFTERCARE

Will seemed like a young man who could successfully transition back to society with social support and a solid aftercare plan. As discussed in Chapter 7, the governor commuted Will's 20-year sentence by 11 years. At that time, he had served more than three years in prison for killing his father and had done well. Unlike many other APOs, he incurred no disciplinary infractions and was considered a model inmate.

Will told me during my evaluation related to his clemency application that he was "tried" by the inmates when he first came to prison. Despite his youth and lack of criminal sophistication, he was able to hold his own in prison and did not encounter difficulties he could not resolve. He was not physically assaulted. Although many sexual remarks were made to him, he was not raped because older inmates advised him on how to avoid such situations. Will "got along" with the correctional officers. He was housed in the Honor Dorm for the two years preceding his clemency application.

While in prison, Will obtained his GED and worked toward getting his first license in waste water management. He learned to play the guitar and to work on computers.

Will's Release from Prison and Return to Prison

Per the governor's executive order, Will was sent to a work release center (WRC) in Newcity, a major city about 90 miles from his home town. The order stipulated that Will was to undergo counseling, including family counseling, if he eventually planned to live with his family. Counseling was to continue until such time as the clemency board determined, upon the recommendation of a licensed mental health professional, that Will was substantially rehabilitated, or upon termination of his probation, whichever occurred earlier. According to the executive order, the counseling was to be approved and monitored by the clemency board on a quarterly basis. The data available to me years later strongly indicated that the WRC staff did not perform as directed.

I conducted a follow-up interview nearly 12 years after Will was sent to the WRC. He was 33 years old and back in prison. I learned then that Will had stayed at the WRC for 18 months before being released back into the community. While there, Will worked at a construction job and did very well, explaining that "there was people watching" him and he was not going to do anything wrong.

For five or six months Will had weekly 45-minute sessions with a therapist he liked at the WRC. When this therapist left, the replacing therapist discontinued therapy. No provisions were made for family therapy. After his release from the WRC, Will went back to his home town for a few weeks. He resumed dating his old girlfriend, Carol, and "hanging out" with his old friend Bobby. Within 13 months, he was rearrested for burglarizing a store.

Will's Reflections on What Went Wrong

Will maintained that he wanted "to do right" when he got out of prison. It was not long, however, before he was breaking probation rules because he was drinking and found it hard to withstand pressure from his old friend, Bobby.

They told me I couldn't drink or nothing. Well, the first, I think I got out on a Tuesday or somethin', and that Friday night, he [Bobby] come and got me. Well, he stopped at the circle K. He said, "Let's go ahead and get some beer." I said, "No, I don't," you know, "I'm on probation." Well, anyway, I ended up—we did get it. He went in. I told him to go in where nobody wouldn't see me. So that started—I started drinking real heavy all during that time. Well, I was in Hometown about three weeks and then we [Will and Carol] found an apartment in Newcity over by the stadium, and we moved there. And I continued to work for my job, but, you know, I just couldn't get into nothin'. I really didn't want to be there, you know. I would show up, and I might [have] just decided [that] I want to leave, and leave. And I was drinking real bad. We [Will and Carol] was visiting the clubs and stuff, so I ended up in downtown Newcity. We got in a wreck. I was drinking; I was drunk that night. And it totaled the car. And I got seven broken ribs, and she got messed up—she had a broken pelvis.

Will was not charged with DUI.[41] Following the accident, he went back to Hometown. Despite my recommendations, he initially went back to live with his mother and stepfather in the home where the killing occurred. Will had mixed feelings about his stepfather. He stated that his stepdad would "do anything" for him and was generous in helping him. At the same time, he recognized that his stepfather was "a heavy drinker" and could be mean at times. Will resented that his stepfather still treated him like a kid. As a result of difficulties with his stepfather, Will moved out and stayed at various locations, including his grandparents' house and Bobby's house. Sometimes he slept in his car.

Will held about five jobs while in Hometown. These jobs included pest control spraying, driving a big tractor, and laying pipes. He was a good worker. Will admitted that he walked off the job because he wanted to be with Carol and was "lazy." He found it hard to stay focused because he was not interested in working. Will admitted that he could not hold a job because of his drinking. Although Will reportedly was "drunk most of the time," nobody seriously confronted him about it.

Will believed that rock music—particularly heavy metal—and TV, along with his heavy drinking, influenced him "to do wrong" when he was first released. He said he watched movies in which the actors did illegal things and he wanted to do those things. The music influenced him to be "rebellious" because that was what it was teaching. "You know, everything that you stand for—I'm against. I dressed in black, you know. I had my nose pierced. I had long hair. I'd dye it. You know, tattoos, and all that."

Will started "doing some illegal activities" with Bobby. On the night that Will was arrested, he had been drinking all day. He was not working at the time and was trying to pay the rent. Will pressured Carol into giving him the combination code to the store where she worked. He broke into the store and stole $2,000. He was sentenced to 11 years for the violation of probation and two years for the burglary.[42]

Carol was convicted of being an accomplice and sentenced to two years on probation. Will said that Carol wanted to get married despite his long sentence. He agreed, and they were married for several years. Their marriage was subsequently annulled because it was never consummated. Will expressed loving feelings toward Carol at the time of the follow-up, but he had no contact with her. Carol remarried and had children.

Will stated several times that he believed his probation officers (POs) were too lax and did not do their jobs. He related that he did not make any payments for eight months or report to the probation office. The PO would come by, but he "didn't do no follow-up."

It don't matter what you do; some people's gonna do wrong anyway. I feel that the pressure of, if somebody woulda been there to guide me .... It's a shame that I need that guidance, but, for some reason, I needed it. I needed some kind of structure, some kind of, to make sure that I was doin' the right thing. I don't know if that's from prison. Like I said, before I went to prison, I didn't have them kind of problems. Then I came, I don't know, I went to prison, and I come out. Now, all of a sudden, I can't keep a job. All of a sudden, I want to do wrong. All of a sudden, I wanna, I'm not doin, I'm not livin' as a regular civilian would .... I needed some kind of supervision or guidance. I needed somebody. Even Ma and them, they, I know, they didn't know a lot that was goin' on. They know I was drinkin' every time I was comin' over there. Somebody just needed to say, "Look, you're coming, you're heading back to prison. You're doin', you're doin' this, you're doin' that," you know. "You're on probation. You got 10 years probation. You ain't even done six months, and you're already doin' this." You know, but nobody never stepped up and said that.

Will contrasted being on probation with being back in prison. He explained that most of the inmates follow the rules in prison because it is "a structured environment" and "there's penalties you're going to pay, if you don't follow 'em." Will emphasized that probation needed to be more strict "at least in the beginning, and maybe longer" to keep probationers on track.

Especially a kid that is, come in and spent a, a large amount of time in the DOC [Department of Corrections]. 'Cause when you're in here, the young kid, we're not hangin' around people that was good people. We're hangin' around people ... all I heard was about the men in there, you know, the crimes they did. And that was sorta exciting to me as a kid. The stories I heard, you know. They didn't tell positive stories. It was about the drinkin', about the women, about the breakin' into stuff, or whatever, you know, always in trouble .... I just feel that they need a, they need some kind of structure, some kind of, somebody to just help them, an environment where they're being watched. I know they don't like to hear that, and I wouldn't like to hear it neither.

Will's Return to Prison on Violation of Probation and Burglary Charges

When Will was returned to prison, he was put in a nine-month drug and alcohol treatment program. He successfully completed the program. Although alcohol and drugs were available in prison, Will did not use them. He explained that it was not hard for him to refrain, " 'Cause if I get caught, I'm in trouble." When asked whether he could see a therapist in prison, Will said that he did not know.

Will learned how to work with sheet metal during his second prison term. However, he felt that the vocational programs were not advanced and did not prepare inmates to get jobs when released. He worked for three years receiving packages at the warehouse and was fortunate to get a paid job at the canteen.

Will said he felt that he was "saved" in prison five years prior to my follow-up meeting. Will was taking Bible correspondence courses and wanted to go to a Bible college when released. Will felt that the pastor would tell him if he "were to step out of bounds." He wanted to become a pastor or evangelist.

Will related that since his return to prison, he had talked to his mother at least twice per week. She and his stepfather visited him monthly. He had occasional visits from his maternal uncle. His maternal grandparents had died. He had had no contact from his father's family. Will has not had contact with Bobby or his other friends in years.

Consistent with his first time in prison, Will was never in trouble in prison during his second term. My check of prison records verified that he was a model inmate.[43] He explained, "I was always, I was able to abide by the rules in here. You know, I knew what I'm supposed to do. And I know that if I break them rules and get in trouble, it's gonna stop me from getting out when I'm supposed to get out."

During his two terms in prison, Will had never been assaulted physically or sexually. He attributed his success to the way he carried himself and the institutions to which he had been sent, which were less violent than others. Will tried to treat people with respect and not to do anything that "would aggravate somebody else."

Will confided that he had felt on edge as his release date drew closer. He said that he was not going back to live in Hometown. Will said that he might look up his old friends, including Bobby, but it would be "like a one-time thing."

Will recognized that he had a drinking problem. He was also aware that his father and his father's side of the family had problems with alcohol. When asked whether he would drink again, Will said he hoped not. He explained, "But I can't, I wouldn't say no, 'cause if I get in, I'm gonna try not to put myself in that situation. I don't want to drink."

Will's Reflections about Killing His Father at Follow-Up

When asked what he thought about the homicide, Will said, "I think that I've done a lot of time because of that one thing." He was not sure whether he regretted shooting his father because of the situation: "I might have been dead if I didn't do it that day, so I don't know." He did not know how the killing could have been prevented because he did not instigate the violence. "As far as the shooting, it would've been up to, it would've been a chance I took. Either I pull the trigger or I don't. Like I said, I don't know what the consequences would have been if I didn't."

Will told me that "the physical abuse was bad; the verbal abuse was bad. He was beatin' on me; he was beatin' on me that day." However, Will related that his father did not sexually assault him, as he had told me 12 years earlier.[44] He said someone told his stepfather when his clemency petition was pending that he had been sexually abused. Will decided to agree with the story in order to increase his chances of getting out of prison. He felt badly that he had lied about his aunt's having knowledge of the made-up sexual abuse. He wrote a letter apologizing to her and hoped that she would forgive him.

Will's Hopes for the Future

At the close of the follow-up interview, Will said he would like to get married and maybe have a child, but he wanted to make sure he was O.K. before he did. He explained, "I wanna make sure that I'm out there and I'm grounded. And I'm doing the right thing for a good amount of time. I don't want to jump into nothing." Will said that he would "raise 'em the Bible way. You know, just love 'em. And no verbal abuse, no physical abuse. You know, just give 'em guidance and instruction."

Will served nearly 10 years during his second time in prison.[45] Three years after I met with Will, I received an unexpected e-mail from him. He wrote that he had been released from prison two years and seven months ago. He said, "All in all everything has been going good for me. I am married and I have a daughter who is 10 months old, and we are currently expecting another child around July. I am enjoying a life as a free man after 16 years in prison." He attached a picture of his beautiful daughter. I learned later that he had become a pastor of a small Baptist church in his hometown and later served in a small city in a neighboring state.[46]

Case Commentary

Prior to Will's release from prison for killing his father, I was asked to make treatment recommendations to help Will deal with his past trauma and adjust successfully to society. The recommendations I made, including his placement in a structured environment, individual counseling, family counseling, quarterly reports to the clemency board, and certification by a licensed mental health professional that Will was rehabilitated prior to discontinuation of therapy, were all ordered by the governor. Unfortunately, despite the efforts of the governor, treatment directives were not followed and Will failed soon after he returned to the community.

In my experience, orders for treatment of parricide offenders are rarely followed. Mental health services in prisons in the United States are woefully inadequate to address the needs of the many inmates who need services. In times of fiscal austerity, treatment and other rehabilitative programs are among the first programs to be cut, because of the necessity of allocating limited funds to the maintenance of institutional security and control in prison.

When I evaluated Will for clemency, he was a good risk offender. As a level 3 passive conformist (Cfm), he was open to the influence of authority figures and capable of advancing if intensive treatment were provided. When I met with him 12 years later, Will seemed very much like the 20-year-old adult I initially evaluated and was functioning at the same level of personality development. As his comments above indicate, Will recognized that he responded well when the structure was clearly defined and he knew what was expected of him. As is characteristic of Cfm individuals, Will had a prosocial image of himself and sought others' approval. If meaningful counseling had been provided to Will while he was in the WRC, he might have come to see that he was vulnerable to behaving impulsively. He might have taken responsibility to ensure that he did not succumb to "temptations" to drink or walk off the job to be with his girlfriend. He might have realized, as I forewarned, that going back to live with his mother and stepfather in the same house where the shooting occurred would not be a good choice for him until he had resolved his past trauma.

Will is correct in suggesting that the POs failed him. If they had actively monitored him, the chances of his getting back into trouble would have been substantially reduced. Will needed a prosocial adult with power to confront him and to help him grow up. His mother was a passive and dependent person. His stepfather, despite his good intentions, was a heavy drinker who still saw Will as a boy rather than as a man who needed to mature.

Will's turning to the Bible appears to have given him the structure he needed. His marriage and his children have anchored him. I would characterize Will as a success based on the information available to me. His success is the result of his own efforts and his faith; the department of corrections can claim little credit for his positive transition to society.

CHAPTER SUMMARY

This chapter challenges the prevailing view that most APOs make a successful adjustment to society. Although the number of previously published studies following up APOs is small, the available literature shows mixed results, with some adolescents making good post-release adjustments and others failing to do so. My follow-up study of 11 APOs appears to be the largest one available to date. The data show that four of the five APOs released from prison failed at least initially and were returned to prison. Four of the six who had not been released from prison when I conducted follow-up interviews spent years being disciplined within the institution for reportedly challenging the institutional authorities.

After studying these people's experiences, I believe three conclusions can be drawn from the disappointing results of these 11 cases. First, prison is not the best environment for APOs. As many of these youths indicated, they were exposed to criminal influences previously unknown to them. They had to figure out a way to survive in a violent, predatory world. Some APOs learned to carry themselves in a way that kept predators away; others fought; and still others accommodated by engaging in homosexual behavior, doing drugs, and "bucking the system." Many became—or feared becoming—institutionalized.

Second, the APOs were rarely provided with treatment, even when it was explicitly ordered. Adult prisons do not have the mental health resources to respond to these youths' needs. As illustrated in the case of Evan Sutton, APOs need to resolve the long-term issues that led them to behave violently. They need in-depth therapy as discussed in the treatment chapter. Behavior modification programs, cognitive restructuring, and anger management courses, available in some prisons, are useful. However, they are rarely sufficient to address the treatment needs of boys and girls who have killed their parents.

Third, aftercare for APOs is critically important. Parricide offenders, perhaps more than other offenders, need help returning to the community. Issues that need to be addressed include the following: (1) whether they should return to their home community; (2) what they will tell others about their conviction offense; (3) what relationship they should have with their family; (4) what behavioral changes they need to make in order to reduce their vulnerability to re-offending; (5) what structural supports they need in order to increase their chances of succeeding; and (6) how they can get effective treatment.

Will Garrison's case illustrates how the failure to address these issues led "a good kid" to take the wrong path shortly after his release from prison. Will was on intensified probation. The PO in Will's case should have monitored him closely and put a program in place to enable him to transition back into society. The PO should have checked to make sure that Will was living independently, reporting consistently for work, continuing individual counseling, and participating in family counseling, given that Will was maintaining contact with his family. Will's alcohol and drug usage should have been monitored and discussed with him. Given his family history, he should have been ordered to attend Alcoholics Anonymous and encouraged to examine his drinking habits.

In closing, it is important to emphasize that many APOs are good risk offenders. When these offenders fail, it is almost always because they did not get the treatment and structural support they needed. The disregard of court orders to treat two parricide offenders, for example, resulted years later in their being arrested again for murder. Clearly there is a greater need for institutional accountability among correctional authorities while offenders are incarcerated and on supervision in the community.

16 Risk Assessment and Prevention

Fortunately, parricide is a rare occurrence in the United States and around the world. Given its low base rate, parricide is not possible to predict.[1] However, risk factors identified from the professional literature reporting on parricide cases in many countries can decrease the risk that parents will be killed by their offspring. As noted by psychologist and legal expert Charles Patrick Ewing, "As with most forms of interpersonal violence, the risk of parricide is greatest where the would-be perpetrator makes an explicit or implicit threat to kill."[2]

Research and clinical reports provide convincing evidence that different models are needed in order to reduce the incidence of parricide. As we have seen, the dynamics leading individuals to kill their parents are often propelled by severe childhood maltreatment, severe mental illness, or antisocial motives.[3] Although age is an important consideration in developing these models, it is not determinative because these dynamics can affect both juveniles and adults. In most cases, individuals who kill their parents in order to end severe abuse are children or adolescents, although young adults might fall into this category, particularly if they remain living in the parents' home. Parricide offenders who kill as a result of severe mental illness are usually adults. However, not all adults who kill their parents suffer from psychosis or other serious mental illness.[4] In addition, cases of psychotic children and adolescents killing parents have been reported in the literature. Although the data are not extensive, the literature indicates that offspring who kill parents to achieve a selfish instrumental end can be either juveniles or adults. The discussion on threat assessment focuses on reducing risk among these three types of parricide offenders.

Offspring who kill their parents to end abuse, as we have seen, rarely have extensive histories of criminal behavior or violence. As a result, the likelihood that they will present as at risk of committing homicide prior to the killing is remote. To date, two studies of adolescent parricide offenders conducted after the murders have found that these youths did not score high on standardized risk assessment instruments such as the Structured Assessment of Violence Risk in Youth (SAVRY), the Psychopathy Checklist: Youth Version(PCL:YV), and the Psychopathy Checklist: Revised(PCL-R).[5]

Heide noted that five factors put youths at higher risk of killing abusive parents or stepparents than when these factors are not present.[6] First, the youth is raised in a home in which parental chemical dependency or other severe family dysfunction is present. Dynamics in these homes generate extreme stress because children do not talk about problems, learn to dissociate from their feelings, and stop trusting adults to help them resolve their difficulties. Second, a pattern of family violence has been ongoing for years. Typically several types of abuse (physical, verbal, psychological, and sexual) and neglect (emotional, physical, and medical) are found in these homes. The abuse, referred to by attorney Mones as "poly-abuse," is best characterized as both "egregious and enduring."[7] When there is a non-abusive parent, this parent often does not protect the children. In many cases, the non-abusive parent, who is typically the mother, is also being abused and does not have the financial resources and emotional strength to extricate herself and her children from this situation. She might lack social support and knowledge of outside agencies to which she can turn for assistance. Despite her personal hardships and stressors, she still has responsibilities to her children. Parents who are themselves abused are not freed from the duty to protect their children from physical and emotional harm. Third, conditions in these homes go from bad to worse, and violence increases. Fourth, over time the youth becomes increasingly vulnerable to the unremitting turmoil in these homes. Fifth, a firearm (handgun, rifle, shotgun) is easily available.[8] Studies spanning more than three decades have shown that in more than 80% of cases in which juveniles killed fathers, the most common parricide victims, they selected guns as their weapons.[9] It is unlikely that had firearms been unavailable, the juveniles would have selected other weapons and had the physical strength and emotional detachment to kill their parents.

When these risk factors are present, certain actions are advisable. First and foremost, guns should be removed from the home.[10] Securing them in locked cabinets or drawers might not be adequate; youths often know where the keys are hidden and can gain access to the guns when motivated to do so. If there is a non-abusive parent, she or he must take action to protect the physical and psychological health of the children. Protecting the children might mean taking the children and leaving the home of the abuser. Leaving the children with the abuser, although often rationalized by the non-abusive spouse, is dangerous for the well-being of the children and constitutes child physical neglect.

Evan Sutton, whose story was highlighted in Chapter 6, described his home environment as dangerous prior to his shooting his father. He and his brother were living at their father's house while their mother stayed at another home with their younger sister. "It was a dangerous environment for this reason, you know, my dad being as strict as he was and abusive. Kind of a tyrant, you know that. There were guns everywhere. All ingredients make a horrible, a horrible outcome or a potential for a horrible outcome, you know. And then I was under a lot of stress too with school. You know, final exams, and stuff, would've totally been ... you know, it was totally a dangerous situation."

Getting therapy for the children is critically important because of the harmful effects that result from being a victim of or witness to prolonged family violence.[11] Youths should be asked directly whether they have had thoughts of killing the abusive parent. As noted by Evans and his colleagues, "Any clinician who is working with abused juveniles is advised to regularly assess for homicidal ideation or intent."[12] Kashani and his colleagues provided specific areas that should be examined in circumstances in which "family discord" is evident. These include the following: "1) the severity of the adolescent's anger/hostility toward the family member, 2) the youngster's degree of impulsiveness, 3) the adolescent's problem-solving abilities, particularly pertaining to conflict; 4) the youth's ability to cope with the family member's potentially provocative behavior, 5) the availability of a weapon, and 6) the specificity of the adolescent's plan."[13] Consistent with other mental health professionals, they recommended that if the youth appears to present a significant risk to an identifiable family member, the treating clinician needs to take appropriate action, including warning the intended victim.[14]

If the family intends to stay together, family therapy with the abusive parent must be undertaken in a safe setting. Substance abuse issues, if present, must be addressed by the parents. Any threats of harm by the abusive parent or by the children, whether to oneself or to others, should be taken seriously.[15] Legal authorities and social services agencies should be utilized if the non-abusive parent is unable to safeguard the children.

SEVERELY MENTALLY ILL PARRICIDE OFFENDER

Severely mentally ill individuals who kill their parents typically have a long-standing history of mental illness and often have an extensive history of psychiatric hospitalization. Green observed more than 30 years ago, in his study of 58 men hospitalized in England for killing their mothers, that "many of the matricides could have been averted by closer psychiatric observation and care."[16] As noted by forensic psychologist Gerald Cooke, in these cases, "the treating mental health professional can be attuned to general psychological deterioration, specific delusional or hallucinatory experiences related to the parents, increased levels of family conflict, and specific threats to parents."[17] Cooke noted further, as have other clinicians and researchers, that certain factors increase the risk that adult patients will kill their parents. These include being male, living with or in close proximity to the parents, being unemployed or financially dependent on their parents, and being unmarried/socially isolated.[18]

Canadian psychiatrist Federic Millaud and his colleagues identified the following as primary risk factors for parricide: psychiatric history (personal and family), history of violence (personal and family), and alcohol and drug use by persons who are psychotic or who present a vulnerability to psychosis.[19] These investigators also noted cessation of psychotropic medication, attempts to get psychiatric help before the assaults, and death in the subject's social and/or familial circle as increasing the risk for parricide.[20] Other researchers have noted essentially the same factors.[21] Following their review of the literature on adult parricide, French clinicians Cornic and Olie advised psychiatrists to be on the alert for these warnings signs: "persecutive delusions, history of a long lasting illness with history of violence during acute states, threats against family and friends, suicidal thoughts, failures of help requests and attempt to escape."[22] A Korean team of researchers identified Capgras syndrome, a delusional disorder whereby patients believe significant others (in this case, parents) have been replaced by doubles or imposters, as a risk factor more common among schizophrenic patients who kill parents than among those who kill strangers.[23]

According to Dr. Jeffrey Metzner, former chair of the American Psychiatric Association Council on Psychiatry and Law, if schizophrenic patients refuse to take their medication and express hostility toward their parents, treating psychiatrists should perform risk assessments on them and possibly involve their parents.[24] When dangerous warning signals are present, patients should be hospitalized. Researchers have noted that psychotic parricide offenders often have expressed feeling emotionally blocked, stifled, and frustrated by their parents and experienced hatred toward them prior to the killings.[25]

University of Pittsburg Professor Christina Newhill outlined an intervention for families at high risk for parricide. She proposed that in addition to psychotropic management for the patient, high-risk families should participate in a psychoeducation program with a family therapist.[26] This approach would be designed to reduce "the negative intensity of the patient's environment," to address directly "the nature and basis for the presence of lethality," and to change the environment as needed.[27] For example, the intervention would reduce contact with parents or other family members whose "expressed emotion" toward the patient is critical, hostile, or emotionally over-involved.

DANGEROUSLY ANTISOCIAL PARRICIDE OFFENDER

As observed by Ewing, the "presence of psychopathy, sociopathy, conduct disorder, or antisocial personality may also be risk factors, but are certainly in no way pathognomonic" (characteristic) of parricide.[28] Many juveniles and adults might meet the diagnostic criteria for conduct disorder (CD) and antisocial personality disorder (APD), respectively,[29] but of these, very few would seriously consider killing their parents. Those diagnosed as high on psychopathy based on empirically validated instruments such as Hare's checklists for adults and youths[30] would likely be at higher risk than those diagnosed as having only CD or APD, because psychopathy instruments take into account dysfunctional affective features of personality in addition to impulsive and antisocial behavior.

Studies on parricide have not specifically identified risk factors that increase the risk that individuals with CD, APD, or psychopath diagnoses will kill parents. However, some can be culled from the existing literature. These include heavy drinking, use of drugs, drug addiction, previous threats of violence against the parents, and previous attacks on the parents.[31] Walsh and Krienert proposed that child–parent violence (CPV) might be part of a complex escalation process leading to parricide. Noting that CPV victims and offenders were significantly younger than parricide victims and offenders in their 11-year study of national data, they suggested that "parricide may be the final stage and culminating action for some, albeit few, families in the violence escalation process."[32]

CPV as a precursor to parricide would seem most applicable to dangerously antisocial children, as noted by the research team.[33] These youths are the ones most likely to come into conflict with parents as a result of the earlier failure of parents to set adequate limits enforced by appropriate discipline strategies. Walsh and Krienert suggested that "identification of an escalation process would provide valuable information that could assist family intervention and nonviolent conflict resolution strategies."[34] The researchers also noted that aggressive and excessive discipline by the parents might have an unintended effect: it could foster intense anger in children and lead to counterattacks by them.[35]

Risk factors identified by researchers with respect to adolescent homicide offenders would seem appropriate to consider in assessing violence potential. A history of antisocial behavior, substance abuse, and psychiatric contact,[36] particularly when combined with threats or acts of violence toward the parents, are important factors that suggest that intervention is needed. A number of warning signs of homicidal aggression proposed by Malmquist based on his evaluations of 20 youths referred for murder also seem relevant in identifying youths at risk of taking lethal action against their parents. These include significant behavioral changes (particularly "deep pessimism about themselves or their predicament"), a "call for help," use of illicit drugs, object losses (particularly with respect to mothers or lovers), threats to their manhood, and "an emotional crescendo" characterized by "an increasing build-up of agitation and energy."[37]

PREVENTION

Clearly, the examination of cases of parricide leaves no doubt that some killings of parents can be prevented. For example, it is likely that Marcus Sanchez (Chapter 1) would not have killed his father if Marcus's mother had acted responsibly. Marcus's parricidal thoughts and behaviors were known to his mother and to his sister. In fact, clinical case notes by Marcus's social worker indicated that this matter had been brought up in counseling more than two years before the shooting. If Marcus had been put in a residential treatment center prior to the killing, he likely would have received the in-depth psychotherapy necessary in order for him to process his strong negative feelings and to deal more effectively with his past. Instead, Marcus's mother sent him to live with his father. She took this action knowing that Marcus had intense ambivalent feelings toward his father and that his father abused drugs and alcohol and could not control him.

The Hillsboro familicide (Chapter 2) is particularly tragic given the facts that emerged after the incident. Review of the hospital, evaluation, and treatment records indicated that Brandon and Derek had independently made statements to mental health professionals that they intended to kill their parents. The police investigation revealed that at least 12 of the Hillsboro brothers' friends had heard one or both of them state that they were going to kill their parents prior to the homicidal event.

There is some disagreement in the literature regarding whether the factors that influence criminal violence also affect parricide.[38] One study that examined parricide in relation to homicide in general and to interpersonal violence was illuminating in this regard. Shon and Targonski noted some differences between the trends in homicide and in parricide.[39] They observed, however, that the declining trend in parricide during the 1990s was similar to that observed in intimate partner homicide (IPV). They suggested societal factors that influence IPV also affect parricides. Accordingly, prevention must look to societal resources and not simply individual factors.[40]

Kashani and his colleagues made several recommendations to reduce family violence by juveniles.[41] They targeted both sociological and psychological factors. They suggested that families de-emphasize status symbols, such as the family car, and that the media stop sensationalizing force and violence. They advised parents to openly communicate with their children, to confront abuse against their children, to give serious consideration to conflict between adolescents and stepparents, and to utilize the extended family to prevent violence. Their recommendations, buttressed by dozens of research studies and clinical reports, underscore the need to address child maltreatment and to provide mental health services to reduce the killing of parents.

Intervention in Cases of Suspected Child Abuse

The undeniable realities and effects of child abuse and neglect in our society are being recognized increasingly as everyone's responsibility. Although few children who are severely abused actually kill their parents, these children are at much higher risk of becoming delinquent or social dependents than children who are treated well by concerned and loving parents or guardians.[42]

Despite the increased public attention given to child mistreatment, many people are unclear about what to do when confronted with this problem. Terry Adams, whose case was profiled in Chapter 1, had a strong message to deliver to teachers almost seven years after he killed his parents:

A kid has a black eye, be inquisitive, don't ask him in front of the other classmates, don't never confront [the child]. You can see the symptoms: black eye, bruised lip, [child seems far away as if he's] just not really there, [may come across as] rebellious, wanting attention …. It's hard on teachers to be personal with classmates, because there's, what, 40 to a class. But, you know, if they detect that, try to find out what's wrong, be questionable [question the child], take the kid home one day. If he's got to take the school bus, yeah, you know, that's a little extra time out of your way, but if down deep inside, you really want to help, [then] *help*, you know. Don't think, I don't want to get involved—what happens if the kid dies. Remember, I think that's the biggest thing, if the kid dies, you could be responsible for that …. That's how I feel—you are just as responsible for it [death] as the person that did it. True enough, you don't want to get involved in the big, long, drawn-out thing, [but] *that's part of life.*

Scott Anders, whose case was mentioned in Chapter 7, expressed bitterness in a follow-up interview four and a half years after his conviction for killing his father when he recalled the number of teachers, neighbors, and relatives whom he had told about the abuse who did nothing to help him.

Just because a kid is young, don't think he's stupid. They don't have to believe him, but at least listen to him. They could check into it. When I told my teachers what was happening, before I got home, they had called my dad, and asked him "Did you beat your son or not?" "I didn't do nothing. I don't know what happened to him." I go to school the next day, I got called a liar. All they had to do is check it out. Neighbors knew about it, but nobody ain't want to call the law and want to get theirselves in trouble.

Will Garrison, who was granted clemency for killing his father (Chapter 7), expressed frustration regarding people who knew about the abuse and did nothing to help him.

But, it's hard for me to believe that things are going on in homes where people don't know. Like I said, there's a lot of people that know, knew some of the things that was goin' on. Even though they might not have known some of the really bad things, they knew that some of the things that were going on, that my dad was abusive. Whether they seen it verbally, some of 'em seen it physically; some of 'em they knew how he was. So, it could've been my aunt could've done somethin'. There's times when my dad had left, and she talked to my mom. "Let him come back." You know, I break down, and I beg 'em, "Don't let him come back." ... And they, you know, she's tryin' to get him back in. There's plenty of times when people, like that, my grandpa, you know, I can't blame none of 'em for what happened. But they knew. People knew that things were goin' on that wadn't right.

If one suspects that a child is being abused or neglected, one should, at a minimum, call the local or state agency that investigates child abuse and neglect cases. The caller's identity is kept confidential by such agencies, and reports in many states can be made anonymously. If the agency determines that the child is in danger, he or she will be removed from the home and placed in a temporary shelter until he or she can be safely returned to the home or other suitable arrangements can be made.

Doctors, teachers, hospital personnel, and law enforcement officers are legally mandated to report suspected cases. Yet even those who are obligated to do so by law are often reluctant to report apparent cases of abuse. I have been contacted by elementary school teachers who have persuasive evidence that children in their classes are being seriously mistreated by their parents. These teachers have pursued school policy by reporting the incident to school administrators and guidance counselors who subsequently took no action because of the "sensitive nature of the topic," beliefs that "that is how those kind of people raise their children" or that "nothing will be done anyway," or heavy caseloads. These teachers were frustrated or too fearful to go further. School administrators need to become more accountable for their responses when cases of suspected abuse are brought to their attention. In the meantime, teachers confronted with such a lack of response should ignore school procedures and make the call themselves to either the respective social service agency or the state attorney in the juvenile division.

In a follow-up interview conducted about one and a half years after she killed her father, Patty Smith (Chapter 9) offered the following advice specifically to teachers: "If you have a student that comes up to you, listen to them, don't turn them away, and talk to them, and call someone—all teachers in junior high, even elementary [schools], and all members of schools should have a list of where kids could go [for help], and automatically, if a kid talks to you, call this center."

When in doubt about what to do, individuals should protect the child's safety and report the suspected case to authorities. In the words of Patty Smith, "Just because there's no [physical] evidence, don't mean the child isn't being abused." As Scott Anders stressed, there are at least two kinds of abuse, physical and emotional. His experience clearly suggested that people seem to want hard evidence of physical abuse and adopt a more complacent attitude toward emotional abuse, often the more damaging of the two.

Prejudice, inertia, defeatism, or a fear of being wrong is insufficient justification to do nothing and hope for the best. Terry Adams offered a litmus test regarding when to act: "Would you let that happen to your kid if you weren't an abusive parent? If you wouldn't let it happen to your kid, then why let it happen to someone else's?"

Those who fear causing undue suspicion of possibly innocent parents are reminded that social service agencies are required to investigate cases thoroughly and to consider the case unfounded if no abuse or neglect is substantiated. The record of social service agencies indicates that they cannot always be trusted to investigate and quickly exonerate parents who have been falsely accused, or to provide help and services to children and families in need.[43] These circumstances need not exist, however, if our society is willing to take two stands: we need to commit the financial resources required in order to provide quality services, and we must employ sufficient numbers of social service personnel, train them adequately, and empower them to discharge their duties. We need to remind ourselves that people who have been cleared of wrongdoing are really not guilty. In order for this end to be achieved, child abuse laws might need to be reexamined and rewritten in some jurisdictions. Laws regarding records kept on parents who have been investigated for child abuse and cleared might need to be changed, particularly regarding confidentiality and expungement.

Support and Education Programs for Parents and Future Parents

The significant reduction of child abuse requires that resources be available to parents and children.[44] Prevent Child Abuse America, initiated more than 40 years ago, has designed a comprehensive strategy to reduce child abuse through a variety of community-based programs.[45] Support programs, including prenatal and postnatal medical care, need to be provided to new parents. Family support programs need to be available on a 24-hour basis to families in stress. As noted by Ann Cohn Donnelly, the former executive director of Prevent Child Abuse America, these should include "telephone hot lines, crisis caretakers, crisis baby-sitters, crisis nurseries, and crisis counseling" to provide help during a crisis.[46] Provisions need to be made for early and regular child and family screening and treatment. In addition, quality childcare options need to be available for all children, regardless of their parents' financial status.[47]

Education for first time parents, those who are facing challenges, and future parents must be easily accessible. Classes should be designed to help parents cope with the stresses of raising children, particularly special needs children. Serious consideration should be given to incorporating child development and parenting skills classes into high school curricula for both boys and girls. Research has indicated that increasing the knowledge of present and future parents about home and child management and enhancing the development of good communication skills, healthy emotional ties, and parent–child bonding help prevent child maltreatment.[48]

Helping individuals learn appropriate parenting skills will reduce child abuse and neglect, simply because many instances of child mistreatment are based on ignorance. Parents and potential parents need to be aware of the importance of setting boundaries for children and disciplining them appropriately. As we have seen, the failure of parents to set limits on their children's behavior can lead to youth becoming antisocial. In extreme cases, youths who have not been taught to respect their parents' authority might respond violently when parents do attempt to enforce limits on their behavior.

Identification of Child Abuse and Delineation of Appropriate Action

In addition to teaching adults and teenagers about child development and good parenting skills, elementary, junior high, and high schools should develop courses on child abuse and neglect. The curricula should be designed to help students recognize child abuse and neglect and encourage them to take appropriate action if victimized or threatened with victimization. The earlier these behaviors are targeted, the earlier they can be stopped and any accompanying damage or difficulties can be addressed therapeutically. The programs should aim to foster the development of self-esteem and conflict resolution skills to aid the youth in self-protection.

Children and adolescents need to learn the difference between functional and dysfunctional families. They should also be informed about the effects of parental alcoholism and chemical dependency on children. They should know that children raised in alcoholic, chemically dependent, or otherwise dysfunctional families appear to be at higher risk of being abused or neglected.[49] They should be told explicitly about support groups, such as Alateen, that help youths cope effectively with problems that arise from living in a home with an addicted parent. These groups should be allowed and encouraged to meet in the schools during lunch, during free periods, and/or immediately following classes. The schools are the most appropriate vehicle for this responsibility, primarily because they might be the only institutions to have any meaningful contact with children from chemically dependent families. Available estimates suggest that one in four children under the age of 18 is exposed to alcohol abuse or dependency in the family.[50]

Immediate Availability of a Supportive Network

Without a supportive network available to guide children through the process of obtaining help, victimization is likely to continue. As Patty Smith said, "After the person [child] comes up to you, for the kid to keep talking, it will be hard, because once she even starts a little bit, she is going to want to shut the door on it. If she knows that she is going to have someone stand by her all the way, like holding her hand and knew the experience, she could continue opening up."

Currently, in most states a mistreated child is on his or her own unless and until the social service agency investigates and files a petition alleging dependency on the basis of its investigation. Once a dependency petition is filed, some assistance for the mistreated child is likely to be forthcoming in most jurisdictions in the United States. The Child Abuse Prevention and Treatment Act enacted by Congress in 1974 required that states seeking federal funds for child protection must enact provisions for the appointment of guardians for children involved in abuse or neglect proceedings.[51] A *guardian ad litem* (a person acting as the child's guardian in a particular action) acts as the child's advocate in court proceedings. Lay volunteers in such states typically receive training through the Court Appointed Special Advocate (CASA) program, a program started in 1977 in Seattle, Washington.[52] There are currently more than 1,000 CASA programs operating in 49 states throughout the United States.[53]

Intervention and assistance by a guardian ad litem at the stage of filing of a dependency petition are good, but they should begin much earlier. Children need an advocate before the filing stage is reached; they need someone to stand by their decision to report the mistreatment. The addition of child advocates in elementary and high schools to help children who are in distress cope with their situations and find solutions is needed in order to prevent youths from taking inappropriate steps to end violence in their homes. A child advocate program is a means to ensure that children's allegations are properly and promptly investigated and that appropriate action is taken. A program of this nature could be implemented either as a separate entity or as an expanded component of existing guardian ad litem programs.

In the model proposed here, a satellite office of a guardian ad litem program based on the CASA model would be placed in every school. Ideally, the person who staffed each satellite office—the school guardian ad litem—would be a full-time salaried employee of the guardian ad litem program in the jurisdiction. The success of existing guardian ad litem programs provides convincing evidence, however, that, with coordination and creativity, satellite offices could be run completely by volunteers.

The school guardian ad litem would be the referral person in each school for teachers, parents, guidance counselors, and, most important, children who might be abused or neglected. It would be the satellite guardian ad litem's role to ensure that each child's case is adequately investigated. The satellite agent would be responsible for assigning a guardian ad litem from the pool of volunteers to ensure that each child is given support as soon as possible.

The volunteer guardian ad litem assigned from the school to the case would also monitor to ensure that court-ordered services were received. The outcome might have been different in the case of Terry Adams had a guardian ad litem actively monitored Terry's case when three petitions alleging neglect, abuse, and physical abuse were filed in the two years preceding the homicide. Had a guardian ad litem brought to the court's attention the failure of Terry's parents to participate in court-ordered counseling, both parents might be alive today. It is disturbing to realize, as Terry Adams said, that "the judge recommended [ordered] all this stuff, but nothing was fulfilled."

The Role of the Media in Preventing Child Maltreatment

Public service advertising through television, radio, and the print media has played a big role in educating the public about the problem of child maltreatment. In addition to informing viewers about what types of behavior and words are abusive, the media can publicize, through traditional venues and the Internet, where abusive parents can get help and what actions concerned citizens can take to help prevent child abuse. The media can alert viewers of the increased risk chemically dependent parents have of abusing and neglecting their children and of support groups and community facilities where they can get help.

Public service announcements advising parents and children who believe they are in danger where they can get *immediate assistance* and temporary shelter are needed in order to prevent violence and continued suffering.[54] James Holt (Chapter 11), who maintained that he was falsely convicted of killing his parents, maintained that the media "dropped the ball" by focusing on "stranger danger" rather than the dangers many children face from their parents at home. "I think the kids still don't know that there's a way they can get help from what's happening at home. Stranger abduction rates" pale in comparison to maltreatment by parents. Existing studies indicating that shelters, legal advocacy programs, and hotlines were associated with lower rates of intimate partner violence suggest that such services for children could likely prevent some parricides.[55] Daniel Culbreath, who pled guilty to killing his parents (Chapter 12), was convinced that parricides could be prevented if young people knew that "if they can't deal with being at home anymore, if they can't deal with their parents anymore driving them nuts … they've got somewhere to go." He believed that he would not have killed his parents if he had had a place to go where he could have stayed as long as needed and not had "the same pressure." Cassie Sparkman, who killed her stepmother (Chapter 1), pleaded for safe places for abused children. When she reported her uncle for sexually abusing her, she was put in foster care, which she found to be a negative experience and was afraid of going back to.

Availability of Mental Health Services

The preceding recommendations point to the importance of having mental health services available for members of abusive and high-stress families. Implications are most direct with respect to the severely abused parricide offender. Abusive parents might need help in understanding their destructive behavior and in learning appropriate ways to manage their anger, cope with stressors, communicate clearly, and discipline effectively. If the abuse is severe, the youth likely will need help in resolving the effects of the trauma, as discussed in the treatment chapter. Younger children also might need treatment to improve their cognitive and developmental skills, which can be adversely affected by childhood maltreatment.[56]

Unlike other recommendations that are mainly targeted at reducing parricide by the severely abused parricide offender, this recommendation has direct applicability to all three types of parricide offenders and their families. If the youth has begun acting out as a result of the parents' abusive behavior or their failure to impose limits when the child was younger, individual and family therapy are likely needed in order to ensure that the youth does not resort to violence against his or her parents. The family members need to recognize the dysfunctional family dynamics and come to an agreement regarding appropriate behavior by the adolescent. If the youth cannot be brought under control with outpatient therapy, inpatient treatment needs to be considered.

Mental health services are critically important in the case of individuals with histories of serious mental illness. In addition to working with the mentally ill parricide offender, who is most likely an adult, clinicians need to be appropriately attuned to the parents of these offspring so that they can prevent violence. When parents present in therapy, clinicians need to inquire about their relationships with their adult children, particularly when the adult children have significant mental health problems and live in the same home with them. Parents need to be asked specifically whether they are afraid of their sons and daughters and whether they fear that their children might harm them physically. Mental health professionals need to inquire directly about whether there has been violence in the home, because many clients are reluctant and embarrassed to provide this information unless specifically asked.

Policymakers need to recognize that extended mental health coverage is a valuable and needed resource for reducing family violence and, in some cases, even homicide. Unlike other types of homicide, the killing of mothers and fathers by their offspring is unlikely to be prevented by putting more police officers on the street or by simply reducing access to firearms. The problems in these families are typically deeply rooted, complex, and private. The literature suggests that access to therapy, hospitalization when indicated, and alternative living homes (e.g., group homes, assisted living facilities) for the mentally ill, when indicated, could help reduce the incidence of parricide and improve the quality of life of the parents and children in many of these families.[57]

SUMMARY AND CONCLUDING REMARKS

This chapter acknowledged that parricide cannot be reliably predicted. However, it is possible to identify factors, based on the accumulating body of research, that, when present, put juveniles and adults more at risk of killing their parents. The risk factors can be targeted for individuals who have histories of severe abuse, mental illness, or antisocial behavior. In addition, serious efforts to prevent parricide can be made through the implementation of recommendations designed to reduce child maltreatment and provide mental health services to individuals and families in need.

Many questions remain unanswered. More in-depth research on long-term outcomes in patricide and matricide cases is needed to guide criminal justice practitioners and policymakers in terms of sentencing and disposition when sons and daughters kill their parents. What is the prognosis in cases of severe mental illness? Do these offenders represent a continuing threat to society? In cases of severe mental illness falling short of the threshold for insanity, is long-term incarceration a just sentence? Decision makers often struggle in cases when adolescents have killed parents after enduring severe abuse over many years.[58] How much consideration should judges and juries in the criminal and juvenile justice systems place on abuse at trial and sentencing?[59] What if the abuse is limited to extreme psychological abuse?

There is a pressing need for long-term follow-up research on juveniles and adults who have killed their parents and been effectively treated. As we have seen, little follow-up data are available on this population. In addition, even when treatment is ordered, it appears that adolescent parricide offenders rarely receive meaningful intervention. Long-term follow-up studies could help judges make informed decisions on whether certain offspring who killed their fathers and mothers can be safely released back into society at the time of disposition, require long-term treatment, or warrant life in prison. In addition, this research could be invaluable in helping corrections personnel, mental health professionals, judges, and clemency boards to evaluate whether incarcerated parricide offenders can be safely released back into society at some point in time.

Sentencing Juvenile Parricide Offenders to LWOP

As we have seen, in 2012, the United States Supreme Court struck down as unconstitutional *mandatory* life sentences without parole for defendants convicted of murders they committed as juveniles. Although the Court did not categorically ban LWOP for juvenile murderers, the ruling in *Miller v. Alabama* is clear that such sentences should be rarely imposed.[60] Writing for the majority, Justice Kagan noted: "But given all we have said in *Roper, Graham*, and this decision about children's diminished culpability and heightened capacity for change, we think appropriate occasions for sentencing juveniles to this harshest possible penalty will be uncommon."[61]

Based on this ruling, it would seem that sentencing juvenile parricide offenders to LWOP will be an unusual disposition in light of the attendant circumstances in many of these cases. Clearly, there are scientific, humanitarian, and fiscal reasons that weigh heavily against imposing life sentences without parole for juvenile murderers. As noted by James Holt (Chapter 11), sentencing juveniles to LWOP "takes away all hope." Prior to the Court's ruling in *Miller v. Alabama,* James made a compelling argument against sentencing juveniles to LWOP in light of our increased understanding of human development and in recognition of current laws in the United States. His essay is reprinted in Box 16-1.

BOX 16-1 TEENAGERS by James Holt (unedited)

A teenager isn't allowed to vote, or go to war, or smoke and drink, or choose their religion, or even see an R-rated comedy, yet this country alone feels it's okay to send us away to prison for life, literally rotting away in a concrete cage for all of eternity. Unlike adults sentenced to Life, a teenager will have never known graduation, proms, a career, marriage, children, travel, and everything else all people take for granted. Let alone those teens whose childhoods were spent in poverty, abuse, and neglect.

Some youth lived sheltered lives and never experienced carefree teenage fun. The poor souls who were virgins when they were locked up probably want to kill themselves (and many do). Most juveniles are also imprinted with any number of criminal deviancies on their descent into madness.

Contrary to the myth of prison preserving you, the reality is years of malnutrition and poor health care (as well as drug use and assaults) along with unimaginable perpetual stress wreak havoc upon your physiology during your formative years. You transition from adolescence into premature middle-age. Yet you never mature; you may age chronologically and physically, but psychologically and emotionally you are trapped in an adolescent limbo, forever viewing life through the distorted prism of a teenager. There is no Peter Pan syndrome of an eccentric, but state-sanctioned arrested development. Psychologists who interviewed me two decades after first meeting me at sixteen testified it was as if they were talking to the same exact teenager they last saw during the Reagan administration; even my physique and voice were unchanged, as if I time-warped to the future.

It is a rare juvenile who can remain true to himself—most are beaten down by the system to become institutionalized, or spend years being victimized and exploited, or to emerge a genuine monster, fueled by hate. Prison officials loathe individuality, no effort or expense is spared to violently suppress all decency, intellect, and creativity. You are relentlessly dehumanized day after day, until you are mired in a deep despair, during which your friends and family have grown up, married, moved away, or died.

Where is the moral outrage—so easily afforded to those with the Death Penalty [that juveniles no longer face]—when the idea of kids languishing in a penal hell of misery for their entire lives is infinitely more cruel? Prison is not "life"—you aren't truly alive in any meaningful sense, you merely exist, a ghost in a zombified state of living death. The irony is these juveniles are usually first offenders who are the most amenable to rehabilitation and the least likely of all prisoners to reoffend, yet they have no hope of release.

Whether victims of self-defense or peer pressure or ignorance, for most these isolated incidents are the result of poor judgment caused by immaturity; criminologists know neurological and sociological/psychological studies verify this. Yet, along with certain murderers like serial killers, these teenagers seem to be among the only prisoners who will never go free. These kids get no second chance at life. The ultimate travesty of justice is the horror of we teenagers who were wrongly convicted of crimes we didn't commit and doomed to an eternity of prison hell.

The case of James Holt is one of many that warrant discussion. The reader will recall that James was determined by the trial court to be mentally ill and sentenced to two consecutive life sentences for killing his parents at age 16, a crime he has consistently maintained he did not commit. He has already been incarcerated for 25 years. Although he has lived in stressful conditions, he has no major health problems (e.g., heart disease, diabetes, cancer). If he lives another 25 years, he will have been incarcerated for 50 years and will be in his mid-60s. Although the average life expectancy for males is 76 in the United States,[62] let's calculate his life expectancy at 66, owing to the stress of incarceration. If the cost of incarcerating an inmate is calculated at $25,000 per year, allowing for no inflation so as to make the numbers easier to comprehend, his state will have spent $1.25 million to maintain him in the prison system. Needless to say, the actual cost will be exponentially higher because inflation is not factored in during the 50-year period. If Holt had been effectively treated, adjudged by mental health professionals not to be a continuing danger to society, and released after 10 years of prison, the state would have saved $1 million. In addition, it is likely that the inmate Larry would not have been killed and that Holt's codefendant Paul would have been released as scheduled on his original charges, potentially saving taxpayers another million dollars. It is possible that James, given his high intelligence, artistic talent and creativity, and passion for helping juvenile offenders, might have made a meaningful contribution to society instead of being a drain on taxpayers' dollars.

A Call to Action

While the justice system struggles with how to deal with the situation of severely abused youths who kill parents, society must take preventive action, as the recommendations above prescribe. In addition to the social issues discussed, there are huge human and financial costs in terms of the toll of childhood abuse on long-term health. These include, for example, the effects of post-traumatic stress disorder (as discussed previously), increased risk for depression,[63] and depressed immune function (leading to increased risk of autoimmune disease).[64]

Child abuse results not only in mental and physical disorders and human carnage, but often in the death of the human spirit.[65] With awareness of the problem comes the opportunity to change the conditions that give rise to child abuse and allow it to continue. The words of Terry Adams alert us to the realization that awareness is not the end but the beginning:

The biggest thing is just being aware. Care, 'cause if you don't, it's not just the little kid you are hurting, you're hurting tomorrow .... because kids are defenseless, they don't have the vocabulary, the mental capacity, the mentality, the strong points to stand up. If somebody won't stand up for them, nobody will. If no one does, then, what's tomorrow?

Each one of us, regardless of our age or station in life, can make a difference in the lives of children. A story attributed to the Minnesota Literacy Council makes this point graphically.

An old fisherman stood on the beach watching a young boy at the shoreline. As the fisherman approached, he saw that the boy was picking up starfish, which had been washed ashore by the waves, and was throwing them back into the sea. When the fisherman caught up with the boy, he asked the boy what he was doing. The boy did not stop his effort as he told the fisherman that he was throwing the starfish back into the sea so that they could live; if left until the morning sun rose, the starfish would die. The fisherman's eyes scanned the beach, noticing thousands of starfish on shore. He said, "But, son, there are thousands upon thousands of starfish on the beach. What difference could your actions possibly make?" As the boy hurled another starfish into the sea, he looked the old man in the eye and said, "It makes a difference to this one."

Afterword

Understanding parricide.

Understanding a horrific crime that flies in the face of human nature, filial attachment, and the first biblical commandment of promise: honor your father and mother so that you may live long upon the earth.

Understanding the incomprehensible by exposing the "back story," the history of abuse, neglect, and significant trauma in the lives of adolescent parricide offenders.

That is what Dr. Heide has accomplished in this remarkable, comprehensive and definitive study of parricide. She has provided not only a meticulously researched history of parricide, and a breakdown by age and gender, but also a tool for preventing parricide and other violent crimes committed by adolescents by identifying and eliminating child abuse.

Fortunately, parricide is rare. Unfortunately, the wish or expressed desire to kill one's parent(s) occurs fairly frequently in juvenile court. In either case, prosecutors, defense attorneys, judges, and other juvenile and criminal justice professionals are ill equipped to deal with it. School employees, neighbors, and friends are squeamish, reluctant to talk about the subject. The underlying abuse suffered by children who kill parents is often so overlooked and unimaginable that when the act occurs, family friends like those of Richard and Deborah Jahnke in the book can only say: "It makes terrible sense."

In my twelve years as a juvenile and family court judge in Florida, I never had a case of parricide, but I had one 11-year-old girl who tried to murder her mother by setting her mattress on fire while she lay drunk, passed out on the bed. Her 15-year-old boyfriend assisted in pouring gasoline around the bed skirt and she lit the match. The fumes woke the mother who then called the police, who had often been to the house because of fights between the mother and daughter. The warning signs were there:

an alcoholic mother, an 11-year-old with a 15-year-old boyfriend, and a history of domestic violence.

Much more often, I learned of adolescents who wanted to kill their parents and/ or themselves, or commit violent acts to others, by reviewing the behavioral evaluations prepared by the three child psychologists who worked alongside the four juvenile judges in our court. Drs. Cindy Zarling, Christine Jaggi, and Adele Solazzo provided detailed information and diagnoses that helped us fashion appropriate treatment and sanctions for violent juvenile offenders. We were the only juvenile court in Florida that had such assistance.

The serious juvenile offenders I saw in court and the parricide defendants in Dr. Heide's book shared a lot in common:

- Significant early trauma, including physical, emotional, and sexual abuse
- Lack of options or alternatives, because they were children and "couldn't get away"
- Availability of weapons, especially guns and knives
- Drug use, on the part of the parents and the youth
- Untreated mental illness
- Built-up rage and anger that become the tipping point
- No adult to talk to, or perhaps no one whom they think will listen
- Adolescent brains still developing, resulting in poor impulse control
- Peer pressure, encouraging or assisting in the crime
- Neglect on the part of the passive parent. Children raising themselves.

In my work in juvenile court, I came to view neglect as one of the most damaging types of abuse. Failure to protect often led to the removal of a child from an abusive home and *both* parents.

I became a "professional affiliate" within Division 56, the trauma division of the American Psychological Association. I learned a lot from Dr. Steven Gold, clinical psychologist and professor at Nova Southeastern University in Ft. Lauderdale. Dr. Gold advocates "taking the drama out of the trauma" for a more complete understanding of the harm of child abuse. What the child *didn't* receive during the years of abuse: guidance, teaching, a moral code, empathy, structure, effective discipline, and of course, love.

The exceptionally thorough, detailed case studies of Patty Smith and Peter Jones in the book reminded me of Dr. Gold's analysis, and all that Patty and Peter *didn't* get while being severely abused and forced to act like the adults in the house, doing most of the chores and protecting younger siblings. If Patty and Peter lacked empathy or disassociated from the terrible acts they committed, no wonder!

The case studies illustrate Dr. Heide's role as a superb clinician as well as a compassionate professional who continued to communicate with the defendants in prison and upon their release, so we could learn about their lives as adults. That's an experience most juvenile judges don't get, but it is so helpful in understanding the big picture.

Sexual abuse is a common thread among parricide offenders. Dr. Heide reports that one in four girls and one in seven boys are sexually abused. That's a shocking statistic but one that mirrors what I saw in juvenile court. This doesn't include the "covert" sexual abuse that Dr. Heide finds harmful, and one that I probably overlooked in court. Yes, there is something wrong about a father parading naked before his wife and sons throughout the home. Disgust, early sexualization, and promiscuity can be expected.

Dr. Heide has a lofty goal that she expresses in her Preface: Reduce family violence to ensure that children today grow up in homes where they are loved and protected by their parents. Resources should be directed to this goal, at the earliest time in a child's life. Elementary school teachers and counselors, child welfare workers, juvenile probation officers, family friends, relatives, and neighbors should be vigilant in watching for abuse. How could the experiences of Patty Smith and Peter Jones go unnoticed?

When former Penn State football assistant coach Jerry Sandusky was found guilty of multiple counts of child sexual abuse, Pennsylvania Attorney General Linda Kelly said that one of the recurring themes in the case was, "Who would believe a kid?" The answer that jumps out of *Understanding Parricide* is that we all should believe, and provide plenty of opportunities for young people to seek help.

Judge Irene Sullivan

Judge Irene Sullivan is a retired circuit court judge in Florida and the author of *Raised by the Courts: One Judge's Insight into Juvenile Justice.*

Notes

PREFACE
1. Ohio boy, 2011.
2 Heide, 1994.

CHAPTER 1
1. Dougherty & O'Connor, 2008.
2. CBS News, 2010.
3. Grinberg, 2006d.
4. McCartney, 2005.
5. Bernstein & Koppel, 2008.
6. Heide, 1992. See, e.g., Janos, 1983; Matthews, 1983; Prendergast, 1983.
7. Janos, 1983; Matthews, 1983; Prendergast, 1983, 1986.
8. See, e.g., Wilson, 1973. Four of the 55 child murderers he profiled using journalistic accounts were implicated in killing their fathers or mothers. Three of these cases involved boys from England; the last case involved two girls from New Zealand. See also Lii Haibo, 2002, outlining lessons to be learned from the murder of a mother and attempted murder of a father by a 16-year-old boy in China.
9. Boots & Heide, 2006; Heide & Boots, 2007.
10. Malmquist, 1980.
11. Borden, 2011; Wertham, 1941b; Newhill, 1991.
12. Shon, 2009, 2010, 2012; Shon & Barton-Bellessa, 2012; Shon & Roberts, 2008, 2010.
13. Strange, 2010.
14. Philbin & Philbin, 2011.
15. Margaret, 2008.
16. Hitchcock, 1960.
17. Hamsher, Murphy, Townsend, & Stone, 1994.
18. Arkoff, Geisinger, Saland, & Rosenberg, 1979; Bay, Form, Fuller, & Douglas, 2005.
19. Cunningham & Marrow, n.d.; Evil Dead, 1989.
20. See, e.g., Davis, 2003; Foucault & Kriegel, 1975; Heron, 2006; Howard, 1994; Kleiman, 1988; Lang, 1995; Lannert, 2011; Leyton, 1990; Linedecker, 1993; McGinnis, 1991; McMurray, 2006, 2009; Mones, 1991; Morris, 1985; Prendergast, 1986; Walker, 1989. Kelleher (1998) briefly discussed a few cases of adolescent parricide offenders in his book.
21. Freud, 1919, 1929; Wertham, 1941b.
22. Freud's works have been instrumental in analyses of patricidal acts and fantasies (see, e.g., Beukenkamp, 1960; Dalma, Knobel, & Fox, 1955; Moulun & Morgan, 1967; Tucker & Cornwell, 1977; Tuovinen, 1973) and matricidal acts and fantasies (see, e.g., Blum, 2001; Jacobs, 2004; Kiremidjian, 1976; Liegner & Motycka, 1981; Lindner, 1948;

Reenkola, 2002; Silberstein, 1998; Tanay & Freeman, 1976). For a critical analysis of Freud's parricidal theories from an evolutionary psychology perspective, see Daly & Wilson, 1988b.

23. In Japan, for example, up until 1973, killing a parent was deemed more morally reprehensible than other homicides under the country's criminal code. Accordingly, parricide offenders were sentenced to either death or life without parole, whereas those involved in "ordinary murders" could be legally sentenced to anything from three years in prison to death. In 1973, the Japanese Supreme Court struck down the criminal code provision mandating more severe penalties for parricide offenders. The relevant case involved a woman who killed her father after he raped her, forced her to live with him, and strongly opposed her marriage to a man she loved. See Matsui, 1987, 2011.

24. Marleau, et al., 2003; Millaud, et al., 1996. Roughhead (1930) discussed the rarity of parricide in Scotland.

25. Heide & Petee, 2007a. For example, the FBI (2011) estimated that 245 parents (107 mothers and 245 fathers) were killed by their offspring in 2010.

26. Boots & Heide, 2006; Heide, 1989; Walsh, Krienert, & Crowder, 2008.

27. Finch, 2001. Biological and adoptive parents constituted approximately 2.4% of all homicide victims in Japan from 1989 to 1995. The Japanese government no longer reports these data, as the category that isolated this particular type of homicide was abolished in 1995.

28. Mouzos & Rushforth, 2003. Percentage calculated by Heide from data provided by authors.

29. Fedorowycz, 1999; Murray, 1999.

30. Dunjic, Maric, Jasovic-Gasic, & Dunjic, 2008.

31. Cornic & Olie, 2006; Fontaine & Guérard des Lauriers, 1994.

32. Dakhlaoui, Khémiri, Gaha, Ridha, & Haffani, 2009.

33. I used the FBI Supplementary Homicide Data victim data base as made available by Fox and Swatt (2009) to compute these statistics. I removed 540 cases with obvious coding errors from the data set (parents incorrectly classified by gender, e.g., fathers coded as female.) With the cases noted removed, the number of victim cases (unweighted) was 8,706. The number of cases weighted to match the U.S. population was 9,621. The estimated number of parents killed (weighted to the U.S. population) should be taken as a good estimate, given the extensiveness of the time period.

34. I used the FBI Supplementary Homicide Data Offender data base as made available by Fox and Swatt (2009) to derive these statistics. I removed 24 cases with obvious coding errors from the data set (parents incorrectly classified by gender, e.g., fathers coded as female.). I also eliminated 17 cases that listed the offenders as unknown. I also examined cases of mothers for errors in coding because, unlike those that might exist with respect to fathers and stepparents, they can be spotted because of trends in reproduction. I excluded nine cases with obvious errors (e.g., age difference between biological mother and child was less than 13 years, mother and child listed as being the same age, biological mother over age 50 when she gave birth). The percentages should be taken as very good estimates, given the number of cases from which the statistics are computed. With the cases noted removed, the number of actual cases (unweighted) was 8,858. The number of cases weighted to match the U.S. population was 9,792. Of the four victim types, fathers were the most likely to be killed in single-victim incidents (86%), followed by stepfathers (84%), mothers (82%), and stepmothers (70%). These differences were statistically significant (χ^2 [9, 9,792] = 188.406, p < .001), meaning

that the probability of achieving these results if the two variables (homicide situation type and victim type) were unrelated was less than 1 in 1,000. However, the relationship between the two variables was weak (Cramer's V =.08).

35. Because of the way the FBI codes homicide data, the most accurate picture of offenders is obtained by looking at single-victim, single-offender incidents, because in these cases the killer is clearly tied to the victim. Given the construction of the FBI data set, it is not possible to link offenders with multiple victims. See Heide, 1993b, 1993c.

36. The percentages of those arrested for killing biological fathers and mothers are slightly lower than reported in previous studies that used shorter time frames (see Heide, 1993b; Heide & Frei, 2010; Heide & Petee, 2007a). For analyses using the same SHR data base that focused on parricide offenders in three age groups up to age 21, see Walsh, Krienert, & Crowder, 2008; for analyses that used another national data base, the National Incident Based Reporting System, see Walsh & Krienert, 2009.

37. Solomon, Berg, & Martin, 2011.

38. As explained above, I used SHR offender data. The numbers reported are based on arrest data weighted for the U.S. population.

39. See, e.g., Shumaker & McGee, 2001; Shumaker & Prinz, 2000.

40. National Criminal Justice Reference Service, 1999.

41. Solomon, Berg, & Martin, 2011.

42. Bender & Curran, 1940.

43. Bender, 1959; Bender & Curran, 1940; Cornell, 1989.

44. Sargent, 1962.

45. Bender, 1959; Zenoff & Zients, 1979. For a more expansive discussion, see Heide, Solomon, Sellers, & Chan, 2011; Shumaker & McGee, 2001; Shumaker & Prinz, 2000.

46. Heide, 1999; Sorrells, 1977; Zenoff & Zients, 1979.

47. *Roper v. Simmons*, 2005.

48. *Graham v. Sullivan*, 2010.

49. Miller v. Alabama, 2012.

50. See, e.g., LawServer (2010) for information on Florida Statutes § 984.085.

51. Infoplease, 2002.

52. U.S. Department of Labor, n.d.

53. "Brief of the American Society for Adolescent Psychiatry," 1986; Grisso, 1996; Grisso & Schwartz, 2000.

54. Heide & Solomon, 2006.

55. On matricide offenders, see, e.g., Abayomi, 2012; Campion et al., 1985; Chiswick, 1981; Dogan, Demirci, Deniz, & Erkol, 2010; Gillies, 1965; Green, 1981; Heide & Frei, 2010; Holcomb, 2000; Clark, 1993; Lipson, 1986; McKnight, Mohr, Quinsey, & Erochko, 1966; O'Connell, 1963; Schwade & Geiger, 1953; Singhal & Dutta, 1992. On patricide offenders, see Cravens, Campion, Rotholc, Covan, & Cravens, 1985; Singhal & Dutta, 1990. On offenders who killed both parents, see Maas, Prakash, Hollender, & Regan, 1984; Raizen, 1960; Weisman, Ehrenclou, & Sharma, 2002.

56. Heide, 1992.

57. See Ewing, 1997, 2001; Hart & Helms, 2003; Hillbrand, Alexandre, Young, & Spitz, 1999; James, 1994; Kashani, Darby, Allan, Hartke, & Reid, 1997; Lennings, 2002; Palermo, 2007; Wasarhaley, Golding, Lynch, & Keller, 2012.

58. Heide, 1992; Mones, 1994.

59. Blais, 1985; Hull, 1987; Kleiman, 1986; Morris, 1985; Rosenthal, 1985; Walker, 1989.

60. American Psychiatric Association, 2000.

61. Benedek & Cornell, 1989; Ewing, 1990; Foucault & Kriegel, 1975; McCully, 1978; Morris, 1985; Newhill, 1991.

62. The American Psychiatric Association is in the process of developing a diagnostic category called "Schizophrenia Spectrum and Other Psychotic Disorders" for inclusion in *DSM-V*. Schizophrenia spectrum disorders share symptoms of schizophrenia. Often included in this rubric are the following: schizoaffective disorder, schizophreniform disorder, schizotypal personality disorder, delusional disorder, brief psychotic disorder, and schizoid personality disorder. See American Psychiatric Association, n.d.

63. "A family's nightmare," 1983.

64. McGraw, 1983.

65. Townsend, 1983; "Man accused of killing," 1983.

66. Dunne, 1990.

67. Callaway, 1989a, 1989b.

68. Callaway, 1989a, p. B13.

69. Callaway, 1989a, p. B13.

70. For case reports in the professional literature, see Lewis, Scott, Baranoski, Buchanan, & Griffith, 1998; Livaditis, Esagian, Kakoulidis, Samakouri, & Tzavaras, 2005.

71. See, e.g., Frith, 2003; Law and Order, 2003.

72. See, e.g., "Metro briefing," 2003.

73. Heide, 1992, 1997.

74. American Psychiatric Association, 2000.

75. Hare, 1999, 2003.

76. Hare, 1999, 2003.

77. American Psychiatric Association, 2000.

78. American Psychiatric Association, 2000.

79. Ewing, 2001; Heide, 1992.

80. The parents also reportedly smoked marijuana.

81. Nora decided not to press charges because there was no room for Karl in her mother's apartment, and Karl was willing to live with his father.

82. Other than failure to supervise an adolescent, there were no data to suggest physical neglect. There was no evidence of medical neglect or emotional incest of either child. There was some suggestion from Karl, Nora, and Mrs. Roberts that Mr. Robert did not meet the child's emotional needs.

83. There were many factors in mitigation in this case. However, Karl's extensive delinquent record and behavior after the shooting were perceived by the defense as very damaging. Evidence suggested that the State likely would be able to prove the elements of felony murder (the armed burglary), even if premeditation were lacking.

84. "It made terrible sense," 1982.

85. "It made terrible sense," 1982.

86. Prendergast, 1986.

87. Prendergast, 1986.

88. Prendergast, 1986.

89. Chambers, 1986; Ewing, 1990; Heide, 1992; Hull, 1987; Shoop, 1993; Siegel, 1983.

90. Cornell, Staresina, & Benedek, 1989, p. 53.

91. Cornell, Staresina, & Benedek, 1989, p. 53.

92. Cornell, Staresina, & Benedek, 1989, p. 53.

93. Shoop, 1993. See also the research study involving mock jurors by Haegerich & Bottoms, 2000.

94. Mones, 1991; see, e.g., Margolick, 1992.

95. Chambers, 1986.

96. Chambers, 1986.

97. Wasarhaley et al, 2012; Stalans & Henry, 1994.

98. For Janet Reese," 1987; Meisol, 1987.

99. See, e.g., Brett, 1997; Douglas, 2010; Fernandez, 2001; Hamilton, 2004; Hull, 1987; "Jeremiah Raymond Berry pleads guilty," 2009; Kaczor, 1989; Siegel, 1983; Reeves, 1993; Timnick, 1986; Toufexis, Bloch, & McDowell, 1992; "Youthful offender status is granted," 1992. The reaction to youths who kill their parents has not been met consistently with sympathy, however. In a time of fiscal austerity, the federal government decided that youths who murdered their parents would no longer be eligible for Social Security benefits under final rules published on September 24, 1982. Social Security officials had previously suspended such payments in January 1982, upon hearing of two cases in California in which individuals adjudicated in juvenile court for the murder of their parents had collected $21,500 and $8,000 upon parole ("Benefits frozen," 1982). The *Financial Times* presented the issue in a rather acidic way in an article titled "Bad Luck for Lizzie Borden" (1982). The article indicated that parricide had become an increasingly popular activity for children in Southern California as a way to make some fast money. In response, the federal government recently formulated a policy that effectively put an end to the lucrative game by ensuring that Social Security benefits were no longer available to adolescent parricide offenders.

100. Springer, 2006.
101. Grinberg, 2006e.
102. Grinberg, 2006e; Karas, 2006.
103. Karas, 2006.
104. Grinberg, 2006b.
105. Grinberg, 2006d.
106. Grinberg, 2006e; Karas, 2006.
107. Grinberg, 2006a.
108. Grinberg, 2006b.
109. Grinberg, 2006d.
110. Grinberg, 2006a, 2006b, 2006c.
111. Grinberg, 2006e.
112. Springer, 2006.
113. Springer, 2006.
114. Romo, 2010.

CHAPTER 2

1. Darby, Allan, Kashani, Hartke, & Reid, 1998; Dent & Jowitt, 1996; Hardwick & Rowton-Lee, 1996; Heide & Solomon, 2009; Heide, Solomon, Sellers, & Chan, 2011; Hughes, Zagar, Busch, Grove, & Arbit, 2009; Lewis et al., 1985; Mones, 1985; Roe-Sepowitz, 2007, 2009; Shumaker & Prinz, 2000; Zagar, Isbell, Busch, & Hughes, 2009.
2. Heide, 1992, 1999.
3. U.S.C.A. Section 5106g, 2003.
4. U.S.C.A. Section 5106g(2), 2003.
5. See U.S. Department of Health and Human Services, 2009.
6. Term introduced by Ackerman (1979).
7. See U.S. Department of Health and Human Services, 2009.
8. Miller (1990) shares a similar viewpoint.
9. There are similarities in the ways that abusive parents and spouses behave. The offending parent, like the battering spouse, might feel guilty and remorseful after the abusive act, ask the child's forgiveness, and promise never to assault the child again. Caution is, however, advised in generalizing from the literature on battered wives/husbands and battered children because the dynamics between victims and offenders are not identical. For further discussion of battered women, the battered wife syndrome, and

the problems these women face in protecting themselves and their children from harm by an abusive mate, see Walker 1979, 1984, 1989; Browne, 1987; Ewing, 1987.

10. Gelles & Straus, 1987.

11. Straus, 2007.

12. Brown, Tierney, & Serwint, 2009; Guandolo, 1985; Jones et al., 1986; Rosen et al., 1983; Rosen, Frost, & Glaze, 1986; Rosenberg, 1987; Sheridan, 2003.

13. Corder et al., 1976; Duncan & Duncan, 1971; Heide, 1994; Mones, 1991; Post, 1982; Sargent, 1962; Tanay, 1973.

14. My discussion of horror and terror was influenced by work of the Lowen (1983).

15. See U.S. Department of Health and Human Services, 2009.

16. Middleton-Moz & Dwinell, 1986; Weiner & Thompson, 1998.

17. Burgess et al., 1978; Groth & Birnbaun, 1979; Groth, 1981. Researchers 30 years later continue to distinguish between child molesters and rapists and have found significant differences between the two groups in terms of offense history, brain functioning, and psychological functioning; see Young, Justice, & Erdberg, 2011.

18. Centers for Disease Control and Prevention, n.d.; Felitti et al., 1998.

19. Heide, 1999.

20. See Weiner & Thompson, 1998.

21. Toufexis, Bloch, & McDowell, 1992.

22. Bass & Davis, 1994; Middleton-Moz & Dwinell, 1986.

23. The concept of covert sexual abuse is a culturally relative one. The norms operating in a particular culture and time period determine what society interprets as sexually explicit or provocative.

24. Bass & Davis, 1994; Bradshaw, 1996; Middleton-Moz & Dwinell, 1986.

25. Weiner & Thompson, 1998.

26. Forward, 2002.

27. Rotter, 1966.

28. Burgess et al., 1978; Groth, 1981.

29. Bass & Davis, 1994; Young, Justice, & Erdberg, 2011.

30. Groth & Birnbaum, 1979; Groth, 1981. See also Young, Justice, & Erdberg, 2011.

31. The sexual assault might provide a way for the parent to project or externalize his own internalized shame. In attacking the child, the parent might be attempting to free himself of fear, helplessness, or rage by acting it out. The parent in this situation seems to be symbolically passing his pain on to the child, who now will have to deal with similar shame-based feelings arising from the victimization (Kaufman, 1992).

32. See, e.g., ABC News, 2002; Johnson, 1997; Kleiman, 1988; Toufexis et al., 1992.

33. Kaufman, 1992.

34. See U.S. Department of Health and Human Services, 2009.

35. Bowlby, 1969; Heide & Solomon, 2009.

36. My definition is consistent with definitions used in many states. See U.S. Department of Health and Human Services, 2009.

37. See U.S. Department of Health and Human Services, 2009.

38. See U.S. Department of Health and Human Services, 2009.

39. Rosenberg, 2007.

40. Bowlby, 1988; Heide & Solomon, 2006.

41. Ackerman, 1979.

42. Heide, 2007.

43. Heide, 1997, 2007.

44. Heide, 2007.

45. Heide, 2007.

46. Solomon & Heide, 1999.
47. Heide & Solomon, 2006; Teicher et al., 2003; van der Kolk, 2006.
48. Heide & Solomon, 2006.
49. American Psychiatric Association, 2000.
50. Cloitre et al., 2009.
51. See Chapter 1 for a discussion of psychopathy. Examples of female juvenile homicide offenders who were not psychopathic, despite appearances, are illustrated in a recently published article by Heide and Solomon (2009).
52. Heide & Solomon, 2006.
53. Amnesty International, 1998; see Chapter 6 for case analysis.
54. See Grisso, 1996; Grisso & Schwartz, 2000; Heide & Solomon, 2006, 2009.
55. Heide, 2007.

CHAPTER 3

1. Smith, 2010.
2. Grodd & Diamond, 2008; TruTV, n.d.
3. Glassberg & Leland, 2005.
4. WTVD-TV/DT ABC, 2008a.
5. WTVD-TV/DT ABC, 2008b, 2008c.
6. CBC News, 2007a; Walton, 2008; Zickefoose, 2008.
7. The court ordered that the first four years be served in a psychiatric institution and be followed by four and a half years of community supervision. She was given credit for 18 months served in custody before trial (CBC News, 2007b).
8. Sunger, 2008.
9. Savill, 2008.
10. Boots & Heide, 2006; Heide & Boots, 2007.
11. See Fox & Swatt, 2009. Numbers in the tables vary slightly because information was not always provided by law enforcement agencies to the FBI for the variable under consideration. Missing data were removed from the analyses.
12. The determination of stepparent status is made by law enforcement. In most cases, the person identified as a stepparent victim by the police was legally married to the offender's parent. However, it is possible in some cases that police recorded the relationship of "stepparent" based on the victim's living circumstances and the duration of the relationship to the offender's parent rather than any legal relationship.
13. The data set I used was constructed by Fox and Swatt (2009). During the 32-year period, the estimated number of offenders arrested for murder or non-negligent homicide was 632,017. The number of offenders arrested each year fluctuated; it averaged 19,751 over the period studied and ranged from a low of 14,856 in 1999 to a high of 26,116 in 1993. Five trends in the number of offenders arrested for homicide were discernible over the 32-year period: increasing trend, 1976–1980; decreasing trend, 1981–1983; increasing trend, 1984–1993; decreasing trend, 1994–1999; and increasing trend, 2000–2007. The victim–offender relationship was known in 65.9% of the 632,017 arrests (N = 416,195).
14. I removed cases that contained obvious errors (e.g., mother coded as male). The number of cases removed was small (n = 50) and would have a negligible effect, given the size of the sample of parricide offenders (unweighted = 8,908, or less than 1/10 of 1%). Numbers in the tables vary slightly because information was not always provided by law enforcement agencies to the FBI for the variable under consideration. Missing data were removed from the analyses.

15. See, e.g., Bourget, Gagné, & Labelle, 2007; Chiswick, 1981; Gillies, 1976; Heide, 1993b; Heide & Petee, 2003; Heide & Petee, 2007a; Hillbrand & Cipriano, 2007; Marleau, Millaud, & Auclair, 2003; McKnight et al., 1966; Walsh, Krienert, & Crowder, 2008; Wick, Mitchell, Gilbert, & Byard, 2008.

16. d'Orbán & O'Connor, 1989.

17. Morris & Blom-Cooper, 1964; Green, 1981.

18. Gillies, 1976.

19. Väisänen & Väisänen, 1983.

20. Devaux, Petit, Perol, & Porot, 1974.

21. Hirose, 1970.

22. Analyses of parents and stepparents focused on cases in which offender gender was known, given its importance. Offender gender was available for 99.8% of offenders who killed biological parents. The exclusion of 20 cases had a slight effect on the estimate; with these cases added in, the estimate would round to 249, rather than 248. Offender gender was also available for 99.8% of offenders who killed stepparents; the exclusion of three cases had no effect on estimates regarding stepparents.

23. Offenders who killed parents constituted 1.2% of all offenders arrested over the 32-year period (estimated N = 632,017) and 1.7% of all arrestees when the victim–offender relationship was known (estimated N = 416,195, amounting to 65.9% of total offenders arrested).

24. My computations are based on the SHR offender data base. Numbers are based on national estimates after cleaning of the data. The number of parents slain was estimated at 7,948; a value of 249 per year was rounded to 250. The number of parents slain should be treated as an estimate, not as an exact number.

25. Data recalculated from Heide (1993b) and from Heide and Petee (2007a). The percentage involvement of females in parricides was slightly lower (13% and 14.5%, respectively).

26. To see whether the percentage involvement of females in killing biological parents had been increasing since the mid-1970s, I did a crosstab of female involvement by year group (1976–1985, 1986–1995, and 1996–2007). Although the percentage involvement of females in parricides increased slightly over the time frames studied (from 14.3% to 14.7% to 15.6%), the differences were not statistically significant (χ^2 [2, 7,950] = 1.911, Cramer's V = .045, p = .385).

27. My computations are based on the SHR offender data base. The numbers are based on national estimates after cleaning of the data. The number of parents slain was estimated at 1,842 per year and averaged about 58 per year. The number of stepparents slain should be treated as an estimate, not as an exact number.

28. Percentages are of course affected by the number of cases considered. When the number of cases is small, such as that of female arrests for killing stepparents, dramatic differences in percentage involvements can be caused by the shifting of a few cases in either direction.

29. To see whether the percentage involvement of females in killing stepparents had been increasing since the mid-1970s, I did a crosstab of female involvement by year group (1976–1985, 1986–1995, and 1996–2007). The percentage involvement of females in parricides did not show an increasing trend over the time frames studied, and no statistically significant differences were found (χ^2 [2, 1,838] = 0.402, Cramer's V = .015, p = .818).

30. Heide, 1992, 1993b; Heide & Petee, 2007a. Analysis of parent killings in Chicago over the period 1870–1930 also found that most offenders were adult males. See Chilton, 2002.

31. The number of cases in Tables 3-2 and 3-3 is less than that in Table 3-1 because offender age data were not available in 111 cases. The effect of removing these cases

on estimating the parameters of parricide and stepparricide arrestees is minuscule (about 1/10 of 1%).

32. Heide, 1993b.
33. χ^2 (1, 9,791) = 44.141, Phi = .067, p < .001.
34. This estimate, based on cases in which offender gender was known, remained the same when all multiple-offender incidents were included.
35. χ^2 (1, 7,863) = 206.735, Phi = −.162, p < .001.
36. χ^2 (1, 1,564) = 82.558, Phi = .230, p < .001.
37. χ^2 (1, 6,298) = 95.784, Phi = .123, p < .001.
38. χ^2 (1, 562) = 5.542, Phi = .099, p < .05.
39. χ^2 (1, 1,266) = 7.338, Phi = .076, p < .05.
40. The SHR victim data base is not easily manipulated, either. Given the complexity of the data base and apparent errors in coding of some of these cases, I decided not to further complicate the statistical discussion.
41. Estimates were based on 126 cases and 491 cases in which offender gender was known.
42. Estimates were based on 23 juvenile cases and 52 adult cases in which offender gender was known.
43. Estimate were based on 21 cases in which offender gender was known.
44. Some of the material discussed in this section was previously published in Heide & Frei, 2010; it is reprinted with the permission of Sage Publications.
45. Schug, 2011.
46. Hillbrand & Cipriano, 2007; Walsh, Krienert, & Crowder, 2008.
47. See, e.g., Baxter, Duggan, Larkin, Cordess, & Page, 2001; Dakhlaoui, Khémiri, Gaha, Ridha, & Haffani, 2009; Devaux, Petit, Perol, & Porot, 1974; Dunjic, Maric, Jasovic-Gasic, & Dunjic, 2008; Gabison-Hermann, Raymond, Mathis, & Robbe, 2010; Hillbrand, Alexandre, Young, & Spitz, 1999; Kirschner, 1992; Kovacevic, Palijan, Radeljak, Kovac, & Golub, 2008; Langer, 2004; LeBihan & Bénézech, 2004; Marleau, Auclair & Millaud, 2006; Millaud, Auclair, & Meunier, 1996; McCarthy et al., 2001; Rozycka & Thille, 1972.
48. Auclair, Marleau, Millaud, & Toutant, 2006; Buyuk, Kurnaz, Eke, Ankarali, & Oral, 2011; Corder, Ball, Haizlip, Rollins, & Beaumont, 1976; Dutton & Yamini, 1995; Ewing, 2001; Heide, 1992; Kashani, Darby, Allan, Hartke, & Reid, 1997; Mones, 1985.
49. Heide, 1992, 1993b, 1993c; Heide & Petee, 2003, 2007a, 2007b.
50. Liettu, Säävälä, Hakko, Räsänen, & Joukamaa, 2009; Weisman & Sharma, 1997.
51. Diaourta-Tsitouridou & Tsitouridis, 2001.
52. Heide, 1992; Marleau, Millaud, & Auclair, 2001.
53. See, e.g., Corder et al., 1976; Holcomb, 2000; Marleau, et al., 2006; Millaud, et al., 1996; Singhal & Dutta, 1990.
54. See, e.g., Holcomb, 2000; LeBihan & Bénézech, 2004; McKnight, Mohr, Quinsey, & Erochko, 1966; Post, 1982.
55. Newhill, 1991.
56. Marleau, et al, 2006. For information about familicide, see Fritzon & Garbutt, 2001; Malmquist, 1980.
57. See, e.g., Cooke, 2001; Maas, Prakash, Hollender, & Regan, 1984; Weisman, Ehrenclou, & Sharma, 2002. For familicides, see Malmquist, 1980.
58. Duncan & Duncan, 1971; Liettu, et al., 2009; Marleau, et al, 2006; Marleau, et al., 2003; Millaud, et al., 1996; Newhill, 1991.
59. Block, 1977; Heide, 1999.
60. Marleau, et al.; Weisman & Sharma, 1997.
61. See, e.g., Buyuk et al., 2011; Marleau, et al., 2003; Shon & Targonski, 2003.

62. Daly & Wilson, 1988a.

63. Heide, 1993b, 1993c; Walsh, Krienert, & Crowder, 2008.

64. See, e.g., Irastorza, 1982; Marleau, et al., 2003; Wick et al., 2008.

65. See Finch, 2001; Kirschner, 1992.

66. Kirschner (1992) proposed that adopted children who killed their parents experienced rejection or perceived rejection that resulted in extreme dissociation that culminated in murder. In some cases, the dissociation might result in the emergence of an alter personality, as found in multiple personality disorder (now referred to as dissociative identity disorder).

67. See, e.g., Baxter, Duggan, Larkin, Cordess, & Page, 2001; Gabison-Hermann et al., 2010; Marleau, 2003; Marleau, et al., 2006; Rozycka & Thille, 1972; Weisman & Sharma, 1997.

68. Auclair, et al., 2006; Buyuk et al., 2011; Corder, Ball, Haizlip, Rollins, & Beaumont, 1976; Heide, 1992; Marleau, et al., 2006; Mones, 1985; Post, 1982.

69. Weisman and Sharma (1997) reported gender differences between male and female offenders in terms of victims killed or attempted to be killed and legal dispositions. Marleau (2003) has called for further investigation regarding gender differences in intrafamily homicides.

70. LeBihan & Bénézech, 2004; Maas, Prakash, Hollender, & Regan, 1984; Millaud, et al., 1996; Weisman, Ehrenclou, & Sharma, 2002.

71. Bourget, Gagné, & Labelle, 2007; Cooke, 2001; Kirschner, 1992; Liettu, et al., 2009; Sadoff, 1971.

72. Heide, 1993c; Heide & Petee, 2003, 2007b.

73. Heide, 1992; Hillbrand & Cipriano, 2007; Marleau, et al., 2006.

74. Heide & Frei, 2010.

75. Marleau, et al., 2006.

76. Cooke, 2001.

77. Marleau, 2002.

78. Cooke, 2001; Hillbrand, Alexandre, Young, & Spitz, 1999; Marleau, et al., 2006.

79. See, e.g., Baxter, Duggan, Larkin, Cordess, & Page, 2001; LeBihan & Bénézech, 2004; Marleau, et al., 2003; Weisman, Ehrenclou, & Sharma, 2002; Weisman & Sharma, 1997.

80. See, e.g., Baxter, Duggan, Larkin, Cordess, & Page, 2001; Campion et al., 1985; Cravens, Campion, Rotholc, Covan, & Cravens, 1985; LeBihan & Bénézech, 2004; Marleau, et al., 2003; Millaud, et al., 1996; West & Feldsher, 2010.

81. Chiswick, 1981.

82. Hillbrand, Alexandre, Young, & Spitz, 1999.

83. Hillbrand and colleagues did not specifically indicate which diagnoses they were including as schizophrenia spectrum disorders. These disorders share symptoms of schizophrenia. Often included in this rubric are the following: schizophrenia; schizoaffective disorder; schizophreniform; schizotypal and schizoid personality disorders; delusional disorder; and brief psychotic disorder.

84. Hillbrand et al., 1999.

85. Bourget, Gagné, and Labelle, 2007.

86. The authors used the term "intoxication" in Table 3; however, it appears that they meant "substance abuse/dependency" given the Axis I designation. They discuss intoxication at the time of the crime separately in the article, although not in terms of offender gender. They noted that 13% of matricide offenders and 19.5% of patricide offenders were intoxicated at the time of the homicide.

87. Menezes, 2010.

88. Walsh, Krienert, & Crowder, 2008.

89. See, e.g., Buyuk et al., 2011; Ewing, 1990, 1997; Heide, 1992, Mones, 1985; Myers & Vo, 2012; Post, 1982; Scherl & Mack, 1966.

90. Auclair, et al., 2006; Corder et al., 1976.

91. Heide, 1994; see Duncan & Duncan, 1971; Evans, McGovern-Kondik, & Peric, 2005; Heide, 1992; Mones, 1985; Sadoff, 1971; Sargent, 1962; Tanay, 1973.

92. Heide, 1992.

93. Anthony & Rizzo, 1973; Corder et al., 1976; Duncan & Duncan, 1971; Heide, 1994; MacDonald, 1986; Mones, 1985; Post, 1982; Russell, 1984; Sadoff, 1971; Sargent, 1962; Scherl & Mack, 1966; Tanay, 1973, 1976.

94. See, e.g., Dutton & Yamini, 1995; Evans, McGovern-Kondik, & Peric, 2005; Myers & Vo, 2012.

95. Buyuk, Kurnaz, Eke, Ankarali, & Oral, 2011.

96. Buyuk et al., 2011.

97. Guttmacher, 1960, p. 51. No age is given; however, it is apparent that the offender was an adult.

98. Guttmacher, 1960, p. 51.

99. Bouchard & Bachelier, 2004 (one case); Cooke, 2001 (two cases); Maas, Prakash, Hollender, & Regan, 1984 (two cases); Raizen, 1960 (one case); Vereeken, 1965.

100. Bourget, Gagné, & Labelle, 2007; Weisman, Ehrenclou, & Sharma, 2002.

101. Raizen, 1960.

102. Maas, Prakash, Hollender, & Regan, 1984.

103. Maas et al., 1984, p. 266.

104. Bouchard & Bachelier, 2004.

105. Cooke, 2001. Cooke described three cases of double parricides committed by two adults and one adolescent (age 16). The two adult cases are discussed in this section; the case of the juvenile is discussed in the section involving double parricides committed by juvenile offenders.

106. Cooke, 2001, p. 42.

107. Cooke, 2001.

108. Vereecken, 1965.

109. Vereecken, 1965, p. 371. "Hebephrenic" is a term that was used in the past to refer to a type of schizophrenia now regarded as the disorganized type. This type of schizophrenia is characterized by disorganized behavior and speech and inappropriate or flat affect. See American Psychiatric Association, 2000.

110. Vereecken, 1965, p. 374.

111. Vereecken, 1965, p. 374.

112. Bourget, Gagné, & Labelle, 2007.

113. Bourget et al., 2007, p. 310.

114. Weisman, Ehrenclou, & Sharma, 2002.

115. The text is inconsistent with Table 3-2. The authors discuss and show their verdict as NGRI, but they show guilt charges and sentence lengths for three of four mentally ill subjects. The fourth defendant was incompetent to stand trial and was civilly committed.

116. Weisman et al., 2002.

117. Weisman et al., 2002.

118. Chamberlain, 1986.

119. Chamberlain, 1986, p. 11.

120. Heide, 1992, 1993a, 1993b; Heide & Petee, 2007a.

121. Gillies (1976), for example, describes a double parricide by an adolescent as follows: "an immature teenager shot his tyrannical parents" (p. 121). No further information is given.

122. Reinhardt, 1970, Chapters 2 and 3.
123. Reinhardt, 1970, Chapter 3.
124. Reinhardt, 1970.
125. Cooke, 2001.
126. Cooke, 2001, pp. 40–41.
127. Cooke, 2001, p. 41.
128. Cooke, 2001.
129. Post, 1982.
130. Post, 1982.
131. Kashani et al., 1997.
132. Kashani et al., 1997, p. 875.
133. Kashani et al., 1997, p. 875.
134. Marleau, et al., 2001.
135. Reinhardt, 1970, Chapter 2.
136. Reinhardt, 1970.
137. Levin & Fox, 1985; Malmquist, 1980.
138. Malmquist, 1980, p. 299.
139. Malmquist, 1980.
140. McCully, 1978; Post, 1982.
141. Malmquist, 1980.
142. Malmquist, 1980, p. 302.
143. Malmquist, 1980, p. 303.
144. McCully, 1978, p. 83.
145. McCully, 1978, p. 83.
146. Although not noted by McCully, the boy's sleeping with his mother appears inappropriate and might have been covertly sexually abusive.
147. McCully, 1978, p. 84.
148. McCully, 1978. Gillies (1976) refers to an adolescent involved in a familicide as follows: "a psychopathic youth stabbed to death his father, brother and sister" (p. 121). No further information is given.
149. Post, 1982.
150. Post, 1982, p. 447.
151. Post, 1982.
152. Baxter, Duggan, Larkin, Cordess, & Page, 2001; McCarthy, Page, Baxter, Larkin, Cordess, & Duggan, 2001.
153. The range was not given; presumably, all admissions were adults.
154. Baxter et al., 2001.
155. McCarthy et al., 2001. A study by Ahn et al. (2008) used medical charts and interviews when needed to obtain information that could be utilized to compare characteristics of schizophrenic patients who killed parents with characteristics of those who killed strangers, in the context of the prevention of homicide. Limited information is available from the English abstract (the article is in Korean).

CHAPTER 4

1. Clary & Moore, 1998.
2. Carlton, French, & Hull, 2000b.
3. Carlton, 1999.
4. Carlton, French, & Hull, 2000a.
5. Fernandez, 2001.
6. Welborn, 2006; "Huntington man," 2006.
7. Mahoney, 1989; Mahoney & Scruton, 1989.

8. Picchi, 1991c.
9. Picchi & Brown, 1990.
10. Picchi, 1991b.
11. Picchi, 1991a.
12. Readers interested in statistical analyses comparing mothers and fathers might wish to consult works by Heide (1993b, 1993c), Heide & Petee (2007a, 2007b), Shon & Targonski (2003), and Walsh, Krienert, & Crowder, 2008.
13. See Fox & Swatt, 2009. Numbers in the tables vary slightly because information was not always provided by law enforcement agencies to the FBI for the variable under consideration. Missing data were removed from the analyses.
14. These tests allow us to determine the likelihood or probability that these differences were obtained by chance and that there is no relationship between the variables (e.g., offender age and weapon used to kill). Conventionally, the probability is set at <.05, meaning that the chances that the differences occurred by chance are less than 5 out of 100. In most of the analyses I did, the tests determined that the likelihood that there was no relationship between the variables and that the results were due to chance was less than 1 out of 1,000 (<.001). The statistical results are reported in the notes or tables when appropriate. Readers who are not interested in the statistical test results may ignore them.
15. Duncan and Duncan (1971) briefly mentioned a case of a 15-year-old who killed his stepmother but gave no specific information about the stepmother or the boy's relationship with her. He told friends on the day of the killing that he was considering shooting someone and that he was angry with his stepmother. The authors commented that interviews with surviving family members indicated that "intra-family strife" predated the homicide and followed it (p. 76).
16. As discussed in Chapter 3, the FBI's Supplementary Homicide Report data base links the offender to the first victim recorded.
17. Based on N = 2,966, the mean was 59.54 with a standard deviation of 14.717; the median was 58.
18. Based on N = 2,983, the racial distribution was as follows: White (72.1%), Black (26.1%), American Indian/Alaskan Native (0.5%), and Asian/Pacific Islander (1.2%).
19. Based on N = 2,944, the mean was 31.84 with a standard deviation of 13.068; the median was 29.
20. χ^2 (1, 2,944) = 6.133, Phi = .046, p < .05. A decreasing pattern was also apparent when equal eight-year periods were examined, and it remained significant; χ^2 (3, 2,943) = 14.813, Cramer's V = .071, p < .05.
21. This finding is consistent with previous studies. See Heide, 1993b; Heide & Petee, 2007b.
22. Based on N = 2,807 mothers. The difference was significant; χ^2 (2, 2,807) = 103.768, Cramer's V = .192, p < .001. Males and females did not differ significantly in their use of the three methods of killing mothers (guns, knives, or other methods [composite]) when examined as a group or within age categories (juvenile and adult).
23. Based on N = 153, the mean was 50.07 with a standard deviation of 14.549; the median was 47.
24. Slight differences seen in percentages are not statistically significant and likely are due to the small number of stepmothers killed over the time frame studied.
25. Based on N = 153.
26. Based on N = 153, the mean was 25.49 with a standard deviation of 13.196; the median was 21.
27. Differences are not significant and likely are due to the small number of cases of juveniles (52) over the 32-year period studied. The percentage involvement of juveniles appears to fluctuate when examined over equal eight-year time frames.

28. χ^2 (2, 2,988) = 8.331, Cramer's V = .053, p < .05.

29. χ^2 (2, 151) = 3.290, Cramer's V = .206, p < .05. Further analyses indicated that the gender differences remained significant for adults, but not for juveniles, when the effect of age was controlled. Relative to adult males, adult women who killed stepmothers were significantly more likely to use knives (53.8% vs. 19.0%) but less likely to use guns (30.8% vs. 48.8%) and other methods to kill (15.4% vs. 32.1%). However, the number of adult female stepmatricide offenders was indeed small (n = 13). The number of adult men was noticeably larger (n = 84). χ^2 (2, 97) = 7.597, Cramer's V = .280, p < .05.

30. Some of this material, including studies mentioned in Tables 4-5, 4-6, and 4-7, was previously published in Heide & Frei, 2010. It is reprinted with the permission of Sage Publications.

31. Campion et al., 1985; Green, 1981; O'Connell, 1963; Singhal & Dutta, 1992.

32. Gillies, 1965, p. 1093. The four matricide offenders in his forensic sample of 66 murder arrestees were all schizophrenic males. Two of these four were teenagers. In a later study, Gillies (1976) reported that of the six matricide offenders in his sample of 400 homicide offenders, all were males and four were schizophrenic. The remaining matricide offenders included one psychopath and one man with "acute alcoholic hallucinosis" (p. 121).

33. Campion et al., 1985; Green, 1981; O'Connell, 1963.

34. Campion et al., 1985; Green, 1981. See also Gillies, 1976.

35. Green, 1981. See also Gillies, 1976.

36. Campion et al., 1985; Green, 1981.

37. Campion et al., 1985; Green, 1981; O'Connell, 1963; Singhal & Dutta, 1992. Schug (2011) drew a similar conclusion from his review of 61 publications about adult and juvenile/adolescent matricide offenders, most of whom were male. West and Feldsher (2010) drew a similar conclusion from their review of the literature.

38. Campion et al., 1985; Green, 1981; McKnight, Mohr, Quinsey, & Erochko, 1966; O'Connell, 1963. Schug (2011) drew a similar conclusion from his review of 61 publications about adult and juvenile/adolescent matricide offenders, most of whom were male.

39. Campion et al., 1985; Green, 1981; O'Connell, 1963.

40. Green, 1981; Singhal & Dutta, 1992. Schug (2011) drew a similar conclusion from his review of 61 publications about adult and juvenile/adolescent matricide offenders, most of whom were male.

41. Campion et al., 1985; O'Connell, 1963. Schug (2011) drew a similar conclusion from his review of 61 publications about adult and juvenile/adolescent matricide offenders, most of whom were male. West and Feldsher (2010) drew a similar conclusion from their review of the literature.

42. McKnight, et al., 1966.

43. Wick et al., 2008.

44. Liettu, et al., 2009.

45. Liettu, et al., 2009, p. 101.

46. Percentages were very similar when restricted to incidents in which the parent died. See Liettu, et al., 2009.

47. Liettu, et al., 2009.

48. Abayomi, 2012; Akuffo, McGuire, & Choon, 1991; Gonzalez Garcia, 1947; Hill, Sargent, & Heppenstall, 1943; Lipson, 1986; Livaditis, Esagian, Kakoulidis, Samakouri, & Tzavaras, 2005; Meloy, 1996; Oberdalhoff, 1974; Revitch & Schlesinger, 1981;

Silberstein, 1998; Sugai, 1999; Tanay & Freeman, 1976. For a detailed listing of case reports of adolescent and adult offenders involving schizophrenia, see Schug, 2011.

49. Aarab, Aalouane, & Rammouz, 2012, citing abstract.
50. Aarab, et al., 2012, citing abstract.
51. Lauerma, Voutilainen, & Tuominen, 2010.
52. Lauerma, et al., 2010, p. 549.
53. Lauerma, et al., 2010, p. 550.
54. Lauerma, et al., 2010. The PCL-R is an instrument developed by Canadian psychologist Robert Hare (2003) and is the most widely used instrument to measure psychopathy.
55. Fontaine & Guérard des Lauriers, 1994.
56. Clark, 1993.
57. Clark, 1993, p. 328.
58. Bourget and colleagues (2007) briefly noted in a study of coroners' records from a 15-year period that only three of 24 mothers were killed by daughters. Two of the offenders, a girl in her late teens and a woman in her mid-30s, were psychotic or presented with psychotic symptoms. The third case involved a severely intoxicated woman who stabbed her elderly mother. All cases occurred in the home where the mother and daughter resided. Weisman and Sharma (1997) noted that eight of the 64 offenders who killed or attempted to kill parents in their sample were daughters whose victims were mothers. No daughters killed or attempted to kill fathers.
59. Bourget et al., 2007.
60. No daughters killed fathers. See Weisman & Sharma, 1997.
61. d'Orbán & O'Connor, 1989.
62. d'Orbán & O'Connor, 1989, p. 20.
63. Marleau, et al., 2001.
64. A case report written in Portuguese described a 28-year-old woman who killed her mother. The daughter was diagnosed as having bipolar disorder and was considered not guilty by reason of insanity. See Valenca, Mezzasalma, Nascimento, & Nardi, 2009.
65. Guttmacher, 1960.
66. Väisänen & Väisänen, 1983.
67. Väisänen & Väisänen, 1983, p. 122.
68. Väisänen & Väisänen, 1983.
69. Abayomi, 2012.
70. Abayomi, 2012.
71. Dogan, Demirci, Deniz, & Erkol, 2010.
72. Dogan et al., 2010, p. 543.
73. Dogan et al., 2010.
74. Guttmacher, 1960.
75. Wertham, 1941a.
76. Wertham, 1941a, p. 26.
77. Wertham, 1941a, p. 27.
78. A psychoanalytic orientation is associated with Sigmund Freud, the founder of psychoanalysis. Briefly, the term refers to Freud's theory that human behavior is largely determined by deep-seated conflicts in the unconscious that stem from childhood fixations and to the therapy that developed from it.
79. Wertham, 1941a, p. 225.
80. Holcomb, 2000.

81. Corder, Ball, Haizlip, Rollins, & Beaumont, 1976; Dutton & Yamini, 1995; MacDonald, 1986; Mack, Scherl, & Macht, 1973; Newhill, 1991; Russell, 1984; Sadoff, 1971; Scherl & Mack, 1966; Wertham, 1941a.
82. Schlesinger, 1999. The boy was in a dissociative state at the time of the killing and was experiencing a catathymic crisis, according to Schlesinger.
83. Heide, 1992; Holcomb, 2000; Malmquist, 2010.
84. Holcomb, 2000.
85. Duncan & Duncan, 1971.
86. Russell, 1984.
87. Russell, 1984.
88. Heide 1992.
89. Mack, et al., 1973; Mohr & McKnight, 1971; Russell, 1984; Sadoff, 1971; Scherl & Mack, 1966; Schlesinger, 1999; Schwade & Geiger, 1953; Tanay, 1973, 1976.
90. Schwade & Geiger, 1953; Winfield & Ozturk, 1959.
91. Benbadis & Lin, 2008.
92. Winfield & Ozturk, 1959.
93. Schwade & Geiger, 1953.
94. Yoshikawa et al., 2006.
95. Asperger's disorder is a pervasive developmental disorder that begins in childhood. It is characterized by difficulties in social interaction and odd behavior that causes difficulties in the individual's ability to interact in social situations and other areas of functioning. See American Psychiatric Association, 2000.
96. Yoshikawa et al., 2006.
97. Mouridsen & Tolstrup, 1988.
98. Slovenko, 2003.
99. Slovenko, 2003, p. 252.
100. Slovenko, 2003. Three defense experts testified that as a result of Robert's mental condition, Robert did not know right from wrong at the time of the killing. The one state psychiatrist opined that he was stabilized on medication prior to becoming intoxicated and knew right from wrong. The jury found the defendant guilty of second-degree murder in a vote of 10–2. The Louisiana Court of Appeals, 4th Circuit, vacated Robert's conviction and ruled that he was not guilty by reason of insanity, stating, "This court cannot imagine a case wherein an insanity defense could possibly be more strong."
101. Marleau, et al., 2001.
102. See, e.g., Strean & Freeman, 1991.
103. Kromm, Vasile, & Gutheil, 1982; Medlicott, 1955; Scherl & Mack, 1966. Klosinski (1996) wrote a detailed case report in German of a 19-year-old girl who killed her mother; the mother was reportedly addicted to alcohol and pills.
104. Medlicott, 1955.
105. Medlicott, 1955.
106. Medlicott, 1955.
107. Medlicott, 1955.
108. Mack, et al., 1973.
109. Mack, et al., 1973, p. 328.
110. Mack, et al., 1973, p. 328.
111. Mack, et al., 1973, p. 329.
112. Kromm, et al., 1982.
113. Kromm, et al., 1982, p. 86.
114. Kromm, et al., 1982, p. 86.
115. Kromm, et al., 1982, p. 86.

116. Lennings, 2002.
117. Lennings, 2002, p. 61.
118. Lennings, 2002, p. 62.
119. Heide & Solomon, 2009.
120. Schug (2011) concluded from his review of 61 publications related to matricide that the rate of schizophrenia among matricide offenders exceeded the rate of schizophrenia in the population. Schug did not analyze and discuss findings in terms of offender age and gender.
121. A case involving a female juvenile who killed her mother and stepfather, largely because of extreme abuse, was reported in the third chapter on double parricide cases.
122. This case was previously published by Heide and Solomon (2009) and is reprinted with the permission of Elsevier.

CHAPTER 5

1. Associated Press, 2008b; "Attorney: Girl accused of," 2007; Ove & McKinnon, 2007.
2. Grazier, 2009; "Report: Son dismembered dad," 2009.
3. "Son charged with stabbing," 2009.
4. Brady-Lunny, 2010a, 2010b, 2010c, 2010d.
5. Gargulinski, 2010.
6. Smith, 2011.
7. Associated Press, 2011.
8. Annese, 2010.
9. Readers interested in statistical analyses comparing mothers and fathers might wish to consult works by Heide (1993b, 1993c), Heide & Petee (2007a, 2007b), Shon & Targonski (2003), and Walsh, Krienert, & Crowder (2008).
10. See Fox & Swatt, 2009. Numbers in the tables vary slightly because information was not always provided by law enforcement agencies to the FBI for the variable under consideration. Missing data were removed from the analyses.
11. These tests allow us to determine the likelihood or probability that these differences were obtained by chance and that there is no relationship between the variables (e.g., offender age and weapon used to kill). Conventionally, the probability is set at <.05, meaning that the chances that the differences occurred by chance are less than 5 out of 100. In most of these analyses, the tests determined that the likelihood that there was no relationship between the variables and that the results were due to chance was less than 1 out of 1,000 (<.001). The statistical results are reported in the notes or tables when appropriate. Readers who are not interested in the statistical test results may ignore them.
12. As discussed in Chapter 3, the FBI's Supplementary Homicide Report data base links the offender to the first victim recorded.
13. Based on N = 3,681, the mean was 55.65 with a standard deviation of 13.045; the median was 54.
14. Based on N = 3,680, the racial distribution was as follows: White (66.6%), Black (31.5%), American Indian/Alaskan Native (0.9%), and Asian/Pacific Islander (1.0%).
15. Based on N = 3,668, the mean was 26.05 with a standard deviation of 10.062; the median was 23.
16. χ^2 (1, 3,668) = 20.683, Phi = .075, p < .001. A decreasing pattern was also apparent when the data were examined in equal eight-year periods, and it remained significant; χ^2 (3, 3,668) = 32.495, Cramer's V = .094, p < .001.
17. χ^2 (2, 3,618) = 16.016, Cramer's V = .067, p < .001.
18. This finding is consistent with previous studies; see Heide, 1993b; Heide & Petee, 2007b.

19. Based on N = 3,580 fathers. The difference was significant; χ^2 (2, 3,580) = 177.108, Cramer's V = .222, p < .001.

20. Daughters under 18, relative to sons under 18, were significantly more likely to use knives (28.9% vs. 12.4%), whereas male offspring under 18 were more likely than their female counterparts to use firearms (81.7% vs. 65.8%) and other weapons (5.9% vs. 5.3%) (χ^2 [2, 793] = 21.370, Cramer's V = .164, p < .001). Adult daughters were significantly more likely than their male counterparts to use knives (29.4% vs. 23.6%). Adult sons were more likely than adult daughters to use other weapons (22.3% vs. 16.6%). The percentages of adult sons and daughters using guns were approximately the same (54.1% vs. 54.0%) (χ^2 [2, 2,786] = 7.457, Cramer's V = .052, p < .05).

21. Based on N = 1,358, the mean was 47.64 with a standard deviation of 13.133; the median was 46.

22. The offender racial distribution was as follows: White (59.8%), Bblack (38.4%), Indian/Alaskan Native (1.3%), and Asian/Pacific Islander (0.5%). Racial differences between offenders who killed fathers and those who killed stepfathers were statistically significant (χ^2 [3, 5,035] = 25.052, Cramer's V = .071, p < .001).

23. Based on N = 1,362.

24. Based on N = 1,353, the mean was 23.33 with a standard deviation of 8.809; the median was 21.

25. $\chi2$ (1, 1,353) = 20.843, Phi = .124, p < .001. A decreasing pattern was also apparent when the data were examined in equal eight-year periods, and it remained significant; $\chi2$ (3, 1,352) = 36.553, Cramer's V = .164, p < .001.

26. $\chi2$ (2, 4,949) = 21.260, Cramer's V = .065, p < .001. Other weapons in this analysis included blunt objects, personal weapons, other (as defined in Table 5-4), fire, strangulation, and asphyxiation.

27. $\chi2$ (2, 1,339) = 40.237, Cramer's V = .173, p < .001.

28. $\chi2$ (2, 1,331) = 30.457, Cramer's V = .151, p < .001.

29. Stepdaughters under 18, relative to stepsons under 18, were significantly more likely to use knives (37.5% vs. 18.5%), whereas male stepchildren under 18 were more likely than their female counterparts to use firearms (74.2% vs. 60.9%) and other weapons (7.3% vs. 1.6%) ($\chi2$ [2, 405] = 13.186, Cramer's V = .180, p < .05). Relative to their male counterparts, adult daughters were significantly more likely to use knives (45.3% vs. 23.9%). Adult sons were more likely than adult daughters to use other weapons (17.3% vs. 3.4%) and guns (58.8% vs. 51.3%) ($\chi2$ [2, 926] = 31.374, Cramer's V = .184, p < .001).

30. Cravens, Campion, Rotholc, Covan, & Cravens, 1985.

31. Cravens et al., 1985, p. 1090.

32. A psychosis with symptoms similar to those of schizophrenia (e.g., delusions, hallucinations, disorganized speech, odd behavior) but of shorter duration. See American Psychiatric Association, 2000.

33. Cravens et al., 1985.

34. Singhal & Dutta, 1990, p. 42.

35. Singhal & Dutta, 1990.

36. One case study written in German by Huth (2009) described a 24-year-old male who killed his father with a Samurai sword. The abstract indicated that he was diagnosed as suffering from borderline personality disorder and polytoxicomania (polysubstance dependence of several psychotropic drugs) . The author reported that the offender was exposed to mental cruelty by his father for years.

37. Lewis & Arsenian, 1977; Lewis, Scott, Baranoski, Buchanan, & Griffith, 1998; Maloney (1994) as cited in Ewing, 2001; Moulun & Morgan, 1967; Roughhead, 1930; Sadoff, 1971; Yusuf & Nuhu, 2010.

38. Moulun & Morgan, 1967; Sadoff, 1971. Newhill (1991) described the father as "a verbally aggressive, large, domineering man" whose "solution to his son's problems was more discipline and regimentation (e.g., military school) rather than counseling. He admitted that he expected 'perfection' from his son …" (pp. 388–389).

39. Roughhead, 1930.

40. Gillies, 1976.

41. Note also that those who attempted to kill parents were more likely to be found not guilty by reason of insanity and more disturbed than those who killed parents. However, the authors did not report whether this finding remained when the effect of victim type was controlled. See Weisman & Sharma, 1997.

42. Liettu, et al., 2009.

43. Analysis excluded attempted homicides and aggravated assaults. See Liettu et al., 2009.

44. Bourget, Gagné, & Labelle, 2007.

45. d'Orbán & O'Connor, 1989.

46. See Chapter 3 for a more expansive discussion of differences identified by d'Orban and O'Connor between adult women who killed mothers and those who killed fathers.

47. d'Orbán & O'Connor, 1989.

48. Marleau, et al., 2001.

49. See "Annex 1," Marleau et al., 2001.

50. Ewing, 1997.

51. Funayama & Sagisaka, 1988. The authors noted that infanticide is not treated severely in Japan unless recurrent. Prison sentences are given when a defendant is convicted of more than one infanticide or, in this case, of killing her father as well as her infant.

52. Lewis, Scott, Baranoski, Buchanan, & Griffith, 1998.

53. Dutton & Yamini, 1995; Malmquist, 1971; Sargent, 1962. These stepfathers were all reportedly abusive.

54. See, e.g., Corder et al., 1976; Duncan & Duncan, 1971; Mones, 1985.

55. Malmquist (2010) raised the question of whether some of the youths he briefly profiled were abused

56. Malmquist suggested that one of the six offenders, a boy who killed his father, was psychotic. Tucker and Cornwall (1977) concluded that the 10-year-old boy who attempted to kill his father shared psychotic delusions with his mother, who was psychotic; these remitted a short time after he began treatment.

57. Reinhardt, 1970, Chapter 10. The father in this case was depicted as an indifferent, lazy man who frequently drank and left home for days.

58. See Duncan & Duncan, 1978; Malmquist, 1971; Sargent, 1962; Tucker & Cornwall, 1977; Tuovinen, 1973. See Myers and Caterine (1990) for a case of attempted patricide by a 9-year-old boy that appeared to have been encouraged by the mother.

59. See, e.g., Duncan & Duncan, 1971; Heide, 1992; MacDonald, 1986; Russell, 1984; Sargent, 1962; Tanay, 1973, 1976.

60. Heide, 1992, 1993c.

61. Heide & Petee, 2007b.

62. Corder et al., 1976.

63. Corder et al., 1976, p. 959.

64. Anthony & Rizzo, 1973 (two cases); Heide, 1992; Mones, 1985. The case in Heide (1992) is presented as a clinical case study with follow-up data. The abstract of an article written in Spanish also suggests that a 15-year-old girl who killed her father was physically and sexually abused by him; see deBagattini, 1993. See Post (1982) for a case involving a 15-year-old girl who killed her stepfather.

65. Anthony & Rizzo, 1973.
66. Anthony & Rizzo, 1973, p. 340.
67. Anthony & Rizzo, 1973, p. 340.
68. Anthony & Rizzo, 1973, p. 341.
69. Anthony & Rizzo, 1973, p. 341.
70. Anthony & Rizzo, 1973, p. 342.
71. Anthony & Rizzo, 1973, p. 343.
72. Anthony & Rizzo, 1973, p. 343.
73. Liettu et al., 2009.
74. Liettu et al., 2009.
75. Marleau and colleagues (2001) identified three. One of the three I discussed, reported by Ewing (1997), overlapped with those addressed by Marleau et al. (2001).

CHAPTER 6

1. The maximum age for original juvenile court jurisdiction in the federal system and in 37 of the states is 18. In the remaining 13 states, the maximum age is 15 (three) or 16 (10) (National Criminal Justice Reference Service, 1999).
2. Dix, 2010.
3. McCord, Widom, & Crowell, 2001.
4. Associated Press, 2009; Oliver, 2009.
5. Beers, 1993; Heide, Boots, Alldredge, Donerly, & White, 2005; Mones, 1991, 1995.
6. For further discussion of applying the criminal law to parricide cases, see Murray (1999).
7. Dix, 2010; 18 U.S.C. § 1111.
8. Dix, 2010; 18 U.S.C. § 1111.
9. After the Sutton home was burglarized, upon the father's instructions, the family kept multiple guns loaded and easily accessible in various locations in case the intruders returned.
10. Cardiopulmonary resuscitation.
11. Dix, 2010; Heide, 1999.
12. Dix, 2010; Heide, 1999.
13. Dix, 2010; Heide, 1999.
14. Dix, 2010.
15. Modern statutes have followed the Model Penal Code's lead in abandoning the distinction between voluntary and involuntary manslaughter and creating a single manslaughter offense. Under this framework, manslaughter is a killing committed recklessly or one that would be murder were it not committed "under the influence of extreme mental or emotional disturbance" for which there is a reasonable excuse or explanation. In addition to delineating degrees of murder and combining types of manslaughter, the Model Penal Code created the new homicide offense of "negligent homicide" to address deaths that resulted from negligence. For a more extensive discussion of voluntary manslaughter, the Model Penal Code's recommendations for homicide laws, derivative homicide laws, and pertinent statute and case citations, see Dix (2010).
16. Heide, 1999; Redding, 2010.
17. Heide, 1999; Redding, 2010; Snyder & Sickmund, 2006.
18. Heide, 1999.
19. ACLU of Michigan, 2004. Note that juveniles convicted of murders they committed as juveniles can still be sentenced to life without parole under the U.S. Supreme Court's ruling in the 2012 case of *Miller v. Alabama*. In this case, the Court ruled that sentencing juvenile homicide offenders to LWOP *under mandatory sentencing structures* was

unconstitutional. The highest court did not strike down LWOP for juvenile murderers as a sentencing option for trial court judges, although the majority opinion did comment that "appropriate occasions for sentencing juveniles to this harshest possible penalty will be uncommon" (p. 17).

20. *Roper v. Simmons*, 2005.

21. *Miller v. Alabama,* 2012. Note that the U.S. Supreme Court consolidated the case of *Jackson v. Hobbs* (No. 10-9647) with *Miller v. Alabama* (No. 10–9646). Inmates affected by this ruling must initiate the resentencing hearing and obtain their own counsel, according to Bryan Stevenson, executive director of the Equal Justice Initiative, a non-profit law firm in Alabama that represented the defendants in the ruling. See Liptak & Bronner, 2012.

22. The section "Juveniles and the Death Penalty" was co-authored with Jessica McCurdy, JD, and was previously published in 2010 in *Victims and Offenders* [Vol. 5(1), pp. 76–99].

23. Pastore & Maguire, 2001; Snell & Maruschak, 2002.

24. See Streib, 1987, 1998, 2003; Streib & Sametz, 1989.

25. Streib, 2005.

26. Streib, 2003.

27. *Roper v. Simmons*, 2005. The U.S. Supreme Court noted that even in the 20 states that did not formally prohibit the execution of juveniles, it was infrequent.

28. Amnesty International, 1998.

29. Amnesty International, 1998.

30. Exposing Satanism, 2010.

31. Exposing Satanism, 2010.

32. Exposing Satanism, 2010.

33. Exposing Satanism, 2010.

34. Exposing Satanism, 2010.

35. Office of the Clark County Prosecuting Attorney, n.d.

36. Exposing Satanism, 2010

37. Office of the Clark County Prosecuting Attorney, n.d.

38. Office of the Clark County Prosecuting Attorney, n.d.

39. Office of the Clark County Prosecuting Attorney, n.d.

40. Exposing Satanism, 2010.

41. Office of the Clark County Prosecuting Attorney, n.d.

42. Office of the Clark County Prosecuting Attorney, n.d.

43. Amnesty International, 1998.

44. Amnesty International, 1998.

45. Lewis et al., 1988; Lewis, Yeager, Blake, Bard, & Strenziok, 2004.

46. Amnesty International, 1998.

47. Amnesty International, 1998.

48. Heide & McCurdy, 2010. For further information on these diagnoses, see American Psychiatric Association, 2000.

49. Amnesty International, 1998.

50. Amnesty International, 1998.

51. *State of Missouri v. Frederick Lashley*, 1984.

52. "Application for grant," 1993.

53. *State of Missouri v. Frederick Lashley*, 1984.

54. National Institute on Drug Abuse, n.d.

55. American Council for Drug Education, n.d.

56. "Application for grant," 1993.

57. Streib, 2005.

58. *McGilberry v. State*, 1999.

59. *McGilberry v. State*, 1999.

60. *McGilberry v. State*, 1999.

61. *McGilberry v. State*, 1999.

62. *McGilberry v. State*, 1999.

63. Streib, 2005.

64. *Roper v. Simmons* Amicus Brief, 2004.

65. *Roper v. Simmons* Amicus Brief, 2004.

66. *Roper v. Simmons* Amicus Brief, 2004.

67. *Roper v. Simmons* Amicus Brief, 2004.

68. *Roper v. Simmons* Amicus Brief, 2004.

69. *Roper v. Simmons* Amicus Brief, 2004.

70. *Roper v. Simmons* Amicus Brief, 2004.

71. *Miller v. Alabama*, 2012, p. 3.

72. *Miller v. Alabama*, 2012, p. 15.

73. Viewing of her body to allow her family to pay respects before burial.

CHAPTER 7

1. Some of the material presented under mental health defenses has been published previously (Heide, 1992).

2. Fitch, 1989; Heide, 1999; Leong, 1989.

3. Petrila & Otto, 1996.

4. Rule 702, 2011.

5. Fitch, 1989; Leong, 1989.

6. Hart & Helms, 2003; Scobey, 1992.

7. Although an adult, Loretta had many of the characteristics of the severely abused parricide offender described in Chapter 1. This type of parricide offender kills a parent to end the abuse.

8. Heide, 1999; Leong, 1989.

9. Cornell, Staresina, & Benedek, 1989; Fitch, 1989; Melton, Petrila, Poythress, & Slobogin, 2007.

10. Melton et al., 2007.

11. Associated Press, 2008a. See Chapter 1 for opening vignette and Chapter 6 for plea and disposition in juvenile court.

12. Melton et al., 2007.

13. Heide, 1992, p. 108.

14. See Heide, 1992, Chapter 8.

15. Melton et al., 2007.

16. *Ford v. Wainwright*, 1986.

17. *Roper v. Simmons*, 2005.

18. Fitch, 1989; Melton et al., 2007.

19. Goldman, 1994.

20. Most of this section was published previously in Heide, Boots, Alldredge, Donerly, and White (2005). It has been updated to reflect legislative changes and cases pertinent to battered child syndrome in recent years with the assistance of A. J. Atchison, JD.

21. Dix, 2010; Fine, 1993; Gillespie, 1988.

22. Dix, 2010; Gillespie, 1988.

23. Dix, 2010; Ewing, 1987; Olla, 2003.

24. Goodwin, 1996, p. 442.

25. Dix, 2010.

26. Browne, 1987.

27. Browne, 1987, p. 174.
28. Dix, 2010.
29. Dix, 2010; Ewing, 1987.
30. Gillespie, 1988.
31. Heide, 1992; James, 1994; Mones, 1993.
32. Ewing, 1987.
33. Dix, 2010.
34. Heide, 1992; Olla, 2003.
35. Noble, 1996; The 'Lectric Law Library, n.d. Earlier versions of this discussion were published in Heide (1995a, 1995b).
36. Kempe, Silverman, & Steele, 1962.
37. Baldwin, 2001; Olla, 2003; Smith, 1992; *State v. Janes*, 1993.
38. See, e.g., Azarcon, 1995; Bjerregaard & Blowers, 1994; Heide, 1992; Mones, 1985, 1993.
39. U.S. Department of Justice, 1996, p. 2.
40. Walker, 1979.
41. U.S. Department of Justice, 1996, p. 21.
42. Ewing, 1997; Walker, 1979, 1984, 1989.
43. Seymour et al., 2000, p. 24.
44. Malmquist (2010) argued that adolescents are more likely to experience "an accumulated sense of humiliation and shame" than "contrite restoration" (p. 77). This shame might fuel rage to the point of murder.
45. Walker, 1979, 1984, 1989.
46. Baldwin, 2001; Hegadorn, 1999.
47. Berliner, 1993; Bjerregaard & Blowers, 1994; Mones, 1993; Olla, 2003.
48. Ewing, 1997.
49. Azarcon, 1995, p. 851.
50. U.S. Department of Justice, 1996, p. 7
51. U.S. Department of Justice, 1996, p. 10.
52. *State v. Nemeth*, 1998; Ohio Evid. R. 702 (2007).
53. *State v. Janes*, 1993, p. 236; Washington statute 9A. 16.050 (Justifiable homicide), 2009.
54. Matter of Appeal in Maricopa County, 1994; Arizona Revised Statutes, 2010 (Arizona's manslaughter statute).
55. Wy. St. Section 6-1-203, 2010.
56. V.A.M.S. 563.033 (2010).
57. Hegadorn, 1999, p. 5.
58. Baldwin, 2001, p. 78.
59. *State v. Janes*, 1993.
60. Baldwin, 2001; Hansen, 1992. Other courts had declined to treat the two as equivalent. See, e.g., *State v. Crabtree* (1991), in which the decision is based "on the record and briefs before us," and *People v. Shanahan* (2001), based on the fact that the validity of the syndrome has not been demonstrated in a Frye-type hearing in Illinois.
61. Hegadorn, 1999, p. 6.
62. "Battered-child syndrome," 1998; *State v. Nemeth*, 1998.
63. "Battered-child syndrome," 1998.
64. *Smullen v. State*, 2003; Magnuson, 2003.
65. Court decision was not published; Magnuson, 2003; see Maryland § 10-916 (2010).
66. Magnuson, 2003.
67. *State v. Smullen*, 2004.
68. *State v. Smullen*, 2004.
69. *State v. MacLennan*, 2005.

70. Minnesota Rules of Evidence Rule 702.
71. In Minnesota, criteria in the Frye-Mack test have been used to evaluate the admissibility of scientific evidence and expert opinion.
72. *State v. MacLennan*, 2005, p. 234.
73. *State v. MacLennan*, 2005, p. 234.
74. *State v. MacLennan*, 2005, p. 235.
75. *State v. Dunham*, 2004.
76. *People v. Jason Victor Bautista*, 2006.
77. *People v. Jason Victor Bautista*, 2006.
78. Matter of Appeal in Maricopa County, 1994.
79. Matter of Appeal in Maricopa County, 1994.
80. Ga. Code Ann., Section 16-5-2 (2010).
81. W. VA. Codes, Section 48-27-1104 (2005).
82. *State v. Janes*, 1993.
83. Mones, 1993.
84. *Chester v. State*, 1996.
85. Chief Judge Benham, concurring specially, *Chester v. State*, 1996, p. 842.
86. *Smith v. State*, 1997, p. 821 (quoting *Chapman v. State*, 1989).
87. Snow, 2003.
88. Ga. Code Ann., Section 16-3-21 (2010).
89. *Smith v. State*, 1997.
90. Ga. Code Ann., Section 16-3-21(d) (2010).
91. *Smith v. State*, 1997.
92. *Freeman v. State*, 1998.
93. *Freeman v. State*, 1998.
94. Wright, 2009.
95. Malmquist, 2010, p. 77. Malmquist believes that rage plays a role in propelling homicidal violence.
96. Goldman, 1994, p. 249.
97. Goldman, 1994.
98. Statements made by all parties indicated that, in contrast to Mr. Garrison's nephew, his siblings did not visit the Garrison home and did not have extensive or frequent contact with Mr. Garrison.
99. Will alleged subsequent to my evaluation and report to the governor that he had been sexually assaulted by his father. There was no corroborative evidence of the alleged sexual assault. Will recanted the allegations pertaining to sexual assault when I met with him in prison 12 years later.
100. Will perceived at I-level 3 in the Interpersonal Level of Maturity personality system. This ego development classification system is discussed in Chapter 8.
101. Dr. Monahan was from a large city 90 minutes away.
102. Melton et al., 2007.
103. Dix, 2010.
104. Dix, 2010; Melton et al., 2007.
105. Dix, 2010.
106. Dix, 2010.
107. Melton et al., 2007; Morris, 1986; Pasewark, 1981. For an excellent discussion of the use of an insanity defense in a parricide case, see Slovenko (2003).
108. Dix, 2010; Melton et al., 2007; Morris, 1986.
109. Dix, 2010; Melton et al., 2007.
110. Rogers, 1986, p. 223.

111. Melton et al., 2007.
112. Melton et al., 2007.
113. Melton et al., 2007; Morris, 1986.
114. Dix, 2010; Melton et al., 2007.
115. Dix, 2010; Melton et al., 2007.

CHAPTER 8

1. Heide, 1999; Moffitt, Lynam, & Silva, 1994; Pincus, 1993.
2. Heide, 1999.
3. Wooden, 2000.
4. Fox & Levin, 2005; Hickey, 2009; Holmes & DeBurger, 1988; Keeney & Heide, 1994; Leyton, 1986; Magid & McKelvey, 1987; Norris, 1988; Ressler, 1992.
5. See Heide, 1986; Heide, 1992, Chapter 5; Heide, 1999, Chapter 4.
6. Following his arrest for scores of murders, Lucas stated that his mother was not his first homicide victim. Although the veracity of Lucas's remarks has been questioned, one fact is certain: if his mother was not his first victim, she was among the first and was far from his last.
7. Darrach & Norris, 1984; Egger, 1990.
8. Cheney, 1976.
9. Hare, 1999, 2003.
10. Fromm, 1973; Heide, 1986, 1992, 1999.
11. Heide, 1986.
12. Heide, 1999.
13. Scott made a good adjustment to prison. He was released after serving three and a half years of his seven-year sentence because the classification team considered him "a good candidate for early termination of sentence." Follow-up conducted two and a half years after his release indicated that he was complying with his probation conditions. See Heide, 1992, Chapter 8.
14. Harris, 1988; Heide, 1992, 1999; Reitsma-Street & Leschied, 1988; Warren, 1969, 1971, 1978, 1983.
15. See Morey, 1996; Pope, Butcher, & Seelen, 1993.
16. Listwan, Van Voorhis, & Ritchey, 2007; Posey, 1988; Van Voorhis, 1988, 2000.
17. Sullivan, Grant, & Grant, 1957; Heide, 1999.
18. Listwan, Van Voorhis, & Ritchey, 2007; Palmer, 2002. For a summary of I-Level development, classification methods, reliability and validity, current status, and future development, see Harris, 1988; Heide, 1999.
19. Heide, 1999.
20. Van Voorhis, 1994; Warren, 1983.
21. Warren, 1983.
22. Heide, 1999.
23. These dimensions were extracted from Harris, 1988; Heide, 1992, 1999; Van Voorhis, 1994; Warren, 1983.
24. Harris, 1983.
25. Harris, 1983.
26. Harris, 1988; Heide, 1992, 1999; Van Voorhis, 1994; Warren, 1983.
27. Harris, 1988; Heide, 1992, 1999; Van Voorhis, 1994; Warren, 1983.
28. Harris, 1988; Heide, 1992, 1999; Van Voorhis, 1994; Warren, 1983. For a more complete discussion of all seven levels, see Heide (1999).
29. Atchison & Heide, 2011; Heide, 1999; Rosenhan & Seligman, 1989; Shipley & Arrigo, 2004.

30. Atchison & Heide, 2011; Heide, 1999; Rosenhan & Seligman, 1989; Shipley & Arrigo, 2004.
31. Atchison & Heide, 2011; Heide, 1999; Rosenhan & Seligman, 1989; Shipley & Arrigo, 2004.
32. American Psychiatric Association, 2000.

CHAPTER 9

1. Harris, 1983, 1988; Heide, 1999; Van Voorhis, 1994; Warren, 1983. The other two behavioral subtypes (*cultural conformist* and *counteractive to power*) are discussed further in Chapter 15.
2. Lowen, 1983.
3. The five types identified by Lowen were the (1) Phallic-Narcissist, (2) Narcissistic Personality, (3) Borderline Personality, (4) Psychopathic Personality, and (5) Paranoid Personality.
4. The effects of horror and terror are discussed in Chapter 2.
5. This incident occurred before cell phones were commonly available.
6. Bass & Davis, 1994; Forward, 2002.
7. Giallombardo, 1966; Heffernan, 1972.
8. State sentencing structures at that time allowed inmates to earn large amounts of "good time," that is, time off their sentences. Laws have since been changed in this state and in most states across the United States. Inmates convicted of violent crimes other than first-degree murder now typically serve 85% of their sentences.

CHAPTER 10

1. Harris, 1983, 1988; Heide, 1999; Van Voorhis, 1994; Warren, 1983.
2. This incident occurred before cell phones were commonly available.
3. See Ackerman, 1979; Cermak, 1988; Cork, 1969; Heide, 1992.
4. See American Psychiatric Association, 2000.
5. State sentencing structures at that time allowed for the generous accumulation of gain time, resulting in substantial time off prison sentences.
6. Cermak, 1986, 1988.

CHAPTER 11

1. Records regarding mental illnesses diagnosed at this hearing were not available. Available data suggest that features of a personality disorder were observable when he was arrested at age 16.
2. The *Diagnostic and Statistical Manual of Mental Disorders*, fourth edition (American Psychiatric Association, 2000), describes personality disorders (PD) as enduring patterns of behavior that begin by early adulthood and are present in a variety of contexts. Each personality disorder has specific diagnostic criteria. Those diagnosed with schizoid PD have "a pervasive pattern of detachment from social relationships and a restricted range of expression of emotions in interpersonal settings." Those diagnosed with schizotypal PD have "a pervasive pattern of social and interpersonal deficits marked by acute discomfort with, and reduced capacity for, close relationships as well as by cognitive or perceptual distortions and eccentricities of behavior." Those diagnosed with narcissistic PD have "a pervasive pattern of grandiosity (in fantasy or behavior), need for admiration, and lack of empathy."
3. Harris, 1983, 1988; Van Voorhis, 1994; Warren, 1983.
4. See Chapter 2 for a discussion of overt and covert sexual abuse.
5. In James's case, "good time" was relatively meaningless, as he had two consecutive life sentences plus 16 years, making his release highly unlikely.

6. For a discussion of intrinsic and extrinsic vulnerabilities found in juvenile murderers, see Lewis, Moy, Jackson, Aaronson, Restifo, Serra, et al., 1985; Lewis, Pincus, Bard, Richardson, Prichep, Feldman, et al., 1988.
7. Palermo, 2010.
8. For a discussion of nihilistic personality, see Fromm, 1973; Heide, 1986, 1992, 1999; Magid & McKelvey, 1987.

CHAPTER 12
1. Harris, 1983, 1988; Heide, 1999; Van Voorhis, 1994; Warren, 1983.
2. For a discussion of types of sexual abuse, see Chapter 2.
3. James Cameron is a Canadian filmmaker, producer, and screenwriter. Major films include *Aliens*, *The Abyss*, and *Titanic*.
4. Marijuana is not dispensed in jails; it is smuggled into jails by visitors, guards, and inmates.
5. I did not evaluate Daniel for psychopathy because I was not trained in the PCL-R at that time. Although he possessed in some degree at least eight of the 20 traits assessed by the PCL-R, it is unlikely that Daniel would have met the threshold requirement of a score of 30 or higher for diagnosis as a psychopath. However, it is important to note that a review of this case indicated the presence of affective traits in addition to behavioral traits.
6. Recall that this case occurred in the British Commonwealth of Nations. Had it occurred in the United States, it is quite likely that the evidence would have been excluded given the illegal nature of the search and the confession.
7. See Wertham, 1941a, 1941b.
8. See Fromm, 1973.

CHAPTER 13
1. Mr. Simpson told police that he had told Ben to call 911.
2. Psychological testing indicated that Ben had a full-scale IQ in the low average range.
3. Harris, 1983, 1988; Heide, 1999; Van Voorhis, 1994; Warren, 1983.
4. Slang term for a White person, typically from rural laboring class in the southern United States, with conservative and sometimes bigoted attitudes.
5. I recommended subsequent neurological and neurophysiological testing.
6. Not counting reception centers.
7. Prisons routinely count all inmates several times per day. At count time, inmates are required to be quiet and still in designated locations. Failure to follow this regimen constitutes count violation.
8. The expression "sex games" typically refers to inmates' making sexual remarks to each other and might include touching each other in a testing way (e.g., touching an inmate's behind). It is often done to test inmates and to explore their interest in sexual behavior.
9. Aggressive behavior is listed as a possible side effect of Xanax. Ben reportedly took "street Xanax." It is unclear exactly what he took and in what amount.
10. Mrs. Kennedy believed that legal changes made in the intoxication defense requiring a mental disease or defect to exist along with the intoxicated state went into effect after Ben killed his father and would not apply. They were investigating this issue with an attorney.
11. See Chapter 14, Box 14-1, for additional reflections of Mrs. Kennedy with respect to the treatment of offenders in prison.
12. For a legal discussion of parricide types, see Murray (1999). Ben's case would fit in the "impulsive" category, with the parent perceived in the child's intoxicated state as an opponent, and would likely be a second-degree murder.

1. Boots and Heide (2006) found eight parricide offenders in 119 incidents who were sentenced to death. Borden (2011) reported the case of a psychotic matricide offender who was sentenced to death for killing his mother at age 18.
2. Hillbrand, 2010, p. 222.
3. Bourget, Gagné, & Labelle, 2007; Cornic & Olie, 2006; Liettu et al., 2010; Palermo, 2010; Shon & Roberts, 2010; Tanay & Freeman, 1976, Chapter 3.
4. Parricide offenders are mostly adults in studies by Bourget, Gagné, & Labelle, 2007; Liettu et al., 2010; Shon & Roberts, 2010.
5. Bourget, et al., 2007. All of the patricide offenders were over 18.
6. Individuals were males who were referred for psychiatric evaluation after reportedly killing, attempting to kill, or committing another violent offense (e.g., aggravated assault) against their mothers or fathers.
7. Liettu et al., 2010. Of the 212 parricide offenders, 94% were over age 18.
8. Perpetrators in the sample studied by Shon and Roberts (2010) ranged in age from 14 to 58 and averaged 31.4 years.
9. Akuffo, McGuire, & Choon, 1991.
10. Akuffo, et al., 1991, p. 108.
11. Hillbrand & Young, 2004, p. 89.
12. Hillbrand & Young, 2008, p. 92.
13. Hillbrand & Young, 2004, p. 89.
14. Hillbrand, 2010; Hillbrand & Young, 2008.
15. Hillbrand & Young, 2008.
16. Gabison-Hermann, Raymond, Mathis, & Robbe, 2010.
17. Bumby, 1994. See Myers & Kemph, 1988.
18. Heide, Spencer, Thompson, & Solomon, 2001; Myers, 1992.
19. See, e.g., Heide, 1992; Myers & Kemph, 1988.
20. Coordinating Council on Juvenile Justice and Delinquency Prevention, 1996; Glick & Goldstein, 1995; Grisso, 1996; Heide, 1999; Howell, 1995; Howell, Krisberg, Hawkins, & Wilson, 1995; Lipsey & Wilson, 1999; Neihart, 1999; Texas Youth Commission, 1996, 1997.
21. Boxer & Frick, 2008; Caldwell, Vitacco, & Van Rybroek, 2006; Heide & Solomon, 2003, 2009; Hubner, 2005; Lipsey, Wilson, & Cothern, 2002; Loeber & Farrington, 2011; Tarolla, Wagner, Rabinowitz, & Tubman, 2002; Texas Youth Commission, 2006; Wainryb, Komolova, & Florsheim, 2010; Zagar, Busch, & Hughes, 2009.
22. Benedek, Cornell, & Staresina, 1989; Loeber & Farrington, 2011; Tarolla, Wagner, Rabinowitz, & Tubman, 2002; Tate, Reppucci, & Mulvey, 1995.
23. Hillbrand, Alexandre, & Spitz, 1999; Myers, 1992.
24. See, e.g., Haizlip, Corder, & Ball, 1984.
25. Myers, 1992.
26. See, e.g., Carek & Watson, 1964; Mouridsen & Tolstrup, 1988; Pfeffer, 1980.
27. Confinement of juvenile homicide offenders in juvenile or adult institutions rather than hospital settings is common practice in the United States (Hagan, 1997; Heide, 1999), England, Wales (Rodway et al., 2011), and the Netherlands (Vries & Liem, 2011).
28. Bumby, 1994.
29. Heide, Spencer, Thompson, & Solomon, 2001. A follow-up study of juvenile homicide offenders (JHOs) in the Netherlands found very similar results in terms of recidivism (59%), and the time to reoffense (median to reoffending) was three years, four months. It was unclear whether JHOs in the Netherlands were confined in juvenile or adult institutions. See Vries & Liem, 2011.

30. Bishop, Frazier, Lanza-Kaduce, & Winner, 1996; Winner, Lanza-Kaduce, Bishop, & Frazier, 1997.
31. Mulvey, 2011, p. 3.
32. Mulvey, 2011, p. 3.
33. Ted Palmer's synthesis of these "meta-analyses" published in 1992 indicated that "behavioral, cognitive behavioral, skill-oriented or life skills, multimodal, and family intervention" were the most successful treatment strategies of those studied in terms of lowering recidivism among juvenile offenders. See also Andrews et al., 1990; Guerra, Kim, & Boxer, 2008; Krisberg, Currie, Onek, & Wiebush, 1995; Lipsey, 1992; Palmer, 1992.
34. Andrews & Bonta, 2006; Viera, Skilling, & Peterson-Badali, 2009.
35. Heide & Solomon, 2003; Howell, 1995; Howell, Krisberg, Hawkins, & Wilson, 1995; Hubner, 2005; Lipsey, 1992; Lipsey & Wilson, 1999; Lipsey, Wilson, & Cothern, 2002; Texas Youth Commission, 1996, 1997, 2006; Townsend, 2010.
36. Caldwell, Vitacco, & Van Rybroek, 2006.
37. Lipsey, Wilson, & Cothern, 2002. The term "teaching family homes" was not defined by the authors.
38. Guerra, Kim, & Boxer, 2008.
39. Zagar, Busch, & Hughes, 2009.
40. Caldwell, Vitacco, & Van Rybroek, 2006.
41. Caldwell, et al., 2006, p. 163.
42. See Heide & Solomon, 1999, Chapter 12; Heide & Solomon, 2003.
43. Agee, 1995. See also Andrews et al., 1990; Gendreau, 1981, 1996; Gendreau & Ross, 1979; Greenwood, 1986; Greenwood & Zimring, 1985; Ross & Fabiano, 1985.
44. See Agee, 1979, 1995.
45. Bailey, 1996a, 1996b.
46. Boxer & Frick, 2008; Goldstein & Glick, 1987; Lescheid & Cummings, 2002; Tate, Reppucci, & Mulvey, 1995.
47. Goldstein, 1988, 1993; Guerra, Kim, & Boxer, 2008; Lipsey & Wilson, 1999; Lipsey, Wilson, & Cothern, 2002.
48. Guerra, et al., 2008.
49. See Heide, Roe-Sepowitz, Solomon, & Chan, 2012; Heide, Solomon, Sellers, & Chan, 2011; Leischeid & Cummings, 2002; Roe-Sepowitz, 2007; Sellers & Heide, 2012.
50. See Box 16.1 for an essay written by James Holt on sentencing juveniles to life without parole.
51. Hale & Scott, 1997.
52. Benedek, Cornell, & Staresina, 1989; Heide, 1999; Heide & Solomon, 2003; Myers, 1992; Tate, Repucci, & Mulvey, 1995.
53. Sargent, 1962.
54. Scherl & Mack, 1966.
55. Duncan & Duncan, 1978.
56. Russell, 1984.
57. Kromm, Vasile, & Gutheil, 1982, p. 94.
58. Kromm, et al., 1982.
59. Neihart, 1999.
60. See Chapter 2 for a discussion of diagnostic criteria.
61. Briere, 1992; Heide & Solomon, 2006, 2009; Herman, 1992; Sanford, 1990; Solomon & Heide, 1999.
62. Cornell, Benedek, & Benedek, 1987, 1989; Myers, 1992.
63. Myers, 1992, p. 55.
64. Myers, 1992.

65. Bettman & Jasperson, 2009.
66. Benedek, Cornell, & Staresina, 1989.
67. Benedek, et al., 1989.
68. Heide, 1992, 1999; Van Voorhis, 2000. The best risk candidates for treatment, meaning those least likely to reoffend, are generally those who are classified as perceiving at the higher levels of Interpersonal Maturity Theory, levels 4 and 5.
69. Hillbrand, Alexandre, Young, & Spitz, 1999.
70. See, e.g., Petit, Petit, & Champeix, 1967; Porot, Couadau, & Petit, 1968. Both works, written in French, appear to describe the case of a 14-year-old boy who killed himself after killing his maternal grandmother. Accounts appear to be discussed in the context of a matricidal event.
71. Solomon & Heide, 2005; Van der Kolk, 1996.
72. Servan-Schreiber, 2000; Shapiro, 1999, 2001; Solomon & Heide, 2005; Solomon, Solomon, & Heide, 2009.
73. Shapiro, 2001.
74. Persons, 2009.
75. Heide & Solomon, 2006.
76. Townsend, 2010.
77. Texas Youth Commission, 2006, p. 1.
78. Texas Youth Commission, 2006.
79. *Miller v. Alabama*, 2012.
80. Benedek, et al., 1989, p. 243.

CHAPTER 15

1. Duncan & Duncan, 1971.
2. Duncan & Duncan, 1971, p. 78.
3. Tanay, 1973, 1976.
4. Corder et al., 1976, p. 959. The authors noted that some of the parricide offenders had undergone very brief periods of hospitalization (p. 960).
5. Corder et al., 1976.
6. Post, 1982.
7. Schlesinger, 1999.
8. Schlesinger, 1999, p. 748.
9. Corder et al., 1976; Heide, 1992; Post, 1982; Schlesinger, 1999; Tanay, 1973, 1976.
10. Corder et al., 1976.
11. Scherl & Mack, 1966.
12. Scherl & Mack, 1966, p. 581.
13. Scherl & Mack, 1966, pp. 581–582.
14. Scherl & Mack, 1966, p. 591.
15. Scherl & Mack, 1966, p. 592.
16. Mack, Scherl, & Macht, 1973, p. 329.
17. Russell, 1984.
18. Reinhardt, 1970, Chapter 10. The father was reportedly indifferent to the needs of his children and his wife, lazy, an alcoholic, and "a portrayal of degradation and a wretched failure" (p. 132).
19. Reinhardt, 1970, p. 127.
20. Reinhardt, 1970, p. 128.
21. Reinhardt, 1970, p. 127.
22. Anthony (1973) described two patricides committed by 13-year-old sons. Both of these cases were reported by Ochonisky and discussed by Lebovici. One of these boys

killed his abusive father and made a successful adjustment many years later. The other boy's story is recounted in the text. (Sources are not provided.)

23. Anthony, 1973, p. 271.
24. Anthony, 1973, p. 271.
25. Anthony, 1973, p. 271.
26. I attempted to follow up on a sample of 20 parricide cases I had evaluated over the years. After receiving approval from the Institutional Review Board on Protection of Human Subjects at the University of South Florida, I succeeded in tracking 18 of these offenders. Eleven agreed to speak with me. Two of the subjects' mothers also agreed to be interviewed.
27. The mean is the average obtained after adding all ages and dividing by 11; the median is the age at the 50th percentile when the ages are lined up in ascending order—in this case, the sixth score.
28. The median was nine years, 10 months; the modal year was seven years (four cases).
29. The median age of the 11 parricide offenders at follow-up was 28 years, one month.
30. Treatment was ordered in the cases of Patty Smith, Peter Jones, Evan Sutton, Will Garrison, James Holt, and Marcus Sanchez.
31. Offenses included defacing state property, manufacturing unauthorized beverages, being in an unauthorized area, committing an obscene act, failing to comply with institutional rules, disobeying a verbal order, failure to comply with count, possession of contraband, disrespect to officials, unauthorized use of drugs, and tattooing.
32. Hagan, 1997 (none of 20); Heide, Spencer, Thompson, & Solomon, 2001 (three of 40); Vries & Liem, 2011 (two of 137). Note, however, that released offenders in all follow-up samples did commit many violent crimes. Vries and Lim noted that there were 16 attempted homicides, and Hagan indicated that three offenders endangered the safety of others to a point that could have resulted in death.
33. See, e.g., Myers and Vo, 2012.
34. See Heide, 1999; Listwan, Van Voorhis, & Ritchey, 2007; Van Voorhis, 1994; Warren, 1983.
35. See Heide, 1999; Warren, 1983. "Antisocial manipulator" was collapsed into the aggressive group; see Listwan, Van Voorhis, & Ritchey, 2007; Van Voorhis, 1994.
36. I contacted Derek Hillsborough and his brother Brandon at the same time. Derek declined to speak with me.
37. See Chapter 6.
38. Bipolar disorder can include both depressive and manic episodes; see American Psychiatric Association, 2000.
39. Inmates had TVs in their individual cells.
40. Convicted felons are not allowed to own or possess firearms.
41. Driving under the influence.
42. The governor's order stipulated that if Will violated his probation, the conditional commutation of sentence (11 years) would be revoked.
43. Verified—no disciplinary reports, no corrective consultations.
44. Will made allegations of sexual assault by his father after I completed my report to the governor. At the request of the director of the clemency administration, I returned to the prison to ask Will about the allegations of sexual assault. Will said that he felt badly that this information had come out and that he would have preferred to serve the remaining portion of his sentence rather than have this information be disclosed. During the two hours we met on my second visit, Will provided details of four incidents of sexual assault. He also described overtly sexually abusive acts by his father (e.g., masturbating on his son). There was some evidence to suggest that Will

was being truthful. I noted at the time that when he provided details of the alleged sexual incidents, his affect and physiology changed and were consistent with an individual who was re-experiencing trauma. His rendition of events was often given in the present tense, again suggesting that he was reliving these events. Prior reports by Will's mother of her husband's sexually abusive and assaultive behavior lend additional support to these allegations. Mrs. Garrison's reports were corroborated in sworn testimony to the prosecutor's office by a family friend. It is unclear whether Will recanted the sexual abuse and rapes because these acts did not happen or for other reasons. However, his explanation that he had no reason to lie to me at the time of the follow-up interview deserves great weight.

45. Will received time off his sentence for good behavior in prison.

46. This information was verified.

CHAPTER 16

1. Evans, McGovern-Kondik, & Peric, 2005; Ewing, 2001; Heide, 1992; Lennings, 2002. Vereecken (1965), for example, reported that a patient admitted for attempting suicide was still in treatment when he later killed both of his parents.

2. Ewing, 2001, p. 192.

3. These three causal elements were noted in studies conducted in many countries. However, they might not apply in all cultures. See LaFontaine's (1967) discussion of how the "Gisu, an agricultural people living in the slopes of Mount Elgon in eastern Uganda" (p. 249), engaged in killing fathers as a result of widespread conflict in their culture.

4. Given the methodological problems cited earlier (see Chapter 3), the percentage of adult parricide offenders who are psychotic or otherwise seriously mentally ill at the time of the killing varies according to the study design.

5. Evans, McGovern-Kondik, & Peric, 2005; Myers & Vo, 2012.

6. Heide, 1992.

7. Ewing, 2001, p. 2001. See also Mones, 1991.

8. Heide, 1992.

9. Heide, 1992, 1993c; Heide & Petee, 2007b. Gun use was also high when juveniles killed stepfathers (75%), mothers (65%), and stepmothers (56%). See Heide (1993c) for data on all parricide victim types.

10. Heide, 1992; Kashani, Darby, Allan, Hartke, & Reid, 1997.

11. Hardwick & Rowton-Lee, 1996; Heide, 1992, 1999.

12. Evans, McGovern-Kondik, & Peric, 2005, p. 48.

13. Kashani et al., 1997, p. 876.

14. Ewing, 2001; Kashani, et al., 1997; Myers & Caterine, 1990.

15. See Ewing, 2001; Hardwick & Rowton-Lee, 1996; Malmquist, 1971; Miller & Looney, 1974.

16. Green, 1981, p. 214.

17. Cooke, 2001, p. 43.

18. Cooke, 2001. See, e.g., Dakhlaoui, Khémiri, Gaha, Ridha, & Haffani, 2009 (16 psychotic patients hospitalized in Tunisia after committing parricide); Dunjic, Maric, Jasovic-Gasic, & Dunjic, 2008 (parricide information taken from autopsy records in Serbia); LeBihan & Bénézech, 2004 (42 male parricide offenders hospitalized in France); Leveillee, Lefebvre, & Vaillancourt, 2010 (parricide information taken from coroners' reports in Canada); Maas, Prakash, Hollender, & Regan, 1984 (two cases of double parricide); Marleau, et al., 2003 (39 psychotic adults who killed or attempted to kill parents); Millaud, et al., 1996 (12 mentally ill men who committed or attempted parricide). Menezes (2010) also identified as risk factors for parricides by mentally

disordered offenders in Zimbabwe being male, living in the same household as the victim, and being psychotic. Nearly half (49%) of these offenders had sought help from "the traditional healer" prior to killing their parents (p. 130).

19. Millaud, et al., 1996.

20. Millaud, et al., 1996. Leveillee, Lefebvre, and Vaillancourt (2010) also noted that one-third of parricide offenders had consulted mental health professionals prior to the killings. Cooke (2001) also noted perceived abandonment and loss as parricide risk factors.

21. See Cornic & Olie, 2006; Marleau, et al., 2003; Newhill, 1991.

22. Cornic & Olie, 2006, p. 452.

23. Ahn et al., 2008.

24. Arehart-Treichel, 2007.

25. LeBihan & Bénézech, 2004.

26. Newhill, 1991.

27. Newhill, 1991, p. 393.

28. Ewing, 2001, p. 193.

29. American Psychiatric Association, 2000.

30. Hare, 2003.

31. See, e.g., Liettu, Säävälä, Hakko, Räsänen, & Joukamaa, 2009.

32. Walsh & Krienert, 2009, p. 1472.

33. Walsh & Krienert, 2009.

34. Walsh & Krienert, 2009, p. 1472.

35. A study by Browne and Hamilton (1998) supports this suggestion. University students who reported being maltreated by their parents when younger were significantly more likely to report being physically violent toward their parents.

36. Labelle, Bradford, Bourget, Jones, & Carmichael, 1991.

37. Malmquist, 1971, pp. 462–464.

38. Young (1993) found that parricide was negatively correlated to criminal violence in the United States, meaning that as crimes of violence rose, murders of parents decreased. Marleau and Webanck (1997), in contrast, found a positive correlation between the two in Canada. Diem and Pizarro (2010) found that previously established findings between social structure and homicide rates did not apply to parricide rates. The effect size measuring the relationship between economic deprivation and parricide, although positive, was minuscule; the relationship between social disorganization (i.e, family disruption, residential instability, etc) was not significant.

39. Shon & Targonski, 2003.

40. Shon & Targonski, 2003.

41. Kashani, et al., 1997.

42. Moore, 1987; Scudder, Blount, Heide, & Silverman, 1993; Sullivan, 2010; Widom, 1989a, 1989b, 1989c, 1989d, 1991.

43. Cases of legal authorities and social services agencies failing to protect children continue to result in children's deaths. See Reyes & Poltilove, 2011.

44. Sullivan, 2010.

45. See Cohn Donnelly, 1997; Prevent Child Abuse America, n.d.

46. Cohn Donnelly, n.d.

47. Cohn Donnelly, n.d.

48. Cohn Donnelly, 1997.

49. Widom & Hiller-Sturmhofel, 2001.

50. Grant, 2000.

51. Flowers, 1986.

52. See Court Appointed Special Advocates for Children, n.d.

53. See Court Appointed Special Advocates for Children, n.d.
54. See Sullivan, 2010, Chapter 25.
55. Dugan, Nagin, & Rosenfeld, 2003.
56. Cohn Donnelly, n.d.; Heide & Solomon, 2006.
57. Heide & Frei, 2010.
58. See Heide, Boots, Alldredge, Donerly, & White, 2005.
59. Heide & Solomon, 2006; Mones, 1993; Walsh, Krienert, & Crowder, 2008.
60. Miller v. Alabama, 2012.
61. Miller v. Alabama, 2012, p. 17. The U.S. Supreme Court referred to *Graham v. Sullivan*, 2010 (life without parole for non-homicide); *Roper v. Simmons*, 2005 (death penalty)
62. Central Intelligence Agency (n.d.), 2011 estimate.
63. Andersen & Teicher, 2008; Heim, Newport, Mletzko, Miller, & Nemeroff, 2008; Widom, Dumont, & Czaja, 2007.
64. Danese, Pariante, Caspi, Taylor, & Poulton, 2007; Dube et al., 2009.
65. Miller, 1990.

References

18 U.S.C. § 1111: U.S. Code—Section 1111: Murder. Retrieved from http://codes.lp.findlaw.com/uscode/18/I/51/1111

42 U.S.C.A. Section 5106g. (2003). Child Welfare Information Gateway. *Definitions of child abuse and neglect.* Retrieved from http://www.childwelfare.gov/systemwide/laws_policies/statutes/define.cfm

Aarab, C., Aalouane, R., & Rammouz, I. (2012). Matricide and chronic hallucinatory psychosis "case report." *l'Information Psychiatrique, 88*(1), 63–69.

Abayomi, A. O. (2012). Matricide and schizophrenia in the 21st century: A review and illustrative cases. *African Journal of Psychiatry,* January, 55–57.

ABC News. (2002, May 30). Woman jailed for killing dad seeks clemency. *Primetime.* New York: American Broadcasting Company.

Ackerman, R. J. (1979). *Children of alcoholics: A guidebook for educators, therapists, and parents* (2nd ed.). Holmes Beach, FL: Learning Publications, Inc.

ACLU of Michigan. (2004). *Second chances: Juveniles serving life without parole in Michigan prison.* Detroit, MI: Author.

Agee, V. L. (1979). *Treatment of the violent incorrigible adolescent.* Lexington, MA: Lexington Books.

Agee, V. L. (1995). Managing clinical programs for juvenile delinquents. In B. Glick & A. Goldstein (Eds.), *Managing delinquency programs that work* (pp. 173–186). Laurel, MD: American Correctional Association.

Ahn, B. H., Choi, S. S., Ahn, S. H., Ha, T. H., Kim, S. B., Kwon, K. H., et al. (2008). Clinical features of parricide in patients with schizophrenia. *Journal of Korean Neuropsychiatric Association, 47*(4), 334–340.

Akuffo, E., McGuire, B. E., & Choon, G. L. (1991). Rehabilitation following matricide in a patient with psychosis, temporal lobe, epilepsy and mental handicap. *British Journal of Hospital Medicine, 45*(2), 108–109.

American Council for Drug Education. (n.d.). *Basic facts about drugs: PCP and LSD.* Retrieved from http://www.acde.org/common/LSD-PCP.pdf

American Psychiatric Association. (2000). *Diagnostic and statistical manual of mental disorders* (4th ed., text revision). Washington, DC: Author.

American Psychiatric Association. (n.d.). *DSM-5 development. Schizophrenia spectrum and other psychotic disorders.* Retrieved from http://www.dsm5.org/ProposedRevision/Pages/SchizophreniaSpectrumandOtherPsychoticDisorders.aspx

Amnesty International. (1998). *USA: Killing hope—The imminent execution of Sean Sellers.* Retrieved from http://web.amnesty.org/library/Index/ENGAMR511081998

Anderson, S. L., & Teicher, M. H. (2008). Stress, sensitive periods and maturational events in adolescent depression. *Trends in Neurosciences, 31*(4), 183–191.

Andrews, D. A., & Bonta, J. (2006). *The psychology of criminal conduct* (4th ed.). Toronto: Lexis/Nexis.

Andrews, D. A., Zinger, I., Hoge, R. D., Bonta, J., Gendreau, P., & Cullen, F. T. (1990). Does correctional treatment work? A clinically relevant and psychologically informed metaanalysis. *Criminology, 28,* 369–404.

Annese, J. M. (2010, September 30). *Mentally ill man kills father at Midland Beach home, incinerates himself in car.* Retrieved from http://www.silive.com/eastshore/index. ssf/2010/09/mentally_ill_man_kills_father.htm

Anthony, E. J. (1973). Editorial comment. In E. J. Anthony & C. Koupernik, *The child in his family* (pp. 267–273). New York: John Wiley & Sons.

Anthony, E. J., & Rizzo, A. (1973). Adolescent girls who kill or try to kill their fathers. In E. J. Anthony & C. Koupernik, *The child in his family* (pp. 333–350). New York: John Wiley & Sons.

Application for grant of reprieve or commutation of sentence. (1993, July 23). Retrieved from http://www.umsl.edu/~phillipsm/dp/Lashley.html

Arehart-Treichel, J. (2007). Most parricides linked to psychotic illness. *Psychiatry News, 42*(23), 24.

Arizona Revised Statutes § 13-ll03(A)(l) (2010).

Arkoff, S. Z. (Executive producer), Geisinger, E. (Producer), Saland, R. (Producer), and Rosenberg, S. (Director). (1979). *The Amityville horror* [Motion picture]. United States: American International Pictures.

Associated Press. (2008a, December 22). Boy, 8, accused of killing father to undergo mental evaluation. *Fox News.* Retrieved from http://www.foxnews.com/story/0,2933,470877,00. html

Associated Press. (2008b, April 11). Girl, 14, gets probation for killing father with shotgun. *Fox News.* Retrieved from http://www.foxnews.com/story/0,2933,350129,00. html

Associated Press. (2009, February 19). Arizona boy, 9, pleads guilty to murdering dad. *Fox News.* Retrieved from http://www.foxnews.com/story/0,2933,496267,00.html

Associated Press. (2011, October 17). Arizona man gets 10 years in father's beating death. *ABC 15: Everything Arizona.* Retrieved from http://www.azcentral.com/news/articles/2 011/10/17/20111017arizona-man-kills-dad-sentence.html

Atchison, A. J., & Heide, K. M. (2011). Charles Manson and the Family: The application of sociological theories to multiple murder. *International Journal of Offender Therapy and Comparative Criminology, 55*(5), 771–798.

Attorney: Girl accused of father's murder was abused. (2007, July 31). *Bucks County Courier Times,* p. C7.

Auclair, N., Marleau, J. D., Millaud, F., & Toutant, C. (2006). Parricidal adolescents : A comparison with homicidal adolescents. *L'Évolution Psychiatrique, 71*(2), 259–267.

Azarcon, C. C. (1995). Battered child defendants in California: The admissibility of evidence regarding the effects of abuse on a child's honest and reasonable belief of imminent danger. *Pacific Law Journal, 26,* 831–879.

Bad luck for Lizzie Borden. (1982, January 19). *Financial Times,* p. 14.

Bailey, S. (1996a). Adolescents who murder. *Journal of Adolescence, 19,* 19–39.

Bailey, S. (1996b). Current perspectives on young offenders: Aliens or alienated? *Journal of Clinical Forensic Medicine, 3,* 1–7.

Baldwin, K. (2001). Battered Child Syndrome as a sword and a shield. *American Journal of Criminal Law, 29,* 59–82.

Baldwin's Kentucky Revised Statutes Annotated, M.G.L.A. 233 § 23F, KRS Section 503.050 (2010).

Bass, E., & Davis, L. (1994). *The courage to heal* (3rd ed.). New York: Harper & Row.

Battered-child syndrome valid in self-defense claim. (1998, July 13). *The National Law Journal,* p. B14.

Baxter, H., Duggan, C., Larkin, E., Cordess, C., & Page, K. (2001). Mentally disordered parricide and stranger killers admitted to high-security care: 1. A descriptive comparison. *Journal of Forensic Psychiatry, 12*(2), 287–299.

Bay, M., Form, A., Fuller, B. (Producers), and Douglas, A. (Director). (2005). *The Amityville horror* [Motion picture]. United States: Platinum Dunes.

Beers, T. (1993). Children who kill their parents: The battered child syndrome. *Children's Legal Rights Journal, 14*(1–2), 2–7.

Benbadis, S. R., & Lin, K. (2008). Errors in EEG interpretation and misdiagnosis of epilepsy. *European Neurology, 59,* 267–271.

Bender, L. (1959). Children and adolescents who have killed. *American Journal of Psychiatry, 116,* 510–513.

Bender, L., & Curran, F. J. (1940). Children and adolescents who kill. *Criminal Psychopathology, 1,* 297–321.

Benedek, E. P., & Cornell, D. G. (1989). Clinical presentations of homicidal adolescents. In E. P. Benedek & D. G. Cornell (Eds.), *Juvenile homicide* (pp. 37–57). Washington, DC: American Psychiatric Press.

Benedek, E. P., Cornell, D. G., & Staresina, L. (1989). Treatment of the homicidal adolescent. In E. P. Benedek & D. G. Cornell (Eds.), *Juvenile homicide* (pp. 221–247). Washington, DC: American Psychiatric Press.

Benefits frozen for kids who kill parents. (1982, October 10). *Juvenile Justice Digest,* 6.

Berliner, L. (1993). When should children be allowed to kill abusers. *Journal of Interpersonal Violence, 8*(2), 296–297.

Bernstein, E., & Koppel, N. (2008, August 16). A death in the family. *Wall Street Journal.* Retrieved from http://online.wsj.com/public/article/SB121883750650245525.html?mod=2_1566_topbox

Bettman, J. E., & Jasperson, R. A. (2009). Adolescents in residential and inpatient treatment: A review of the literature. *Child Youth Care Forum, 38,* 161–183.

Beukenkamp, C. (1960). Phantom patricide. *Archives of General Psychiatry, 3,* 282–288.

Bishop, D. M., Frazier, C. E., Lanza- Kaduce, L., & Winner, L. (1996). The transfer of juveniles to criminal court: Does it make a difference? *Crime & Delinquency, 42*(2), 171–191.

Bjerregaard, B., & Blowers, A. N. (1994). Chartering a new frontier for self-defense claims: The applicability of the battered person syndrome as a defense for parricide offenders. *University of Louisville Journal of Family Law, 33*(Fall), 843–873

Blais, M. (1985, March 10). The twisting of Kenny White. *Tropic (The Miami Herald),* pp. 10–17.

Block, R. L. (1977). *Violent crime: Environment, interaction, and death.* Lexington, MA: Lexington Books.

Blum, H. P. (2001). Matricide and the Oedipus complex. In P. Hartocolis (Ed.), *Mankind's oedipal destiny: Libidinal and aggressive aspects of sexuality* (pp. 209–228). Madison, CT: International University Press.

Boots, D. P., & Heide, K. M. (2006). Parricides in the media: A content analysis of available reports across cultures. *International Journal of Offender Therapy and Comparative Criminology, 50*(4), 418–445.

Borden, W. A. (2011). Classically insane. *Journal of the American Academy of Psychiatry & Law, 39*(2), 255–257.

Bouchard, J. P., & Bachelier, A. S. (2004). Schizophrenia and double parricide: About a clinical observation. *Annales Medico Psychologiques, 162,* 626–633.

Bourget, D., Gagné, P., and Labelle, M. -E. (2007). Parricide: A comparative study of matricide versus patricide. *Journal of the American Academy of Psychiatry and Law, 35*(12), 306–312.

Bowlby, J. (1969). *Attachment and loss: Vol. 1. Attachment.* New York: Basic Books.

Bowlby, J. (1988). *A secure base: Parent–child attachment and healthy human development.* New York: Basic Books.

Boxer, P., & Frick, P. J. (2008). Treatment of violent offenders. In R. D. Hoge, N. G. Guerra, & P. Boxer (Eds.), *Treating the juvenile offender* (pp. 147–170). New York: Guilford Press.

Bradshaw, J. (1996). *Bradshaw on: The family.* Pompano, FL: Health Communications.

Brady-Lunny, E. (2010a, July 27). *Judge finds McCauley guilty, mentally ill in father's death.* Retrieved from http://www.pantagraph.com/news/local/crime-and-courts/article_d14972f6-99ba-11df-af03-001cc4c002e0.html

Brady-Lunny, E. (2010b, September 20). *Local man gets 27 years for father's killing.* Retrieved from http://www.pantagraph.com/news/local/crime-and-courts/article_9878c362-c509-11df-88a6-001cc4c03286.html

Brady-Lunny, E. (2010c, July 21). *Psychiatrist: B-N man was insane when he killed his dad.* Retrieved from http://www.pantagraph.com/news/local/crime-and-courts/article_e6bcf852-94f5-11df-998b-001cc4c002e0.html

Brady-Lunny, E. (2010d, July 22). *Testimony: LSD use triggered violent psychotic episode.* Retrieved from http://www.pantagraph.com/news/local/crime-and-courts/article_371757a2-95b9-11df-8a0d-001cc4c002e0.html

Brett, R. (1997, March 21). A judge's sentence keeps teen out of jail. *The Times Union,* p. D1. Retrieved from Lexis Nexis™ Academic.

Brief of the American Society for Adolescent Psychiatry and the American Orthopsychiatric Association as Amici Curiae in support of petitioner. (1986, October). *William Wayne Thompson v. State of Oklahoma.* Retrieved from http://findarticles.com/p/articles/mi_qa3882/is_200201/ai_n9032510/

Briere, J. (1992). *Child abuse trauma: Theory and treatment of the lasting effects.* Newbury Park, CA: Sage.

Brown, P., Tierney, C., & Serwint, J. R. (2009). Munchausen by proxy. *Pediatrics in Review, 30,* 414–415.

Browne, A. (1987). *When battered women kill.* New York: The Free Press.

Browne, K. D., & Hamilton, C. E. (1998). Physical violence between young adults and their parents: Associations with a history of child maltreatment. *Journal of Family Violence, 13*(1), 59–79.

Bumby, K. M. (1994). Psycholegal considerations in abuse-motivated parricides: Children who kill their abusive parents. *Journal of Psychiatry and Law, 22*(1), 51–90.

Burgess, A. W., Groth, A. N., Holmstrom, L. L., & Sgroi, S. M. (1978). *Sexual assault of children and adolescents.* Lexington, MA: Lexington Books.

Buyuk, Y., Kurnaz, G., Eke, S. M., Ankarali, H. C., & Oral, G. (2011). Medico-legal evaluation of adolescent parricide offenders: Thirty nine cases from Turkey. *Journal of Family Violence, 26,* 1–7.

Caldwell, M. F., Vitacco, M., & Van Rybroek, G. J. (2006). Are violent delinquents worth treating? A cost-benefit analysis. *Journal of Research in Crime and Delinquency, 43*(2), 148–168.

California Evidence Code 1107 (2009).

Callaway, J. D. (1989a, March 17). Son's list of things to do included killing mom. *Tampa Tribune,* pp. B1, B13.

Callaway, J. D. (1989b, March 18). Man given life term in slaying. *Tampa Tribune,* pp. B1, B6.

Campion, J., Cravens, J. M., Rotholc, A., Weinstein, H. C., Covan, F., & Alpert, M. (1985). A study of 15 matricidal men. *American Journal of Psychiatry, 142*(3), 312–317.

Carek, D. J., & Watson, A. S. (1964). Treatment of a family involved in fratricide. *Archives of General Psychiatry, 11,* 533–542.

Carlton, S. (1999, December 18). Judge seals Davis' fate: Death. *St. Petersburg Times.* Retrieved from http://www.sptimes.com/News/121899/TampaBay/Judge_seals_Davis__fa.shtml

Carlton, S., French, T., & Hull, A. (2000a, April 22). A lesser degree. *St. Petersburg Times.* Retrieved from http://www.sptimes.com/News/webspecials/robinsonmurder/day12/index.shtm

Carlton, S., French, T., & Hull, A. (2000b, April 14). The lost boy. *St. Petersburg Times.* Retrieved from http://www.sptimes.com/News/webspecials/robinsonmurder/day6/index.shtml

CBC News. (2007a, July 9). *Medicine Hat girl guilty of first-degree murder.* Retrieved from http://www.cbc.ca/canada/calgary/story/2007/07/09/med-hat.html

CBC News. (2007b, November 8). *Teen gets maximum sentence for Medicine Hat killings.* Retrieved from http://www.cbc.ca/canada/calgary/story/2007/11/08/girl-sentence.html

CBS News. (2010, May 27). *Did twins kill mother? Victim "afraid" of girls, says neighbor.* Retrieved from http://www.cbsnews.com/8301-504083_162-20006143-504083.html

Center for Disease Control and Prevention. (n.d.). *Adverse childhood experiences.* Retrieved from http://www.cdc.gov/nccdphp/ace/prevalence.htm

Central Intelligence Agency. (n.d.). *CIA World Factbook.* Retrieved from https://www.cia.gov/library/publications/the-world-factbook/

Cermak, T. (1986). *Diagnosing and treating co-dependence.* Center City, MO: Hazelden.

Cermak, T. (1988) *A time to heal.* Los Angeles: Jeremy P. Tarcher, Inc.

Chamberlain, T. J. (1986). The dynamics of a parricide. *American Journal of Forensic Psychiatry, 7*(3), 11–23.

Chambers, M. A. U. (1986, October 12). Growing number pleading self-defense in murder of parent. *New York Times,* p. Y23.

Chapman v. State, 259 706, 708, 386 S.E.2d 129 (1989).

Cheney, M. (1976). *The co-ed killer.* New York: Walker and Company.

Chester v. State, S96A0236, Supreme Court of Georgia, 267 Ga. 9; 471 S.E.2d 836 (1996); Ga. Lexis 219; 96 Fulton County D. Rep. 1748, May 6, 1996, decided, as amended. Reconsideration denied July 12, 1996.

Chilton, R. (2002). Homicides among Chicago families. *The Journal of Criminal Law and Criminology, 92*(3/4), 899–916.

Chiswick, D. (1981). Matricide. *British Medical Journal, 283,* 1279–1280.

Clark, S. A. (1993). Matricide: The schizophrenic crime? *Medicine Science & Law, 33,* 325–328.

Clary, S., & Moore, A. (1998, July 3). Missing teens captured in Texas. *St. Petersburg Times.* Retrieved from http://www.sptimes.com/TampaBay/07039/Missing_teens_capture.html

Cloitre, M., Stolbach, B. C., Herman, J. L., van der Kolk, B., Pynoos, R., Wang, J., et al. (2009). A developmental approach to complex PTSD: Childhood and adult cumulative trauma as predictors of symptom complexity. *Journal of Traumatic Stress, 22*(5), 399–408.

Cohn Donnelly, A. (1997). *An approach to preventing child abuse.* Chicago: National Committee to Prevent Child Abuse.

Cohn Donnelly, A. (n.d.). *Fact sheet: An approach to preventing child abuse.* Retrieved from http://member.preventchildabuse.org/site/DocServer/an_approach_to_prevention.pdf?docID=121

Cooke, G. (2001). Parricide. *Journal of Threat Assessment, 1*(1), 35–45.

Coordinating Council on Juvenile Justice and Delinquency Prevention. (1996). *Combatting violence and delinquency: The National Juvenile Justice Action Plan.* Washington, DC: U.S. Department of Justice, Office of Justice Programs, Office of Juvenile Justice and Delinquency Prevention.

Corder, B. F., Ball, B. C., Haizlip, T. M., Rollins, R., & Beaumont, R. (1976). Adolescent parricide: A comparison with other adolescent murder. *American Journal of Psychiatry, 133*(8), 957–961.

Cork, R. M. (1969). *The forgotten children.* Ontario, Canada: PaperJacks Ltd.

Cornell, D. G. (1989). Causes of juvenile homicide: A review of the literature. In E. P. Benedek & D. G. Cornell (Eds.), *Juvenile homicide* (pp. 3–36). Washington, DC: American Psychiatric Press.

Cornell, D., Benedek, E., & Benedek, D. (1987). Juvenile homicide: Prior adjustment and a proposed typology. *American Journal of Orthopsychiatry, 57,* 383–393.

Cornell, D., Benedek, E., & Benedek, D. (1989). A typology of juvenile homicide offenders. In E. P. Benedek & D. G. Cornell (Eds.), *Juvenile homicide* (pp. 59–84). Washington, DC: American Psychiatric Press.

Cornell, D. G., Staresina, L., & Benedek, E. P. (1989). Legal outcome of juveniles charged with homicide. In E. P. Benedek & D. G. Cornell (Eds.), *Juvenile homicide* (pp. 163–182). Washington, DC: American Psychiatric Press.

Cornic, F., & Olie, J. P. (2006). Psychotic parricide: Prevention. *Encephale, 32*(4 Pt 1), 452–458.

Court Appointed Special Advocates for Children. (n.d.). *About us.* Retrieved from http://www.casaforchildren.org/site/c.mtJSJ7MPIsE/b.5301303/k.6FB1/About_Us__CASA_for_Children.htm

Cravens, J. M., Campion, J., Rotholc, A., Covan, F., & Cravens, R. A. (1985). A study of men charged with patricide. *American Journal of Psychiatry, 142*(9), 1089–1091.

Cunningham, E., & Marrow, T. L. (n.d.). Momma's gotta die tonight [Recorded by Ice-T]. On *Body count* [CD] Lyrics retrieved from http://www.lyricsfreak.com/b/body+count/mommas+gotta+die+tonight_20022081.html

Dakhlaoui, O., Khé miri, O., Gaha, N., Ridha, R., & Haffani, F. (2009). Le parricide psychotique: etude clinique et analytique a propos de 16 cas [Psychotic parricide: Clinical and analytic study of 16 cases]. *La Tunisie Médicale, 87*(12), 824–828.

Dalma, J., Knobel, M., & Fox, M. (1955). Paternal pressure as a criminogenic factor. *Acta Neuropsiquitrica Argentina, 1,* 491–499.

Daly, M., & Wilson, M. (1988a). Evolutionary social psychology and family homicide. *Science, 242*(Oct. 28), 519–524.

Daly, M., & Wilson, M. (1988b). *Homicide.* Hawthorne, NY: Aldine de Gruyter.

Danese, A., Pariante, C. M., Caspi, A., Taylor, A., & Poulton, R. (2007). Childhood maltreatment predicts adult inflammation in a life-course study. *Proceedings of the National Academy of Science, 104,* 1319–1324.

Darby, P. J., Allan, W. D., Kashani, J. H., Hartke, K. L., & Reid, J. C. (1998). Analysis of 112 juveniles who committed homicide: Characteristics and a closer look at family abuse. *Journal of Family Violence, 13*(4), 365–375.

Darrach, B., & Norris, J. (1984). An American tragedy. *Life,* August, pp. 58, 60, 63, 64, 66, 68, 70–74.

Davis, C. A. (2003). *Children who kill.* London: Allison & Busby Limited.

deBagattini, C. M. (1993). A hole in the wall. *Revista Uruguaya De Psicoanalisis, 77,* 87–109.

Dent, R. J., & Jowitt, S. (1996). Homicide and serious sexual offences committed by children and young people: Findings from the literature and a serious case review. *Journal of Adolescence, 19,* 263–276.

Devaux, C., Petit, G., Perol, Y., & Porot, M. (1974). Enquete sur le parricide en France [Investigation of the parricide in France]. *Annales Medico-Psychologiques, 1,* 161–168.

Diaourta-Tsitouridou, M., & Tsitouridis, S. (2001). Patricide and matricide among psychiatric patients [Abstract]. *Encephalos: Archives of Neurology and Psychiatry, 38*(3). Retrieved from http://www.encephalos.gr/38-3-01e.htm

Diem, C., & Pizarro, J. M. (2010). Social structure and family homicides. *Journal of Family Violence, 25,* 521–532.

Dix, G. E. (2010). *Criminal law* (18th ed.). New York: Thomson West.

Dogan, K. H., Demirci, S., Deniz, I., & Erkol, Z. (2010). Decapitation and dismemberment of the corpse: A matricide case. *Journal of Forensic Sciences, 55*(2), 542–545.

d'Orbán, P. T., & O' Connor, A. (1989). Women who kill their parents. *British Journal of Psychiatry, 154,* 27–33.

Dougherty, J., & O' Connor, A. (2008, November 10). Prosecutors say boy methodically shot his father. *New York Times.* Retrieved from http://www.nytimes.com/2008/11/11/us/11child.html

Douglas, M. (2010, March 10). No jail in burning-bed case after 'lifetime of abuse.' Retrieved from http://www2.tbo.com/news/news/2010/mar/08/no-jail-burning-bed-case-after-lifetime-abuse-ar-71612/

Dube, S. R., Fairweather, D., Pearson, W. S., Felitti, V. J., Anda, R. F., & Croft, J. B. (2009). Cumulative childhood stress and autoimmune diseases in adults. *Psychosomatic Medicine, 71*(2), 243–250.

Dugan, L., Nagin, D. S., & Rosenfeld, R. (2003). Exposure reduction or retaliation? The effects of domestic violence resources on intimate-partner homicide. *Law & Society Review, 37*(1), 169–198.

Duncan, J. W., & Duncan, G. M. (1971). Murder in the family: A study of some homicidal adolescents. *American Journal of Psychiatry, 127*(11), 1498–1502.

Duncan, J. W., & Duncan, G. M. (1978). Murder in the family. In I. L. Kutash, S. B. Kutash, & L. B. Schlesinger (Eds.), *Violence: Perspectives on murder and aggression* (pp. 171–186). San Francisco: Jossey-Bass Publishers.

Dunjic, B., Maric, N., Jasovic-Gasic, M., & Dunjic, D. (2008). Parricide: Psychiatric morbidity. *Srpski Arhiv Za Celokupno Lekarstvo, 136*(11–12), 635–639.

Dunne, D. (1990, November). Nightmare on Elm Drive. *Vanity Fair.* Retrieved from http://www.vanityfair.com/magazine/archive/1990/10/dunne199010

Dutton, D. G., & Yamini, S. (1995). Adolescent parricide: An integration of social cognitive theory and clinical views of projective-introjective cycling. *American Journal of Orthopsychiatry, 65*(1), 39–47.

Egger, S. A. (1990). *Serial murder: An elusive phenomenon.* New York: Praeger.

Evans, T. M., McGovern-Kondik, M., & Peric, F. (2005). Juvenile parricide: A predictable offense? *Journal of Forensic Psychology Practice, 5*(2), 31–50.

Evil Dead. (1989). Parricide. On *Annihilation of civilization* [CD]. Lyrics retrieved from http://www.metrolyrics.com/parricide-lyrics-evil-dead.html

Ewing, C. P. (1987). *Battered women who kill.* Lexington, MA: Lexington Books.

Ewing, C. P. (1990). *When children kill.* Lexington, MA: Lexington Books.

Ewing, C. P. (1997). *Fatal families: The dynamics of intrafamilial homicide.* Thousand Oaks, CA: Sage.

Ewing, C. P. (2001). Parricide. In G.-F. Pinard & L. Pagani (Eds.), *Clinical assessment of dangerousness: Empirical contributions.* New York: Cambridge University Press.

Exposing Satanism. (2010). *Who was Sean Sellers?* Retrieved from http://www.exposingsatanism.org/seansellers.htm

A family's nightmare in posh Palos Verdes. (1983, April 4). *Newsweek,* 27.

Federal Bureau of Investigation. (2011). *Uniform crime reports for the United States 2010.* Washington, DC: Government Printing Office.

Fedorowycz, O. (1999). L'homicide au Canada—1998 [Homicide in Canada—1998]. *Juristat, 19,* 1–15.

Felitti, V. J., Anda, R. F., Nordenberg, D., Williamson, D. F., Spitz, A. M., Edwards, V., et al. (1998). Relationship of childhood abuse and household dysfunction to many of the leading causes of death in adults. *American Journal of Preventive Medicine, 14*(4), 245–258.

Fernandez, L. (2001, August 8). 19-year-old Fremont man slashed his abusive mother in January 2000, guilty plea in killing. *San Jose Mercury News* [Alameda County edition], p. 1B. Retrieved from Lexis Nexis™ Academic.

Finch, A. (2001). Homicide in contemporary Japan. *The British Journal of Criminology, 41*, 219–235.

Fine, S. A. (1993). Do not blur self-defense and revenge. *Journal of Interpersonal Violence, 1993*(8), 299–301.

Fitch, W. L. (1989). Competency to stand trial and criminal responsibility in the juvenile court. In E. P. Benedek & D. G. Cornell (Eds.), *Juvenile homicide* (pp. 143–162). Washington, DC: American Psychiatric Press.

Florida Statutes 921.0026 (2011). Retrieved from http://www.flsenate.gov/laws/statutes/2011/921.0026

Flowers, R. B. (1986). *Children and criminality.* New York: Greenwood Press.

Fontaine, I., & Guérard des Lauriers, A. (1994). A propos de trios observations de matricide [About three observations of matricide]. *Annales Médico-Psychologiques, 152*, 497–510.

Ford v. Wainwright, 106 S. Ct. 2595 (1986).

For Janet Reese, death seemed her only way out. (1987, February 1). *St. Petersburg Times*, pp. 1A, 16A.

Forward, S. (2002). *Toxic parents.* New York: Bantam Books.

Foucault, M., & Kriegel, B. (1975). *I, Pierre Riviere, having slaughtered my mother, my sister, and my brother: A case of parricide in the 19th century.* New York: Pantheon Books.

Fox, J. A., & Levin, J. (2005). *Extreme killing.* Thousand Oaks, CA: Sage.

Fox, J. A., & Swatt, M. L. (2009). *Uniform crime reports [United States]: Supplemental homicide reports with multiple imputation, cumulative files 1976–2007* [Data file]. Ann Arbor, MI: Inter-university Consortium for Political and Social Research. Available at http://icpsr.umich.edu/

Freeman v. State, S97A1959, Supreme Court of Georgia, 269 Ga. 337; 496 S.E.2d 716 (1998) Ga. Lexis 336; 98 Fulton County D. Rep. 818, March 9, 1998, decided, reconsideration denied April 2, 1998.

Freud, S. (1919). *Totem and taboo* (A. A. Brill, Trans.). London: George Routledge & Sons, Limited.

Freud, S. (1929). Dostoevski and parricide (D. R. Tait, Trans.). *The Realist, 1*(4), 18–33.

Frith, M. (2003, May 17). Judge frees lonely son who killed his parents after a life of caring for them. *The Independent.* Retrieved from http://www.independent.co.uk/news/uk/crime/judge-frees-lonely-son-who-killed-his-parents-after-a-life-of-caring-for-them-538636.html

Fritzon, K., & Garbutt, R. (2001). A fatal interaction: The role of the victim and function of aggression in intrafamilial homicide. *Psychology Crime & Law, 7*(4), 309–331.

Fromm, E. (1973). *The anatomy of human destructiveness.* Greenwich, CT: Fawcett Publications, Inc.

Funayama, M., & Sagisaka, K. (1988). Consecutive infanticides in Japan. *The American Journal of Forensic Medicine and Pathology, 9*(1), 9–11.

Furman v. Georgia, 408 U.S. 238 (1972).

Gabison-Hermann, D., Raymond, S., Mathis, D., & Robbe, G. (2010). Psychotic parricide: Description and evolution of patients hospitalized in the Henri-Colin secure unit. *L'Evolution Psychiatrique, 75*, 35–43.

Ga. Code Ann., Section 16-3-21(d) (2010).

Ga. Code Ann., Section 16-5-2 (2010).

Gargulinski, R. (2010, September 24). Murder of Thomas Tucker: Drugs, deep resentment recipe of killing father, cousin says. *Tuscon Citizen.* Retrieved from http://tucsoncitizen.

com/rynski/2010/09/24/the-murder-of-thomas-tucker-drugs-deep-resentment-is-recipe-for-son-killing-father-cousin-says/

Gelles, R. J., & Straus, M. (1987). Is violence toward children increasing? A comparison of 1975 and 1985 national survey rates. In R. J. Gelles (Ed.), *Family violence*. Beverly Hills, CA: Sage.

Gendreau, P. (1981). Treatment in corrections: Martinson was wrong. *Canadian Psychology, 22,* 232–338.

Gendreau, P. (1996). The principles of effective intervention with offenders. In A. T. Harland (Ed.), *Choosing correctional options that work: Defining the demand and evaluating the supply* (pp. 117–130). Thousand Oaks, CA: Sage.

Gendreau, P., & Ross, R. R. (1979). Effective correctional treatment: Bibliography and cynics. *Crime & Delinquency, 25,* 463–489.

Giallombardo, R. (1966). *Society of women: A study of a women's prison*. New York: Wiley.

Gillespie, C. K. (1988). *Justifiable homicide: Battered women, self-defense, and the law*. Columbus: Ohio State University Press.

Gillies, H. (1965). Homicide in the west of Scotland. *British Journal of Psychiatry, 111,* 1087–1094.

Gillies, H. (1976). Homicide in the west of Scotland. *British Journal of Psychiatry, 128,* 105–127.

Glassberg, R., & Leland, E. (2005, May 21). Grisly murders baffle town. *Charlotte Observer*, p. 1A.

Glick, B., & Goldstein, A. P. (Eds.). (1995). *Managing delinquency programs that work*. Laurel, MD: American Correctional Association.

Goldman, L. E. (1994). Nonconfrontational killings and the appropriate use of Battered Child Syndrome testimony: The hazards of subjective self-defense and the merits of partial excuse. *Case Western Reserve Law Review, 45,* 185–249.

Goldstein, A. P. (1988). *The Prepare curriculum*. Champaign, IL: Research Press.

Goldstein, A. P. (1993). Interpersonal skills training interventions. In A. P. Goldstein & R. C. Huff (Eds.), *The gang intervention handbook* (pp. 87–157). Champaign, IL: Research Press.

Goldstein, A. P., & Glick, B. (1987). *Aggression replacement training: A comprehensive intervention for aggressive youth*. Champaign, IL: Research Press.

Gonzalez Garcia, F. (1947). A psychiatric study of a parricide. *Revista De Medicina Legal De Columbia, 9,* 111–124.

Goodwin, M. R. (1996). Parricide: States are beginning to recognize that abused children who kill their parents should be afforded the right to assert a claim of self-defense. *Southwestern University Law Review, 25,* 429–460.

Graham v. Sullivan, Slip Opinion, decided, May 2010. Retrieved from http://www.supremecourt.gov/opinions/09pdf/08-7412.pdf

Grant, B. F. (2000). Estimates of US children exposed to alcohol abuse and dependence in the family. *American Journal of Public Health, 90*(1), 112–115.

Grazier, S. (2009, September 26). Berry receives 3 years. *Cortez Journal*. Retrieved from http://www.cortezjournal.com/main.asp?SectionID=1&SubSectionID=1&ArticleID=8101

Green, C. M. (1981). Matricide by sons. *Medicine, Science and the Law, 21,* 207–214.

Greenwood, P. W. (1986). *Correctional supervision of juvenile offenders: Where do we go from here?* Santa Monica, CA: RAND.

Greenwood, P. W., & Zimring, F. E. (1985). *One more chance: The pursuit of promising intervention strategies for chronic juvenile offenders*. Santa Monica, CA: RAND.

Gregg v. Georgia, 428 U.S. 153 (1976).

Grinberg, E. (2006a, January 27). Psychologist: In killing his family, Cody Posey took the only road available to him. *Court TV.* Retrieved from http://news.findlaw.com/court_tv/s/20060127/27jan2006165056.html

Grinberg, E. (2006b, February 1). Psychologist: A lifetime of abuse, depression led teen shooter to despair. *Court TV* [Television broadcast]. Atlanta, GA: Turner Broadcasting.

Grinberg, E. (2006c, February 1). Psychiatrist: Teen took responsibility for killing family. *Court TV.* Retrieved from http://news.findlaw.com/court_tv/s/20060131/31jan2006172943.html

Grinberg, E. (2006d, February 1). Teen who killed his family describes years of torture at his father's hand. *Court TV* [Television broadcast]. Atlanta, GA: Turner Broadcasting.

Grinberg, E. (2006e, February 8). Teen Cody Posey convicted of murder, manslaughter for killing his family. *Court TV.* Retrieved from http://news.findlaw.com/court_tv/s/20060208/08feb2006103242.html

Grisso, T. (1996). Society's retributive response to juvenile violence: A developmental perspective. *Law and Human Behavior, 20*(3), 229–246.

Grisso, T., & Schwartz, R. G. (2000). *Youth on trial.* Chicago: University of Chicago Press.

Grodd, E. R., & Diamond, J. L. (2008, August 13). *Primetime crime: Teen charged with parents' gruesome murder.* Retrieved from http://abcnews.go.com/TheLaw/story?id=3451371&page=1

Groth, A. N. (1981). *Chart of sexual offenders against children.* Webster, MA: Forensic Mental Health Associates, Inc.

Groth, A. N., & Birnbaum, H. J. (1979). *Men who rape: The psychology of the offender.* New York: Plenum.

Guandolo, V. L. (1985). Munchausen Syndrome by Proxy: An outpatient challenge. *Pediatrics, 75*(3), 526–530.

Guerra, G., Kim, T. E., & Boxer, P. (2008). What works: Best practices with juvenile offenders. In R. D. Hoge, N. G. Guerra, & P. Boxer (Eds.), *Treating the juvenile offender* (pp. 79–102). New York: Guilford Press.

Guttmacher, M. S. (1960). *The mind of the murderer.* New York: Farrar, Straus and Cudahy.

Haegerich, T. M., & Bottoms, B. L. (2000). Empathy and jurors' decisions in patricide trials involving child sexual assault allegations. *Law and Human Behavior, 24*(4), 421–428.

Hagan, M. P. (1997). An analysis of adolescent perpetrators of homicide and attempted homicide upon return to the community. *International Journal of Offender Therapy and Comparative Criminology, 41*(3), 250–259.

Haizlip, T., Corder, B. F., & Ball, B. C. (1984). Adolescent murderer. In C. R. Keith (Ed.), *Aggressive adolescent* (pp. 126–148). New York: Free Press.

Hale, R., & Scott, D. (1997). Sociological jurisprudence for parricide. *Journal of Contemporary Criminal Justice, 13*(3), 279–293.

Hamilton, T. I. (2004). Experts describe kids who kill parents. *San Antonio Express-News*, p. 1B. Retrieved from Lexis Nexis™ Academic.

Hamsher, J., Murphy, D., Townsend, C. (Producers), & Stone, O. (Director). (1994). *Natural born killers* [Motion picture]. United States: Warner Bros. Pictures.

Hansen, M. (1992). Battered child's defense. *ABA Journal, 78,* 28.

Hardwick, P. J., & Rowton- Lee, M. A. (1996). Adolescent homicide: Towards assessment of risk. *Journal of Adolescence, 19,* 263–276.

Hare, R. D. (1999). *Without conscience: The disturbing world of the psychopaths among us.* New York: Guilford Publications.

Hare, R. D. (2003). *Hare PCL-R (2nd ed.).* North Tonawanda, NY: MHS.

Harris, P. W. (1983). The interpersonal maturity of delinquents and nondelinquents. In W. S. Laufer & J. M. Day (Eds.), *Personality theory, moral development and criminal behavior* (pp. 145–64). Lexington, Mass: D.C. Heath and Company.

Harris, P. W. (1988). The Interpersonal Maturity Level Classification System: I-Level. *Criminal Justice and Behavior, 15,* 58–77.

Hart, J. L., & Helms, J. L. (2003). Factors of parricide: Allowance of the use of battered child syndrome as a defense. *Aggression and Violent Behavior, 8,* 671–683.

Heffernan, E. (1972). *Making it in prison: The square, the cool, and the life.* New York: Wiley-Interscience.

Hegadorn, R. (1999). Clemency: Doing justice to incarcerated battered children. *Missouri Bar Journal.* Retrieved from http://www.mobar.org/journal/1999/marapr/hegadorn. htm

Heide, K. M. (1986). A taxonomy of murder: Motivational dynamics behind the homicidal acts of adolescents. *The Journal of Justice Issues, 1,* 4–19.

Heide, K. M. (1989). Parricide: Incidence and issues. *The Justice Professional, 4*(1), 19–41.

Heide, K. M. (1992). *Why kids kill parents: Child abuse and adolescent homicide* Columbus: Ohio State University Press.

Heide, K. M. (1993a). Juvenile involvement in multiple offender and multiple victim parricides. *Journal of Police & Criminal Psychology, 9*(2), 53–64.

Heide, K. M. (1993b). Parents who get killed and the children who kill them. *Journal of Interpersonal Violence, 8*(4), 531–544.

Heide, K. M. (1993c). Weapons used by juveniles and adults to kill parents. *Behavioral Sciences & the Law, 11*(4), 397–405.

Heide, K. M. (1994). Evidence of child maltreatment among adolescent parricide offenders. *International Journal of Offender Therapy and Comparative Criminology, 38*(2), 151–162.

Heide, K. M. (1995a). The Menendez Murders: Parricide in perspective. In C. Block & Richard Block (Ed.), *Proceedings of the Third Annual Meeting of the Homicide Research Working Group* (pp. 191–194). Washington, DC: National Institute of Justice.

Heide, K. M. (1995b). *Why kids kill parents: Child abuse and adolescent homicide* (paperback ed.). Thousand Oaks, CA: Sage.

Heide, K. M. (1997). Dangerously antisocial kids who kill their parents: Understanding the phenomenon better. In P. Latimore (Ed.), *Proceedings of the 1996 Meeting of the Homicide Research Working Group* (pp. 228–233). Washington, DC: National Institute of Justice.

Heide, K. M. (1999). *Young killers: The challenge of juvenile homicide.* Thousands Oaks, CA: Sage.

Heide, K. M. (2007). Parricide. In N. Jackson (Ed.), *Encyclopedia of domestic violence* (pp. 530–536). New York: Routledge.

Heide, K. M., & Boots, D. P. (2007). A comparative analysis of media reports of U.S. parricide cases with officially reported national crime data and the psychiatric and psychological literature. *International Journal of Offender Therapy and Comparative Criminology, 51*(6), 646–675.

Heide, K. M., Boots, D., Alldredge, C., Donerly, B., & White, J. R. (2005). Battered Child Syndrome: An overview of case law and legislation. *Criminal Law Bulletin, 41*(3), 219–239.

Heide, K. M., & Frei, A. (2010). Matricide: A critique of the literature. *Trauma, Violence, & Abuse, 11*(1), 3–17.

Heide, K. M., & McCurdy, J. L. (2010). Juvenile parricide offenders sentenced to death. *Victims & Offenders, 5*(1), 76–99.

Heide, K. M., & Petee, T. (2003). Parents who get killed and the children who kill them: An examination of 24 years of data. In C. R. Block & R. L. Block (Eds.), *Proceedings of the 2003 Homicide Research Working Group Annual Symposium* (pp. 319–335). Chicago, IL: Homicide Research Working Group.

Heide, K. M., & Petee, T. A. (2007a). Parricide: An examination of 24 years of data. *Journal of Interpersonal Violence, 23*(10), 1382–1399.

Heide, K. M., & Petee, T. A. (2007b). Weapons used by juveniles and adult offenders in U.S. parricide cases. *Journal of Interpersonal Violence, 23*(10), 1400–1414.

Heide, K. M., Roe-Sepowitz, D., Solomon, E. P., & Chan, H. C. (2012). Male and female juveniles arrested for murder: A comprehensive analysis of U.S. data by offender gender. *International Journal of Offender Therapy and Comparative Criminology, 56*(3), 356–384.

Heide, K. M., & Solomon, E. P. (1999). Treating young killers. In K. M. Heide (Ed.), *Young Killers* (pp. 221–238). Thousand Oaks, CA: Sage.

Heide, K. M., & Solomon, E. P. (2003). Treating today's juvenile homicide offenders. *Youth Violence and Juvenile Justice, 1*(1), 5–31.

Heide, K. M., & Solomon, E. P. (2006). Biology, childhood trauma, and murder: Rethinking justice. *International Journal of Law and Psychiatry, 29*(3), 220–233.

Heide, K. M., & Solomon, E. P. (2009). Female juvenile murderers: Biological and psychological dynamics leading to homicide. *International Journal of Law & Psychiatry, 32,* 244–252.

Heide, K. M., Solomon, E. P., Sellers, B. G., & Chan, H. C. (2011). Male and female juvenile homicide offenders: An empirical analysis of U.S. arrest data by offender age. *Feminist Criminology, 6*(1), 3–31.

Heide, K. M., Spencer, E., Thompson, A., & Solomon, E. P. (2001). Who's in, who's out, and who's back: Follow-up data on 59 juveniles incarcerated for murder or attempted murder in the early 1980s. *Behavioral Sciences and the Law, 19,* 97–108.

Heim, C., Newport, D. J., Mletzko, T., Miller, A. H., & Nemeroff, C. B. (2008). The link between childhood trauma and depression: Insights from HPA axis studies in humans. *Psychoneuroendocrinology, 33*(6), 693–710.

Herman, J. L. (1992). Complex PTSD: A syndrome in survivors of prolonged and repeated trauma. *Journal of Traumatic Stress, 5*(3), 377–391.

Heron, L. (2006). *Inherited rage.* Amazon Digital Services: Lucky Egg Publishing.

Hickey, E. W. (2009). *Serial murderers and their victims* (5th ed.). Belmont, CA : Cengage Learning.

Hill, D., Sargent, W., & Heppenstall, M. E. (1943). A case of matricide. *Lancet, 244,* 526–527.

Hillbrand, M. (2010). Commentary: Addressing suicidality in the treatment of parricidal offenders. *Journal of the American Academy of Psychiatry and Law, 38,* 221–222.

Hillbrand, M., Alexandre, J. W., Young, J. L., & Spitz, R. T. (1999). Parricides: Characteristics of offenders and victims, legal factors, and treatment issues. *Aggression and Violent Behavior, 4*(2), 179–190.

Hillbrand, M., & Cipriano, T. (2007). Commentary: Parricides—Unanswered questions, methodological obstacles, and legal considerations. *Journal of the American Academy of Psychiatry and Law, 35*(3), 313–316.

Hillbrand, M., & Young, J. L. (2004). Group psychotherapy for parricides: The Genesis group. *Forensische Psychiatrie und Psychotherapie Werkstattschriften, 11,* 89–97.

Hillbrand, M., & Young, J. L. (2008). Instilling hope into forensic treatment: The antidote to despair and desperation. *Journal of the American Academy of Psychiatry and the Law, 36,* 90–94.

Hirose, K. (1970). A psychiatric study of female homicides: On the case of parricide. *Acta Criminologiae et Medicinae Legalis Japonica, 36,* 29.

Hitchcock, A. (Producer/Director). (1960). *Psycho* [Motion picture]. United States: Paramount Pictures.

Holcomb, W. R. (2000). Matricide: Primal aggression in search of self-affirmation. *Psychiatry, 63*(3), 264–287.

Holmes, R., & DeBurger, J. (1988). *Serial murder.* New Park, CA: Sage.

Howard, C. (1994). *Love's blood.* New York: St. Martin's Press.

Howell, J. C. (Ed.). (1995). *Guide for implementing the comprehensive strategy for serious, violent, and chronic juvenile offenders.* Washington, DC: U.S. Department of Justice, Office of Justice Programs, Office of Juvenile Justice and Delinquency Prevention.

Howell, J. C., Krisberg, B., Hawkins, J. D., & Wilson, J. J. (Eds.). (1995). *A sourcebook: Serious, violent, & chronic juvenile offenders* (pp. 275–277). Thousand Oaks, CA: Sage.

Hubner, J. (2005). *Last chance in Texas.* New York: Random House.

Hughes, J. R., Zagar, R. J., Busch, K. G., Grove, W. M., & Arbit, J. (2009). Looking forward in records of youth abused as children: Risks for homicidal, violent, and delinquent offenses. *Psychological Reports, 104,* 103–127.

Hull, J. D. (1987, October 19). Brutal treatment, vicious deeds. *Time,* 68.

Huntington man who killed mom sentenced. (2006, December 16). *The Orange County Register*, p. County B. Retrieved from Lexis Nexis™ Academic.

Huth, M. (2009). Patrizid mittels eines Samuraischwertes [Patricide using a samurai sword]. *Trauma & Gewalt, 3*(3), 260.

Infoplease. (2002). *State Compulsory School Attendance Laws.* Retrieved from http://www.infoplease.com/ipa/A0112617.html

Irastorza, A. P. (1982). Homicidios, asesinatos y parricidios en psiquiatría forense [Killings, assassinations, and parricides in forensic psychiatry]. *Revista del Hospital Psiquiátrico de La Habana, 23*(2), 303–314.

It made terrible sense. (1982, December 13). *Time,* 34.

Jackson v. Hobbs (No. 10-9647). (2011, March 23). Retrieved from http://www.supreme-court.gov/Search.aspx?FileName=/docketfiles/10-9646.htm

Jacobs, A. (2004). Towards a structural theory of matricide: Psychoanalysis, the *Oresteia* and the maternal prohibition. *Women: A Cultural Review, 15*(1), 19–34.

James, J. R. (1994). Turning the tables: Redefining self-defense theory for children who kill abusive parents. *Law & Psychology Review, 18,* 393–408.

Janos, L. (1983, March 7). On a windswept Wyoming prairie. *People Weekly,* 34–36.

Jeremiah Raymond Berry pleads guilty to feeding abusive father to coyotes. (2009, October 29). *The Huffington Post.* Retrieved from http://www.huffingtonpost.com/2009/09/28/jeremiah-raymond-berry-pl_n_301757.html?view=screen

Johnson, B. (1997, July 10). Abuse outlined during teen's murder trial. *Rolling Meadows Review*, p. 9.

Jones, J. G., Butler, H. L., Hamilton, B., Perdue, J. D., Stern, H. P., & Woody, R. C. (1986). Munchausen by Proxy. *Child Abuse and Neglect, 10,* 33–40.

Kaczor, B. (1989, July 1). Precedent-setting defense gets girl cleared in slaying. *Tampa Tribune*, pp. B1, B5.

Karas, B. (2006, January 12). Anchor memo: New Mexico v. Cody Posey. *Court TV* [Television broadcast]. Atlanta, GA: Turner Broadcasting.

Kashani, J. H., Darby, P. J., Allan, W. D., Hartke, K. L., & Reid, J. C. (1997). Intrafamilial homicide committed by juveniles: Examination of a sample with recommendations for prevention. *Journal of Forensic Sciences, 42*(5), 873–878.

Kaufman, G. (1992). *Shame: The power of caring* (3rd. ed.). Cambridge, MA: Schneckman Publishing Company, Inc.

Keeney, B., & Heide, K. M. (1994). Gender differences in serial murderers: A preliminary analysis. *The Journal of Interpersonal Violence, 9*(3), 383–398.

Kelleher, M. D. (1998). *When good kids kill.* Westport, CT: Praeger.

Kempe, C. H., Silverman, F. N., & Steele, B. F. (1962). The battered child syndrome. *Journal of the American Medical Association, 181,* 17–24.

Kiremidjian, D. (1976). Crime and punishment: Matricide and the woman question. *American Imago, 33*(4), 403–433.

Kirschner, D. (1992). Understanding adoptees who kill: Dissociation, patricide, and the psychodynamics of adoption. *International Journal of Offender Therapy and Comparative Criminology, 36*(4), 323–333.

Kleiman, D. (1986, September 14). Murder on Long Island. *The New York Times Magazine,* pp. 52, 56, 58, 62, 64, 65.

Kleiman, D. (1988). *A deadly silence.* New York: The Atlantic Monthly Press.

Klosinski, G. (1996). Murder of the mother by the daughter: Family dynamics and mythology. *Praxis der Kinderpsychologie und Kinderpsychiatrie, 45*(6), 217–222.

Kovacevic, D., Palijan, T. Z., Radeljak, S., Kovac, M., & Golub, T. L. (2008). Domestic homicide cases related to schizophrenic offenders. *Collegium Antropologicum, 32*(2), 115–122.

Krisberg, B., Currie, E., Onek, D., & Wiebush, R. G. (1995). Graduated sanctions for serious, violent, and chronic juvenile offenders. In J. C. Howell, B. Krisberg, J. D. Hawkins, & J. J. Wilson (Eds.), *A sourcebook: Serious, violent, & chronic juvenile offenders* (pp. 142–170). Thousand Oaks, CA: Sage.

Kromm, J., Vasile, R. G., & Gutheil, T. H. (1982). Occupational therapy in the assessment of a woman accused of murder. *Psychiatric Quarterly, 54*(2), 85–96.

Labelle, A., Bradford, J. M., Bourget, D., Jones, B., & Carmichael, M. (1991). Adolescent murderers. *Canadian Journal of Psychatry, 36*(8), 583–587.

La. Code Evid. Ann. art. 404A(2)(a) (1994).

LaFontaine, J. S. (1967). Parricide in Bugisu: A study in inter-generational conflict. *Man, New Series, 2*(2), 249–259.

Lang, D. (1995). *The dark son.* New York: Avon Books.

Langer, L. M. (2004). Matricide or patricide: Profile of inpatients. *Enfermagem Atual, 4*(23), 39–41.

Lannert, S. (2011). *Redemption.* New York: Crown Publishers.

Lauerma, H., Voutilainen, J., & Tuominen, T. (2010). Matricide and two sexual femicides by a male strangler with a transgender sadomasochistic identity. *Journal of Forensic Sciences, 55*(2), 549–550.

Law & Order. (2003, January 16). Prosecutors appeal killer's sentence. *Tampa Tribune,* p. 6. Retrieved from Lexis Nexis™ Academic.

LawServer. (2010). *Florida Statutes § 984.085—Sheltering unmarried minors; aiding unmarried minor runaways; violations.* Retrieved from http://www.lawserver.com/law/state/florida/statutes/florida_statutes_984-085

LeBihan, P., & Bénézech, M. (2004). Degree of organization of pathological parricide: Modus operandi and criminological profile of 42 cases. *Annales Medico-Psychologiques, 162*(8), 626–633.

Lennings, C. J. (2002). Children who kill family members: Three cases from Australia. *Journal of Threat Assessment, 2*(2), 57–72.

Leong, G. B. (1989). Clinical issues for the forensic examiner. In E. P. Benedek & D. G. Cornell (Eds.), *Juvenile homicide* (pp. 115–141). Washington, DC: American Psychiatric Press.

Leischeid, A. W., & Cummings, A. L. (2002). Youth violence: An overview of predictors, counseling interventions, and future directions. *Canadian Journal of Counseling, 36*(4), 256–264.

Leveillee, S., Lefebvre, J., & Vaillancourt, J. -P. (2010). Parricide committed by adults men: Descriptive variables and motivations. *L'Evolution Psychiatrique, 75*(1), 77–91.

Levin, J., & Fox, J. A. (1985). *Mass murder: America's growing menace.* New York: Plenum Press.

Lewis, C. N., & Arsenian, J. (1977). Murder will out: A case of parricide in a painter and his writing. *Journal of Nervous & Mental Disorders, 164*(4), 273–279.

Lewis, D. O., Moy, E., Jackson, L. D., Aaronson, R., Restifo, N., Serra, S., et al. (1985). Biopsychosocial characteristics of children who later murder: A prospective study. *American Journal of Psychiatry, 142,* 1161–1166.

Lewis, D. O., Pincus, J. H., Bard, B., Richardson, E., Prichep, L. S., Feldman, M., et al. (1988). Neuropsychiatric, psychoeducational, and family characteristics of 14 juveniles condemned to death in the United States. *American Journal of Psychiatry, 145*(5), 584–589.

Lewis, D. O., Yeager, C. A., Blake, P., Bard, B., & Strenziok, M. (2004). Ethics questions raised by the neuropsychiatric, neuropsychological, educational, developmental, and family characteristics of 18 juveniles awaiting execution in Texas. *Journal of American Academy of Psychiatry and Law, 32*(4), 408–429.

Lewis, M. E., Scott, D. C., Baranoski, M. V., Buchanan, J. A., & Griffith, E. E. H. (1998). Prototypes of intrafamily homicide and serious assault among insanity acquittees. *Journal of the American Academy of Psychiatry and the Law, 26*(1), 37–48.

Leyton, E. (1986). *Compulsive killers: The story of modern multiple murder.* New York: New York University Press.

Leyton, E. (1990). *Sole survivor: Children who murder their parents.* New York: Pocket Books.

Liegner, E., & Motycka, R. (1981). James Joyce's *Ulysses* revisited: Matricide and the search for the mother. *The Psychoanalytic Review, 68*(4), 561–579.

Liettu, A., Mikkola, L., Säävälä, H., Räsä nen, P., Joukamaa, M., & Hakko, H. (2010). Mortality rates of males who commit parricide or other violent offense against a parent. *Journal of the American Academy of Psychiatry and Law, 38*(2), 212–220.

Liettu, A., Säävälä, H., Hakko, H., Räsä nen, P., & Joukamaa, M. (2009). Mental disorders of male parricidal offenders: A study of offenders in forensic psychiatric examination in Finland during 1973–2004. *Social Psychiatry and Psychiatric Epidemiology, 44*(2), 96–103.

Lii, H. (2002). Lessons from a matricide. *Beijing Review, 45*(27), 7.

Lindner, R. M. (1948). The equivalents of matricide. *The Psychoanalytic Quarterly, 17,* 453–470.

Linedecker, C. (1993). *Killer kids.* New York: St. Martin's Press.

Lipsey, M. W. (1992). Juvenile delinquency treatment: A meta-analytic inquiry into the variability of effects. In T. D. Cook (Ed.), *Meta-analysis for explanation: A casebook* (pp. 83–127). New York: Russell Sage Foundation.

Lipsey, M. W., & Wilson, D. B. (1999). Effective intervention for serious juvenile offenders. In R. Loeber & D. P. Farrington (Eds.), *Serious & violent juvenile offenders* (pp. 313–345). Thousands Oaks, CA: Sage.

Lipsey, M. W., Wilson, D. B., & Cothern, L. (2002). *Effective intervention for serious juvenile offenders.* Washington, DC: U.S. Department of Justice, Office of Juvenile and Delinquency Prevention.

Lipson, C. T. (1986). A case report of matricide. *American Journal of Psychiatry, 143,* 112–113.

Liptak, A., & Bronner, E. (2012, June 25). Justices bar mandatory life terms for juveniles. Retrieved http://www.nytimes.com/2012/06/26/us/justices-bar-mandatory-life-sentences-for-juveniles.html?_r=1

Listwan, S. J., Van Voorhis, P., & Ritchey, P. N. (2007). Personality, criminal behavior, and risk assessment. *Criminal Justice and Behavior, 34*(1), 60–75.

Livaditis, M. D., Esagian, G. S., Kakoulidis, C. P., Samakouri, M. A., & Tzavaras, N. A. (2005). Matricide by person with bipolar disorder and dependent overcompliant personality. *Journal of Forensic Sciences, 50*(3), 658–661.

Loeber, R., & Farrington, D. (2011). *Young homicide offenders and victims: Development, risk factors and prediction from childhood.* New York: Springer.

Lowen, A. (1983). *Narcissism: Denial of the true self.* New York: Macmillan Publishing Company.

Maas, R. L., Prakash, R., Hollender, M. H., & Regan, W. M. (1984). Double parricide— Matricide and patricide: A comparison with other schizophrenic murders. *Psychiatric Quarterly, 56*(4), 286–290.

MacDonald, J. M. (1986). *The murderer and his victim* (2nd ed.). Springfield, IL: Charles C. Thomas.

Mack, J. E., Scherl, D. J., & Macht, L. B. (1973). Children who kill their mothers. In E. J. Anthony & C. Koupernik (Eds.), *The child in his family* (pp. 319–332). New York: John Wiley & Sons.

Magid, K., & McKelvey, C. A. (1987). *High risk: Children without a conscience.* New York: Bantam Books.

Magnuson, C. (2003, April 2). Teen wins chance to use Battered Child Syndrome. *The Daily Record.* Retrieved from http://web.lexis-nexis.com/universe.

Mahoney, J. (1989, July 22). 2 sisters jailed in slaying stepmother killed in Schodack home. *Albany Times Union.* Retrieved from http://www.highbeam.com/doc/1G1-156076731. html

Mahoney, J., & Scruton, B. A. (1989, July 21). Stepdaughters charged in murder. *Albany Times Union.* Retrieved from http://www.highbeam.com/doc/1G1-156076782.html

Malmquist, C. P. (1971). Premonitory signs of homicidal aggression in juveniles. *American Journal of Psychiatry, 128*(4), 93–97.

Malmquist, C. P. (1980). Psychiatric aspects of familicide. *Bulletin of the American Academy of Psychiatry & Law, 13,* 221–231.

Malmquist, C. P. (2010). Adolescent parricide as a clinical and legal problem. *Journal of the American Academy of Psychiatry and Law, 38,* 73–79.

Man accused of killing of mother placed in hospital. (1983, May). *Los Angeles Times,* p. II 1.

Margaret. (2008, November 21). Notorious sisters: Lizzie & Co. *Sisterpedia.* Retrieved from http://thesisterproject.com/sisterpedia/

Margolick, D. (1992, February 14). When child kills parent, it's sometimes to survive. *New York Times,* p. A1. Retrieved from http://www.nytimes.com/1992/02/14/news/wh en-child-kills-parent-it-s-sometimes-to-survive.html

Marleau, J. D. (2002). Parricide et Caracteristiques de la Fratrie des Agresseurs [Parricide and characteristics of the aggressors]. *Canadian Journal of Criminology, 44,* 77–96.

Marleau, J. D. (2003). Methods of killing employed by psychotic parricides. *Psychological Reports, 93,* 519–520.

Marleau, J. D., Auclair, N. S., & Millaud, F. (2006). Comparison of factors associated with parricide in adults and adolescents. *Journal of Family Violence, 21*(5), 321–325.

Marleau, J. D., Millaud, F., & Auclair, N. S. (2001). Parricide commis par des femmes: Synthèse de la littérature [Parricide committed by females : Synthesis of the literature]. *Revue Quebecoise de Psychologie, 22*(3), 99–110.

Marleau, J. D., Millaud, F., & Auclair, N. S. (2003). A comparison of parricide and attempted parricide: A study of 39 psychotic adults. *International Journal of Law and Psychiatry, 26*(3), 269–279.

Marleau, J. D., & Webanck, T. (1997). Parricide and violent crimes: A Canadian study. *Adolescence, 32*(126), 357–359.

Maryland § 10-916 (2010).

Matsui, S. (1987). A comment upon the role of the judiciary in Japan. *Osaka University Law Review, 35,* 17–28.

Matsui, S. (2011). Why is the Japanese Supreme Court so conservative? *Washington University Law Review, 88,* 1375–1423.

Matter of Appeal in Maricopa County, Juvenile Action No. JV-506561 (App. Div. 1) (1994). 182 Ariz. 60, 893 P.2d 60, review denied.

Matthews, J. (1983, April 28). Girl molested by father faces prison term for killing him. *Washington Post,* p. A2.

McCarthy, L., Page, K., Baxter, H., Larkin, E., Cordess, C., & Duggan, C. (2001). Mentally disordered parricide and stranger killers admitted to high-security care: 2: Course after release. *Journal of Forensic Psychiatry, 12*(3), 501–514.

McCartney, A. (2005, November 29). Family killed 1 by 1 in home. *Tampa Tribune,* pp. 1, 6.

McCord, J., Widom, C. S., & Crowell, N. A. (2001). *Juvenile crime, juvenile justice.* Washington, DC: National Academy Press.

McCully, R. S. (1978). The laugh of Satan: A study of a familial murderer. *Journal of Personality Assessment, 42*(1), 81–91.

McGilberry v. State. 741 So. 2d 894 (1999).

McGinnis, J. (1991). *Cruel doubt.* New York: Simon & Schuster.

McGraw, C. (1983, April 2). Man held in killing of mother called suicidal. *Los Angeles Times,* p. II 6.

McKnight, C. K., Mohr, J. W., Quinsey, R. E., & Erochko, J. (1966). Matricide and mental illness. *Canadian Psychiatric Association Journal, 11*(2), 99–106.

McMurray, K. F. (2006). *If you really loved me.* New York: St. Martin's Press.

McMurray, K. F. (2009). *Desire turned deadly.* New York: St. Martin's Press.

Medlicott, R. W. (1955). Paranoia of the exalted type in a setting of folie a deux: A study of two adolescent homicides. *British Journal of Medical Psychology, 28,* 205–223.

Meisol, P. (1987, March). Charges dropped in killing of father. *St. Petersburg Times,* p. 1A.

Meloy, J. R. (1996). Orestes in Southern California: A forensic case of matricide. *Journal of Psychiatry & Law, 24*(1), 77–102.

Melton, G. B., Petrila, J., Poythress, N. G., & Slobogin, C. (2007). *Psychological evaluations for the courts* (3rd ed.). New York: Guilford Press.

Menezes, S. B. (2010). Parricides by mentally disordered offenders in Zimbabwe. *Medicine, Science and the Law, 50,* 126–130.

Metro briefing: New York: White Plains: Former prosecutor pleads guilty. (2003, June 13). *New York Times,* p. B5.

M.G.L.A. 233 § 23F (2010).

Middleton-Moz, J., & Dwinell, L. (1986). *After the tears: Reclaiming the losses of childhood.* Pompano Beach, FL: Health Communications.

Millaud, F., Auclair, N., & Meunier, D. (1996). Parricide and mental illness: A study of 12 cases. *International Journal of Law and Psychiatry, 19*(2), 173–182.

Miller, A. (1990). *For your own good* (3rd. ed.) New York: Noonday.

Miller, D., & Looney, J. (1974). The prediction of adolescent homicide: Episodic dyscontrol & dehumanization. *American Journal of Psychoanalysis, 34,* 187–198.

Miller v. Alabama (No. 10-9646) (2012, June 25). Retrieved from http://www.supremecourt.gov/opinions/11pdf/10-9646g2i8.pdf

Minnesota Rules of Evidence Rule 702. (2006). Retrieved from https://www.revisor.mn.gov/court_rules/rule.php?name=ev-702

Moffitt, T. E., Lynam, D. R., & Silva, P. A. (1994). Neuropsychological tests predicting persistent male delinquency. *Criminology, 2*(32), 277–300.

Mohr, J. W., & McKnight, C. K. (1971). Violence as a function of age and relationship with special reference to matricide. *Canadian Psychiatric Association Journal, 16*(1), 29–32.

Mones, P. (1985). The relationship between child abuse and parricide: An overview. In E. H. Newberger & R. Bourne (Eds.), *Unhappy families: Clinical and research perspectives on family violence* (pp. 31–38). Littleton, MA: PSG Publishing.

Mones, P. (1991). *When a child kills: Abused children who kill their parents.* New York: Pocket Books.

Mones, P. (1993). When the innocent strike back: Abused children who kill their parents. *Journal of Interpersonal Violence, 8*(2), 297–299.

Mones, P. (1994, February). Battered child syndrome; Understanding parricide. *Trial,* pp. 24–29.

Mones, P. (1995). Parricide: Opening a window through the defense of teens who kill. *Stanford Law and Policy Review, 7,* 61–64.

Moore, M. H. (1987). *From children to citizens.* New York: Springer-Verlag.

Morey, L. C. (1996). *An inventory guide to the Personality Assessment Inventory (PAI).* Odessa, FL: Psychological Assessment Resources.

Morris, G. (1985). *The kids next door: Sons and daughters who kill their parents.* New York: William Morrow & Company, Inc.

Morris, N. (1986). *Insanity defense: Crime file study guide.* Rockville, MD: U.S. Department of Justice, National Institute of Justice/National Criminal Justice Reference Service.

Morris, T., & Blom-Cooper, L. (1964). *A calendar of murder.* London: Michael Joseph.

Moulun, R., & Morgan, R. F. (1967). Sibling bondage: A clinical report on a parricide and his brother. *Bulletin Menninger Clinic, 31*(July), 229–235.

Mouridsen, S. E., & Tolstrup, K. (1988). Children who kill: A case study of matricide. *Journal of Child Psychology and Psychiatry, 29*(4), 511–515.

Mouzos, J., & Rushforth, C. (2003). Family homicide in Australia. *Trends & Issues in Crime and Criminal Justice, 255,* 241–260. Retrieved from http://www.aic.gov.au/publications/current%20series/tandi/241-260/tandi255/view%20paper.aspx

Mulvey, E. P. (2011). Highlights from pathways to desistance: A longitudinal study of serious adolescent offenders. *OJJDP Juvenile Justice Fact Sheet.* Washington, DC: U.S. Department of Justice, Office of Justice Programs, Office of Juvenile Justice and Delinquency Prevention. Retrieved from http://www.ncjrs.gov/pdffiles1/ojjdp/230971.pdf

Murray, D. C. (1999). Parricide in Canada. *Criminal Law Quarterly, 43,* 110–144.

Myers, W. C. (1992). What treatments do we have for children and adolescents who have killed? *Bulletin of the American Academy of Psychiatry and the Law, 20*(1), 47–58.

Myers, W. C., & Caterine, A. (1990). Tarasoff and threats of patricide by a 9-year-old boy [letter]. *American Journal of Psychiatry, 147*(4), 535–536.

Myers, W. C., & Kemph, J. P. (1988). Characteristics and treatment of four homicidal adolescents. *Journal of the American Academy of Child and Adolescent Psychiatry, 27*(5), 595–599.

Myers, W. C., & Vo, E. J. (2012). Adolescent parricide and psychopathy. *International Journal of Offender Therapy and Comparative Criminology, 56*(5), 715–729.

National Criminal Justice Reference Service. (1999, December). State statutes define who is under the jurisdiction of juvenile court. *1999 National Report Series, Juvenile Justice Bulletin: Juvenile Justice: A century of change.* Retrieved from https://www.ncjrs.gov/html/ojjdp/9912_2/juv3.html

National Institute on Drug Abuse. (n.d.). *Research reports: Hallucinogens and dissociative drugs.* Retrieved from http://www.drugabuse.gov/publications/research-reports/hallucinogens-dissociative-drugs

Neihart, M. (1999). The treatment of juvenile homicide offenders. *Psychotherapy, 36*(1), 36–46.

Nevada Rev. Stat. 48.061 (2009).

Newhill, C. E. (1991). Parricide. *Journal of Family Violence, 6*(4), 375–394.

Noble, K. B. (1996, March 21). Menendez brothers guilty of killing their parents. *New York Times.* Retrieved from http://www.nytimes.com/1996/03/21/us/menendez-brothers-guilty-of-killing-their-parents.html

Norris, J. (1988). *Serial killers: The growing menace.* New York: Doubleday.

Oberdalhoff, H. E. (1974). Matricide in a schizophrenic psychosis: Case report. *Confinia Psychiatrica, 17*(2), 122–131.

O' Connell, B. (1963). Matricide. *Lancet, 1,* 1083–1084.

Office of the Clark County Prosecuting Attorney. (n.d.). *Sean Richard Sellers #512.* Retrieved from http://www.clarkprosecutor.org/html/death/US/sellers512.htm

Ohio boy, 10, charged with mom's murder. (2011, January 4). *USA Today.* Retrieved from http://www.usatoday.com/news/nation/2011-01-03-mother-killed_N.htm

Ohio Evid. R. 702 (2007).

Okla. Stat. Ann. Tit. 22 Sect. 40.7 (2006).

Oliver, K. (2009, January 18). 8-year-old killer gets residential treatment for shooting dad and friend. *48 Hours.* Retrieved from http://www.cbsnews.com/8301-504083_162-6100584-504083.html

Olla, R. A. (2003). Redefining the objectively reasonable person in Texas: A case for battered child syndrome as pure self-defense for parricide. *Texas State Bar Section Report Juvenile Law, 17*(4), 6–25.

Ove, T., & McKinnon, J. (2007, July 31). Elizabeth Township girl charged in dad's killing. *Pittsburg Post-Gazette.* Retrieved from http://www.post-gazette.com/pg/07212/805648-55.stm

Palermo, G. B. (2007). Homicidal syndromes: A clinical psychiatric perspective. In R. N. Kocsis (Ed.), *Criminal profiling: International theory, research, and practice.* Totowa, NJ: Human Press Inc.

Palermo, G. B. (2010). Parricide: A crime against nature. *International Journal of Offender Therapy and Comparative Criminology, 54*(1), 3–5.

Palermo, G. B. (2012). *Severe personality-disordered defendants and the insanity plea in the United States.* Southport, UK: Boom Juridische uitgevers.

Palmer, T. (1992). *The re-emergence of correctional interventions.* Newbury Park, CA: Sage.

Palmer, T. (2002). *Individualized intervention with young multiple offenders.* New York: Routledge.

Pasewark, R. A. (1981). Insanity plea: A review of the research literature. *Journal of Psychiatry and Law, 9,* 357–401.

Pastore, A. L., & Maguire, K. (2001). *Bureau of Justice statistics: Sourcebook of criminal justice statistics.* Washington, DC: Department of Justice.

People v. Jason Victor Bautista, G035436, Court Of Appeal Of California, Fourth Appellate District, Division Three, 2006 Cal. App. Unpub. LEXIS 11714, December 28, 2006, Filed.

People v. Shanahan, 753 NE 2d 1028 (Ill Appellate Court, 1st Dist.) (2001).

Persons, R. W. (2009). Art therapy with serious juvenile offenders: A phenomenological analysis. *International Journal of Offender Therapy and Comparative Criminology, 53*(4), 433–453.

Petit, G., Petit, G., & Champeix, J. (1967). Parricide committed by an adolescent followed by suicide (apropos of a case). *Annales De Médecine Légale, Criminologie, Police Scientifique Et Toxicologie, 47*(6), 685–690.

Petrila, J., & Otto, R. K. (1996). *Law and mental health professionals—Florida.* Washington, DC: American Psychological Association.

Pfeffer, C. R. (1980). Psychiatric hospital treatment of assaultive homicidal children. *American Journal of Psychotherapy, 34*(2), 197–207.

Philbin, T., & Philbin, M. (2011). *The killer book of infamous murders.* Naperville, IL: Sourcebooks, Inc.

Picchi, J. (1991a, September 21). Finkle acquitted of cover-up in 1989 murder. *Albany Times Union.* Retrieved from http://www.highbeam.com/doc/1G1-156218498.html

Picchi, J. (1991b, January 9). The maximum Lisa Finkle gets 25 to life in murder. *Albany Times Union.* Retrieved from http://www.highbeam.com/doc/1G1-156257570.html

Picchi, J. (1991c, September 14). Weeping Finkle escorted from court. *Albany Times Union.* Retrieved from http://www.highbeam.com/doc/1G1-156217793.html

Picchi, J., & Brown, P. (1990, December 1). Lisa Finkle guilty of murdering stepmother. *Albany Times Union.* Retrieved from http://www.highbeam.com/doc/1G1-156098906. html

Pincus, J. H. (1993). Neurologist's role in understanding violence. *Archives of Neurology, 8,* 867–869.

Pope, H. S., Butcher, J. N., & Seelen, J. (1993). *The MMPI, MMPI-2 & MMPI-A in court: A practical guide for expert witnesses and attorneys.* Washington, DC: American Psychological Association.

Porot, M., Couadau, A., & Petit, G. (1968). Reflections on parricide. *Annales Medico Psychologiques, 2*(1), 110.

Posey, C. D. (Ed.). (1988). Correctional classification based upon psychological characteristics [Special issue]. *Criminal Justice and Behavior, 15*(1).

Post, S. (1982). Adolescent parricide in abusive families. *Child Welfare Journal, 61*(7), 445–455.

Prendergast, A. (1983, May 26). It's you or me, Dad. *Rolling Stone,* pp. 41–44, 66–67.

Prendergast, A. (1986). *The poison tree.* New York: Avon Books.

Prevent Child Abuse America. (n.d.). *Prevent Child Abuse America: About us.* Retrieved from http://www.preventchildabuse.org/about_us/index.shtml

Raizen, K. H. (1960). A case of matricide and patricide. *British Journal of Delinquency, 10*(4), 277–294.

Redding, R. E. (2010). *Juvenile transfer laws: An effective deterrent to delinquency?* Washington, DC: U.S. Department of Justice, Office of Justice Programs, Office of Juvenile Justice and Delinquency Prevention.

Reenkola, E. (2002). Matricide. In *The veiled female core* (pp. 91–122). New York: Other Press.

Reeves, P. (1993, September 19). Why the boys killed Daddy; when Lonnie Dutton's killers walked free no one complained: His sons had suffered enough. *The Independent,* p. 15. Retrieved from Lexis Nexis™ Academic.

Reinhardt, J. M. (1970). *Nothing left but murder.* Lincoln, NE: Johnsen Publishing Co.

Reitsma-Street, M., and Leschied, A. W. (1988). The Conceptual Level matching model in corrections. *Criminal Justice and Behavior, 15,* 92–108.

Report: Son dismembered dad after being raped. (2008, May 16). *The Denver Channel.* Retrieved from http://www.thedenverchannel.com/news/16301415/detail.html

Ressler, R. (1992). *Whoever fights monsters.* New York: St. Martin's Press.

Reyes, R., & Poltilove, J. (2011, June 3). Reports fault agencies. *The Tampa Tribune,* pp. 1, 4.

Revitch, E., & Schlesinger, L. B. (1981). *Psychopathology of homicide.* Springfiled, IL: Charles C. Thomas, Publisher.

Rodway, C., Norrington-Moore, V., While, D., Hunt, I. M., Flynn, S., Swinson, N., et al. (2011). A population-based study of juvenile perpetrators of homicide in England and Wales. *Journal of Adolescence, 34,* 19–28.

Roe-Sepowitz, D. E. (2007). Adolescent female murderers: Characteristics and treatment implications. *American Journal of Orthopsychiatry: Interdisciplinary Perspectives on Mental Health and Social Justice, 77*(3), 489–496.

Roe-Sepowitz, D. E. (2009).Comparing male and female juveniles charged with homicide: Child maltreatment, substance abuse and crime details. *The Journal of Interpersonal Violence, 24*(4), 601–617.

Rogers, R. (1986). *Conducting insanity evaluations.* New York: Van Nostrand Reinhold.

Romo, R. (2010, October 10). Posey released from custody. *Albuquerque Journal.* Retrieved from http://www.abqjournal.com/news/state/10235632state10-10-10.htm

Roper v. Simmons, 543 U.S. 551 (2005).

Roper v. Simmons amicus brief. (2004). Retrieved from http://www.juvjustice.org/publications_amicus.html

Rosen, C. L., Frost, J. D., Bricker, T., Tarnow, J. D., Gilette, P. C., & Duniavy, S. (1983). Two siblings with recurrent cardiorespiratory arrest: Munchausen Syndrome by Proxy or child abuse? *Pediatrics, 71*(5), 715–720.

Rosen, C. L., Frost, J. D., & Glaze, D. G. (1986). Clinical and laboratory observations: Child abuse and recurrent infant apnea. *Journal of Pediatrics, 109*(6), 1065–1067.

Rosenberg, D. (2007). Non-organic failure to thrive. In R. Meadow, J. Mok, & D. Rosenberg (Eds.), *ABC of child protection* (4th ed.) (pp. 56–59). Malden, MA: Blackwell Publishing.

Rosenberg, D. A. (1987). Web of deceit: A literature review of Munchausen Syndrome by Proxy. *Child Abuse and Neglect, 11,* 547–563.

Rosenhan, D. L., & Seligman, M. E. P. (1989). *Abnormal psychology* (2nd ed.). New York: W.M. Norton and Company.

Rosenthal, D. (1985, April 16). When a child kills a parent. *Parade,* pp. 6–9.

Ross, R. R., & Fabiano, E. (1985). *Time to think: A cognitive model of delinquency prevention and offender rehabilitation.* Johnson City, TN: Institute of Social Sciences and Arts.

Rotter, J. (1966). Generalized expectancies for internal versus external control of reinforcement. *Psychological Monographs: General and Applied, 80,* 1–28.

Roughhead, W. (1930). The edge of circumstance: A problem in parricide. *Judicial Review, 42,* 99–135.

Rozycka, M., & Thille, Z. (1972). The psychopathological aspect of parricide. *Psychiatria Polska, 6*(2), 159–168.

Rule 702, Testimony by expert witnesses. *Federal Rules of Evidence,* Article VII (2011).

Russell, D. H. (1984). A study of juvenile murderers of family members. *International Journal of Offender Therapy & Comparative Criminology, 28*(3), 177–192.

Sadoff, R. L. (1971). Clinical observations on parricide. *Psychiatric Quarterly, 45*(1), 65–69.

Sanford, L. T. (1990). *Strong at the broken places: Overcoming the trauma of childhood abuse.* New York: Random House.

Sargent, D. (1962). Children who kill: A family conspiracy? *Social Works, 7,* 35–42.

Savill, R. (2008, December 17). Parents killed by mentally ill son "could have been saved." *The Telegraph.* Retrieved from http://www.telegraph.co.uk/news/uknews/law-and-order/3814787/Parents-killed-by-mentally-ill-son-could-have-been-saved.html

Scherl, D. J., & Mack, J. E. (1966). A study of adolescent matricide. *Journal of the American Academy of Child Psychology, 5*(4), 569–593.

Schlesinger, L. B. (1999). Adolescent sexual matricide following repetitive mother-son incest. *Journal of Forensic Sciences, 44,* 746–749.

Schug, R. A. (2011). Schizophrenia and matricide: An integrative review. *Journal of Contemporary Criminal Justice, 24*(2), 204–229.

Schwade, E. D., & Geiger, S. G. (1953). Matricide with electroencephalographic evidence of thalamic or hypothalamic disorder. *Diseases of the Nervous System, 14,* 18–20.

Scobey, J. N. (1992). Self-defense parricide: Expert testimony on the battered child syndrome. *Hamolnie Journal of Public Law and Policy, 13,* 181–198.

Scudder, R. G., Blount, W. R., Heide, K. M., & Silverman, I. J. (1993). Important links between child abuse, neglect, and delinquency. *International Journal of Offender Therapy and Comparative Criminology, 37*(4), 315–323.

Sellers, B. G., & Heide, K. M. (2012). Male and female child murderers: An empirical analysis of U.S. arrest data. *International Journal of Offender Therapy and Comparative Criminology, 56*(5), 691–714.

Servan-Schreiber, D. (2000). Point: Eye Movement Densitization and Reprocessing. Is psychiatry missing the point? *Psychiatric Times, XVII, (7)*. Retrieved from http://faculty.uml.edu/darcus/47.474/EMDR_point_2000.pdf

Seymour, A., Murray, M., Sigmon, J., Hook, M., Edmunds, C., Gaboury, M., et al. (Eds.). (2000). Domestic violence. *2000 National Victim Assistance Academy*. Retrieved from https://www.ncjrs.gov/ovc_archives/academy/welcome.html

Shapiro, F. (1999). Eye movement desensitization and reprocessing (EMDR) and the anxiety disorders: Clinical and research implications of an integrated psychotherapy treatment. *Journal of Anxiety Disorders, 13*(1–2), 35–67.

Shapiro, F. (2001). *Eye movement desensitization and reprocessing: Basic principles, protocols, and procedures* (2nd ed.). New York: Guilford Press.

Sheridan, M. S. (2003). The deceit continues: An updated literature review of Munchausen by Proxy. *Child Abuse and Neglect, 24*(4), 431–451.

Shipley, S. L., & Arrigo, B. A. (2004). *The female homicide offender: Serial murder and the case of Aileen Wuornos.* Upper Saddle River, NJ: Pearson Prentice Hall.

Shon, P. C. (2009). Sources of conflict between parents and their offspring in nineteenth-century American parricides: An archival exploration. *Journal of Forensic Psychology Practice, 9*, 249–279.

Shon, P. C. (2010). Weapon usage in attempted and completed parricides in 19th century America: An archival exploration of the physical strength hypothesis. *Journal of Forensic Sciences, 55*(1), 232–236.

Shon, P. C. H. (2012). Existential boundary crossings: An archival exploration of identity projects in nineteenth-century American parricides. *Human Studies*. Retrieved http://www.springerlink.com/content/464741u883u77653/fulltext.pdf

Shon, P. C. H., & Barton- Bellessa, S. M. (2012). Pre-offense characteristics of nineteenth-century American parricide offenders: An archival exploration, *Journal of Criminal Psychology, 2*(1), 51–66.

Shon, P. C., & Roberts, M. A. (2008). Post-offence characteristics of 19th century American parricides: An archival exploration. *Journal of Investigative Psychology and Offender Profiling, 5*, 147–169.

Shon, P. C., & Roberts, M. A. (2010). An archival exploration of homicide-suicide and mass murder in the context of 19th century American parricides. *International Journal of Offender Therapy and Comparative Criminology, 54*(1), 43–60.

Shon, P. C. H., & Targonski, J. R. (2003). Declining trends in U.S. parricides, 1976–1998: Testing the Freudian assumptions. *International Journal Of Law and Psychiatry, 26*(4), 387–402.

Shoop, J. G. (1993). Self-defense claims gain acceptance in parricide cases. *Trial, 29*(3), 11–12.

Shumaker, D. M., & McKee, G. R. (2001). Characteristics of homicidal and violent juveniles. *Violence and Victims, 16*(4), 401–409.

Shumaker, D. M., & Prinz, R. (2000). Children who murder: A review. *Clinical Child and Family Psychology Review, 3*(2), 97–115.

Siegel, B. (1983). Kids and the law: When tortured kids strike back. In *Juvenile Justice: Getting behind the stereotypes.* Washington, DC: American Bar Association.

Silberstein, J. A. (1998). Matricide: A paradigmatic case in family violence. *International Journal of Offender Therapy and Comparative Criminology, 42*(3), 210–223.

Singhal, S., & Dutta, A. (1990). Who commits patricide? *Acta Psychiatrica Scandinavica, 82*(1), 40–43.

Singhal, S., & Dutta, A. (1992). Who commits matricide? *Medicine Science & Law, 32*(3), 213–217.

Slovenko, R. (2003). The insanity defense: Matricide in a French Quarter hotel. *Journal of Psychiatry & Law, 31*(2), 251–284.

Smith, K. (2011, September 2). Sahuarita man convicted in beating death of dad, 58. *Arizona Daily Star.* Retrieved from http://azstarnet.com/news/local/crime/article_da237bc9-1e67-531a-8296-222345d83821.html

Smith, S. C. (1992). Abused children who kill abusive parents: Moving toward an appropriate legal response. *Catholic University Law Review, 42,* 141–178.

Smith, T. (2010, December 9). Sheriff says Johnson acted alone. *Idaho Mountain Express.* Retrieved from http://www.mtexpress.com/vu_breaking_story.php?bid=96165

Smith v. State, S96G1914, Supreme Court of Georgia, 268 Ga. 196, 486 S.E.2d 819 (1997). Ga. Lexis 426; 97 Fulton County D. Rep. 2590, July 14, 1997, decided.

Smullen v. State, Md. Spec. App., No. 1179 (April 1, 2003).

Snell, T., & Maruschak, L. M. (2002). *Bureau of Justice statistics bulletin: Capital punishment 2001.* Washington, DC: Department of Justice.

Snow, A. (2003). *Battered Person Syndrome: A research guide to common evidentiary issues & specific treatment in Georgia.* Atlanta, GA: Georgia State University College of Law, Advanced Legal Research.

Snyder, H. N., & Sickmund, M. (2006). *Juvenile offenders and victims: 2006 national report.* Washington, DC: U.S. Department of Justice, Office of Justice Programs, Office of Juvenile Justice and Delinquency Prevention.

Solomon, E. P., Berg, L. R., & Martin, D. W. (2011). *Biology* (9th ed.). Belmont, CA: Brooks/Cole/Cengage.

Solomon, E. P., & Heide, K. M. (1999). Type III trauma: Toward a more effective conceptualization of psychological trauma. *International Journal of Offender Therapy and Comparative Criminology, 43*(2), 202–210.

Solomon, E. P., & Heide, K. M. (2005). The biology of trauma: Implications for treatment. *Journal of Interpersonal Violence, 20*(1), 51–60.

Solomon, E. P., Solomon, R., & Heide, K. M. (2009). EMRD: An evidence-based treatment for victims of trauma. *Victims & Offenders, 4*(4), 391–397.

Son charged with stabbing father more than 40 times, using bat. (2009, August 22). *Pantagraph.* Retrieved from http://www.pantagraph.com/news/local/article_692921c0-8f53-11de-9736-001cc4c03286.html

Sorrells, J. M., Jr. (1977). Kids who kill. *Crime & Delinquency, 16,* 152–161.

Springer, J. (2006, February 23). Teen killer Cody Posey spared prison, sentenced to juvenile center. *Court TV.* Retrieved from http://news.findlaw.com/court_tv/s/20060223/23feb2006170303.html

Stalans, L. J., & Henry, G. T. (1994). Societal views of justice for adolescents accused of murder: Inconsistency between community sentiment and automatic legislative transfers. *Law and Human Behavior, 18,* 675–696.

Stanford v. Kentucky, 492 U.S. 361 (1989).

State of Missouri v. Frederick Lashley. (1984). Retrieved from http://websolutions.learfield.com/deathrow/gestalt/go.cfm?objectid=6FBB22D2-6D7F-473A-AF77EF2803092AB3

State v. Crabtree, 805 P. 2d 1, 6 (Kansas Supreme Court) (1991).

State v. Dunham, Tenn. Court of Appeals (2004), No. M2003-02802-CCA-R3-CD.

State v. Gachot, 609 So. 2d 269 (LA Court of Appeals, 3rd Circuit) (1992).

State v. Gachot, 620 So. 2d 830, LA Supreme Court (1993) (reconsideration denied).

State v. Janes, 121 Wash. 2d 220; 850 P.2d 495, 501; 22 A.L.R. 5th 921 (1993).

State v. MacLennan, 702 N.W.2d 219 (Minn.) (2005).

State v. Nemeth, 82 Ohio St. 3d. 202 (1998).

State v. Smullen, 844 A. 2d 429, 380 Md. 233 (Md: Court of Appeals) (2004).

Strange, C. (2010). The unwritten law of executive justice: Pardoning patricide in Reconstruction-era New York. *Law and History, 28*(4), 891–930.

Straus, M. A. (2007). Conflict tactics scales. In N. A. Jackson (Ed.), *Encyclopedia of domestic violence* (pp. 190–197). New York: Routledge: Taylor & Francis Group.

Strean, H. S., & Freeman, L. (1991). *Our wish to kill.* New York: St. Martin's Press.

Streib, V. L. (1987). *Death penalty for juveniles.* Bloomington: Indiana University Press.

Streib, V. L. (1998). Moratorium on the death penalty for juveniles. *Transnational Law and Contemporary Problems, 61*(4), 55–87.

Streib, V. L. (2003). Executing juvenile offenders: The ultimate denial of juvenile justice. *Stanford Law and Policy Research, 14,* 121–139.

Streib, V. L. (2005). *The juvenile death penalty today: Death sentences and executions for juvenile crimes, January 1, 1973 to December 31, 2004.* Ada: Ohio Northern University Pettit College of Law.

Streib, V. L., & Sametz, L. (1989). Executing female juveniles. *Connecticut Law Review, 22*(1), 3–59.

Sugai, K. (1999). A case of schizophrenia with a "dream occurrence" episode as "arrest coloring" in a prisoner after committing matricide. *Seishin Igaku (Clinical Psychiatry), 41*(4), 429–431.

Sullivan, C. L., Grant, M. Q., & Grant, J. D. (1957). The development of interpersonal maturity: Application to delinquency. *Psychiatry, 20,* 373–385.

Sullivan, I. (2010). *Raised by the courts.* New York: Kaplan.

Sunger, S. (2008, December 15). Judge hands Jeremy Steinke life sentence. *CTV Edmonton.* Retrieved from http://edmonton.ctv.ca/servlet/an/local/CTVNews/20081214/EDM_steinke_sentence_081214/20081215?hub=EdmontonHome

Tanay, E. (1973). Adolescents who kill parents: Reactive parricide. *Australian and New Zealand Journal of Psychiatry, 7*(4), 263–277.

Tanay, E. (1976). Reactive parricide. *Journal of Forensic Sciences, 21*(2), 76–81.

Tanay, E., & Freeman, L. (1976). *The murderers.* Indianapolis, IN: Bobbs-Merrill Company, Inc.

Tarolla, S. M., Wagner, E. F., Rabinowitz, J., & Tubman, J. G. (2002). Understanding and treating juvenile offenders: A review of current knowledge and future directions. *Aggression and Violent Behavior, 7,* 125–143.

Tate, D. C., Reppucci, N. D., & Mulvey, E. P. (1995). Violent juvenile delinquents: Treatment effectiveness and implications for future action. *American Psychologist, 50*(9), 777–781.

Teicher, M. H., Andersen, S. L., Polcari, A., Anderson, C. M., Navalta, C. P., & Kim, D. M. (2003). The neurobiological consequences of early stress and childhood maltreatment. *Neuroscience and Biobehavioral Reviews, 27*(1–2), 33–44.

Texas Youth Commission. (1996). *Review of treatment programs.* Austin, TX: Author.

Texas Youth Commission. (1997). *Specialized treatment recidivism effectiveness summary.* Austin, TX: Author.

Texas Youth Commission. (2006). *Treatment and case management. Capital & serious violent offender treatment program manual.* Austin, TX: Author.

The 'Lectric Law Library. (n.d.). *Menendez II Penalty Phase 4/17/96 jury verdict transcript.* Retrieved from http://www.lectlaw.com/files/case11.htm

Thompson v. Oklahoma, 487 U.S. 815 (1988).

Timnick, L. (1986, August 31). Fatal means for children to end abuse parricide cases evoke conflict in sympathy, need for punishment. *Los Angeles Times.* Retrieved from http://articles.latimes.com/1986-08-31/local/me-15039_1_child-abuse

Toufexis, A., Bloch, H., & McDowell, J. (1992, November 23). When kids kill abusive parents. *Time.* Retrieved from http://articles.latimes.com/1986–08–31/local/me-15039_1_child-abuse

Townsend, C. K. (2010). *2010 Annual Review of Treatment Effectiveness.* Texas Youth Commission. Retrieved from http://204.65.113.10/about/Annual_Treatment_Effectiveness_Review2010.pdf

Townsend, D. (1983, April 30). Miller declared unfit for trial. *Los Angeles Times,* p. I 31.

TruTV. (n.d.). *Sara Johnson murder trial evidence.* Retrieved from http://www.trutv.com/library/crime/photogallery/johnson-evidence.html

Tucker, L. S., & Cornwall, T. P. (1977). Mother-son folie à deux: A case of attempted patricide. *American Journal of Psychiatry, 134*(10), 1146–1147.

Tuovinen, M. (1973). On parricide. *Psychiatria Fennica, 2,* 141–146.

U.S. Department of Health and Human Services. (2009). Definitions of child abuse and neglect. *Administration for Children and Families child welfare information gateway.* Retrieved from http://www.childwelfare.gov/systemwide/laws_policies/statutes/define.cfm

U.S. Department of Justice. (1996). *The validity and use of evidence concerning battering and its effects in criminal trials.* Retrieved from http://www.http://www.ncjrs.org/txtfiles/batter.txt

U.S. Department of Labor. (n.d.). *Youth and labor—Age requirements.* Retrieved from http://www.dol.gov/dol/topic/youthlabor/agerequirements.htm

Utah Crim. Code 76-2-402(5) (2010).

Väisänen, L., & Väisänen, E. (1983). Matricide where the daughter was an instrument for the suicide of her mother. *Psychiatria Fennica,* Suppl, 119–122.

Valenca, A. M., Mezzasalma, M. A., Nascimento, I., & Nardi, A. E. (2009). Matricídio e transtorno bipolar [Matricide and bipolar disorder]. *Revista de Psiquiatra Clínica, 36*(4), 170–174.

V.A.M.S. 563.033 (2010).

van der Kolk, B. A. (1996). The body keeps the score. Approaches to the psychobiology of posttraumatic stress disorder. In B. A. van der Kolk, A. C. McFarlane, & L.Weisaeth (Eds.), *Traumatic stress: the effects of overwhelming experience on mind, body, and society* (pp. 214–241). New York: Guilford Press.

van der Kolk, B. A. (2006). Clinical implications of neuroscience research in PTSD. *Annals of the New York Academy of Sciences, 1071*(1), 277–293.

Van Voorhis, P. (1988). A cross classification of five offender typologies: Issues of construct and predictive validity. *Criminal Justice and Behavior, 15,* 109–124.

Van Voorhis, P. (1994). *Psychological classification of the adult prison male.* Albany: State University of New York Press.

Van Voorhis, P. (2000). An overview of offender classification systems. In P. Van Voorhis, M. Braswell, & D. Lester (Eds.), *Correctional counseling and rehabilitation* (pp. 81–105). Cincinnati, OH: Anderson.

Vereecken, J. L. (1965). A case of parricide. *Psychotherapy and Psychosomatics, 13*(5), 364–379.

Vernon's Ann. Texas C.C.P. Art. 38.36 (2009).

Viera, T. A., Skilling, T. A., & Peterson-Badali, M. (2009). Matching court-ordered services with treatment needs: Predictive treatment success with young offenders. *Criminal Justice and Behavior, 36*(4), 385–401.

Vries, A. M., & Liem, M. (2011). Recidivism of juvenile homicide offenders. *Behavioral Sciences and the Law, 29*(4), 483–498.

Wainryb, C., Komolova, M., & Florsheim, P. (2010). How violent youth offenders and typically developing adolescents construct moral agency in narratives about doing harm. In

K. C. McLean & M. Pasupathi (Eds.), *Narrative development in adolescence: Advancing responsible adolescent development* (pp. 185–206.) New York: Springer Science + Business Media.

Walker, L. (1989). *Sudden fury*. New York: St. Martin's Press.

Walker, L. E. (1979). *The battered woman*. New York: Harper & Row.

Walker, L. E. (1984). *The battered woman syndrome*. New York: Springer.

Walker, L. E. (1989). *Terrifying love*. New York: Harper & Row.

Walsh, J. A., & Krienert, J. L. (2009). A decade of child-initiated family violence: Comparative analysis of child-parent violence and parricide examining offender, victim, and event characteristics in a national sample of reported incidents, 1999–2005. *Journal of Interpersonal Violence, 24*(9), 1450–1477.

Walsh, J. A., Krienert, J. L., & Crowder, D. (2008). Innocence lost: A gender-based study of parricide offenders, victim, and incident characteristics in a national sample, 1976–2003. *Journal of Aggression, Maltreatment, & Trauma, 16*(2), 202–227.

Walton, D. (2008, December 6). Steinke convicted in murder of girlfriend's family. *The Globe and Mail* [summarized by *Religion News Blog*]. Retrieved from http://www.religionnewsblog.com/23026/jeremy-steinke

Warren, M. Q. (1969). The case for differential treatment of delinquents. *Annals of the American Academy of Political and Social Science, 381*, 47–59.

Warren, M. Q. (1971). Classification of offenders as an aid to effective management and effective treatment. *The Journal of Criminal Law, Criminology and Police Science, 62*, 239–258.

Warren, M. Q. (1978). The "impossible child," the difficult child, and other assorted delinquents: Etiology, characteristics and incidence. *Canadian Psychiatric Association Journal, 23*(Special Supplement), SS41–SS60.

Warren, M. Q. (1983). Applications of interpersonal maturity level theory to offender populations. In W. S. Laufer & J. M. Day (Eds.), *Personality theory, moral development and criminal behavior* (pp. 23–50). Lexington, MA: D.C. Heath and Company.

Wasarhaley, N. W., Golding, J. M., Lynch, K. R., & Keller, P. S. (2012). The impact of abuse allegations in perceiving parricide in the courtroom. *Psychology, Crime & Law*. Retrieved http://www.tandfonline.com/doi/abs/10.1080/1068316X.2012.684056

Washington Statute 9A. 16.050 (2009).

Weiner, K. E., & Thompson, J. K. (1998). Overt and covert sexual abuse: Relationship to body image and eating disturbance. *International Journal of Eating Disorders, 22*(3), 273–284.

Weisman, A. M., Ehrenclou, M. G., & Sharma, K. K. (2002). Double parricide: Forensic analysis and psycholegal implications. *Journal of Forensic Science, 47*, 313–317.

Weisman, A. M., & Sharma, K. K. (1997). Forensic analysis and psycholegal implications of parricide and attempted parricide. *Journal of Forensic Science, 42*(6), 1107–1113.

Welborn, L. (2006, June 29). Man found sane in mother's murder. *The Orange County Register*, p. Central B. Retrieved from Lexis Nexis™ Academic.

Wertham, F. (1941a). *Dark legend: A study in murder*. New York: Duell, Sloan and Pierce.

Wertham, F. (1941b). The matricidal impulse. *Journal of Criminal Psychology, 2*, 455–464.

West, S. G., & Feldsher, M. (2010, November). Parricide: Characteristics of sons and daughters who kill their parents. *Current Psychiatry*, pp. 20, 22, 28, 29, 38.

West's Ann. Cal. Fam. Code 6211 (2012).

Wick, R., Mitchell, E., Gilbert, J. D., & Byard, R. W. (2008). Matricides in South Australia. *Journal of Forensic and Legal Medicine, 15*(3), 168–171.

Widom, C. S. (1989a). Child abuse, neglect, and adult behavior: Research design and findings on criminality, violence, and child abuse. *American Journal of Orthopsychiatry, 59*(3), 355–366.

Widom, C. S. (1989b). Child abuse, neglect, and violent criminal behavior. *Criminology, 27,* 251–271.

Widom, C. S. (1989c). Does violence beget violence? A critical examination of the literature. *Psychological Bulletin, 106*(1), 3–28.

Widom, C. S. (1989d, April 14). The cycle of violence. *Science, 244,* 160–166.

Widom, C. S. (1991). A tail on an untold tale: Response to "Biological and genetic contributors to violence"—Widom's untold tale. *Psychological Bulletin, 109*(1), 130–132.

Widom, C. S., DuMont, K., & Czaja, S. J. (2007). A prospective investigation of major depressive disorder and comorbidity in abused and neglected children grown up. *Archives of General Psychiatry, 64*(1), 49–56.

Widom, C. S., & Hiller- Sturmhofel, S. (2001). Alcohol abuse as a risk factor for and consequence of child abuse. *Alcohol Research & Health, 25*(1), 52–57

Wilson, P. (1973). *The children who kill.* London: Michael Joseph Ltd.

Winfield, D. L., & Ozturk, O. (1959). Electroencephalographic findings in matricide. *Diseases of the Nervous System, 20,* 176–180.

Winner, L., Lanza- Kaduce, L., Bishop, D. M., & Frazier, C. E. (1997). The transfer of juveniles to criminal court: Reexamining recidivism over the long term. *Crime & Delinquency, 43*(4), 548–563.

Wooden, K. (2000). *Weeping in the playtime of others* (2nd ed.). Columbus: Ohio State University Press.

Wright, N. (2009). Voice for the voiceless: The case for adopting the "domestic abuse syndrome" for self defense purposes for all victims of domestic violence who kill their abusers. *4 Crim. L. Brief 76.*

WTVD-TV/DT ABC. (2008a, January 25). *Plea deal for teen accused of killing parents.* Retrieved from http://abclocal.go.com/wtvd/story?section=news/local&id=5914689

WTVD-TV/DT ABC. (2008b, February 9). *Sapikowski sentenced to another 20 years.* Retrieved from http://abclocal.go.com/wtvd/story?section=news/local&id=5945716

WTVD-TV/DT ABC. (2008c, February 8). *Sapikowski sentenced to at least 20 years.* Retrieved from http://abclocal.go.com/wtvd/story?section=news/local&id=5928770

W. VA. Codes, Section 48-27-1104 (2005).

Wy. St. Section 6-1-203 (2010).

Yoshikawa, K., Fukui, H., Noda, T., Yoshizumi, M., Matsumoto, T., & Okada, T. (2006). Matricide of Asperger syndrome caused by brain tumor. *Acta Criminologiae et Medicinae Legalis Japonica, 72*(4), 105–109.

Young, M. H., Justice, J., & Erdberg, P. (2011)). *A comparison of rape and molest offenders in prison psychiatric treatment. International Journal of Offender Therapy and Comparative Criminology.* Retrieved from http://ijo.sagepub.com/content/early/2011/09/09/030662 4X11417361.full.pdf+html

Young, T. J. (1993). Parricide rates and criminal street violence in the United States: Is there a correlation? *Adolescence, 28*(109), 171–172.

Youthful offender status is granted based on mitigating circumstances. (1992, June 2). *New York Law Journal,* Court Decisions, p. 21. Retrieved from Lexis Nexis™ Academic.

Yusuf, A. J., & Nuhu, I. T. (2010). Consequences of untreated severe psychiatric disorders in northern Nigeria. *African Journal of Psychiatry,* May, 92–93.

Zagar, R. J., Busch, K. G., & Hughes, J. R. (2009). Empirical risk factors for delinquency and best treatments: Where do we go from here? *Psychological Reports, 104,* 279–308.

Zagar, R. J., Isbell, S. A., Busch, K. G., & Hughes, J. R. (2009). An empirical theory of the development of homicide within victims. *Psychological Reports, 104,* 199–245.

Zenoff, E., & Zeints, A. (1979). Juvenile murderers: Should the punishment fit the crime? *International Journal of Law and Psychiatry, 2,* 53–55.

Zickefoose, S. (2008, December 6). Steinke convicted of killing girlfriend's family. *Religion News Blog.* Retrieved from http://www.religionnewsblog.com/23026/jeremy-steinke

Index

About the Author

Kathleen M. Heide is a Full Professor in the Department of Criminology, University of South Florida (USF), Tampa. She received her B.A. in Psychology from Vassar College and her M.A. and Ph.D. in Criminal Justice from the University at Albany, State University of New York. Professor Heide is an internationally recognized consultant and lecturer on homicide and family violence. She has authored or co-authored more than 100 scholarly publications in the areas of homicide, parricide, family violence, personality assessment, and juvenile justice. Dr. Heide is the author of two widely acclaimed books on juvenile homicide (*Why Kids Kill Parents: Child Abuse and Adolescent Homicide* and *Young Killers: The Challenge of Juvenile Homicide*). She is the co-author (with Linda Merz-Perez) of *Animal Cruelty: Pathway to Violence against People*. Requests for copies of Dr. Heide's publications have come from scholars and practitioners around the world.

Dr. Heide is a licensed mental health professional and court-appointed expert in matters relating to homicide, children, and families. She has evaluated adolescents and adults charged with parricide in 12 states and Canada. Dr. Heide has been qualified as an expert to testify in several areas, including psychology, criminology, adolescent homicide and parricide, child abuse, personality assessment, and forensic evaluation, in Florida circuit courts and in various jurisdictions across the United States. She is a frequent consultant to the national print and electronic media and to numerous international newspapers and magazines. She has also appeared as an expert on many national talk and news shows, including *Larry King Live*, CNN, *Good Morning America*, *Fox News*, and *20/20*.

Dr. Heide has been the recipient of many honors and awards. She was granted full membership status in the American Psychological Association in light of her accomplishments in the field of psychology. She was recognized as a Distinguished Alumna by the School of Criminal Justice, University at Albany. Professor Heide was one of a handful of experts invited by Queen Sofia of Spain to present her research on juvenile homicide offenders in Valencia.

Professor Heide enjoys teaching both undergraduate and graduate students and has received six awards for teaching excellence. She has served as a consultant to the National Institute of Justice, the National Institutes of Health, and many state agencies, and she currently serves on the editorial boards of three professional journals. Dr. Heide is a member or former member of more than 10 community and state boards of directors, councils, or task forces and is an active participant in the U.S. Coast Guard Auxiliary in port security, marine safety, and search and rescue operations.